International accounting and transnational decisions

International accounting and transnational decisions

Edited by
S. J. Gray
University of Glasgow, Scotland

Butterworth
London Boston Durban Singapore Sydney Toronto Wellington

First published 1983

© **Butterworth & Co. (Publishers) Ltd 1983**

British Library Cataloguing in Publication Data

International accounting and transnational
  decisions
  1. Accounting
  I. Gray, S. J.
  657   HF5657

  ISBN 0-408-10841-X

Library of Congress Cataloging in Publication Data

Main entry under title:

International accounting and transnational
  decisions
  Bibliography: p.
  Includes index.
  1. International business enterprises—Accounting—
Addresses, essays, lectures. I. Gray, S. J.
HF5686.I56I55 1983   657′.95   83–2026

  ISBN 0-408-10841-X

New typesetting by Butterworths Litho Preparation Department
Printed and Bound in Great Britain by Whitstable Litho Ltd,
Whitstable, Kent

Preface

International accounting is in a stage of rapid development. This is so much so that there is a shortage of textbooks that bring together material relevant to the wide range of accounting issues that concern those involved in international business. Professor Gerhard Mueller's pioneering book entitled *International Accounting* (1967) stood virtually by itself for many years and only relatively recently, with the growth of international accounting courses, has there been a serious attempt to remedy this situation.

This book aims to contribute to the development of the subject by providing a collection of readings that should usefully supplement material in the few international accounting textbooks now available or serve in the development of independent courses at senior undergraduate and postgraduate level.

The selection is based largely on my experience of teaching and research in the international aspects of accounting. The structure chosen reflects a personal perception of significant areas of study. Naturally, the most difficult problem, given the limitation of space, has been to restrict the range of topics covered and the number of articles selected to within manageable proportions. Many useful articles have been omitted in the process but hopefully the chosen readings will encourage further study and lead to an appreciation of the wider range of material available. A further limitation is that some of the factual content is in the process of being superseded by events. This is unavoidable given the dynamic nature of the subject. However, the readings have been chosen largely on the basis of their more durable analytical content and contribution to issues of current and likely future substance.

As editor, I wish to express my appreciation to all of the authors and publishers who have granted permission to reprint the articles included here and to my colleagues and others who have helped me with suggestions concerning the structure and content of this collection.

S. J. G.
University of Glasgow

Contributors

Jane O. Burns
Indiana University
A. Louis Calvet
University of Ottawa
Frederick D. S. Choi
New York University
Clive R. Emmanuel
University of Kansas
Adolf J. H. Enthoven
University of Texas, Dallas
Werner G. Frank
University of Wisconsin, Madison
Sidney J. Gray
University of Glasgow
William P. Hauworth II
Arthur Andersen & Co, Chicago
Thomas Horst
Taxecon Associates
Laurent L. Jacque
University of Pennsylvania
Sanjaya Lall
University of Oxford
Donald R. Lessard
Massachusetts Institute of Technology
Peter Lorange
Massachusetts Institute of Technology
Desmond McComb
University of Southampton

L. Brendan McSweeney
Association of Certified Accountants
Gerhard G. Mueller
University of Washington
R. D. Nair
University of Wisconsin, Madison
Christopher W. Nobes
University of Strathclyde
Robert H. Parker
University of Exeter
Lee H. Radebaugh
Brigham Young University
J. Timothy Sale
University of Cincinnati, Ohio
Robert W. Scapens
University of Manchester
Hein Schreuder
Free University of Amsterdam
Alan C. Shapiro
University of Southern California
John C. Shaw
University of Glasgow
Hans B. Thorelli
Indiana University
Robert G. Walker
University of New South Wales

Contents

Introduction

The purpose of this book is to explore a wide range of significant international accounting issues with special reference to the comparative development of national systems of accounting, international accounting standards, transnational financial reporting issues and financial planning and control in the multinational corporation.

Whilst international accounting is by no means a new area of study its significance has grown enormously along with the explosion in international business activity over the last two decades. The complexity and diversity of the subject has also increased with the result that no single book is likely to embrace satisfactorily all aspects which may be of concern to those involved in international business. An attempt has been made, however, to cover many important areas of international accounting and to offer a selection of readings that will not only inform about major issues, ideas and developments but also stimulate further enquiry and debate.

The book is divided into five parts. The first part explores the international dimensions of accounting including both the financial reporting and managerial decision-making perspectives. The second part is concerned with the comparative international aspects of accounting. The third part examines developments and questions relating to international accounting standards. The fourth part considers a number of selected transnational financial reporting issues of concern both to managers and financial statement users. The fifth part takes a managerial perspective in its coverage of important problems of transnational financial decision-making and control.

Part I: The international dimensions of accounting

The introductory articles by Parker and Choi provide a stimulating overview of the international dimensions of accounting. Parker identifies four main reasons for studying international accounting. The first three, namely, the historical, multinational and comparative reasons are widely applicable. The fourth, the European reason, is more specifically related to the UK and other EEC countries but is of larger significance given the likely influence of EEC harmonization experiences for policy-making in other countries. Choi provides a development of the managerial perspective with an overview of relevant issues including foreign exchange risks, consolidations and group accounts, financial planning, external financing, international taxation, transfer pricing, performance evaluation and information systems.

Part II: Comparative international accounting

A selection of studies are presented which attempt to describe, explain and compare the development of accounting systems at national level including an assessment of systematic differences and similarities between countries with a view to identifying accounting patterns. The article by Radebaugh develops an extremely useful analytical framework for identifying factors likely to influence the development of accounting objectives, standards and practices at national level. This is applied specifically to the case of Peru but many other countries including the USA are referred to by way of comparison and illustration. Mueller, in a pioneering article, groups countries according to their business, economic, political and legal environments and provides some evidence to suggest a likely correlation with national systems of accounting. Nair and Frank, on the other hand, group countries according to their accounting practices and then attempt to explain such groupings by reference to economic and cultural factors. A significant finding is that major differences exist in country groupings between the measurement and disclosure sub-sets of accounting practices and related factors, with greater diversity in respect to disclosure practices. In overall terms, this study confirms the relationship between accounting practices and environmental factors. Gray explores further the relationship between measurement practices and environmental factors, with special reference to France, Germany and the UK, and concludes that a major impact on accounting patterns is the relative development of national stock markets and the corresponding influence of investors in comparison with creditors, bankers and other long-term financiers. Research that attempts to identify accounting patterns is of growing interest and concern especially in the context of international harmonization but is still in the early stages of development; major problems are the need to develop criteria for comparison and the lack of comprehensive data relating to national systems of accounting.

Part III: International accounting standards

The development of international accounting standards is taking place in a variety of forms. The article by Nobes concerns accounting harmonization in the EEC which provides an important case study of the development of international standards of accounting at regional level. Included is discussion of the major differences in national systems of accounting in the EEC, the purpose of harmonization and the development of the EEC Company Law harmonization programme with special reference to an evaluation of the Fourth Directive on Annual Accounts which is now being implemented in all of the community countries. Enthoven presents the case for international accounting standards in the context of world-wide economic development but with special reference to the less developed countries. McComb examines the objectives underlying pressures for international harmonization from professional accounting organizations, for example the International Accounting Standards Committee (IASC) and the International Federation of Accountants (IFAC). Whilst there is a strong case for the further development of international accounting standards it is suggested that more attention should be given to understanding the reasons for the continuing existence of national differences and hence the problems of attempts to impose uniform standards internationally. Finally, the article by Gray, Shaw and McSweeney explores issues relating to the development of accounting standards for multinational corporations. It is concluded that multinational corporations are a primary focus for international standards and that standard-setting is a political/social choice process involving supranational intergovernmental as well as international professional accounting organizations.

Part IV: Transnational financial reporting issues

Major issues identified for examination in the context of transnational financial reporting include: group accounting, segmental reporting, foreign currency accounting, inflation accounting and social reporting.

In an article on group accounting, Parker provides a comparative analysis of concepts of consolidation together with a survey of reporting practices in the EEC. Walker examines the problem of consolidation accounting in the context of the development of the IASC's international accounting standard No. 3 with the conclusion that it may be more confusing than helpful as a basis for international accounting harmonization.

Segmental reporting is an issue which is relatively new in terms of its international significance. Gray examines this problem in the EEC context with special reference to an empirical study of disclosure practices by multinational corporations. Factors likely to explain country differences include corporate structure and organization as well as the differential stimulus to disclosure provided by the regulatory environment of legal, professional and stock market requirements. This study confirms that a critical financial reporting problem concerns the lack of effective criteria for the identification of segments. This issue is taken up by Emmanuel and Gray with an analysis of different approaches to segment identification and the development of a proposal for disclosure by multinational corporations which attempts to reconcile managerial and external user interests.

Foreign currency accounting is an issue unique to interntional business and is closely related to foreign exchange risk management which is covered in Part V. Considerable controversy exists concerning the concept and method of translation to be used in the consolidation of foreign currency financial statements. The article by Nobes provides a useful historical and comparative international review of the arguments for and against alternative approaches including the use of purchasing power parities. Choi analyses further the alternatives in response to the complex and controversial question of how to account for price-level changes, both specific and general, in the context of foreign currency translation and foreign subsidiary accounting.

Accounting for inflation is a problem of world-wide significance with a growing number and variety of recent developments at national level. Hauworth provides a wide-ranging review of recent developments internationally including the USA, UK, Continental Europe and South America. Sale and Scapens explore the nature of recent experiments in the USA and UK in greater depth with a comparative analysis of SFAS33 and SSAP16 respectively.

Social reporting is an issue of growing significance in the corporate reporting context. Schreuder reports on research into the response of employees to information disclosure in the Netherlands where it is rapidly becoming normal business practice to issue additional social reports. At the level of the multinational corporation, information of a social nature is perhaps especially significant in the context of relationships with host governments. Thorelli discusses the development of economic and social indicators of performance for multinational corporations and reveals the problems and challenges facing accountants in this emerging area of concern.

Part V: Transnational financial decisions and control

Major areas for examination in the context of managerial decision-making include: foreign investment decisions, capital budgeting and long-term financing, foreign exchange risk management, international taxation, transfer pricing, and perform-ance evaluation and control systems.

In an article on foreign investment decisions, Calvet provides a useful review of foreign direct investment theories and recent research relating to the development of a theory of multinational corporations in the context of the theory of the firm.

International aspects of capital budgeting, financial structure and cost of capital for the multinational corporation are very effectively dealt with in articles by Shapiro. First, problems that distinguish capital budgeting in the international context are identified. Secondly, the cost of capital issue is explored with reference also to questions concerning financial structure, risk and diversification, and the impact of tax and regulatory factors.

Foreign exchange risk management is a unique problem of international business which has grown rapidly in significance with continuing exchange rate fluctuations. The article by Jacque provides a useful review of theory and evidence in this area with particular reference to the forecasting of exchange rates and the measurement of exposure to exchange risk.

International taxation is a vast and extremely complex subject. Horst analyses the behaviour of the multinational corporation, especially in its relationships with foreign subsidiaries, in the context of the taxation system in the USA. It is concluded that the interaction between tax policy and multinational financial behaviour is significant and warrants further attention. Nobes introduces a comparative perspective with expositions of the UK, French and West German imputation systems of corporation tax. Some comparative discussion of inflation adjustments for tax purposes and a review of proposals for EEC harmonization are also provided.

Transfer pricing is a significant issue for multinational corporations and govern-ments alike. Lall reviews the factors influencing the transfer pricing policy of multinational corporations, examines the evidence available and explores the implications with special reference to host governments. Burns reports on the results of a recent empirical study of transfer pricing decisions in US multinational corporations with the conclusion that a number of external pressures are influen-tial, including taxation at home and abroad, and that these pressures are positively related to the size of corporation involved.

The final issue included under the heading of transnational financial decisions concerns problems of performance evaluation and control. Shapiro provides a wide-ranging overview and guide to questions concerning the design and imple-mentation of evaluation and control systems for foreign operations. Lessard and

Lorange take up the highly significant issue of exchange rate changes in the context of budgeting and control with the argument that over-reactions to exchange risks by foreign subsidiaries with decentralized responsibility can be avoided if exchange rates can be agreed for the translation of future foreign currency revenues and expenses.

This concludes the selection of readings which it is hoped will have provided much to inform and stimulate the reader about major issues, ideas, developments and problems in this exciting and rapidly growing area of study.

PART I

The international dimensions of accounting

CHAPTER 1

Some international aspects of accounting*
R. H. Parker

The theme of this chapter is the growing importance of the international aspects of accounting. The chapter is divided into four parts since one can, I think, distinguish four different reasons why we in Britain should be interested in international accounting. I shall call them the historical reason, the multinational reason, the comparative reason and the European reason.

The historical reason

The historical reason is the least important, but it is worth remembering that modern accounting is not the invention of any one country. A number of countries have made important contributions.

   Not surprisingly leadership in accounting and financial affairs has tended to coincide with leadership in trade and industry. In so far as we can fix a date at all, modern accounting began in the Italian city states round about the year 1300. The Italians remained the leaders for over two centuries and it was as the 'Italian method of bookkeeping' that the techniques of double entry accounting spread slowly throughout Europe. The direction of the flow is neatly summed up in the second half of the title of the English edition (1547) of Jan Ympyn's *Nieuwe Instructie (New Instruction):*

> A Notable and very excellente woorke, expressyng and declaryng the maner and forme how to kepe a boke of accomptes or reconynges . . . Translated with greate Diligence out of the Italian toung into Dutche, and out of Dutche, into Frenche, and now out of Frenche into Englishe.

By the sixteenth century commercial supremacy had in fact moved to Flanders and the Netherlands, and in the writings of Simon Stevin of Bruges we find the beginnings of discounted cash flow and investment analysis. In an appendix to his *Tables of Interest* (Antwerp, 1582) he describes 'a general rule for finding which is the most profitable of two or more conditions, and by how much it is more profitable than the other'. The rule is to find the present value of each proposed condition in respect to a given rate of interest, the difference between these present values showing by how much one condition is better than the other[1].

* This article is reprinted, with permission, from *Journal of Business Finance* (Winter 1971) pp 29–36. Revised by the author in August, 1979

By the nineteenth century Britain had become the leader and it was, of course, in Scotland that the accountancy profession as we know it today first began. During the first half of the century, Scottish accountants were active as trustees of sequestrated and deceased estates. They were also engaged in the winding up of partnerships, and in the keeping and balancing of merchants' account books. The close links with the legal profession are apparent and Sir Walter Scott in a letter written in 1820 described accountancy as one of the 'branches of our legal practice'[2]. It soon became rather more than that and lawyers were no doubt no more numerate then than they are today. In any case, a Society of Accountants in Edinburgh was granted a royal charter in 1854. The Glasgow accountants followed in 1855 and the Aberdeen accountants in 1867. The English were slower[3]. Societies of accountants were formed in Liverpool and London in 1870, in Manchester in 1871 and in Sheffield in 1877. In 1880 they came together as The Institute of Chartered Accountants in England and Wales. Like the Scots their main work at first was in the field of bankruptcies, liquidations and trusteeships.

As the century progressed there was an increased emphasis on auditing, the first important text being Pixley's *Auditors: Their Duties and Responsibilities* published in London in 1881. In 1905 Richard Brown, a leading Scottish accountant, asked: 'Why should not the adjustment of an Income Tax Return of profits, where a difficulty has arisen, be left to an accountant?'[4] and during the First World War taxation replaced bankruptcy as the most important branch of work, after auditing, in most accountants' offices.

At the same time there was a growing interest in accounting as an aid to management. The most important early British work on costing, Garcke and Fells' *Factory Accounts*, written jointly by an engineer and an accountant, was first published in 1887. After the War, in 1919, associations of cost accountants were established both in Britain (the Institute of Cost and Works Accountants) and in the United States (the National Association of Cost Accountants). It was in fact to the United States that accounting as well as commercial leadership was now passing. The American accountancy profession was at first very much an offshoot of the British one[5], but it grew very quickly, especially in the fields of cost accounting and education. Richard Brown, though describing (in 1905) the US accounting profession as only about 20 years old, could yet state that:

Withal a good deal may be learned from our American cousins in matters of Accounting, more especially in the working of costing systems and in the devising of methods of bookkeeping by which the results of the trading of huge concerns are shown with a frequency and a rapidity which would astonish accountants or bookkeepers of the old-fashioned school[6].

The world owes both standard costing and direct costing mainly to the Americans[7]. The phrase 'direct costing' is used in both the French and German languages to describe the technique known in Britain by the equally misleading name of 'marginal costing'.

When the first American business school – the Wharton School of Finance and Commerce at the University of Pennsylvania – was founded in 1881, it included a professor of accounting on its staff and today there are almost certainly more university teachers of accounting and allied subjects in the United States than in the rest of the world put together.

Accounting has thus always been international in scope. My second reason, the multinational reason, is ensuring that it will become even more so.

Companies have traded outside their own national boundaries for centuries but it is only comparatively recently that the term 'multinational company' has come into common use. It is difficult to provide a precise definition of the term. A broad definition is that a multinational company is any firm which performs its main operations, either manufacture or the provision of a service, in at least two countries[8].

As soon as companies begin to trade and manufacture outside their home country accounting and financial problems arise. Some of the problems are peculiar to international operations, others are simply new versions of ones already existing at home.

The most obvious accounting problem peculiar to international activity is that of foreign currencies. Rules of 'translating' from one currency to another have had to be established. In general, one can distinguish between the 'closing rate' method in which all amounts in foreign currencies are translated at the rate ruling at the date of the balance sheet; and the 'historic rate' method in which fixed assets, depreciation, permanent investments, long-term receivables, long-term liabilities and share capital are translated at acquisition rates, current assets at closing rates, remittances at 'actual', and revenue and expenses other than depreciation at average rates.

It is interesting to note that whilst the former method appears to be growing in popularity among British companies, it has made little headway among American ones. I have suggested elsewhere the reasons for this[9]. The historic rate method is only satisfactory for major currency devaluations and revaluations at infrequent intervals if we make rather heroic assumptions about changes in local replacement costs. British companies increasingly hold their foreign assets in North America and Western Europe, where periodic rather than continual devaluation and revaluation is the norm. On the other hand, the closing rate method works very badly – and the historic rate method reasonably well – where the home country is one like the United States and the foreign country one in which inflation and devaluation are continual, as they are in those Latin American countries that invariably provide the American textbook examples.

This is an example of accounting principles being influenced by the local environment. A more universal approach, the combining of the use of current replacement costs with closing exchange rates, has been adopted by the Philips company of the Netherlands[10] and also, less systematically I suspect, by some British companies using the closing rate method.

The preceding paragraphs were written in 1971. In 1979 the position was still confused. There was no British accounting standard on a subject which became increasingly important through the 1970s. The American Financial Accounting Standards Board had (sensibly) embraced the 'temporal principle' that translations should not change underlying principles but (with much less sense) applied it to historical costs rather than current costs.

An example of a national accounting problem made more difficult by international operations is the setting of transfer prices. A great deal has been written about the problems of setting such prices within national firms. Some writers have stressed an approach based on marginal analysis; others have thought behavioural considerations to be more important[11]. At the international level, with the foreign subsidiary replacing the national division, new factors are added[12].

First, and most obviously, transfer prices can be used to minimize taxes on a world-wide basis. For example, the Report of the Committee of Enquiry into the Relationship of the Pharmaceutical Industry with the National Health Service (the 'Sainsbury Report') includes the following paragraph:

> The second difficulty about foreign-owned firms, the transfer price of raw materials or intermediates procured from foreign affiliates, is likewise an intricate one and we have reason to believe from the results of our financial questionnaire that it is of considerable importance. Foreign firms reported a much higher cost of materials as a percentage of the total cost of manufacture than did British firms and we believe that the propriety of such costs should be investigated. We are aware that the United Kingdom tax authorities have a right to investigate these transfer prices in order to ensure that foreign-owned manufacturing or distributing companies in this country (no matter in what industry) are not improperly reducing the apparent amount of their profits in the United Kingdom by inflating the transfer prices that they pay to their foreign parents. The tax authorities of other countries have and operate similar powers. We recommend that the attention of the British tax authorities should be drawn to the transfer prices of pharmaceutical raw materials or intermediates, and that the Ministry, in assessing the Standard Cost Returns of foreign-owned manufacturing companies, should make use of the ability of chemical engineers to form reasonable assessments of the production costs of chemical materials. They should be unwilling to accept the prices noted on Standard Cost Returns unless the foreign-owned firm offers confirmation of the reasonableness of its transfer prices, and the Ministry's own professional staff consider them reasonable.

Tables in the financial appendix to the report showed that British companies imported 21.6% of their materials in 1965, subsidiaries of American companies 39.0%, subsidiaries of Swiss companies 74.1% and subsidiaries of other European companies 47.1%. Materials consumed were 49.2% of the total cost of manufacture for British companies, 57.7% for American subsidiaries, 85.5% for Swiss subsidiaries and 60.0% for other European subsidiaries. For British companies profits before interest and taxation were 22.5% of sales, royalties, service charges and other trading income, for American subsidiaries 23.2%, for Swiss subsidiaries 8.7% and for other European subsidiaries 15.3%[13].

One disadvantage of relatively high transfer prices is that the larger the transfer price, the larger the import duty payable. The holding company's net gain may not therefore be very great, especially as there is a tendency, at least among the advanced industrial countries of Western Europe and North America, for tax differentials to narrow.

Secondly, transfer prices can be used to reduce exchange losses. A country suffering from balance of payments difficulties may restrict remittances of dividends, but not remittances in payment of materials or machinery imported by the subsidiary. Brooke and Remmers give the example of a financial director who explained that no dividend had been received from a couple of subsidiaries for a number of years, 'but do they ever pay through the nose when they have a mechanical breakdown!'[14].

Thirdly, transfer prices may be deliberately set low in order to provide finance for a subsidiary.

Fourthly, transfer prices can be used to shift profits, for political just as much as for tax reasons, from country to country. •

The opportunities mentioned above have their drawbacks: the expense of administration; possible trouble with tax and customs authorities; and, very importantly, adverse repercussions on the company's control system.

Arbitrary transfer prices combined with intercountry differences in accounting principles may make the reported profits of foreign subsidiaries meaningless:

> The truth is that profitability exercises in [the pharmaceutical] industry are meaningless. More than anything else profitability tends to reflect accounting practice . . .
>
> What does the rapid fall in foreign subsidiary profits since 1954 tell us? Simply that firms have begun to realize (rather late in life in some instances) that the British M.P. is extremely badly informed. He is happier with large remissions of royalties, inflated raw material costs (which effectively cheat the Exchequer) and transfer of profits to the parent represented as cost items, than he is with high profits here, with 50% going into the Exchequer and 25% going into capital investments in Britain's future[15].

The comparative reason

The third reason for studying international accounting is the comparative one. We can learn by observing how others have reacted to accounting problems which, especially in industrial nations, often do not differ very markedly from our own. We shall take just three examples.

Companies Acts

It is sometimes suggested in Britain that accounting principles and valuation methods should be written into the Companies Act or that companies should follow exactly the same rules in reporting to shareholders as they do in reporting to the Inland Revenue.

The former suggestion has already been put into practice in the German Federal Republic where the Companies Act (*Aktiengesetz*) of 1965 sets out in legal terms the familiar accounting philosophy of historical cost modified by conservatism. Section 153, for example, provides that fixed and financial assets shall be carried at the cost of acquisition or construction less depreciation or diminution in value. Section 155 prescribes the valuation of current assets at the costs of acquisition or manufacture or a lower valuation if the latter

(1) is necessary in accordance with reasonable business judgment in order to prevent the valuation of these assets from being changed in the near future as a result of fluctuations of values, or

(2) is held permissible for purposes of taxation.

It is expressly stated that such lower valuation may be retained even if the reasons for it have ceased to exist![16]

The influence of taxation law on the accounts prepared for shareholders varies from country to country. In France the rule that all deductions claimed for tax purposes must be similarly recorded in the accounts has meant that there is almost no difference between the financial statements prepared for the shareholders and those prepared for tax purposes.

In the United States, the last-in first-out method of inventory valuation can be used for tax purposes only if it is also used in the published financial statements, whereas the Canadian Anaconda case[17] has had the effect of ruling out LIFO for shareholders as well as for tax not only in Canada but also in Britain. The omission of all overheads when valuing stock-in-trade is not an accepted accounting practice in North America but it is in Britain where its use for tax purposes was approved by the House of Lords in the Duple Motor Bodies case[18].

National accounting plans

In the current debate in Britain about comparability of financial statements and uniformity of accounting principles, suggestions of reform are sometimes made which could lead to some kind of national plan or chart of accounts.

Writing in 1946, Professor Lauzel, a leading promoter of the French national accounting plan, stated that 'if one wants accounting to be a valid instrument for measuring and making comparisons over time and in space, it has to fulfil a certain number of conditions and, especially, the following:

—it must use a terminology based on precise definitions;
—it must classify facts logically according to well defined criteria;
—it must supply a general method for the recording of movements between classes of accounts;
—it must state rules as general as possible for determining the values to be recorded'[19].

A national accounting plan drawn up on lines such as these would clearly be rather more than just an exercise in bookkeeping.

The French accounting plan was first published in 1947 and revised in 1957. Its requirements are imposed by law on the nationalized industries and on state-controlled or subsidized firms and organizations. Decrees of 28 December 1959 and 13 April 1962 prescribe the eventual extension of its field of application to all industrial and commercial enterprises. A *guide comptable professionel* will be drawn up for each industry[20].

I shall not attempt to argue here whether or not we in Britain should move towards such a national accounting plan. It is worth pointing out, however, as an illustration that uniformity by itself is not enough, some of the weaknesses of French accounting.

First, as has already been noted, the influence of taxation on French accounts is much too strong. To quote Lauzel once more:

From this point of view it can appear regrettable, for example, that the accounts must obligatorily record 'fiscal' depreciation . . . that is either too low or too high in relation to standards reasonably taking account of the real factors of the wearing out of the plant and equipment. There is a similar problem for stocks, which, it must be admitted, are sometimes undervalued, sometimes overvalued, in the tax return, in relation to the principles which seem to flow from rational management concepts[21].

Secondly, uniformity has been stressed at the expense of disclosure. French balance sheets have remained very conservative documents, and consolidated financial statements were very rare until quite recently.

Thirdly, there has tended to be uniformity of method rather than of principle. For example the plan provides, without explanation, for stocks to be valued at the lower of weighted average cost and net selling price. (But this is not always observed in practice.)

Accounting for inflation

Accountants throughout the world have grappled unsatisfactorily with accounting for inflation. Nothing is finally settled yet but it does look as if the UK, the USA and France will opt for varying versions of current replacement costs based mainly on specific indices. All appeared at one stage to be moving instead towards current purchasing power accounting based on general indices[22].

The position in the UK and the USA will be familiar to readers. The German[23] and French[24] experiences have been rather different. Both demonstrate a tendency to return to historical cost accounting after the inflationary blizzard has passed.

At the end of the Second World War the German economy had collapsed completely and the then existing monetary unit, the Reichsmark (RM), was virtually worthless. It continued, however, to be used in financial statements and departure from historical cost was legally impossible. In 1948 the currency was reformed and a new monetary unit, the Deutschemark (DM) was introduced. It was followed by the DM *Eröffnungsbilanzgesetz* (literally the DM opening balance sheet law) which gave every German company a fresh start from a valuation point of view. The basic objective of the law was to restate all assets at amounts approximating current replacement cost as closely as possible. After the reform had been achieved German financial reporting reverted to the system of historical cost modified by conservatism already described. Holzer and Schönfeld comment as follows on one result of the law:

It made possible tax deductible depreciation on the basis of revalued assets; i.e., expenses could be deducted which had never been cash outlays. The resulting tax savings (the corporate tax rate was 50%) produced substantial benefits for industry and were more effective and of a more permanent nature than those accruing from accelerated depreciation measures. It goes without saying that businesses with relatively large capital investments were the main beneficiaries[25].

As is well known the German Federal Republic now has one of the strongest currencies and lowest inflation rates in the world. There seems very little likelihood that any form of inflation accounting will be permitted in West Germany.

In France from 1945 to 1959 companies were permitted (but not compelled) for tax purposes to revalue most fixed assets and also receivables and payables in foreign currencies. The revaluation had to be achieved through the use of revaluation coefficients published in the *Journal officiel*. Depreciation was based on the restated book values and was fully deductible for tax purposes. Stocks could not be revalued but a tax-free reserve for stock replacement could be established. During the 1960s French financial statements reverted to historical cost, the rise in the price level having slowed down.

The inflation of the 1970s has once again brought a limited form of inflation accounting to France. As usual it is closely linked with taxation rules.

In contrast to Germany and France, the main influence on Dutch accounting is economic theory rather than legislation. Replacement costs rather than historical costs are used by a number of important companies, although the majority use historical costs in their published accounts[26].

The European reason

These remarks lead to my fourth reason for looking at international aspects of accounting: the *European* reason. As a member of the European Economic Community Britain is increasingly affected by the EEC's progress towards harmonization of tax law and company law. The former is not very advanced but Britain's adoption of a value-added tax[27] and an imputation system of corporation tax[28] were both influenced by European models.

Harmonization of corporate financial reporting by shareholders and other users has been a long drawn out process. The Council of Ministers approved a first directive on company law harmonization in 1968[29]. The first section of the directive dealt with publicity and provided, *inter alia*, for the publication of a balance sheet and a profit and loss account for each financial period. Harmonization of the contents of these documents was, however, postponed. A draft directive on these matters was prepared and published in 1969 by a study group under the Chairmanship of Dr W. Elmendorff of the German Federal Republic[30].

The study group considered that its task was not to work out completely new regulations but rather to investigate the extent to which the various national laws could be harmonized. Their proposals, which formed the basis for the first draft of the directive, followed the German pattern of compulsory layouts and valuation rules and of disclosure varied according to company size (measured by balance sheet total, turnover and number of employees). There was no reference to a 'true and fair view'. This was added in a revised draft published after the enlargement of the Community to include the UK, Ireland and Denmark. After almost a decade of discussions the 'Fourth Council Directive of 25 July, 1978 based on Article 54(3)(g) of the Treaty on the annual accounts of certain types of companies' was at last adopted. It is an interesting compromise of German, British, French and Dutch views on company financial reporting. It has still to be incorporated into the national laws of the ten member states.

Meanwhile, second and third directives on other company law matters have also been adopted by the Council and not far away on the horizon are directives of great importance to accountants on consolidated financial statements and auditors.

British accounting is being pulled closer to continental European accounting. On the other hand, American accounting practices influence all the member states and an International Accounting Standards Committee has been formed. Other international bodies such as the United Nations are also increasingly interested in accounting.

I have tried in this chapter to give some idea of the scope of the international aspects of accounting. I have not been comprehensive. If I have left the reader with the impression of a new, exciting and relatively unexplored field of great practical importance and much academic interest, then I have succeeded in what I set out to achieve.

References

1 Stevin Simon, *Tafalen van Interest*, Antwerp: Christoffel Plantijn, 1582. The original is reprinted with a facing translation in D. J. Struik (ed.), *The Principal Works of Simon Stevin, Vol. 11A, Mathematics*, Amsterdam: C. V. Swets & Zeitlinger, 1958, pp. 25–117. The passage quoted is on p. 107 of the translation.

2 Brown, R. (ed.), *A History of Accounting and Accountants*, Edinburgh: Jack, 1905, p. 197

3 Partly because the law of bankruptcy was more advanced in Scotland than in England. See A. C. Littleton, *Accounting Evolution to 1900*, New York: American Institute Publishing Co., 1933, pp. 285–286

4 Brown, op. cit. pp. 339–340

5 Murphy, M. E., *Advanced Public Accounting Practice*, Homewood, Ill.: Irwin, 1966, Chapters 1 and 2

6 Brown, op. cit. pp. 271, 279–280

7 Solomons, D. 'The Historical Development of Costing' in his *Studies in Cost Analysis*, London: Sweet & Maxwell, 2nd end, 1968; C. Weber, *The Evolution of Direct Costing*, Urbana, Ill.: Center for International Education and Research in Accounting, 1966

8 Brooke, M. Z. and Remmers, H. L. *The Strategy of Multinational Enterprise*, London: Longman, 1970, p. 5

9 Parker, R. H. 'Principles and Practice in Translating Foreign Currencies', *Abacus*, **6**(2), December, 1970

10 Breek, P. C. 'Accounting Problems Peculiar to International Enterprises', *The New Horizons of Accounting*, Proceedings of 9th International Congress of Accountants, Paris, 1967

11 See, for example, the papers by Hirschleifer and Shillinglaw in C. P. Bonini, R. K. Jaedicke and H. M. Wagner (eds), *Management Controls*, New York: McGraw-Hill, 1964

12 Brooke and Remmers, op.cit. (note 8), especially pp. 172–176

13 *Report of the Committee of Enquiry into the Relationship of the Pharmaceutical Industry with the National Health Service 1965–1967*, London: HMSO, 1967, Cmnd. 3410. Paragraph 310, p. 84; Appendix 1, Tables 6,8, 16, pp. 102–103, 108

14 Brooke and Remmers, op.cit. p. 173

15 Cooper, M. H. *Prices and Profits in the Pharmaceutical Industry*, Oxford: Pergamon, 1966, pp. 39–40

16 The text of the Act in German and English can be found in R. Mueller and E. G. Galbraith (eds and translators), *The German Stock Corporation Law*, Bilingual edition with Introduction, Frankfurt am Main: Fritz Knapp Verlag, 1966

17 Minister of National Revenue v. Anaconda American Brass, Ltd. (1956) A.C. 85 P.C.

18 Ostime v. Duple Motor Bodies, Ltd. (1961) 1 W.L.R. 739 (H.L.)

19 *Conseil national de la comptabilité, Plan comptable général*, Paris: Imprimerie nationale, 1965, Introduction, p. 11; also, P. Lauzel, *Le plan comptable français*, Paris: Presses Universitaires de France, 2nd edn, 1967, pp. 15–16

20 The text of the decrees is given in the 1965 printing of the Plan. See also Lauzel, op.cit. (note 19), Chapter 4

21 Lauzel, op.cit. pp. 103–104

22 Kirkman, P. R. A. *Accounting under Inflationary Conditions*, London: George Allen & Unwin, 2nd ed. 1978, especially Chapters 13 and 14

23 Holzer, H. P. and Shönfeld, H. M. 'The German Solution of the Post-War Price Level Problem', *Accounting Review*, April 1963, reprinted in Berg, Mueller and Walker, *Readings in International Accounting*, Boston: Houghton Mifflin, 1969

24 See, for example, L. Petit, *Le bilan dans les entreprises*, Paris: Presses Universitaires de France, 5th ed, 1967, Chapter 2

25 Berg, Mueller and Walker, op.cit. p. 251

26 Beeny, J. H. and Chastney, J. G. *European Financial Reporting. 4. The Netherlands*, London: Institute of Chartered Accountants in England and Wales, 1978. Chapter III

27 Value-added Tax, Cmnd. 4621, 1971

28 Reform of Corporation Tax, Cmnd. 4630, 1971, para. 10

29 *Journal officiel*, No. L.65, 14 March, 1968

30 *Proposal for a directive to coordinate, with a view to making them equivalent, the guarantees demanded in the Member-States from companies within the meaning of article 58, 2nd paragraph, of the Treaty of Rome for the purpose of protecting the interests both of the members of such companies and of third parties. Annual financial reports (form and valuation); contents of the notes and the report of management; audit by an accountant and publication.* Dusseldorf: Verlagsbuchhandlung des Instituts der Wirtschaftsprüfer GmbH., 1969. See also W. Elmendorff's article, 'Coordination of the legal accounting requirements in the various countries of the European Economic community', *Journal UEC*, October, 1967.

CHAPTER 2

Multinational challenges for managerial accountants*
Frederick D. S. Choi

Accounting traditionally has been a dynamic discipline. Historically, accounting responded in positive fashion to environmental developments such as the industrial revolution, the growth of the joint-stock form of business organization and, more recently, to developments in the areas of management and computer science. Since accounting is also a service activity designed to facilitate the information needs of decision makers, both internal and external to the firm, it must remain responsive to the ever-changing needs of its users if it is to maintain its social utility.

An environmental phenomenon which currently is testing the vitality of the accounting discipline is the multinational company. Spawned within the past two decades, these companies today are confronting accountants with problems of no small proportion. But, while the external reporting dimensions of multinational business have received much attention in the literature,[1] little has been accorded the attendant managerial accounting dimensions.[2] This paper accordingly seeks to fill this void by identifying some of the problem areas and issues which the multinational company is posing for managerial accountants.

MULTINATIONAL COMPANY AND MANAGEMENT ACCOUNTING

Before proceeding to specific issues, it might be good to define what it is we are talking about. Just what is a multinational company and what do we mean by the term "management accounting"?

Put simply, a multinational company is one which engages in business or financing transactions which transcend national boundaries. In an expanded sense, a multinational concern is one in which global thinking

* This article is reprinted, with permission, from *Journal of Contemporary Business* (Autumn 1975) pp 51–67

and organization supplants a purely domestic orientation, where international matters often assume a "low profile." From this enlarged perspective, subsidiary companies are viewed not as mere appendages or independent satellites of the parent company, but as parts of an integrated system whose aims are to optimize both global and local objectives. Productive resources--financial, human and natural--are secured wherever in the world they are the least expensive and employed in those locations where their productivity is greatest.[3]

However, this description is idealistic, as few companies today meet these criteria in their entirety. In fact, one should envision a spectrum of degrees of multinationalism with extreme points representing entirely domestic enterprises and "pure" multinational enterprises. An evolutionary movement is apparent along the spectrum as companies acquire more of the attributes of multinationalism."[4]

It also should be noted at the outset that the concept of managerial accounting entertained here does not incorporate the traditional notion of accounting for enterprise costs. For cost accounting concepts are, to a large extent, the same both domestically and internationally. Instead, we are concerned with the newer strategic area of managerial planning and control systems, for it is here that significant international challenges are making themselves felt.

The foregoing implies that managerial accounting exists to provide information inputs to some decision process. Therefore, it would seem appropriate to examine managerial accounting issues from the perspective of enterprise managers in the multinational company.

INTERNATIONAL FINANCIAL MANAGEMENT

In this respect, the spread of business beyond national boundaries has fostered mutations of domestic management specialities. These have been necessitated by the additional variables and constraints which typify the international dimension. Foreign currency exchange risks; restrictions on fund remittances across national borders; conflicting national tax laws; interest rate differentials in various national financial markets; the global shortage of money capital; and the effects of worldwide inflation on enterprise assets, earnings and capital costs are just a sample of variables calling for specialized knowledge among financial executives.

A direct response to such environmental complexities has been the
emergence of the international financial management function. A recent
conference board study reveals that more than half of the companies queried
reported having a specially designated executive concerned solely with
financial management of international operations. What is more, the
trend in this direction is definitely on the increase.[5]

In view of the recent emergence of this managerial speciality, the scope
of the present paper will be limited to a description of some of the
major international financial management issues and their accounting
implications. As engineers of information support systems for financial
decision-making within the firm, managerial accountants have a strategic
interest in the resolution and outcome of such issues.

Specific problem areas examined in the following sections include those
dealing with (1) foreign exchange risk management, (2) consolidation
of enterprise accounts, (3) investment planning, (4) external financial
sourcing, (5) international taxation, (6) transfer pricing, (7) performance
evaluation and (8) information and control systems.

FOREIGN EXCHANGE RISKS

A risk dimension unique to international business is the risk of loss
due to changes in the value of national currencies in which financial
transactions are denominated. Thus, a U. S. parent operating a wholly
owned subsidiary in France, whose assets are denominated in French francs,
experiences a foreign currency translation gain or loss in terms of U. S.
dollars whenever the value of the French franc appreciates or depreciates
relative to the dollar. Since foreign currency amounts typically are
translated to their domestic currency equivalents, either for management
review or external financial reporting purposes, the "translation"
gain or loss in this case would be reflected on the financial statements
of the U. S. parent.

Currency fluctuations often have been quite pronounced in the past.
Consequently, a major objective of international financial management
is to minimize such risks. Risk management techniques in this regard
include (1) those used to forecast exchange rate movements and the

magnitude of possible losses and (2) compensating strategies designed to hedge such exchange risks. However, great disagreement exists as to which device is best. Those supporting exchange rate forecasting as the superior risk management technique operate under the premise that decision makers in the firm have the capability to outperform the market as a whole when it comes to predicting exchange rate movements. However, those opposing this alternative argue that foreign exchange markets, in a world where exchange rates are free to fluctuate, are "efficient" markets. Accordingly, attempts to predict future rate movements are, for all practical purposes, futile.[6]

Hedging techniques are equally controversial as financial managers and accountants still do not agree on how best to measure the concept of exposure. For example, under conventional translation methods, a foreign subsidiary's current assets and liabilities are translated to their domestic currency equivalents using the rate of exchange prevailing at the time the financial statements are prepared. Noncurrent items are translated using the rate which prevailed when those items were acquired/incurred.[7] Under these translation rules, a parent company's exposure would be measured by the net current asset position of the foreign subsidiary. Assuming that the rate of exchange between the foreign currency (FC) and the dollar were to decline from FC4 to $1 to FC5 to $1, the potential foreign exchange loss on a firm's exposed current assets of FC100 would be $5. This is illustrated below:

Current Assets	FC 150	
Current Liabilities	50	
Exposure	FC 100	
Predevaluation rate (FC4 to $1)	FC100 =	$25
Postdevaluation rate (FC5 to $1)	FC100 =	20
Potential foreign exchange loss		$ 5

Appropriate hedging policies then would be taken to offset this potential loss. This would be accomplished by decreasing FC-denominated assets and/or increasing FC-denominated liabilities. Any remaining exposure then might be covered in the forward exchange market.

However, critics of such an exposure concept are quick to point out that while the foregoing measures "accounting" exposure, it may not really measure a firm's exposure in an "economic" sense.[8] Thus, assume that

the foregoing example refers to a foreign subsidiary which obtains all
of its labor and materials in its domestic economy and, in turn, sells
its entire output abroad. In this instance, a significant devaluation
might very well improve the subsidiary's FC revenues by making its goods
cheaper in terms of other foreign currencies. That is, the firm either
could maintain its product prices in terms of the foreign currency,
thereby increasing its FC receipts by the devaluation percentage, or
it could lower the FC price and, presumably, increase its sales volume.
In turn, the devaluation would have no appreciable effect on the cost
of its factor inputs. Thus, the profitability of the subsidiary conceivably would increase rather than decline because of the devaluation,
and there would be little economic justification for the translation
loss shown.

Controversies such as these, while far from settled, have direct managerial accounting implications. Subscription to exchange rate forecasting
as a promising risk reduction technique entails development of comprehensive information systems. These systems must be capable of gathering
and processing substantial amounts of information relating to factors
affecting currency stability to ensure financial managers a "superior"
source of information on which to base their forecasts. On the other
hand, hedging techniques call for the construction of measurement
techniques which reflect more realistic approaches to the valuation of
assets and liabilities after changes in exchange rates. Therefore,
much remains to be done in this facet of multinationalism by the management accountant.

CONSOLIDATION ISSUES

Coupled with the problem of measuring foreign exchange risks is the
need to consolidate the results of a multinational company's foreign
operations. Shareholders, creditors and other external user groups
desire, in general, a single frame of reference for company operations
regardless of geographic origin. Since consolidated statements can be
presented only in terms of a single currency unit, currency translation
procedures are called for that transform foreign currency into domestic
currency statements.

During the "premultinational era," foreign operations generally were
conceived of from a national point of view. International activities

during this period were confined largely to import and export operations. The limited investments existing outside the home country generally were made to facilitate trading activities or to participate in profits that could be remitted readily in dollars to the U. S. parent. Under these circumstances, currency translation techniques favoring a "home country perspective" seemed both logical and desirable.

Assumptions such as these no longer appear tenable for the multinational company. As mentioned earlier, foreign subsidiaries are no longer being viewed as mere "step-child" operations; rather, they are seen as strategic components of an integrated corporate network. Worldwide economies of operation and organizational control are increasingly becoming primary influences affecting the distribution policies of foreign direct investments abroad. In short, foreign investments are being viewed as permanent in nature, with remittances of foreign earnings no longer being a primary objective. Given these developments, existing translation methods are becoming increasingly suspect.[9]

Even if one could resolve the foregoing issue, the problem of how to account for translation adjustments which arise during the consolidation process still would exist. Translation adjustments refer to the effects, in the reporting currency, of a change in foreign exchange rates on the carrying value of enterprise net assets denominated in terms of the foreign currency. While the mechanics of translation adjustments are straightforward, the nature of the resultant figure is obscure. Thus, is a translation adjustment arising from a change in the translation rate (1)a gain or a loss, (2)an adjustment of the costs of imports or revenue from exports, (3)an adjustment of borrowing costs or returns from lending or (4)an adjustment of owners' equity? If one regards the adjustment as a "gain or loss," should it then be taken immediately into income or should it be deferred? Advocates of immediate recognition are generally frustrated by the absence of any clear-cut criterion on which to base the needed attendant realization concept. Those advocating deferral of foreign exchange gains, for lack of realization, are usually in a quandry as to the amount of the gain to be deferred. Indeed, in those instances where foreign affiliates have no intention of repatriating funds to the parent company, the concept of realization becomes extremely nebulous. In cases such as these one wonders whether the realization concept has any meaning at all!

Another consolidation problem which promises to test the ingenuity of
managerial accountants is how to incorporate the effects of foreign inflation in the consolidated accounts. Foreign inflation is of particular
interest to statement readers concerned with multinational operations
as (1)it often occurs at different rates from those of the parent country,
(2)the prices that are changing are foreign prices rather than domestic
prices and (3)inflation abroad is related to movements in foreign exchange rates. In these circumstances, is it better first to restate
foreign account balances to reflect the effects of foreign inflation
and then to translate the results to the currency of the parent country?
Or, is it better first to translate the accounts to their domestic
currency equivalents and then adjust the accounts to reflect the effects
of inflation? The issue remains unsettled, with proponents of each
approach continuing to argue the conceptual merits of one construct over
the other.[10]

FINANCIAL PLANNING

Financial planning in the multinational enterprise also poses additional
challenges for the managerial accountant. While financial planning
processes at home are conceptually similar to those in the international
sphere, the latter are much more difficult to administer because of the
expanded number of decision variables that make up the financial manager's
decision set.

Consider, for example, the area of investment planning. Owing to significant advances in the areas of financial management theory, sophisticated procedures now exist for determining a firm's optimum capital
structure; measuring a firm's cost of capital; and evaluating investment
alternatives under conditions of uncertainty. When we enter the international arena, investment planning quickly becomes a "mission impossible."
Considerations such as differential tax laws, differential rates of
inflation, risks of expropriation, fluctuating exchange rates, exchange
controls, restrictions on the transferability of foreign earnings and
language and intercultural differences all add a degree of complexity
not usually found under more homogeneous and stable domestic conditions.
Add to this the difficulty of quantifying such data and the problem
quickly magnifies. For example, how does one adjust and measure the
expected returns of a foreign investment opportunity where inflation,
a depreciating foreign currency, and exchange controls are the rule

rather than the exception? Assuming this problem is resolved, should the investing company then consider local country rates of return, investor country rates of return or both? If foreign investments are evaluated in the context of the present value model, then an appropriate discount rate must be developed. While a company's cost of capital is utilized in the domestic decision model, should the same hold in the multinational case? If a substantial portion of the money capital required to undertake a foreign investment were supplied by the parent corporation, should the cost of capital of the parent company be used or should this discount rate be altered to reflect the additional risk associated with the foreign investment? To cite another consideration, if a foreign affiliate's financing plan calls for more expensive debt or equity financing than is available to the parent firm elsewhere, should this additional cost be reflected in a higher company-wide cost of capital, or should the incremental financing cost be absorbed by the subsidiary in the form of higher required periodic cash returns? Indeed, does debt financing abroad which exceeds borrowing norms in the home country necessarily raise the company-wide cost of capital when under- taken to hedge against foreign exchange risks abroad?

Considerations such as these are far from academic. In the absence of information systems which capture these extranational considerations, it is not surprising that many firms investing abroad have been forced to rely on tools designed for domestic analyses. This would appear to be a less than satisfactory state of affairs.

EXTERNAL SOURCING

Multinational investment plans necessitate the accumulation of massive sums of money capital for their implementation. Owing to a shortage of money capital internationally, planning for external financing sourcing is assuming a strategic role in the competitive calculus of the multi- national enterprise.

Sources of funds for direct investments abroad can be classified into the familiar internal/external framework. As one might expect, internal financing modes internationally are generally not unlike those employed in a strictly uninational setting. However, once external financing is entertained, multinational financing alternatives are expanded quickly both in number and scope. In addition to borrowing in domestic financial markets, external sourcing can take the form of joint business venture arrangements with foreign owners, borrowing in the financial markets of foreign affiliates and entry to the international capital markets.

Raising funds abroad offers certain opportunities to borrowing enterprises, the benefits of which need to be measured and communicated to financial managers. However, foreign borrowing is not without attendant risks. Thus, a Belgian subsidiary of a U. S. parent borrowing deutch marks from a German bank and then converting the proceeds to Belgian francs for working capital purposes would experience a significant increase in its debt burden if the German mark appreciated in value relative to the franc prior to the loan's maturity. While such risks may be hedged in the forward exchange markets, these facilities are not always available when needed. Therefore, such risks require constant appraisal on the part of international financial managers and their accountants.

Borrowing in foreign financial markets also requires an awareness of the diversity of financing instruments which exist internationally. While many of these instruments are common to several countries, their availability, relative costs and repayment terms can vary significantly between countries. For example, an overdraft is essentially a short-term line of credit arrangement, popularized in Europe, which allows a borrower to write checks in excess of existing deposit balances up to some predetermined limit. But while this credit facility is probably the cheapest and most extensively used form of short-term credit in the United Kingdom, it is probably the most expensive form of short-term credit in Belgium.

A recent innovation in the international financial environment has been the emergence of the Euro-currency market; Euro-currencies refer to foreign currencies owned and held outside the country of issue. The market has expanded rapidly and now offers most of the credit facilities available in most sophisticated money and capital markets, with the exception that it is unregulated, international in scope and multicurrency in nature! Borrowing in such a market adds another dimension to the financial manager's information needs. Sophisticated answers must be sought for questions ranging from the choice of a particular financing instrument to desirable financial reporting formats for transnational investor

groups, not to mention the choice of currencies in which to denominate
one's debts.

The spectrum of external financing possibilities just identified are
far from exhaustive because financial markets are in a constant
state of flux. Indeed, within just a short time after the market's
inception, many of the conditions giving rise to the Euro-currency
capital market have ceased to exist.[11] Newer developments in international finance, such as the massive cash payments flowing to the OPEC
nations and the recent emergence of an "Asia-dollar" market, suggest
that the Middle East and Pacific Basin are assuming importance as
new financial centers to be reckoned with. In an area where *change* is
likely to be the only *constant*, the burden is on management accountants
to monitor constantly new developments on the international financial
scene.

INTERNATIONAL TAXATION

Tax planning is undoubtedly one of the most difficult yet vitally important aspects of a financial executive's job as it impacts on so many
business activities of a firm. This process becomes an even more complex
affair when extended to multinational business operations. Being an
instrument of national economic policy, tax systems worldwide are understandably as diverse as the political entities which create them.

For example, a company operating abroad incurs a variety of taxes ranging from direct taxes, such as the corporate income and capital gains
taxes, to numerous indirect taxes, such as value-added taxes, border
taxes, net worth taxes and withholding taxes. In addition, tax rates
vary from country to country. Thus, while the corporate income tax
rate is close to 50 percent in the United States, it may range any-
where from as low a figure as zero in Bermuda and other tax-haven countries
to as high as 60 percent in a country like Libya.[12] Tax collection
systems also vary internationally. Systems which appear most prevalent
include (1)the classical system--where corporate taxes are levied at
a single rate and dividends then are taxed as income to shareholders
at their personal income tax rates, (2)the split-rate system--where
corporate taxes are levied at two different rates depending on whether
enterprise earnings are distributed or retained and (3)the tax credit

or imputation system--whereby a corporate tax is levied on enterprise income at one rate with part of the tax paid being allowed as a tax credit against the income tax on dividends.[13]

To add to the complexity, financial managers need to be aware of special tax provisions applicable to international operations as they often help or hinder multinational companies. Included here would be things such as bilateral tax treaties between countries which seek to avoid double taxation of the same corporate income by each country and regional tax incentives granted by host governments to encourage certain kinds of businesses to locate within their borders.

Therefore, a necessary ingredient of any successful tax planning program is an information system which is capable of keeping financial managers apprised of all relevant international tax variables that impact on their decisions. This' is especially important in the international sphere as tax laws and regulations of individual countries are changing constantly. Changes in one country's tax provisions often affect the relative advantages and disadvantages in a multinational tax network. And, since tax minimization policies of one subsidiary often can have unintended consequences elsewhere in the network, the effects of such policies need to be traced throughout the entire system before final decisions are made. Computerized tax simulation models designed to optimize a company's global tax bill are promising innovations in this regard.

As a minimum, tax planning information systems should enable financial managers to access information on variables such as features of the various domestic and foreign tax systems, tax base definitions employed internationally, tax treaties, legal structure of the parent and subsidiaries, policies on the movement of funds within the corporate system and risks of currency inconvertibility. Without such support systems, it is little wonder that many view the complexities of international tax planning as overwhelming. Until this situation is corrected, effective international tax planning will continue to be a major bottleneck for many multinational companies.

A problem area which parallels the taxation issue in complexity is the pricing of goods, services and technology between affiliates of the multinational enterprise. The dimensions of the problem become readily apparent when one recognizes that international transfer pricing (1)lacks any theoretical or operationally optimum solutions, (2)is affected by a larger number of environmental variables than is true of a strictly domestic setting, (3)affects social, economic and political relation-ships in entire countries, (4) varies from company to company, industry to industry and country to country and (5)is conducted on a relatively larger scale internationally than it is domestically.

In a uninational setting, transfer pricing is employed to facilitate the control and evaluation of operations and to motivate divisional managers toward achieving corporate-wide goals. In the multinational sphere, added considerations such as taxes, tariffs, fluctuating currencies, inflation, economic restrictions on fund transfers and political insta-bilities, complicate transfer pricing policy objectives. In addition, the aforementioned considerations involve tradeoffs that need to be weighed and decided carefully.

Consider the influence of the corporate income tax. Other things being the same, profits for the corporate system can be maximized by using high transfer prices to siphon profits out of subsidiaries domiciled in coun-tries with high taxes and by using low transfer prices to move profits to subsidiaries located in low tax countries. Unfortunately, other things are not the same, and this practice often evokes problems which may offset any perceived advantages. Governments faced with a potential loss of tax revenues, owing to the tax avoidance policies of corporate taxpayers, often will take steps to counteract such measures. For example, Section 482 of the U. S. Internal Revenue Code gives the U. S. Treasury the right to reallocate gross income, deductions, credits or other allowances among related corporations in order to prevent tax evasion or to reflect more clearly a "proper" allocation of income. Many other countries have allocation provisions similar to those of the United States. Internally, transfer pricing schemes designed to mini-mize global taxes often cause abberations in subsidiary operating re-sults. This, in turn, often leads to conflicting goals and dysfunctional decisions on the part of subsidiary managers.[14]

In similar fashion, currency exchange restrictions may be sidestepped
and losses from currency devaluations may be avoided by shifting funds
to the parent or related affiliates through inflated transfer prices.
Here again, tradeoffs need to be considered as expected benefits of the
action and need to be weighed against the higher taxes resulting from
increased revenues accruing to the parent or related affiliates.

When the simultaneous effects of environmental factors on transfer
prices are considered, additional problems arise. Thus, how should
transfer prices be established? Is a standard market price preferable
to full cost or cost plus a percentage markup? Or, is a negotiated
price the only feasible alternative? Assuming this problem is solved,
should transfer pricing policies then be standardized among all countries,
or should they be country-specific? Should there be different transfer
prices for different purposes? Here again is another challenge to the
management accountant.

Performance Evaluation

In the domestic case, company activities typically are organized as
independent profit or investment centers. Under these decentralized
systems, subsidiary managers are accorded the necessary authority to
engage in decisions directly affecting their spheres of activity. Under
these conditions, numerical measures of performance, such as rate of
return statistics, are highly useful and appropriate.

Internationally, such evaluation systems are seldom functional. To
begin, foreign operations often are established for strategic reasons,
many of which do not lend themselves to precise quantitative measures.
For example, a manager of a major oil company might not want to risk
being left out of a foreign market that one of the competitors is exploring even if the expected returns may prove to be negative when discounted
to their present value equivalents. In addition, many of the major
decisions affecting the profitability of the foreign subsidiary often
are made by central headquarters. Centralized control over investment
policy, external financial sourcing and transfer prices are examples
in this regard. Then, too, many variables affecting the reported
performance of subsidiary operations are usually beyond the control of
the respective manager. For example, government restrictions on remittances on invested capital may greatly affect some subsidiaries and

not others. Required minimum capitalization ratios in various countries often bias subsidiary rate-of-return calculations by inflating the investment base against which earnings are compared. As a final example, fluctuating exchange rates which are beyond a subsidiary manager's control also may have a significant effect on reported performance

Under these conditions, alternative evaluation schemes for appraising foreign operations appear necesssary. And yet, empirical studies have revealed that most companies operating abroad continue to evaluate their foreign subsidiaries on precisely the same basis as their domestic subsidiaries![15] Additional research and experimentation seem urgently needed on this aspect of managerial accounting for the multinational company.

Information Systems

Previous sections of this paper suggest that international financial managers require an expanded and more sophisticated information base than their domestic counterpart. This is attributable largely to environmental complexities--cultural, social, economic and political--which often impede simple and effective financial information flows. Language barriers and geographical distances complicate these flows even further. Therefore, financial executives are concerned not only with the type of information they receive, but also with the related systems through which such information is gathered and communicated.

Here again financial managers confront a dilemma. On the one hand, a firm entering the multinational arena desires information systems facilitating centralized control over its new international empire. Yet, for political, motivational and perhaps cultural reasons, it wants (and needs) to be oriented locally. Business climates and earnings potentials abroad are often better if foreign affiliates shed the image of foreign control. In some instances, a host country orientation even may be required by local statute.[16]

Thus, differences of opinion exist as to the type of information system needed to facilitate multinational business information flows. For example, some business experts argue that information and control systems employed domestically are equally applicable abroad.[17] For all practical purposes, this may very well be a good starting point for firms just venturing into the multinational business arena. It makes good sense from a financial consolidation perspective and is no doubt cheaper to install than an entirely new system designed from scratch.

However, others feel that what is needed are tailor-made information systems which are developed to accommodate the enlarged outlook of the multinational enterprise.[18] An extention of this proposal incorporates a "fresh start" approach which attempts to develop systems with truly global orientations (systems not oriented to decentralized parent-country operations) almost from the ground up. From this perspective, "financial control in multinational companies is more than control, it is financial coordination."[19]

However, these positions appear ill-suited to the polycentric modes (host-country orientation) which presently characterize the organizational patterns of the great majority of international business firms. These organizations recognize and thrive on international diversity. Their policies permit substantial degrees of local autonomy for foreign affiliates, with communications being largely of the two-way variety. In these circumstances, local managers in host countries need different decision information than headquarters management is likely to require for control purposes.[20] Therefore, what seems needed are expanded accounting systems capable of satisfying different but parallel information needs. Management accountants should aid in designing information systems which incorporate data retaining their local characteristics and, yet, which can be aggregated to satisfy more global points of view. Such systems, in short, should be programmed to enable enterprise managers to optimize centralized financial control as well as local autonomy and comparability. This would appear to be far better than adoption of a single, centralized global information system which is strange to everyone, particularly those at the subsidiary level.

CONCLUSIONS

Multinational enterprises differ in many respects from their purely domestic counterparts and are calling forth new innovations in business and financial management processes. Management accountants as information specialists internal to the firm are in an excellent position to assist in developing and implementing information systems which will aid in resolving many dilemmas currently confronting international financial executives.

34 Whether accountants will respond to their new managerial challenges remains to be seen. However, we observe that only a decade and a half ago most accountants were, by and large, indifferent to the international dimensions of accounting and financial reporting. This seems a far cry from the present environment in which international financial reporting standards are being courted seriously by the leading professional accountancy bodies worldwide! Thus, there is every reason to expect that accounting will hurdle successfully the challenges posed by the development of multinational companies.

FOOTNOTES

[1]For example, see K. Kubin and G. G. Mueller, *A Bibliography of International Accounting* (Seattle, Washington: University of Washington, Graduate School of Business Administration, 1974).

[2]A noteworthy exception is the recent report of the Committee on International Accounting of the American Accounting Association, reprinted as *An Introduction to Financial Control and Reporting in Multinational Enterprises*, ed., G. M. Scott (University of Texas at Austin, Graduate School of Business, Bureau of Business Research, 1973).

[3]H. Perlmutter, "The Tortuous Evolution of the Multinational Company," *Columbia Journal of World Business* (January-February 1969), pp. 9-18.

[4]Scott, *Financial Control,* p. 5.

[5]I. W. Meister, *Managing the International Financial Function* (New York: The Conference Board, 1970), pp. 1-2.

[6]G. Dufey, "Corporate Financial Policies and Floating Exchange Rates," (unpublished manuscript).

[7]American Institute of Certified Public Accountants, *Accounting Research Bulletin No. 43* (New York: AICPA, 1953), Ch. 12, pars. 8 & 9.

[8]For an excellent description of the concept of economic versus accounting exposure, see G. Dufey, "Corporate Finance and Exchange Rate Variations," *Financial Management* (Summer 1972), pp. 51-57.

[9]G. G. Mueller, "Are Traditional Foreign Exchange Translation Methods Obsolete?" *California Management Review* (Summer 1965), pp. 41-46.

[10]The dimensions of this controversy are treated in another piece by the author entitled, "Price Level Adjustments and Foreign Currency Translation-- Newlyweds or Reluctant Bedfellows?" *The International Journal of Accounting.* (Fall 1975).

[11]W. T. Gregor, et al., "Changes in International Capital Markets," *Financial Executive* (November 1974), pp. 50-62.

[12]Ernst and Ernst, *Foreign Corporate Income and Withholding Tax Rates, January 1975* (International Business Series, Author, 1975).

[13]J. F. Chown, *Taxation and Multinational Enterprises* (London: Longman Group Ltd., 1974).

[14]J. S. Shulman, "Transfer Pricing in the Multinational Firm," *European Business* (January 1969), pp. 46-54.

[15]S. M. Robbins and R. B. Stobaugh, "The Bent Measuring Stick for Foreign Subsidiaries," *Harvard Business Review* (September-October 1973).

[16]G. G. Mueller, "Accounting for Multinational Companies," *Cost and Management* (July-August 1971), p. 2.

[17]H. C. Knortz, "Controllership in International Corporations," *Financial Executive* (June 1969), pp. 54-60.

[18]D. E. Hawkins, "Controlling Foreign Operations," *Financial Executive* (February 1965), p. 26.

[19]G. M. Scott, "Financial Control in Multinational Enterprise," *International Journal of Accounting* (Spring 1972), pp. 55-68.

[20]Mueller, "Multinational Companies."

PART II

Comparative international accounting

CHAPTER 3

Environmental factors influencing the development of accounting objectives, standards and practices in Peru*

Lee H. Radebaugh

Accounting is a multifaceted discipline that is often divided into three major areas: enterprise accounting (both financial and managerial), government accounting, and social or macro accounting (that is, national income accounts). Specialized facets of accounting — such as tax accounting — also can be accorded special status. Not only do objectives, standards, and practices vary somewhat among these major areas in a given country, but they also vary in any given area — such as enterprise accounting — when comparing different countries. The purpose of this paper is to discuss the major environmental factors that influence the development of accounting objectives, standards, and practices and to illustrate these ideas with current developments in Peru.

The study of accounting in other countries can be of a descriptive, conceptual, or hypothesis-testing nature.[1] The descriptive approach is by far the most common and involves a discussion of the current state

* Lee H. Radebaugh is an assistant professor of international business at the Pennsylvania State University. He earned his B.S. degree at Brigham Young University, and M.B.A. and D.B.A. degrees at Indiana University. Professor Radebaugh has written extensively in the international business and accounting fields and has had overseas experience. The accounting disclosure of foreign currency transactions constitutes a major part of his current research. Professor Radebaugh has just completed an extensive educational assignment in accounting in Peru.
[1] B. L. Jaggi, "Accounting Studies of Developing Countries: An Assessment," *International Journal of Accounting* (Fall 1973): 160-61.

* This article is reprinted, with permission, from *The International Journal of Accounting: Education and Research* (Fall 1975) pp 39–56

of the art. Current developments in enterprise accounting as well as a discussion of the accounting profession are most frequently presented. The development of a conceptual framework adds a level of sophistication by permitting dynamic as well as static comparisons of accounting. Hypothesis testing is more difficult to employ and involves testing against reality certain hypotheses about which principles and practices ought to be in a country.

A CONCEPTUAL FRAMEWORK

Accounting is basically a process of identifying, recording, and interpreting economic events, and its goals and purposes should be clearly stated in the objectives of any accounting system. The Financial Accounting Standards Board (FASB) is currently wrestling with a discussion memorandum entitled "Conceptual Framework for Accounting and Reporting." The basis for the discussion memorandum is a report of the study group on the *Objectives of Financial Statements* released by the American Institute of Certified Public Accountants (AICPA) in October 1973.

As pointed out by the study group, these objectives provide the basis for developing accounting and reporting standards which in turn lead to specific practices. The objectives, standards, and practices are or should be heavily influenced by the definitive needs of users.[2] Exhibit 1 illustrates how this process is linked. The process is dynamic in that needs often change over time, leading to changes in objectives, standards, and practices. As emphasized by AlHashim, "If the purpose changes, economic events can be defined differently and alternative accounting methods and reports prescribed."[3]

The question of whether a uniform set of accounting standards and practices exists for all classes of users worldwide or even for one class of users worldwide has been widely discussed, and no consensus of opinion has been reached. The answer to this question depends a great deal on understanding the major factors that influence the development of accounting objectives, standards, and practices. Exhibit 2 is an attempt to identify these major factors.[4] The first four factors deal

---

[2] Accounting Objectives Study Group, *Objectives of Financial Statements* (New York: American Institute of Certified Public Accountants, 1973), p. 15.
[3] Dhia D. AlHashim, "Accounting Control through Purposive Uniformity: An International Perspective," *International Journal of Accounting* (Spring 1973): 21.
[4] The author acknowledges the efforts of Professor Reginald Jägerhorn in a preliminary attempt to develop a model on factors having an impact on financial reporting practices. See Reginald Jägerhorn, "Some Aspects of Inter-

Exhibit 1. The Evolution of Accounting and Reporting Practices

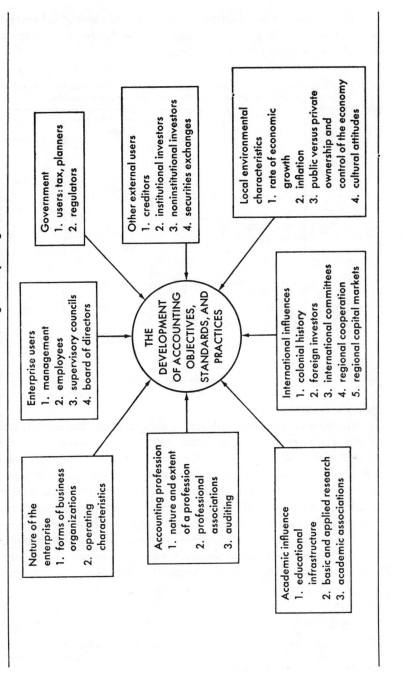

41

Nature of the enterprise
1. forms of business organizations
2. operating characteristics

Enterprise users
1. management
2. employees
3. supervisory councils
4. board of directors

Government
1. users: tax, planners
2. regulators

Other external users
1. creditors
2. institutional investors
3. noninstitutional investors
4. securities exchanges

Local environmental characteristics
1. rate of economic growth
2. inflation
3. public versus private ownership and control of the economy
4. cultural attitudes

THE DEVELOPMENT OF ACCOUNTING OBJECTIVES, STANDARDS, AND PRACTICES

Accounting profession
1. nature and extent of a profession
2. professional associations
3. auditing

Academic influence
1. educational infrastructure
2. basic and applied research
3. academic associations

International influences
1. colonial history
2. foreign investors
3. international committees
4. regional cooperation
5. regional capital markets

42

with the nature of the enterprise and the direct users of information, whereas the last four represent other major factors that affect accounting objectives, principles, and practices.

Exhibit 2. Major Factors Influencing the Development of Accounting Objectives, Standards, and Practices: Domestically and Worldwide

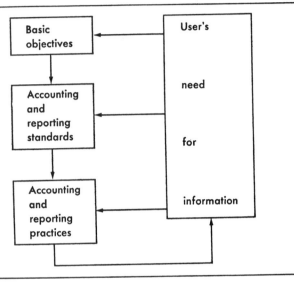

Nature of the Enterprise

The same major forms of business organizations exist in most parts of the world: proprietorships, partnerships, and corporations. Ownership of enterprises can be either broadly based as is characteristic of the United States, state owned, or family centered as is the case in many developing countries. Historically, Peru fits in the latter category. Family-owned businesses tend to be very secretive and rely more on a bookkeeping type of accountability. Very few firms have broad investor ownership. Government enterprises are becoming a more important part of the economy as the military regime continues to nationalize major industries. The increasingly prevalent role of the government in the economy and eventually in accounting will be the final of the eight major factors to be discussed.

Enterprises vary in size as well as form. Although it can be argued

national Accounting with Special Emphasis on Scandinavian Reporting Practices," *Preliminara Forskningsrapporter* (Helsinki, Finland: Swedish School of Economics and Business Administration, 1973).

that information is required for all firms regardless of size or form of organization, the nature and extent of that information may be quite different. Different types of industries as well as different operating techniques give rise to special problems. There is a vigorous debate among professionals in accounting as well as in taxation on proper methods of treating discovery costs in extractive industries.[5] In Peru special accounting rules exist for three types of industries that are crucial to the Peruvian economy: mining, petroleum, and fishing. In the United States the prevalence of leasing requires special standards and principles to account for this type of operating technique, just as special principles exist for installment sales and for revenue recognition in long-term projects where percentage of completion is relevant.

Enterprise Users

Within the enterprise there are many users of information. The quantity and quality of information provided depends on the level of sophistication of the users as well as the technical competence of the accountants. Managers require specialized information to assist in decision making, and a whole branch of accounting has resulted from this need.

Employees have a vested interest in the enterprise and may have an impact on the disclosure of financial data. This can be made manifest through unions that require certain types of information prior to the negotiation of labor contracts. An important social change that has taken place in Peru is the development of the worker's community. The community is an organization composed of all workers employed in a firm. Fifteen percent of the profits of the enterprise goes to the community and is used to purchase equity in the firm until the workers have 50 percent of the ownership. The community elects members of the board of directors based on the voting power of its shares of stock. As the community increases in its size and influence on the board of directors, it could influence the disclosure of financial data in order to protect its interests.

In some countries, such as West Germany, Norway, and Finland, supervisory or works councils are organized with special supervisory and auditing functions. A good example "is the German law which requires that the Works Council (Betriebsrat) be a party to company decisions as they relate to working conditions, training, and all methods of payment. The council must agree to savings, profit-sharing, a stock

---

[5] For example, see Joseph E. Connar, "Discovery Value: The Oil Industry's Untried Method," *Journal of Accountancy* (May 1975): 54-63.

ownership, and all other employee benefit plans. . . ."[6] In the United States as well as other countries, the board of directors is a powerful policy-making group that can have a strong impact on the nature and quality of reported information. The board also requires certain types of information to assist it in making good decisions.

Other External Users

This category includes users other than internal to the firm or the government. In many countries creditors are the most important users of corporate financial data. This is especially true in West Germany and Japan where banks are institutional investors or provide very high leverage for expansion. In the United States, institutional investors such as insurance companies have an influential voice in the development of accounting principles and practices because they are an important source of funds for corporate expansion and often control large blocs of votes in the annual shareholders' meeting. Noninstitutional investors in a broadly based capital market need quality information on which to base investment decisions. They are often represented by their stockbrokers who are able to perform a more sophisticated analysis of financial data. In many countries, securities exchanges help protect the investor by setting requirements for statement preparation and presentation.

In Peru, banks are becoming more sophisticated and are requiring better information to help them make decisions. In addition, most of the banking system has now come under government control, adding one more dimension to the public sector of the economy. However, the banks still operate with a certain degree of autonomy and request information from firms based on their needs rather than on a specific government format.

Individual and nongovernmental institutional investors do not play an important role in the development of accounting principles and practices. A member of the Comision Nacional Supervisora de Empresas y Valores (CNSEV) — a government agency responsible for supervising enterprises and the securities market — recently remarked that the securities market in Peru does the volume of business in one year that is conducted on the securities exchange in Sao Paulo, Brazil, in two days. Many would argue that the lack of a Peruvian securities market is partly a result of poor accounting data. The basic hypothesis is that better accounting data will stimulate the growth of a securities

---

[6] Richard D. Robinson, *International Business Management* (New York: Holt, Rinehart, and Winston, 1973), p. 182.

market; as the market grows, there is pressure to develop accounting principles that will provide even better information.[7] The problem with the Peruvian situation is the lack of confidence in the growth of the private sector of the economy due to the attitudes of the current regime toward socialism and the increased implementation of the worker's community.

Accounting Profession

As is the case in countries such as the United States, Canada, the United Kingdom, and the Netherlands, the accounting profession can be an important influence on the development of accounting objectives, standards, and practices. Three phases of the profession are important: the nature and extent of the profession, the existence of professional associations, and the auditing function. The mere existence of a profession is not as important as the level of sophistication of that profession.

The major problem in Peru is that accounting is not recognized as a profession. Because of the relatively low status of the profession, it is very difficult to attract high-quality students. The major accounting professional association is the Colegio de Contadores Publicos de Lima. The colegio in Lima is the largest of the colegios instituted in various localities in Peru. Each colegio names delegates to the Federación Nacional de Colegios de Contadores Publicos del Peru. Each contador publico is required by law to join the colegio in the locality in which he resides.[8] Collectively, the colegios have a very large membership and have a strong voice in regulating the accounting profession, but they are not active in research or in the development of accounting principles. The staffs of the various colegios receive little remuneration and thus do not devote full-time effort to research activities.

The Instituto de Contadores del Peru is an older and more selective organization than the various colegios, but it also is not very influential. The members of the instituto are also members of the colegios.

Auditing as a discipline exists but until recently has not been very important. With the passage of regulations by the CNSEV (as will be

---

[7] For a discussion of this idea, see Frederick D. S. Choi, "Financial Disclosure in Relation to the European Capital Market," *International Journal of Accounting* (Fall 1973): 53-66.
[8] Edward L. Elliott, *The Nature and Stages of Accounting Development in Latin America* (Urbana-Champaign, Ill.: Center for International Education and Research in Accounting, University of Illinois at Urbana-Champaign, 1968), pp. 118-20. See pages 110-38 for a comprehensive historical discussion of the accounting profession in Peru.

discussed later) independently audited financial statements of most large Peruvian enterprises will be required by law. An auditor must be a registered contador publico in order to officially sign audited financial statements. Most of the large U.S. public accounting firms are currently operating in Peru.

Academic Influence

The academic infrastructure refers to the quality of the education offered as well as the access of students to an education. One of the typical problems in Latin America is the shortage of qualified professors in accounting, and Peru is no different. By economic necessity, teaching is a part-time occupation in most cases. Complicating the education issue is the requirement that a student graduate in accounting from an accredited university in order to receive the title of contador publico. Thus the Escuela de Administracion de Negocios para Graduados (ESAN), a graduate business school in Lima, has a very good accounting program, but its graduates cannot become contadores publicos as long as ESAN is not an accredited university for accounting purposes.

Since instruction in accounting is not considered a full-time profession and is generally not at a very high level, little academic research is done. There are no active educational associations, such as the American Accounting Association in the United States, and all professors are also professionals and thus belong to the instituto and/or one of the colegios.

International Influences

There are many international forces of an institutional rather than environmental nature that have strongly influenced accounting principles worldwide. A prime example of this is the geographical influence of England and France in the colonial era. Each of these countries took their business and accounting philosophies to their colonies and instituted similar systems. The United States has tended to do this as its economic influence has spread through foreign direct investment. Peruvian accounting strongly reflects the influence of the United States not only through investment but also through U.S. participation in the Inter-American Accounting Conferences (IAAC) held periodically.

Many international accounting committees are currently active in the attempt to harmonize accounting principles. The International Congress of Accountants (ICA) is the major forum for the accounting professions of various countries to exchange views on a wide variety of topics. In 1972, the delegates to the ICA formed the International Coordination Committee for the Accountancy Profession (ICCAP) in an effort to improve intercountry cooperation. Five standing committees have been organized by ICCAP: (1) regional bodies, (2) ethics committee, (3) professional education and training committee, (4) future international organization, and (5) publicity. In addition, the ICA has set up the International Accounting Standards Committee (IASC) in an effort to formulate standards to be observed in the audited accounts and financial statements of firms worldwide. Peruvian accounting has been and continues to be influenced more directly by the IAAC, as mentioned previously.

The European Economic Community (EEC) has taken several steps toward the harmonization of accounting principles including the issuance of three directives and the completion of two drafts of a fourth directive. However, the variance in accounting objectives, standards, and practices among France, West Germany, the Netherlands, and the United Kingdom has made harmonization very difficult. The emergence of a regional capital market in the EEC has certainly enhanced the need for more uniformity.

Even though Peru is a member of the Andean Common Market (ANCOM), and the Latin American Free Trade Association (LAFTA), there is little pressure from within these regional economic groups to harmonize accounting standards. The major reason for this is that there is no regional capital market. Most of the countries in ANCOM, for example, have very strict currency controls which preclude the free flow of capital. The only aspect of ANCOM that could affect accounting principles in the near future is decision 46, the approval of an Andean subregional enterprise. This enterprise would be an Andean company owned jointly by investors from two or more countries in ANCOM. In order to make wise investment decisions, these investors would need comparable accounting data. Even though Spanish is the official language in all ANCOM countries, accounting terminology varies considerably. Thus far, decision 46 has not been ratified by all members of ANCOM, so its potential impact on accounting principles is fairly distant.

Local Environmental Characteristics

Local environmental characteristics belong to the broadest and most important of all of the categories. This category contains diverse factors such as the nature and state of the economy as well as cultural attitudes. The four factors listed in exhibit 2 are certainly not exhaustive. Even though the characteristics are referred to as "local," they are not independent of the world economy. The rate of economic growth and inflation depends on a country's major trading partners as well as internal economic conditions.

Geographically, Peru is the third largest country in South America, and with 14.9 million people, it ranks fourth in population. The gross national product (GNP) was estimated to be $7 billion in 1973 or an annual per capita GNP of $469.[9] Compared to other Latin American countries, Peru fits in the intermediate level in terms of social indicators such as per capita GNP, population growth rate, and literacy.[10] In terms of income distribution, Peru falls in the high inequality area. In 1971, the top 20 percent of the population earned 60 percent of the income while the bottom 40 percent of the population earned only 6.5 percent of the income.[11] It was estimated that in 1969 25.5 percent of the population earned less than $75 per year compared with 17.4 percent earning less than $75 per year in all of Latin America.[12] Peru is a developing country that suffers from most of the economic problems facing all developing countries. The military took over the government in a coup in 1968 with General Juan Velasco Alvarado as the head of the regime. The new government (the Revolutionary Government of the Armed Forces) has begun to effect broad social and economic changes, such as nationalization of key industries and the initiation of workers' communities alluded to previously. The following reflects the government's attitude toward economic development: "In economic policy, the government's avowed intention was to avoid both capitalism and communism as models and to push pragmatically along a unique path of state-directed development."[13] The country is now a mix of state-owned, privately owned, and collective enterprises.

Due to the strict control of the economy by the government, it is difficult to get current, reliable information. In a discussion of government-released statistics, the following comments were made:

There was an ample flow of this kind of percentage figure but their overall usefulness is questioned by bankers and economists who have become increasingly worried in the past few years by the unavailability of the regular

[9] *Peru in Figures 1974* (Lima, Peru: Banco Continental).
[10] Charles T. Goodsell, *American Corporations and Peruvian Politics* (Cambridge, Mass.: Harvard University Press, 1974), pp. 29-30.
[11] Montek S. Ahlwalia, "Income Inequality: Some Dimensions of the Problem," *Finance and Development* (September 1974): 4.
[12] Ibid., p. 5.
[13] Goodsell, *American Corporations,* p. 43.

low of economic information and straightforward statistics which used to be vailable. This preoccupation becomes especially acute when the few figures hat are given out during ministers' speeches tend to chop and change for no pparent reason.[14]

Because of the lack of reliability of government-published data, it is lifficult to know what shape the economy is in. Inflation is running etween 18.7 percent (government figures) and 30 percent (estimates) er year — a problem that has brought on price controls. Those firms uffering most from price controls are those which must rely heavily n imports of materials for production. Import prices obviously cannot e regulated.

Although Peru had a balance of trade surplus in 1973, even govern- nent experts had forecast a trade deficit for 1974. This fact is impor- ant since imports are already strictly regulated. Including services, lebt repayments, and profit remissions by foreign investors, Peru has ad to rely on substantial long-term and short-term international orrowing. In 1973, for example, short-term borrowing increased 500 ercent over 1972 levels. Even though the Peruvian currency is very trictly regulated by the government and is not freely convertible into ther currencies, the government has maintained that all is well in the oreign sector. Privately, however, the government has been concerned bout the foreign sector of the economy and has reflected this attitude n its most recent recommendations for a general accounting plan, s will be discussed later.

In terms of the ownership of factors of production and control of he economy, the Peruvian government is taking an increasingly active ole. This, of course, has had a dampening effect on the private sector, ut it has also meant that the government is becoming a more impor- ant user of financial data.

Government

The government is one of the most persuasive forces in the develop- ment of accounting objectives, standards, and practices. For the pur- pose of this discussion, the government can be divided in two groups: users and regulators. Users are tax authorities, planning commissions such as GOSPLAN in the Soviet Union, and various government agencies such as the Bureau of Labor Statistics in the United States, that compile statistics for general use.

[14] "Heavy Borrowing Financing Record Imports," *Andean/Peruvian Times,* 8 November 1974, p. 9.

Government regulators often act in response to the needs of government users. A good example of this would be the Cost Accounting Standards Board in the United States, which is generating uniform cost accounting standards that must be used by government defense contractors. Regulators also act in response to the best interests of the general public, such as the Securities and Exchange Commission (SEC) in the United States.

The extent to which the government becomes involved in the setting of objectives, standards, and practices depends on the interaction of all of the factors listed in exhibit 2. A weak and relatively unsophisticated government will probably not be too concerned about the development of accounting. If the accounting profession in a country is relatively sophisticated and appears to be meeting the needs of the users, the government may not interfere very much. Where the government is an important user of information, does not feel that the accounting profession is meeting the needs of users, and does not foresee much change in the near future, it will probably take a much more active role in setting or influencing the development of accounting objectives, standards, and practices.

Two factors have led to heavy government influence in the accounting sector: a relatively weak and unsophisticated accounting profession and, more importantly, the increasing need for uniform financial data by government users and regulators. There are three major areas of accounting requirements as formulated by the government: Company Law, the CNSEV, and the Plan Contable. The Company Law was most recently formulated in 1966, prior to the Velasco regime. It imposes minimum disclosure and presentative requirements as well as giving general guidelines on the basis for stating assets.

In the mid-1960s a new government agency under the direction of the Ministry of Economy and Finance, the CNSEV (Comision Nacional Supervisora de Empresas y Valores) was organized to function as a watchdog over enterprises as well as the securities market. In 1973, the Comision released a resolution applying to:

(1) enterprises with a net worth of ten million soles ($250,000) or more, annual gross revenues of 50 million soles ($1,250,000), or
(2) enterprises making public offerings of stock, those with shares registered on the exchange, and/or those requesting registration and quotation of their shares on the exchange.[15]

---

[15] Arthur Andersen & Co. (Peru), "Regulations for Reporting on Financial Statements in Peru" (February 1973), p. 2.

The resolution sets out five basic requirements: (1) the general
requirements for presentation and auditing of statements, (2) the disclosure requirements in the financial statements, (3) the notes to the
financial statements, (4) supplementary information and the contents
of the auditor's report, and (5) the auditing requirements.[16] The preamble to the resolution highlights the importance of the new guidelines:

Financial statements prepared in accordance with uniform rules and appropriately examined constitute a basic element for the analysis of the financial situation and the results of operations of an enterprise and an indispensable source for the global study of important sections of the national economy.
At the same time such statements contribute fundamentally to aid in judgment on decisions by banks, financial institutions, and others as to the operations they may enter into, as well as to provide adequate information to
investors. . . .[17]

One of the key problems emphasized in the Arthur Andersen & Co.
translation of the CNSEV document is the auditing requirement. The
auditing firms argue that if statements are prepared by the enterprises
to which the resolution applies (as defined above), these statements
must be audited. The enterprises themselves argue that the statements
must be presented to an outsider in order to qualify for an audit. In
early 1975 the CNSEV called for statements to be furnished for all
firms that qualify under the resolution, thus necessitating an audit of
those statements.

PLAN CONTABLE GENERAL

Concurrent with the CNSEV proposals and under the direction of
the Ministry of Economy and Finance, a Plan Contable General was
developed. The plan is a uniform system of accounting for enterprises
and was designed with three things in mind: (1) managerial needs,
(2) macroeconomic needs, and (3) customs that apply to accounting
in Peru. It is intended that the plan will form a base of reliable information on which the national accounts (macro statistics) can be prepared, as well as provide useful information for managers, shareholders,
workers, creditors, and others.

A series of governmental commissions took four years to complete
the project. Several representatives of the accounting profession served
with government personnel on the commission; conspicuously absent

---

Comision Nacional Supervisora de Empresas y Valores, *Reglamento de Audi-
toria y Certificacion de Balances* (Lima, Peru, 1974).
Arthur Andersen & Co., "Regulations," p. 1.

were any representatives of the private industrial sector of the economy. Three main reasons are given for instituting the plan:

1. The contemporary world economy is developing along the path o
integration, that is, COMECON, EEC, ANCOM;
2. Countries need to have significant forces for planning and developing their economies in order to gain the maximum out of integration
and
3. There seems to be a lack of uniform accounting practice which
inhibits the ability of the government to get high-quality information
for decision making.

There are two volumes to the study. The first volume was released
in early 1975; volume 2 was due for release sometime in 1975. Volume
1 begins with background information on the plan, as well as a discussion of the national accounts. Generally accepted accounting principles are then discussed and include such principles as historical cost
the going-concern concept, objectivity, the realization principle, materiality, and so forth — principles very similar to those accepted in
the United States. Apparently there was no attempt to question the
acceptance of these principles. Instead, the emphasis was on the gen-
eration of data, given these principles. A list of accounting terminology
was also presented. One of the big problems in Peruvian accounting
is the lack of uniform terminology.

The majority of volume 1 is devoted to the chart of accounts and
supporting data. Exhibit 3 presents the chart of accounts and exhibit
4 lists the detail in the structure of the accounts.[18] Each class of accounts is discussed in detail in volume 1. For example, under class 2 and
account 20 (merchandise), the following information would be given
content, valuation, presentation, and special notes and commentary
This is presented for each account. The Peruvian chart of accounts is
very similar to the French chart; the French were consulted on the
organization and implementation of the Peruvian system. However
there are two major differences between the systems. The French plan
is organized in typical continental fashion in order of increasing liquidity. The Peruvian system presents the accounts in the same sequence
that Peruvian accountants are accustomed to — current assets then
noncurrent assets.

A second major difference is that the Peruvian plan provides special

[18] *Plan Contable General* I (Lima, Peru: Ministerio de Economia y Finanzas
1973). Portions of the volume were translated by the author for use in the paper

Exhibit 3. Chart of Accounts

General accounting								Analytical accounts	Accounts of order
Balance sheet accounts					Revenue and expense		Results		
Class 1	Class 2	Class 3	Class 4	Class 5	Class 6	Class 7	Class 8	Class 9	Class 0
Current assets		Noncurrent assets	Current liabilities	Noncurrent liabilities and net worth	Expenses	Revenues	Profit and loss		
10-19	20-29	30-39	40-49	50-59	60-69	70-79	80-89	90-99	00-09

Total asset balance plus the debit
balance of classes 4 and 5   XX
Less total liabilities plus the
credit balance of class 1   XX
Net income (or loss) = balance of
     account 89   XX

Total of class 7   XX
Total of class 6   XX
The difference is the
results of operations   XX   (balance of account 80)
Plus gains (or losses)
(accounts 81-88)   XX
Net income or loss: XX   (balance of account 89)

information about the foreign sector. As noted in exhibit 4, all accounts preceded by an asterisk separate foreign and domestic components. In some cases this is clear from the two-digit classification, such as account 71 which is foreign sales. In other cases, distinction is made between items derived from Peru, ANCOM countries, and other foreign countries. This information is useful in helping the government keep track of the import and export of goods, services, and capital.

Volume 2 had not been published when the author was in Peru in February 1975, but it is really the implementation volume. It will explain how the plan can be used to generate financial statements for special purposes. When the two volumes have been released and the plan goes into effect, compliance will be required of all firms with gross revenues of 50 million soles ($1,250,000) or more. According to an official of the CNSEV, which will administer the plan, this will affect approximately 1,200 of the 60,000-70,000 firms in Peru. Eventually, the plan will affect more firms than currently anticipated.

SUMMARY

Accounting can and should be a dynamic discipline; many different systems exist around the world to suit different circumstances. The analysis of accounting in a given country should present not only a description of the current state of the art, but a discussion of the changes in accounting objectives, standards, and practices, what factors led to those changes, and how these changes were accomplished. This type of analysis will help identify accounting practices that can assist a country in resolving specific types of problems. The U.S. approach to disclosure has been a good starting point for countries developing a broadly based capital market. Peru's need for uniform data to assist in national planning gave rise to a Peruvian version of the French general accounting plan. A more thorough investigation of the factors leading to the principles and practices of a country will help identify common situations where universal principles can be adopted, and unique situations where compromise may be necessary or where uniform standards and practices are simply impracticable.

Exhibit 4. Peruvian Plan Contable General: Structure of the Accounts 55

Class 1: Current assets

  10 cash and bank accounts
  11 negotiable securities
*12 trade accounts receivable
*13 notes receivable
  16 accounts receivable from shareholders, partners, and management
  17 other accounts receivable
  19 allowance for doubtful accounts

Class 2: Inventory

  20 merchandise
  21 finished goods
  22 by-products and scrap
  23 goods in process
  24 raw materials
  25 packaging materials
  26 miscellaneous supplies
  28 goods in transit
  29 allowance for inventory write-down

Class 3: Noncurrent assets

  30 accounts of branches and affiliates
  31 investments in securities
  33 land, machinery, and equipment
  34 intangible assets
  36 land, machinery, and equipment under incentive laws
  37 intangible assets under incentive laws
  38 deferred charges
  39 accumulated depreciation and amortization

Class 4: Current liabilities

  40 taxes payable
  41 expenses payable
*42 trade accounts payable
*43 notes payable
  46 dividends payable
  48 miscellaneous allowances

Class 5: Noncurrent liabilities, deferred income, and net worth

*50 long-term debt
  52 provisions for social benefits
  53 deferred income
*54 capital stock
  55 capital rights of the workers' community
  56 capital surplus
  57 revaluation of assets
  58 reserves
  59 retained earnings

Class 6: Expenses

60 domestic purchases
*61 foreign purchases
62 salaries and labor expenses
63 services by domestic third parties
*64 services by foreign third parties
65 taxes
66 miscellaneous expenses
67 financial expenses
68 current period expense portions of allowances (depreciation, etc.)
*69 selling expenses

Class 7: Revenues

70 domestic sales
*71 foreign sales
72 returns of domestic sales
*73 returns of foreign sales
74 discounts, rebates, etc., on domestic sales
*75 discounts, rebates, etc., on foreign sales
76 other revenues
77 financial revenues
*78 discounts, rebates, etc., from suppliers
79 allocated expenses

Class 8: Profit and loss

80 operating income
81 extraordinary gains
82 extraordinary losses
83 gains from prior periods
84 losses from prior periods
85 legal distribution of net income
88 income taxes
89 net income for the period

---

* All accounts with an asterisk before them separate foreign and domestic components. In some cases, this is clear from the two-digit classification, such as account 71 which is foreign sales. In other cases, distinction is usually made between items derived from Peru, Andean Common Market countries, and other foreign countries.

CHAPTER 4

Accounting principles generally accepted in the United States versus those generally accepted elsewhere*
Gerhard G. Mueller

Substantial evidence exists to support the claim that material differences characterize generally-accepted accounting principles as applied in various countries.[1] While these differences are significant for a number of individual concepts and practices, they should not obscure the equally important observation that there are also a great many similarities between the generally-accepted accounting principles of different countries. The differences, however, are the source of frequent and substantive problems in accounting practice.

With a steadily increasing volume of international business and in-

* Support from the Price Waterhouse Foundation for the preparation of this article is gratefully acknowledged.

** Gerhard G. Mueller, Ph.D., is Professor of Accounting in the Graduate School of Business Administration at the University of Washington. He is also a consultant to the American Institute of CPAs (Accounting Research Division), Price Waterhouse & Co., and several private business firms. Professor Mueller is a past chairman of the Committee of International Accounting of the American Accounting Association and a former consultant to the U.S. Treasury Department of accounting matters relating to international taxation. He was an International Accounting Research Fellow with Price Waterhouse & Co. in New York. His articles have been published in professional journals in the U.S. and abroad, and he is author of *International Accounting* (Macmillan, 1967) and a series of monographs on accounting practices in various countries (University of Washington, 1962-67). He also is co-editor of *Readings in International Accounting* (Houghton-Mifflin, 1968).

[1] For instance, *Professional Accounting in 25 Countries* (American Institute of Certified Public Accountants, 1964).

* This article is reprinted, with permission, from *The International Journal of Accounting: Education and Research* (Spring 1968) pp 91–103

vestments, national differences in accounting principles have a growing impact. From a practical point of view, these national differences cause difficulties in at least these areas:

1. Reporting for international subsidiaries whose financial statements are to be consolidated or combined with United States parent-company statements.

2. Reporting for international subsidiaries which lie beyond the consolidation or combination requirements — separate reports being required by the United States parent company.

3. Reporting for independent companies located in countries other than the United States where the statements are for local use and a standard United States form of opinion is to be furnished.

4. Reporting for independent companies in countries outside the United States where the statements and the opinions are likely to be read and used in the United States, *e.g.,* for SEC filings, use by bankers, and possible acquisitions or general publication in English to stockholders residing in the United States.

This paper has as its main purpose the empirical evaluation of the complexities of varying accounting principles among different countries. While it is recognized that conceptual considerations are only one aspect of the over-all problem, a better perspective should be possible by limiting the focus of the discussion.

ECONOMIC AND BUSINESS ENVIRONMENTS DIFFER AMONG VARIOUS COUNTRIES

Experience and observation tell us that the business environment normally varies from one country to the next. Indeed, some parts of an overall business environment may well differ between individual regions of a single country. On the other hand, there are instances where two or more countries have essentially the same environmental conditions. This reduces to the proposition that the dimensions of a business environment are primarily economic in nature whereas borders of a country are drawn because of political factors. Thus, political boundaries are not necessarily the only or the best lines of distinction for differing business environments.

What separates one business environment from another? Primarily, there are four marks of separation:

1. States of economic development — A highly developed economy provides an environment different from an undeveloped economy. In

an African country, workers at a plant had to walk three hours twice each day to get to and from work. An AID program provided them with bicycles, after which they quit work. Possession of a bicycle was the sole motive for their accepting employment in the first place.

2. Stages of business complexity — Business needs as well as business output are functions of business complexity. An example of this is that West Germany in a recent year imported approximately DM 600 million (net) of industrial know-how in the form of Research and Development services outside Germany.

3. Shades of political persuasion — Political tendencies clearly affect business environments. Among the better known international examples are the expropriations of private property by central governments in South America and the Near and Far East. Forms of social legislation also affect business environments directly.

4. Reliance on some particular system of law — Differences between common law and code law are widely known. There are other differences as well. Detailed companies legislation may inhibit or protect business, as the case may be. The United States has rather stringent unfair trade and antitrust laws. The legal systems of some European countries tolerate market share agreements and cartel arrangements.

Using principally these four elements of differentiation, a quick analysis of business environments existing in different countries can be undertaken. This yields, in the author's opinion, ten distinct sets of business environments. Each differs from all others in at least one important respect. The ten are:

1. United States/Canada/The Netherlands — There is a minimum of commercial or companies legislation in this environment. Industry is highly developed; currencies are relatively stable. A strong orientation to business innovation exists. Many companies with widespread international business interests are headquartered in these countries.

2. British Commonwealth (Excluding Canada) — Comparable companies legislation exists in all Commonwealth countries and administrative procedures and social order reflect strong ties to the mother country. There exists an intertwining of currencies through the so-called "sterling block" arrangement. Business is highly developed but often quite traditional.

3. Germany/Japan — Rapid economic growth has occurred since World War II. Influences stemming from various United States military and administrative operations have caused considerable imitation

of many facets of the United States practices, often by grafting United States procedures to various local traditions. The appearance of a new class of professional business managers is observable. Relative political, social, and currency stability exists.

4. Continental Europe (Excluding Germany, The Netherlands and Scandinavia) — Private business lacks significant government support. Private property and the profit motive are not necessarily in the center of economic and business orientation. Some national economic planning exists. Political swings from far right to far left, and vice versa, have a long history in this environment. Limited reservoirs of economic resources are available.

5. Scandinavia — Here we have developed economies, but characteristically slow rates of economic and business growth. Governments tend toward social legislation. Companies acts regulate business. Relative stability of population numbers is the rule. Currencies are quite stable. Several business innovations (especially in consumer goods) originated in Scandinavia. Personal characteristics and outlooks are quite similar in all five Scandinavian countries.

6. Israel/Mexico — These are the only two countries with substantial success in fairly rapid economic development. Trends of a shift to more reliance on private enterprise are beginning to appear; however, there is still a significant government presence in business. Political and monetary stability seem to be increasing. Some specialization in business and the professions is taking place. The general population apparently has a strong desire for higher standards of living.

7. South America[2] — Many instances are present of significant economic underdevelopment along with social and educational underdevelopment. The business base is narrow. Agricultural and military interests are strong and often dominate governments. There is considerable reliance on export/import trade. Currencies are generally soft. Populations are increasing heavily.

8. The Developing Nations of the Near and Far East[2] — Modern concepts and ethics of business have predominantly Western origins. These concepts and ethics often clash with the basic oriental cultures. Business in the developing nations of the Orient largely means trade only. There is severe underdevelopment on most measures, coupled with vast population numbers. Political scenes and currencies are most shaky.

---

[2] These areas are obviously treated very generally; exceptions exist for a few given countries.

Major economic advances are probably impossible without substantial assistance from the industrialized countries.

9. Africa (Excluding South Africa)[2] — Most of the African continent is still in the early stages of independent civilization and thus little or no native business environment presently exists. There are significant natural and human resources. Business is likely to assume a major role and responsibility in the development of African nations.

10. Communist Nations — The complete control by central governments removes these countries from any further interest for the purpose of this article.

The above categorization suggests that each country does not necessarily have a separate and distinct environment for its business. It also suggests a manageable way of viewing the existing differences.

One additional general observation on business environments seems worthwhile. In the ten categories listed above, little likelihood of change may be expected in the near future. Of course, details and specifics constantly change in the economic surroundings of business. But the overall philosophy and character that distinguish the ten separate cases seem rather well established, perhaps for as long as a quarter of a century. Therefore, relative stability appears to be one of the properties of different business environments. This means two things: (1) business concepts and practices, including accounting concepts and practices, do not necessarily require rapid changes if they are based on environmental conditions, and (2) business environments are probably more difficult to change than is sometimes assumed.

ACCOUNTING AND THE ECONOMIC/BUSINESS ENVIRONMENT

In society, accounting performs a service function. This function is put in jeopardy unless accounting remains, above all, practically useful. Thus, it must respond to the ever-changing needs of society and must reflect the social, political, legal, and economic conditions within which it operates. Its meaningfulness depends upon its ability to mirror these conditions.

The history of accounting and accountants reveals the changes which accounting consistently undergoes. At one time accounting was little more than a recording system for certain banking services and tax collection plans. Later it responded with double-entry bookkeeping procedures to meet the needs of trading ventures. The industrialization and division of labor made possible cost and management-type accounting. The advent of modern corporation stimulated periodic financial reporting and auditing. Most recently, accounting has revealed a greater social awareness by assuming public-interest responsibilities together with the providing of decision information for the larger public-securities markets and management-consulting functions. Accounting is clearly concerned with its environment. Its developmental processes are often compared with that of common law.

From an environmental point of view, various developments in society affect accounting. What else would have caused, for instance, the very serious preoccupation of United States accountants with the needs of United States security analysts? Similar influences are present in recent U.S. efforts concerning lessor and lessee accounting, accounting for business combinations, and the wholesale extension of accounting to international business problems.

But accounting also affects its environment. Many economic resources are allocated to specific business uses on the basis of relevant accounting information. In some measure, national economic policies are formulated on the contents or message of corporate financial statements, and unions often base wage demands on similar information. Rate cases of regulated companies are based primarily on accounting data, and so are most antitrust cases initiated by governmental agencies. Therefore, accounting both reflects environmental conditions and influences them.

Dudley E. Browne touches on the relationship of accounting to its environment in his review of *Corporate Financial Reporting in a Competitive Economy,* by Herman W. Bevis:

The financial accounting and reporting of any corporation are subject to a variety of external influences. A larger number of common approaches to accounting and reporting problems can be found in a given industry or other relatively homogeneous group of corporations than in all of industry, but the internal relationship of its operations and programs with external influences will continue to make each corporation different from every other.

The necessity that corporate financial accounting and reporting be sufficiently unrestricted to respond readily to change should be kept in mind . . . the principle of full and fair disclosure must remain the keystone of successful corporation-stockholder and corporate-society relationships.[3]

THE ISSUE OF DIFFERENT ACCOUNTING PRINCIPLES

If we accept that (1) economic and business environments are not

---

[3] Dudley E. Browne, *Financial Executive,* January 1966, p. 50.

the same in all countries, and (2) a close interrelationship exists between economic and business environments and accounting, it follows that a single set of generally-accepted accounting principles cannot be useful and meaningful in all situations. This conclusion admits the possibility of some honest and well-founded differences in accounting principles that find general acceptance in certain national or geographic-area circumstances.

Let us postulate for a moment that accounting principles generally accepted in the United States were enforced in all countries of the free world. This would create an international uniformity which would have some intellectual appeal and would ease many problems in international accounting practice and international financial reporting.

At the same time, such uniformity would lack meaning. It would have to assume that business conditions are the same in all parts of the free world and that the same stage of professional, social, and economic development has been reached everywhere. This is certainly not the case. In fact, enforced international uniformity on the basis of United States accounting principles alone would probably lead to misinformation or inaccurate results in many instances. The same types of calamity which have characterized so many U.S. foreign aid problems in the past would result.

Nevertheless, the issue of international differences in accounting principles does not resolve itself into a complete laissez-faire approach. A strong theoretical argument can be made for consistency of generally-accepted accounting principles between those countries or geographic areas where economic and business environments are substantially similar. In other words, from a theoretical viewpoint, generally-accepted principles in the United States should be the same as those in Canada, but may differ in some respects from those used in South America or Pakistan or India. The business and economic environments of the United States and Canada are very similar; the respective environments of the United States and India are very dissimilar.

ENVIRONMENTAL CIRCUMSTANCES AND APPROPRIATE ACCOUNTING PRINCIPLES

Reference to environmental conditions is subjective. It is not possible, therefore, to develop a conclusive list of those circumstances which permit or require differing accounting principles from one country or area to the next, but some of the circumstances affecting the determination of appropriate accounting principles in an international framework can be identified. Such circumstances include:

1. Relative stability of the currency of account — If a currency is quite stable over time, historical cost accounting is generally indicated. Significant currency instability calls for some form of price index adjustment, with the form of adjustments depending largely on the type of indexes available and reliable.

2. Degree of legislative business interference — Tax legislation may require the application of certain accounting principles. This is the case in Sweden where some tax allowances must be entered in the accounts before they can be claimed for tax purposes; this is also the situation for LIFO inventory valuations in the United States.

Furthermore, varying social security laws may affect accounting principles. Severance pay requirements in several South American countries illustrate this.

3. Nature of business ownership — Widespread public ownership of corporate securities generally requires different financial reporting and disclosure principles from those applicable to predominantly family or bank-owned corporate equities. This is in essence a difference because public and closely held companies do not need to capitalize small stock distributions at market value whereas publicly held companies do.

4. Level of sophistication of business management — Highly refined accounting principles have no place in an environment where they are misunderstood and misused. A technical report on cost variances is meaningless unless the reader understands cost accounting well. A sources and uses of funds statement should not be prepared unless it can be read competently.

5. Differences in size and complexity of business firms — Self-insurance may be acceptable for a very large firm where it is obviously not for a smaller firm. Similarly, a large firm mounting an extensive advertising campaign directed at a specific market or season may be justified in deferring part of the resultant expenditure, whereas smaller programs in smaller firms may need to be expensed directly.

Comparable conclusions apply to complexity. Heavy and regular Research and Development outlays by a United States corporation may require accounting recognition, especially when long-range projects are involved. Incidental development costs of a firm producing only oil additives in Mexico normally have no such requirement.

6. Speed of business innovations — Business combinations became

popular in Europe only a few years ago. Before that, European countries had little need of accounting principles and practices for this type of business event. Very small stock distributions occur most generally in the United States. Again, this produces differences in accounting principles. Equipment leasing is not practiced in a number of countries with the consequent absence of a need for lease accounting principles.

7. Presence of specific accounting legislation — Companies acts containing accounting provisions are found in many countries. While these acts change over time (for example, there were new acts recently in both Germany and the United Kingdom), their stipulations must be observed when in force and legally binding. The German act requires setting aside certain earnings as a "legal reserve." It also stipulates when and how consolidated financial statements are to be prepared. The British act defines how the term "reserve" is to be used in accounting. Many other examples of this type exist.

8. Stage of economic development — A one-crop agricultural economy needs accounting principles different from a United States-type economy. In the former, for instance, there is probably relatively little dependence on credit and long-term business contracts. Thus, sophisticated accrual accounting is out of place and essentially cash accounting is needed.

9. Type of economy involved — National economies vary in nature. Some are purely agricultural, while others depend heavily on the exploitation of natural resources (oil in the Near East, gold and diamonds in South Africa, copper in Chile, etc.). Some economies rely mainly on trade and institutions (Switzerland, Lebanon), whereas still others are highly diversified and touch on a great variety of economic and business activities. These are reasons for different principles regarding consolidations, accretion or discovery of natural resources, and inventory methods, among others.

10. Growing pattern of an economy — Companies and industries grow, stabilize, or decline. The same applies to national economies. If growth and expansion are typical, the capitalization of certain deferred charges is more feasible than under stable or declining conditions. Stable conditions intensify competition for existing markets, requiring restrictive credit and inventory methods. Declining conditions may indicate write-offs and adjustments not warranted in other situations.

11. Status of professional education and organization — In the absence of organized accounting professionalism and native sources of account-

ing authority, principles from other areas or countries may be needed to fill existing voids. The process of adaptation, however, will be unsuccessful unless it allows for circumstantial factors of the type identified here.

12. General levels of education and tool processes facilitating accounting — Statistical methods in accounting and auditing cannot be used successfully where little or no knowledge of statistics and mathematics exists. Computer principles are not needed in the absence of working EDP installations. The French general accounting plan has enjoyed wide acceptance in France because it is easily understood and readily usable by those with average levels of education and without sophisticated accounting training.

The reader will recognize that several of the factors listed above may apply to a national situation as well as the international scene. This is not surprising since national variations in accounting concepts and practices are increasingly analyzed in terms of their respective environmental backgrounds, particularly in the United States. A relationship seems to exist between accounting flexibility within a country and among countries or areas. The topic of such a possible relationship, however, falls beyond the scope of this paper.

SOME EXAMPLES

As a limited test of the applicability of the list of environmental circumstances referred to in the preceding section, several different accounting principles are related to this list in order to evaluate at least some of the underlying environmental relationships. A complete diagnosis of this type would be a substantial undertaking and is not attempted here.

Different Circumstances Resulting in Different Accounting Principles

Investments in marketable securities are generally carried at the lower of cost or market, stock exchange quotations being used as indications of "market." A different principle needs application where no national stock exchange exists, for example, in Guatemala.

Severance payments are normally at the option of the employer and thus are customarily expensed at the time of payment. If severance payments of material amounts are required by law, however, they should be accrued in some fashion before actual severance occurs.

In the United States, owners' equity is recorded, classified, and reported as to source. Interest in dividend potential is one reason for this. It results in basic distinctions between contributed capital, retained earnings, and capital from other sources.

On the other hand, a single owners' equity principle of legal capital dominates accounting in some European countries, *e.g.*, Germany. This is based on a balance-sheet accounting orientation to creditor protection.

Similar Circumstances Resulting in (Largely Unexplained) Different Accounting Principles

The circumstances of inventory valuation are highly similar in the United States and the United Kingdom. In the lower of cost or market test, "market" means essentially replacement value in the United States and net realizable future sales value in the United Kingdom.

Despite close similarities of circumstances, deferred income tax "liabilities" are generally recognized in the United States and only sparingly recognized in Canada. Deferred tax accounting is not a generally-accepted accounting principle in Canada.

Accounting terminology varies internationally to a considerable degree without good reason. United States and United Kingdom usage of the terms "reserve" and "provision" differs, French use of the term "depreciation" differs from that in other European countries, and "goodwill" means nearly all things to all people. This is largely unexplainable.

CHANGE IN ACCOUNTING PRINCIPLES

For the time being, meaningful international uniformity of generally-accepted accounting principles should have full regard for differences existing in the environments in which accounting operates. While complete differentiation for each politically recognized country is undesirable and unwarranted, fundamentally different conditions between different countries or areas conceptually call for separate recognition.

Assuming that this can be achieved, a most important mandate of accounting is to respond to any changes in environmental conditions as soon as they occur. Accounting can actually further the cause of change since it has, as we have seen, some influence on its environment in addition to reacting to its environment. Therefore, identification with desirable efforts toward change, and quick and full response to accomplished change are probably the primary leverage factors available to accounting in resolving justifiable international differences in generally-accepted accounting principles.

Three practical examples illustrate the force of change in accounting. First, the revised German companies law enacted in 1965 contains several financial disclosure provisions which are definitely patterned after United States SEC requirements. As Germany moves closer to a corporate business society that has much in common with the United States business society, tested SEC-type legislation would seem to be a valid response to the changes occurring.

Second, more comprehensive general financial-disclosure requirements are in evidence in the United Kingdom via the widely discussed 1964 London Stock Exchange memorandum as well as the recent new companies legislation. For some time the Swiss business press has carried repeated strong appeals for greater disclosure in the financial statements of Swiss companies. These and similar admonitions for wider general disclosures seem to be a consequence of widening securities markets in the countries concerned. Here again, an environmental condition has changed and accounting should respond.

Third, there is a notable increase in consolidated financial reporting on the part of larger corporations in countries outside of North America. In many instances, consolidated financial statements are presented even though applicable laws do not require such presentations. The cause of this move toward greater use of consolidated financial reports undoubtedly lies in the ever growing extent of intercorporate investments and the steady growth of portfolio investments beyond the domicile countries of respective investors. The companies affected may have changed somewhat, but the far greater change has occurred in the environment of their operations.

In summary, a particular responsibility which accounting has in relation to change seems to exist. Awareness of this responsibility and concentrated efforts in connection with it are theoretically the most effective ways in which accounting principles between countries can be brought into greater harmony.

CONCLUSIONS

The three main conclusions of this paper are:

1. *United States generally-accepted accounting principles should not be enforced arbitrarily in other countries.* There is a theoretical incompatibility between the economic and business environments prevailing in different countries and an arbitrary imposition of any single set of generally-accepted accounting principles would run counter to environmental differences which exist.

Only where environments are alike or similar can meaningful results be achieved by the use of a particular single body of accounting principles. At the same time, the overall theoretical framework of accounting itself needs to be general and permit analysis in terms of applicable environmental circumstances.

2. *Complete international diversity of accounting principles is undesirable and unnecessary.* The author has attempted to define ten different areas in which comparable environmental conditions exist and which therefore would gain from a particular approach to generally-accepted accounting principles. The ten-fold classification is highly subjective; nevertheless, it demonstrates a frame of reference with regard to limited international diversity of accounting principles.

Free international exchange and cooperation with regard to accounting principles would avoid unnecessary duplications in accounting research and provide the latest accounting knowhow for application when conditions demand it.

3. *Accounting is dynamic and operates in an atmosphere of change.* Even though the basic character of a given business environment seems slow to change, the continuing evolution of the accounting discipline affords means toward more international harmony in generally-accepted accounting principles. Efforts to change unnecessary international diversities in accounting in response to changing economic and business conditions appear to hold greater promise, in theory, than legislation or another form of enforcement of dictated international accounting uniformity.

CHAPTER 5

The impact of disclosure and measurement practices on international accounting classifications*

R. D. Nair and Werner G. Frank

ABSTRACT: This article examines whether the classification of countries into groups based on their accounting practices is the same whether measurement or disclosure practices are used to do the grouping. Data from the Price Waterhouse & Co. survey relating to these two subsets of accounting practices for 38 countries in 1973 and 46 countries in 1975 formed the data base. The groupings yielded by analyzing disclosure practices were found to be different from groupings based on measurement practices. A further analysis was then done to determine whether the same underlying environmental variables (such as the structure of the economy and trading affiliations of each country) were associated with the two groupings. It was found that although economic variables were related to the groupings, the specific variables most closely related to each subset were different. Because of these differences, it may be more difficult for policy makers to achieve harmonization of accounting practices than was previously realized.

S EVERAL attempts have been made to classify countries into groups based on the accounting practices that they follow. Examples of such efforts include Previts [1975], Seidler [1967], Buckley [1974], Mueller [1967, 1968], and Frank [1979]. In all of these studies, accounting practices were treated as a single group and no attempt was made to determine whether the clustering of countries was dependent on the composition of the set of accounting practices under study.

One important way of disaggregating accounting practices into two subsets is to distinguish whether they deal with disclosure or with measurement practices. The importance of this distinction in the United States can be seen by referring to the report of the American Institute of Certified Public Accountants' Committee on Generally Accepted Accounting Principles for Smaller and/or Closely Held Businesses ["Report," 1976]. The committee recommended that measurement principles should apply to all businesses regardless of their size or number of shareholders, while, on the other hand, the applicability of disclosure principles should vary depending on a number of factors and should not be required in all circumstances. A similar dichotomy has also served as a basis for distinguishing between the roles of the Securities and Exchange Commission and the Financial Accounting Standards Board (FASB), with the former concerning itself with disclosure practices and the

R. D. Nair is Assistant Professor of Accounting and Werner G. Frank is Professor of Accounting, University of Wisconsin—Madison.

Manuscript received April, 1979.
Revision received August, 1979.
Accepted November, 1979.

* This article is reprinted, with permission, from *The Accounting Review* (July, 1980) pp 426–450

latter with measurement practices. Beaver [1978] notes that the current jurisdictional controversy between these two bodies is the result of each encroaching on the other's role.

This article reports the results of a study which groups countries first by their measurement practices, and then by their disclosure practices. We also attempted to find whether different economic and cultural variables were associated with each subset of practices. It was found that the two subsets yield very different results. The number of groupings, the alignment of countries, and the underlying environmental variables associated with the practices were all different between the two subsets. The next section describes and compares the groupings of countries on each subset for 1973 and then this comparison is repeated for 1975. Section II describes and compares the environmental variables most closely associated with each subset of practices, while Section III points out the limitations of the analyses. Section IV presents the conclusions of the study and its implications for policy making.

I. COUNTRY GROUPINGS

The reasons why we expected measurement and disclosure practices to yield different country groupings were as follows. As noted above, disclosure and measurement practices sometimes fall in the province of two different rule-making bodies. Besides the United States, this disclosure/measurement regulatory dichotomy can also be observed in the United Kingdom, as pointed out by Benston [1975]. The administration of the Companies Acts of 1948 and 1967 which govern disclosure is largely the responsibility of the Department of Trade and Industry while measurement practices are addressed mainly by the Accounting Standards Committee. Second,

measurement practices sometimes may have application over a wider range of business enterprises than disclosure practices, as is the case, for example, with respect to reporting segmented and earnings per share data in the United States. Third, the criteria brought to bear in the choice of measurement practices may be different from those used in choosing among disclosure practices. While factors such as relevance, verifiability, and objectivity may be important in the choice of the former, cost considerations in preparing the data may predominate in the choice of the latter. Finally, some may argue that given efficient capital markets, those disclosure practices dealing with format are much less substantive than most measurement practices. If this last line of argument is followed, one would expect disclosure practices to exhibit more diversity and yield more country groupings than measurement practices.

A. Data

The data for this part of the analysis consisted of the results of two surveys conducted by the accounting firm of Price Waterhouse & Co. on accounting principles and reporting practices. In 1973, the survey covered 233 principles and practices in 38 countries. The 1975 survey constitutes a richer data source, with eight countries being added and 264 principles and practices being covered. The eight new countries were Bermuda, Denmark, Greece, Iran, Malaysia, Nigeria, Norway, and Zaire. The 164 practices reported on in 1975 included all but 22 of the practices reported on in 1973. The samplings of countries in both years have a bias towards Western Hemisphere countries—a not unimportant group in their own right. Also, while the 1973 survey had six categories (Required, Majority, About Half, Minority, No Application, and Not Permitted), the

1975 survey added a seventh category: Not Found in Practice. The categories were numerically coded in this research as follows:

Survey Category	Numerical Code (Percentage Usage)
Required	100%
Majority	75%
About Half	50%
Minority	25%
Not Found in Practice	0% (not used in 1973)
Not Permitted	0%
No Application	0%

The reason for the percentage coding was to permit input of the data into a factor analysis program. The possibility of measurement error being introduced into the analysis by this transformation is taken up in Section III.

The principles and practices for both years were classified as either measurement practices or disclosure practices independently by the two researchers. The criterion used for the classification was the following. If the application of a specific practice would result in the recording of a different value in a given account, then it was classified as a measurement practice. If it did not, or if the practice dealt explicitly with disclosure, then it was classified as a disclosure practice. For example, Item 12 from the 1975 survey deals with whether "A note is appended to historical cost financial statements, disclosing the effects of price level changes." This item was classified as a disclosure practice. On the other hand, Item 13 from the same survey asks whether "In preparing current purchasing power financial statements, a general price-level index is used and not an index or indices which measure the level of particular goods or services." Since this item measures how the figures appearing in the statements are determined, it was classified as a measurement practice. In most cases, the choice was clear-cut. In a few cases (not exceeding 15 in either year), different classifications initially were made by the two researchers. These were then resolved by mutual discussion until a consensus emerged. This procedure resulted in the following classification:

Year/Classification[1]	Disclosure	Measurement
1973 (38 countries)	86 practices	147 practices
1975 (46 countries)	102 practices	162 practices

The data from the 1973 and 1975 surveys were used as inputs into a factor analysis program. There were two objectives of the factor analysis procedure. One was to see whether the groupings yielded by the two subsets of data for each year were the same, or whether the disaggregation of accounting practices into disclosure and measurement subsets caused the composition of groups to change. The second objective was to use the groupings obtained with the 1975 subsets as inputs into a discriminant analysis. In this second step of the overall analysis, we wanted to see whether the same economic, social, and cultural variables would predict the membership of countries in the different accounting groups. The remainder of this section describes the results of applying the factor analysis procedure four times (two years of data × two subsets of practices). Section II describes the results of the discriminant analysis.

B. 1973 Analysis:

1. Measurement practices. Percentage data on the extent of acceptance of the 147 practices in 38 countries were used as 147 observations in a factor analysis based on a correlation matrix to identify common patterns among the 38 countries. Factor analysis is a statistical technique which uses a measure of similarity between variables, such as the coefficient

---

[1] The list of practices falling into each group for each year is available from the authors.

of correlation, to search for variables which are like each other and collapses these variables into more compact groups or factors. The strength with which each of the original variables is associated with these new basic variables or factors is measured by a statistic called factor loading. A statistic called the eigenvalue helps determine the number of factors to be extracted, while the percentage of the variance in the original data which is accounted for by the extracted factors is a measure of the overall success of the

which it had the highest loading. The countries within each group or factor are those which are quite similar to each other in terms of accounting practices and quite different from the countries which are members of other groups or factors. As can be seen no country had its highest loading on the fifth factor, and no logical grouping appears to exist for the countries with relatively high loadings on that factor. That factor is, therefore, not used in the subsequent analysis. The remaining four factors yield the following groupings of the 38 countries:

Group I	Group II	Group III	Group IV
Australia	Argentina	Belgium	Canada
Bahamas	Bolivia	France	Japan
Fiji	Brazil	Germany	Mexico
Jamaica	Chile	Italy	Panama
Kenya	Colombia	Spain	Philippines
Netherlands	Ethiopia	Sweden	United States
New Zealand	India	Switzerland	
Pakistan	Paraguay	Venezuela	
Republic of Ireland	Peru		
Rhodesia	Uruguay		
Singapore			
South Africa			
Trinidad & Tobago			
United Kingdom			

factoring procedure. Using the usual criterion that only those factors whose eigenvalues exceeded 1.0 would be considered, five factors were identified. Each factor represents a different common pattern of acceptance of measurement practices. These five factors accounted for approximately 71 percent of the variance in the data. To provide an intuitive interpretation of the groups, the factor matrix was rotated using a varimax rotation procedure. This procedure associates the various individual variables or countries in the strongest way possible with a single factor. A complete listing of the loadings of the countries on the rotated factors is given in Table 1. Each country was assigned to the factor on

By noting the overall composition of each group and the alignment of countries, the following intuitively appealing characterizations can be made:

Group I: British Commonwealth model
Group II: Latin American model
Group III: Continental European model
Group IV: United States model

A comparison of these groupings with those obtained by Frank [1979] when he used all 233 principles from the same period reveals little difference. The number of factors stays the same as does the general overall composition and character of each group. Five countries—Ethiopia, Pakistan, Colombia, Netherlands, and Germany—do change group membership, but some of these shifts are understandable since in three of the five

Table 1
Rotated Factor Matrix Based on Measurement Practices
(1973 Survey Data)

	Variable/Factor	1	2	3	4	5
1	Argentina	.154	.814	.130	.144	−.013
2	Australia	.664	.115	.237	.235	.592
3	Bahamas	.662	.228	.101	.410	.051
4	Belgium	.329	.355	.726	−.004	.100
5	Bolivia	.085	.845	.187	.080	.169
6	Brazil	.215	.674	.249	−.074	−.094
7	Canada	.535	.057	.199	.627	.050
8	Chile	.249	.662	.250	.129	−.008
9	Colombia	.210	.500	.406	.384	.329
10	Ethiopia	.419	.438	.286	.246	.259
11	Fiji	.653	.138	.253	.255	.577
12	France	.316	.247	.650	.150	.059
13	Germany	.339	.213	.619	.484	.070
14	India	.402	.496	.470	.108	.184
15	Italy	.041	.302	.676	.290	.073
16	Jamaica	.731	.275	.293	.179	.250
17	Japan	.339	.337	.475	.476	.040
18	Kenya	.647	.225	.321	.262	.173
19	Mexico	.301	.309	.241	.561	.128
20	Netherlands	.690	.146	.241	.363	−.213
21	New Zealand	.643	.143	.263	.273	.587
22	Pakistan	.492	.472	.331	.075	.285
23	Panama	.313	.393	.316	.436	.270
24	Paraguay	.114	.717	.261	.214	.107
25	Peru	.084	.843	.187	.084	.177
26	Philippines	.426	.247	.207	.712	.183
27	Republic of Ireland	.815	.176	.207	.140	.170
28	Rhodesia	.739	.234	.277	.199	.092
29	Singapore	.765	.327	.139	.127	.086
30	South Africa	.765	.160	.136	.289	.205
31	Spain	.299	.433	.600	−.052	.121
32	Sweden	.423	.294	.609	.121	.055
33	Switzerland	.373	.145	.571	.291	.034
34	Trinidad & Tobago	.761	.223	.274	.205	.081
35	United Kingdom	.784	.026	.233	.231	−.052
36	United States	.328	.018	.049	.831	.068
37	Uruguay	.202	.696	.189	.196	−.067
38	Venezuela	.133	.462	.606	.151	.251

(Highest factor loading for each country is underlined)

cases the loadings on the two groups are approximately equal.

2. *Disclosure Practices.* A similar factor analytic procedure was applied to the 86 observations on reporting practices in the same 38 countries for 1973. The same criteria for extracting and rotating factors were used. Seven factors, *i.e.*, country groupings, were identified, accounting for 73.2 percent of the total variance in the data. A complete listing of the load-ings of the countries on the rotated factors is given in Table 2. Each country again was assigned to the factor on which it had the highest loading. The seven factors yield the following groupings of the 38 countries. (Factors 6 and 7 both yield separate single-country "groups", but this treatment seems valid since each country's loading on its individual factor is much greater than its loading on any other factor.)

TABLE 2

ROTATED FACTOR MATRIX BASED ON DISCLOSURE PRACTICES
(1973 Survey Data)

Variable/Factor	1	2	3	4	5	6	7
1 Argentina	.210	.444	.320	.266	.473	.363	.047
2 Australia	.867	.091	.142	.183	.173	.067	.078
3 Bahamas	.473	.275	.161	.444	.055	−.264	−.089
4 Belgium	.392	.152	.616	.063	.087	.127	.083
5 Bolivia	.227	.731	.382	.169	.250	.071	−.117
6 Brazil	.130	.217	.763	−.147	.271	−.003	−.081
7 Canada	.431	.319	−.016	.697	.014	−.024	−.148
8 Chile	.164	.377	.232	.148	.537	.284	−.118
9 Colombia	−.028	.354	.699	.047	−.064	.160	.077
10 Ethiopia	.373	.313	.028	.042	.602	.012	−.061
11 Fiji	.817	.120	.213	.260	.196	.007	.007
12 France	.083	.108	.724	−.168	−.140	.332	−.047
13 Germany	.208	.768	.070	.196	−.025	.054	.240
14 India	.435	.681	.196	.181	.123	.150	.086
15 Italy	.081	.043	.646	.220	.024	−.141	.457
16 Jamaica	.790	.438	.133	.120	.136	−.015	.062
17 Japan	.078	.673	.282	.249	.192	.089	.150
18 Kenya	.711	.341	.041	.065	.327	.089	.259
19 Mexico	.271	.389	.167	.522	.353	−.062	−.060
20 Netherlands	.384	.090	−.026	.672	.081	.111	.290
21 New Zealand	.855	.204	.168	.145	.205	.050	.189
22 Pakistan	.397	.640	.077	.231	.210	.231	.191
23 Panama	.143	.288	.217	.480	.380	3.12	.017
24 Paraguay	.076	.226	.639	.057	.331	.302	−.066
25 Peru	.125	.711	.339	.237	.224	.083	−.108
26 Philippines	.194	.189	.173	.639	.183	.434	.210
27 Republic of Ireland	.794	.014	.131	.206	−.110	−.140	−.177
28 Rhodesia	.749	.165	.112	.116	.221	.219	.299
29 Singapore	.670	.266	−.001	.027	.026	.404	.022
30 South Africa	.643	.237	−.036	.106	.023	.477	.125
31 Spain	.166	−.055	.786	.095	.276	−.154	.070
32 Sweden	.175	.173	.288	.136	.118	.649	.028
33 Switzerland	.284	.204	.207	.035	−.138	.073	.695
34 Trinidad & Tobago	.568	.508	.145	.234	.263	.067	.216
35 United Kingdom	.659	−.097	−.049	.280	−.187	.368	−.182
36 United States	.151	.416	−.065	.741	−.167	0.90	.010
37 Uruguay	.091	.061	.414	−.203	.732	−.017	.005
38 Venezuela	−.024	.228	.708	.265	.226	.025	.238

Group I	Group II	Group III	Group IV	Group V	Group VI	Group VII
Australia	Bolivia	Belgium	Canada	Argentina	Sweden	Switzerland
Bahamas	Germany	Brazil	Mexico	Chile		
Fiji	India	Colombia	Netherlands	Ethiopia		
Jamaica	Japan	France	Panama	Uruguay		
Kenya	Pakistan	Italy	Philippines			
New Zealand	Peru	Paraguay	United States			
Republic of Ireland		Spain				
Rhodesia		Venezuela				
Singapore						
South Africa						
Trinidad & Tobago						
United Kingdom						

TABLE 3

TRANSFORMATION MATRIX

Disclosure and Measurement Groupings for 1973

Measurement Groups \ Disclosure Groups	I	II	III	IV	V	VI	VIII
I	.95046	.01836	−.24363	.09157	.03178	.15910	−.02553
II	.00219	.51636	.42280	.07120	.57897	.15573	−.20126
III	−.15747	−.00932	.69828	−.13866	−.20452	.40454	.42632
IV	−.24282	.38358	−.11821	.81579	.00990	.04072	.07050
V	.44992	.12042	.12218	−.10335	.13736	−.12002	.01576

Comparing these results with the groupings obtained in the previous section reveals that the clusterings of countries can change depending upon the subset of accounting practices used. The impact, however, is different on the various groups. For example, the British Commonwealth group (Group I) and the United States group (Group IV) are basically unchanged in character and composition between the two comparisons. The countries which are affected by the differences between reporting and measurement practices are the Latin American and Continental European countries. The previously identified Latin American model disintegrates, with Bolivia and Peru joining Germany and Japan in a grouping (Group II) which has no ready intuitive identification; Argentina, Chile, and Uruguay break off to form a predominantly "South" Latin American group (Group V), while Brazil, Colombia, and Paraguay join a group of European countries (Group III). Similarly, in the previously identified Continental European model, a group of Central and Southern European countries—Belgium, France, Italy, and Spain —join with the above-mentioned Latin American countries, while Germany, Sweden, and Switzerland, on the other hand, go in different directions. The groupings obtained here do not lend themselves to an intuitive basis for differentiation, and it is difficult to characterize these groups.

The difference in the factor structures between those obtained for measurement practices and those obtained for disclosure practices were quantified by the transformation analysis procedures suggested by Rummel [1970]. This is a method for comparing the structures of factor matrices yielded by two different factor analyses. The method yields a transformation matrix, the elements of which can be interpreted as regression coefficients. The coefficients give the best prediction of each factor of one factor matrix in terms of each factor of the second matrix. The transformation matrix is given in Table 3, with factors from the analysis of measurement practices as the rows and the factors from the analysis of disclosure practices as the columns. The U.K. group (Group I in both) and to a slightly lesser extent the U.S. group (Group IV in both) are similarly delineated in both factor analyses. The latter shows some similarity with Group II from the disclosure practices, perhaps because of the shift of Japan. Observing the elements for the rows dealing with the

Latin American group (Group II) and the Continental European group (Group III) it can be seen that both lose their clearcut distinctiveness and the outlines of both groups become blurred as each becomes positively associated with two or more groups on the disclosure dimension. These observations tend to bolster the conclusions drawn earlier about the lack of cohesiveness in the Latin American and Continental European groups when disclosure practices are considered.

Rummel also suggests the computation of an index of deviation for each variable, *i.e.*, country. This index would measure the overall (factor loading) similarity of a country from one factor analysis to the next. The index is zero if a country has identical loadings on all factors in both factor analyses. A level of 0.1 was arbitrarily picked as the level at which a change in factor loadings would be studied to identify outliers. (The average index was 0.17 and the range was from 0.02 to 0.36.) Using this criterion, all but 11 countries had significant shifts in their overall factor loadings between the two factor matrices. The 11 which did not shift significantly in overall factor loadings were: Argentina, Australia, Belgium, Chile, Fiji, Jamaica, Mexico, New Zealand, Rhodesia, United States, and Venezuela. These countries exhibit the greatest stability between the two sets of practices. The fact that most countries registered a shift in loadings between the factor analyses of the two sets of practices again confirms that the groupings achieved are quite different.

C. 1975 Analysis

The above analyses which had been performed with the data from the 1973 Price Waterhouse survey were all replicated using data from the 1975 survey.

1. *Measurement Practices.* The 162 practices relating to measurement in the 46 countries surveyed in 1975 were analyzed using the same criteria as before for the extraction and rotation of factors. Six factors accounting for approximately 72 percent of the variance were isolated and a complete listing of the loadings of the 46 countries is given in Table 4. For the purpose of grouping, each country was assigned to the factor on which it loaded the highest. Since no country loaded highest on the sixth factor, it was ignored in the subsequent analysis. The remaining five factors yielded the following groups (including a single-country "group"):

Group I	Group II	Group III	Group IV	Group V
Australia	Argentina	Belgium	Bermuda*	Chile
Bahamas	Bolivia	Denmark*	Canada	
Fiji	Brazil	France	Japan	
Iran*	Colombia	Germany	Mexico	
Jamaica	Ethiopia	Norway*	Philippines	
Malaysia*	Greece*	Sweden	United States	
Netherlands	India	Switzerland	Venezuela	
New Zeland*	Italy	Zaire*		
Nigeria*	Pakistan			
Republic of Ireland	Panama			
Rhodesia	Paraguay			
Singapore	Peru			
South Africa	Spain			
Trinidad & Tobago	Uruguay			
United Kingdom				

* Countries not included in the 1973 survey.

TABLE 4

ROTATED FACTOR MATRIX BASED ON MEASUREMENT PRACTICES

(1975 Survey Data)

	1	2	3	4	5	6
1 Argentina	.125	.735	.085	.193	.465	.132
2 Australia	.785	.136	.204	.260	.136	.378
3 Bahamas	.603	.344	.053	.438	−.134	−.010
4 Belgium	.293	.408	.648	.124	.053	−.208
5 Bermuda	.485	.169	.241	.650	.115	−.087
6 Bolivia	.145	.851	.106	.122	.173	−.036
7 Brazil	.122	.541	.360	.133	.349	.016
8 Canada	.384	.145	.153	.808	.118	−.025
9 Chile	.242	.292	.308	.035	.632	−.048
10 Colombia	.199	.698	.294	.169	.008	.132
11 Denmark	.385	.212	.558	.166	.300	.084
12 Ethiopia	.467	.628	.231	.069	−.010	−.001
13 Fiji	.756	.171	.222	.274	.124	.397
14 France	.375	.258	.557	.200	.286	.207
15 Germany	.297	.368	.664	.300	.031	−.026
16 Greece	.154	.501	.400	.265	.113	−.387
17 India	.449	.575	.388	.029	.005	−.227
18 Iran	.373	.372	.244	.346	.199	−.294
19 Italy	.158	.565	.420	.238	−.107	−.074
20 Jamaica	.777	.252	.272	.116	.115	−.084
21 Japan	.274	.274	.380	.554	−.037	−.162
22 Kenya	.674	.308	.198	.973	−.038	.052
23 Malaysia	.653	.233	.423	.292	.068	−.102
24 Mexico	.443	.234	.250	.596	.220	−.028
25 Netherlands	.583	.145	.277	.429	.148	−.100
26 New Zealand	.764	.146	.239	.268	.129	.376
27 Nigeria	.628	.442	.242	.281	−.083	−.045
28 Norway	.230	.253	.636	.302	.251	.049
29 Pakistan	.543	.636	.114	.067	−.114	−.159
30 Panama	.326	.589	.162	.339	−.024	.237
31 Paraguay	.138	.824	.187	.125	.087	−.039
32 Peru	.131	.727	.231	.229	.195	−.145
33 Philippines	.403	.385	.186	.575	.168	.149
34 Republic of Ireland	.747	.017	.212	.408	.147	−.114
35 Rhodesia	.765	.247	.174	.238	.214	−.173
36 Singapore	.754	.157	.318	.204	.050	−.030
37 South Africa	.753	.162	.135	.325	.095	−.075
38 Spain	.100	.582	.476	.032	.008	.065
39 Sweden	.404	.232	.623	.160	.209	.049
40 Switzerland	.223	.185	.732	.195	−.007	.163
41 Trinidad & Tobago	.658	.414	.194	.051	.061	−.071
42 United Kingdom	.736	.058	.166	.414	.167	−.112
43 United States	.311	.115	.141	.806	−.047	.180
44 Uruguay	.196	.652	.127	.228	.472	.035
45 Venezuela	.272	.436	.328	.584	.024	−.101
46 Zaire	.272	.450	.516	.188	.080	−.241

A comparison with the measurement grouping obtained in 1973 indicates that the overall composition and character of the groups has remained stable over time. Although the number of groups has changed they can be characterized as follows:

Group I: British Commonwealth model
Group II: Latin American/South European model
Group III: Northern and Central European model
Group IV: United States model
Group V: Chile

Of the 38 countries common to both surveys, the major change between 1973

TABLE 5

ROTATED FACTOR MATRIX BASED ON DISCLOSURE PRACTICES

(1975 Survey Data)

	1	2	3	4	5	6	7	8
1 Argentina	.366	.229	.377	.058	.526	.278	.217	-.118
2 Australia	.172	.874	.176	.232	.042	.021	.138	.024
3 Bahamas	.140	.386	.505	.396	-.011	.046	.159	-.154
4 Belgium	.747	.109	-.080	.211	.049	.244	.014	.130
5 Bermuda	.010	.210	.334	.701	.137	.048	.278	.131
6 Bolivia	.775	.222	.228	.061	.212	.039	.211	-.155
7 Brazil	.624	.047	.209	-.023	.226	.193	.354	-.069
8 Canada	.037	.203	.366	.749	.113	.036	.220	.098
9 Chile	.629	.139	.234	.240	.315	.209	.281	.056
10 Colombia	.675	.059	.402	-.024	.146	-.041	-.140	.155
11 Denmark	.217	.252	.108	.198	.147	.693	.165	-.007
12 Ethiopia	.309	.569	.368	-.005	.010	.300	.188	.108
13 Fiji	.238	.832	.214	.266	.021	.022	.079	.044
14 France	.578	.148	.184	.151	-.065	.507	-.228	.058
15 Germany	.089	.147	.603	.036	.238	.306	.159	.207
16 Greece	.694	.129	.083	.044	.065	.050	.025	.041
17 India	.295	.262	.235	.170	.482	.337	.274	.242
18 Iran	.171	.174	.081	.135	.708	.180	-.055	-.051
19 Italy	.506	.029	.253	-.018	.058	.188	-.077	.514
20 Jamaica	.208	.409	.207	.582	.107	.215	.139	.055
21 Japan	.333	.158	.643	.115	.212	.228	.188	.115
22 Kenya	.188	.741	.127	.121	.345	.262	.048	.098
23 Malaysia	.114	.558	.128	.323	.346	.243	-.089	.383
24 Mexico	.256	.370	.531	.301	.279	.093	.106	.166
25 Netherlands	.056	.374	.375	.492	.183	-.092	-.007	.056
26 New Zealand	.175	.876	.155	.254	.039	.126	.070	.093
27 Nigeria	.025	.598	.070	.347	.290	.330	-.060	.227
28 Norway	.287	.072	.191	.123	.161	.567	.459	.175
29 Pakistan	.265	.310	.213	.162	.470	.066	.301	.409
30 Panama	.298	.247	.728	.224	-.027	.003	.129	.037
31 Paraguay	.804	.208	.263	.064	.222	.121	.099	.054
32 Peru	.360	.274	.352	.285	.540	.019	.272	.032
33 Philippines	.156	.182	.591	.251	.479	.021	.038	.214
34 Republic of Ireland	.241	.250	.164	.750	.107	.107	-.180	-.111
35 Rhodesia	.063	.491	.189	.638	.105	.076	.038	.105
36 Singapore	.092	.790	.155	.266	.253	.110	-.151	.042
37 South Africa	.069	.514	.178	.362	.260	.277	.095	-.097
38 Spain	.859	.033	-.038	.021	-.024	.045	-.035	.206
39 Sweden	.192	.112	.142	.094	.188	.754	-.034	.139
40 Switzerland	.303	.290	.272	.129	-.090	.184	.171	.587
41 Trinidad & Tobago	.355	.502	.121	.259	.136	.161	.470	.217
42 United Kingdom	-.011	.295	-.005	.674	.036	.381	-.101	.019
43 United States	.040	.097	.723	.454	.175	.032	-.035	.147
44 Uruguay	.520	.260	.290	.216	.338	.189	.319	-.220
45 Venezuela	.132	.203	.690	.288	.030	.237	-.187	-.020
46 Zaire	.863	.187	.065	.052	.065	.089	.042	.064

and 1975 in the measurement groupings is the expansion of the Latin American group. Pakistan (from the British Commonwealth group), Panama (from the United States group), and Italy and Spain (both from the Continental European group) join it, while only Chile leaves it to become its own "group." The only other change is Venezuela, going from the Continental European model to the United States model.

Another point to note is the affiliation of the eight countries included for the first time in the 1975 survey. Most of them are linked with those groups which one would have expected on the basis of Seidler's "spheres-of-influence" classification [1967]. Denmark and Norway are to be found in the North/Central Euro-

the factor on which it had the highest loading. Factor 7 on which no country loaded the highest is ignored in the subsequent analysis. The seven remaining factors yield the following groupings of the 46 countries:

Group I	Group II	Group III	Group IV
Belgium	Australia	Bahamas	Bermuda*
Bolivia	Ethiopia	Germany	Canada
Brazil	Fiji	Japan	Jamaica
Chile	Kenya	Mexico	Netherlands
Colombia	Malaysia*	Panama	Republic of Ireland
France	New Zealand	Philippines	Rhodesia
Greece*	Nigeria*	United States	United Kingdom
Paraguay	Singapore	Venezuela	
Spain	South Africa		
Uruguay	Trinidad & Tobago		
Zaire*			

	Group V	Group VI	Group VII
	Argentina	Denmark*	Italy
	India	Norway*	Switzerland
	Iran*	Sweden	
	Pakistan		
	Peru		

* Not included in the 1973 survey.

pean group, which also includes Sweden. Zaire (formerly the Belgian Congo) is also included in that group, which is not anomalous considering that that group also included Belgium. Nigeria and Malaysia also follow colonial patterns by exhibiting an affiliation with the British Commonwealth model. Greece is associated with the Latin American/South European group, while Iran and Bermuda are linked with the British Commonwealth and United States models, respectively.

2. *Disclosure practices.* The same factor analytic procedure was applied to the 102 observations on disclosure practices in the 46 countries. The factor analysis yielded eight factors accounting for 73 percent of total variance in the data. A complete listing of the loading of the countries on the rotated factors is given in Table 5. Each country was assigned to

A comparison of the groupings ob-

tained here with those obtained with the 1975 measurement practices reveals the same lack of clear-cut groups that was observed with the 1973 data. It is apparent that the pattern underlying measurement practices in different countries is quite different from the pattern underlying disclosure practices. It is interesting to note that Chile is not an outlier with respect to disclosure practices as it was with measurement practices. The major point to note in comparing these groupings with the 1975 measurement groupings is the same disintegration of the Continental European model that was observed with the 1973 data. Denmark and Norway, both new to the survey in 1975, join Sweden, which was a single-country "group" in 1973, to form a Scandinavian cluster; France and Belgium (and also Zaire) join the Latin American/South European clustering which was apparent in the 1973 disclosure clusters. Germany, on the other hand,

TABLE 6

TRANSFORMATION MATRIX

Disclosure and Measurement Groupings for 1975

Disclosure Groups	Measurement Groups					
	I	II	III	IV	V	VI
I	.03471	.62300	.33670	.00283	.16781	−.13457
II	.73277	.10673	.04313	−.05188	−.06535	.28554
III	−.01699	.32644	.12510	.58064	−.07843	.21107
IV	.54843	−.15385	.07851	.52763	.18130	−.26455
V	.03742	.43512	−.14613	.06364	.22529	−.29476
VI	.24183	.00069	.63196	.03558	.22162	−.07316
VII	−.13349	.10818	−.08318	−.19601	.15844	.12999
VIII	.12464	−.01960	.52809	.06689	−.37418	−.01581

joins Japan as it had in the 1973 clusters, while Italy joins Switzerland as a separate "group."

The other major point to be noted is that while the U.S. group stays largely intact across the two sets of methods, the British Commonwealth cluster splits into two groups. This split was not observed with the 1973 data; it may be speculated that it is the result of the entry of the United Kingdom into the European Common Market during the intervening period. However, in general, there is no clear-cut basis for systematically differentiating between the various groups and offering intuitively appealing characterizations.

The lack of agreement between the factor structures can also be seen in the transformation matrix given in Table 6. The rows indicate the factors obtained from the analysis of disclosure practices, while the columns give the factors obtained from the analysis of measurement practices. None of the elements of the matrix is above 0.8, and only one (between the "Eastern Commonwealth" group—group II on disclosure practices and the British Commonwealth group—Group I on measurement practices) is above 0.7. Since 1.0 would indicate con-

gruence of two factors, the results here indicate that the clusters of countries obtained with measurement practices are not similar to the clusters of countries obtained with measurement practices are not similar to the clusters obtained with disclosure practices. Examination of the index of deviation indicated that nine of the 46 countries had significant (index greater than 0.1) shifts in their overall factor loadings. These nine countries were: Argentina, Bahamas, Chile, Ethiopia, Germany, Greece, Japan, Nigeria, and Pakistan.

The preceding analysis answers the first question raised in this study. It shows that the groupings achieved on different subsets of accounting practices are, in fact, different. Also, disclosure practices exhibit greater diversity than the factors obtained from the analysis of measurement practices. In the second part of the analysis, we attempted to see whether different underlying economic and cultural variables were associated with the groupings.

II. ASSOCIATION OF ECONOMIC AND CULTURAL VARIABLES WITH GROUPINGS

It has long been argued by accountants that accounting is shaped by its environment. APB Statement No. 4 [1970, para. 209] states, "Generally accepted accounting principles change in response to changes in economic and social conditions, to new knowledge and technology, and to demands of users for more serviceable financial information." A similar line of argument can be found in the FASB's Objectives of Financial Reporting by Business Enterprises [1978, para. 9], "Accordingly, the objectives in this Statement are affected by the economic, legal, political, and social environment in the United States." Following this line of reasoning would lead one to believe that countries with similar environments, in the sense of similar economies and cultures, should have similar accounting practices and those with different environments should exhibit differences in accounting practices. As Choi and Mueller [1978, p. 22] state, "If we then accept the proposition that the environments in which accounting operates are not the same in different countries . . . it stands to reason that accounting must necessarily differ from case to case if it is to retain the sharp cutting edge of social utility."

The earlier study by Frank [1979] confirmed that an association between environmental variables and accounting groupings exists. However, it is of interest to investigate whether the environmental variables associated with disclosure practices are different from those associated with measurement practices. For example, one might expect factors such as extent of similarity between legal structures to be more important in the determination of disclosure practices since many disclosure requirements are laid down in laws such as the Securities Acts of 1933 and 1934 in the United States. Similarly, the degree of separation of ownership from management and the overall state of economic development might have an

impact more on the determination of disclosure issues as would the degree of public ownership of business enterprises since disclosure issues become more urgent as ownership is diffused. Similarity in measurement practices, on the other hand, might be affected more by a similar economic experience, such as rapid inflation or the emergence of firms with significant overseas investments. In such cases, we would expect the countries to draw upon each other's experiences in formulating approaches to measuring such economic events.

A. *Data*

In this, the second step of the analysis, discriminant functions were first constructed using data from 36 countries. Four countries (Bahamas, Bermuda, Malaysia, and Rhodesia) were excluded from this part of the study since the United Nations source for the economic and cultural variables did not provide data for these countries. Six countries (Denmark, Greece, Iran, Nigeria, Norway, and Zaire) were kept as a hold-out sample to test the predictive power of the discriminant functions. These countries were chosen to form the hold-out sample since they were new to the 1975 sample.

The major cultural variable used was the country's official language. This variable should capture similarities in legal systems, since colonizing countries usually bequeathed their own legal system and official language to the colonies. Use of English, French, Spanish, Portuguese, German, and Italian was indicated through use of a separate (0, 1) dummy variable for each of these countries.

Eight economic structure variables were included to capture the importance of the degree of industrialization and the state of development. These were: (1) per capita income, (2) private sector consumption relative to gross national product, (3) relative gross capital formation, (4) relative balance of trade (exports less imports), (5) agricultural sector output relative to gross national product, (6) geometric (average) annual growth rate of real gross national product, (7) average annual change in the country's foreign exchange rate for U.S. dollars, and (8) average annual change in consumer prices. Averages were computed over the period 1962–1970 inclusive.

Three bilateral trade variables were constructed for this analysis to capture trading ties between countries: imports, exports, and total trade (imports plus exploits). Two differences exist in terms of how these variables were measured in this study as compared to Frank's earlier study [1979] of 1973 accounting practices. In the earlier study, country A's imports from country B were assumed to be equal to B's exports to A. Because of differences in how duties are assigned, the point in time when warehoused goods are included in the import/export category, etc., the equality mentioned above does not strictly hold. In this study, separate import and export data were gathered and used in constructing the trade variables. Differences due to this alternative measurement procedure are minor.

The major difference in the construction of the trade variables between this and the Frank study [1979] is how the data were summarized for use in the discriminant analysis. In the earlier study, the trade statistics for individual countries were aggregated by country groupings, as determined from the factor analysis. The same country groupings were thus assumed to be known for the dependent variable (country groups with similar accounting principles and reporting practices) and for the independent trade variables. This was not a major concern in that study since the discriminant analysis was used in the earlier

study primarily for the descriptive purposes to show the close association between a country's economic and cultural characteristics and the accounting principles and practices it followed. In this study, we use the discriminant functions for prediction, as well as classification, purposes. To make unbiased prediction tests requires that information incorporated in the dependent variable not be used in constructing the independent, explanatory variables. To avoid creating such a bias, we used the Gutman-Lingoes smallest space analysis technique, SSA-I, to construct three sets of six trading blocks, one based on imports, a second based on exports, and a third based on total trade.

Smallest space analysis (SSA) is a technique whose objective is similar to factor analysis, i.e., to reduce a large number of variables into a more compact set. Instead of "loadings" and "factors," this technique yields "coordinates" and "dimensions" which can be interpreted analogously. Each dimension represents a block of countries closely linked to each other through their trading ties. As mentioned above, three sets of six dimensions or trading blocks were identified. The scores or coordinates of each country on each dimension obtained after a varimax rotation procedure similar to factor analysis were then used as additional variables in a stepwise multiple discriminant analysis.

B. Measurement Practices

To separate the five groups identified from the 1975 measurement practices, four discriminant functions incorporating 14 variables were developed. These are the variables which are most helpful in distinguishing one group from another. Variables having an F-value of less than 1.0 were excluded from the functions to ensure that each new variable

TABLE 7

STATISTICS AND COEFFICIENTS FOR DISCRIMINANT FUNCTIONS

(Five Country-Groups Based on 1975 Measurement Practices)

Discriminant Function	Eigenvalue	Relative Percentage of Variance Explained
1	20.28123	72.14
2	5.54915	19.74
3	1.79360	6.38
4	.48847	1.74

Standardized Discriminant Function Coefficients

Variable*	Func. 1	Func. 2	Func. 3	Func. 4
PCINC	−.15783	−.03425	−.70824	−.23241
PVTCOM	.02090	−.42862	−.15204	.28516
BOT	.12204	−.13515	−.40640	−.17116
AGSEC	−.36588	−.22393	.02271	−.30652
GNPGR	.17815	.03300	−.66175	−.04788
IMPORT2	.03758	−.53581	−.38788	−.29477
IMPORT5	−.11883	−.02301	.49665	−.70039
TOTTR2	−.04576	−.11889	.08155	.93717
TOTTR5	.30093	−.06241	−.52312	.50142
TOTTR6	.15269	−.20809	−.43914	−.21185
ENGLISH	.43462	.05506	−.56149	.28497
FRENCH	−.56961	−.06400	−.22521	−.11773
GERM	−.55298	.01100	−.13039	−.04819
ITAL	.03094	−.29792	.00304	−.05797

(Largest Coefficient for each function is underlined)

Centroids of Groups in Reduced Space

	Func. 1	Func. 2	Func. 3	Func. 4
Group 1	.45353	1.08409	.56911	.18319
Group 2	.13371	−.98595	.43719	−.29004
Group 3	−2.33724	.30685	−.32964	.07103
Group 4	.73674	.19949	−1.60335	−.28097
Group 5	.53867	−1.83878	−.67534	3.08613

* See Table 8 for names of variables

added a significant amount of separation above and beyond the variables already included in the functions. The number of discriminant functions to be used in further analysis was determined by examining the relative percentage of variance explained by each function. The functions themselves can be interpreted like the factors in factor analysis, and clues to the dimension each function represents can be found by looking to the variable whose standardized coefficient has the largest absolute value on that function. The standardized discriminant function coefficients are given in Table 7 along with other summary statistics on the four functions. Table 8 lists the names of the variables entering the analysis.

The first two of these functions represent approximately 92 percent of the discriminatory power, and are significant at the .001 level. All three types of variables—cultural, economic structure, and trading block data play a role in the

TABLE 8

LIST OF VARIABLES

PCINC:	per capita income
PVTCOM:	private sector consumption relative to Gross National Product
BOT:	relative balance of trade
AGSEC:	agricultural sector relative to Gross National Product
GNPGR:	geometric annual growth rate of real Gross National Product
IMPORT2:	Trading block of Argentina, Bolivia, Brazil, Chile, Mexico, Paraguay, Peru, and Uruguay
IMPORT5:	Trading block of Denmark, Greece, Iran, and Ireland
EXPORT1:	Trading block of Belgium, France, Italy, Netherlands, Nigeria, Republic of Ireland, South Africa, Spain, United Kingdom, United States, Uruguay, and Zaire
EXPORT2:	Trading block of Argentina, Brazil, Chile, Colombia, Denmark, Panama, Paraguay, Sweden, Trinidad, and Venezuela
EXPORT4:	Trading block of Ethiopia, Japan, Mexico, Peru, and Philippines
EXPORT6:	Trading block of India, Iran, Pakistan, Singapore, and Switzerland
TOTTR2:	Trading block of Brazil, Canada, Chile, Denmark, Colombia, Germany, Norway, and Switzerland
TOTTR5:	Trading block of Argentina, Paraguay, and Peru
TOTTR6:	Trading block of Mexico, Panama, and Trinidad & Tobago
ENGLISH:	Dummy variable for use of the English language
FRENCH:	Dummy variable for use of the French language
GERM:	Dummy variable for use of the German language
ITAL:	Dummy variable for use of the Italian language

discriminant functions. The five economic structure variables are: per capita income, private sector consumption, balance of trade, role of the agricultural sector, and the GNP growth rate. The four cultural variables are English, French, German, and Italian. The trade variables include two of the import trading blocks and three of the total trade trading blocks. Based on the absolute value of the standardized discriminant function coefficients, the single most important variable for each of the functions are:

Function 1: French
Function 2: Trading block of Mexico, Peru, Paraguay, Uruguay, Argentina, Bolivia, Brazil, and Chile based on imports
Function 3: Per capita income
Function 4: Trading block of Argentina, Paraguay, and Peru based on total trade.

There are two ways of judging the success of discriminant analysis—first, how well the functions classify the cases which had been used in constructing those functions, and second, and also

more importantly, how well it predicts the membership of new cases excluded from the function-building process. Discriminant functions may be outstanding successes by the first test, but may fail the stronger second test. In such instances, as happens in this study, the results of the analysis should be treated with caution and any conclusions that may be drawn are only tentative in nature.

The four functions classified all of the 36 countries used to construct the functions correctly, as shown in Table 9. The predictive results with respect to the six countries in the hold-out sample, which had not been used to construct the discriminant functions, however, were not as impressive. Only three out of the six countries were classified correctly. These were Greece, Nigeria, and Zaire. Denmark (actually in Group III) was classified in Group II; Iran (actually in Group I) was classified in Group IV, and Norway (actually in Group III) was classified in Group I.

TABLE 9

PREDICTION RESULTS—MEASUREMENT PRACTICES
(Countries Used to Construct Discriminant Functions)

Actual Group	No. of Cases	Predicted Group Membership				
		Group 1	Group 2	Group 3	Group 4	Group 5
Group 1	11	11	0	0	0	0
		100.0%	0%	0%	0%	0%
Group 2	13	0	13	0	0	0
		0	100.0%	0%	0%	0%
Group 3	5	0	0	5	0	0
		0%	0%	100.0%	0%	0%
Group 4	6	0	0	0	6	0
		0%	0%	0%	100.0%	0%
Group 5	1	0	0	0	0	1
		0%	0%	0%	0%	100.0%

Percentage of "grouped" cases correctly classified: 100.0%

C. Disclosure Practices

A similar discriminant procedure was run to identify the variables associated with the seven groups present in the 1975 disclosure data. Six discriminant functions incorporating 13 variables were developed. The standardized discriminant function coefficients are given in Table 10 along with other summary statistics on the six functions.

In this case, the first three of these functions are the most important ones since they represent approximately 92 percent of the discriminatory power, and are significant at the .02 level (or better). Again, all three types of variables play a role in the discriminant functions. The four economic structure variables are: per capita income, private sector consumption, balance of trade and the role of the agricultural sector. The two cultural variables are English and German, while the trade variables include four of the export trading blocks and three of the total trade trading blocks.

Based on the absolute value of the standardized discriminant function coefficients, the single most important variable for each of the functions are:

Function 1: English
Function 2: Importance of the agricultural sector
Function 3: Trading block of Mexico, Panama, and Trinidad & Tobago based on total trade
Function 4: Trading block of India, Iran, Pakistan, Singapore, and Switzerland based on exports
Function 5: Germany
Function 6: Trading block of Brazil, Canada, Chile, Colombia, Denmark, Germany, Norway, and Switzerland based on total trade.

It should be noted that none of the variables found to have the greatest association with disclosure clusters had the same dominant position with respect to measurement groups. This result would suggest that measurement and disclosure practices in countries may be determined by different underlying environmental variables. It is difficult, however, to distinguish between the two sets of environmental variables on any con-

TABLE 10

STATISTICS AND COEFFICIENTS FOR DISCRIMINANT FUNCTIONS

(Seven Country Groups Based on 1975 Disclosure Practices)

	Discriminant Function	Eigenvalue	Relative Percentage of Variance Explained
	1	11.72267	58.12
	2	3.99413	19.80
	3	2.86354	14.20
	4	.76771	3.81
	5	.54109	2.68
	6	.27982	1.39

Standardized Discriminant Function Coefficients

Variable*	Func. 1	Func. 2	Func. 3	Func. 4	Func. 5	Func. 6
PCINC	.39505	−.28494	−.02571	−.48939	.22529	−.39951
PCTCOM	.21276	.57404	.03531	−.32088	−.30422	−.22466
BOT	−.15062	.15253	−.24851	.17354	.25479	.11367
AGSEC	.58180	−.66993	.33218	.27298	.06118	.32783
EXPORT1	.14490	.25057	.27401	−.44714	−.40396	−.21583
EXPORT2	.67356	−.24167	.31235	.19114	−.18493	−.41792
EXPORT4	.19721	−.22063	−.26943	.12212	.26166	−.26464
EXPORT6	.44322	−.00375	−.09753	.76185	−.08608	−.41329
TOTTR2	−.38305	−.19641	.16900	.13527	−.12939	.91950
TOTTR5	−.06748	.35371	−.25224	.63948	−.08820	−.22954
TOTTR6	−.40387	.24153	−.64160	−.24475	.29130	.07630
ENGLISH	−.77968	.35789	−.02730	.36794	−.31581	−.32416
GERM	.07383	−.21313	−.49613	−.24463	−.82295	0.01277

Centroids of Groups in Reduced Space

	Func. 1	Func. 2	Func. 3	Func. 4	Func. 5	Func. 6
Group 1	.74584	.84687	.40572	−.06867	−.07152	.41290
Group 2	−1.20260	−.69315	.51180	.45512	−.18182	.25944
Group 3	−.20234	−.17771	−1.24025	−.23496	.77264	.09474
Group 4	−.43695	.02123	.53887	−1.22565	−.25167	−.62538
Group 5	.22810	.80079	−.27398	1.16953	−.08310	−.89321
Group 6	2.40021	−3.42810	1.59997	.31260	.92131	−.38827
Group 7	1.45102	−1.56073	−2.66827	−.17208	−2.56927	.22025

* See Table 8 for variable names.

ceptual basis. Our *a priori* reasoning had led us to believe that the cultural and economic variables might be associated with disclosure practices, while the trading variables might be more important for measurement practices. This, however, does not seem to be the case.

With respect to the classification of countries into similar disclosure groups, the discriminant functions classified all but one of the 36 countries correctly. Thus, the analysis was very successful by the first, weaker test. The exception was Japan, which was actually in Group III but was classified in Group V. The classification results are given in Table 11. The predictive results with respect to the six hold-out countries was poor. Only one out of the six, Greece, was classified correctly, reflecting the lack of any clear-cut systematic basis for differentiating between the disclosure groups. Nigeria (Group II) and Denmark (Group VI) were both predicted to belong to

TABLE 11

PREDICTION RESULTS—DISCLOSURE PRACTICES

(Countries Used to Construct Discriminant Functions)

Actual Group	No. of Cases	Predicted Group Membership						
		Group 1	Group 2	Group 3	Group 4	Group 5	Group 6	Group 7
Group 1	10	10 100.0%	0 0%	0 0%	0 0%	0 0%	0 0%	0 0%
Group 2	8	0 0%	8 100.0%	0 0%	0 0%	0 0%	0 0%	0 0%
Group 3	7	0 0%	0 0%	6 85.7%	0 0%	1 14.3%	0 0%	0 0%
Group 4	5	0 0%	0 0%	0 0%	5 100.0%	0 0%	0 0%	0 0%
Group 5	4	0 0%	0 0%	0 0%	0 0%	4 100.0%	0 0%	0 0%
Group 6	1	0 0%	0 0%	0 0%	0 0%	0 0%	1 100.0%	0 0%
Group 7	1	0 0%	0 0%	0 0%	0 0%	0 0%	0 0%	1 100.0%

Percentage of "grouped" cases correctly classified: 97.22%.

Group I; Iran (Group V) and Zaire (Group I) were predicted to belong to Group II and Norway (Group VII) was predicted as a Group III country. Thus, the analysis was quite unsuccessful as judged by this second, stronger, test.

III. LIMITATIONS

The analyses described above suffer from several limitations; the purpose of this section is to describe the more prominent of these shortcomings and the steps taken to deal with them. These limitations should be kept in mind when drawing conclusions from this study.

First, the primary data source for this study)—the Price Waterhouse & Co. Survey—may be a source of potential error. In its favor, it should be pointed out that uniform procedures are used worldwide in collecting, compiling, editing, and checking the consistency of the data. Also, the firm tries not to bias the survey in favor of the accounting practices of their own clients but tries to develop an overall consensus about the accounting practices used in presenting financial statements to shareholders in a given country.[2] This process entails the use of considerable judgment when there is diversity of practice within a country. A similar situation arises when there are not many published financial statements in a given country. The last two considerations have an impact on the validity of the data. Another point to be noted is that

[2] Details on the procedures used to collect, process, and check the consistency of the survey data were obtained from Alan D. Stickler of Price Waterhouse & Co., Toronto.

the companies whose practices are surveyed may not be comparable across countries. For example, the companies whose practices are reported on in the the survey may not all meet the same criteria such as being listed on a stock exchange, or even being publicly held. While these drawbacks of our data source are all quite important, there was no feasible way to make alterations to the published data.

A second possible source of error is the transformation of the original categorical data into percentages which represent the mid-points of intervals, as described above in Section II. To assess the possible error from this source, each factor analysis for 1975 was replicated by SSA using counts of category codes in common between all possible pairs of countries as input. The reason for this replication is that while factor analysis requires that the data be measured on an interval scale, SSA is satisfied with nominally scaled data, a weaker level of measurement. SSA is, therefore, useful in validating the results of factor analysis when, as was done in this study, data which are measured on a scale intermediate between a nominal and interval scale is input into factor analysis. In this analysis, six dimensions were recovered from the original data. Both the disclosure and the measurement analysis yielded a Kruskal stress coefficient value of 0.07. This value is usually interpreted as indicating goodness of fit to the data, much like the R-square statistic in regression analysis. This coefficient can take on values from 0.0 to 1.0 with lower values indicating better fits. A value of .05 is usually considered to indicate a good fit.

As pointed out earlier, SSA yields coordinates and dimensions which can be used to prepare graphic plots of the original variables (i.e., countries) with respect to these dimensions. The degree of similarity between the original variables is revealed by their distances from each other. The results of the analysis are displayed in Figures 1 and 2. For ease in presentation, each country is plotted using only its scores on the first two of the six dimensions. Countries are numbered with the same numerical code used in Table 4, and each group of countries identified in the factor analysis is identified by a Roman numeral. The robustness of the groupings yielded by the factor analysis on the 1975 survey data confirms a similar finding by Frank [1979] with respect to the 1973 survey data. The implication of this finding is that measurement error in coding the data is not a limitation of this analysis.

A third possible source of concern is the lack of predictive power of the discriminant functions, especially those fitted to the disclosure groupings. Several possibilities exist which could account for the weak predictive performance of this set of discriminant functions, other than an inherent lack of distinctiveness of the disclosure groups. The (assumed correct) original assignment of the misclassified countries to common disclosure practices groups could have been in error. We discount this possibility since all of the countries in the hold-out samples had relatively high loadings on only a single factor. A partial explanation might relate to the removal of Denmark and Norway from the set of 42 countries used to form the seven disclosure groups. This transfer reduced the Scandinavian group (Group VI) to a single country, Sweden. The two single-country groups (Groups VI and VII) accordingly show an unrealistic degree of homogeneity, and might account for the misclassification of Denmark and Norway. Another explanation is the "overfitting" of the discriminant function to the sample data occurred. The relatively large number of groups

90

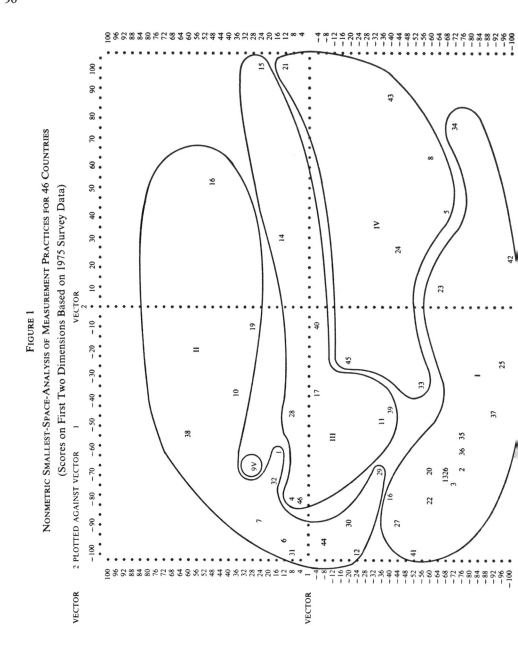

FIGURE 1

NONMETRIC SMALLEST-SPACE-ANALYSIS OF MEASUREMENT PRACTICES FOR 46 COUNTRIES

(Scores on First Two Dimensions Based on 1975 Survey Data)

NONMETRIC SMALLEST-SPACE-ANALYSIS OF DISCLOSURE PRACTICES FOR 46 COUNTRIES
(Scores on First Two Dimensions Based on 1975 Survey Data)

VECTOR 2 PLOTTED AGAINST VECTOR 1

(seven), small number of countries per group (from one to ten), and large number of variables in the discriminant function (13) may have combined to yield an excellent fit to the sample of 36 countries from which the six discriminant functions were constructed, but poor predictive power to new countries not in the original sample of 36. A final possible explanation is that the number of countries (six) on which the prediction tests were made is too small to be representative. Some of these possibilities were pursued further and the discriminant analysis was rerun with (a) changes in the F-level for inclusion of variables in the analysis, (b) an increase in the number of countries in the hold-out sample to a randomly selected set of 14, and use of the remaining 28 to construct the discriminant functions, and (c) a reduction in the number of variables in the analysis to two economic structure variables (per capita income and change in the foreign exchange rate), the six total trade variables, and three language variables (English, French, and German). None of these changes had the effect of improving the predictive power of the discriminant functions or changing their form in any significant way.

The fourth limitation to be kept in mind is the possibility of omitted variables in the discriminant analysis. As pointed out by Benston [1975] and Zeff [1972], a variety of factors can have an impact on the similarities and differences between the accounting principles of countries. Many of them are factors which are difficult to quantify (and hence were excluded from the analysis). These omitted factors include the prospect of governmental intervention in the establishment of accounting standards, the professional and regulatory environment, the existence of a sophisticated and demanding financial press, the prevalence of widespread stock ownership, and the vulnerability of accountants to lawsuits. Also, in Third World countries the presence of U.S.- or U.K.-based multinational firms may be a powerful homogenizing influence.

IV. SUMMARY AND CONCLUSIONS

This study attempted to determine whether the classification of countries suggested by various authors applies equally well to the measurement and disclosure subsets of accounting practices. Observations on both the disclosure and measurement practices in 1973 for a sample of 38 countries were factor-analyzed, and the resulting factor structures for disclosure and measurement were compared. The environmental variables most closely associated with each set of groupings were determined by discriminant analysis. The analyses were then replicated for the same two subsets of practices using 1975 data on the measurement and disclosure practices for 46 countries. It was found that the number of groupings, the character and composition of each group, and even the underlying environmental variables most closely associated with the practices were quite different between the two subsets of accounting practices.

The major implication of these findings is that the groupings of countries and the classification schemes offered by authors such as Seidler [1967] and Frank [1979] may have only limited validity. The clear-cut distinctions that they propose are found to apply primarily to the measurement subset of practices. The disclosure practices do not seem to conform to any such conceptual classification schemes. They present a picture of greater diversity where the boundary lines between different groups become blurred and indistinct. A less direct implication is that greater care needs to be exercised in cross-country comparisons. Since the affiliation of a given country with others is dependent upon the set of accounting practices selected, the validity of cross-country comparisons depends upon the nature of the practice on which the comparison is made. For example, the financial statements of Belgian and Swiss firms are much more comparable on the measurement subset than on the disclosure subset.

Both the earlier Frank [1979] research and this study have established a clear association between economic and cultural variables and accounting groupings. The next step in this line of research would be to establish empirically a direction of causation with a longitudinal study of a sample of countries over a sufficiently long period of time. The objective would be to see whether, as economic structure and trade and cultural affiliations change over time, they are accompanied by a change in accounting affiliations. Another direction that research could take is that of using the methodology presented in the first part of the study, factor analysis, as a tool for evaluating the success of harmonization measures. A decreasing number of groups over time would be an indicator of success in reducing the diversity of accounting practices. This kind of research could further help policy makers by isolating the specific practices which cause the most difference between groups of countries. For instance, the differences between groups may be caused by differences in a small set of practices such as those dealing with inflation. The attention of policy makers attempting to harmonize accounting practices could then be directed toward these practices.

Since this research was largely aimed at empirically assessing the validity of international classifications proposed repeatedly in the accounting literature rather than researching specific issues of policy alternatives, it is difficult to make definite policy prescriptions. This task is complicated further by the fact that the basic thrust of our empirical results is that the situation is more complex than has generally been assumed by accountants and may not be amenable to easy manipulations by policy makers. The findings do suggest that policy-making bodies concerned with the harmonization of international accounting standards should concern themselves with reducing diversity in disclosure practices, since it it is with respect to them that the greatest dispersion exists. Our findings, however, tend to confirm the conclusions drawn by Frank [1979] that underlying environmental variables are closely associated with the groupings obtained from accounting practices. The implications of this are that reaching the goal of harmonization may be difficult because, given the above association, countries may be reluctant to make a change in accounting practices so long as the underlying environmental variables are significantly different. If this is the case, then the issuance of authoritative standards by policy-making bodies may be a less effective force for harmonization of accounting practices than is the growing commonality of world-wide economic interests.

REFERENCES

Accounting Principles Board (APB) (1970), "Basic Concepts and Accounting Principles Underlying Financial Statements of Business Enterprises," *Statement No. 4* (AICPA, 1970).

Beaver, W. H. (1978), "Current Trends in Corporate Disclosure," *Journal of Accountancy* (January 1978), pp. 44–52.

94   Benston, G. J. (1975), "Accounting Standards in the United States and the United Kingdom: Their Nature, Causes and Consequences," *Vanderbilt Law Review* (January 1975), pp. 235–68.

Buckley, J. W. and M. H. Buckley (1974), *The Accounting Profession* (Melville, 1974).

Choi, F. D. S. and G. G. Mueller (1978), *An Introduction to Multinational Accounting* (Prentice-Hall, 1978).

Financial Accounting Standards Board (FASB) (1978), "Objectives of Financial Reporting by Business Enterprises," *Statement of Financial Accounting Concepts No. 1* (FASB, 1978).

Frank, W. G. (1979), "An Empirical Analysis of International Accounting Practices," *Journal of Accounting Research* (Autumn 1979).

Mueller, G. G. (1967), *International Accounting* (Macmillan Company, 1967).

———, "Accounting Principles Generally Accepted in the United States Versus Those Generally Accepted Elsewhere," *The International Journal of Accounting Education and Research* (Spring 1968), pp. 91–103.

Previts, G. J. (1975), "On The Subject of Methodology and Models of International Accountancy," *The International Journal of Accounting Education and Research* (Spring 1975), pp. 1–12.

Price Waterhouse International, *Accounting Principles and Reporting Practices* (Price Waterhouse, 1973).

———, *Accounting Principles and Reporting Practices* (Price Waterhouse, 1975).

"Report of the Committee on Generally Accepted Accounting Principles for Smaller and/or Closely Held Businesses," *Journal of Accountancy* (October 1976), pp. 116–20.

Rummel, R. J. (1970), *Applied Factor Analysis* (Northwestern University Press, 1970).

Seidler, L. J. (1967), "International Accounting—The Ultimate Theory Course," THE ACCOUNTING REVIEW (October 1967), pp. 775–81.

Zeff, S. A. (1972), *Forging Accounting Principles in Five Countries: A History and an Analysis of Trends* (Stipes Publishing Company, 1972).

CHAPTER 6

The impact of international accounting differences from a security-analysis perspective: some European evidence*

S. J. Gray

While there has been an awareness that international accounting differences exist, with differential impact on the measurement of company profits as between countries, there have been few studies which have attempted to determine empirically the quantitative significance of such differences. The comparative studies by Davidson and Kohlmeier[1] and Abel[2] certainly provided some indications of the significance of country differences for profit measurement purposes, but this was limited by their reliance on simulation exercises as a basis for analysis. In contrast, the more recent work of Choi[3] and Barrett[4] has been concerned with quantitative issues relating to the extent of overall financial disclosure and its correlation with the development of capital markets, rather than with the differential effect of accounting practices on the measurement of profits.

This paper specifically explores the question of impact and the extent to which the measurement of company profits is correlated with national characteristics. These characteristics can be expected to reflect the dif-

* Professor, University of Glasgow. [Accepted for publication May 1979.]
[1] Sidney Davidson and John M. Kohlmeier, "A Measure of the Impact of Some Foreign Accounting Principles," *Journal of Accounting Research* (Autumn 1966): 183–212.
[2] Rein Abel, "A Comparative Simulation of German and United States Accounting Principles," *Journal of Accounting Research* (Spring 1969): 1–11.
[3] Frederick Choi, "Financial Disclosure and Entry to the European Capital Market," *Journal of Accounting Research* (Autumn 1973): 159–75.
[4] M. Edgar Barrett, "Annual Report Disclosure: Are American Reports Superior?" *Journal of International Business Studies* (Fall 1975): 15–24; "Financial Reporting Practices: Disclosure and Comprehensiveness in an International Setting." *Journal of Accounting Research* (Spring 1976): 10–26.

* This article is reprinted, with permission, from the *Journal of Accounting Research* (Spring 1980) pp 64–76

ferential influence of factors, such as managerial philosophy, the structure and development of capital markets, legal requirements, professional accounting standards, and tax law, which constitute a country's accounting policy-making system. Is there support for the hypothesis that country factors are significant in determining quantitatively the relative amount of profits disclosed? Are some countries more "conservative" in their approach to profits measurement than others? If so, what is the nature of the differences discovered? Is there, for example, a correlation between profits-measurement behavior and the efficiency and development of national equity markets?

These questions are investigated by a comparative empirical study of profits reported by large companies in France, West Germany, and the United Kingdom and of adjustments to such published results carried out by European security analysts, for the period 1972–75. The study is limited to these three European countries because of the current lack of relevant comparative data. Subsequent to the statistical analysis, an attempt is made to explain the situation discovered and to analyze the reasons for any differences in measurement behavior. Finally, some implications arising from the findings of the study are discussed.

Criteria for Comparison: A "Conservatism" Index

A fundamental problem in any comparative study is to establish the criteria for comparison. This is even more complex when the focus is on profits reported by companies in different countries, where the outcome is determined by the application of differing sets of national accounting practices. If the differential impact of accounting systems and practices on profits is to be gauged in an international context, then a common yardstick for the purposes of evaluation is an essential prerequisite to the analysis.

In the European context, a candidate with some potential for this task can be found in the standardized method of analysis and presentation of company accounts which has been developed by the European Federation of Financial Analysts Societies (EFFAS). This "European Method" of financial analysis is the outcome of a project (set up in 1963 and completed in 1967) for the special purpose of overcoming the problems of making international comparisons of company performance. The essential aim of the "European Method" is "to arrive at a figure which can be used as a basis for earnings forecasts and for the calculation of ratios."[5] As a consequence, several adjustments are made to a company's reported profits (after tax) in an attempt to eliminate subjective and nonrecurring elements and so reveal a relatively objective measure of current profits

---

[5] European Federation of Financial Analysts Societies, *Report of the Permanent Commission on Standardisation* (Oslo: Noordwijk, 1967), p. 11. See also Dennis Weaver, *Investment Analysis* (New York: Longman, 1971).

attributable to ordinary shareholders on a standardized basis. This requires the exclusion from the profit result of any extraordinary/exceptional items, of any discretionary transfers to or from reserves, and of any provisions which are of a purely expectational nature or which are designed mainly to obtain short-term tax advantages. The latter two items are especially problematic in France and Germany.[6] Further, if the disclosed depreciation figure is different from that allowed for tax purposes, an appropriate estimated transfer is made, if necessary, to or from a tax equalization account in order to preserve some consistency between depreciation and tax charged in the accounts. But no attempt is made to standardize the depreciation charge itself. Finally, any hidden or "secret" reserves (e.g., undervaluation of stocks, special depreciation) are eliminated from profits in cases where analysts are able to ascertain their existence.

It must be recognized, of course, that while the security analysts' approach represents a useful attempt at dealing with the diversity of company accounting practices, it is by no means ideal or necessarily representative of a "true" result. It is also biased in favor of the analysts' needs. A further limitation is that no amount of standardization by security analysts can remove defects or adjust for differences in data for which there is no knowledge about its compilation or underlying quality. This applies with special reference to the valuation of stocks and to charges for the depreciation of fixed assets, where the influence of tax law may be highly significant, especially in France and Germany. Moreover, the analyst, as an outsider, cannot directly remedy any lack of data about other items which are of interest in making adjustments to the accounts, for example, the consolidation of subsidiaries, the treatment of associated companies, and the impact of inflation. As a consequence, the analysts' adjustments to company accounts can only remove the impact of some of the more obvious differences in accounting treatment and are thus likely to provide a somewhat modest assessment of the full position.

Despite these limitations, the European Method does provide a common yardstick, for comparative purposes, which is perceived to be of significance to security analysts in the process of making investment decisions. As such, it would seem reasonable to employ it as an exploratory yardstick for the purposes of this study. It is not, of course, the sole yardstick that could be used to assess the impact of international accounting differences.

Using the European security analysts' approach as a base, it is relative-measurement behavior which is significant for the purposes of my study, and hence the relevant indicator is the difference between a company's

---

[6] See, for example, J. H. Beeny, *European Financial Reporting—West Germany* (London: Institute of Chartered Accountants in England and Wales, 1975); and *European Financial Reporting—France* (London: Institute of Chartered Accountants in England and Wales, 1976).

disclosed profits and its adjusted profits as calculated in accordance with the European Method. An assessment of this relationship is clearly feasible, whatever the national context. The use of a ratio or index to express the relationship between disclosed and adjusted profits provides a neutral indicator of measurement behavior of companies located in different countries. If one takes the European Method adjusted profit as the yardstick, it is possible to calculate the ratio of disclosed profit to adjusted profit as:

$$1 - \left(\frac{R_A - R_D}{|R_A|} \right),$$

where R_A = adjusted profit and R_D = disclosed profit. The resulting ratio can be termed a "conservatism" index in that companies with a ratio of more than one would appear to employ accounting practices with outcomes which are relatively optimistic in relation to the yardstick, whereas companies with a ratio of less than one would appear to be relatively pessimistic or "conservative." Profits-measurement behavior, which is the net outcome of the set of accounting practices employed, can thus be assessed along a continuum of conservatism. More conservative reporting behavior can be distinguished from less conservative behavior among both companies and countries. This is not to say that all of the items adjusted by the analysts are entirely discretionary in nature, but that this is the case in terms of their overall emphasis, with the consequence that the conservatism index is likely to be a useful indicator of different attitudes to the measurement of profits. Conservatism or "prudence" is indeed a basic principle of accounting in France, Germany, and the United Kingdom and is explicitly incorporated in the EEC's *Fourth Directive regarding Annual Accounts.*[7] But what is the effect of conservatism in application? Are there significant differences between countries? How can this situation be explained?

Profits-Measurement Behavior: A Comparative Analysis

The data base for the study was provided by DAFSA Analyse of Paris, a financial and economic research organization which is building up a data bank of European company accounts adjusted according to its interpretation of the European Method of financial analysis. The data bank is currently composed of mainly French, German, and United Kingdom (U.K.) companies, but includes a small number of Belgian, Italian, and Dutch companies. Data for a total of ninety companies (thirty French, thirty German, and thirty U.K.), selected on the basis of being the largest companies ranked by sales turnover in 1975, were

---

[7] Commission of the European Communities, *Fourth Council Directive for Coordination of National Legislation regarding the Annual Accounts of Limited Liability Companies* (Luxembourg, July 1978).

provided by DAFSA covering the five-year period 1971–75. But as the data were incomplete for some companies, for reasons which included company mergers and a lack of adjusted accounts for earlier years, it was necessary to reduce the number of companies in each national sample and to shorten the time period covered to four years. The French sample was that most affected by the lack of data, with consequent potential for sample bias, but the companies remaining were not significantly different in character from those omitted. The final sample thus comprised seventy-two companies—fifteen from France, twenty-eight from Germany, and twenty-nine from the United Kingdom—with a total of 288 profits disclosures over the period 1972–75.

I calculated conservatism ratios for each company, using the formula described earlier, and prepared a frequency distribution. A summary of the findings for 1972–75 is given in table 1, where the ratios have been classified into nine categories from the highly conservative or pessimistic category of <0.50 to the less conservative or optimistic category of >1.50. In addition, three subgroups have been identified which are labeled pessimistic, neutral, and optimistic. The pessimistic grouping is for conservatism ratios of <0.95, whereas the optimistic grouping is for ratios of >1.05. While a strictly neutral ratio would be unity, it seems appropriate to allow some measure of tolerance—hence the neutral grouping for ratios of 0.95–1.05.

There appears to be some differences among the countries, but are these differences statistically significant? The null hypothesis can be

TABLE 1

A Comparative Analysis of Profits-Measurement Behavior in France, Germany, and the United Kingdom, 1972–75

Reported Profits Classified Using an Index of Conservatism	France	Germany	United Kingdom	Total Disclosures
I. 0.50	12	12	2	26
II. 0.50–0.74	20	35	10	65
III. 0.75–0.94	14	37	5	56
Pessimistic (< 0.95)	46 (77%)	84 (75%)	17 (14%)	147
IV. 0.95–0.99	4	4	11	19
V. 1.00	1	1	4	6
VI. 1.01–1.05	0	4	17	21
Neutral (0.95–1.05)	5 (8%)	9 (8%)	32 (28%)	46
VII. 1.06–1.25	3	6	37	46
VIII. 1.26–1.50	2	6	20	28
IX. 1.50	4	7	10	21
Optimistic (>1.05)	9 (15%)	19 (17%)	67 (58%)	95
Total Disclosures	60 (100%)	112 (100%)	116 (100%)	288

stated formally as: the proportion of company profits disclosures which are classified in each of the categories of conservatism is the same for all countries. This hypothesis is tested using the nonparametric chi square (χ^2) test.[8] It would seem that this is the most appropriate test for assessing the significance of differences among the countries, given the nature of the samples and the need to use nominal data, owing to the presence of some large and sometimes negative ratios.

To avoid any problem of interdependence in the data between years, I decided to carry out tests on a year-by-year basis. To do this, it was necessary to regroup the data into two groups only, to insure that the expected frequencies in each group would not be too small. This was done by classifying ratios of ≤1 as "pessimistic" and those of >1 as "optimistic." The resulting chi square statistics of 13.80, 25.67, 28.30, and 19.00 for 1972, 1973, 1974, and 1975, respectively, are all statistically significant at the 0.01 level, with the 1973–75 statistics significant at the 0.001 level. Similar results were obtained using the alternative classification scheme of <1 and ≧1. These findings reject the null hypothesis and support the conclusion that country factors are significant in determining profits-measurement behavior.

But what is the nature and significance of differences between the countries examined? The chi square (one-tailed) test was applied to 2 × 2 analyses of the data in order to assess the situation for each of the years 1972–75 using the same classification scheme of ≤1 and >1 outlined above. The results are given in table 2, which shows that profits-measurement behavior in France and Germany is significantly different from that in the United Kingdom. An evaluation of the direction of these differences shows that French and German companies are significantly more conservative or pessimistic than U.K. companies. In contrast, it is evident that no statistically significant differences exist between France and Germany.

It also seems that there is some stability in this relationship from year to year, in that companies within each country tend to adopt consistent measurement behavior. An assessment of the Kendall coefficient of

TABLE 2

A Comparative Analysis of Profits-Measurement Behavior: Chi Square Test Statistics 1972–75 (2 × 2 Analysis, One-Tailed Test)

Comparative Analysis	1972	1973	1974	1975
1. France/United Kingdom	6.67**	10.40***	16.30***	11.54***
2. Germany/United Kingdom	9.27***	19.36***	16.97***	9.53***
3. France/Germany	0.05	0.003	0.30	0.67

** Significant at the 0.01 level.
*** Significant at the 0.001 level.

[8] See Sidney Siegel, *Non-Parametric Statistics for the Behavioral Sciences* (New York: McGraw-Hill, 1956).

concordance (W), which indicates the degree of association between rankings, was carried out after ranking the conservatism ratios for each year within each country sample. The coefficients for France, Germany, and the United Kingdom were 0.469, 0.410, and 0.581, respectively. The significance of W can be established using the chi square test, and in all cases the association is significant at the 0.05 level, though in the case of the United Kingdom this is significant beyond the 0.001 level.

Explanations

This exploratory study of profits-measurement behavior in France, Germany, and the United Kingdom indicates that the quantitative impact of international differences in accounting practices on profits is statistically significant with particular reference to comparisons between the United Kingdom and either France or Germany. While this would seem only to confirm general tendencies which may be expected from an a priori analysis of the situation in the countries concerned (as will be evident from the subsequent discussion), this is an important result because it demonstrates that perceived differences in accounting practice do have a significant quantitative impact on relative performance when taken as a whole. After all, there could just as easily have been some compensating factors in the differences identified.

These findings must be kept in perspective, however, as they reflect the impact of only those accounting differences which European analysts (represented by DAFSA) have been able to identify and adjust for in the European Method of analysis. Although this assessment by security analysts is not comprehensive, it clearly is considered by them to be significant for investment decision-making purposes. Moreover, the statistical results support the view that the analysts have indeed been successful in identifying some important differences. Of course, the possible existence of potentially confounding variables, such as an industry factor or differences in economic stability, must be considered. However, industry is unlikely to be significant in explaining the country differences discovered, since the samples were not biased in favor of any particular industry or group of industries. With regard to economic differences, although there is a nondiscretionary element with respect to some of the items adjusted by analysts (e.g., extraordinary items), this would seem to be of relatively minor significance in relation to the emphasis of the European Method, which focuses on the discretionary aspects of content, valuation, and presentation.

But there are a number of other important differences, pointed out in the earlier discussion of the European Method, which the analysts have not been able to deal with satisfactorily. This must be borne in mind in any attempt to explain the results of this study. It seems likely that most of these differences will serve only to reinforce the conclusion that French and German companies are significantly more conservative in their profits-measurement behavior than are U.K. companies. But whether this is so remains the subject of further empirical investigation.

First, the analysts are not able, in the normal course of events, to adjust stock valuation and depreciation figures to a comparable basis. These are notorious areas of managerial discretion, but in France and Germany it seems that a strong motivation toward conservatism is given by the influence of tax law, which requires valuations and adjustments for tax purposes to be consistent with the published accounts.[9] Tax advantages dictate that write-downs of stocks and accelerated rates of depreciation are written into company accounts to an extent quite alien to U.K. commercial orientation and experience. It would seem then that the analysts' European Method does not reflect what is perhaps the most important impact of tax law. Any special write-downs or provisions relating to stocks and depreciation are, however, eliminated if disclosed in the accounts. But the task of allowing for differences between tax-oriented valuations in France and Germany and those in the United Kingdom is generally too fraught with problems to be a worthwhile exercise. The full impact of the differential influence of tax law thus remains to be assessed, though the tendency toward a generally more conservative outcome in France and Germany than in the United Kingdom seems clear.

Second, quite apart from taxation, the analysts face problems of consolidation and inflation. In France, there is no requirement to provide consolidated accounts, though more and more large companies are doing so following pressure from the French Stock Exchange Commission (*Commission des Opérations de Bourse*). Even where consolidated accounts are provided, there is considerable diversity of practice compared with the United Kingdom, where consolidations are usually required for all subsidiaries, including those overseas, and where the equity accounting treatment of associates is a professional standard.[10] In Germany, however, only domestic subsidiaries are required to be consolidated by law and equity accounting is prohibited. This situation suggests further potential for a more conservative bias in French and German profits results. With regard to inflation, there has been no attempt by the analysts to make any adjustments on a comparative basis, despite the generally accepted view that inflation distorts profits and gives them an optimistic bias when measured under the conventional historical cost system. With inflation in the United Kingdom running at a much higher average rate than in France or Germany over the past few years, it seems likely that this is another significant factor worthy of detailed investigation. But so far as the analysts are concerned, both theoretical and practical problems

[9] See n. 6.

[10] R. H. Parker, "Explaining National Differences in Consolidated Accounts," *Accounting and Business Research* (Summer 1977): 203–7.

inhibit the making of adjustments which would be satisfactory on an international basis.

This discussion of the limitations of the European Method would seem to permit a more perceptive assessment of the findings of this study and of the influential factors involved. For the main thrust of the analysts' efforts is effectively aimed at adjusting items which involve management discretion as to nature or presentation. While many of these items are no doubt motivated by tax advantage to some degree, with particular reference to special provisions in France and Germany which allow tax deferral benefits to be obtained, other influential factors are involved and require explanation. This does not deny the significant influence of tax law on managerial behavior or the distorting effects of inflation. But the analysts do seem to have isolated to an important degree those discretionary areas where other factors besides taxation are likely to have an impact on accounting policy decisions. Much more work needs to be done to assess the relative impact of all the factors influencing profits-measurement behavior. But with the focus now on managerial discretion in the accounting policy-making process let us try to identify those environmental influences which could account for the biases discovered.

There are certainly differences in philosophy towards the development of accounting systems. A much more legal orientation prevails in France and Germany compared to the United Kingdom, where professional standards dominate, though within the constraints of a general framework of disclosure provided by legal requirements. Relatively detailed and uniform requirements about valuation, classification, and presentation are prescribed in French and German company law, while in the United Kingdom such matters are left largely to the profession. There seems to be a macroeconomic rationale underlying the French and German uniform approaches, whereas in the United Kingdom there is more of a philosophy of flexibility to suit the circumstances of individual companies and of reverence for the qualities of independence and judgment.[11] All of the foregoing suggests that discretion is likely to be the preserve of the United Kingdom with its emphasis on flexibility. But although uniform accounting principles and forms of presentation are specified in France and Germany, there remains considerable scope for flexibility in application and for such discretion to manifest itself in a more conservative view of profits. The most significant areas of flexibility are indeed those identified by the analysts and concern transfers to and from reserves, and the creation and write-back of provisions for various risks and special purposes including those which are designed to gain tax advantages. These can be used to create hidden or secret reserves and to smooth or

[11] See, for example, Gerhard G. Mueller, *International Accounting* (New York: Macmillan, 1967); Adolf J. H. Enthoven, *Accountancy and Economic Development Policy* (Amsterdam: North-Holland, 1973).

bias fluctuations in profits.[12] The treatment of extraordinary and exceptional items poses further problems of flexibility with respect to identification and valuation. A final point here is that the impact of flexibility in France and Germany is highlighted by the fact that all discretionary adjustments must be passed through the profit and loss account. In the United Kingdom there has until recently been considerable scope for bypassing the profit and loss account altogether. Extraordinary, exceptional, and other items, including capital gains and losses and foreign exchange differences, could thus be dealt with as adjustments to balance sheet reserves or as constituents of the profit and loss account with the potential for an optimistic view of profits to be taken. Attempts to standardize treatment in this area by requiring extraordinary items to be stated separately in the profit and loss account have met with only partial success, as it is still a matter of judgment about whether or not an item is to be classified as extraordinary.

While it is possible to see how different biases in profits disclosures may become effective, it is an altogether more important, and possibly more contentious, question to determine why such pessimistic or optimistic biases exist in the first place. To assess this requires a perspective which includes factors relating to the business and investment environment within which managers, financiers, and investors appraise the performance, security, and prospects of companies in which they are interested. It is in this wider context that the work of Choi[13] and Barrett[14] seems relevant and suggests a possibly important explanation. They have argued and demonstrated empirically that there is a correlation between the extent of financial disclosure and the develpment and efficiency of capital markets. A greater extent of disclosure seems to be found in the more well developed equity markets of the United Kingdom and the United States compared to continental markets. Could it be that there is also a correlation between profits-measurement behavior and equity market development? But why should relatively conservative measurement behavior be associated with relatively less developed and narrow equity markets such as exist in France and Germany? Why should profits-measurement behavior in a relatively well developed equity market such as the United Kingdom be relatively optimistic? The answers are perhaps to be found to some extent in the different user orientations of published company accounts in France, Germany, and the United Kingdom, which in turn reflect different patterns of company financing and national financial development.[15] The historical emphasis in the United Kingdom

---

[12] See n. 6.

[13] See n 3.

[14] See n. 4.

[15] See, for example, Peter Readman ey al., *The European Money Puzzle* (London: Michael Joseph, 1973); J. M. Samuels, R. E. V. Groves, and C. S, Goddard, *Company Finance in Europe* (London: Institute of Chartered Accountants in England and Wales, 1975).

is on the equity investor and equity finance, while in France and Germany the pattern of development has placed the emphasis more on debt financiers, creditors, bankers, and government as major suppliers of finance and users of information. Associated with this is the suggestion that there tends to be a short-term financial orientation in the United Kingdom, in contrast to France and Germany where there is more concern for long-term investment and production.

Differences in the relative conservatism of profits disclosures may thus be explained by examining the different needs of these two major groups of users and by ascertaining their likely influence on company managers and accountants. Equity investors are presumably primarily interested in profits available for distribution, in the enhancement of share prices, and in an active secondary market. Thus an optimistic influence is likely to be generated by the demands of equity investors where there is an emphasis on the equity market. This finds support in the relative optimism evident in profits reported by U.K. companies. In contrast, debt financiers, creditors, and bankers are likely to be more concerned with the security of their investment and the capacity of the company concerned to fund its interest payments. Generous measures of distributable profits would be contrary to their interests just as much as conservative profits would tend to be a disservice to the equity investor. In the French and German contexts, a conservative influence is thus likely to be generated and such an explanation is indeed supported by the relative conservatism or pessimism evident in the profits reported.

Implications

Having examined some of the factors which may explain intercountry differences in measurement behavior, I will now consider some of the implications for accounting harmonization, international performance comparisons, and inflation accounting policy.

On the question of accounting harmonization, both at the EEC and wider international level, it would seem that success will require careful consideration of the differential influence of the various user groups interested in company accounts in each of the countries concerned. A uniformity of general accounting principles, especially the fundamental conservatism or prudence principle, can only give a false sense of progress when what is significant is the way in which such a principle is applied. Until there is a more rigorous and common approach to the treatment of items such as provisions, reserves, extraordinary and exceptional gains and losses, stock valuation, and depreciation, harmonization will be an illusion. Indeed, the EEC's *Fourth Directive* is in danger of becoming just such an example of harmonization at the superficial level. Its flexibility in key areas, where the exercise of differential attitudes to conservatism is likely to be significant, tends to undermine the aim of providing a basis for comparison of company financial performance across countries. The influence of tax law on company reporting practice does, of course, provide an additional major obstacle. Indeed, harmonization may not serve any useful purpose when different user groups with different interests are involved at the national level. But with the growth of international finance and investment, a purely national orientation no longer seems sufficient, if all interested parties are to have access to relevant information.

The significance of international performance comparisons may also be suspect. The work of groups such as EFFAS would seem to warrant much closer attention, albeit that they have a special interest in security analysis. Reliable comparisons may be possible, but only if an appropriate allowance is made for differences in the conservatism of profits-measurement behavior across countries. This has implications for many groups of users concerned with making international comparisons in connection with financing, investment, employment, and regulatory decisions. These include supranational bodies (such as the United Nations, OECD and EEC), national governments, economists and statisticians, company managers and accountants, and employees and trade unions, as well as investors and financiers.

This study also has implications for inflation accounting policy. Since U.K. accounting practices appear to have a relatively optimistic impact on profits compared to France and Germany, there may be a stronger case, in the context of promoting comparison, for an inflation accounting system to be introduced in the United Kingdom than in the other countries. This is also further supported by the fact that the effect of inflation on company profits is to some extent already taken into account in France and Germany because of the influence of tax law on company accounts. That is, tax allowances are often designed to motivate investment and, in the process, to alleviate the effects of inflation. This is the case in the United Kingdom, too, but with the difference that valuation adjustments for taxation purposes are not required to be incorporated in the published accounts. Moreover, the relatively greater conservatism of management in France and Germany means that measures have already been taken to conserve resources against inflation. But this has probably been done in the traditional manner, that is, through the medium of adjustments to provisions and reserves. Any attempt at the harmonization of inflation accounting policy in the EEC could be harmful without a consideration of these differential aspects of accounting practice.

A final implication concerns the scope for further research into the impact of international differences in accounting practices. The potential for studies in a wider or different international context is clear. The impact of taxation and inflation differences certainly requires detailed assessment. A consideration of the effect of company size, growth, industry activity, and geographical diversification on behavior both within and between countries is another likely area of interest. The behavioral aspects also require further investigation so as to discern more clearly why different managerial approaches to reporting profits exist.

Summary and Conclusions

This exploratory empirical study of the impact of some international differences in accounting practices on company profits in France, Germany, and the United Kingdom from a security-analysis perspective has provided some results which are of significance in assessing the effect of the different accounting systems and sets of accounting practices employed. These results, which are based on adjustments to company accounts made by European security analysts for investment decision-making purposes, suggest that profits-measurement behavior is correlated with national characteristics. The country in which a company is located is a statistically significant factor in quantitatively determining the relative amount of profits disclosed. It is clear from the analysts' yardstick that large companies in France and Germany are significantly more conservative or pessimistic in their measurement behavior than are large companies in the United Kingdom, which are relatively optimistic.

There are a number of factors arising out of the regulatory and capital-market environment which may explain or reinforce this conclusion. Of course, there is the influence of tax law, but another important factor directly relevant to the empirical results is related to the different user orientations of the countries concerned. The relative emphasis on equity investors in the United Kingdom, in contrast to the creditor, financier, banker emphasis in France and Germany provides support for the hypothesis that the behavior of company management is likely to be strongly influenced by user demands in their respective national environments. The consequence is that accounting principles tend to be applied in practice in such a way that the disclosure of company performance is biased in the direction of relative conservatism or optimism as user needs indicate and hence managerial interests dictate.

The implications of these empirical results and possible explanations suggest additional perspectives to be taken into account with special reference to issues such as international accounting harmonization, performance comparisons in the context of decisions bearing on international finance and investment, and inflation accounting policy. The importance of these issues indicates potential for further research into the impact of international differences in accounting practices.

PART III

International accounting standards

Harmonization of accounting within the European communities: the Fourth Directive on Company Law*

C. W. Nobes

The pages of this journal have previously carried articles concerning accounting differences between the United States and various European countries.[1] Also, harmonization within the European Economic Community (EEC) has been discussed.[2] However, much has happened in the last few years which merits additional comment. This article summarizes the main causes of present national differences in accounting, discusses the purposes of harmonization, examines the EEC proposals for harmonization, and, finally, outlines the British government's response, particularly to the EEC's Fourth Directive on Company Law of July 1978.

CAUSES OF DIFFERENCES

One basic cause of international differences in accounting is differing legal systems. The common law system of England and of most states in the United States involves a limited number of statutes supplemented by a large volume of case law. However, continental legal systems, such as those of France and Germany, are based on a civil code which is prescriptive in a much more detailed manner than is the

---

*C. W. Nobes is lecturer in accountancy at the University of Exeter, England.
[1] N. M. Bedford and J. P. Gautier, "An International Analytical Comparison of the Structure and Content of Annual Reports in the EEC, Switzerland and the United States," *International Journal of Accounting* (Spring 1974); and P. E. M. Standish, "Accounting Responses to Inflation in the EEC," *International Journal of Accounting* (Fall 1975).
[2] R. A. Burnett, "The Harmonization of Accounting Principles in the Member Countries of the EEC," *International Journal of Accounting* (Fall 1975).

* This article is reprinted, with permission, from the *International Journal of Accounting: Education and Research* (Spring 1980) pp 1–16

common law system. In such countries, the law precisely prescribes rules of asset valuation, income measurement, and the format of financial statements. Thus, there is little room for the "fair" presentation which relies on more flexible rules and on an accounting profession trained and permitted to use judgment. Another reason for the comparative lack of importance of "fair" presentation in French and German accounting is that there are only approximately 900 listed corporations in France and 500 in West Germany, compared to more than 3,000 in the United Kingdom and 2,500 in the United States.[3] In addition, much of the stock in the relatively few listed corporations in France and Germany is controlled by banks, governments, or families, all of whom have internal sources of information. Consequently, the remaining small number of private stockholders means a reduced need for the "fair" presentation.

Traditionally, accounting in France and Germany has been performed primarily for the purposes of the revenue authorities and for government economic and statistical agencies. To a large extent, the profit amounts are the same for published accounting reports and taxation purposes, and auditing is mainly concerned with ensuring that the law has been obeyed and that taxable profit is correct. Partly for these reasons, the accounting profession in France and Germany is much smaller and performs different tasks from those of the profession in the United States or the United Kingdom.[4]

The remarks concerning France and Germany apply, broadly speaking, to other continental European countries except for the Netherlands, where accounting and auditing are performed in a way which approximates the Anglo-Saxon approach.[5] It will be useful to recall this major difference between the accounting practices of continental countries and the Anglo-Saxon world (plus the Netherlands) for the next section of the article.

MAIN DIFFERENCES

One fundamental difference in approach between continental and Anglo-Saxon accounting has already been mentioned: the importance of "fair" presentation in Anglo-Saxon accounting developed in part from the need to provide useful and comparable information to outside stockholders. Continental accounting involves many rigid

---

[3]*New York Stock Exchange Fact Book* (1977). See also M. Lafferty, *Accounting in Europe* (London: Woodhead-Faulkner, 1975).
[4]C. W. Nobes, "Some Topics in International Accounting," *International Accountant* (February 1978 and April 1978).
[5]J. H. Beeny and J. G. Chastney, *European Financial Reporting—Netherlands* (London: ICAEW, 1978).

rules and the operation of "uniform accounting" which are useful for government and tax officials. The rigid rules are those established mainly by revenue law in France and by company law in Germany, for example, standardized formats, prescribed rates of depreciation, and rules of asset valuation. "Uniform Accounting," as described by Mueller,[6] for example, consists of detailed charts of accounts and many standardized definitions and measurement rules. In France, these are contained in the Plan Comptable Général (General Accounting Plan) which is compulsory for companies and is supervised by a government body.[7]

A further important difference is the degree of conservatism. The strong influence of law and the importance of bankers and governments as controllers of corporations help to explain the prevailing conservatism in continental accounting. Manifestations of this include the general illegality of revaluing fixed assets; the compulsory increase of legal reserves from profit, typically 5 percent of yearly profit until reserves reach 10 percent of capital; and the prevalence of other reserves and allowances for price rises, risks, and possible losses in value. In Germany, for example, although income figures are not rounded to the nearest thousand as might be the case in the United States, they are often declared as round numbers ending in several zeros, making it clear that profit is a contrived figure and that reserves have been manipulated. Beeny uses the examples of several German companies, such as BASF, Salzgitten, and Feldmühle, to illustrate this. For the information of investors and analysts, some German companies make more realistic estimates of income which may be many times higher.[8]

A third important difference has already been mentioned, that is, that continental corporate accounts must reflect any charges against taxable income in the accounting calculations. For example, although continental depreciation charges allowed for tax purposes are usually based on the lengths of useful lives of assets, there are occasions when a depreciation charge in the financial accounts is above what is "reasonable," in order to take advantage of accelerated tax allowances. In addition, tax regulations allow a variety of write-offs and special reserves which must be reflected in the financial accounts if they are to be allowed for tax.

Another important difference from the point of view of interpreta-

[6]G. G. Mueller, *International Accounting* (New York: Macmillan, 1967), pt. 1.
[7]J. H. Beeny, *European Financial Reporting—France* (London: ICAEW, 1976), ch. 4; and Lafferty, *Accounting in Europe*, ch. 2.
[8]J. H. Beeny, *European Financial Reporting—Germany* (London: ICAEW, 1976), ch. 4.

tion of published accounts concerns consolidation.[9] Many French and most Italian groups do not provide consolidated financial statements. Those which do consolidate use a variety of practices, including variants of the parent company and equity methods, and completely different methods such as proportional consolidation. This situation results from a lack of legislation in the area and the absence of a strong accounting profession capable of formulating and enforcing its own rules. German groups are required by law to consolidate, but this extends only to domestic subsidiaries. There is no consolidation for foreign subsidiaries (unless the group voluntarily prepares additional statements) or for any associated companies (see following sections and note 16).

These differences mean that great care must be used in comparing the accounts of, for example, Standard Oil, British Petroleum, and Total Oil (France). Such international comparisons between companies will usually involve the use of consolidated accounts. To a large extent, it is not possible to adjust accurately for the differences in consolidation techniques using only the information in company accounts from different countries. Clearly, the harmonization of consolidation practices is very important. This is considered in a later section.

Publication requirements also vary by country. Those of the United Kingdom and Ireland are unusual in Europe because they do not exempt small companies from any publication of audit requirements. This will probably be remedied when the Fourth Directive is brought into national law, as discussed later.

Finally, the positions of the professions and governments throughout the EEC toward inflation accounting[10] vary widely. The British government is in favor of inflation accounting, but the profession finds it difficult to agree upon an acceptable version; some Dutch companies have been voluntarily using current value accounting for decades; the French government has recently rejected a proposal concerning supplementary current purchasing-power information and the German government was so against inflation accounting for Germany and any other EEC country that approval of the Fourth Directive (which allows governments to introduce it) was placed in jeopardy. As yet, no government or professional body in the EEC has promulgated any standard practice in this area. This might be an area

---

[9]R. H. Parker, "Concepts of Consolidation in the EEC," *Accountancy* (February 1977).
[10]Following common (though inexact) practice, the expression "inflation accounting" is used to include systems which adjust for specific price changes as well as general inflation.

which will cause even greater problems of harmonization. However,
it is expected that a standard (SSAP 16) on supplementary current cost
accounting will be issued in the United Kingdom March 31, 1980.

THE PURPOSES OF HARMONIZATION

Harmonization of accounting is a process whereby the size and
number of differences in practice between countries are reduced. It
does not imply complete standardization that would require uniform
and rigid rules throughout the EEC. General arguments for the international harmonization of accounting practices[11] include the usefulness that this would have for investors, financial analysts, and credit
agencies (for example, the World Bank) in assessing and comparing
the performance and prospects of companies from different countries.
Multinational corporations and international accounting firms would
gain from having financial statements based on similar systems
throughout the world to audit, consolidate, compare, and so on. Tax
authorities would find it easier to assess foreign companies. Also
governments, economic and statistical agencies, and trade unions
would be better able to collect information and monitor the activities
of corporations.

On a worldwide basis, the International Accounting Standards
Committee (IASC), the United Nations, and the Organization for
Economic Cooperation and Development (OECD)[12] are among bodies
interested in the harmonization of accounting for the reasons mentioned earlier and, also, in the case of the latter two bodies, to enable
greater control of multinational corporations.

Within the EEC, in particular, harmonization of corporate
accounting and taxation is an aim of the commission due to the
objectives of the Treaty of Rome. These include the promotion of the
free movement of persons, capital, goods, and services throughout
the EEC. The free movement of capital requires the supply of reliable,
homogeneous accounting information from EEC companies. This
implies the harmonization of accounting. The free movement of
persons and capital also requires the harmonization of direct taxation. The commission, therefore, intends that companies of the same
form which are in competition within the EEC will be subject to the
same laws, taxes, accounting, and disclosure requirements.

---

[11]International Centre for Research in Accounting, *International Financial Reporting
Standards*, Occasional Paper No. 13 (Lancaster: ICRA, 1977).
[12]J. P. Cummings and M. N. Chetkovich, "World Accounting Enters a New Era,"
Journal of Accountancy (April 1978).

Although the professional bodies of many countries in the EEC belong to the IASC, harmonization in the EEC will not be due to IASC's work, because company and revenue law in such countries as France and Germany is sufficiently weak that accounting standards can have little power in those countries. Therefore, harmonization results from new company law brought into effect as a result of EEC directives. The present list of relevant directives and draft directives is shown in exhibit 1. The most important directives for accounting are the fourth and the seventh (still in draft).

Exhibit 1. Directives Relevant to Corporate Accounting

Directives on Company Law	Draft dates	Date approved	Purpose
First	1964	1968	Ultra vires rules
Second	1970, 1972	1976	Separation of private from public companies, minimum capital, limitation on distributions and interim dividends
Third	1970, 1973, 1975	1978	Mergers
Fourth	1971, 1974	1978	Formats and rules of accounting
Fifth	1972		Structure, management, and audit of companies
Sixth	1972, 1975		Prospectuses
Seventh	1976, 1978		Group accounts
Eighth	1978		Qualifications and work of auditors
Regulations on Company Law			
Societas Europea	1970, 1975		Proposals for a European company subject to EEC laws
European cooperation grouping	1973, 1978		Proposals for a business form facilitating multinational joint ventures
Directives on corporate taxation			
Company taxation	1975		Harmonization of system of company taxation and of withholding taxes
Collective investment institutions	1978		Extends the 1975 directive to these special companies

The Fourth Directive on Company Law was approved by the Council of Ministers of the EEC in July 1978. The first stage that the directive passes through is translation and checking by the "jurists and linguists" group. An example of the problems faced during this stage is that the British prefer the word "prudence" to the rather stricter "conservatism." However, the obvious translation of "conservatism" into French would be the French word *prudence*. The directive must then be passed into law by the member states within two years. There is a further period of eighteen months for the national legislation to come into force.

The original 1971 draft of the Fourth Directive and its much amended successor of 1974 which followed the accession of the United Kindgom, Denmark, and Ireland have been discussed elsewhere.[13] The gradual move away from the domination of Franco-German, legalistic, uniform, conservative, creditor- and tax-based accounting continued between 1974 and 1978. The governments of the United Kingdom, the Netherlands, and Ireland successfully proposed that the "fair" presentation notion should predominate. Support for this view came from the Groupe d'Etudes (Accountants' Study Group, representing professional accountancy bodies in the EEC).

The directive applies to all limited companies (and limited partnerships), except banks and insurance companies for which there will be special directives. It proposes minimum standards only. For example, many member states of the EEC will require statements of the source and application of funds, even though the Fourth Directive does not. The directive's main concerns are valuation rules, formats, and contents of published financial statements, and publication requirements. Consolidation is left to the proposed Seventh Directive.

Valuation will be performed using the historical cost basis. The conventions of the going concern, prudence, accruals, and consistency will be applied. The explicit statement of these conventions has been a change in the drafting. It parallels British and U.S. accounting standards.[14] There are detailed rules concerning the valuations of inventories, measurement of depreciation, and other similar matters. In general, these will not necessitate changes in practice. However, there is a requirement to write off purchased goodwill over five years (or a longer period, up to its useful economic life, if allowed by member states). This may change British practice. Also, exceptional

---

[13]Burnett, "Harmonization."

[14]Accounting Standards Committee, *Disclosure of Accounting Policies: SSAP 2* (U.K. Accountancy Bodies, 1972); and Accounting Principles Board, *Basic Concepts and Accounting Principles, APB Statement No. 4* (U.K. Accountancy Bodies, 1970).

value adjustments must be separately disclosed. This includes any accelerated depreciation shown in the financial statements because this is necessary if it is to be allowed for tax purposes. This will lead to useful additional information in French and German financial statements. Similarly, the importance of secret reserves is diminished because all changes in valuation must pass through the income statement.

One of the great problems encountered when trying to reach agreement among the member states of the EEC was inflation accounting. The different governmental attitudes have already been mentioned. The Fourth Directive compromises by allowing member states to ban, permit, or require inflation accounting. It may be as a replacement or as a supplement to historical cost accounting. No system is specified. In all cases, historical cost balance-sheet figures must still be disclosed. Thus, the directive allows the development of financial statements with dual sets of accounts, with different versions of inflation accounting used in different member states. This casts serious doubt on whether "reliable, homogeneous accounting information" will be available throughout the EEC.

Published financial statements in the United Kingdom and the Netherlands (as in the United States) show very little standardization, whereas most continental European countries impose a considerable measure of uniformity. The Fourth Directive will force greater uniformity on the United Kingdon and the Netherlands with the objective of enhancing comparability. There will be one basic format for balance sheets, though member states may choose vertical or horizontal versions, or may allow both. Certain items must be shown on the balance sheet; other items may be grouped together (see next section). The income statement may be organized by type of expenditure or by stage of production. In each case, a horizontal or vertical format is allowed by the directive. The detail required will considerably exceed that published at present by British companies in their profit and loss accounts. In particular, the cost of goods sold will have to be shown. This will be welcomed by financial analysts. The general increase in uniformity, without complete rigidity, should make comprehension of accounts by nonaccountants somewhat easier.

As for disclosure in notes, there are many disclosures in U.S. and British financial statements not provided by those in most EEC countries. Many of these become necessary under the Fourth Directive, for example, average number of employees, financial commitments, directors' benefits, and turnover by category and area.

Throughout most of the EEC (but not in the United Kingdom),

publication requirements are relaxed for small or private companies. The directive (unlike the earlier drafts) makes no distinction between public and private companies. However, there are important distinctions based on size. Small companies are those which satisfy at least two of the following criteria: balance-sheet total < 1m units of account (u.a.),[15] turnover < 2m u.a., employees < 50. Such small companies may be permitted by member states to publish an abridged balance sheet without an income statement, and to avoid an audit. Medium-sized companies are those which satisfy at least two of these: balance-sheet total < 4m u.a., turnover < 8m u.a., employees < 250. These companies may be permitted to abridge their balance sheets and to omit the detail of the calculation of gross earnings in their income statements. If the British government takes advantage of these provisions, there will be considerable advantages for smaller companies.

An important new provision in the final directive is the establishment of a "contact committee" to deal with problems arising with the implementation, and suggestions for amendments. This may help to reduce the problems of inflexibility, which have been a particular concern of British accountants not accustomed to detailed prescriptions in company law. Nevertheless, the directive has already been criticized in the United Kingdom for being too creditor biased, and doubt has been cast on the usefulness of harmonizing historical cost accounting.

The important remaining aspect of the harmonization of consolidation practices awaits the approval of the Seventh Directive. The present draft proposes that subsidiaries (both domestic and foreign) shall be consolidated using the parent-company concept, and that associated companies[16] shall be treated by the equity method.

This appears very similar to British practice, but there are some important differences. The definition of an associated company is in line with British practice (that is, a 20 percent or higher holding, or a joint-venture arrangement). However, the concept of a subsidiary follows German practice and relies on the existence of control "on a unified basis," rather than on percentages of stockholdings. Also, proportional consolidation may be allowed by member states for joint ventures.

Finally, it is proposed that "horizontal consolidation" will be

---

[15]The European unit of account is based on a basket of EEC currencies. For approximations, the unit of account may be taken to be between 1 and 1.5 U.S. dollars.
[16]"Associated company" is a British expression used to denote those companies which are treated by the equity method of consolidation.

necessary for companies within the EEC which are independent of each other but are owned by the same parent outside the EEC. For example, if a U.S.-based multinational company has subsidiaries in the United Kingdom, France, and Germany, these subsidiaries jointly would have to prepare one set of "consolidated" EEC accounts even though none of them had any control over any other.

NEW BRITISH COMPANY LAW

In September 1979, the British government issued a Consultative Document (or "Green Paper") called "Company Accounting and Disclosure."[17] Its purpose is to announce the government's proposals on the reform of company law, in particular those changes which will be necessary to implement the Fourth Directive. It is intended that British companies shall have the maximum flexibility permitted by the directive (Green Paper, part B, II, iii). This is evidenced, for example, by the proposals on formats. Both of the two balance-sheet formats in the directive, and any of the four profit and loss formats are to be allowed (see exhibits 2 and 3).

To understand the Green Paper's proposals on formats, two further concepts which are quite new for the United Kingdom must be discussed. As mentioned in the previous section, the directive allows member states to introduce reduced disclosure for smaller companies. The British government intends to take advantage of this. The suggested definitions can be seen in the first row of exhibit 4. The second concept is the difference between financial statements which are "drawn up" for shareholders, and those which are "published" and sent to the registrar of companies. Small companies will be required to disclose less than large companies; there are to be greater relaxations for published accounts than for drawn up accounts. Exhibit 4 summarizes the publication proposals.

This new proposed distinction between companies, based on size, will be a major innovation for British company law. The expression "proprietary company" will provide a useful label for small private companies. It is not yet clear whether the government will take advantage of the option in the directive to reduce the scope of audits for proprietary companies. If it does, a "review" will still be necessary (part A, chapter II).

The Green Paper announces the intention to introduce extra disclosure requirements for *large* companies: funds-flow statements

---

[17]Department of Trade, *Company Accounting and Disclosure* (London: H.M.S.O. 1979).

Exhibit 2. A Proposed U.K. Balance Sheet 121

	£	£
A. Subscribed capital called but not paid		xxxx
C. Fixed assets		
I. Intangible assets		
Preliminary expenses	x	
1. Costs of development	x	
2. Concessions, patents, licences, trademarks, etc.	x	
3. Goodwill	x	
4. Payments on account	x	
	xx	
II. Tangible assets		
1. Land and buildings	x	
2. Plant and equipment	x	
3. Other fixtures and fittings, tools, and equipment	x	
4. Payments on account, and tangible assets in course of construction	x	
	xx	
III. Investments		
1. Shares in group companies	x	
2. Loans to group companies	x	
3. Participating interests	x	
4. Loans to undertakings with which the company is linked by virtue of participating interests	x	
5. Investments held as fixed assets	x	
6. Other loans	x	
7. Own shares	x	
	xx	
D. Current assets		
I. Stocks		
1. Raw materials and consumables	x	
2. Work in progress	x	
3. Finished goods and goods for resale	x	
4. Payments on account	x	
	xx	
II. Debtors*		
1. Trade debtors	x	
2. Amounts owed by group companies	x	
3. Amounts owed by undertakings with which the company is linked by virtue of participating interests	x	
4. Other debtors	x	
5. Subscribed capital called but not paid	x	
6. Prepayments and accrued income	x	
	xx	

	£	£
III. Investments		
1. Shares in group companies	x	
2. Own shares	x	
3. Other investments	x	
	xx	
IV. Cash at bank and in hand	xx	
E. Prepayments and accrued income	xx	
	xxx**	
F. Creditors: amounts becoming due and payable within one year		
1. Debenture loans, showing convertible loans separately	(x)	
2. Bank loans and overdrafts	(x)	
3. Payments received on account of orders	(x)	
4. Trade creditors	(x)	
5. Bills of exchange payable	(x)	
6. Amounts owed to group companies	(x)	
7. Amounts owed to undertakings with which the company is linked by virtue of participating interests	(x)	
8. Other creditors, including tax and social security	(x)	
9. Accruals and deferred income	(x)	
	(xx)	
G. Net current assets/liabilities	xxx***	
H. Total assets less current liabilities		xxxx
I. Creditors: amounts becoming due and payable after more than one year		
1. Debenture loans, showing convertible loans separately	(x)	
2. Bank loans and overdrafts	(x)	
3. Payments received on account of orders	(x)	
4. Trade creditors	(x)	
5. Bills of exchange payable	(x)	
6. Amounts owed to group companies	(x)	
7. Amounts owed to undertakings with which the company is linked by virtue of participating interests	(x)	
8. Other creditors, including tax and social security	(x)	
9. Accruals and deferred income	(x)	
		(xxxx)

Exhibit 2. (cont.)   123

	£	£
J. Provisions for liabilities and charges		
1. Provisions for pensions and similar obligations	(x)	
2. Provisions for taxation, including deferred tax	(x)	
3. Other provisions	(x)	
		(xxxx)
K. Accruals and deferred income		(xxxx)
		xxxx
L. Capital and reserves		
I. Subscribed capital called up (of which £ has been paid up)		x
II. Share premium account		x
III. Revaluation reserve		x
IV. Reserves		
1. Capital Redemption Reserve Fund	x	
3. Reserves provided for by the Articles of Association	x	
4. Other reserves	x	x
V. Profit (loss) brought forward		x
VI. Profit (loss) for the financial year		x
		xxxx

*Amounts due in less than one year and more than one year to be shown separately in respect of each heading.
**Total current assets.
***Current assets less creditors becoming due and payable within one year.
Source: Department of Trade, *Company Accounting and Disclosure* (London: H. M. S. O., 1979), Chapter III.
Note: The lettering and numbering in exhibits 2 and 3 are those adapted by the British government from the fourth directive. Hence certain letters or numbers are omitted or repeated.

(not required by the directive), and notes on short-term borrowings, leasing arrangements, pension commitments, and disaggregation of turnover (sections v to vii of chapter VI). As expected, the government intends to allow revaluations of assets and full current cost accounting, as permitted by Article 33 of the directive.

OTHER DIRECTIVES AND REGULATIONS

Exhibit 1 shows a considerable list of EEC directives and regulations, which are mainly still in draft form. The most important directives on company law are the fourth and seventh, discussed earlier. The others are briefly described in exhibit 1.

Exhibit 3. A Proposed U.K. Profit and Loss Account

	£	£
1. Turnover		xxx
2. Cost of sales		(xxx)
3. Gross profit/loss		xxx
4. Distribution costs		(xxx)
5. Administrative expenses		(xxx)
6. Other operating income		xxx
— Operating profit/loss		xxx
7. Dividends from subsidiaries	x	
7. Dividends from participating interests	x	
	xx	
8. Interest on loans to group companies	x	
8. Interest on other loans	x	
	xx	
10. Amounts written off investments		(xxx)
11. Interest payable to group companies	(x)	
11. Other interest payable	(x)	(xxx)
— Profit/loss before tax		xxx
12. Corporation Tax		(xxx)
13. Profit/loss after tax		xxx
14. Extraordinary income	x	
17. Less: tax thereon	(x)	xxx
19. Profit/loss for the year		xxx

Source: Department of Trade, *Company Accounting and Disclosure* (London: H.M.S.O., 1979), Chapter III.

Regulations become law throughout the EEC without the need of action by the legislatures of member states. There are two draft regulations of relevance here. The draft regulation for a European company (Societas Europea) is moving slowly, particularly because of disagreements as to employees on boards of directors. It would create a business form subject to EEC law and taxation rather than to those of member states. No agreement is in sight. There is more likely to be agreement on the draft regulation on the European Cooperation Grouping. This regulation would facilitate the creation of a business form suitable for multinational temporary joint ventures within the EEC.

The draft directive on the harmonization of corporate taxation proposes the adoption of an imputation system of corporation tax throughout the EEC with rates between 45 and 55 percent, and tax credits between 45 and 55 percent of the underlying corporation tax. Progress will also be slow on this directive. There are no plans to

Exhibit 4. Green Paper's Publication Proposals 125

	Large	Medium	Small "proprietary"
1. Definitions	All listed	All public not large	Turnover <£1.3m B.S. <£0.65m
2 out of 3 size	Others with: Turnover >£5m B.S. >£2.5m Employees >250	All private not small	Employees <50
2. Balance sheet drawn up for shareholders	May show Arabic numeral headings in notes	May show Arabic numeral headings in notes	May omit some Arabic numeral headings
3. Balance sheet published	As above	As above	May omit Arabic numeral headings
4. Profit and loss account drawn up for shareholders	Flexible arrangement	Flexible arrangement	Possibly combine 1-5 in exhibit 3
5. Profit and loss account published	As above	As above, and possibly combine 1-5 in exhibit 3	Exempt

harmonize the calculation of taxable income, which is defined very differently in different member states. The latter point renders the proposals somewhat cosmetic. This draft directive is discussed by this author elsewhere.[18]

SUMMARY

The passing of the Fourth Directive into national company law throughout the EEC should narrow some of the important differences in accounting outlined earlier. The "fair" presentation should take precedence over detailed rules; conservative allowances in excess of reasonable estimates will be separately declared; and the effects of taxation on accounting expenses will also be separately declared. In addition, the formats of published financial statements will become

---

[18]C. W. Nobes, "Corporation Taxes in the EEC, and Their Harmonization," *Accountancy* (October 1978).

more standardized throughout the EEC, and corporations of similar sizes will be subject to similar publication requirements. When the Seventh Directive is finalized by the Council of Ministers, there should be considerable harmonization of practices within the important area of consolidation.

Nevertheless, it is likely that substantial diversity (both between and within countries) will still be possible within the national laws which will eventually be passed. Supporters of the view that rigid uniformity merely masks a multitude of differences will be happy with this. However, the possibility of different inflation accounting systems of varying prominence in difference EEC countries may destroy any hopes of simple comparability.

Standardized accountancy and economic development*
Adolf J. H. Enthoven

A greater degree of standardization in accounting would be of particular benefit to developing countries. They are often faced with deficient and disorganized economic and financial data, and may lack, at all levels of the economy, both effective accounting systems and related administrative skills. Because of limited natural, financial and human resources, their governments may need to undertake increasingly centralized cost–benefit analyses and to involve themselves, through planning and control systems, in all socioeconomic activity.

Effective uniform standards of accounting are therefore required throughout the economies of developing countries – in enterprise accounting, government administration, social accounting, in national and international evaluations of industrial structures, in project and sectoral appraisals, and in the assessment of capital markets and development finance.

We should first make clear the scope for standardization in accounting. Standardization generally aims to simplify and unify all aspects of accounting information systems in order to improve the reliability and consistency of information. It involves establishing methodological standards of definition and terminology; criteria for the identification, collection, measurement, and processing of data, and for the layout of accounts and tables; procedures for integrating information into cohesive accounting models; and standards for evaluating and communicating such information.

Standardization by functions

One way to approach standardization is to examine the particular function or branch involved, whether it be enterprise, government, or social accounting. Although all three work with the same socioeconomic raw material they use it differently for their specific functions.

Enterprise accounting

Enterprise accounting deals with microeconomic planning and control. It is increasingly concerned with the more sophisticated management techniques – operations research, for example – necessary in taking decisions in an enterprise. However, a distinction must be made between financial accounting and management (or cost) accounting although both deal with the administration of microeconomic activities. Financial accounting is primarily concerned with providing

* This article is reprinted, with permission, from *Finance and Development* (March, 1973) pp 28–31

outsiders with financial information. Because of this it largely describes – in a manner complying with statutory requirements – the enterprise's economic activity in its immediate past. Management accounting is less governed by such constraints. Since its function is to provide information for operational decisions, it has to correspond more closely with economic reality. In practice, unfortunately, management accounting is often practised little differently from conventional financial accounting.

Although income determination is the central function of enterprise accounting, it is also closely linked to the normal presentation of balance sheets and information about the sources and uses of funds within the enterprise. Income determination, indicating the enterprise's activities and use of resources, is needed for rational decision making (e.g., investment policy), taxation, reporting on stewardship, and the preparation of social accounts.

However, what 'income' is, and how it should be measured, still causes a major schism within the accounting profession and between accountants, on the one hand, and economists and statisticians on the other. For example, should real or money income be measured; should capital gains be treated as income?

Here, then, is a clear need for standardization; we need an interdisciplinary concept for income measurement which would be widely accepted by accountants and economists alike. This would benefit all people who use public and private enterprise income measurements – either in collecting data from enterprise revenue and expense statements for national (social) accounting purposes, or in the preparation of national economic, fiscal, and monetary policies.

The unfortunate truth is that, at present, enterprise accounting lacks consistency in both its current practice and its theory, which is often merely the sum total of prevailing practices. This makes it extremely hard to compare and assess financial statements; to pinpoint capital needs; to construct effective budgets; to measure the overall efficiency and performance of enterprises and industry; to design and appraise effective industry, sector, and national economic plans; and to set out reliable social accounts. None of these activities – so important to developing countries – will be much improved until comprehensive and consistent patterns of thought, borrowing from other disciplines, are applied to the process of standardizing accounting principles and practices.

Standardization of enterprise accounting should also be matched by standardization of company legislation. Since the function of accounting has a major bearing on capital market activities, finance, and capital formation, the laws affecting commercial reporting, disclosure requirements, and overall company operations should themselves be standardized. Furthermore, accountants – whether working independently or under government supervision, in either the public or private sector – themselves need legislative protection for their activities. Finally, legal status should be given to both the accounting profession and to an accountant's report in standardized form.

Government accounting

Extensive government involvement in national affairs is now normal in industrialized and developing countries alike. It has created a demand for sound systems and techniques of accounting, essential for the responsible and effective administration of, for example, public finance or fiscal policy. Government accounting deals with

the collection, measurement, processing, communication, control of, and accountability for, all receipts and expenditures and related activities in the public sector.
The distinctive aspects of accounting information, classification, and procedures
applicable in government sector transactions make it desirable to treat this as a
separate – but interrelated – branch of accounting, although governments make
extensive use of the records of entries, techniques, and procedures used in
enterprise accounting.

A standardized system for recording, measuring, and processing information in
the government sector is necessary to ensure (a) effective coordination with other
branches of accounting; (b) greater accountability, e.g., compliance with legal
provisions and budgetary commitments; (c) greater efficiency in management,
planning, and policy; and (d) greater validity in domestic and international
comparisons, analyses, evaluations, and measurements (for example, Fund and
UN statistics).

An improved classification system for government transactions is of extreme
importance for giving a clear effective outline to the government's activities, for
making governmental and national economic appraisals, and for their effective
integration with the system of social accounts. The conventional classification
system, which mostly consists of listing receipts by various types of taxes, and
stating expenditures by object, is not very meaningful and prohibits effective
planning, decision making, and managerial and economic analysis.

A better system shows government receipts and, particularly, expenditures
classified by *economic categories*, and split into current and capital items (for
example, current expenditure on goods and services, interest payments, and social
security payments). Services should also be *functionally* classified (for example,
community service or social service expenditure); and particular functions further
classified into 'programmes', 'activities', and 'projects'.

However good a standardized government accounting classification model, it
may yet need refinement and improvement to unify the accounting framework.
However, it is not only the system of classification that needs standardization, but
also the data that have to be classified. Often the identification, valuation, and
recording of data, which is to be transformed into information, is poorly carried
out; standardization to make data more useful is a difficult but vital task.

The government budget, in which government accounting is reflected, sets forth
the financial programme for the year; it should thus be an integral part of a
country's economic development plan. Budgeting is increasingly becoming a
decision-making process and an exercise in planning to ensure the effective
allocation and application of resources to economic needs and objectives. This
change from conventional government budgeting to plan-oriented budgeting
challenges traditional historical cost accounting standards and procedures.

Budgeting also increasingly utilizes the refined quantitative decision-making
techniques used in management accounting; it examines the costs (inputs) and
benefits (outputs) of particular economic functions, programmes, and projects.
Thus budgeting tries to assess how limited resources can be allocated to many
possible competing claims. To compare such claims, a standardized information
and classification system is necessary to ensure realistic and accurate measurement.
An authentic set of inputs and outputs must be collated into a coherent decision
model, which has to take account not only of present and future income and
expenditure flows but also of external effects on the economy. Such processes

present a tremendous challenge to accounting which, at present, finds difficulty in coping with the demand for the more standardized accounting structures and procedures required.

Accounting also plays a part in taxation; its role affects both the formulation of tax structures and policies and tax administration. It should assist in choosing the most suitable forms of taxation and in ensuring that more equitable and effective tax policies and procedures are carried out. The effective administration of a tax system depends on the development of a sound body of accounting standards and practices covering, for example, expense deductions and depreciation. Furthermore, standardization would facilitate the application of computers to taxation.

Social accounting

The third branch of accounting, social (or macro) accounting, aims to describe systematically and quantitatively the structure and activities of an economy, region, or sector during a certain time span, and also of stocks (assets and liabilities) at a particular time. All economic transactions between groups of individuals (households), business enterprises, government agencies and with the outside world, are dealt with. The mass of quantitative data is recorded, measured, processed, and consolidated into various systems designed to display the principal national aggregates (such as national product and income), and their interrelations, in accounts and tables. Units dealt with – whether an industry, sector, or the whole economy – are much larger in social than in enterprise or government accounting.

Both aggregate and individual data recorded in social accounts are needed for measuring economic progress and for the design of national – and even international – economic, monetary, and fiscal harmonization policies; they also play an essential role in setting national goals, in economic planning and budgeting, and in structuring econometric models required for such purposes.

Standardization of social accounting has in fact progressed fairly adequately; we find that the system of classification (into sectors, accounts, and transactions), and the procedures used are quite well harmonized. However, when information from governmental and enterprise accounts is needed in the preparation of social accounts, tremendous gaps occur. Above all, when we realize that the source of a large proportion of social accounting information (especially in national income and product accounts) comes from business operations it is obvious that the three accounting branches should be more cohesively coordinated.

One particular standardization problem lies in methods of quantifying and evaluating data. Once again the question is – how good is a classification scheme when the data it deals with are not uniformly measured? It is an essential function of all accounting to ensure that techniques, procedures, and data, at all levels of the economy, are accurate.

Although many basic techniques for the treatment of data are common to social, government, and enterprise accounting, the underlying procedures may vary. In social accounting current (market) values are used, capital gains and losses are not recognized, certain items – for example, research and development expenditure – are charged to the income account (as against the capital account in enterprise accounting), value-added and intertemporal adjustments are necessary, and, in general, estimates involving subjective criteria are more widely utilized.

Since accounting procedures are also crucial in other spheres of economic analysis and policy-making the scope for standardization is not limited to the three branches discussed above.

Development planning

Economic development planning utilizes, in the process of resource allocation, measurement tools which would themselves be more effective if subject to greater accounting standardization.

Among the most important are capital-output ratios, dynamic input–output analyses, and shadow pricing. Capital-output ratios – which reflect the relationship between capital investment and the likely resulting growth of real national product – serve as a crucial guide for economic policy. However, their use is restricted unless the composition and value of such items as fixed assets, inventories, and output can be accurately analysed. Dynamic input–output models – reflecting altered economic and technical conditions – also form an important element of planning. To be effective, cost inputs and outputs should be put on a standardized basis – preferably using current market or replacement value criteria. Shadow pricing attempts to price the various factors of production as if market equilibrium existed in an economy in order to try to show society's preference for, and relative scarcity of, factors of production. It thus constitutes an important tool in framing a development plan. For all three development tools, deficiencies in measurement, and inconsistent or nonstandard data, may prevent developing countries from making more rational decisions.

Project appraisals

Every plan consists of a series of activities or projects involving the production of specific goods and services. Appraising the feasibility and justification of such projects and their components requires extensive use of past, present and future data, and their measurement in the form of direct and indirect benefits and costs. The necessary cost–benefit calculations demand information which has an economically realistic, comprehensive standardized content. It is desirable and feasible to use tables to incorporate information regarding, for example, standardized labour inputs per production process; raw material requirements, power and fuel needs for each scale of output; and installation costs. Such standardized capital investment and operating data improve the reliability of project studies and also requires greater uniformity in the classification and valuation system itself.

Other socioeconomic studies

Accounting will also play an increasingly important role in socioeconomic studies of problems of ecology, poverty, social security, and human resource development. Any examination of such areas demands effective cost-benefit analysis; there is great scope for standardizing the way in which the direct and indirect effects of any programme designed to tackle such problems are measured.

So far we have discussed the scope and methods for standardization within particular activities: enterprise, government, and social accounting. These accounting activities are, however, interrelated in that they form an overall framework. We, therefore, need to consider standardization in such a broader context in order to ensure consistency in both the theory and practice of the interrelated systems and activities.

The overall accounting system should indeed be concerned with general economic behaviour, with its own techniques helping in the solution of specific socioeconomic problems. Accounting as a discipline should thus be conceived of, and practised as, a dynamic quantitative information system within the economic environment. It deals with the identification of data, its analysis, selection, measurement, evaluation, and its communication in the form of direct and indirect socioeconomic costs and benefits. As a result it facilitates the planning and control of activities and processes. All this must be done in accordance with certain fundamental criteria, such as usefulness, verifiability, and quantifiability.

Existing standardization schemes

A number of schemes for standardizing accounting are already in practice.

The French Plan Comptable Général

This is a standardized plan for enterprises, but is also geared toward broader economic needs. Its major characteristics are a uniform terminology; a uniform classification of accounts; a standardized method of registration; and generalized rules of valuation, albeit on a historical cost basis only. It is designed to improve fiscal administration, to provide systematic information for social accounting, and to standardize company rules on the presentation of financial statements. Not only has the system proved extremely useful for social accounting and public administration but it has also been of great benefit to French national economic planning; to industries and industrial associations in making necessary economic analyses and forecasts; for structural analyses and for measuring and comparing industrial productivity; and, generally, for improving efficient enterprise administration. Many former French territories, and several other developing countries, have adopted this model in modified form.

The German framework of accounts (Kontenrahmen)

This system differs from the French in that it is aimed more at microeconomic activity and less at the needs of social accounting or economic planning. Essentially its purpose is to improve comparative industrial data. The system sets forth both standard accounting charts and also industrial flow charts – for integration with the accounting charts – which show all transactions taking place within the enterprise.

Standardization of accounting in the United States largely focuses on three microaccounting aspects: 'generally accepted accounting principles', the layout of accounts, and a uniform pattern of reporting and costing, required by federal agencies for utilities and certain other industries.

More recently, the US government has outlined uniform cost accounting standards for defence contract purposes in order to ensure comparability, reliability, and consistency of cost data. Such standards will undoubtedly be extended to other public and private economic sectors.

Although each of the above models for accounting standardization contains elements worthy of consideration in developing economies, we feel that a more comprehensive uniform plan, along the lines of the French system, is most relevant and useful for them.

Conclusions and recommendations

Standardization of accounting has been criticized on economic and political grounds; it is claimed to be unwieldy, static, unimaginative, and very expensive, and is said to hamper accounting theory. Its advocates claim, however, it will ensure better comparability, more effective consolidation and integration, sounder economic and fiscal policies, better control, easier education and training, and the development of a more unified overall accounting theory.

A realistic appraisal of accounting standardization should take into account the objectives and methods of accounting in the whole socioeconomic process, and of the particular needs of developing countries for whom the advantages of standardization are more pronounced. The following section offers some suggestions for improvements in accounting standardization.

Identifying the need for standardization

The need for standardization should first be analysed according to the particular branch of accounting concerned, the requirements of the users of the accounting information, and to the economic functions involved. More standardized accounting information will be useful for government administration, taxation purposes, economic planning, project appraisals, shareholders, financial institutions, management, trade unions, and for consumers. From such a comprehensive body of requirements, common characteristics should be identified and utilized.

Approach to standardization

This should take place – both nationally and internationally – within an overall information system of accounting, composed of various subsystems applicable to all types of socioeconomic activities. Sound standardization therefore demands sound overall accounting theory and methodology.

Flexibility in standardization systems

A large degree of variation and flexibility – for example, between developing and developed countries – may prevail without hampering the objectives. Measurement, for example, may vary considerably in different detailed classification and evaluation models. Different value systems, furthermore, will dictate variations because of different needs, economic circumstances, data available, and skills at hand. Such diversity as may prevail should, however, not detract from the need to design effective current value criteria and standardized systems applicable to national and international operations.

Studies of accounting change

Before better standards and systems can be devised, extensive studies – involving all recognized accounting bodies working in close liaison with economists, statisticians, government administrators, and lawyers – are necessary. Furthermore, it is imperative that such appraisals be carried out in coordination with international agencies, such as the International Monetary Fund and the World Bank Group. On an international scale, the implementation of standards, conventions, and systems of accounting may require a vast degree of technical assistance and transfer of knowledge.

Accounting training

The establishment of international standards and conventions would greatly assist in developing methodology and curricula for accountancy training. It would also encourage skills needed in the economic development process and would facilitate the international transfer of accounting knowledge.

To conclude, a profound need exists for the development of effective international accounting standards and conventions for all the great range of socioeconomic activities with which accountants are concerned. The adoption of such standards would help to promote economic growth and development.

Social accounting already shows what can be done by standardization developed on an international basis; organizations such as the United Nations and the Organization for Economic Cooperation and Development have been very active in working up sound and systematic social account structures[1]. Although systems in some countries (e.g., the United States) deviate from these international standards, the models are largely similar and can be easily compared.

However, an international body to coordinate all areas of accountancy, supported by professional and international development institutions, is urgently required to ensure better harmonization and to make accounting more effective in the economic development process.

Reference

1 See, for example, OECD, *A Standardized System of National Accounts*, Paris, 1959; United Nations, *A System of National Accounts*, New York, 1968.

CHAPTER 9

The international harmonization of accounting: a cultural dimension*
Desmond McComb

Although there has been sporadic professional ventilation on the issue of international standards for accounting since at least the turn of the century, the development of a uniform international framework for corporate financial reporting did not exert any very strong claim to professional, or indeed academic, interest before the nineteen fifties.[1] As we approach the eighties, efforts to establish international standards of accounting are achieving a momentum which has brought the issue to the forefront of public interest.

This paper proposes a pause to examine the conceptual justification for national differences in accounting standards and practices before attempting to promote uniformity in the supposed interests of international understanding. It is claimed that, while some such differences may be accidental historical survivals, there is nevertheless an identifiable pattern of national accounting systems reflecting local information demands. In this context, alterations in accounting standards and practices which have a primary objective, other than one of improving the quality or quantity of information at a national level, require careful analysis to establish their effects.

---

* Desmond McComb is chairman of the Graduate Program of the Department of Accounting and Management Economics, University of Southampton, England.

[1] An early comparison of international accounting practice and standards appears in evidence given before the *Select Committee on Joint Stock Companies, 1841-1844: British Parliamentary Papers (1844) VII*. International accounting standards were also discussed at the International Congresses of Accountants at St. Louis in 1904, at New York in 1929, and at London in 1933.

* This article is reprinted, with permission, from *The International Journal of Accounting: Education and Research* (Spring 1979) pp 1–16

There can be little criticism of the aim of improving the intelligibility of corporate financial reporting at an international level. It would indeed be admirable if we could lift an American, British, French, German, or Japanese set of accounts and feel confident that, using our own background of accounting principles, we should be equally at home in understanding them all. Unfortunately, that is not possible at the present time. If our reaction to that situation is that it should be possible, then it is but a short step in the rational evaluation of that unsatisfactory situation to conclude that a remedy should be found. However, it constitutes a long and unjustifiable leap in logic if we conclude that the solution to the problem of resolving the difficulties of international understanding of corporate financial reports lies in the acceptance, and establishment, by the worldwide accounting profession of an internationally agreed set of accounting standards. Before this could be justified as a rational conclusion, it would be necessary to pass through a number of intermediate propositions and conclusions relating to the objectives of corporate financial reporting. It might very well be maintained that this would be no great problem and that a coherent, internationally acceptable objectives framework could be readily identified and acted upon. In practice, however, the usual interpretation of this belief is that it should be possible to restate accounts prepared in a foreign country so that they will be in accord with generally accepted principles in the user's home country. In so far as certain technical standards could be agreed upon internationally, there is no doubt that this would make the restatement process easier. However, the case for the harmonization process goes more deeply than that and ultimately involves unified accounting objectives.[2] It is only if accounting models based upon such objectives are compatible with one another that there is any real prospect of arriving at meaningful common standards. If any two national accounting models are irreconcilable, then either one or both must be fundamentally changed if common standards are assumed to be a primary goal.

PRESSURES FOR HARMONIZATION

The thrust of the movement towards the harmonization of accounting standards on the international level has come mainly from accountants in public practice rather than from academic accountants. Those who

---

[2] "One of the chief, and least recognized, misconceptions which occurs in international accounting is the assumption that accounting objectives are uniform." Irving L. Fantl, "The Case Against International Uniformity," *Management Accounting (N.A.A.)* (May 1971).

teach and research accounting in universities and other institutes of learning are normally in the vanguard of developments in their disciplines. However, while a few academic accountants may claim to have thought about, discussed, and perhaps even published[3] on this topic, the honors for making it a live issue must go to the practitioners. In particular, the late Jacob Kraayenhof, onetime president of the Netherlands Institute of Accountants, and Sir Henry Benson, onetime president of the Institute of Chartered Accountants in England and Wales, can be credited with having respectively sown the seed and husbanded the crop which so many today wish to harvest.[4]

That having been said, it remains questionable whether a sufficiently perceptive approach has been taken in the attempts to narrow the areas of differences in international accounting and financial reporting. In a situation such as that facing the various national professional organizations once they had become convinced that international uniformity was a desirable goal, the natural response was to produce visible evidence of their intention to make progress. The establishment of the International Accounting Standards Committee (IASC) had in turn a built-in need to be productive and has, between its establishment in 1973 and the time of writing, produced the following standards:

IAS 1   Disclosure of Accounting Policies;

IAS 2   Valuation and Presentation of Inventories in the Context of the Historical Cost System;

IAS 3   Consolidated Financial Statements;

IAS 4   Depreciation Accounting;

IAS 5   Information to Be Disclosed in Financial Statements;

IAS 6   Accounting Responses to Changing Prices;

IAS 7   Statement of Changes in Financial Position;

IAS 8   Treatment in the Income Statement of Unusual Items and Changes in Accounting Estimates and Accounting Policies;

IAS 9   Accounting for Research and Development;

---

[3] T. K. Cowan, "Harmonization of Accounting Principles," *New Horizons of Accounting* (Paris: 9th International Congress of Accountants, 1967), pp. 206-10; Norton M. Bedford, "The International Flow of Accounting Thought," *International Journal of Accounting* (Spring 1966); Mary E. Murphy, "Need for International Documentation in Management Accounting," *Accountants Journal (U.K.)* (February 1962): 43-45; and Gerhard G. Mueller, *International Accounting* (New York: Macmillan Company, 1967), pp. 235-46.

[4] Jacob Kraayenhof, "International Challenges for Accounting," *Journal of Accountancy* (January 1960): 34-38; Sir Henry Benson, "The Story of International Accounting Standards," *Accountancy* (July 1976): 34-39.

IAS 10 Contingencies and Events Occurring after the Balance Sheet Date;

IAS 11 Accounting for Construction Contracts;

IAS 12 Accounting for Taxes on Income; and

IAS 13 Presentation of Current Assets, and Current Liabilities.

It is suggested that most of the above standards represented an attempt to lead the various member countries of IASC into adopting what was existing good practice in some other member countries. It is, in fact, possible to identify a strong Anglo-American influence in the standards issued. Most of them also were concerned with technical issues which were not highly contentious. However, the scope for the issue of further remedial standards is decidedly limited. It is therefore at this point in the evolution of international accounting standards that we may be obliged to pause and to give more consideration to investigating the possibility of designing a conceptual framework within which international standards can or should be developed.

The emphasis which the author has placed upon the activities of IASC reflects the dominant influence which that committee has exercised in what has been implied here to have been a remedial phase in the development of international accounting standards. However, the processes of harmonization have involved a number of other groups and organizations which are the product of international cooperation by the accounting profession.

THE INTERNATIONAL FEDERATION OF ACCOUNTANTS

The International Federation of Accountants (IFAC) came into existence as the result of proposals agreed upon at the eleventh International Congress of Accountants in 1977. It is the successor of an earlier committee, the International Coordination Committee for the Accountancy Profession, formed at the 1967 Congress. The constitution of IFAC states that it:

1. Initiates, coordinates, and guides efforts that have as their goal the achievement of international, technical, ethical and educational guidelines for the accounting profession and reciprocal recognition of qualifications for practice, and works toward this purpose by establishing appropriate committees through cooperative effort with regional organizations for implementation.

2. Encourages and promotes the development of regional organizations with common objectives and develops guidelines for the structure and constitution of such regional organizations.

3. Arranges the holding of International Congresses of Accountants so as to:
   a) Enable members of the accountancy profession to meet one another in

an environment that facilitates discussion and the interchange of ideas on accounting and related matters.

b) Direct attention to and inform accountants of developments in selected fields of accountancy thought and practice.

c) Reach broad conclusions on desired common aims.

Regional groups, such as the Union Européene des Expertes Comptables Economiques et Financieres (UEC), the Confederation of Asian and Pacific Accountants (CAPA), the Inter-American Accounting Association (IAA) and the Accountants International Study Group (AISG), have also had a significant role to play.

Ultimately, however, it is only through organizations such as IFAC and IASC which carry some degree of international acceptability and authority that implementation procedures could be established.

ROLE OF NATIONAL INSTITUTES OF ACCOUNTANTS

National professional institutes are, it may be assumed, fully aware of the social framework within which their indigenous accounting standards are developed. By definition, they will aim to, and hopefully achieve, systems of accounting measurement which can provide users of financial reports in their home country with relevant information. Although their scope for influencing or initiating developments in accounting is more limited in some countries than in others, it is not unreasonable also to assume that national accounting organizations could be expected to endeavor to establish standards of accounting which would give the most acceptable results possible in the context of what they see as user needs. It follows that any deviation from such standards could result in some deterioration in the quality of financial reporting. If the logic of the above propositions is accepted, it would, of course, seem that the acceptance of international standards which differed from national standards might have a detrimental influence on the quality of financial reporting. Indeed, it may be assumed that the approach taken to the IASC Standards in the United States is, in part, a reflection of such a view. Thus the AICPA is committed to using its "best endeavors" to bring about compliance with international standards. However, the standard-setting body, the FASB makes no such commitment and neither it nor the SEC has shown any evidence of intent to be led into altering existing U.S. standards in order to achieve accord with international standards. For the most part, these latter are considered to have fallen short of generally accepted accounting standards in the United States so that one could hold that existing

U.S. practice was already in compliance with the international standard concerned. However, if, as seems likely, the remedial phase of the work of IASC is drawing to a close, then the next phase must inevitably become one of harmonizing "good" accounting practice at an international level. What has until now been little more than a program of encouraging countries with plainly deficient accounting standards to bring their practice into line with that of countries with more highly developed systems of financial reporting must inevitably be followed by a second phase in which the problems of the harmonization of accounting standards where national philosophies of accounting are at variance, or where national social institutions create distinctive pressures, should be faced squarely.

A THEORY OF DISPARATE ACCOUNTING

A rational evaluation of the justification for differences between theories of accounting and corporate financial reporting in an international context should be an essential primary stage in a program of international harmonization of accounting principles and practice. Few people believe that national differences in accounting have come about as part of a random process. Rather all the evidence would suggest that the various national accounting systems have each evolved in response to societal need and demands within the countries concerned.[5] If this is accepted as an explanation and a justification for difference, it would be useful to identify those factors which may have contributed to each singular national accounting system. Hopefully in the process of doing that, those factors common to each national economic and social framework will also be identified. A further possibility favoring the process of harmonization is that some of the factors which originally contributed to national differences in accounting may have ceased to be relevant, even though their effects continue to be encountered. Clearly in that context, their identification and their demise as an influence should be associated events.

Here discussion is restricted to accounting for private-sector, profit-oriented firms. A case can be made for the application of international

---

[5] The literature evidencing this view is, by the nature of the issue involved, frequently scattered among articles and papers dealing with other topics. The most comprehensive survey is that in Frederick D. S. Choi and Gerhard G. Mueller, *An Introduction to Multinational Accounting* (Englewood Cliffs, N.J.: Prentice Hall, 1978). The issue is also discussed in Desmond McComb, "The Environment of Accounting Development, U.K. and U.S. Comparative Views," 63rd Annual American Accounting Association Convention 1978, Collected Papers.

accounting standards to other types of organization, but it would be a much less powerful one, and there is little evidence of any great demand for, or interest in, the international standardization of accounting for, say, public sector commercial and industrial organizations, or not-for-profit organizations.

ACCOUNTING FOR THE FIRM

Any system of accounting for business organizations must inevitably be built around an economic and/or social theory of the firm. Such a theory should in turn reflect its political, legal, and financial environment.

U.K. accounting theory provides an example. It developed during the nineteenth century in an atmosphere in which the entrepreneurial proprietor was seen as the dynamic force that made the other factors of production (land, labor, and capital) productive. In that context, accounting for the firm meant accounting to the owners or shareholders. The entrepreneur was also normally assumed to be a major provider of capital, although each role could be distinguished for purposes of economic analysis. Within that scenario, the idea that it was a function of the firm to maximize profits for its owners seemed perfectly rational, and was readily accepted. Accounting for the firm meant satisfying the information needs of the principal owners who had provided both capital and entrepreneurial skills. The proprietary theory of accounting was indeed a reflection of the classical economic theory which had found ready acceptance in the Western world, more especially in those countries such as the United Kingdom and the United States, where open capital markets encouraged corporate shareholding.

However, while the proprietary theory is highly appropriate to a firm in which there is a close relationship between ownership and the entrepreneurial function, it is patently less so when used as a basis of accounting for large organizations, in which owners and management have become separate groups.

The concept of a business entity having an economic life as distinct from a legal existence, separate from its owners, later made the proprietorship theory seem inappropriate to many accountants and gave rise to an "entity theory" in which the focus of accounting became value to the business and profits of the firm, rather than proprietorship worth and profits.

The implications of these two theories for the valuation of assets and liabilities, and for the recognition of revenues and expenses, have been widely discussed in the literature.[6] They will not be elaborated upon here. Suffice to say that it is generally agreed that the choice of one or other approach might have a marked effect upon the values placed upon assets and liabilities, and upon the measurement of profits.

The question which arises is the relevance of all this to the issue of international harmonization of accounting. The fact is, however, that some countries appear to lean more towards one or other theory. (To truncate the argument, variants of the proprietorship and equity theories such as the "Funds" and "Commander" theories will be ignored.) Reverting to a comparison between the United States and the United Kingdom, the following quotations from eminent professional committees in each country are of interest as indicating the different attitudes which can be found as between countries.

The primary and continuing goal of every commercial enterprise is to increase its monetary wealth so that over time it can return the maximum cash to its owners.[7]

In reviewing the relevance of the conventional view of the aim of published financial reports to current conditions and attitudes we note the trend towards the acceptance by business enterprises of multiple responsibilities and conclude that distributable profit is no longer the sole or premier indicator of performance in the corporate reports of such entities. . . .[8]

Clearly, the two committees do not agree on the goals of a business enterprise. Perhaps their views are not representative of those commonly held in their respective countries, but the balance of the evidence would suggest that they at least reflect widely held views.

While the view of corporate goals expressed in the U.S. report is fully in accord with the view of the firm upon which the proprietory theory of accounting is based, that could not be said of the corresponding perception of corporate goals expressed by the U.K. committee. Accounting measures designed to gauge the degree to which a firm is achieving a goal of returning the most cash to its owners could not be expected to provide a suitable measure of the less clear-cut corporate objectives postulated in the U.K. report. However much we might

---

[6] Useful contributions on the topic are A. N. Lorig, "Some Basic Concepts of Accounting and Their Implications," *Accounting Review* (July 1964): 563-73; R. S. Gynther, "Accounting Concepts and Behavioral Hypotheses," *Accounting Review* (April 1967): 274-90.

[7] American Institute of Certified Public Accountants, *Report of the Study Group on the Objectives of Financial Statements* (New York: AICPA, 1973), p. 21.

[8] Accounting Standards Steering Committee, *The Corporate Report* (London: ASSC, 1975), p. 79.

desire the more readily attainable measures called for by the U.S. committee's concept, it is obvious that there is inherent in the U.K. model a belief that the company has aims and responsibilities distinct from those of its owners.

One is tempted to surmise that a reflection of differing political and social ideologies exists in these two different attitudes toward what is basically the same institution. For instance, Milton Friedman, a firm believer in classical economic capitalism, might almost have been the inspiration for the U.S. committee's view when, writing on corporate responsibility, he says, "Few trends could so thoroughly undermine the very foundations of our free society as the acceptance by corporate officials of a social responsibility other than to make as much money for the stockholders as possible."[9]

If social and political ideologies are reflected in our accounting measurement systems, clearly it would be beneficial if they were made explicit. It is generally accepted that the objectives of accounting under Communism would be different from those in a capitalist economy. However, even if we confine ourselves to the non-Communist countries of the West, it is equally true that their so-called mixed economies range from those in which state intervention in economic affairs is highly pervasive to others in which it is minimal. This author suggests that the public perception of the aims of any ubiquitous institution such as the commercial corporation will always reflect accepted social and political norms. The commercial company is a pervasive institution in the Western world but perceived by the public in each country somewhat differently. Thus, in some places companies have almost the same freedoms and responsibilities as have individuals, whereas in others they may be more closely circumscribed by legal and societal restrictions. In every country those who control companies will, it is here contended, conform to what society expects from them. This conformity will also extend to influence corporate reporting. Basically, the view that corporate financial reporting should be specifically directed to meeting the information needs of shareholders and potential investors is based upon an abstract economic model of the firm rather than upon the mode of operation by actual companies in the developed industrial countries. Nevertheless, the U.S. "Objectives Study Group" adhered closely to this classical economic model of the firm so that it must be presumed that they regarded it as a valid descriptive model of

[9] M. Friedman, *Capitalism and Freedom* (Chicago: The University of Chicago Press, 1962), p. 133.

corporate organization. It is seriously doubted whether it would be equally acceptable in all the other developed countries currently represented on IASC or IFAC. This author suggests that in a number of such countries, the classical capitalist theory of the firm would be regarded as a naive model of the motivational forces which operate within large corporate groups. That is particularly so because few such countries could be said to have either capitalist or socialist economies. In fact, in greater or lesser degree, all the wealthy industrial countries of the Western world have mixed economies. In these countries, it is customary to regulate the activities of large commercial and industrial groups in a variety of ways which influence their freedom of action. Since the unrestrained operations of these groups are often considered to be inimical to the free operation of market forces, their actions may be circumscribed in accordance with the teachings of classical economic theory, while correspondingly and paradoxically, they may at the same time find their operations controlled in the interests of socioeconomic planning by the state. It is inconceivable that corporate organizations operating within such diverse socioeconomic frameworks as are found even among the developed countries of the Western world should see their corporate objectives as being independent of the societal norms of the particular countries in which they operate. Rather it is to be expected that such corporate objectives would in some way reflect the expectations of the wider community within whose national boundaries they operate. To the extent that multinational companies tend to reflect the attitudes of their parent rather than those of their host countries, we may also perhaps find some explanation of the suspicions, strained relations, and general adverse social reactions which many such companies have experienced abroad.

In this author's opinion, it is reasonable to say that if a corporate organization has objectives amenable to financial evaluation, then they should become the subject of accounting measurement and reporting. Unless such objectives are trivial, there can be no case for ignoring them or considering them unworthy of evaluation. If it is accepted that corporate objectives may vary, or have differing priorities or rankings from one country to another, it follows that accounting standards may also vary as they relate to those diverse objectives. Any attempt to achieve absolute uniformity between national accounting practices without giving due weight to the reasons for differences both of substance and of emphasis would, I suggest, result in a serious reduction in the quality of information provided. The scope for the harmonizaion of accounting as between countries is therefore limited by the degree of compatability which exists between corporate objectives in each of them.

LEGAL AND INSTITUTIONAL CONSTRAINTS

In the foregoing comments, the opinion has been expressed that corporate objectives and, therefore, corporate accounting and financial reporting may be expected to reflect societal expectations. These latter may in turn be derived from generally accepted political and economic theories in the countries concerned. Where there are wide differences in societal norms arising from such beliefs, those differences must inevitably act as a deterrent to establishing an internationally acceptable framework of accounting.

Of comparable significance are the differences which exist in legal systems and in financial institutions. Some of these may be a reflection of diverse political and economic systems, others no more than an accident of history. For whatever reason diversity of legal systems or financial institutions may exist, it is incontrovertible that it can exercise an immense influence upon accounting. Not only is this influence felt in respect to its effect upon the quality of financial reporting, but it is also to be seen in the way by which the organization of the accountancy profession has responded to the demands of the legal and institutional frameworks of the countries concerned.

Two major European nations, France and West Germany, provide an excellent example of countries whose legal systems and financial institutions differ greatly both from each other and from those of the United Kingdom and the United States. It is, of course, beyond the scope of this paper to describe accounting in France and West Germany in any detail.[10] Nevertheless, reference to some aspects of the legal and institutional background to the practice of accounting may be sufficient to demonstrate the difficulties inherent in attempting to harmonize accounting in those countries with one another and with the United Kingdom and the United States.

France

France has always lacked an effective capital market such as is found in the United Kingdom and United States. The Paris stock exchange

---

[10] The most comprehensive English-language descriptions of accounting in France and Germany are J. H. Beeny, *European Financial Reporting*, vol. 1, *West Germany*, vol. 2, *France* (London: Institute of Chartered Accountants in England and Wales).

is the most active in Europe apart from that in London, but it does not compare in the scale of operations with its London counterpart, either as a secondary market for dealing in securities, or as an essential aim of the market for the issue of new securities. In general, therefore, French industrial and commercial companies have traditionally relied much less upon an active new issue market as a source of long-term funds than have U.K. and U.S. companies. This has resulted in a low emphasis being given to the provision of investor-oriented corporate financial reporting and to the audit function as a safeguard for investors. Arising from that situation, the auditing profession has, at least until recently, been weakly organized and lacking in the influence exercised by the profession in either the United Kingdom or United States. As a result, pronouncements by the main professional institute (L'Ordre des Experts Comptables) have had little influence upon accounting practice unless they were also incorporated in recommendations by the government-appointed national accounting council (Consel National de la Comptabilité).

The primary influence upon the development of accounting principles and practice in France has been the general accounting plan (Le Plan Comptable General) first effectively developed in 1947. The essence of French national economic organization is that it is state planned. The accounting plan is designed as a tool of that economic planning and is intended to be used by all major companies. It is kept under review by the National Accounting Council which derives its authority from the government. The Council, rather than the accounting profession, is the real power in the implementation of change in accounting and financial reporting. Apart from being designed to provide information useful for purposes of the National Economic Plan, the Plan Comptable is also intended to form a basis for the taxation of companies. In fact, fiscal uses take priority over shareholder information needs in the design of accounts. This in turn gives rise to accounting methods related to the provisions of tax laws rather than to the commercial and industrial realities of a company's operations.

West Germany

West Germany has a somewhat inactive capital market which is dominated by the major banks which are the main dealers in securities and are also heavily involved as providers of loan finance. The ratio of long-term liabilities of German companies to their shareholders' funds is, for example, over 4 to 1, a situation contrasting dramatically with the very much lower proportion of borrowing by U.K. and U.S. companies. This is reflected in the very strong emphasis upon solvency and a tendency towards highly conservative methods of asset valuation and revenue recognition, which characterize German accounting.

Accounting and financial reporting by corporations is regulated by the Company Law, the Commercial Code, and the Income Tax Law. Together, these specify in considerable detail the accounting records which must be maintained and the information which must be published. The Income Tax Act in particular is highly specific regarding records and methods, and many expenses are allowable for tax purposes only if they appear in exactly the same fashion in the financial accounts. The principle of a common base for financial reporting, and taxation of profits, often results in tax planning considerations taking precedence over the concept of a "true and fair" presentation of financial affairs. This is not to imply that financial reporting in West Germany is inferior to that of say the United Kingdom or the United States, but rather that the basis for such reporting is different from that of the latter two countries.

Again, although the accounting profession in West Germany is well organized and highly skilled, it must work within the rigid legal framework established for corporate financial reporting. It is not, therefore, in a strong position with regard to furthering the adoption of standards of accounting practice which do not already coincide with current laws.

HARMONIZING ACCOUNTING PRACTICE IN THE CONTEXT OF DISPARATE OBJECTIVES

Disparate objectives of accounting, such as those outlined above in respect to France and West Germany and implied in the U.S. Accounting Objectives Study and the U.K. Corporate Report, have clear implications for accounting measurement. In that context, two factors which operate as constraints upon the processes of the international harmonization of accounting theory and practice can be identified:

1. Variations in perception of the objectives of corporate business organizations; and
2. Differences in what are regarded as the ranking of the objectives of accounting for corporate business organizations.

The latter factor is likely to be of greater significance in practice, although the former is more fundamental. There is a natural tendency to assume that since accounting must be concerned with reflecting the objectives of corporate business organizations, it is necessary to attempt to devise systems which, by attaining such ends, can act as an infor mation base for decision making. The problem with this approach i that it is entirely inward looking. It views the company either as ai entity in its own right or as a projection of its shareholders' interest.

Corporate financial reporting is, however, increasingly acquiring wider societal dimension. It is not simply that the public is becomin, more interested in corporate behavior but rather that, in some coun tries at least, governments and the public also display evidence of . desire to influence the activities of the corporate private sector. At governmental level, this tendency to exert influence may be reflecte in a highly structured manner as is the case in France where each suc cessive "National Plan" has direct relevance to corporate activity, o it may be exhibited in a more haphazard fashion as witnessed by th activities of the various arms of the U.S. federal government. Eithe way, corporate public reporting is increasingly expected to meet th information demands of a growing bureaucracy.

The power of the general public to influence the corporate privat sector for its own ends is naturally more limited than that of govern ments. Nevertheless, the information claims of such groups as thos concerned with ecological and environmental interests provide evi dence of pressures which can be exercised.

National differences in ranking of the objectives of accounting ar an aspect of the problem of improving mutual understanding of cor porate reporting which should repay careful study. International har monization of accounting will not come about as the result of th imposition of uniform accounting practices — even if any group o institution had the will, the authority, or the power to impose sucl uniformity. Rather, it will result from an awareness of the cultural anc societal reasons for such differences as exist in the underlying philos ophy of accounting and corporate financial reporting in each country In this context, I do not, for example, regard the uniformity whicl will be imposed by the E.E.C. Fourth Directive on Company Accounts[1] as being something which will add much to real international under standing. The Directive should have benefits as a remedial device foi standardizing and improving corporate financial reporting in some o the member countries, but it in no way affects national rankings o the uses which should be made of such reports. It is the contentior

---

[1] *E. E. C. Fourth Directive for Co-ordination of National Legislation Regardin, the Annual Accounts of Limited Liability Companies* (Brussels, Belgium E.E.C., 1978). (Also published in full English-language version in *Trade an Industry* [U.K.] [11 August 1978].)

of this author that such rankings have a major qualitative influence on the information content of accounts.

CONCLUSION

In conclusion, we are entering upon a phase of the process of the internationalization of accounting in which attention should be directed toward achieving an understanding of the reasons for the continuing existence of national differences in accounting principles and practices. In that context, emphasis should be upon investigation, analysis, and education rather than upon speeding the processes of promulgating further international accounting standards.

The author realizes that what has been said here could risk being interpreted as an argument against the further development and issue of international accounting standards. It is not intended to be so. The case for harmonizing accounting principles and practice on an international level is stronger today than it ever has been. True accord can be achieved, however, only if there is mutual international understanding, both of corporate objectives and the rankings attached to them.

BIBLIOGRAPHY

Accountants International Study Group. *International Financial Reporting.* London: AISG, 1975.

American Accounting Association. *A Statement of Basic Accounting Theory.* Sarasota, Fla.: AAA, 1966.

———. *Statement on Accounting Theory and Theory Acceptance.* Sarasota, Fla.: AAA, 1977.

M. Edgar Barrett. "Financial Reporting Practices: Disclosure and Comprehensiveness in an International Setting." *Journal of Accounting Research,* Spring 1976.

Norton M. Bedford. *The Future of Accounting in a Changing Society.* Champaign, Ill.: Stipes Publishing Co., 1970.

———. *Extensions in Accounting Disclosure.* Englewood Cliffs, N.J.: Prentice-Hall, Inc., 1973.

R. Andrew Burnett. "The Harmonization of Accounting Principles in the Member Countries of the European Economic Community." *International Journal of Accounting,* Fall 1975: 23-30.

R. J. Chambers. "Accounting Principles and Practices — Negotiated or Dictated?" Accounting Research Convocation 1976, The University of Alabama, Gary John Previts, ed.

Frederick D. S. Choi. "Financial Disclosure in Relation to the European Capital Market." *International Journal of Accounting,* Fall 1973: 121-43.

———. "European Disclosure: The Competitive Disclosure Hypothesis." *Journal of International Business Studies,* Fall 1974: 15-23.

Sidney Davidson and John Kohlmeier. "A Measure of the Impact of Some

150   Foreign Accounting Principles." *Journal of Accounting Research,* Autumn 1966: 183-212.

D. M. Gilling. "Accounting and Social Change." *International Journal of Accounting,* Spring 1976: 59-71.

Louis Goldberg. *An Inquiry into the Nature of Accounting.* Iowa City, Iowa: American Accounting Association, 1965.

George Gorelik. "Soviet Accounting, Planning, and Control." *Abacus,* June 1974: 13-25; also in Gerhard F. Mueller and Charles H. Smith, eds. *Accounting: A Book of Readings.* 2nd ed. Hinsdale, Ill.: The Dryden Press, 1977.

Charles T. Horngren. *Setting Accounting Standards in the 1980s.* Proceedings of the Arthur Young Professors Roundtable, University of Illinois 1976. Norton M. Bedford, ed.

International Congress of Accountants, Proceedings, Munich, 1977.

Joint Organization of African Malagasy and Mauritian States, OCAM General Accounting Plan.

Harvey Kapnick. "Conflicts in Standard Setting for Financial Reporting." *Journal of Contemporary Business,* Spring 1973.

A. T. McLean. *Business Finance and Accounting in the E. E. C.* Farnberough: Saxon House, 1973.

Maurice Moonitz. *Obtaining Agreement on Standards.* Sarasota, Fla.: American Accounting Association, 1974.

Gerhard G. Mueller and Lauren M. Walker. "The Coming of Age of Transnational Financial Reporting." *Journal of Accountancy,* July 1976.

Edward Stamp. "Uniformity in International Accounting Standards." *Journal of Accountancy,* April 1972: 64-67.

Survey of Accounting Principles and Reporting Practices in 46 Countries. London: Price Waterhouse International,

Ross L. Watts and Jerold L. Zimmerman. "Towards a Positive Theory of the Determination of Accounting Standards." *Accounting Review,* January 1978: 112-34.

Stephen A. Zeff. *Forging Accounting Principles in Five Countries.* Champaign, Ill.: Stipes Publishing Co., 1972.

CHAPTER 10

Accounting standards and multinational corporations*

S. J. Gray, J. C. Shaw and L. B. McSweeney

Abstract. The power of MNCs and corresponding pressures, especially from governments and trade unions, for higher levels of accountability has brought into focus the need for more information about MNCs as a basis for policy making at national and international levels. However, the problem of developing accounting standards of disclosure and measurement for MNCs is complex, multidimensional, and dynamic. This paper attempts to clarify some of the issues involved and to identify significant trends. The analysis centers on three fundamental questions: Should there be standards for MNCs? What should be required by the standards? Who should set the standards?

INTRODUCTION

■Accounting standard-setting is controversial and problematic at the national level but at the international and multinational level it becomes even more complex, multidimensional, and dynamic. This paper attempts to identify and evaluate emerging issues and trends relating to accounting standards and multinational corporations. This is likely to be an area of growing importance to accountants not least because of the economic significance of MNCs and the sensitive political issues generated by their activities.

Multinational corporations are significant economic entities, both in aggregate worldwide situations and within most individual countries[1] where they operate.

*Sidney J. Gray is Professor of Accountancy and Head of Department in The University of Glasgow, Scotland. He received his economics degree from the University of Sydney, Australia and Ph.D. in accounting from the University of Lancaster, England. His publications include a recent book on Value Added Reporting and articles on financial reporting by MNCs and the impact of national differences in profit measurement practices.

**Jack C. Shaw is the Johnstone Smith Professor of Accountancy, (established 1925), in the University of Glasgow, Scotland. As a condition of tenure he continues as senior partner of the Edinburgh office of Deloitte Haskins & Sells. His publications include books on group accounts and on auditing. Current research interests besides MNCs include the analysis of national differences in financial reporting practices.

***L. Brendan McSweeney is Senior Technical Officer, the Association of Certified Accountants, UK. He received his commerce degree from University College, Dublin, Ireland. His research interests besides MNCs include reporting to employees.

An earlier version of this paper was presented to the European Accounting Association, Third Congress, Amsterdam, March 1980.

The financial support of the European Centre for Study and Information on Multinational Corporations (E.C.S.I.M.) is gratefully acknowledged.

* This article is reprinted, with permission, from the *Journal of International Business Studies* (Spring/Summer 1981, Tenth Anniversary Special Issue) pp 121–136

Their distinctive economic, social, and political impact arises from their power to control and move resources internationally and has resulted in growing pressures for higher levels of accountability. Such pressures are exerted by host governments (the governments of countries which are recipients of foreign direct investment) and others, in part from a desire for information which may be the means of regulating, constraining, or analyzing the local activities of MNCs. It would appear that the dissolution of political imperialism during the last quarter century (for example: the Belgian, British, French, Portuguese, and Netherlands Empires and Colonies) has given rise to a deeply felt and sometimes strongly expressed economic nationalism.[2] The host governments that are apparently most vociferous in the pressure toward greater accountability by MNCs are those of the developing nations. These pressures complement attempts by home governments[3] to control large companies — operating and particularly headquartered or based in their territories — many of which are the center of multinational operations.

Information about corporate behavior is recognized increasingly as an essential prerequisite to policy making at the national level. At the supranational and intergovernmental level, forms of accountability by MNCs are now being actively promoted, for example, by the United Nations (UN), by the Organization for Economic Cooperation and Development (OECD), and by the European Economic Community (EEC).[4] These activities are a relatively recent phenomenon with most of the developments taking place since 1975 and in the case of the UN and OECD within the broader framework of Codes of Conduct. Each of these organizations, of course, is constituted differently and has different objectives and varying powers of enforcement. All, however, demonstrate the political sensitivity and significance of MNC accountability and of questions concerning financial and nonfinancial disclosure. The development of such political pressures has been spurred by both the relative lack of comparability of corporate reporting in an international context and the apparent deficiencies in the information usually provided.[5]

These pressures for increased MNC accountability and disclosures have also been supported by international trade unions — such as, the International Confederation of Free Trade Unions, European Trade Union Confederation, World Confederation of Labour, and the International Metal Workers Federation.[6] The international investment and banking community and the accounting profession (for example: International Accounting Standards Committee) also appear to be anxious to improve the comparability of corporate reporting at the international level.[7] Managements of MNCs are naturally sensitive to these developments, with responses varying according to their perception of the costs and benefits involved.[8] Many are aware of the potential benefits of greater harmonization in terms of removing the current multiplicity of reporting requirements[9]; however, there is a proliferation of bodies claiming to have authority as standard-setting agencies — national and supranational, political and professional. Hence the managerial response to or acceptance of the need for harmonization of standards is to some extent confused and perhaps inhibited by these multiple claims to authority.

SOME FUNDAMENTAL QUESTIONS

It would seem useful to pose some fundamental questions, which, incidentally, are relevant in the national context just as much as in the multinational, as a means of structuring this inquiry into emerging issues and trends relating to accounting standards and MNCs. Questions which would appear to concern all interested parties include the following: Should there be standards for MNCs? What should be required by standards? Who should set standards? Before addressing these questions, however, we must first define the terms used in the analysis because they are subject to many interpretations.

What are standards? What are MNCs? The term "standard" may be used in a variety of ways but here it is used broadly to mean a set of statements which may include reference to disclosure or measurement issues to be dealt with by MNCs. Such statements may range from those intended to achieve strict uniformity to those capable of more flexible interpretation; from those derived from statutory authority, to those which are effectively advisory. The fact that they exist as guidelines or criteria against which MNC accountability can be assessed qualifies such statements to be described as "standards" in the context of this discussion. The relevant questions are thus concerned not only with the rationale for standards but also with their scope and force. The discussion is not restricted to standards which are associated exclusively with mechanisms to monitor compliance or impose penalties for noncompliance. A major problem in the international context is that the scope of standards is not always clearly specified, posing consequent potential for confusion.

The term "multinational corporation," or alternatives such as "transnational" corporation, may also be used in a variety of ways; but here it is defined broadly to mean any corporation that controls economic resources, in terms of production or service facilities, in two or more countries.[10] If MNCs are to be affected by standards set exclusively for them, then clearly questions of definition become crucial and will involve criteria such as overall size, relative economic significance in countries of operation, number of geographical locations, and the extent of foreign as compared to domestic operations. In this regard, it is instructive to note the focus of existing proposals/requirements. In the UN proposals [1977][11] the emphasis is on all large MNCs (broadly defined as above) but application to uninational companies is recommended. The OECD guidelines[12] [1976] refer to all MNCs irrespective of size but again wider application is expected. The EEC deals in the main with all corporate activities within the EEC territories, including those by MNCs, but with the emphasis on large companies. The accounting profession, through the International Accounting Standards Committee (IASC) attempts to prescribe for all companies without distinguishing between those that are uninational and multinational. Any attempt to evaluate the relevance of international standards requires specification of those enterprises for which such standards are primarily intended. The definition of the enterprise will indicate the range and nature of user groups involved and hence the rationale for the standards. It is only by reference to user groups and to their decision requirements that the effectiveness and relevance of standards can be judged.

Should There Be Standards for MNCs?

In the context of reporting financial information, it has to be recognized that there have been significant changes in the perceptions of the use to which accounts are put. In the past the emphasis was on legal concepts — accounts demonstrated the ability of the enterprise to satisfy those who had legally enforceable claims on its resources. Accounts were referred to primarily as a means of confirming that legally defined constraints on the disposition of resources and allocation of results had been complied with. Currently, a widely held view of the use of financial statements is that they serve as a basis for economic decisions. These decisions include not just the legality but also the fairness and effectiveness of managerial actions. The wide community of stakeholders interested in the modern corporate enterprise demands information not only about the conduct of the enterprise as a whole, but about the ways in which any particular sectional stakeholders' interests in the enterprise have been dealt with relative to the treatment afforded to other sectional interests. If there are difficulties in discerning how best to provide for the information needs of those varied stakeholder interests in the context of single-state, uninational enterprise, there are added degrees of complexity in confronting the problem of standards for MNCs.

Traditionally, ideas of information disclosure and in particular financial reporting have been developed within the concept of the legal entity — the corporation — whose boundaries coincided with those of an economic entity. Increasingly the boundaries of the economic entity do not coincide with those of a legal entity; the economic activity may be within only a part of the legal entity (for example: the "group") or may extend beyond the boundaries of an individual legal entity (for example: single company). This problem is sharply demonstrated by the nature, structure, and organization of the MNC.

It may be, of course, that there is no case for standards of any kind; for example, where the content of existing published annual reports satisfies the needs of the community of users without the intervention of a standard-setting body. To some extent at least, the arguments of the agency-theorists may be relevant here.[13] If the management of an MNC perceives it to be in the interests of either the MNC as an entity or its management to respond to the information demands of users, then management will strive to assure satisfaction of those demands. Such a line of argument leads to the proposition that no separate standard-setting mechanisms are needed; the normal pressures of demand and supply will operate to achieve equilibrium.[14] If those who demand information from MNCs also exert influence over the environment within which the MNC operates, then there will be a strong influence on the MNC to move toward satisfying these information demands in exchange for the maintenance of existing rights or the avoidance of potential constraints to the operations of the enterprise. If those responsible for meeting demands for information (that is, the management) conclude that the information requirement is unreasonable or inimical to the interests of the MNC, they have to achieve some compromise with the interest group exerting pressure for disclosure. On this basis, the actual level of accountability achieved is a constantly shifting compromise between the perception of user needs on the one hand and the view taken about the interests of the corporate enterprise as a whole on the other hand. In this context it can be suggested that where MNC managements respond to pressures for increased disclosure then this demonstrates their recognition of the need to maintain reasonable operating environments in the face of political pressures for legal and economic constraints on MNC operations in many countries. Similarly they may recognize that the investor in the MNC, in national and international capital markets, seeks information about differential risks within the MNC and that labor relations in any locality may be affected by a local trade union's response to international trade union views or pressures.

It would seem, however, that the perception of some users and organizations such as the UN, OECD, and EEC is that market forces cannot be relied upon to ensure the provision of sufficient comparable information about MNCs. The emphasis in the UN proposals on more extensive disclosure by large MNCs[15] is directed toward a wide range of users but appears strongly influenced nevertheless by the needs of individual national governments, particularly in developing countries, for information about the economic, social, and political impact of MNCs.[16] A similar demand for information is expressed by trade union organizations, who would appear to support strongly the UN initiatives, both at national and international levels.

The OECD seems to have a range of users in mind similar to the UN. But in contrast to the UN proposals, which are detailed and cover individual subsidiary as well as group accounts, the OECD guidelines are limited to group accounts and incorporate disclosure requirements which are more general in nature.[17] This probably reflects the OECD's greater concern with and sensitivity to business interests.

It is perhaps not unfair to suggest that within the UN the influence of developing third world nations appears to be relatively powerful as compared to the largely developed and substantially westernized membership of OECD. To date, neither the UN nor the OECD statements appear to have achieved much in the way of encouraging MNCs to provide additional informaion disclosures in practice; but these developments are, of course, still at an early stage. They do, however, provide powerful indications of expectations at the supranational political level, and within the terms set for the present discussion these statements do constitute standards against which to measure the performance of MNCs with regard to information disclosure and corporate conduct.

The position of the European Economic Community (EEC) and of EEC Directives is distinguishable. The EEC is what its name says — a supranational community; moreover, it is a community of nations committed to achieving, ultimately, political and economic union.[18] Member states have accepted treaty obligations to enact local legislation giving effect to the decisions of the Council of Ministers as reflected in the Directives approved by the Council. As regards company laws, the object of the EEC harmonization program is to facilitate freedom of establishment of companies within member countries and to protect the interests of shareholders, employees, and third parties. The company law harmonization program is seen as an important contribution to an economic environment within which finance and investment can move freely and where equality of competition is achieved. It is also seen as a means by which proper supervision of corporate activity can be attained. Observation of the consequences in the United States of fragmented, state-based company legislation suggested that individual states might seek to encourage corporations to establish headquarters in their territory by imposing only minimal regulatory and disclosure requirements. EEC harmonization is intended to achieve the highest common factor of disclosure and corporate conduct generally — not the lowest common denominator. The EEC company law directives are substantially prescriptive and become embodied in statutorily defined requirements.

In practice, the EEC directives and proposals relating to accounting achieve some degree of compromise between a perspective of legal prescription and one related to economic decision making; for example, the Fourth Directive[19] adopts the predominantly UK concept of a "true and fair view" but in the context of a rigorously defined financial reporting framework. The EEC Directives apply to all large companies and extend to those whose operations are restricted to the territories of the member states as well as MNCs which are based within one or other of the member states, but whose operations extend well beyond EEC boundaries. The proposed Seventh Directive[20] dealing with group accounts is particularly relevant to MNCs based outside but with operations within EEC territorial limits. This particular directive, if approved, would require the same disclosure for such MNCs with regard to their EEC activities as would be required from EEC-based MNCs. The important difference, of course, is that the latter must meet EEC reporting requirements with regard to their worldwide activities but the MNC based outside the EEC must report only those aspects of its operations relating to its business entities based in the EEC. Such MNCs will, however, be required to provide subgroup consolidations for each holding company within the EEC or, alternatively, a consolidation of its EEC operations as a whole.

Apart from such legislative harmonization within the relatively narrow confines of the EEC, there are other potent influences on most MNCs toward harmonization, indeed uniformity, through the medium of Stock Enchanges — perhaps the strongest influences being the UK and U.S. Stock Exchanges.[21] In the UK, for example, it is obvious that any British-based MNC has to comply with UK-defined disclosure requirements with respect to its worldwide activities. The significance of the disclosure requirements of the UK Stock Exchange is that these will apply to any non-UK-based MNC which seeks a listing for its shares in the UK — either to provide access to UK stock markets for its existing shareholders or to raise funds through the UK capital markets; for example, a Japanese-based MNC seeking a UK listing for its share capital must report in the UK as if it were UK-based including worldwide consolidation of results and translation of accounts into the UK domestic currency. Recent years indicate growth of the transnationality of sources of capital and increasing numbers of MNCs seeking Stock Exchange listings outside the country of their base or headquarters.

Such influence tends to achieve a restricted uniformity rather than harmony because the prescription of Stock Exchange requirements in any individual country depends upon the local national legislative arrangements and professional accountancy influences in defining appropriate financial disclosure. The trend, noted earlier, toward multiple stock exchange listings demonstrates the problem of achieving harmonization. Philips, a Netherlands-based MNC, reports, for example, in terms of replacement values, a basis of measurement not accepted by regulatory agencies in the United States and, thus, to support its New York Stock Exchange listing, Philips has to provide a reconciliation translating its Netherlands figures into the U.S.-required historical cost equivalent. Senior executives of Royal Dutch Shell, a Netherlands-UK-based MNC, have commented publicly on the consequences of the present U.S. prescription for foreign currency translation (FAS #8) which has to be followed to support the U.S. listing of Shell shares but imposes on Shell the need either to provide two sets of financial statements — FAS #8 for the U.S. and, say, closing rate for UK — or to maintain the use, for reporting outside the U.S., of a method of currency translation which may not be the most appropriate representation of Shell's financial performance.

Other areas of particular interest and concern to MNCs with regard to financial performance and measurement, besides inflation accounting and foreign currency translation, include consolidation techniques and the identification of groups, segmental reporting, accounting for taxation, and the treatment of provisions and reserves. These are areas where significant differences exist in national practice and prescription.[22] The managements of many MNCs certainly seem anxious to eliminate such differences and achieve harmonization without the need for complex supplementary or reconciliation statements to meet differently defined reporting requirements.

The problem is, of course, that the perception of the management of an MNC as to what is the most appropriate reporting or measurement formula will be very strongly influenced by the social and professional perceptions of the country in which the MNC is headquartered. At least in the English-speaking world, detailed perceptions of disclosure and of reporting tend to be developed through social mechanisms, and legislation gives expression to what should be disclosed. Questions of how disclosure should be made and the measurement methods adopted for reporting events and transactions in financial terms have been left, in the main, to the professional accountancy bodies — with greater or less advice from and control by nonaccountants. Non-English-speaking traditions are, of course, somewhat different and developments within the EEC touched on previously demonstrate these: that is, a more prescriptive, legalistic approach is evident.

Harmonization of legislatively defined disclosure can perhaps be achieved only at the political level. The need in the U.S. to create an SEC to deal at the federal level with the lack of harmonization in individual states' legislation can be pointed to in support of such a suggestion. Within the EEC it seems to have been recognized that political structures are needed to deal with legislatively defined matters. The professional accountancy-orientated views about how to measure and how to disclose reflect less immediately the concerns of trade unions, consumers, and governments. But to the extent to which all such questions relating to the use to which information is put by users of financial statements, even the accountancy professional bodies are responsive to such "external," nonaccountant pressures. Harmonization of such local standards defined by professional accountancy societies need not necessarily involve political mechanisms — the self-regulatory stock exchange in the UK demonstrates this.

Transnational groupings of accountancy bodies — for example: IASC, IFAC, UEC, CAPA, IAA, and AFA[23] — are also seeking to make progress in this area. Perhaps the major organization involved is the International Accounting Standards Committee (IASC),[24] where the aim is to improve the comparability of measurement and reporting by all enterprises, worldwide. But there is very much less emphasis at IASC on extensions in disclosure and virtually no concern specifically with the problems of MNCs as distinct from uninational enterprises.

Professionally developed IASC standards would seem to be influenced very largely by the needs of the investment and banking community, with special reference to best practice in developed equity markets such as the UK and U.S.[25] The specific interests of governments and of trade unions, on the other hand, are not directly recognized. Little real progress has been achieved toward harmonization, for example, on foreign currency translation, on inflation accounting, on research and development, or consolidations, because IASC has to accommodate the different established laws and professional practices of the United States and of Western Europe. It is not surprising, therefore, that IASC standards tend to be somewhat bland compromises which are generally ignored either because they are easily accommodated or cannot be enforced.

It continues to be difficult to provide a simple answer to the question "Should there be standards for MNCs?" Many MNCs are already subject to standards — imposed by legislation and defined by professional accountancy organizations — because MNCs based in any country have to follow at least the same degree of disclosure and accountability as any other domestic enterprise based in that same country. One set of problems arising from the lack of consistency of accountability among MNCs based in different countries is not really related to MNCs at all; they derive from the lack of consistency or harmonization of national standards and apply to the lack of comparability of disclosure by all large companies based in different countries. For MNCs there might be problems arising from substantially different disclosure requirements. There are difficulties for governments and for elements within domestic societies in relating information about the local units of an MNC to that provided about the worldwide activities of locally based MNCs. For the governments and societies of host countries there are problems in relating information about local units to the aggregated information of the worldwide MNC activities, particularly when there is no consistency in the provision of the aggregated data for MNCs based in different countries. For the MNCs themselves, or at least their management, there is the complication of maintaining records and providing information to satisfy distinguishable local demands as well as being able to provide the level of accountability expected in their home base. There is also an arguable case for international standards to the extent that MNCs are not providing information demanded and apparently needed by users. The demands from organizations such as the UN, OECD, EEC, International Trade Unions, and IASC, indicate the quantity and quality of information currently disclosed by MNCs is less than satisfactory and warrants some form of standard-setting; however, whether or not the precise content of the demands identified can be justified in that the benefits outweigh the costs involved is a question which has yet to be answered despite the convictions of the groups involved.

Perhaps there is a case for standards applicable to MNCs only as opposed to all large companies worldwide, at least in the short term. The present lack of consistency in MNC accountability and the proliferation of national standards may lead to the conclusion that worldwide harmonization of MNC reporting — disclosure and measurement — is needed. Equally, there may be a supportable argument that international harmonization should not be considered a major priority for uninational (domestic) enterprises with no foreign operations, because the needs of the international investment community, the main group involved and relatively expert, could be met to a large extent by accounting policy disclosures. It is only when uninational companies become units of a supranational economic entity, the MNC, that arguments of consistency and comparability in the interests of international constituencies of users become persuasive. If this line of argument is to be pursued, then it would seem that the UN and OECD have embarked on a potentially more fruitful path than has the IASC; the important point being to emphasize and develop supranational standards for MNCs rather than to seek at this stage the ideal of a harmonization of national standards for all corporations.

Ideally the answer to this question would seem to depend on the decision requirements of the user groups involved, taking into consideration the costs and benefits arising. In practice, the outcome is likely to result from a political process involving both MNC managements and the accounting profession as suppliers and verifiers of information in addition to international groups of users such as investors, creditors, trade unions, governments, and society at-large.

There is, of course, a fundamental problem, as in the national context, of defining user information needs. A positive approach would be to ask users what they need with the danger, however, that responses may well be conditioned by experience, and hence less than imaginative in dealing with new situations. There is also the danger that users may be encouraged to compile shopping lists of information, including anything that might conceivably be useful, especially when they do not bear the cost, at least directly, of providing the information. Can users then be trusted to articulate their needs, and are MNCs to respond unquestioningly to stated needs without challenging the relevance of the information demanded? An alternative normative approach to defining user needs is to attempt to construct models of the decision processes of users and thereby deduce what information they should need to satisfy their objectives. It may be that more attention should be paid to this approach in the MNC context where new situations have arisen with the corresponding potential for new forms of reporting to be developed and for information needs to be shaped by policy-makers at the supranational level.

An important issue in the supranational context is the extent to which the separate needs of users are to be satisfied by general purpose reports or by special purpose reports.[26] It appears at present that the UN, with special reference to the developing nations and trade unions, at the national and international levels, is concerned to obtain as much information as possible in a general purpose report. The interests of these groups appear to be initially to obtain information as a step toward developing policies and strategies for dealing with and regulating MNCs. The governments of developing countries and those involved in trade unions (nationally and internationally) feel themselves to be at a severe disadvantage in their dealings with MNCs. The relative transnational freedom of MNCs and the mechanisms available to them, especially transfer pricing, to modify the impact of national economic, fiscal, and social policies have been discussed extensively elsewhere.[27]

Those who seek to constrain and regulate, or at the very least to influence, the activities of MNCs, tend to suspect the existence of abuse by MNCs in their supranational powers and flexibility. Part of the pressure for MNC accountability is to assist the perception of the existence of abuse or, more positively, to confirm its absence. In the context of the single company, the various stakeholders (investors, creditors, employees, customers) are concerned to preserve their own individual interests; with the MNCs, individual governments are concerned to protect the interests of their own nationals as against other nationals; at the trade union level, there is ideological commitment to eliminate exploitation of any one group of employees in favor of another, or in favor of other stakeholders.

"Special" reports, however, may be more pertinent to specific needs and these could be tailored to meet the requirements of individual countries or individual interest groups. In this case, the onus of specification is shifted directly to the user group seeking information; there has to be definition of the data needed, and desirably an explanation of why it is needed.

A key element of the UN emphasis on general purpose reports is the provision of nonfinancial information relating to employment, production, investment, social policies, and pollution,[28] which would seem to be relevant mainly to governments. If so, then there is the question of whether some of this information could be presented better in special reports.

Other disclosure and measurement issues which are regarded as especially significant (and often sensitive) in the context of MNCs include: (a) segmental information, particularly on a geographical basis, or multianalysis by activity and by country[29]; (b) transfer pricing policies and their impact[30]; (c) employment conditions and prospects[31]; (d) foreign currency transactions and the translation of foreign currency financial statements.[32] Additional MNC financial reporting issues, which are nonetheless controversial, include accounting for groups and the consolidation of financial statements, accounting for inflation, and accounting for taxation.[33] Consideration also needs to be given to the form of presentation of financial information.

It may be that the conventional Income Statement and Balance Sheet for consolidated groups or for individual companies is not the most appropriate, say, for government and employee users. Statements of Value Added[34] — segmented as required — might be a more useful method of presentation. Statements of funds or cash flow may also be useful — again segmented. The present perception of the bases on which governments and trade unions are seeking additional disclosure certainly suggests that such forms of accounting are worthy of further investigation in that they might meet more fully the needs of these groups for information from MNCs. Both the UN and the OECD are at the moment striving for acceptance of their ideas with regard to a minimum list of items of disclosure but, at this early stage of their activities, have given relatively little attention to issues concerning classification, presentation, and measurement; thus, there is much work to be done if standards for MNCs are to be developed. This effort will require cooperation from the accountancy profession and a substantial research effort, as well as political will.

Who Should Set the Standards?

The very fact that one has to discuss the need for standards of MNC disclosure and measurement implies that the definition of such standards cannot be left to the MNCs themselves. Reference was made earlier to the proposition that standards as such would be unnecessary if the process of enlightened self-interest, in the long run, assured that managements of MNCs meet the information needs of all the multinational interest groups who establish claims to disclosure by the MNC about its worldwide and/or local activities. On the one hand, there is the local community — whether host or home government, or national elements of employees, investors, consumers, or others within the nation — anxious to supervise, influence, or at least be informed about the MNC's operations. On the other hand, there is the management of the MNC, anxious to achieve the most congenial operational environment possible and to minimize costs of preparing and producing information for external (to the management) consumption. This assures that there are two strong parties to the bargaining process by which equilibrium may be achieved.

If one rejects the argument that natural balance will be achieved and accepts the argument that MNCs themselves cannot be relied on or expected to develop appropriate standards, one is forced to consider the two alternative agencies referred to earlier — the political or the professional. This choice, or tension, between these two types of agency exists, of course, at the national level. As with so many other aspects of this discussion it may be that there are few new problems with MNCs; many similar problems can be found at the domestic level, but with MNCs there is an extra multinational dimension of complexity.

On the whole, accountants prefer the professionally orientated IASC type of approach whereby auditors and, to a lesser extent, financial executives agree on procedures of measurement and disclosure. The weaknesses of this approach have already been touched on. Accountancy bodies cannot legitimately claim to identify exclusively the effect of accounting reports on the decision-making behavior of users nor the sole right to choose between reporting alternatives which may influence actions by some users to the detriment of others.

The auditing bias of many of the professional accountancy organizations also leads to preoccupation with the validation aspects of disclosure and a reluctance to develop ideas for disclosure of information which cannot be validated other than by the passage of time. There is a tendency for such efforts also to concentrate on how to achieve disclosure rather than to examine ideas of what should be disclosed to meet the needs of users. Further, the needs of users other than shareholders and creditors have received little attention. Ideas for alternative methods of disclosure are not examined enthusiastically; alternative measurement bases — for example: current cost accounting in the UK — are seldom initiated except under "encouragement" from political agencies. As noted earlier, only very limited progress has been made with difficult technical issues — for example: foreign currency translation — and very little harmonization has been attained. Last, the close relationships between professional firms, which are increasingly multinational, and their clients (the MNCs) together with the apparent acquiescence of management generally in any professionally based program is seen by some, at least, as a valid basis for challenging the validity of such an approach. Perhaps self-regulation is too suspect to succeed.

It may be then that a political approach is inevitable. In the United States, a political solution in the creation of the SEC was seen as the only way of achieving harmonization at an acceptably high level of disclosure. Until recently the SEC was content to leave to professional accountancy agencies the determination of technical accountancy matters. Now the accounting standard-setting agencies (notably FASB) involve directly many more influences other than accountants, and the SEC itself has challenged and even reversed procedures approved by FASB; for example: oil and gas accounting.[35] Matters of accountancy appear to have become too important to be left to accountancy bodies. If the levels of accountability are to be defined at the national level in the first instance and ultimately some form of supranational harmonization is to be achieved, then it is difficult to see any alternative to political agencies. At this stage, it also seems likely that such agencies will concentrate on the philosophy of information disclosure — why information is needed and in what form it is required — leaving detailed aspects to be worked out in cooperation with professional accountancy organizations.[36]

Whereas the UN and OECD approach to MNC standards seems inevitable, it may well succeed only in the long term because it is difficult to see how anything other than "guidelines" as opposed to "requirements" can be provided at this stage.[37] Mechanisms for reviewing and enforcing compliance can operate only at the national level — applicable to corporations within the jurisdiction of nation-states and exercised by local regulatory, legislative, and judicial agencies. If different supranational agencies issue competing guidelines then individual nation-states have to decide which, if any, set of guidelines matches their information needs; the harmonization sought by the management of MNCs is frustrated and they have to respond to differently defined information needs. Even if guidelines emanate from only one supranational agency, unless a sufficient degree of commonality is achieved in the specification of information, it is likely that nation-states will individually vary the guidelines, again arriving at the frustration of the desire for simple, unequivocal, and uniform disclosure. The relative success of the EEC in achieving enforceable standards with a fair degree of commonality cannot be expected to be repeated worldwide. As has already been noted, the EEC is a relatively homogeneous, cultural grouping of nations committed (even if less than wholeheartedly in some instances) to ultimate total political and economic unity. But presumably from the standpoint of the UN and OECD some attempt at standards is better than none at all. Nevertheless, the paradox remains: supranational requirements cannot be enforced; supranational guidelines may lead to so many national variants that standardization will be frustrated. There may be more rapid progress to be made by achieving initially some degree of harmonization among smaller, perhaps regional groupings of nations sharing at least some common cultural and economic characteristics and ultimately achieving harmonization of that smaller number of regionally defined standards.

Such a regional approach could also simplify the attainment of adequate representation of various user groups. The better the user representation, the more confident one could be that the information being sought was relevant to user needs, and the easier it would be to distinguish what should be conveyed in general purpose reports from that confined to special reports.

In practice, a gradualist approach may therefore be preferable to the attempt to arrive at a total solution for MNC standards, though clearly there are some aspects of MNC activities which may lend themselves to universal solutions; such as, transfer pricing, segmental information, and foreign currency translation.

CONCLUSIONS

The power of MNCs and corresponding pressures, especially from governments and trade unions, for higher levels of accountability has brought into focus the need for more information about MNCs as a basis for policy making at national and international levels. To some extent the conflict expresses the shift in the balance between the economic power of MNCs, still largely based in developed nations, and the growing political influence of developing nations. It is generally recognized that calls for greater accountability must be accompanied by consideration of what and how disclosure is to be made; some degree of consistency or standardization is needed. However, the problem of developing accounting standards of disclosure and measurement for MNCs is complex, multidimensional, and dynamic.

An attempt has been made in this paper to clarify some of the issues involved and to identify trends. The analysis has centered on three fundamental questions: Should there be standards for MNCs? What should be required by the standards? Who should set standards? Some tentative conclusions follow.

Despite the many similarities in the problems associated with accounting standards for MNCs and those restricted to wholly domestic companies, MNC problems are more complex, in terms of identifying user groups involved, in defining their information needs and in considering the factors determining the standard-setting process. The confusion of boundaries between economic, legal, and political entities raises special issues when considering standards for MNCs.

If the bargaining processes between MNCs and users were to result in the provision of information which was acceptable, in terms of quantity and quality, both to management and the user groups concerned — such as, governments, trade unions, investors, lenders/bankers — there might be no need to consider further the issue of standard setting.

Where MNCs are unwilling (or unable because of difficulties in defining user needs) to meet the demands of governments, trade unions, investors, and others for information there is an arguable case for MNC standards at the supranational level. The current activities of the UN, OECD, EEC, International Trade Unions, IASC, and others indicate a strongly perceived need for improvements in information disclosure and the comparability of reporting by MNCs.

The content of MNC standards will depend on the user groups involved, their decision requirements, and their need for general purpose or special reports. It may be that special reports would be more pertinent in some instances to the specific needs of individual governments and interest groups; however, the problem of identifying and validating user needs and resolving conflicts, where they exist, between these needs is unsettled and warrants further investigation. The fears and problems of management concerning the effects of government interference, better informed competition, and changes in employee relations must also be evaluated, together with the costs and complexities believed to be associated with implementing standards.

Significant disclosure and measurement issues in the context of the development of MNC accounting standards are: (a) nonfinancial information relating to employment conditions and prospects, organization, production, investment, and the environment; (b) segmental information, particularly on a geographical basis, or multianalysis by activity and country; (c) transfer pricing policies and their impact; (d) foreign currency transactions and the translation of foreign currency financial statements. Additional MNC financial reporting issues include accounting for groups and the consolidation of financial statements, accounting for inflation, and accounting for taxation.

The setting of MNC standards is essentially a political process and it seems inevitable that corporate reporting objectives and standards of disclosure will be harmonized only at the supranational or intergovernmental level; for example, the UN, OECD, and EEC. The accounting profession and the IASC are likely to play a more supportive role in terms of providing the detailed development and assisting practical implementation of desired standards of disclosure and measurement.

The development of MNC standards by the UN, OECD, and other supranational political agencies seems likely to be both more supportable, at least in the short term, and to have better prospects for success than the professional IASC attempt to seek the ideal of international harmonization of national standards for all corporations. The relative preference for the UN and OECD approach is due, at least in part, to the emphasis on MNCs which are in many important respects distinguishable from domestic corporations.

MNC standards may be developed as "requirements" or as indicative "guidelines." It is difficult to see them as anything other than guidelines because compliance can be enforced only at the national level or in regional groupings equivalent to the national level such as the EEC. The paradox is that supranational "requirements" cannot be enforced without national adoption, and supranational "guidelines" may lead to so many national variants that simple specification of universally relevant MNC standards is frustrated. A gradualist approach may be preferable with MNC standards implemented initially on a regional basis.

FOOTNOTES

1. The relative importance of MNCs to individual country economies is not confined to developing nations. There is a high level of MNC penetration of many developed countries which accounts for nearly three-quarters of MNCs' foreign activities. See OECD [1977], UN Economic and Social Council [1978].

2. See Turner [1974]; Wallace [1976]; and Vernon [1977].

3. By home government is meant the government of a country from which ultimate control is exercised. Home and host countries are not discrete categories because the major home countries are also major host countries. The extent to which MNCs are centralized or decentralized is discussed extensively in the literature but is not considered here. See Stopford and Wells, Jr. [1972]; Robbins and Stobaugh [1974]; Vernon and Wells, Jr. [1976]; and Vernon [1977].

4. The principal statements are: OECD [1976]; UN [1977]; and Commission of the European Communities [1976 and 1978].

5. See for example Lea [1971]; UN Economic and Social Council [1974]; Choi and Mueller [1978]; and Fitzgerald and Kelley [1979].

6. For an account of the role of international trade union organizations and international trade union centers see, for example, Northrup and Rowan [1974]; Roberts and Liebhaberg [1977]; and Wilms-Wright [1977].

7. The object of the International Accounting Standards Committee (IASC) is ". . . to formulate and publish in the public interest standards to be observed in the presentation of audited financial statements and to promote their world-wide acceptance and observance." [IASC 1977].

8. Resistance to increased disclosure by many MNCs is based on a variety of objections including the cost, the limited comprehension of recipients, and the possible utilization of the additional disclosure by others to the detriment of the MNC. (From private interviews with a number of UK and U.S.-based MNCs. Also USA-Business Industry and Advisory Committee [1974]; Behrman [1976]; Mautz and May [1978]; International Chamber of Commerce [1978]; and OECD [1979].)

9. See for example de Bruyne [1980].

10. There is an extensive literature on defining MNCs. See for example American Accounting Association [1973]; Confederation of British Industry [1975]; and Wallace [1976].

11. The UN proposals — UN [1977] — are contained in a report prepared for the Commission on Transnational Corporations by an Expert Group on "International Standards of Accounting and Reporting." The Group, serving in their individual capacities, came from various disciplines (accounting, law, social sciences) and backgrounds (including the accounting profession, home and host government, trade unions, and MNCs).

12. The OECD guidelines referred to here are those relating to information disclosure in the OECD's wide-ranging code of conduct: "Guidelines for Multinationals" in OECD [1976].

13. An agency relationship between managers and shareholders is postulated whereby managers in their capacity as agents have market incentives to disclose information con-

sistent with their own and shareholders' interests. See Jensen and Meckling [1976]; Watts [1977]; and Watts and Zimmerman [1978].

14. Watts [1977]; Watts and Zimmerman [1978]; and Benston [1969].

15. UN Economic and Social Council [1977] recommends that smaller companies be excluded from its proposed reporting requirements. The requirement for consolidated reports of the MNC as a whole would apply if it met two of the three specified criteria (p. 47). No criteria for size are stated for individual subsidiaries or intermediate parent companies.

16. The UN proposals refer to a number of different user groups including 'governments,' 'the general public,' 'the international community,' consumer groups, labor, trade unions and company employees, investors, creditors, local authorities. They have been criticized for neither specifying nor justifying their perception of the information needs of these users nor relating their proposals to these needs. See International Chamber of Commerce [1978].

17. OECD [1976] refers primarily to "the enterprise as a whole" thereby avoiding a major source of tension: the extent to which an MNC's subsidiaries' reports may be influenced by or reflect its relationship with the group as a whole. See Robbins and Stobaugh [1974] and Vernon [1977].

18. Treaty establishing the European Economic Community, signed at Rome, 25th March 1957.

19. Commission of the European Communities [1978]. The Fourth Directive has as its object the harmonization of the content and format of annual accounts (Art. 2) of individual companies. This directive does not require absolute uniformity because options are provided in certain clearly defined areas.

20. Commission of the European Communities [1976], amended [1979].

21. See for example Watson [1974]; AISG [1975]; and Zeff [1979].

22. See for example Fitzgerald, Stickler, and Watts [1979] and Gray [1980].

23. International Accounting Standards Committee, International Federation of Accountants, Union Europeenne des Experts Comptables, Confederation of Asian and Pacific Accountants, Inter-American Accounting Association and Asean Federation of Accountants. See Choi and Mueller [1978].

24. The International Accounting Standards Committee was founded in 1973 by accounting bodies from Australia, Canada, France, the Federal Republic of Germany, Japan, Mexico, Netherlands, the UK, Ireland, and the U.S. Fifty-six accounting bodies from 43 countries are represented in the Committee. Its controlling board is composed of the founders plus Nigeria and South Africa.

25. The narrowness and relatively minor role of the equity markets in most developing countries and in some developed countries restricts the relevance of the IASC's current work even further. See Scott [1970] and Lowe [1974].

26. Special purpose reports may be confidential or publicly available but are tailored to the information needs of a single user. See for example Confederation of British Industry [1975]; International Chamber of Commerce [1978]; and UN Economic and Social Council [1977].

27. Robbins and Stobaugh [1973]; UN Economic and Social Council [1974]; Barnet and Mueller [1975]; Vernon [1977]; and UN Conference on Trade and Development [1978].

28. UN Economic and Social Council [1977] suggests a wide range of nonfinancial disclosures at both individual company and group levels but states "that this aspect of general purpose reporting requires further study." (p. 27) OECD [1976] requests disclosure of only one item of nonfinancial information, the average number of employees in each geographical area (p. 15). The IASC has not considered nonfinancial information.

29. U.S. Business Industry and Advisory Committee [1976]; Gray [1978]; OECD [1979]; and IASC [1980].

30. The Monopolies Commission [1973]; U.S. Business Industry and Advisory Committee [1976]; UN Economic and Social Council [1977]; UN Conference on Trade and Development [1978]; and OECD [1979].

31. UN Economic and Social Council [1976]; International Labour Office [1977]; International Confederation of Free Trade Unions; European Trade Union Confederation, World Confederation of Labour [1977]; and International Chamber of Commerce [1978].

32. FASB [1975]; Morris [1975]; and Choi and Mueller [1978].

33. Choi and Mueller [1978]; Center for International Education and Research in Accounting [1977 and 1979]; and Scott and Drapalik [1978].

34. By a 'value added statement' is meant a statement which reports, in financial terms, the output of an enterprise less external inputs (that is, its value added) and the distribution of the value added to the various stakeholders. See for example Gray and Maunders [1980] and UN Economic and Social Council [1976].

35. Zeff [1978].

36. In identifying complementary but separate roles for political and professional agencies in the development of standards for MNCs we are rejecting the view of some commentators who consider the political and the professional to be mutually exclusive alternatives and who usually favor the professional. See for example International Chamber of Commerce [1978] and Fitzgerald and Kelley [1979].

37. This conclusion is based on the recognition of a number of political and technical constraints including: the divergent interests of the involved parties; the difficulty of defining MNCs; the diversity of existing national laws/requirements; the experience of agreeing and implementing existing multilateral conventions.

REFERENCES

Accountants International Study Group. *International Financial Reporting*. New York, 1975.

American Accounting Association. "Report of the Committee on International Accounting." *The Accounting Review,* Supplement, 1973.

Barnet, R. J., and Mueller, R. E. *Global Reach: The Power of the Multinational Corporation.* London: Jonathan Cape, 1975.

Behrman, J. N. *Demand for Information from Multinational Enterprises.* New York: Fund for Multinational Management Education/Council of the Americas, 1976.

Benston, G. J. "The Value of the SEC's Accounting Disclosure Requirements." *Accounting Review,* July 1969.

Center for International Education and Research in Accounting. *The Multinational Corporation: Accounting and Social Implications.* University of Illinois, 1977.

_____. *The Impact of Inflation on Accounting: A Global View.* University of Illinois, 1979.

Choi, F. D. S., and Mueller, G. G. *An Introduction to Multinational Accounting.* Englewood Cliffs: Prentice-Hall, 1978.

Commission of the European Communities. *Proposal for a Seventh Directive on Group Accounts.* Brussels, 1976, amended 1979.

_____. *Fourth Council Directive for Co-Ordination of National Legislation Regarding the Annual Accounts of Limited Liability Companies.* Brussels, 1978.

Confederation of British Industry. *The Provision of Information by Multinational Enterprises in the UK.* London, 1975.

de Bruyne, D. "Global Standards: A Tower of Babel." *Financial Executive,* February 1980.

Financial Accounting Standards Board. *Statement of Financial Accounting Standards No. 8, Accounting for the Translation of Foreign Currency Transactions and Foreign Currency Financial Statements.* Stamford, CT, 1975.

Fitzgerald, R. D., and Kelley, E. M. "International Disclosure Standards — the United Nations Position." *Journal of Accounting, Auditing and Finance,* Fall 1979.

Fitzgerald, R. D.; Stickler, A. D.; and Watts, T. R. *International Survey of Accounting Principles and Reporting Practices.* Butterworths and Price Waterhouse International, 1979.

Gray, S. J. "Segment Reporting and the EEC Multinationals." *Journal of Accounting Research.* Autumn 1978.

_____. "The Impact of International Accounting Differences from a Security Analysis Perspective: Some European Evidence." *Journal of Accounting Research,* Spring 1980.

_____, and Maunders, K. T. *Value Added Reporting: Uses and Measurement.* London: Association of Certified Accountants, 1980.

International Accounting Standard No. 1, Disclosure of Accounting Policies, London, 1975.

_____. *The Work and Purpose of the International Accounting Standards Committee,* London, 1977.

_____. *International Accounting Standard No. 3, Consolidated Financial Statements,* London, 1976.

_____. *Exposure Draft 15, Reporting Financial Information by Segment.* London, 1980.

International Chamber of Commerce. *ICC Comments on the Report of the UN Expert Group on Accounting Standards and Reporting.* Paris, 1978.

International Confederation of Free Trade Unions, World Confederation of Labour, European Trade Union Confederation. *Trade Union Requirements for Accounting and Publication by Undertakings and Groups of Companies.* Brussels, 1977.

International Labour Office. *Tripartite Declaration of Principles Concerning Multinational Enterprises and Social Policy.* Geneva: ILO, 1977.

Jensen, M. C., and Meckling, W. H. "Theory of the Firm: Managerial Behaviour, Agency Costs and Ownership Structure." *Journal of Financial Economics,* October 1976.

Lea, D. "International Companies and Trade Union Interests." In *The Multinational Enterprise,* edited by J. H. Dunning. London: Allen and Unwin, 1971.

Lowe, J. W. "Financial Markets in Developing Countries." *Finance and Development,* December 1974.

Mautz, R. K., and May, R. G. *Financial Disclosure in a Competitive Economy.* New York: Research Foundation of the Financial Executives Institute, 1978.

The Monopolies Commission (UK). *Chlordiazepoxide and Diazepam.* London: HMSO, 1973.

Morris, R. C. "The Financial Reporting Problems of Multinational Companies." *The Accountant's Magazine,* September 1975.

Northrup, H. R., and Rowan, R. C. "Multinational Collective Bargaining Activity: The Factual Record in Chemicals, Glass and Rubber Tyres." *Columbia Journal of World Business,* Spring and Summer 1974.

Organization for Economic Co-Operation and Development. *International Investment and Multinational Enterprises.* Paris, 1976, revised 1979.

_____. *Penetration of Multinational Enterprises in Manufacturing Industry in Member Countries.* Paris, 1977.

_____. *International Investment and Multinational Enterprises — Review of the 1976 Declaration and Decisions.* Paris, 1979.

Robbins, S. M., and Stobaugh, R. B. "The Bent Measuring Stick for Foreign Subsidiaries." *Harvard Business Review,* September/October 1973.

_____ *Money in the Multinational Enterprise.* New York: Basic Books, 1974.

Roberts, B. C., and Liebhaberg, B. "International Regulation of Multinational Enterprises: Trade Union and Management Concerns." *British Journal of Industrial Relations,* November 1977.

Scott, G. M. *Accounting and Developing Nations.* Washington, DC: International Accounting Studies Institute, 1970.

_____., and Drapalik, J. F. "Financial Control and Reporting in Multinational Enterprises." In *Accounting for Multinational Corporations,* edited by D. D. Al Hashim and J. W. Robertson. Indianapolis: Bobb-Merrill, 1978.

Stopford, J. M., and Wells, L. T., Jr. *Managing the Multinational Enterprise.* London: Longman, 1972.

Turner, L. *Multinational Companies and the Third World.* London: Allen Lane, 1974.

United Nations Conference on Trade and Development. *Dominant Positions of Market Power of Transnational Corporations — Use of the Transfer Pricing Mechanism.* New York: UN, 1978.

United Nations Economic and Social Council. *The Impact of Multinational Corporations on the Development Process and on International Relations — Report of the Group of Eminent Persons.* New York: UN, 1976.

_____. *Some Aspects of Corporate Accounting and Reporting of Special Interest to Developing Countries.* New York: UN, 1976.

168   _____ *International Standards of Accounting and Reporting for Transnational Corporations.* New York: UN, 1977.

_____. *Transnational Corporations in World Development: A Re-Examination.* New York: UN, 1978.

United States of America — Business and Industry Advisory Committee, Committee on International Investment and Multinational Enterprise. *A Discussion of Provision of Data on MNC Operations.* New York: USA-BIAC, 1974.

_____. *A Review of the OECD Guidelines for Multinational Enterprises: Disclosure of Information.* New York, USA-BIAC, 1976.

Vernon, R. *Storm Over the Multinationals — the Real Issues.* London: Macmillan Press, 1977.

_____., and Wells, L. T., Jr. *Economic Environment of International Business.* 2nd ed. Englewood Cliffs: Prentice Hall, 1976.

Wallace, D. *International Regulation of Multinational Corporations.* New York, Praeger, 1976.

Watson, W. H., Jr. "Global Role for US Stock Exchange." *Columbia Journal of World Business,* Spring 1974.

Watts, R. L. "Corporate Financial Statements, A Product of the Market and Political Processes." *Australian Journal of Management.* April 1977.

_____., and Zimmerman, J. L. "Towards a Positive Theory of the Determination of Accounting Standards." *Accounting Review,* January 1978.

Wilms-Wright, C. *Transnational Corporations: A Strategy for Control.* London: Fabian Society, 1977.

Zeff, S. A. "The Rise of 'Economic Consequences.'" *Journal of Accountancy,* December 1978.

_____. "Greater Disclosure Fever Spreading Across the Globe." *World Accounting Report.* February 1979.

PART IV

Transnational financial reporting issues

GROUP ACCOUNTING

CHAPTER 11

Concepts of consolidation in the EEC*
R. H. Parker

Consolidated accounts are of great practical importance, but are often regarded, especially by academics, as mere exercises in mechanical ingenuity. It can be shown not only that they involve interesting conceptual problems, but that the choice of concepts to be adopted in practice is by no means as straightforward as textbooks suggest. This article offers a theoretical analysis of concepts of consolidation (not including so-called merger accounting) and then surveys actual practice in the UK, West Germany, France and the Netherlands. The analysis is carried out using 'Anglo-Saxon' terminology, and it should be mentioned that goodwill on consolidation does not exist, as such, in the pure forms of French and German consolidation accounting.

Many (but not all) 'investees' have two kinds of shareholders: the parent company and the others, usually referred to collectively as the 'minority interest'.

One possible approach is to regard the parent company and the minority interest as co-shareholders of equal importance, and to credit *both* of them with a proportionate share not only of the net tangible assets (including identifiable intangibles), but also with a share of goodwill on consolidation. This is the 'entity' concept of consolidation[1].

An alternative approach is the 'parent company' concept. The parent company is regarded as the dominant shareholder, and the minority interest is credited with its share of the investee's net tangible assets, but *not* with a share of goodwill on consolidation. This concept is supported by the Accountants International Study Group[2].

Where it is not possible to distinguish a parent company and a minority interest, a third concept is relevant. The investor brings into its consolidated balance sheet a proportionate part only of the investee company's assets and records no minority interest at all. This can be termed the 'proprietary' concept[3] and may be divided into 'proportional consolidation' and 'equity consolidation'.

The difference between proportional consolidation and equity consolidation is that under the latter the investment is shown as one item (e.g., investment in associated companies), while under the former the same amount in total is distributed over the relevant assets and liabilities. The definition of net assets under the proprietary concept may or may not include goodwill on consolidation.

Under each of the three concepts, the investee's net assets may be brought in either at historic values or at book values.

* This article is reprinted, with permission, from *Accountancy* (February 1977) pp 72–75

The entity and parent company concepts can thus be subdivided as in *Figure 11.1*, and the proprietary concept as in *Figure 11.2*.

The practical consequences of adopting one or other concept of consolidation are best shown by means of a simple example. Consider the situation illustrated in *Figure 11.3*. Investor Ltd has just acquired for £960 cash 75% of the equity share

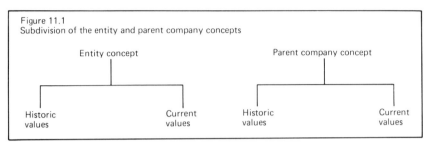

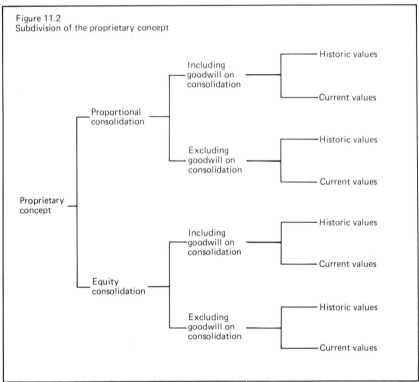

capital of Investee Ltd, at which date the latter has net tangible assets (including identifiable intangibles) with an historic value of £800 and a current value of £900.

If the parent company concept is adopted, the calculations are as shown in *Figure 11.4*. And if the entity concept, the calculations are as in *Figure 11.5*. It will be seen that, compared with the parent company concept, both goodwill and minority interest are increased by £95 if current values are used, that is by the minority share

Figure 11.3
Graphical illustration of net assets of an investee (not drawn to scale)

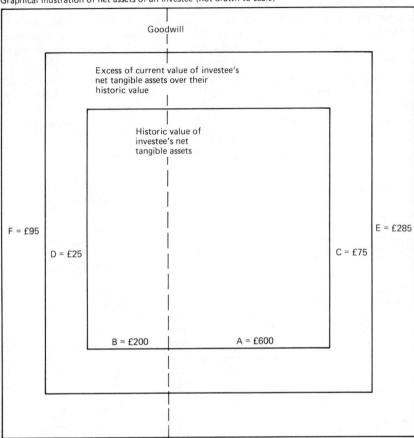

Goodwill

Excess of current value of investee's
net tangible assets over their
historic value

Historic value of
investee's net
tangible assets

F = £95

D = £25

E = £285

C = £75

B = £200

A = £600

Figure 11.4
Calculations for the parent company concept

	Historic values £	Current values £
Investee net tangible assets brought in	A+B = 800	A+B+ C+D = 900
Goodwill	C+E = 360	E 285
	1,160	1,185
Minority interest	B = 200	B+D = 225
Investor interest = A + C + E =	£960	£960

of goodwill on consolidation, and by £120 if historic values are used, i.e., by the minority share of both goodwill on consolidation and the excess of current over historic value of the investee's net tangible assets.

If proportional consolidation is adopted, the position is as shown in *Figure 11.6*. Note that if goodwill is excluded, its place is taken by 'difference on consolidation'; and that if it is included, the amount is the same as under the parent company concept. There is, of course, no minority interest.

Equity consolidation gives the same results in a different form. The Anglo-Saxon 'investment in associated companies', which includes goodwill, would be £960. The French *participation mise en équivalence* would be £600 (historic values) or £675 (current values) with the balance (£360 or £285) in difference on consolidation.

11.5
Calculations for the entity concept

	Historic values £	Current values £
Investee net tangible assets brought in	A+B = 800	A+B+ C+D = 900
Goodwill	C+D+ E+F = 480 ‾‾‾‾‾ 1,280	E+F = 380 ‾‾‾‾‾ 1,280
Minority interest	B+D+F = 320	B+D+F = 320
Investor interest	£960	£960

Figure 11.6
Calculations for the proportional consolidation concept

	Historic values £	Current values £
Investee net tangible assets brought in	A = 600	A+C = 675
Goodwill on 'difference on consolidation'	C+E = 360	E = 285
Investor interest	£960	£960

As an additional illustration of the practical effect of choosing among the three concepts, it is instructive to consider the problem of eliminating inter-company profits. Assume that the investor company has in stock goods acquired from a 60% held investee for £120, the original cost to the investee having been £100.

Under the entity concept, it will be remembered, assets are brought in 100% and the minority interest is regarded as a co-shareholder with the parent company and credited with its share of goodwill on consolidation. It follows that neither of the co-shareholders can be regarded as making a profit out of an intra-group sale, and the elimination on consolidation of such a profit must therefore be 100% – i.e. in the consolidation worksheet the closing stock will be credited with £20, and profits attributable to the parent company and minority shareholders will be debited with £12 and £8 respectively.

Under the parent company concept, assets are brought in 100%, but the minority interest is regarded as an outsider. The elimination of inter-company profit should therefore be partial (60%), not total. In the consolidation worksheet, closing stock is credited with £12, and profits attributable to the parent company debited with £12. The minority interest is *not* debited with £8.

Where proportional or equity consolidation is appropriate, there is no parent company and no minority interest, merely several investors. The 'other' investors are clearly 'outsiders', and elimination of inter-company profit should therefore be partial, not total.

Which concept ought we to use?

The appropriate concept for use in practice is that which in any given circumstances most faithfully reflects and discloses the underlying reality. In most cases, the minority interest (where it exists) will *not*, in fact, be in the position of a co-shareholder with the parent or investor company.

The consequent case against the entity concept has been put concisely and clearly by the Accountants International Study Group[4]: 'The report of the independent auditor accompanying consolidated statements is addressed either to the shareholders of the parent company or to the directors who are responsible for reporting to the shareholders. Non-shareholders, such as management, creditors, and governmental bodies, may find the statements useful and informative, but generally these groups are primarily interested in more detailed or supplementary information prepared in response to their particular needs.

'Outside or minority shareholders do not receive any information of direct benefit to them from consolidated statements. They must look to a particular company for the determination of their equity, the likelihood of dividends and their prospects in the event of liquidation. The shareholder of the parent company is interested in consolidated statements which give the overall results of operations attributable to the investment which he has in the parent corporation and in the earnings per share, funds flow and similar information related thereto.

'For these reasons, it is considered that the parent company concept is the more appropriate and useful basis of preparation.'

Current values are to be preferred to historic values for the kinds of reasons set out in the Sandilands Report.

The proprietary concept is appropriate only where there is no minority interest. There may, for example, be several investors, each of which has an element of control, i.e. the investee is what the French call a *société fermée* (closed company)[5]. No investor controls 100% of the net assets, so bringing them in proportionately reflects the real situation.

Where there is no element of control, but significant influence is exercised, then there is an argument for equity consolidation, i.e. the Anglo-Saxon equity method, or the French *mise en équivalence* can be used (the latter, it will be remembered, excludes the goodwill on consolidation element in the calculation).

All three concepts, and many of their subdivisions, can be found in practice within the EEC:

United Kingdom. Current practice in the UK is a compound of the parent company concept for subsidiaries and the equity method for associated companies. The entity concept intrudes slightly in that inter-company profits are sometimes eliminated 100%, even where there is a minority interest, but this is probably the result of conservatism and a desire for simplicity.

Methods of treating inter-company profits are seldom disclosed in publishing company accounts, so it is difficult to be certain what the usual practice is. Most companies still use historic values, but a changeover to current values is on the way.

Proportional consolidation is rare, but not entirely unknown, in the UK. For several years, up to and including 1972, the British Petroleum Company's offshore production interests in Abu Dhabi were jointly owned by *Compagnie Françoise de Pétroles* (CFP) with the proportion two-thirds/one-third applying strictly throughout in every regard as to crude oil fittings, provision of finance etc. In the BP accounts, the one-third interest of CFP was excluded. From 1973 onwards, after a sale of part of the two-thirds interest, the group's interest in the company concerned (Abu Dhabi Marine Areas Ltd) has been treated as an equity accounted investment in an associated company[6].

The equity method is now standard British accounting practice for associated companies even where the investee, as in the case, for example, of Mardon Packaging International Ltd, of Bristol, which is jointly and equally owned by two companies only (Imperial Group Ltd and British-American Tobacco Investments Ltd).

France. French practice is notable for the relative importance attached to the proprietary concept. The National Accounting Council recommends that proportional consolidation be adopted for *Sociétés fermées* (closed companies) in which the investor has a participation of more than 10%. The parent company concept is to be applied to *sociétés ouvertes* (open companies) which are subsidiaries, subsubsidiaries, or *participations multiples*, (i.e. the parent company, its subsidiaries and subsubsidiaries have a majority of the votes). *Mise en équivalence* is to be applied to other *sociétés ouvertes* in which the investor company has a participation of more than 33%.

Consolidation is not yet compulsory in France, but is becoming increasingly common. Although some companies (e.g. *Saint-Gobain-Pont-à-Mousson*) use Anglo-Saxon methods of consolidation, most follow the National Accounting Council's recommendations reasonably closely. For example, *Compagnie Française des Pétroles's* consolidation practices may be summarised as follows:

(a) for a company to be included in the consolidation, CFP's interest must be at least 10%, and also represent a minimum value of F5 million;
(b) companies in which the CFP group has an interest exceeding 50% or, if the group has majority policy control, less than 50%, are consolidated fully (i.e. the net assets are brought in 100% and minority interests are shown);
(c) proportional consolidation is used for 'joint interests' companies (in which operations are shared on the basis of each partner's interest) and for companies controlled jointly on a 50/50 basis by the group and a single other shareholder;
(d) all other companies included are consolidated by *mise en équivalence*.

In 1975, 184 companies were consolidated by CFP – 116 fully, 44 proportionately and 24 by *mise en équivalence*.

Not all French companies practise proportional consolidation. The 'proportion' may vary considerably; *Carnaud-Bass-Indre* consolidates by this method a 3.12% holding; Ferodo consolidates proportionately a 70% holding. Some French companies, e.g. *l'Oreal*, do not use *mise en équivalence*.

West Germany. West Germany is the only EEC country in which a group of companies (a *Konzern*) constitutes a legal entity, and German consolidation law and practice in general have been influenced by the entity concept (*Einheitstheorie*)[7]. No distinction is made between subsidiaries and associated companies, and neither proportional nor equity consolidation is used. The treatment of inter-company profits is laid down by company law; with certain exceptions, they must be eliminated 100% (s 331(4)(2), Companies Act 1965).

Netherlands. Dutch practice is very similar to British, except that the use of current values is more common. There are also rather more examples of proportional consolidation. The following extracts from the explanatory notes to Heineken's consolidated balance sheet and statement of income for 1974/75 are of interest:

'In the consolidated annual account, the participations in which Heineken NV has a direct or indirect interest of more than 50% are shown as fully consolidated. The minority interests in the group funds and in the group profit are indicated separately.

Partial consolidation has taken place in the case of these participations in which an interest of 50% or less is held, if the influence exerted by Heineken on management policy is at least equal to that of the other partners combined. The amounts of assets and liabilities and of items in the statement of income respectively, have been stated in proportion to our interest in the total issued capital.'

Assets are valued by Heineken on the basis of replacement value, and participations are stated at their 'intrinsic value', i.e. using the equity method.

Harmonisation

An EEC draft Directive on consolidated accounts has recently been published[8]. A distinction is made between an 'associated undertaking', i.e. an undertaking over which another undertaking exercises, directly or indirectly, a significant influence (article 1) and a 'dependent undertaking', i.e. an undertaking over which another undertaking, referred to as a 'dominant undertaking', is able, directly or indirectly, to exercise a dominant influence (article 2). Subject to the proviso stated in the next paragraph, associated undertakings are to be brought into the consolidated balance sheet using the Anglo-Saxon equity method (article 17).

Member States may, however, authorise proportional consolidation 'where a group undertaking manages another undertaking jointly with one or more undertakings which do not form part of the group' (article 18). An undertaking managed jointly within the meaning of article 18 will usually be an associated undertaking.

The draft Directive in general appears to follow, though not explicitly, the parent company concept, except in relation to inter-company profits which are to be eliminated in total (article 14).

The explanatory memorandum attached to the draft directive states: 'Profits accruing from group undertakings must be entirely excluded. The Directive does not allow them to be excluded on a *pro rata* basis in proportion to the percentage of capital held. The possible existence of shareholders outside the group does not alter the fact that profits accruing from undertakings within the group are unrealised. The "principle" may be departed from, however, for practical reasons in certain cases.'

The international accounting Standard on consolidated financial statements[9] follows Anglo-Saxon practice. The parent company concept is not specifically mentioned, but is supported by such statements as: 'Certain parties with interests in the parent company of a group . . . are concerned with the fortunes of the entire group. Consequently, they need to be informed about the results of operations and financial position of the group as a whole. This need is served by consolidated financial statements . . . The needs of those interested in the financial position of a parent company or of individual subsidiaries, in particular, creditors and minority interests, are served by the separate financial statements of those subsidiaries' (paras. 5, 6, 7). 'The minority interest in the equity of consolidated companies . . . should not be shown as part of shareholders' equity' (para 3).

The Anglo-Saxon equity method (i.e. including a share of goodwill on consolidation) is supported (para 22). No mention is made of proportional consolidation.

The inter-company profit problem is not dealt with in the Standard as finally agreed. The relevant paragraph (38) in the Exposure Draft was vague: 'The portion of unrealised profits arising in the current period should be charged against consolidated income after giving appropriate recognition to minority interests'.

Summary and conclusions

Three concepts of consolidation – entity, parent company, proprietary – have been analysed. Practice in EEC countries follows all of them, including their subdivisions, in varying degrees. Harmonisation will thus not be easy. The way forward, it is suggested, is to define carefully in which circumstances a particular concept, or subdivision thereof, most faithfully reflects and discloses the underlying reality.

References

1 M. Moonitz. *The Entity Theory of Consolidated Statements*. American Accounting Association, 1944.
2 Accountants International Study Group, 'Consolidated Financial Statements' (1973), para 24.
3 cf G. C. Baxter and J. C. Spinney. 'A Closer Look at Consolidated Statement Theory'. *C. A. Magazine*, Jan and Feb 1975. I am greatly indebted to this article.
4 'Consolidated Financial Statements', para 26. The AISG does not mention the proprietary concept.
5 Conseil National de la Comptabilité *Consolidation des Bilans et des Comptes* (Paris, 1973) p. 24.
6 Information kindly supplied by the chief accountant of the British Petroleum Co Ltd. See also the company's annual reports for the relevant years.
7 See Adler, Düring, Schmaltz, *Rechnungslegung und Profung der Aktiengesellschaft*, vol 3, 4th ed. 1972, pp. 4–8.
8 Proposal for a seventh Directive pursuant to Article 54(3)(g) of the EEC Treaty concerning group accounts (28 April 1976).
9 'Consolidated Financial Statements', International Accounting Standards Committee, June 1976.

CHAPTER 12

International accounting compromises: the case of consolidation accounting*

R. G. Walker

The International Accounting Standards Committee (IASC) was formed in 1973. Since then it has published a series of exposure drafts and International Accounting Standards. The third International Accounting Standard (IAS3) was titled 'Consolidated Financial Statements' and appeared in June 1976. This paper reviews IAS3 and the exposure draft which preceded it, and relates this material to a 1973 report [1] of the Accountants International Study Group (AISG) and to some national rules or practices concerning the preparation of consolidated statements and the use of equity accounting. This examination leads to an assessment of the quality of the IASC's analysis of technical issues in this area. And the comparison of national rules and successive IASC documents constitutes a case study of how the IASC has obtained agreement on accounting standards.

Authority of the IASC

When the IASC was formed in 1973, the founder-members agreed to use their best endeavours to ensure that published financial statements complied with forthcoming International Standards (IASC [25]). The IASC's objectives were widely supported in professional journals in several countries. Much store was placed on the supposed desirability of international co-operation and of achieving 'harmonization of rules'.

The support subsequently afforded the IASC was variable. In the U.S.A., for example, the AICPA's 'best endeavours' amounted to a policy that International Standards must be specifically adopted by the FASB before they could be regarded as acceptable (AICPA [5]). In the U.K., the professional associations advised their members that they were expected to conform to International Accounting Standards to the extent that they did not conflict with local standards. This policy was put into effect by a requirement that auditors were to draw attention to instances of non-compliance, and, if necessary, to state the extent to which a given set of reports did not comply [6]. Australian professional associations similarly professed strong support for International Standards (see, e.g., Statement K1/300 [12] and Statement K3/300 [13]). However in practice they declined to modify local standards when they conflicted with the IASC's rulings, stating that conformity with more-restrictive local rules would be sufficient to 'ensure compliance' with International Standards, or that

R. G. WALKER is a Professor of Accountancy, University of New South Wales. He wishes to acknowledge the helpful comments of Greg Whittred on an earlier draft of this paper.

* This article is reprinted, with permission, from *Abacus* (December, 1978) pp 97–111

an IASC disclosure rule was 'not necessary for Australian practice' (see, e.g. Statement DS2/307 supp., November 1976; Statement DS5/302 supp., June 1977) And they did not adopt those International Standards which dealt with matters which were not covered by Australian rules.

These examples indicate the limited extent to which the IASC's rulings were followed by local professional associations. Perhaps because of this experience, the 1973 Agreement was abandoned. A revised agreement was approved in October 1977 for publication in March 1978 [30]. The 1977 version acknowledged that the IASC's pronouncements would not override local regulations, and described the IASC's task as that of 'adapting' existing national standards so that agreement could be obtained on 'essentials'.

It would seem that the IASC has little authority. The status of its pronouncements is determined by local rule-making bodies. The major significance of the IASC's operations seems to lie in their influence upon the agendas of the standard-setting committees of several professional associations. (See, Canadian Institute [15]; Vieler [41], p. 10; ASA and ICAA, Statement K3/300 [13].)

Of course, the authority of the IASC is irrelevant if one looks at International Standards in terms of their contribution to the technical literature. The status of IASC pronouncements is only of significance if one is interested in examining aspects of the process of regulating accounting practice. The IASC may be a paper tiger. But this in itself suggests that examination of IASC activities may contribute to the development of an overall picture of the process of standard-setting. Several studies of U.S. rule making activities have described or examined the significance of external political pressures on this process (e.g., Zeff [44]; Watts and Zimmerman [43]). Political pressures may or may not dominate the rule-making process in some jurisdictions however it seems unlikely that an analysis of lobbying activities can provide a complete explanation of how the content of accounting standards is determined. Because International Standards would be of little interest to potential lobbyists, it seems reasonable to suppose that the IASC has been largely insulated from political pressures. An examination of IASC activities may thus provide the opportunity to focus on the way that rule-making committees develop solutions to technical issues — without these observations being biased by the influence of lobbyists.

Background to IAS3

As noted above, IAS3 was published in 1976; it followed the publication eighteen months earlier of an exposure draft under the title, 'Consolidated Financial Statements and the Equity Method of Accounting' [26]. This draft was in turn preceded by a report of the Accountants International Study Group [1].

Presumably both the AISG and the IASC would have compared the accounting standards and disclosure rules which were operative in different countries. In the course of this comparison, both organizations would have encountered inconsistencies in rules dealing with the use and preparation of consolidated reports. These inconsistencies relate to fundamental questions: when should consolidated statements be prepared and published; should they be presented alone or in conjunction with parent company reports; what firms should be included or excluded from the scope of consolidation — and so forth.

To illustrate the diversity of national rules it is sufficient to outline the major features of the practices adopted or required in the three regions from which the AISG drew its membership: U.K., U.S.A. and Canada.

In the U.S. and Canada consolidated statements are usually published as the sole vehicle for reporting financial data to holding companies' shareholders. In the U.K., consolidated statements appear in conjunction with parent company data. Moreover, the publication of consolidated statements is not compulsory and is only one way of complying with the U.K. Companies Act's requirements for reports to supplement the financial statements of holding companies. The legislation requires the publication of 'group accounts'. These may consist of consolidated statements, or the separate statements of individual subsidiaries, or a combination of consolidated statements and separate reports. It appears to be customary for British firms to prepare all-encompassing consolidated statements. (See, e.g., Robson and Duncan [40], p. 102; ICAEW [24], p. 89.) But the fact remains that consolidated reports are regarded in the legislation as supplements to (or amplifications of) parent company statements.

These differences in rules are readily understandable in the light of the background of the North American and British use of consolidated reports. Consolidated reporting was initially adopted under significantly different circumstances in different countries. Consolidated reporting was regarded as a *substitute* for parent company statements in the U.S., and as a *supplement* to parent company statements in the U.K. It appears that Canadian practices were largely patterned on those adopted by U.S. firms (Mulcahy [34], p. 65); from the meagre sources available in the journal literature it is difficult to discern any distinctive Canadian perspective on the use of consolidated reports.

American accountants adopted consolidated reporting at a time when there were no effective disclosure rules requiring alternative presentations, and when the use of the holding company form appeared attractive as a means of consummating mergers. Given that consolidated statements typically encompassed subsidiaries which were substantially-owned, this form of report was viewed as a useful vehicle for reflecting the aggregate financial standing and profitability of a group as an economic entity. The alternative of presenting only holding company statements was less attractive since it meant that the profitability of subsidiaries could be concealed through cost-based valuation; and the pattern of investment within the group could remain undisclosed, while the liquidity of the holding company could be distorted by the presence of inter-company loans. (See, e.g., Dickinson [17], pp. 175-6; Esquerre [18], p. 448; Finney [19], p. 11; Newlove [35], p. 7.)

On the other hand, the British accounting profession first considered the use of consolidated statements at a time when the legislation required companies to file accounting data for public inspection but afforded relief from these rules to 'private' companies (a category which included the subsidiaries of firms whose securities were publicly traded). There is evidence to suggest that the incorporation of private companies was motivated at times by a desire to conceal the affairs of business firms from public scrutiny; certainly some commentators were critical of the obscurity of many company reports which simply reflected intercorporate investments at net cost and which reported gains on investments in subsidiaries to the extent of dividends received (while losses were ignored). (See Walker [42], pp. 42ff.) In this setting, consolidated statements were not regarded as a means of reporting on an 'economic entity' consisting of a parent and its substantially-owned subsidiaries, but simply as a device to provide more information than the balance sheet item, 'Investments in subsidiaries — at cost'. And those who supported consolidated reporting acknowledged that other presentations or devices (such as the separate publication of subsidiaries' statements, or the publication of a statement aggregating the affairs of subsidiaries but not including the parent company) would be equally acceptable. (See, e.g., Garnsey [20], pp. 13-26; Cash [16], p. 651; Robson [39], p. 63.)

With this background North American and British accountants developed differing rationales for the presentation of consolidated statements. To American (and Canadian) accountants, consolidated reports were reports on holding company organizations, and were improvements on (and substitutes for) the reports of parent companies. To British accountants, consolidated statements were one way of amplifying the representations contained in parent company reports — and support for the use of these documents (rather than other forms of group accounts) stemmed from a belief that they were the best way of supplying information to a variety of users. The current diversity of consolidation rules and practices appears in a large measure to be attributable to long-standing differences in views about the role and status of consolidated reporting.

The Function of Consolidated Reports

It appears that when the AISG examined consolidated reporting, it devoted no attention to the background to the adoption of specific rules and practices in different countries. Its report was largely descriptive. It focused on matters on which member-associations agreed, and disregarded the fact that different sets of accounting standards or disclosure rules were based on dissimilar assumptions. The AISG asserted that 'in all but rare circumstances, financial statements of companies with subsidiaries *should be prepared on a consolidated basis*'. It claimed that consolidated statements 'are likely to be the most informative presentation'. But it gave no reasons why consolidated statements were 'likely' to be more informative, and offered no evaluation of the utility of consolidated statements relatively to other presentations.

It seems likely that the AISG report was studied closely by the IASC. The report did in fact document inconsistencies in rules, and made some allusions to disagreements within the literature. It also seems likely that the IASC would have encountered further evidence of differences in national perspectives on the use of consolidated statements. Its response is now a matter of record.

The IASC steering committee charged with the preparation of the exposure draft on consolidated reporting was drawn from professional associations in Australia, Germany and the U.S.A. The steering committee made no reference to evidence of conflicting rules or views in this area. Nor did it provide an analysis of the objectives of consolidated reporting. The Committee simply asserted that there was a 'need' for a form of document — the consolidated report. It avoided specifying what that document was intended to show — and to whom. In lieu of analysis, the IASC offered assertion.

The preamble to IAS3 contains four propositions. The first is:

1. Certain parties with interests in the parent company of a group, such as present and potential shareholders, employees, customers, and in some circumstances, creditors, are concerned with the fortunes of the entire group.

It is easy enough to claim that various parties are 'concerned' with the overall fortunes of a group of companies. It is harder to justify this position. It may be that customers or employees are concerned with the profitability of *particular* industry divisions, rather than the profitability of an entire group. Creditors may be concerned with the financial strength of the firm against which they hold claims and of the firms which have guaranteed the loan of the borrowing corporation. The shareholders of parent companies may be directly concerned with the profitability of those firms alone. Hence the IASC statement seems to be, at best, a very broad generalization.

The IASC's text continues:

2. Consequently, they need to be informed about (i) the results of operations and (ii) the financial position of the group as a whole.

This is a *non sequitur*. It may be possible to establish that various parties are 'concerned' with aspects of the affairs of a so-called 'group'. It does not follow that they need aggregative reports on (i) the income, or (ii) the position of a set of companies (let alone that they need *both* (i) and (ii)). Indeed, it seems highly likely that certain participants are primarily interested in fairly limited aspects of an enterprise's performance or financial position. One way of identifying these 'information needs' would be to carefully investigate the decision-situations faced by various parties and to examine the relevance of different types and arrangements of data to those situations. The IASC made no such investigation. Nor did it use other methods to identify 'information needs'. Nor did it refer to the findings of other investigators. This second proposition is nothing more than an unsupported assertion.

It is then asserted that:

3. This need is served by consolidated statements.

This amounts to the claim that the 'information needs' of various parties are all satisfied by a particular form of presenting data. Since no attempt was made to spell out the 'needs' of any particular set of users, it is impossible to decide whether or not consolidated statements do in fact meet the needs of shareholders, employees, customers *or* creditors — let alone the needs of shareholders *and* employees *and* customers *and* creditors. Proposition 3 is another unsupported assertion.

On the basis of this chain of argument, the IASC offered the following judgement:

4. A parent company should issue consolidated financial statements, except that it need not do so when it is a wholly-owned subsidiary.

This simply does not follow from the IASC's analysis. To illustrate, suppose for the moment that the objections raised in the preceding paragraphs were in fact satisfied.

Suppose that the IASC had in fact (i) identified the 'information needs' of various parties, (ii) demonstrated that these 'needs' included information concerning a holding company and its subsidiaries, and (iii) demonstrated that the information contained in consolidated statements met the needs of a specified range of parties. Even so, there could be alternatives to consolidated statements, alternatives which might be more useful to various classes of participants. For example, creditors might find it more convenient to refer to schedules detailing the security which supported their loans to specific corporations; employees might be satisfied with analyses of rate of return or earnings per share statistics; and so forth. Indeed, it seems likely that consolidated statements are not the optimum form of reporting to any particular set of participants. What the IASC has done is to suggest that consolidated statements are the optimum way of meeting the 'information needs' of not one class of users, but several. It has reached this 'conclusion' without detailing the costs and benefits of alternative forms of presentation and without indicating the decision-rule it has used to arrive at a solution.

It may seem unfair to subject the IASC to criticism for its espousal of a line of reasoning that has appeared in the accounting literature for decades. But the IASC was well placed to take note of anomalies and inconsistencies in the conventional rationale for this form of reporting and glossed over them.

Moreover the Committee made some unusual contributions of its own to an already unsatisfactory literature. For example IAS3 included a clause (not previously contained in an exposure draft) that 'better information for the parent company shareholders and other users . . . may be provided by presenting *sepa,ate* financial statements in respect of subsidiaries engaged in dissimilar operations' (para. 37). This statement is open to several interpretations. It could be taken as an acknowledgement that, in some situations, shareholders and others do not 'need' information about overall group operations. This interpretation contradicts the IASC's claim summarized in proposition 2 above. On the other hand, if one assumes that shareholders and others 'need' information about the position and performance of a group of companies, then the suggestion that one form of data is 'better' than another could be taken as indicating that those needs are *not* fully satisfied by consolidated statements — an interpretation which directly contradicts proposition 3. A third interpretation is that the IASC is suggesting that consolidated statements are not necessarily the optimum way of reporting on the affairs of parent companies — an interpretation which is inconsistent with proposition 4. Whichever way one interprets the IASC's claim that 'better information' may be provided by the publication of separate statements for certain subsidiaries, the claim is inconsistent with the main part of the IASC's statement. The Committee did not provide any outline of the conditions under which the publication of separate statements would be more informative than the publication of all-encompassing consolidated reports. It seems reasonable to suppose that this clause was included for the sole purpose of accommodating conflicting national views about the appropriate area of consolidation.

Which firms' financial statements should be encompassed by a consolidated statement? Should consolidated statements cover a holding company and all of its subsidiaries and sub-subsidiaries? Or should they only incorporate the reports of firms that the holding company actively controls? Or only those firms which are engaged in similar (or complementary) activities?

This list of questions could be extended. Should consolidated statements only deal with 'material' investments of the holding company? Should consolidated statements only deal with incorporated firms — and exclude partnerships and joint-venture arrangements? Should foreign subsidiaries be excluded? What of subsidiaries which are slated for sale, or which are financed by outside debts, or which are insolvent?

One way of answering these questions would be to consider the aims of consolidated reporting and then decide what criteria for determining the scope of consolidated reports are consistent with those aims. Unfortunately, the literature on the subject is not very precise. Many writers have claimed there is a need to report on the affairs of an 'economic entity' or 'group' without spelling out in any detail why specific users would require or employ such data.

However, some broad lines of argument are readily discernible in the literature. The AISG acknowledged this when it distinguished 'two general concepts of consolidated financial statements' — 'the parent company concept' and the 'entity concept'. According to the Study Group, the key difference between the two concepts was that consolidated statements were viewed either as an 'extension' of a parent's financial statements, or as reports of a separate entity. Unfortunately the AISG only alluded to these two concepts in the course of categorizing competing arguments about the choice of technical processes for the compilation of consolidated data. The different perspectives on the aims of consolidated reporting were entirely ignored by the AISG when it came to analyse differences in rules dealing with the status and scope of consolidated statements.

For example, if consolidated statements were regarded as 'extensions' or 'amplifications' of parent company statements, so that these reports were primarily intended to furnish information to a holding company's shareholders, then one might suppose that the ambit of consolidation would be linked in some way with the materiality of inter-corporate investments or the materiality of revenues or expenses derived from inter-corporate investments. Alternatively, if one viewed consolidated statements as a means of amplifying a holding company's reports for the benefit of creditors, then the appropriate ambit of consolidation might be determined by the pattern of inter-company guarantees and might have regard to the distorting effect on the apparent liquidity of those firms through the inclusion of insolvent firms, banking subsidiaries, etc. On the other hand, if consolidated statements were intended to depict the affairs of a 'group' of companies operating under common managerial direction then the area of consolidation might be determined by reference to the capacity of firms to control the affairs of others. And if consolidated statements were supposed to deal with the activities of 'economic entities' then one might determine the area of consolidation by reference to both the presence of 'controlling' relationships and the similarity or complementarity of the activities engaged in by the firms concerned. Exhibit 1 illustrates the way in which different criteria for identifying the ambit of consolidation might be suggested by the acceptance of different propositions about the status and purpose of consolidated reports. The first three are consistent with the general statement that consolidated reports are 'extensions' of parent-company statements; the latter two relate to claims that consolidated statements reflect the affairs of a separate 'economic' or 'group' entity. (The five propositions dealing with the supposed purposes of consolidated statements roughly summarize the main arguments that may be found in the accounting literature as to the aims of this form of reporting. It is not suggested that propositions of this form are adequate statements of 'function'.)

EXHIBIT 1

Status and supposed function	*Possible area of consolidation*
1. Primary documents -- to depict the financial position and performance of holding companies.	Holding company plus 'substantially owned' subsidiaries.
2. Supplementary reports — to amplify the financial statements of holding companies.	Substantially owned subsidiaries only — excluding holding company *or* A series of group statements each covering those subsidiaries engaged in a particular line of business *or* A series of group statements each covering domestic subsidiaries, foreign subsidiaries *or* Holding company and all 'material' subsidiaries.
3. Supplementary reports — to facilitate assessments of the ability of firms to meet their debts.	Holding company and all 'controlled' subsidiaries *or* All companies which have guaranteed the indebtedness of other companies, plus the companies subject to those guarantees *or* Some other combination — depending upon pattern of inter-company loans (e.g., all subsidiaries involved in inter-company loans but excluding the holding company, if it was not involved in loans). (N.B. foreign subsidiaries might be excluded on ground that currency restrictions and/or jurisdictional limitations make resources unavailable to creditors; banking, finance or insurance subsidiaries might be excluded to avoid 'distortion' of liquid ratios.)
4. Supplementary statements — to depict position and performance of 'group entities'.	All corporations (or unincorporated associations) subject to (actually exercised) control. (N.B.: tests of control might be based on voting power or contractual rights.)
5. Supplementary statements — to depict position and performance of 'economic entities'.	All 'controlled' corporations (or unincorporated associations) engaged in some specified business activity or activities.

The AISG asserted that 'the parent company concept is the most appropriate and useful basis' for preparing consolidated statements. Presumably one can interpret this allusion to the 'parent company concept' as indicating support for one or more of the first three propositions listed in the Exhibit — those which spell out ways in which consolidated reports may be regarded as 'extensions' of a holding company statement. However, the AISG went on to state that 'control of companies is an important prerequisite to their inclusion in consolidated statements'. Note that the test of 'control' is inconsistent with the first two statements of the status and function of consolidated statements listed in the Exhibit, and is consistent with only one interpretation of how to achieve the suggested aim of providing information which will facilitate assessments of the ability of firms to meet their debts. To that extent, the AISG's conclusion about the significance of the criterion of 'control' was unrelated to its discussion of the 'appropriate basis' for preparing consolidated statements.

Further, the AISG implied that the presence of a controlling relationship was a necessary but not a sufficient condition for a given company's financial statements to be consolidated. Indeed, the Study Group noted that in U.S. and U.K. practice, firms were occasionally omitted from consolidation because their operations were not homogeneous with those of their parent companies. But should the scope of consolidated statements be determined by the dual tests of control and similarity (or complementarity) of operations? The AISG avoided analysing this question, and simply concluded that control was the key criterion.

However, the IASC took a much firmer stand than the AISG. In its 1974 exposure draft [26], the IASC claimed that 'a parent company should consolidate all subsidiaries, foreign and domestic' and proposed that the only firms which might be excluded were those subsidiaries over which control was likely to be temporary, and those subject to 'severe long term restrictions on the transfer of funds ' such that the parent's capacity to exercise control was in jeopardy. Dissimilarity of operations was not to warrant non-consolidation.

These proposals were consistent with the aim of reporting on the affairs of a 'group entity'. But the proposals conflicted drastically with several national standards. When the Committee finally produced IAS3 it had changed its position on the conditions justifying the exclusion of particular subsidiaries from consolidation. IAS3 incorporated several caveats which had the effect of re-specifying the ambit of consolidation in terms of multiple criteria. The exposure draft's emphasis on 'control' was retained, and in one respect made more stringent by the addition of a test to the effect that firms controlled in terms of specific agreements should also be consolidated. At the same time, IAS3 stated that firms could be excluded from consolidation if their business activities were inconsistent with those of their parent company or their fellow subsidiaries. These caveats suggested that the IASC had changed its views about the aims of consolidation: the new rules were consistent with attempts to accumulate data regarding those elements of a multi-corporation enterprise which were engaged in some 'common economic activity' (rather than the formerly-implied aim of representing the aggregate profitability of all firms which were operating under unified direction and control).

On the other hand, the IASC introduced a further test to the effect that majority-owned firms which were *not* controlled should also be included in a consolidation. This was utterly inconsistent with attempts to report on an 'economic entity'.

The outcome of the IASC's deliberations about the appropriate area of consolidation was a set of rules which accommodated the major points of difference that arose between the disclosure rules and accounting standards of different nations. At the same time, the rules were not consistent with any of the major claims that have been made (in the English-language literature) about the objectives of consolidated reporting.

The Use of Equity Accounting

The IASC's exposure draft was titled 'Consolidated Financial Statements and the Equity Method of Accounting'. IAS3 bore the briefer title, 'Consolidated Financial Statements'. The issues surrounding the use of equity accounting were de-emphasized. Why?

It may be helpful to trace the lines of argument from the AISG's report through to the published standard, and to relate these to the views which appear to hold sway in the accounting standards of several nations.

The AISG claimed that 'the equity method is not a valid substitute for consolidation' (para. 73). How the AISG managed to reach this conclusion is not at all clear. Possibly the Study Group merely *assumed* that consolidated statements were more useful presentations than parent company statements which incorporated the product of equity accounting calculations (and which were unaccompanied by any supplementary schedules relating to the affairs of subsidiaries).

Had the AISG examined the history of the use of consolidated statements it may have been less hasty in making such an assumption. This history indicates that the choice of consolidated reporting was largely a response to the inadequacies of cost-based valuation of inter-corporate investments and dividend-based recognition of revenues derived from those investments. Consolidated statements were introduced into North American, and later British accounting practice, at a time when the recording of 'unrealized' gains was often regarded as unacceptable — so that equity accounting was not a suitable method of handling inter-corporate investments.

The AISG's claim that 'equity accounting is not a valid substitute for consolidation' may be supportable — but only in terms of specific assumptions about what either procedure is intended to achieve. For example, if consolidated statements were intended to overcome the deficiencies of conventional methods of handling inter-corporate investments so as to obtain a 'better' impression of a parent's overall earnings, then equity accounting would seem to be a perfectly adequate substitute for consolidated reporting. Presumably the AISG assumed that consolidated statements were intended to provide something other than an indication of parent company income; unfortunately the Study Group neglected to spell out its assumptions or to provide an outline of how it evaluated the relative merits of the two procedures.

The seriousness of these omissions is apparent when one notes that equity accounting is no longer widely regarded as taboo. Equity procedures have been (and still are) expressly banned in some jurisdictions — for example, by German corporation laws and in terms of U.S. public utilities legislation. Otherwise the lack of attention afforded equity accounting until recently seems to be the product of differing factors in different countries. In the U.K., equity accounting was regarded as a substitute for consolidated statements by some observers in the 1920s; but when the 1948 Companies Act specified a variety of methods for reporting on the affairs of holding companies, equity accounting was not included. It seems that equity accounting slipped into disuse. In the U.S., equity accounting has had a longer history. For example, texts by Finney (1922) [19], Newlove (1926 and 1948) [35, 36], Lewis (1942) [32], Noble et al. (1941) [38], and Mason (1942) [33] all alluded to equity accounting. Newlove, and Noble et al. provided alternative illustrations of consolidation procedures, depending upon whether the parent valued investments in subsidiaries by the net cost or the equity method. Finney provided forthright support for equity accounting, which he described as the 'approved method'. But consolidated statements rapidly became the customary medium for corporate reporting by American companies — and these statements typically were unaccompanied by the reports of parent companies. Consequently the adoption of net cost or equity methods did not affect reported balance sheet or income statement figures. The acceptance or rejection of equity accounting became a non-issue.

In view of the fact that in both the U.S. and the U.K. the use of equity accounting took second place to the use of consolidated statements, it is something of a paradox that interest in equity accounting was revived by efforts to avoid anomalies arising from the application of consolidation accounting. The American Institute's Accounting Research Bulletin 51 [2] stated that equity accounting was the 'preferable method' for handling unconsolidated subsidiaries. Subsequently the Accounting Principles Board expressed its support more strongly, asserting that equity methods should be used for all unconsolidated domestic subsidiaries (APB 10, [3]). Evidently this ruling proved to be inadequate, for the Board later extended the application of equity methods to investments in associated companies and joint ventures (APB 18, [4]).

In 1971 the British profession similarly approved the use of equity methods for the treatment of investments in unconsolidated subsidiaries and associated companies (ICAEW [23]) — a move which in some respects was a retreat from the widely held British view that 'unrealized gains' should not be regarded as revenues. In Australia, support for the use of equity methods can be directly linked with a concern about manipulations of consolidated data. During the late 1960s the Australian financial press gave some prominence to the practice of 'de-consolidation' whereby small parcels of shares changed hands in order to ensure or avoid an investee-firm being deemed a 'subsidiary' in terms of the statutory rules in force at that time. The Australian Society of Accountants' concern at this practice led eventually to the preparation of draft rules involving the use of equity methods for 'controlled' (but not majority-owned) subsidiaries and also for associated companies. (See ASA [8, 9, 10]; ASA and ICAA [11].)

Support for the use of equity accounting was also extended by accounting associations in Canada (1972) [14] and New Zealand (1974) [37]; these statements seemed to have been based on statements previously issued in the U.S. and U.K. respectively.

Now the fact that equity accounting has become a feature of national accounting standards might suggest that the process of achieving 'international harmonization' would be a straightforward and uncomplicated process. However, on analysis, it is apparent that the *basis of the support* for equity accounting is substantially different in different countries.

In the U.S. the application of equity methods to the reports of parent companies was a 'non-issue' since consolidated statements are the primary method of reporting and typically are unaccompanied by the separate reports of parent companies. (APB 18 did extend the application of equity methods to parent statements, but only when these were 'prepared for issuance to stockholders as the financial statements of the primary reporting entity'.) In Australia, a 1973 exposure draft provided for equity methods to be used to record investments in subsidiaries and associated companies in *both* consolidated statements and the published statements of 'the investor company as a legal entity'. In the U.K. and New Zealand, equity methods were only to be used in consolidated statements (or if another form of 'group accounts' was prepared, in supplementary reports); the use of equity methods to record the undistributed profits of investee companies was said to be 'in breach of the principle that credit should not be taken for investment income until it is received or receivable'.

The fact that different national standards embody such different approaches to a single issue underlines the potential of comparative studies as a means of focusing on unresolved issues in accounting. Unfortunately the IASC avoided such matters. It seems that in trying to reach a consensus the IASC was concerned to emphasize points of agreement rather than points at issue. Thus, IAS3 asserted that equity methods should be used *in consolidated statements*. On that, at least, there was 'agreement'. But should equity methods be used in parent company statements? Such an application of equity accounting was favoured by the Australian profession, opposed in the U.K. and New Zealand (and also in Germany) and seems to have been met with indifference in the U.S.A. and Canada. IAS3 made no reference to this issue.

Compromise by Committee

The IASC issued some comments on the difference between the exposure draft and the final text of IAS3. It reported that 'a large volume of comments was received in response to the exposure draft' and that 'every comment was examined in detail and *wherever practicable* changes were made to incorporate in IAS3 the substance of these comments' ([7], p. 45, emphasis added).

Wherever practicable? It appears that the IASC wanted to accommodate every view, regardless of whether those views were consistent or not with a particular analytical framework. Indeed the IAS3 rules on the ambit of consolidation appear to reflect the outcome of such a strategy, for these rules are not consistent with any of the commonly-outlined rationales for consolidated reporting.

Presumably the proposals which the IASC would deem 'impracticable' to adopt were those which conflicted with other proposals. The manner in which IAS3 avoided discussing the relatively contentious issue of the use of equity accounting by parent companies is consistent with such a notion of 'impracticability'.

Conclusion

Three main conclusions emerge.

First, IAS3 has serious technical deficiencies. The rationale for the use of consolidated reporting in IAS3 constitutes little more than a series of vague generalizations. The 'argument' is illogical, inconsistent, and lacks supporting analysis or evidence.

Second, the content of IAS3 seems to have been determined by a process aimed at achieving agreement; theoretical considerations appear to have been afforded little attention. This indicates that the manner in which committees deliberate on technical issues may be a significant influence on the *content* of accounting standards. One reservation about the generality of these findings may be that the IASC is not typical of rule-making committees. IASC members appear to have 'agreed to agree'. Members of other rule-making bodies may be less inhibited.

Third, the process used to achieve agreement in IAS3 suggests that the IASC is not meeting its stated objectives of formulating and publishing 'basic standards' (IASC, [25]) or of concentrating on 'essentials' (IASC [30]). 'Agreement' on procedures in IAS3 was accomplished by ignoring the conflict between the rationale underlying this or that national standard. Instead, the IASC catalogued those technical procedures on which representatives of different national accounting bodies could agree. This plan of action may seem to be diplomatic. It may encourage the view that progress is being made in resolving disputes in accounting. But it may also have deleterious effects. The rules which emerge may add to the difficulty of unravelling inconsistent lines of argument about the aims of specific accounting techniques — and hence foster confusion in the practice of accounting in different countries.

Dale Gerboth borrowed from the literature on policy-making to suggest that the APB's process of formulating accounting standards could be looked upon as a rational and useful task of 'muddling through' (Gerboth [21]). One wonders whether the IASC could be said to be 'muddling through'.

Or just plain muddling.

REFERENCES

1. Accountants International Study Group, *Consolidated Financial Statements*, 1973.
2. American Institute of Certified Public Accountants (AICPA), Accounting Research Bulletin 51, 1959.
3. ———, Accounting Principles Board Opinion 10, 1966.
4. ———, Accounting Principles Board Opinion 18, 1971.
5. ———, 'AICPA Reaffirms Support for International Standards', *The CPA Letter*, August 1975.
6. Anon., 'Introduction to International Accounting Standards', *The Accountant*, 16 January 1975.
7. ———, 'Consolidated Financial Statements', *Accountancy Ireland*, August 1976.

8. Australian Society of Accountants (ASA), 'Consolidated Financial Statements and the Practices of De-consolidation and Non-consolidation' (exposure draft), 1969.

9. ———, 'Omission of Subsidiaries from Consolidated Statements' (exposure draft), *The Australian Accountant,* November 1969.

10. ———, 'Accounting for Material Investments in other Companies by Consolidation and by the Equity Method' (exposure draft), *The Australian Accountant,* July 1971.

11. Australian Society of Accountants and Institute of Chartered Accountants in Australia (ASA and ICAA), 'The Use of the Equity Method in Accounting for Investments in Subsidiaries and Associated Companies', 1973.

12. ———, Statement K1/300, 'Conformity with Accounting Standards', 1976.

13. ———, Statement K3/300, 'Compatibility of Australian Accounting Standards and International Accounting Standards', 1976.

14. Canadian Institute of Chartered Accountants, 'Long Term Inter-Corporate Investments', October 1972, Members *Handbook* Section 3050.

15. ———, 'International Accounting Standards' (exposure draft), July 1975.

16. Cash, W., 'Consolidated Balance Sheets', *Proceedings — International Congress on Accounting,* New York 1930.

17. Dickinson, A. L., *Accounting Practice and Procedure,* Ronald Press, New York 1914.

18. Esquerre, P. J., *The Applied Theory of Accounts,* Ronald Press, New York 1914.

19. Finney, H. A., *Consolidated Statements for Holding Company and Subsidiaries,* Prentice Hall, New York 1922.

20. Garnsey, G., 'Holding Companies and their Published Accounts', *The Accountant,* January 1923.

21. Gerboth, D. L., '"Muddling Through" with the APB', *The Journal of Accountancy,* May 1972.

22. Institute of Chartered Accountants in England and Wales (ICAEW), 'Treatment of Investments in the Balance Sheets of Trading Companies', Recommendation N20, 1958.

23. ———, 'Accounting for the Results of Associated Companies', Statement of Standard Accounting Practice 1, 1971.

24. ———, *Survey of Published Accounts 1969-1970,* 1971.

25. International Accounting Standards Committee (IASC), 'An Agreement to Establish an International Accounting Standards Committee', London 1973.

26. ———, 'Consolidated Financial Statements and the Equity Method of Accounting' (exposure draft), 1974.

27. ———, 'The Work and Purpose of The International Accounting Standards Committee', 1975.

28. ———, 'Preface to International Accounting Standards', 1975.

29. ———, 'Consolidated Financial Statements', IAS3, 1976.

30. ———, 'Preface to Statements of International Accounting Standards', 1978.

31. International Centre for Research in Accounting (ICRA), *International Financial Reporting Standards: Problems and Prospects,* Occasional Paper 13, 1977.

32. Lewis, E. J. B., *Consolidated Statements,* Ronald Press, New York 1942.

33. Mason, P., *Fundamentals of Accounting,* The Foundation Press, Chicago 1942.

34. Mulcahy, G., 'History of Holding Companies and Consolidated Financial Statements', *Canadian Chartered Accountant,* July 1956.

35. Newlove, G. H., *Consolidated Balance Sheets,* Ronald Press, New York 1926.

36. ———, *Consolidated Statements,* D. C. Heath, Boston 1948.

37. New Zealand Society of Accountants, 'Accounting for Associated Companies (Equity Accounting)', Statement of Standard Accounting Practice 2, 1974.

38. Noble, H. S., W. E. Karrenbrock and H. Simons, *Advanced Accounting,* South-Western Publishing, Cincinnati 1941.

39. Robson, T. B., *Consolidated Accounts,* Gee & Company, London 1946.

40. Robson, T. B. and S. N. Duncan, *Consolidated and Other Group Accounts,* 4th edn, Gee & Company, London 1969.

41. Vieler, D. E. G., 'Generally Accepted Accounting Practice', *The South African Chartered Accountant*, January 1976.
42. Walker, R. G., *Consolidated Statements: A History and Analysis*, Arno Press, New York 1978.
43. Watts, R. J. and J. L. Zimmerman, 'Towards a Positive Theory of the Determination of Accounting Standards', *The Accounting Review*, January 1978.
44. Zeff, S. A., 'Developing Accounting Principles: A Summary Review and Analysis of the U.S. Experience', *Journal of Contemporary Business*, Spring 1973.

SEGMENTAL REPORTING

CHAPTER 13

Segment reporting and the EEC multinationals*
S. J. Gray

An integral part of the evolution of large companies has been the diverse nature of their business and geographical activities. It is this diversity which has raised the question of whether a more comprehensive form of accountability and disclosure is to be desired. In this regard, the potential of segment reporting as an appropriate form of disclosure seems to have achieved some recognition, both at the national and international level.[1] But there is a major difficulty with many of the requirements which have been introduced. The criteria by which to identify the segments to be reported upon are not always well specified, with lack of disclosure a possible consequence.[2] The nature of this problem has been recognized in the United States, where the Financial Accounting Standards Board (FASB) has recently issued a standard which provides a detailed framework for disclosure, incorporating a set of quantitative significance criteria for the purpose of identifying reportable segments.[3] While the efficacy of these re-

* Lecturer, University of Lancaster. I wish to express my gratitude to Professor Edward Stamp and the International Centre for Research in Accounting, University of Lancaster, for providing the financial support for this study. [Accepted for publication August 1977.]

[1] Some examples are: Canada (1976 Business Corporations Act); France (1966, 1967 Companies Acts); South Africa (1973 Companies Act); United Kingdom (1967 Companies Act); United States (1970 Securities and Exchange Commission, 1976 Financial Accounting Standards Board); EEC (1974, 1976 Proposals); OECD (1976 Guidelines for Multinationals).

[2] See, for example, United Kingdom Department of Trade, *Aims and Scope of Company Reports* (June 1976): para. 12(c). Also see C. R. Emmanuel and S. J. Gray, "Segmental Disclosures and the Segment Identification Problem," *Accounting and Business Research* (Witner 1977).

[3] Financial Accounting Standards Board, *Financial Reporting for Segments of a Business Enterprise* (December 1976).

* This article is reprinted, with permission, from *Journal of Accounting Research* (Autumn 1978) pp 242–253

quirements may be open to doubt,[4] they could well indicate the scope for developments in other countries should the need for such a regulatory framework be perceived to exist.

It is against this background that this paper will examine the situation in the EEC context, with special reference to disclosure by its multinational companies. The EEC is of interest because of its economic significance and because there is some concern to standardize and develop disclosure requirements as a necessary part of the process of economic integration. To what extent, then, are segment reports provided in practice? Are there differences in disclosure between companies based in different countries in the EEC, and if so, how can this situation be explained? Answers to these questions may help determine whether there is a case for a more comprehensive set of rules such as those currently prevailing in the United States.

1. The Extent of Disclosure: A Comparative Analysis

A survey was made of the segment-reporting practices of the 100 largest industrial multinational companies based in the EEC, and listed on stock exchanges, in 1973. The companies were selected on the basis of sales turnover as reported in *Fortune* (September 1973) and comprised forty-five companies based in the United Kingdom, twenty-three in the Federal Republic of Germany, twenty in France, four each in Italy and the Netherlands, three in Belgium, and one in Luxembourg. All of these companies were operating in two or more countries.

The data base of the survey was provided by the 1972/73 Annual Reports and Accounts of the companies concerned, which were collected in 1973/74, with a cut-off date of July 1, 1974 and then analyzed during 1974/75 as part of a project to assess the full range of disclosure practices by EEC companies.[5] The Annual Reports used were primarily the English-language versions, provided that they were unabridged. Also included, however, were some original French and German versions. The bias toward the English versions of Annual Reports by continental EEC companies tended to have the effect of focusing on the international investor user, but this is consistent with the international scope of the EEC situation.

The survey results revealed that 95 percent of the largest 100 EEC multinationals provided segment reports of one kind or another. Table 1 shows that while sales, profits, production, and assets analyses were provided by quite a few companies, only in the case of sales analyses was disclosure provided by a majority of companies.

---

[4] See C. R. Emmanuel and S. J. Gray, "Corporate Diversification and Segmental Disclosure Requirements in the U.S.A.," *Journal of Business Finance and Accounting* (Autumn/Winter 1977).

[5] See S. J. Gray, "Company Financial Reporting Standards and the European Community" (Ph.D. diss., University of Lancaster, 1975).

TABLE 1

Segmental Disclosures: Analysis by Country of Companies Providing Segment Information

Disclosure Practice Country	Sales			Profits			Production			Assets			Capital Expenditure		
	Yes	No	Total	Yes	No	Total	Yes	No	Total	Yes	No	Total	Yes	No	Total
Belgium	3	—	3	—	3	3	3	—	3	1	2	3	—	3	3
France	16	4	20	8	12	20	8	12	20	7	13	20	—	20	20
Germany	21	2	23	—	23	23	12	11	23	3	20	23	6	17	23
Italy	4	—	4	—	4	4	—	4	4	1	3	4	—	4	4
Luxembourg	1	—	1	—	1	1	1	—	1	1	—	1	—	1	1
Netherlands	3	1	4	—	4	4	1	3	4	2	2	4	—	4	4
United Kingdom	44	1	45	41	4	45	3	42	45	11	34	45	1	44	45
Total Companies	92	8	100	49	51	100	28	72	100	26	74	100	7	93	100

These results lead to the question of whether there are statistically significant differences in disclosure between companies in the EEC, both at the general level of a particular type of analysis (i.e., sales, profits) and with respect to the dimensions of both business (product or industry) and geographical activity. In attempting a statistical comparison, I decided to group together all of the fifty-five continental EEC companies. While I recognize that the continental companies do not necessarily form a homogeneous group, they do seem to provide a contrast with the forty-five United Kingdom companies. Such a grouping may also be supported by the argument that the U.K. equity market is more efficient than the continental national equity markets. As a consequence, it can be hypothesized that there is likely to be significantly greater disclosure by U.K. companies. Barrett has shown in a recent international survey that the extent of overall disclosure, including segment reports, does tend to be correlated with national equity market efficiency.[6] What, then, is the situation with respect to this survey of a large sample of EEC companies on the specific issue of segment reports?

Table 2 sets out the detailed results of the survey with respect to analyses of sales, profits, production, and assets provided by the U.K. and continental groups of companies.

A statistical analysis of this data does provide some support for the hypothesis that the extent of disclosure is related to national equity market efficiency – but only to a degree. The analysis was performed using the Chi-square (one-tailed) test[7] to assess the significance of differences between the U.K. and continental groups of companies for each type of segmental analysis provided. This seemed to allow a more sensitive and detailed analysis of the situation, in contrast to the weighted-index approach used by Barrett. The results are set out in table 3. Capital expenditure analyses are excluded because of the very low level of disclosure. As can be seen, there are statistically significant differences in five cases, but not for (1) sales analyses in general (i.e., either by business or geographical activity), (2) business analyses of sales, and (3) assets analyses. In the five cases where there were differences, the U.K. companies exhibited a greater extent of disclosure, except for production analyses, where the situation was reversed.

While the differences in the extent of disclosure between U.K. and continental EEC companies need to be examined, tables 1 and 2 suggest that the overall extent of disclosure may require some explanation as well. For only with respect to segmental analyses of sales did a majority of the 100 largest EEC multinationals provide disclosures. This ranged from a 92-percent disclosure level with respect to

---

[6] M. Edgar Barrett, "Financial Reporting Practices: Disclosure and Comprehensiveness in an International Setting," *Journal of Accounting Research* (Spring 1976): 10–26.

[7] For details, see Sidney Siegel, *Nonparametric Statistics for Behavioral Sciences* (New York: McGraw-Hill, 1956), pp. 104–11.

TABLE 2

Segmental Disclosures: Comparative Analysis of Disclosure by United Kingdom and Continental EEC Companies

Disclosure Practice / Companies			United Kingdom ($n = 45$)	Continental ($n = 55$)	Total Companies ($n = 100$)
A1.	Sales Analyses (either business or	Yes	44	48	92
	geographical activity)	No	1	7	8
A2.	Sales-Business Analyses	Yes	39	42	81
		No	6	13	19
A3.	Sales-Geographical Analyses	Yes	42	39	81
		No	3	16	19
B1.	Profits Analyses (either business or	Yes	41	8	49
	geographical activity)	No	4	47	51
B2.	Profits-Business Analyses	Yes	35	7	42
		No	10	48	58
B3.	Profits-Geographical Analyses	Yes	34	2	36
		No	11	53	64
C.	Production Analyses (by volume) ..	Yes	3	25	28
		No	42	30	72
D.	Assets Analyses	Yes	11	15	26
		No	34	40	74

sales analyses by either business or geographical activity, to an 81-percent level in the case of both business and geographical analyses when separately assessed. However, segmental analyses of profits (49 percent), production (28 percent), assets (26 percent), and capital expenditure (7 percent) all fell below 50 percent.

To what degree can the overall extent of segment reporting, together with differences in disclosure between U.K. and continental EEC companies, be explained? Explanatory variables which appear worthy of some consideration can be included under the headings of the managerial environment, the legal and political environment, the professional environment, and the stock market and investment environment.

2. The Managerial Environment

This is composed of (1) the strategic aspects of managerial behavior and the organization structures which are the outcome of this process and (2) the cost and competition aspects of managerial behavior.

2.1 CORPORATE STRATEGY AND ORGANIZATION STRUCTURE

The overall lack of segmental disclosures could be explained by the absence of a major diversification strategy on the part of corporate

TABLE 3

Results of Chi-square Tests (One-Tailed) for the Significance of Differences between U.K. and Continental Companies

Segmental Disclosures Practices	χ^2 Statistic
A1. Sales analyses (either business or geographical activity).......	2.42
A2. Sales–business analyses	1.10
A3. Sales–geographical analyses	6.69**
B1. Profits analyses (either business or geographical activity)	55.04***
B2. Profits–business analyses	40.36***
B3. Profits–geographical analyses	52.48***
C. Production analyses (by volume)	16.60***
D. Assets analyses	0.01

** Significant difference at the 0.05 level.
*** Significant difference at the 0.01 level.

management. From a study of additional information provided in the company reports of the sample companies, it seems that eight continental EEC companies and one U.K. company were concentrated in a single basic industry (e.g., steel, automobiles).[8] While this could explain the lack of disclosure, it can only account for part of it here and a small part at that in all cases except sales analyses. As far as the comparative statistical analysis is concerned, the nine companies identified would, if excluded, have no effect on the differences evident from the results already reported. Moreover, all of the sample companies were multiproduct in operation, and it could be argued that different products may well have different markets within an industry which could be identified for disclosure purposes. With regard to the geographical dimension, all of the companies operated multinationally, judging from additional information provided about the activities of subsidiaries. Hence there seems to be no immediate explanation of the lack of geographical analyses.

Of course, the mere existence of a diversification strategy covering different business and geographical activities does not mean that disclosure is desirable or feasible. This depends on the company's situation as well as on management's perceptions of the advantages and disadvantages of disclosure. A major problem in this regard concerns the nature of the organization structure of the companies concerned. In the case of a company which is integrated or highly coordinated for economic reasons, the relevance of segmental disclosures must be questioned. Thus, a prerequisite to meaningful segment reporting is an organization structure which reflects a degree of decentralization sufficient to recognize business or geographical seg-

[8] This observation tends to confirm the view that large U.K. companies have adopted a more aggressive diversification strategy than their continental counterparts. See Gareth P. Dyas and Heinz T. Thanheiser, *The Emerging European Enterprise: Strategy and Structure in French and German Industry* (New York: Macmillan, 1976); and Lawrence G. Franko, *The European Multinationals* (New York: Harper & Row, 1976).

T A B L E 4

Segmental Disclosures: Intragroup Sales as a Percentage of Total Sales

<5%	5–10%	11–25%	>25%	Total Companies Disclos-ing Sales Data
8 (38%)	4 (19%)	8 (38%)	1 (5%)	21 (100%)

ments.[9] Such a structure would also be useful from a feasibility standpoint, since the information required will be readily available at no extra cost of processing by the company. Note also that just as the nature of the organization structure will differ between companies, so will the nature and extent of the information produced internally and hence potentially available for disclosure. Any regulatory framework should be sufficiently flexible to accommodate such a situation.

The extent to which the EEC multinationals used in the sample are in fact integrated or coordinated is difficult to ascertain from their company reports. But some indication is given by the minority of companies that disclose the value of their intragroup sales. Only twenty-one companies provided this information; but as can be seen from table 4, eight companies had intragroup sales of between 11–25 percent of total sales, and a single company had intragroup sales of more than 25 percent.

Without additional information about the extent of sales between the various units making up a group, it is, of course, difficult to make an assessment of the degree of integration or coordination; quite apart from the fact that the situation with respect to the majority of companies is unknown. But from the evidence given, it seems that while total intragroup trade is often significant, it is not significant enough to prevent the provision of segment reports of one kind or other by these twenty-one disclosing companies. Whether those companies which do not provide segmental disclosures can justify their policy by the existence of a higher proportion of internal trade remains to be seen.

2.2 COST AND COMPETITION ASPECTS

An important disadvantage which might lead to the lack of disclosure relates to the increased competition which can result from segmental disclosures revealing those parts of the business with desirable profit prospects, whether they be industrially or geographically based. Such a view is likely to be common across all the EEC countries, though it has been suggested that the tendency to be secretive about business affairs is more pronounced in the continental

---

[9] C. R. Emmanuel and S. J. Gray, "The Segment Reporting Issue: Analysis and Proposal" (Paper presented to the Workshop on Accounting in a Changing Social and Political Environment, European Institute for Advanced Studies in Management, Oxford, April 1977)

EEC countries than it is in the U.K.[10] If this in fact is a prevalent attitude, then there is unlikely to be any change in this situation without some regulatory stimulus affecting all companies in the EEC.

Another more tangible cost is that of preparing and providing the segment reports, and it may be that management is in many cases unconvinced that the benefits outweigh the costs. The benefits are after all largely intangible, given our present state of knowledge, though they are persuasive. Some exploratory empirical work done in the United States by Kinney and Collins suggests that the forecasting performance of investors may be improved.[11] A more efficient allocation of financial resources could thus be promoted by the provision of segment data. Of course, these arguments may not be sufficient for managers who are concerned with the maintenance of their company's relative competitive position, though the company's capacity to raise finance may be directly affected by the quality of disclosure in developed national equity markets, such as in the United Kingdom.

3. The Legal and Political Environment

An important factor which may explain the differences in disclosure between U.K. and continental EEC companies is that of legal regulation. Only in the U.K.[12] and France[13] are there currently any requirements to provide segmental analyses, but these are restricted to business analyses of sales turnover in France and sales turnover and profits (before tax) in the U.K. The geographical dimension is not incorporated. Moreover, the French requirement relates only to large companies and necessitates disclosure in an official bulletin, the *Bulletin des Annonces Légales Obligatoires,* rather than in the company report itself. This legal situation seems to account for the differences with respect to business analyses of profits and, moreover, provides a partial explanation of why no differences exist with respect to business analyses of sales. But it does not account for differences in the disclosure of geographical or production analyses. A factor which may explain the lack of disclosure by some U.K. companies, in spite of the law and in addition to those managerial factors already discussed, is that the criteria to be used to identify segments are not well specified. As a consequence, managerial discretion reigns and, with it, the potential for a lack of disclosure.

---

[10] See, for example, Peter Readman et al., *The European Money Puzzle* (London: Michael Joseph, 1973).

[11] William R. Kinney, Jr., "Predicting Earnings: Entity versus Sub-Entity Data," *Journal of Accounting Research* (Spring 1971): 127-37; and Daniel W. Collins, "Predicting Earnings with Sub-Entity Data: Some Further Evidence," *Journal of Accounting Research* (Spring 1976): 163-77.

[12] *Companies Act* (1976): sec. 17.

[13] *Law on Commercial Companies* (July 24, 1966); *Decree on Commercial Companies* (March 23, 1967).

While legal requirements at the national level are limited, there are some interesting developments at the international level of the EEC and OECD. At the EEC level, segmental disclosure requirements have been incorporated into the European Commission's *Fourth* and *Seventh Directive Proposals on Annual Accounts and Group Accounts* respectively.[14] The motivation for this legal activity, which has yet to be approved, is to standardize and improve disclosure requirements in the EEC in a way which will promote the integration of its constituent economies through the encouragement of competition and the free flow of resources to their most efficient uses. This is an ideal, but it does provide a rationale for segment reporting in an international context. Hovever, an important difficulty with the EEC proposals, as with the national requirements, is that segment identification criteria are lacking, so that the stimulus to make disclosure is likely to be muted. As regards content, the proposals do go further than national law in that turnover and profits analyses are to be provided by both business and geographical activity. But a further difficulty is the vague specification of content with reference to profit results. Exactly which measure of profit to use (e.g., profit contribution, trading profit, profit before tax) is at the discretion of management.

Developments at the OECD level provide further support for the disclosure of segmental analyses, but in this case, the rationale seems to be that of promoting the control of multinational companies by making them more accountable for their activities.[15] Disclosure guidelines are provided which include the provision of geographical analyses of sales and profit results together with business analyses of sales only. An additional item to be disclosed is that of "significant new capital investment" by both business and geography. Further, the policies followed with respect to transfer pricing are to be disclosed. This is important because it is well known that transfer prices may be manipulated for taxation or commercial reasons. But without information on the extent of intersegment trade, it is still not possible to assess the impact of transfer-pricing policy.

4. The Professional Environment

The absence of significant professional activity in the EEC in the area of segment reporting is another factor which may explain the overall lack of disclosure. There is no evident stimulus at the level of professional standards. There is, however, some perception, at least in the

---

[14] Commission of the European Communities, Brussels, *Amended Proposal for a Fourth Council Directive for Coordination of National Legislation regarding the Annual Accounts of Limited Liability Companies* (February 21, 1974), and *Proposal for a Seventh Directive Concerning Group Accounts* (May 4, 1976).

[15] Organisation for Economic Cooperation and Development, *International Investment and Multinational Enterprises* (Paris, 1976).

United Kingdom, that a problem may exist and that professional action is desirable. For example, a 1975 discussion paper entitled *The Corporate Report* stated that there was a need to improve the implementation of the 1967 Companies Act,[16] but it also argued that it was necessary to recognize the difficulties of imposing a set of comprehensive requirements on companies. The profession is now in the process of developing an accounting standard on the subject.[17]

5. *The Stock Market and Investment Environment*

Finally, the differences in disclosure with respect to geographical analyses between U.K. and continental EEC companies may be because of stock market requirements. Only in the U.K. does the Stock Exchange authority require disclosure of geographical analyses of sales turnover and trading profits.[18] These are additional to the requirements of the 1967 Companies Act but are consistent with current proposals at the EEC level.

However, the requirements are couched in such general terms as to provide considerable scope for managerial discretion. This is not to say that a better alternative is readily available. But it may explain the failure of some companies to provide analyses with particular reference to profits, despite the fact that all of the U.K. companies surveyed had subsidiary operations in other countries.

While there is significantly less disclosure of geographical analyses by continental EEC companies, a considerable proportion (71 percent) do provide geographical analyses of sales. Moreover, with respect to business analyses of sales, there is no statistically significant difference. In the stock market context, a partial explanation may be found in the fact that in France, the Commission des Operations de Bourse (COB) recommends the disclosure of both business and geographical analyses of sales.

Another relevant factor which relates to the investment environment in general is the influence of financial analysts on disclosure. The European Federation of Financial Analysts Societies, for example, indicated the desirability of segment reports as long ago as 1963.[19] They have continuously pressed for such disclosures, and it may be that those companies and/or countries which are more perceptive to the needs of investors have responded to this to some extent. It is, of course, easy for financial analysts to request information when they do not bear the

---

[16] Accounting Standards (Steering) Committee, *The Corporate Report* (July 1975).

[17] Note the study by Coopers & Lybrand, "Analysed Reporting" (Research paper prepared for the Research Committee of the Institute of Chartered Accountants in England and Wales, 1977).

[18] Federation of Stock Exchanges in Great Britain and Ireland, *Admission of Securities to Listing* (as amended), para, 9(*b*) and n. 29.

[19] European Federation of Financial Analysts Societies, *Proceedings of the Second Congress* (Cambridge, July 1963).

cost. But at the same time, their interests as major consumers of information in developed equity markets such as the United Kingdom presumably cannot be ignored. Even if the information is used only occasionally, there is no less justification for providing it than that underlying the mass of data which is disclosed already. In less developed equity markets such as France and Germany, the interests of financial analysts are of much less significance as there are other more important sources of finance, such as the banks, outside the equity market.[20] This seems to provide some explanation of the current disclosure situation at the national level, but does not necessarily justify it from the standpoint of the investor who is concerned with diversifying internationally across the EEC countries.

6. Summary and Conclusions

The results of this empirical study of segmental disclosure practices by EEC multinational companies in 1972–73 suggest that the overall level of disclosure is low apart from sales analyses. Statistically significant differences also existed in the extent of disclosure between U.K. and continental EEC companies, with U.K. companies exhibiting a greater disclosure of business analyses of profits and geographical analyses of sales and profits. However, there were no significant differences found with respect to business analyses of sales and assets analyses. Moreover, continental EEC companies exhibited a significantly greater disclosure of production analyses.

These findings provide some support for the hypothesis that the extent of financial disclosure is correlated with the efficiency of national equity markets; that is, United Kingdom disclosure is greater than that prevailing in the continental EEC countries. However, this is not always the case, the most noteworthy exception being the disclosure of production analyses. The latter may be an indication of a more production-oriented philosophy, in contrast to the usual financial orientation of countries with developed and relatively efficient equity markets.

A number of factors can provide some explanation of the overall extent of segmental disclosures and of the differences existing between U.K. and continental EEC companies. These can be grouped under the headings of managerial, legal and political, professional, and stock market and investment environments.

The most important explanatory variables seem to be those relating to (1) the structure of the company with respect to the extent of its economic integration and managerial coordination, and (2) the differential stimulus to disclosure provided by the regulatory environment of legal, professional, and stock market requirements. The impact of the

---

[20] See, for example, J. M. Samuels, R. E. V. Groves, and C. S. Goddard, *Company Finance in Europe* (London: Institute of Chartered Accountants in England and Wales, 1975).

former variable is difficult to assess from company reports, and further research into this aspect would seem useful to determine the feasibility of disclosure. With regard to the impact of the latter variable, there is little doubt about the unsatisfactory nature of existing disclosure requirements, such as they are. The critical problem is that of defining appropriate criteria for the identification of reportable segments. This is a difficulty which is currently thwarting the development of segment reporting in the EEC, given that a case for providing such information is perceived to exist by some of the rule-making bodies concerned.

Whether a detailed regulatory framework for segment reporting, such as that established in the United States, is to be desired warrants further investigation. But any proposed formulation should include a careful consideration of company structure, the identification issue, and the differing emphases on disclosure currently prevailing in the EEC context.

CHAPTER 14

Segmental disclosures by multibusiness multinational companies: a proposal*

C. R. Emmanuel and S. J. Gray

Introduction

The Companies Act, 1967[1] requires UK companies to disclose the turnover and profit (before tax) of the substantially different classes of business in which they are engaged. The Stock Exchange Listing Agreement[2] also requires a geographical analysis of turnover and profit before tax. These disclosure requirements are supported by the EEC[3] and the OECD.[4] However, none of these documents defines a segment and, in the case of the British legislation, this task is delegated to the directors of the companies concerned.

This paper attempts to indicate the deficiencies of the current segmental disclosure requirements in the UK and refers to empirical evidence which reveals the wide variety of practices presently being followed. The alternative bases of identifying segments are examined and, finally, a proposal to promote the recognition of reportable segments is made. At this stage, the primary concern of the research is related to the feasibility of *identifying* reportable segments and not with the information content of the disclosure requirements. This latter aspect would seem to be of secondary importance whilst companies are in a position to consciously or inadvertently manipulate the means of identifying segments in order to avoid or minimise disclosure.

The need for segmental disclosure

Several empirical studies of user needs support the disclosure of financial information by segments. A sample of financial analysts, commercial bankers and government agencies in the USA[5] indicated that there was an important need for information about the operating results of major segments of diversified companies. In particular the sales and contributions to company profit are wanted so as to forecast consolidated profits, and are also needed to appraise the success of the management of the company. A later study[6] found that financial analysts attempted to disaggregate consolidated information even when they felt that the information available was less than was needed to perform the task adequately. British studies[7] have also found that certain groups of external users (viz. financial analysts, bankers) regard the provision of effective segmental disclosure as being of prime importance. More recently, *The Corporate Report*[8] has approved the concept of disaggregation and has drawn attention to the need for a generally applicable and practical basis for disaggregation. This has been supported by the Department of Trade in its recent Green Paper *The Future of Company Reports* where it is stated that existing legal requirement 'has not worked well because it leaves too much to the discretion of

---

[1] *The Companies Act 1967.* Section 17 relates to disclosure of turnover and profit by class of business. Section 20 relates to disclosure of exports in terms of turnover.

[2] *Stock Exchange Listing Agreement – Companies.* Paragraph 9 (b) requires a geographical analysis of turnover and profit (before tax).

[3] Commission of the European Communities, *Proposal for a Fourth Council Directive for Coordination of National Legislation regarding the Annual Accounts of Limited Liability Companies* (Brussels, 1974) Article 40; *Proposal for a Seventh Directive concerning Group Accounts* (Brussels, 1976) Article 20.

[4] Organisation for Economic Co-operation and Development, *International Investment and Multinational Enterprises* (Paris, 1976) pp. 14–15.

[5] Backer, M. B. and McFarland, W. B., *External Reporting for Segments of a Business* (New York: NAA, 1968) pp. 6–14.

[6] Mautz, R. K., *Financial Reporting by Diversified Companies* (New York: Financial Executives Research Foundation, 1968) chapter IV.

[7] Peasnell, K. V., The Fundamental Nature and Purposes of Published Accounts of Companies, with particular reference to the needs of users and potential users, unpublished Ph.D. thesis (University of Lancaster, 1975) Appendix 1, Table 4 and Nicholson, J., 'Why Annual Reports Misfire', *Management Today*, December, 1971.

[8] Accounting Standards Committee, *The Corporate Report* London, 1975) paragraph 6.51.

---

* This article is reprinted, with permission, from *Accounting and Business Research* (Summer, 1978) pp 169–177

directors and as a result the information disclosed has been of only limited value'.[9]

The need for information on a segmental basis by a large section of the external users of annual accounts would appear to be significant. Financial analysts need separate sales and profit figures for segments in order to understand the business, to make forecasts of consolidated profit and to appraise management's diversification strategy. The primary characteristic which makes a segment significant to investors and creditors is homogeneity in the effect of economic conditions on earnings.[10] This implies that reportable segments should have differing rates of profitability, growth and risk over time. Thus activities should be grouped together if their earnings respond to changes in economic conditions in the same way.

Alternative bases for identifying segments

Several bases are available for identifying segments. The company may be segmented in terms of the industries in which it operates, the product lines or services offered, the markets served, or the geographical areas in which it is involved. Alternatively the segments may be identified in accordance with the organisation structure of the enterprise such as by division, department, branch or subsidiary. We will examine each of these alternatives and will introduce empirical evidence[11] from our earlier research to assess whether they are feasible in the light of present-day UK disclosure practices.

Industry and Product Line

The distinction between industry and product line is blurred in practice because industrial classification reflects an aggregation of related products and services. Sometimes the industry and product bases will identify segments consistently as in the case when a company produces tobacco and paint. Conversely, if the company produces paint and soap products, only one industry segment may be recognised or two product segments.

The Standard Industrial Classification in the UK categorises establishments according to industry. The authors found from a study of the disclosure practices of the 100 largest UK industrial companies that of the

78 companies providing a full or partial analysis of sales and/or profits by segments, only 11 were not at all consistent with the SIC Order Level (1 digit), whilst 25 were not consistent with the SIC Minimum List Heading Level (3 digit). The number of companies which were only partially consistent also increased as the more specific industrial classification was applied. Therefore the SIC broadly accorded with the way in which the majority of the participating companies identified and disclosed segment information.

Further information about the activities of a company can usually be found elsewhere in the annual report. For example, there is a legal requirement to disclose the principal activities and a listing of subsidiaries.[12] Increasingly, annual reports illustrate the organisation structure and managerial responsibilities within the enterprise and an indication of activities is also given in the presentation of the Chairman's Review. These supplementary sources were used in comparison with the SIC to gauge whether the legal requirement of segmental disclosure could be improved. At the SIC 1 digit level, all but 2 of the 78 companies concerned could have disclosed segments consistent or partially consistent with this classification. Only 5 companies could not have complied with the SIC at the 3 digit level as judged by the supplementary information available.

The practice of minimum disclosure was highlighted in the case of the 22 companies which did not comply with the legal requirement imposed by the Companies Act. The Chairman's Review or Directors' Report of 19 of these companies suggested that segment disclosure was appropriate and that a single class of business was not being operated. At the SIC 1 digit level, all of these companies could have disclosed more than one industrial activity.

Before the implications of these findings are examined, the stringency of the analysis must be questioned. Firstly, the companies which could have identified more industrial segments than they actually did may argue that the activities are co-ordinated centrally. As a result the companies are not truly diversified but have a single dominant product. A second line of argument relates to the accuracy of the SIC itself and whether it reflects distinct, industrial activities. There is also the difficulty that the SIC relates to establishments which may or may not be consistent with the individual company's organisation.

Further research and up-dating of the SIC is necessary to refute or substantiate these latter arguments. In respect of the first point, the authors are aware of the problem of central co-ordination

[9]Department of Trade, *The Future of Company Reports*, Cmnd 6888 (HMSO, 1977) paragraph 39.

[10]Backer, M. B. and McFarland, W. B., op. cit., pp. 21–2.

[11]Emmanuel, C. R. and Gray, S. J., 'Segmental Disclosures and the Segment Identification Problem', *Accounting and Business Research*, Winter 1977. The empirical evidence is drawn from the 100 largest quoted industrial companies ranked by turnover in *The Times 1000*, 1975/76.

[12]*The Companies Act* 1967, Sections 16 and 3 respectively.

across industrial boundaries and have adopted a conservative view in categorising these firms. Broad categories such as wholesaling, manufacturing, retailing are regarded as indicators of functional activities unless specifically linked to separate products or services.

Notwithstanding these arguments, the evidence suggests that the practice of reporting by industry or product line is widespread. The supplementary information relating to industrial and product line activities suggests that the quality of this disclosure can be improved and the potential confusion resulting from a seeming mis-match of the legal disclosure and the other information contained in the annual report may thereby be avoided. However, those companies which did not disclose on an industrial basis may have adopted an alternative basis, such as by the markets served.

Markets

It can be argued that different markets have different degrees of risk attaching to them and hence the use of markets as the basis of identifying segments is suggested. The dependence of a company upon a single or a relatively small number of customers, or a particular industry or a government agency as major purchasers of the firm's product may be particularly useful information for investors, creditors and analysts. But only 3 companies in the survey supplied sufficient information to indicate that they did or could segment their activities on this basis. Hence the practicability of such an approach seems doubtful though its desirability remains an open question.

Geographical Area

As regards geographical segmentation it was discovered that only one of the companies in the authors' survey provided no disclosure by geographical area because, in fact, no overseas operations existed. Twelve provided no analysis without any comment at all and a further 12 companies disclosed a partial analysis on a UK/Overseas basis only. A mixed analysis was disclosed by 9 companies where turnover may be segmented on a country or continental basis but profit information was disclosed on a UK/Overseas basis only. Therefore 66 companies disclosed financial information by country or continent. Practice relating to partial or full analysis varied within this group.[13] Whilst the majority identified geographical segments by continent, a significant number, 17 companies, aggregated continents and a further 7 mixed continents and countries in their presentations of the analysis.

Again the supplementary information about geographical areas was examined and compared with the actual segmental disclosure. For those companies providing an analysis by geographical segments, only 27 were consistent with the categories presented in the Directors' Report or Chairman's Review; whilst only 15 were consistent when the comparison was made with the grouping of subsidiaries information. Of significance is the fact that only 52 per cent of the total number of companies sampled disclosed both turnover and profit information for the UK as distinct from overseas performance. But, as emphasised by the Department of Trade, information about the geographical location of a company's business and its contribution to trading results is 'important for a true appreciation of its financial situation and prospects'.[14]

Organisational Lines

The identification of segments consistent with the company's subsidiaries, divisions, departments or branches offers an alternative basis for disclosure. However, when the organisational unit does not coincide with an industry, product line, market or geographical area, disclosure by this means may be regarded as inconsistent with the needs of external users. The managerial responsibilities highlighted in the internal accounting system may be of dubious worth when reporting for external users. Product lines or markets assigned to a division may not be homogeneous in terms of risk, profitability or growth.[15] Divisions or legal entities may be created for other than economic reasons, for example to take advantage of provisions in tax laws.[16] If a division of a company is producing ice cream and ball-bearings, the previous arguments call for a product line segmentation because this would provide relevant information for external users. But there is a difficulty with this line of reasoning. For it implies that user needs can be satisfied without regard to the way in which the company is managed.

There are several reasons why a company may consciously combine diverse activities under a single manager's responsibility. Firstly, the products concerned may have a common demand elasticity and are therefore treated as a single activity. Secondly, the products may use joint production facilities making separation of the activities meaningless for control purposes. Thirdly, one of the activities or

---

[13]Emmanuel, C. R. and Gray, S. J., op. cit., p. 19.

[14]Department of Trade, op. cit., paragraph 40.

[15]Backer, M. B. and McFarland, W. B., op. cit., p. 20.

[16]Financial Accounting Standards Board, *Financial Reporting for Segments of a Business Enterprise: Discussion Memorandum* (Connecticut, 1974) paragraph 59.

products may dominate the others to the extent that diversification is superficial. Fourthly, the activities may be sequentially or reciprocally interdependent and separation would involve inter-segment transfers which are substantial in terms of volume and value. This list is not exhaustive but serves to indicate that there may be tenable managerial arguments for placing seemingly diverse activities under the control of one man. The needs of the external users for product line or industry segments will not be effectively served if, for example, the breaking up of an organisational unit involves substantial allocations of common costs. Nor will the reportable segments reflect the strategy and philosophy which the company is following. The need to report for segments which display differences in risk, profitability and growth profiles is not denied by these arguments but the real problem is to determine who is in the best position to gauge these differences. Solomons[17] argues that if the internal accounting reports are 'the best that management can produce to guide their own decisions, then there is an initial presumption that the same statements, or less detailed versions of them, are likely best to serve the investor in making his investment and dis-investment decisions.' In fact, segmental disclosure on other than organisational lines can misguide the external users as to the extent to which the company is actively following a diversification strategy. The unconsistency of the argument favoring the needs of external users to the exclusion of managerial realities is indicated by the conclusions of the Backer and McFarland and FASB documents where it is ultimately recognised that the management of a company is best placed to define the segments on which to report.[18] If the organisation structure reflects the way in which the company is being managed in response to its product/market environment, should not segmental disclosure be required on a basis consistent with this situation? If this is accepted then the identification of segments which exhibit homogeneity with regard to the effect of economic conditions upon results should be a managerial prerogative verified by the company's organisation structure.

Interestingly, the survey of disclosure practices showed (see Table 1) that 77 companies provided information sufficient to identify their organisation structures, some of which gave the names of the managers responsible for the individual divisions or subsidiaries. The majority of these companies indicated that their organisational units are organised on a basis broadly consistent with the SIC.

All of the alternative bases for identifying segments outlined here have some relevance in practice. In fact a combination of bases may provide the most meaningful presentation. For example, 18 companies illustrate

---

[17]Solomons, D., 'Accounting Problems and Some Proposed Solutions', in A. Rappaport, P. A. Firmin, and S. A. Zeff (editors) *Public Reporting by Conglomerates* (Prentice-Hall, 1968).

[18]Backer, M. B. and McFarland, W. B., op. cit., p. 100 and Financial Accounting Standards Board, *Financial Reporting for Segments of a Business Enterprise, Statement of Financial Accounting Standards No. 14* (Connecticut, 1976) paragraph 12.

TABLE 1
Segmental disclosures: identification of the company's management organisation structure from supplementary disclosures provided in the company report

Supplementary Disclosures	Organisation Structure	Business Dominated	Geographically Dominated	Mixture of Business and Geography	Functional	Total Companies
Explicit		17	6	23	2	48
Indicative		8	7	13	1	29
Total Identified		25	13	36	3	77
Indeterminate						23
Total Companies						100

TABLE 2
Matrix analysis: segmental disclosure of business and international activities in matrix form

Full Matrix	Business Oriented Matrix		Internationally Oriented Matrix		No Matrix	Total Companies
	Full	Partial	Full	Partial		
1	—	6	3	8	82	100

their segments' results by means of a matrix (see Table 2) where industrial and geographical classifications form the axes. Amongst those companies which comply with the legislation, the disclosure of segments by industry or product line, or by organisational lines seems to be most popular. Segmental disclosure by geographical area also seems to be feasible in practice and is generally given in addition to a business analysis. However, a tightening of the disclosure requirement along these lines is unlikely to be universally acceptable because the ways of identifying segments do not incorporate any measure of materiality.

Materiality and segmental disclosure

The provision of segment reports based on product lines would involve some companies in producing literally hundreds of additional financial statements. The costs incurred in this exercise are unlikely to be outweighed by the subsequent benefits to external users partly because of the user's inability to assimilate and understand the mass of information which would then become available. Hence a significance criterion must be found.

The present UK legislation allows the directors' opinion to determine whether or not the financial results of a segment are material and therefore worthy of disclosure. The question of what is a *substantial* contribution to sales or profits is open to wide interpretation. In the USA, the recent *Statement of Financial Accounting Standards No. 14*[19] defines a reportable segment as one which contributes 10 per cent or more to combined revenues, operating profits or losses, or identifiable assets. However, a practical limit of 10 reportable segments is seen as generally appropriate for disclosure purposes. In Canada, the SIC is the means of identifying segments and a quantitative significance criterion is then applied to

isolate reportable segments. The North American approach is therefore more prescriptive than that embodied in the UK legislation but it is not without its shortcomings.

Firstly, the quantitative significance criteria which determine whether a segment is material and therefore requires disclosure are arbitrary. Secondly, the American Standard requires back-up rules to ensure that the reportable segments identified reflect a substantial proportion of the consolidated results. These rules are sometimes inconsistent and may lead to alternative interpretations being applied.[20] Finally, the quantitative significance criteria do not eliminate the use of managerial discretion. The determination of industry segments under the American Standard 'must depend to a considerable extent on the judgement of the management of the enterprise'. The significance criteria are only applied, in fact, after industry segments have been identified.

It seems, therefore, that any solution to the problem of identifying reportable segments involves the satisfaction of two major constraints if external user needs are to be met:

A. That the activities of the reportable segments as determined by the company's management exhibit homogeneity in regard to the effect of economic conditions upon results.

B. That the identified reportable segments are material in relation to the total company's results.

The proposal which follows seeks to satisfy both of these constraints by developing a method of identifying reportable segments which can be applied to any company situation.

A dual yardstick

The organisation of a company reflects a continuing process of adaptation to the uncertain business

---

[19]Financial Accounting Standards Board, ibid., paragraphs 15–20.

[20]Emmanuel, C. R. and Gray, S. J., 'Corporate Diversification and Segmental Disclosure Requirements in the USA', *Journal of Business Finance and Accounting*, Winter, 1977.

environment with respect to products, technology, and industry, and with respect to the location of its businesses and the markets they serve. Segmental disclosure must necessarily reflect the nature of the business if it is to inform users about different rates of growth, profitability and risk perceived by management as pertaining to its various activities. But if such disclosure is to be useful to external users in assessing a company's prospects and comparing it with other companies then some *external* yardstick for identification purposes would also seem necessary. Only then will there be a discipline on the disclosure made: something approaching an objective criterion which is verifiable. Without this the matter would be left entirely to the unfettered discretion of directors, notwithstanding the need to justify the disclosure by showing consistency with the organisation structure which is also under the directors' control. Moreover, an external yardstick could help to determine at what level of a company's organisation the disclosure cut-off point is material. Clearly, too much information would pose a burden on both those providing and those receiving it. Hence the organisation structure of the individual firm is suggested as an internal yardstick for the identification of segments to be used in conjunction with the Standard Industrial Classification (at the 3 digit level) as the external criterion for purposes of verification and interpretation.[21] Segmental disclosures can then be more easily related to other relevant external data such as aggregate market, production and financial statistics for the sectors concerned. The potential for auditor authentication is also enhanced.

The application of these criteria is perhaps best illustrated by the means of some examples by which the feasibility of our proposal can be examined

[21]Note that our choice of the SIC as the appropriate external yardstick does not mean that it is necessarily superior to alternatives such as the FT – Actuaries Index. In fact, improvements to both of the systems would seem desirable but in the absence of an ideal classification it would seem to us that the SIC is more widely recognised and offers greater potential for future development.

subsequently. Consider, first, the organisatoin of Company X.

These segments of the organisation structure are consistent with the SIC at the 3 digit level. Therefore disclosure for each class of business could be required. This, however, ignores the manner in which the company is being managed. This structure is fairly frequently found in retail chains. If the activities of the transport and property segments are co-ordinated 'primarily' for the benefit of the retail outlet segment, then no segmental disclosure would be required. The problem now becomes one of defining 'primarily'. We would suggest a decision criterion to the effect that an organisational unit is a segment for reporting purposes if *all* of the following apply:

(i)   over 50 per cent of its physical sales volume is sold externally;

(ii)   revenue and profitability information is accumulated regularly for this unit;

(iii)   responsibility for the unit's operating performance resides with the immediate manager of the unit.

Effectively the conditions of a profit centre are applied to the organisational units of the company. Due to the size of the company, different organisational units must be recognised but this should not be taken as meaning that each is run as a separate business activity. The extent of the co-ordination of the activities may be roughly gauged by the degree of internal versus external trade. Let us now apply our proposal to an organisation structure such as that of Company Y.

At the first organisational level, the identified units are not consistent with the SIC at the 3 digit level. At the next tier, there is partial consistency. In respect to the Paper and Packaging Division, if less than 50 per cent of the sales volume of the paper and board department is sold internally and the units are treated as profit centres for internal purposes, then two reportable segments can be identified. For the engineering division, a further tier of the organisation structure must be uncovered. The electronics and telephone units are consistent with the SIC and if

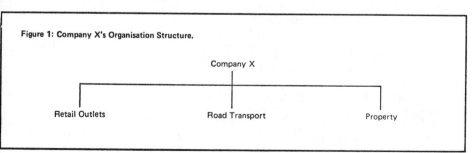

Figure 1: Company X's Organisation Structure.

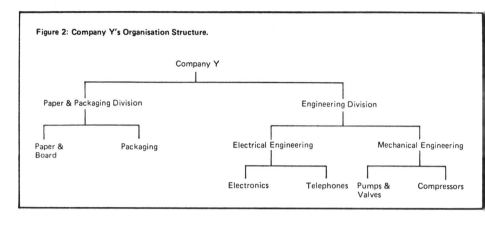

Figure 2: Company Y's Organisation Structure.

the three conditions for a profit centre are satisfied, two further reportable segments are discovered. On the mechanical engineering side, however, the company's organisation is inconsistent with the SIC, where pumps, valves and compressors constitute a single heading at the 3 digit level. The company now has a choice regarding the identification of reportable segments given that the sub-units conform with the definition of a profit centre. The company's executives can decide whether the gains from disclosing information for pumps, valves and compressors separately will outweigh any possible competitive disadvantages. Should separate disclosure not take place, the results of a reportable segment called Mechanical Engineering: pumps, valves and compressors will be given. For Company Y, given the assumptions about the individual unit's degree of dependence on internal trade, five segments can thus be identified and reported upon.

Before examining further the practical feasibility of the proposal, the conditions assumed to be sufficient for the identification of a profit centre must be inspected. The 50 per cent plus figure for external sales is arbitrary. Arguments about the materiality of the output as an input for other sub-units may arise. For instance, in the case of Company Y, the paper and board unit's internal sales may represent less than 50 per cent of that unit's physical sales volume but for the packaging unit these internal sales may represent more than 50 per cent of that unit's total demand for that input. But it is important to note that the internally traded commodity will be only one of perhaps several inputs that it needs. To have a symmetrical condition for the input or purchasing unit would ignore this fact and the focus of attention on external activities.

The rule therefore emphasises the output activity of the individual identifiable units. When the unit produces more than one type of output, the 50 per cent rule applies to the average external sales to total physical sales. In situations where a physically diverse range of products is manufactured, the opinion of the auditors may decide whether disclosure is required or not. The relative *sales value* of the products may provide useful supplementary information in allowing the auditors to express an opinion.

With regard to the practical feasibility of the proposal, doubts must be expressed about the verifiability of the third condition that responsibility for the unit's performance resides with the immediate manager of the unit.

Along with our dual yardstick for identifying segments we would suggest, therefore, the desirability of a requirement for *all* companies to provide information about managerial responsibilities, organisation structure (preferably in the form of a chart showing both the business and geographical elements), and volume of internal transactions. This seems feasible judging by the best examples of current practice and would also facilitate auditor verification of the quality of segmental disclosures. Such additional information may also be significant in its own right as an indicator of company strategy.

The proposal therefore attempts to identify reportable segments by combining the management's method of operating a company's diverse activities with the SIC at the 3 digit level. The rigid use of the SIC to identify reportable segments is avoided by initially focusing on the company's organisation structure and hence a balance is struck between the use of managerial discretion and a potentially inflexible classification system. The reportable segments identified under the proposal are significant for external users because of the identification process. Successive tiers of the organisation structure are uncovered only when disclosure is not consistent with the SIC. The process of disaggregation starts at the top and proceeds downwards which is in marked contrast with the FASB Statement which requires profit centres to be first identified, then industrial segments and finally reportable industrial segments. It is also unlikely that our proposed process of disaggregation will stop short of identifying segments which have a material effect on the enterprise's operating results. Furthermore, the absence of a quantitative significance criterion reduces the scope for manipulation inasmuch that modifications of the organisation structure will carry serious implications for internal control and behaviour. The proposal therefore appears to satisfy the twin constraints relating to the identification of realistic, material segments.

In addition to the discussion of business activity so far considered, an international analysis, both by location and markets, also requires consideration. What we suggest here is that again the primary yardstick to be used should be the organisation structure, identified in the same way as outlined earlier, but that disclosure should be made consistent with the geographical areas considered significant by management. In this respect a clear-cut disclosure by continent or country should be made depending on the organisation of the company concerned and the emphasis of its activities; though clearly there is a limit on the number of segments which could be identified without information overload. A mixing-up of geographical locations with the markets served from such locations should obviously be avoided.

We acknowledge that this approach to identifying reportable geographical segments is not entirely satisfactory because of the discretion given to management. However, the use of significance criteria or other arbitrary rules is unlikely to be of universal application and could thus result in the provision of misleading information.

Considerations of integration on an international scale must also be accounted for so that if external sales, in terms of physical volume, for any international segment corresponding to a specific organisational unit are less than 50 per cent the separate disclosure of that segment may be omitted. A more complex situation arises when more than one organisational unit appears within an identified geographical segment. When the external sales of each unit are less than 50 per cent, only the total geographical segment need be disclosed. This indicates that our proposal in respect to business analyses can be applied primarily to the organisation structure if that structure initially identifies business activities, or it can be applied secondarily to the case where the organisation structure initially shows geographical locations. Hence an international analysis should also be disclosed irrespective of whether the organisation structure is business dominated as opposed to being geographically dominated or is some mixture/combination of both. A crucial distinction to be made concerns the disclosure of UK (or home country) performance from that overseas since this will assist the monitoring of national performance. In exceptional cases the 50 per cent rule would need to be relaxed in order that UK or home country performance could be distinguished from other geographical reportable segments.

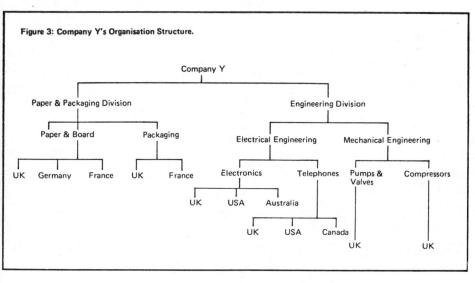

Figure 3: Company Y's Organisation Structure.

An application of geographical disclosure relating to location can be illustrated with reference to the business-dominated organisation structure of Company Y.

It is first necessary to establish whether or not geographical segments exist relating to the business segments already identified from the organisation structure. If less than 50 per cent of the sales volume of the German or French locations of the Paper and Board department is sold internally and the units are treated as profit centres for internal purposes then three reportable geographical segments, including the UK, can be identified. A similar identification procedure can be adopted in the case of packaging, electronics, telephones and pumps, valves and compressors. If, say, in the case of telephones the Canadian unit was selling internally more than 50 per cent of its volume to the USA unit then a choice has to be made as to whether to aggregate Canada with the USA into a segment entitled North America or to disclose the Canadian unit separately with other similar units as 'non-segmented operations'. What is appropriate would seem to depend on the nature of the firm's other activities in the USA, and since there is a separate electronics operation it could be more informative to keep USA activities as a separate disclosure.

Clearly, the task of the auditor is an important one in this context, just as in the case of business analyses, for it rests on him to judge the meaningfulness of the segmental disclosures in the light of the company's international activities and its organisation of responsibilities to match such activities.

We have thus demonstrated the application of our proposal with special reference to the identification of business segments. We have also considered the additional perspective of international operations. It should be emphasised, however, that the examples given serve only to illustrate our proposal. In practice, a complex variety of organisation structures will be found which will challenge both judgment and ingenuity to a greater degree than exhibited here. It is hoped, however, that our proposal will provide guidelines capable of meeting such a challenge.

Conclusion

The proposals made here in regard to business and international analyses would generally call for more information in order that segmental disclosure could be verified by auditors and their usefulness to external users enhanced. Information about organisation structure and some indication of the internal control system would be called for. However, the net result would be the disclosure of segment information which is meaningful and consistent with the way in which a company is operated. The proposal attempts to provide flexibility to facilitate the disclosure of comparable segment information but not at the expense of disguising the individual company's underlying philosophy and strategy. The materiality concept is therefore linked to managerial perceptions and not user perceptions, largely on the grounds that management are better placed to understand the nature of the business. A matching of the organisation structure and the SIC at the 3 digit level, or some other suitable classification, may help to identify segments in a way which is relevant, comparable and material for the purposes of investor decisions.

CHAPTER 15

A review of the translation debate*
C. W. Nobes

There are many linked but separable matters which might reasonably be included within the problem of currency translation. The concern of this article will be mainly with the translation for consolidation of foreign currency balance sheet items, and the relationship of this to adjustments for specific or general price changes. This leaves the translation of income items and the treatment of foreign currency transactions largely untouched. However, the bulk of controversy and past discussion has been in the area of the translation of balance sheet items and its effects.

I intend here to review critically the premises, arguments and conclusions of academic and professional bodies on both sides of the Atlantic. The literature contains much to mislead the unwary: inconsistent premises, confused argument and straightforward errors of definition. I hope to make it clear how the various issues in the translation debate are connected, and how and why writers differ.

Consolidation and translation

Many of the differences in approach suggested by accountancy bodies and writers stem from differences of view with respect to the purpose of consolidation and translation, and indeed the purpose of financial statements. In some cases, there seems to be little consideration for any underlying principle. Such fundamental confusion has been noted by several writers (e.g. Parker, 1970; Patz, 1977, 1).

In *Accounting Research Study No. 12* (ARS12), Lorensen suggests that translation is a 'measurement conversion process' which should, therefore, preserve the original accounting principles (AICPA, 1972). Many of the criticisms of translation methods are really criticisms of the results of translation, which are imperfect because of the original accounting principles. Further, some arguments in favour of particular methods involve attempts to 'improve' the original principles by taking account of inflation or the *future* effects of a devaluation. For example, one American writer suggests that, when choosing a currency translation method, 'selection ... should be based upon the most probable (economic) impact of a movement in exchange rates' (Smith, 1978). Since most systems of accounting in use, particularly historic cost which was the context of the above quotation, do not intend to reflect economic reality, the suggested selection criterion seems somewhat bizarre.

More generally, much of the argument for and against particular methods, on both sides of the Atlantic, seems to be based on the acceptability of their effects on the consolidated historic cost profits of large companies under the exchange rate and inflation conditions that exist in that particular country at that particular time. Partly for this reason, there are several recent writings in the US (where the temporal method has been in use) against the temporal method (e.g. Smith, 1978; Seidler, 1978).

It should be noted that the next five sections are written in the context of historic cost accounting. Even if this is seen as an unattractive context, it is fairly clearly the one that most multinationals have been and still are in.

Definitions and recent history of methods

One of the problems with the definition of translation methods is that many of them have, in practice, been impure versions of more fundamental methods. However, there might be said to be four underlying translation methods on which variations have been built.

The *closing rate* method translates all balance sheet items at the rate ruling on the balance sheet date (which will be referred to as the 'closing' rate, not the 'current' rate which can be ambiguous). The other three methods involve a mixture of closing and historic rates. The *monetary/non-monetary* (MNM) method uses closing rates for monetary assets and liabilities, and the historic rates relevant to the date the balance was established for other balances. The *current/non-current* (CNC) method uses closing rates for current assets and liabilities, and the relevant historic

Table A

Translation Rates used for Balance Sheet Items Under Historic Cost

	Closing rate	CNC	MNM	Temporal
Fixed assets and long term investments: cost	C	H	H	H
Stocks and short-term investments:				
cost	C	C	H	H
market	C	C	H*	C
Debtors	C	C	C	C
Cash	C	C	C	C
Long-term debt	C	H	C	C
Current liabilities	C	C	C	C

C = closing rate
H = historic rate

*Some variants of MNM translate current items held at NRV using the closing rate

Table B

An Example of Translation

Foreign HC balances in Picos	Balances	Translated Balances for Consolidation			
		Closing Rate £	CNC £	MNM £	Temporal £
10,000	Fixed Assets	5,000	2,500	2,500	2,500
3,000	Stock (Cost)	1,500	1,500	1,000	1,000
2,000	Stock (NRV)	1,000	1,000	667	1,000
3,000	Debtors	1,500	1,500	1,500	1,500
1,000	Cash	500	500	500	500
19,000	Total Assets	9,500	7,000	6,167	6,500
12,000	Equity	6,000	4,500	2,667	3,000
4,000	Loans	2,000	1,000	2,000	2,000
3,000	Creditors	1,500	1,500	1,500	1,500
19,000	Total Capital	9,500	7,000	6,167	6,500

Historic rate for fixed assets and loans: 4 picos = £1
Historic rate for stocks: 3 picos = £1
Closing rate: 2 picos = £1

rates for others. The *temporal* principle is that translation rates should be determined by the measurement basis. Balances carried at historic cost will be translated using the relevant historic rate; balances carried at present or future values will be translated at the closing rate. The effect of these definitions is summarised and illustrated in Tables A and B.

It can be seen that, under a system of historic cost accounting which did not allow revaluation, the MNM method would be the same as the temporal method, with the exception of such current assets as inventory held at net realisable value (NRV). In practice, some variants of the MNM method have translated current assets held at NRV at closing rates.

As far as current value (CV) accounting is concerned, the temporal principle would clearly give the same results as the closing rate method. Indeed, if the date on which balances are established under a CV system is taken to be the balance sheet date, the MNM method might also give the same result. The original writings are not entirely clear on this point.

Attempts at understanding the nature and effects of these multitudinous translation methods have not been assisted by the evident confusion even in high places. For example, *Accountancy* (published by the Institute of Chartered Accountants in England and Wales) recently contained an article misleadingly describing the monetary/non-monetary method as the temporal method (Kettel, 1978); whereas *The Accountant's Magazine* (published by the Institute of Chartered Accountants of Scotland) carried an article wrongly describing the current/non-current method as the temporal method (McMonnies and Rankin, 1977). Further, the 1978 *Survey of Published Accounts* (ICAEW, 1979, p. 50) states incorrectly that the temporal method 'is the use of the historical exchange rate ruling at the date when the asset or liability was acquired or the book value established'. This is wrong for liabilities and misleading for assets. Even a distinguished American textbook on accounting theory can quite erroneously report that 'ARB No. 43 also recommends that capital stock, long-term debt and long-term receivables should likewise be translated in terms of the exchange rates prevailing at the date of the balance sheet' (Hendriksen, 1970). In fact, ARB 43 recommended historic rates.

The recent vacillatory history of translation theory and practice reflects this confusion and the expediency mentioned before. A brief chronology is presented as Table C. As for the dates of origin of the various methods used, the closing rate seems to be the oldest. It was certainly used by British accountants for overseas branches in the nineteenth century (e.g. Plumb, 1891). Long periods of fixed exchange rates remove most of the arguments against the closing rate method. As Table C shows, the CNC method was formally recommended in the United States as early as 1931. However, it was advocated even earlier (Dicksee, 1911). The MNM method can be traced back to 1956. The temporal principle is much more recent and has its first clear expression in 1972.

Table C

History of Statements and Studies

	US	UK	Method
1931	AICPA Bulletin No. 92		CNC
1934	AICPA Bulletin No. 117		CNC
1939	ARB 4		CNC
1953	ARB 43		CNC
1956	S.R. Hepworth		suggests MNM
1960	NAA Research Report No. 36		discusses MNM
1965	APB Opinion 6		MNM
1968		ICAEW, N25	closing or historic rates
1969	APB Statement 3		translate-restate
1970		ICAS, Research Study	closing rate
1972	ARS 12		'temporal'
1972	APB draft Opinion		about losses on long-term liabilities under MNM
1973	FAS 1		about disclosure
1975		ED16	non-committal
1975	FAS 8		'temporal'
1977		ED21	closing rate or 'temporal'
1977	E11		closing rate or 'temporal'
1980		ED27	closing rate (situational)

CNC	= current/non-current
MNM	= monetary/non-monetary
AICPA	= American Institure of Certified Public Accountants
ARB	= Accounting Research Bulletin
APB	= Accounting Principles Board
ARS	= Accounting Research Study
FAS	= Financial Accounting Standard
ICAEW	= Institute of Chartered Accountants in England and Wales
ICAS	= Institute of Chartered Accountants of Scotland
ED	= Exposure draft published by the Accounting Standards Committee
E	= Exposure draft published by the International Accounting Standards Committee

The early use of the closing rate method

The earliest method of translation was the closing rate method. This evolved in the UK and the US when their currencies and those of other developed trading nations were exchanged at fixed rates, and when the currencies of underdeveloped countries were weaker. Therefore, for most important currencies, the problem of choosing an exchange rate did not arise and, for the others, the closing rate was reassuringly conservative. In addition, the closing rate seems obvious at first sight and is simple to use.

However, in a world where exchange rates fluctuate about their fixed parities or, worse, are freely floating, it has been necessary to address the problem of choosing exchange rates. Some of the arguments for using various methods which involve historic rates are looked at in the following sections. Nevertheless, there are still arguments for the closing rate method; but they have to take account of the different world. These latter arguments are also examined later.

Arguments for and against the CNC and MNM methods

The CNC method was common in the inter-war years (see Table C) when exchanged rates were not continually moving in the same direction but were fluctuating reasonably gently. (See Appendix for exchange rate movements.) The argument supporting the CNC method against the closing rate method was that, with fluctuating currencies, the closing rate at any time was unlikely to be the same as the future rate ruling when non-current liabilities had to be repaid. The consequent practical difference from the closing rate method is that gains or losses on non-current items are not recognised (see Table B). This is justified on the ground that any exchange rate movement is quite likely to reverse (several times) in the following months or years.

The effect of the method is also to link fixed assets with related long-term liabilities. Gains and losses on neither of them are reported, unlike the MNM method, below. However, there has been little backing for the CNC method in recent years, not least because exchange rates no longer fluctuate about fixed parities. Consequently, it is unreasonable to hold that exchange rate movements are likely to reverse. The closing exchange rate is probably the best estimate of the future exchange rate for non-current liabilities (Henning et al., 1978). Further, it is reasonably argued that

the definition of current assets and liabilities is a matter of classification, which implies no underlying accounting or economic difference which could be used to determine the appropriate rate of translation (Baxter and Yamey, 1951). These conclusions led to the alternative MNM method as proposed by Hepworth (1956).

As with the CNC method, the MNM method translates non-monetary fixed assets at historic rates and monetary assets at the closing rate. Assets and liabilities are defined as 'monetary' if their amounts are fixed by contract in terms of the currency of the foreign entity. In practice, this tends to include inventories valued at net realisable value (and quoted securities) (Kettel, 1978). This latter exception, which is necessary on the grounds of expediency because of the strange effects of using the historic rate with such assets, suggests that the theory underlying the MNM method is weak. As Lorensen notes (ARS 12, p. 35), inventory cannot be a monetary asset under any reasonable definition, including those used by Hepworth and the National Accounting Association. Inventory is not worth a fixed number of units of the subsidiary's currency.

The difference between the two methods is that MNM exposes long-term liabilities rather than inventories to exchange rate fluctuations. This has been opposed by some, not on theoretical accounting grounds but because of its effect on profits when the parent's currency loses value. In this case, there will be losses shown as a result of long-term liabilities but no gains on fixed assets or inventories. This, it was argued, will be against the real effects of such an exchange rate change, which will actually cause the foreign subsidiary to make larger profits (and dividends) in terms of the parent's currency (Kettel, 1978; APB, 1972; Connor, 1972). However, such a criticism about *future* profits seems hardly relevant under most systems of accounting, let alone historic cost, in the context of which the arguments were made.

It is clear, however, that the practical acceptability of exchange rate methods depended then, as now, mainly on their effects on consolidated profit figures under the economic conditions that happened to be ruling. The above criticisms of the MNM method arose in the US under the novel circumstances of the early 1970s when the dollar was falling against several other currencies (see Appendix). The lack of underlying theory was recognised at this time, and an accounting research study (ARS 12) was commissioned and produced. It was followed by a new financial accounting standard, FAS 8 (FASB, 1975). These documents proposed the temporal principle and incorporated fundamental theoretical reasoning in its favour. Parts of the following discussion can also be used as a justification for the use of historic rates by the MNM method.

Arguments for the temporal principle

ARS 12 and FAS 8 were attempts to provide a logical basis for the choice of rates of exchange for translation, which was not to be restricted to a pure historic cost system of accounting. To start with, at least, economic effects (see later) and the degree to which gains or losses were implied by particular methods were considered less important than a coherent financial accounting theory.

The purpose of consolidation was discussed and concluded to be the presentation of the results of a group as if they were those of a single entity (FAS 8, Appendix D). This leads to the conclusion that the accounting principles of the parent company should be used throughout the group and that the parent's currency should be the single currency used. Under historic cost accounting, the purchase of a foreign subsidiary or the purchase of an asset by a foreign subsidiary should be measured at cost in dollars at the moment of purchase. Each transaction of the foreign subsidiary should have the same effect as if it had been a transaction of the parent. For a US parent, for example, the objective will be to measure and express the assets and liabilities of a foreign subsidiary in dollars and in conformity with US GAAP.

This means that where the parent holds balances at historic cost, for example a machine, then a subsidiary's balances on similar accounts should also be held at historic cost, and translated at historic rates. This will express what it would have cost to buy the asset in the parent's currency on the date of purchase. On the other hand, cash is clearly valued at current value and should therefore be translated at closing rates.

Many balances expressed in money terms imply future amounts of money; for example, debtors, creditors and long-term liabilities. These might be said to require the appropriate *future* rates of exchange. However, fortunately, reality as well as objectivity can be satisfied by using closing rates on the grounds that the present rate of exchange is the best predictor of future rates. This suggestion, that present rates embody expectations, is linked to the efficient market hypothesis (Henning et al. 1978). Lorensen in ARS 12 raises other arguments. For example, the loss or gain on exchange

is said to belong to the future period when the exchange rate changes, so the closing rate should be used for present balance sheets. This seems a false argument. If the rate change can be predicted, accountants might be expected to provide now for foreseeable losses. If the rate change cannot be predicted, such provision is impossible rather than inappropriate. Further, Lorensen argues that receivables and payables are stated now at current (rather than future) purchasing power. Under historic cost, this surely tells us little about which exchange rate to use. It is the argument at the start of this paragraph which is convincing, and strong enough by itself.

Various details of the application of the temporal principle can be seen to be consistent with the underlying theory. For example, FAS 8 makes it clear (para. 46) that the 'lower of cost and market' rule for inventory valuation should involve a comparison of historic cost at historic exchange rates with net realisable value at closing exchange rates.

Another consistent detail is the choice of the remittance rate when there are multiple rates. In order to explain this it should be noted that it is the proprietary theory which is dominant behind the temporal method. Foreign subsidiaries are seen as existing in order to provide domestic cash flows by remittance (FAS 8, para. 227). Thus, the remittance rate is appropriate for earnings, for assets measured at market values (which could be sold for remittance) and for assets measured at historic cost because this measures the historic sacrifice in remittances in order to incur the cost of the asset. However, Flower (1976, p. 59) suggests that the investment rate would be more logical for the cost of fixed assets.

There are several supporters of the temporal principle, including Lorensen (in ARS 12), Flower (1976) and Hinton (1978). The arguments, that the translation method should not distort the underlying accounting principles so that consolidation can take place on a consistent basis, and that the method should not be expected to correct for the inadequacies of underlying principles in particular accounting systems, seem sound.

Arguments against the temporal principle are contained in the next section.

Arguments for and against the closing rate method

Acknowledging that we do not now live in a world of fixed exchange rates and that we are prepared to use more respectable criteria than simplicity of operation (and, in the UK, familiarity), do there remain any good arguments for the closing rate method?

It is the objectives of consolidation and translation which are crucial here. Suppose that the aim is 'to represent to decision-makers ... foreign investments and operations in a familiar currency framework and ... to facilitate comparisons' (AAA, 1975). The arguments against the temporal principle and in favour of the closing rate method follow from this. Perhaps such arguments have been more readily accepted in such countries as the UK and Canada, rather than the US, because of greater familiarity with the concept of foreign parents.

The initial plank of the argument is that foreign subsidiaries do *not* exist mainly in order to make remittances to parents. A foreign subsidiary is a separate entity and it is only its net worth which is at risk, not each individual balance. This 'entity' argument is rehearsed in FAS 8 (para. 140 onwards) and seriously advanced by Parkinson (1972) for 'independent' operations as part of a 'situational' approach, and by Patz (1977, 1, pp. 319–321; and 1977, 2).

In this case, it can be argued that all the balances should be translated at the same rate, which should be the rate ruling at the balance sheet date. It can be further argued that, unless this is done, the original relationships between the various balances and profit items will be upset by using more than one rate. Also, there are fewer problems caused by gains or losses on long-term liabilities because there are similar movements on the assets that were financed by them.

It is argued that the economic and commercial environments of foreign subsidiaries may be quite different from that of the parent. Assets were not bought by the parent in its currency, and in many cases could not have been bought at the historic prices translated at historic rates. In this sense, assets do not have an historic cost in terms of the parent's currency. Further, the assets were not bought at the expense of remittance, for the money would otherwise have been used for some other foreign purpose.

At this point, the supporters of the temporal method might reply that if the foreign subsidiary is 'independent' and not for remittances, it should not be consolidated but treated by the *equity* method. In those cases where a subsidiary is centrally controlled and should be consolidated, the temporal arguments about consistency of principles should apply.

It seems clear that there is no precise consensus about the purpose of consolidation. Are consolidated statements intended to amplify parent company statements, to be a more realistic form of parent company statements, to represent the group as if it were a single entity, or to perform some other purpose? The genesis of consolidation and the influence of these competing purposes is very well described by Walker (1978). He points out that it is not at all obvious that full consolidation is the correct approach for subsidiaries, let alone for partially owned foreign subsidiaries. This vagueness of purpose contributes to the confusion of the translation debate.

Returning to the arguments of supporters of the temporal method, they would further hold that a foreign subsidiary's historic cost balances which are translated at closing rates become a meaningless combination which is neither historic cost nor a valuation. The closing rate for historic cost accounting is said to lead to 'conceptual and practical nonsense' (Hinton, 1978). It leads to 'nothing except the product of multiplying two unrelated numbers' (Storey, 1972).

If these dismissals of the theoretical arguments for the closing rate are accepted, there is still further 'economic' argument to hear. For example, Seidler (1972) supports the closing rate method on the basis that, unlike the temporal or MNM methods, it moves profit in the same direction as future earnings streams in the parent's currency. Smith (1978) argues that same point, that subsidiaries in a country with a strong currency show a loss under the temporal method because of long-term liabilities, but actually represent a good investment. However, these are imprecise arguments based on what happens to be expedient under temporary conditions. They are partly criticisms of the underlying historic cost accounting. As Flower (1976, p. 28) says: 'If ... the historic rate method ... produces unacceptable translated accounts, then the deficiency may well rest with the historic cost based accounts ... The underlying problem will not be solved by changing the method of translation to the closing rate method, which ... is not theoretically consistent with ... accounts based on historic cost'.

It has been noted that the clamour against the temporal method seems to have much to do with the effects on the income statement. A survey has found that 80 per cent of US multinationals were already taking exchange differences to income *before* FAS 8 was introduced (Evans and Folks, 1979). The strength of opposition seems to be related to the fact that, because of the weakness of the dollar, the practice imposed by FAS 8 is now inexpedient.

Recent developments in standard practice

There is currently (June, 1980) no standard practice in the UK. Exposure Draft 21 was much criticised for allowing either closing rates or the temporal principle. The latter was allowed because some UK companies file their financial statements with the SEC, and hence must obey FAS 8 at least for that version of their statements. However, during 1977/78, 94 per cent of the top 300 companies used the closing rate method (ICAEW, 1979, p. 53). The new exposure draft of October 1980 makes its preference for the closing rate method more obvious but allows use of the temporal method under certain circumstances.

In the US, FAS 8 has come under heavy criticism, particularly from practical men rather than from academics. In March 1980 the FASB concluded that the closing rate method had a number of advantages, and announced an intention to prepare a new exposure draft on that basis (issued August 1980).

In Canada, there has been similar uncertainty about the existing proposals for the introduction of the temporal method. However, in Australia, an exposure draft based on the temporal method was issued during 1979. Not surprisingly, the exposure draft of the IASC proposes to allow both the temporal and the closing rate methods. However, it would be unrealistic to expect a standard until the FASB has resolved its difficulties.

Inflation and specific price changes

A somewhat analogous problem to the choice of rates of exchange for foreign currency translation is the choice of 'rates of exchange' for translation of units of a domestic currency over time. Historic cost accounting is a sort of MNM method, and current purchasing power (CPP) accounting might be compared to the closing rate method. Current value accounting, however, is not directly analogous, because it is not the 'rate of exchange' between pounds of different dates which is being adjusted for.

Naturally, when dealing with the financial statements of foreign subsidiaries in periods of changing prices, the above problem is combined (and sometimes confused) with the problem of translation. Many writers on CPP in this context have recommended restatement of the subsidiary's financial statements to CPP using a foreign index, followed by translation at the closing rate of exchange (Zwick and Zenoff, 1969; Parkinson, 1972; Shwayder, 1972; Choi, 1975; AAA, 1975). The restate-translate method is better for resource

allocation and performance comparison, it is argued.

However, the sounder arguments from a financial accounting theory point of view appear to be on the other side, and thus for translate-restate (CPP) using a parent country index. (Rosenfield, 1971; Lorensen and Rosenfield, 1974; APB, 1965; Flower, 1976, p. 51). It is argued that restate-translate is wrong because it leads to foreign balances which have been adjusted for foreign inflation being added to domestic balances adjusted for domestic inflation. Since CPP is a historic-cost based system, historic rates should be used to translate the foreign balances. This should be followed by restatement to CPP for consolidation using the price indices of the parent country. Thus, balances which are all expressed in historic units of the domestic currency will all be adjusted for domestic inflation before being added together. Consistency of accounting principles will have been achieved. However, Patz (1977, 1, p. 317) rightly notes that translate-restate is only obviously theoretically correct once a proprietary assumption has been made.

There are criticisms of the *usefulness* of the answers given by translate-restate (CPP). These have not only been made by those who support restate-translate. Perhaps a greater consensus exists when dealing with current value (CV) accounting. There is general support for restate (CV)-translate. (Goudeket, 1960; Parker, 1970; Flower, 1976; IASG, 1976). Here the foreign subsidiary restates its financial statements using some form of current value accounting (perhaps CCA). This is followed by translation using closing rates of exchange. This approach seems less vulnerable to attacks on theoretical or practical grounds.

Purchasing power parities

An alternative approach for dealing simultaneously with translation and inflation uses purchasing power parities (PPPs). The purchasing power parity theory has been developed by economists studying the moments of exchange rates (e.g. Balassa, 1964). It has been adapted by accountants as an alternative to exchange rates, initially particularly for measuring foreign exchange exposure (NAA, 1960; AAA, 1974; Aliber and Stickney, 1975; Patz, 1977, 1, p. 321; Patz, 1977, 2). Supporters of PPPs concede that translate-restate (CPP) might be satisfactory if exchange rate movements and relative price level movements cancelled out. However, it is clear that exchange rates are not only affected by relative inflation rates but also by political factors, interest rates, balances of payments, and so on. Considerable stress is placed upon the suggestion that this renders exchange rates 'inaccurate' and unsuitable for translation, for which they were not designed. Some writings are just assertions, which offer no reasoned argument about why it matters what determines exchange rates (AAA, 1974). This question needs to be answered, for we do not reject an historic cost or a current value on the basis of which particular elements of supply or demand have determined a price. It is possible to guess that the above assertions are based on the assumptions of Scott (1975) who sat on the appropriate AAA Committee. If so, the reasoning is based on the idea that the objective of translation is to enable a better prediction of the future. This has already been criticised, particularly in the context of historic cost. Many of Scott's arguments in favour of PPPs and against exchange rates are answered by Clarke (1977), who thinks that neither may be appropriate for many balances.

Fortunately, some arguments in favour of PPPs are more clearly stated. Patz (1977, 1) makes it clear that under proprietary theory of the sort which leads to the temporal method, exchange rates seem sensible. He claims, however, that an entity approach is more suitable and that, in order to preserve the original local meaning of foreign financial statements, PPPs are more appropriate than exchange rates. It is also argued that foreign balances awaiting translation have a 'place significance' which is somewhat similar to the 'time significance' of balances being adjusted for inflation (Patz, 1977, 2, p. 19). The coefficients necessary for translation are based upon ratios of the general purchasing power of the currencies involved. Exchange rates could be used if it can be proved that they approximate to such PPPs. This entity-based theory suggests that a UK parent should be interested in its worldwide command over goods and services not over pounds sterling.

The response to this is that a UK holding company's shareholders *are* interested in command over pounds sterling, and that the local subsidiary's financial statements still remain for other uses (Flower, 1978). However, this does not seem to fit with the idea that consolidation presents the accounts of the *group* rather than amplifying the holding company accounts. As for the 'place significance', Clarke (1978) suggests that domestic goods and foreign goods are just as heterogeneous as domestic money and foreign money,

because of transportation costs and other reasons. Therefore, adjusting by PPPs does not provide balances which may sensibly be summed.

There is, no doubt, considerable mileage left in the PPP debate. However, it seems unlikely that Table C will need to be updated on this account in the near future.

Economic effects

It has been noted several times in this paper that some writers have argued for or against particular translation methods at particular times on grounds of the economic effects of resulting profit and asset figures. The late 1970s has seen the development of a considerable literature (mainly American) on the subject of economic and political effects of accounting standards. One of the areas which is often used as an example is currency translation.

Many have argued that accounting standards have considerable effects on profit and asset figures and that, therefore, they have economic effects (Rappaport, 1977; Wyatt, 1977; Solomons, 1978). Zeff (1978, pp. 57–59) has charted the influence of 'economic consequences' on accounting pronouncements in the US since 1941. He says that 'on each of the occasions ..., outside parties intervened ... by an appeal to criteria that transcended the traditional questions of accounting measurement and fair presentation'.

The arguments have gone even further, to suggest that accounting rules should be set democratically by politically responsive institutions (Gerboth, 1973; Horngren, 1973; May and Sundem, 1976). There is clearly considerable pressure for such 'democratic' involvement by interested parties. Such pressures hastened the demise of the APB (Zeff, 1978, p. 60). Consequently, the FASB is less dependent on the accounting profession, and has added 'probable economic or social impact' to its conceptual framework (FASB, 1976).

In the case of currency translation, it has been shown that some methods have been criticised because they can cause profits to be smaller or more volatile (Scott, 1975, p. 61; Smith, 1978). The arguments are often not concerned with whether or not this is a better presentation but with any effects on the decision-making of multinationals. However, the arguments against allowing accounting rules to be influenced by political pressures based on probable economic consequences seem very strong. Solomons (1978, p. 69) notes that 'critics of the FASB are asserting that economic behaviour, such as ... hedging, which would not have been rational under the old accounting rules becomes rational under the new ones. Such an assertion is difficult to defend because the new rules have not changed the underlying cash flows or risks.... Only if significance is attached exclusively to *the bottom line*, rather than to the present value of the enterprise, can the change in behaviour be defended'. Solomons goes on to give several examples where manipulating a measuring device soon gives rise to loss of neutrality, loss of reliability and, then, loss of usefulness. Zeff (1978, p. 63) agrees that 'the FASB would surely preside over its own demise if it were to...make decisions primarily on other than accounting grounds'.

It should not be regretted that different accounting gives rise to different economic decisions. Perhaps some of the decisions made by Rolls Royce and its shareholders in the late 1960s would have been different if SSAP 13 on R & D expenditure had been in operation. To claim that such a standard inhibits R & D expenditure would not prove that the standard should be changed.

Summary

The purpose of this article is to try to clarify the differences in translation methods, and their causes. Some differences are due to different underlying assumptions; others appear to be due to a lack of *consistent* assumptions. The debate has been confused by the use of erroneous definitions and faulty argument. Many translation methods have been advanced in theoretical writings and several have been recommended by professional bodies and used in practice in the UK and the US. A chronology of the development of these methods is provided.

The current/non-current and the monetary/non-monetary methods were attempts to provide a method which was thought to be more suitable than the closing rate method in a world of fluctuating exchange rates. However, the former has attracted particularly heavy criticism on theoretical grounds. The desire to have a consistent underlying financial accounting theory, which would cope with both historic cost accounting and other systems, led to ARS 12 and FAS 8 which introduced the temporal principle. This seems acceptable to many financial accounting theorists on both sides of the Atlantic. However, some practitioners, specialists in business finance and management accountants are opposed to it because of its effects on profits.

Also, alternative accounting assumptions to the proprietary method (on which ARS 12 was based) can be used to favour the closing rate method.

In practice, it might appear that the translation method used in a particular country at a particular time depends little on theories but more on its effects on profits under the ruling exchange rate conditions.

The underlying assumptions about the purpose of financial statements, consolidation and translation affect the way in which adjustments for inflation and specific price changes are linked with a translation method. For CPP, translate-restate seems to fit with the proprietary assumption and the temporal principle. The weight of theoretical arguments appear to be on this side. For CCA, restate-translate is fairly clearly correct.

There is, however, a more fundamental suggestion that exchange rates are not suitable for translation. Some writers propose purchasing power parities, but these have failed to gain general acceptance. There are, also, arguments that suggest that neither exchange rates nor PPPs are suitable for most balances and that, since the proprietary theory is questionable for many multinationals, consolidation is not suitable either.

More recently, the intensity of the debate on the economic consequences of accounting rules about such matters as translation has increased. However, the arguments in favour of 'integrity' and 'neutrality' for accounting standards seem to be the stronger, even if expediency and short-term political matters are beginning to affect more seriously the setting of standards in practice.

References

AICPA, 1972, *ARS 12-Reporting Foreign Operations of US Companies in US Dollars.*
Aliber, R. Z. and Stickney, C. P., 1975, 'Measures of foreign exchange exposure', *Accounting Review*, January.
American Accounting Association, 1974, 'Report of the Committee on International Accounting', *Accounting Review Supplement*, pp. 259–262.
American Accounting Association, 1975, 'Report of the Committee on International Accounting', *Accounting Review Supplement*, pp. 91–95.
APB, 1972, *Proposed Opinion, Translating Foreign Operations.*
Baxter, W. T. and Yamey, B. S., 1951, 'Theory of foreign branch accounts', *Accounting Research*, April.
Balassa, B., 1964, 'The purchasing-power parity doctrine: a reappraisal', *Journal of Political Economy*, December.
Choi, F. D. S., 1975, 'Foreign currency translation', *International Journal of Accounting*, Fall.
Clarke, F. L., 1977, 'A note on exchange rates, purchasing power parities and translation procedures', *Abacus*, June.
Clarke, F. L., 1978, 'Patz on parities, exchange rates and translation', *Accounting and Business Research*, Winter, p. 75.
Connor, J. E., 1972, 'Accounting for the upward float of foreign currencies', *Journal of Accountancy*, June.
Dicksee, L. R., 1911, *Advanced Accounting*, Gee and Co, p. 30.

Evans, T. H. and Folks, W. R., 1979, 'SFAS 8: conforming, coping, complaining, and correcting!', *International Journal of Accounting*, Fall, p. 36.

FASB, 1975, *Accounting for the Translation of Foreign Currency Transactions and Foreign Currency Financial Statements FAS No. 8*.

FASB, 1976, *Conceptual Framework for Financial Accounting and Reporting*—discussion memorandum, para 367.

Flower, J., 1976, *Accounting Treatment of Overseas Currencies*, ICAEW.

Flower, J., 1978, 'A price parity theory of translation: a comment', *Accounting and Business Research*, Winter.

Gerboth, D. L., 1973, 'Research, intuition and politics in accounting enquiry', *Accounting Review*, July.

Goudeket, A., 1960, 'An application of replacement value theory', *Journal of Accountancy*, July.

Hendriksen, E. S., 1970, *Accounting Theory*, Irwin, Homewood, Illinois, p. 232. It should be mentioned, however, that Hendriksen states correctly on another page (233) that the *historical* rate was recommended. References to ABR 43 are omitted in later editions.

Henning, C. N., Piggott, W. and Scott, R. H., 1978, *International Financial Management*, McGraw Hill, New York, pp. 375–377.

Hepworth, S. R., 1956, *Reporting Foreign Operations*, University of Michigan.

Hinton, R. P., 1978, 'Foreign currency transactions', *Accountant*, May 4.

Horngren, C. T., 1973, 'The marketing of accounting standards', *Journal of Accountancy*, October.

IASG (1976) *Guidance Manual on CCA*, London, p. 200.

ICAEW, 1979, *Survey of Published Accounts—1978*, ICAEW, London.

Kettel, B., 1978 'Foreign exchange exposure', *Accountancy*, March, p. 86.

Lorensen, L. and Rosenfield, P., 1974, 'Management information and foreign inflation', *Journal of Accountancy*, December.

May, R. G. and Sundem, G. L., 1976, 'Research for accounting policy: an overview', *Accounting Review*, October.

McMonnies, P. N. and Rankin, B. J., 1977, 'Accounting for foreign currency translation', *Accountant's Magazine*, June, p. 241.

National Accounting Association, *Research Report No. 36*, 1960.

Parker, R. H., 1970, 'Principles and practice in translating foreign currencies', *Abacus*, December.

Parkinson, R. M., 1972, *Translation of Foreign Currencies*, Canadian Institute of Chartered Accountants.

Patz, D. H., 1977 (1), 'The state of the art in translation theory', *Journal of Business Finance and Accounting*, 4, 3.

Patz, D. H., 1977 (2), 'A price parity theory of translation', *Accounting and Business Research*, Winter.

Plumb, H. A., 1891, 'The treatment of fluctuating currencies in the accounts of English companies', *Accountant*, April 4, p. 259.

Rappaport, A., 1977, 'Economic impact of accounting standards—implications for the FASB', *Journal of Accountancy*, May.

Rosenfield, P., 1971, 'General price level accounting and foreign operations', *Journal of Accountancy*, February.

Scott, G. M., 1975, 'Currency exchange rates and accounting translation: a mis-marriage?', *Abacus*, June, p. 59.

Seidler, L. J., 1972, 'An income approach to the translation of foreign currency financial statements', *CPA Journal*, January.

Seidler, L. J., 1978, 'Accounting for foreign currency translation', in *Accounting for Multinational Enterprises*, Eds. D. D. AlHashim and J. W. Robertson, Bobbs-Merrill.

Shwayder, K., 1972, 'Accounting for exchange rate fluctuations', *Accounting Review*, October, p. 749.

Smith, A. F., 1978, 'Temporal method: temporary mode', *Management Accounting* (US), February, p. 25.

Solomons, D., 1978, 'The politicization of accounting', *Journal of Accountancy*, November.

Storey, R., 1972, Appendix to *ARS 12*.

Walker, R. G., 1978, *Consolidated Statements*, Arno Press, especially ch. 15.

Wyatt, A. R., 1977, 'The economic impact of financial accounting standards', *Journal of Accountancy*, October.

Zeff, S. A., 1978, 'The rise of economic consequences', *Journal of Accountancy*, December.

Zenoff, D. B. and Zwick, J., 1969, *International Financial Management*, Prentice-Hall, p. 500.

Appendix

Selected exchange rates

	US $ to £1	French francs to £1	French francs to $1	German marks to £1	German marks to $1	Brazil cruzeiro to £1	Brazil cruzeiro to $1
1870		25.1	4.98				
Pre-war	4.867	25.22	5.18	20.429	4.198	15	3.080
1914		25.3	5.19				
1915	4.86	25.12	5.24		4.59	17.75	3.17
1916	4.77	28	5.90		5.36	20	4.04
1917	4.76	27.8	5.86		5.53	20	4.27
1918	4.76	27.18	5.72			17.75	3.72
1919	4.76	26	5.47			18.5	3.92
1920	3.7	41	11	340	100.5	13.75	3.72
1921	3.8	54	14	215	57	25.25	6.78
1922	4.2	51.4	12.15	790	186	32	7.87
1923	4.65	62	14	32,000	6890	40	8.60
1924	4.25	84	20	19 billion	4.47 billion	40	9.41
1925	4.74	88	18.57	20	4.22	40	8.44
1926	4.85	129.25	26.59	20.3	4.18	34.25	6.64

Year							
1927	4.85	122	25.10	20.4	4.2	41.75	8.6
1928	4.87	124	25.52	20.45	4.21	40	8.23
1929	4.85	124	25.52	20.4	4.20	40	8.36
1930	4.87	123.9	25.50	20.4	4.20	43.5	8.95
1931	4.87	123.67	25.43	20.4	4.20	53.3	10.97
1932	3.38	86	25.59	14.25	4.24	60	17.86
1933	3.34	86	25.59	14.10	4.2	43.5	12.95
1934	5.0	83	16.6	13.6	2.61	60	16
1935	4.93	74.5	15.31	12.1	2.45	84.9	17.22
1936	4.93	75	15.31	12.25	2.48	86.3	17.33
1937	4.91	105	21.43	12.25	2.48	79.6	16.08
1938	5.0	147	29.4	12.4	2.49	83.5	18.17
1939	4.63	176.5	39.8	11.5	2.49	81.9	19.71
1940	4.03	176.5	43.8		2.5	73.7	19.79
1941	4.03						
1942	4.03					83.6	19.64
1943	4.03					83.6	19.63
1944	4.03					83.6	19.57
1945	4.03	203	49.72			82.8	19.50
1946	4.03	480	119.3			79	18.72
1947	4.03	480	119.3			79	18.72
1948	4.03	864	214.7	13.4	3.33	79	18.72
1949	4.03	1093	350	13.4	3.33	52	18.72
1950	2.80	980	350	11.76	4.2		
1951	2.80	979	349.95	11.76	4.2		
1952	2.79	981	349.95	11.5	4.2		
1953	2.81	982	349.95	11.70	4.2		
1954	2.81	981	349.95	11.73	4.2		
1955	2.79	978	349.95	11.74	4.2		
1956	2.80	982	350	11.71	4.2		
1957	2.79	984	350	11.73	4.2		
1958	2.81	1117	420	11.72	4.2		
1959	2.81	1374	490	11.74	4.18		
1960	2.81	13.74	4.90	11.71	4.17		
1961	2.81	13.7	4.9	11.17	3.99		
1962	2.81	13.7	4.9	11.20	3.99		
1963	2.80	13.7	4.9	11.11	3.97		
1964	2.79	13.7	4.9	11.09	3.97	4400	1610
1965	2.80	13.7	4.9	11.22	4.0	6216	2220
1966	2.79	13.8	4.9	11.09	3.97	6216	2220
1967	2.79	13.8	4.9	11.22	4.01	6130	2200
1968	2.4	11.8	4.9	9.5	3.98	7.6	3.2
1969	2.4	11.8	4.9	9.58	4.01	9.0	3.5
1970	2.4	13.2		8.7		10.4	
1971	2.42	13.3		8.7		11.9	
1972	2.6	13.3		8.3		14.4	
1973	2.4	12.0		7.5		14.6	
1974	2.3	11.2		6.0		14.2	
1975	2.2	9.5		5.4		17.0	
1976	1.8	8.6		4.6		18.3	
1977	1.7	8.5		4.0		21.0	
1978	1.9	9.1		4.1		30.6	
1979	2.0	8.5		3.7		42.5	

Sources: R. L. Bidwell, *Currency Tables*, Rex Collings, London, 1970; CSO, *Financial Statistics* February 1973 and December 1979, HMSO, London, Table 102.

When several rates are quoted in the sources, the rate noted above is the earliest given for the particular year.

CHAPTER 16

Price-level adjustments and foreign currency translation: are they compatible?*

Frederick D. S. Choi

Someone long ago remarked on the certainty of two things — death and taxes. A contemporary version of that saying should include two additional considerations: namely (1) the growth of multinational business and (2) the phenomenon of global inflation. Indeed, the activities of today's multinational corporations have expanded to such an extent that their combined output is estimated now at nearly one-sixth of world economic output. Inflation, once thought to characterize the economies of underdeveloped countries, is now a common problem of the industrialized world. In fact, this modern-day disease has reached such proportions that *double-digit inflation* is a term generally accepted by economists throughout the world. These two phenomena, which reflect whirlwind developments of the 1960s and early 1970s, have significant accounting implications and promise to present accountants with some of the greatest challenges they will encounter during the balance of this decade.

A particular problem in this regard (and one which this paper addresses) concerns consolidation of the financial accounts of a firm's foreign subsidiaries in inflationary environments. In the face of rising

* Frederick D. S. Choi is a native of Hawaii and is assistant professor of accounting at the University of Hawaii. He received his bachelor's and master's degrees in the area of finance from that same university. Currently Professor Choi is serving as a visiting professor at the University of Washington where he earned his doctorate in accounting. He has had business experience in banking and real estate and is particularly interested in international dimensions of accounting and its relationship to the development of broadly based and integrated capital markets.

* This article is reprinted, with permission, from *The International Journal of Accounting: Education and Research* (Fall 1975) pp 121–143

price levels worldwide, traditional financial statements have been challenged increasingly as inappropriate and even misleading. Not surprisingly, more and more accountants subscribe to the view that the statement effects of changing price levels ought to be accounted for.[1]

Coupled with the problem of accounting for changing price levels is the need to express the results of foreign operations in terms of a single currency. Shareholders, creditors, and other external user groups desire in general a single frame of reference for company operations, regardless of geographic origin. In most cases, however, accounts of foreign subsidiaries are denominated typically in the currency of a host country; whereas, accounts of a parent company are denominated in the currency of its home country. Since consolidated statements can be presented only in terms of a single currency unit, currency translation procedures are called for that transform foreign currency into domestic currency statements.

Under these circumstances, is it better, first, to restate the accounts of foreign subsidiaries for foreign inflation and then translate the adjusted amounts into the currency of the home country? Or is it preferable, first, to translate subsidiary accounts into home country currency units then adjust for inflation? Preliminary evidence from an actual case study — prepared for the author by Carlaw and Raleigh, two MBA students at the University of Washington — suggests that the differential effect of either approach on consolidated financial statements is significant.[2] Still, the issue remains unsettled and proponents of each approach continue to argue the "conceptual superiority" of one construct over the other.

This paper reexamines issues underlying the budding controversy with the objective of placing them in proper perspective. The restate-translate versus translate-restate controversy is viewed along with arguments supporting each model. The problem is put into perspective by drawing on recent recommendations of the AICPA's Accounting Objectives Study Group; that is, the issues underlying the translation-restatement controversy are discussed from the perspective of a norma-

---

[1] When speaking about accounting for price-level changes, however, we must be careful to distinguish between two kinds of price changes; namely, general price-level changes and specific price changes. In view of the confusion that surrounds each, the distinction between them will be clarified in the following section. For an excellent survey of extant accounting treatments of inflation internationally, see R. W. Scapens, "The Treatment of Inflation Overseas," *Accountancy* (September 1973): 10-16.

[2] Details of the case study are included in the Appendix to this paper.

tive decision-framework. Conclusions, additional insights, and policy implications then follow.

GENERAL VERSUS SPECIFIC PRICE-LEVEL CHANGES

Before proceeding, it may be instructive to clarify the distinction between general and specific prive-level changes since the term *inflation* often is applied indiscriminately to both. A *general price-level change* occurs when the prices of all goods and services in the economy move on the average, that is, the purchasing power of the monetary unit changes in terms of its ability to command goods and services in general. A *specific price-level change,* on the other hand, refers to a change in the price of a specific commodity. In the context of a business enterprise, it refers to changes in the specific prices of a firm's economic resources. Each type of price change has a differing effect on measures of a firm's financial status and operating performance, and is accounted for, consequently, with different objectives in mind. Hereafter, accounting adjustments for general price-level changes will be referred to as the general price-level model and accounting for specific price changes will be referred to as the current cost model.[3]

The general price-level model measures income such that it represents the amount of resources a firm could distribute to various income claimants during a given period of time leaving the firm able to command as many goods and services (in general) at the end of the period as it could at the beginning. To achieve this result, net assets at the beginning and end of a given accounting period are adjusted to their end-of-period purchasing power equivalents using a general price-level index such as the U.S. GNP implicit price deflator or the United Kingdom (U.K.) consumer expenditure deflator.

The current cost model, on the other hand, holds that income is the amount of resources a firm can distribute during a given period while maintaining its capability of replacing physical capital, for example, inventories and plant and equipment, which it uses to produce goods and services for sale to the consuming public. This may be achieved by adjusting a firm's beginning and ending net asset position (usually via appropriate specific price indexes) to reflect changes in specific price levels during the period. Thus, while the general price-level model

---

[3] For an expanded discussion of the concepts treated here, the reader is referred to Robert G. May, Gerhard G. Mueller, and Thomas H. Williams, *A New Introduction to Financial Accounting* (Englewood Cliffs, N.J.: Prentice-Hall, 1973).

strives to preserve the general purchasing power of the enterprise's original money capital, the current cost model seeks to preserve the firm's physical capital or operating capability.

TRADITIONAL METHODS OF CURRENCY TRANSLATION

Traditional methods of translation have not dealt explicitly with the phenomenon of changing price levels. Attention has focused instead on the appropriate foreign exchange rates to use in the translation process and the appropriate treatment of gains and losses resulting from foreign currency exchange rate changes. Alternatives generally accepted in the United States include the long-standing current-non-current method, and a variant thereof, and the monetary-nonmonetary method.

The current-noncurrent method, essentially, translates current assets and current liabilities at rates of exchange prevailing at the balance sheet date while long-term assets, liabilities, and capital are translated at rates prevailing when the assets were acquired, the liabilities incurred, and the capital contributed. Realized gains or losses on foreign exchange typically are charged or credited to operations. Unrealized losses are also charged against current operations; whereas, unrealized gains are preferably deferred.[4] A variant of this approach, however, is permitted by Accounting Principles Board (APB) Opinion No. 6, in which long-term receivables and payables also may be translated at the current rate.[5] The monetary-nonmonetary approach distinguishes between monetary and nonmonetary items which many feel is more appropriate. Under this approach, monetary items are translated at the current rate while nonmonetary items are translated at the historical rate. While Hepworth[6] would favor recognizing all gains and losses immediately, accounting practice, for the most part, conforms to the treatment recommended under the method previously described.

THE RESTATE-TRANSLATE PROPOSAL[7]

While all translation methods described find support in practice,[8]

---

[4] American Institute of Certified Public Accountants, *Accounting Research Bulletin No. 43* (New York: AICPA, 1953), chap. 12, pars. 8 and 9.
[5] American Institute of Certified Public Accountants, "Status of Accounting Research Bulletins," *Accounting Principles Board Opinion No. 6* (New York: AICPA, 1965), par. 18.
[6] Samuel R. Hepworth, "Accounting Problems in Foreign Operations," *NAA Research Report No. 36* (New York: National Association of Accountants, 1960).
[7] While the following comments may be generalized to any country, we will adopt

they are being criticized more and more for producing financial statement effects which distort a subsidiary's financial picture. To begin, traditional translation techniques assume that foreign inflation is offset exactly by depreciation in the value of that country's currency. Thus, if a long-lived asset were transferred from a U.S. parent to one of its foreign subsidiaries at a cost of $100, with the foreign exchange rate at $1 to 2 units of foreign currency (FC2), the asset would be recorded on the subsidiary's books at FC200. If the general price level of the foreign country should rise 100 percent, traditional translation methods assume that the foreign exchange rate would depreciate, proportionately, to $1 to FC4. Thus, a restated asset of FC400 still would retain its original dollar valuation of $100. Empirical evidence, however, suggests that inflation and devaluation are not perfectly negatively correlated.[9] The direct implication of this finding is that the financial position statements of foreign affiliates, translated in conformity with traditional methods of translation, may be subject to significant distortion.

Traditional translation techniques produce distortions on the income statement as well. It has been demonstrated, for example, that inventories — held by a foreign subsidiary during an accounting period in which the foreign currency depreciates relative to the U.S. dollar and which is resold during a subsequent period — will result usually in an understatement of first-period profits and an overstatement of profits reported in the subsequent period.[10]

Traditional translation methods are suspect, also, from a managerial viewpoint. Foreign exchange losses and gains are said to provide managers with little insight unless they are adjusted to reflect changing internal price levels. Local pricing decisions, capital expenditure policies, inter- and intracountry comparisons, external sourcing decisions, and the like, are difficult without such information.[11]

To remedy these shortcomings, Zenoff and Zwick propose, for consolidation purposes, that the financial accounts of foreign subsidiaries

the perspective of a U.S. parent which operates a number of foreign subsidiaries abroad.

[8] See Thomas G. Evans, "Diversity in Foreign Currency Translation Methods: A Proposal for Uniformity," *CPA* (February 1974): 41-45.

[9] Robert L. Aliber and Clyde P. Stickney, "Accounting Measures of Foreign Exchange Exposure: The Long and Short of It," *Accounting Review* (January 1975): 44-57.

[10] See Gerhard G. Mueller, *International Accounting* (New York: Macmillan Co., 1967), p. 182.

[11] David B. Zenoff and Jack Zwick, *International Financial Management* (Englewood Cliffs, N.J.: Prentice-Hall, 1969), p. 500.

be restated, first to reflect changes in the purchasing power of the foreign currency unit and then translated into their U.S.-dollar equivalents, using a single foreign currency exchange rate — the rate of exchange in effect at the financial statement date.[12]

The purported advantages of the restate-translate proposal are that it:

1. Enables statement readers to assess ordinary operating results in terms of local currency as well as the effect of foreign inflation on these results.
2. Enables management to better gauge the performance of a subsidiary after providing for "maintenance" of affiliate assets.
3. Enables management to evaluate the performance of a subsidiary in terms of the environment in which the subsidiary's assets are domiciled.
4. Enables management to ascertain the effect of currency devaluation on a subsidiary's operating results if devaluation occurs.

Other proposals that appear to be consistent with the restate-translate construct (or some variant thereof) include a recent study by the Financial Executives Research Foundation,[13] a study on foreign accounting by Parkinson of the Canadian institute,[14] another by Schwayder,[15] and a report by the Committee on International Accounting of the American Accounting Association.[16]

THE TRANSLATE-RESTATE PROPOSAL

The restate-translate proposal was challenged first in an article by Rosenfield[17] and more recently in an article coauthored by Lorensen and Rosenfield.[18] Rosenfield argues that the restate-translate method results in a unit of measure that reflects multiple standards in terms

---

[12] Ibid.
[13] Edward C. Bursk, John Dearden, David F. Hawkins, and Victor M. Longstreet, *Financial Control of Multinational Operations* (New York: Financial Executives Research Foundation, 1971), p. 43.
[14] R. MacDonald Parkinson, *Translation of Foreign Currencies* (Toronto: Canadian Institute of Chartered Accountants, 1972), p. 111.
[15] Keith R. Schwayder, "Accounting for Exchange Rate Fluctuations," *Accounting Review* (October 1972): 759-60.
[16] Committee on International Accounting, *Report to the Financial Accounting Standards Board on Accounting for Foreign Currency Translation* (Sarasota, Florida: American Accounting Association, June 1974), p. 7.
[17] Paul Rosenfield, "General Price-Level Accounting and Foreign Operations," *Journal of Accountancy* (February 1971): 58-65.
[18] Leonard Lorensen and Paul Rosenfield, "Management Information and Foreign Inflation," *Journal of Accountancy* (December 1974): 98-102.

of general purchasing power — that is, translating the restated accounts of foreign affiliates domiciled in a number of different countries results in dollars of mixed foreign purchasing power. This, in turn, results not only in information that is ambiguous, but unintelligible and noncomparable as well. One reason for this is due purportedly to the fact that goods and services generally purchased by a unit of money in one country, are seldom the same as those generally purchased by a unit of money in another (the type of goods and services and the quantities purchased differ in each country). "Even if the same goods and services were purchased in the same quantities in the two countries the two units of money would almost certainly not buy the same quantities of goods and services in general."[19] Thus, five Argentine pesos ($a5) may equal $1 in foreign exchange markets. However, $a5 might purchase five hours of labor in Argentina while $1 might purchase less than one-half hour in the United States. In a more recent article, Lorensen and Rosenfield continue their case against the Zenoff and Zwick model, arguing that neither headquarters management nor U.S. investors are interested in foreign purchasing power; nor is either group interested in purchasing foreign goods and services. They are more interested in purchasing goods and services in the United States and, since they are interested really in U.S. purchasing power, this is the information that should be provided.[20]

Restate-translate critics support adoption of what may be called the translate-restate proposal, originally recommended in APB statement 3.[21] Statement 3 advocates that the financial accounts of U.S. foreign subsidiaries should be translated first into U.S. dollars, then restated to U.S. purchasing power equivalents, using the index of changes in the general price level in the United States. The merit of the proposal, according to Lorensen and Rosenfield, is that it not only reveals the financial statement effects of changes in foreign currency exchange rates but discloses the effect of U.S. inflation on the prospective returns to U.S. investors. In short, consolidated accounts, prepared accordingly to the prescriptions of APB statement 3, would be expressed in terms of a single standard of measure (namely, dollars of U.S. purchasing power), and would provide a perspective more germane to U.S. investors and management.

---

[19] Rosenfield, "Price-Level Accounting," p. 60.

[20] Lorensen and Rosenfield, "Management Information," pp. 100-101.

[21] American Institute of Certified Public Accountants, "Financial Statements Restated for General Price Level Changes," *Statement of the Accounting Principles Board No. 3* (New York: AICPA, 1969) : 18-19.

Restate-translate proponents, however, would question the assertion that U.S. investors and managers are not interested in foreign inflation. Envision, for example, an extreme case where a U.S. parent company possesses a single wholly owned subsidiary domiciled in a strongly inflationary economy like present-day England. Under such circumstances, would conventional accounting performance measures of the British subsidiary, translated by using the widely employed monetary-nonmonetary translation method and then restated to U.S. general purchasing power equivalents, really provide U.S. investors with information useful for forecasting their future return streams (which necessarily emanate from sterling transactions)? From a managerial perspective, would not disregard of foreign price-level changes lead to decisions possibly detrimental to the continued well-being of foreign operations, for example, unrealistic pricing and replacement decisions? Or, take the case of a U.S. multinational company with a worldwide network of foreign affiliates. Would not foreign inflation adjustments facilitate (1) inter- and intracountry comparisons of relative subsidiary performance, and (2) resource allocation decisions with respect to the various subsidiaries? Questions such as these suggest that the Lorensen-Rosenfield proposal is not without shortcomings.

THE CONTROVERSY IN PERSPECTIVE

In view of the many features associated with these competing proposals, how does one choose between them? Is the restate-translate construct conceptually superior to the translate-restate alternative? Or is the converse true? Proponents on both sides of the controversy thus far have refused to give ground.

In the author's opinion, arguing in this vein is apt to prove fruitless; for, in the absence of explicit choice criteria, it is impossible to resolve the issue in a satisfactory way. Arguing that a General Motors Cadillac is better than a Volkswagen Beetle, without specifying some decision criteria, is likewise pointless.

It might be best at this point to consider the broader picture by asking the question, What is it that we ought to be measuring? On a more fundamental level, What is the purpose of the accounting measurement process?

In October 1973 the American Institute of Certified Public Accountants published a significant piece of literature. Entitled *The Objectives of Financial Statements,* the study, chaired by the late Robert M. Trueblood, makes explicit the objectives of the external financial reporting process.[22] One of the specified objectives of the study is "to provide information useful to investors and creditors for predicting, comparing, and evaluating potential cash flows to them...."[23] Thus, one of the fundamental objectives of accounting is to provide information which is useful to investors, that is, information that is decision-relevant. Determining what is relevant, in turn, requires examination of an investor's decision model. Only by examining decision models can we really identify what measurement attributes are called for by these models.[24] Note that the concern here is with information relevant to an investor's decision model rather than information relevant to the decision maker. While the two can and should be the same, they need not be. Sterling offers a beautiful example in this regard:

We service a large number of decision-makers (e.g., investors and potential investors), many of whom have demonstrably erroneous ideas about which attributes are relevant to their decisions. For example, despite the fact that the efficient market research has demonstrated that "technical analysis" (price charting) is of no use in trading the market, many investors and financial analysts still use it. Others use other attributes. It is impossible for us to supply measures of all the attributes that all investors think are relevant. Worse, such attributes are of no help in making the decision despite the fact that decision makers use them and think that they are relevant. Hence we must define relevance in relation to decision models, not decision-makers.[25]

A NORMATIVE INVESTOR DECISION MODEL[26]

Finance literature suggests that the value of a firm's stock is a function of its discounted future dividend stream and the perceived riskiness of that returned stream.[27] *Dividends* are defined as any monies paid to the holder of a security as a consequence of ownership. Dividends are, in turn, primarily a function of a firm's net operating cash flows. Thus, the higher a firm's net operating cash flows the higher the po-

[22] *The Objectives of Financial Statements* (New York: American Institute of CPAs, October 1973).
[23] Ibid., p. 20.
[24] For example, see Robert R. Sterling, "Decision-Oriented Financial Accounting," *Accounting and Business Research* (Summer 1972).
[25] Robert R. Sterling, "Relevant Financial Reporting in an Age of Price Changes," *Journal of Accountancy* (February 1975): p. 44.
[26] The following draws on the model developed by Lawrence Revsine in his *Replacement Cost Accounting* (Englewood Cliffs, N.J.: Prentice-Hall, 1973).
[27] While some portfolio theorists imply that accounting information may not be useful in assessing the risk of an individual security, this can be shown to be incorrect. For a demonstration of the consistency between the single security partial equilibrium model and the single period capital asset pricing model, see Frederick D. S. Choi, "Financial Disclosure in Relation to a Firm's Capital Costs," *Accounting and Business Research* (Autumn 1973).

tential dividend streams to investors, and conversely. Since managers reportedly are reluctant to lower dividends once established, for fear of an adverse effect on the company's share prices in the marketplace, they are understandably interested in maintaining the level of a firm's net operating cash flows over time.

Net operating cash flows of a firm are a function of both the firm's physical and technological capacity to produce goods and services, and the prevailing prices of its factor and product markets. Since management has limited, if any, control over the latter, maintaining the firm's physical capacity to produce is extremely important. It is the one strategic variable that management can control in striving to maintain operating cash flows at some minimum level over time.[28]

The foregoing model thus enables us to derive a criterion for evaluating competing inflation accounting options such as the restate-translate versus translate-restate proposals. Specifically, the proposal that generates an operating performance measure that best reflects the preservation of a firm's physical capacity to produce goods and services (and, hence, future dividend-generating potential) is the better alternative from management's viewpoint. And, as long as an income concept reflects the maximum dividend that can be paid during a given period of time without impairing the firm's operating capability, an investor also has a basis for estimating the growth potential of his return stream, based on a given dividend policy (payout percentage).

In the context of our earlier discussion regarding price-level changes, it follows that specific price-level adjustments, rather than general price-level adjustments, are what investors are interested in primarily. For specific price-level adjustments, our current cost model produces a measure of income, disposable cash flows, that is consistent with the criterion just developed.

To sum up, investors — and, therefore management — are interested primarily in the specific purchasing power of a firm rather than its ability to command goods and services in general. Specific purchasing power is what determines the amount of gross operating flows that can be distributed as dividends without reducing a firm's physical capacity to produce. To the extent that general price-level movements are not perfectly positively correlated with specific price behavior, the current cost model provides investors with more reliable information.

---

[28] This assumes that the margin between input and output prices remains the same. See Revsine, *Replacement Cost Accounting*, p. 99.

What implications can we draw from the previous discussion? We have learned that investors are primarily interested in the financial statement effects of specific price changes on the operating performance of a firm. This provides a measure of the firm's operating performance which, in turn, enables investors to formulate realistic expectations regarding cash flows that interest them. We also know that the main purpose of consolidated financial statements is to apprise investors of the achievements of the parent company and its foreign subsidiaries as a whole. Viewed from this perspective the translate–restate–restate–translate competing constructs dilemma becomes trivial. Both models essentially reflect a historical cost orientation. Neither restatement for general price-level changes abroad and translation to U.S. dollars, nor translation to U.S. dollars and restatement for U.S. inflation, changes the valuation framework. A historical cost model, adjusted for changes in the general purchasing power of the monetary unit (whether it be foreign general purchasing power or domestic general purchasing power) is still a historical cost model!

The price-level adjustment procedure which we recommended and which is consistent with our previous decision criterion may be outlined as follows:

1. First restate the financial statements of all subsidiaries, as well as the statements of the parent, to reflect changes in specific price levels.
2. Translate the accounts of all foreign subsidiaries into U.S. dollars using a constant — the current foreign currency exchange rate.

Restating both foreign and domestic accounts into their current cost equivalents is consistent with recommendations of the Accounting Objectives Study Group in that such information is decision-relevant. This information reflects the maximum amount of potential dividend flows an investor can expect to receive in dollars; thus facilitating predictions of future cash flows. This overcomes fundamental shortcomings of the earlier translation–restatement constructs. The translation process, in turn, is simply a neutral process which transforms amounts expressed in foreign money units to a more familiar currency framework — U.S. dollars. This proposal would also facilitate an investor's comparison and evaluation processes since the consolidation results of all firms would be expressed in terms of a common scale — current cost equivalents.

While this study has not explicitly addressed the decision models of management, the current proposal would also appear germane to them. Since managers would report to external decision makers in terms of the standards identified, it would seem logical to manage in these terms as well. In the words of Lorensen and Rosenfield: [29]

The standards of measurement for overall management of all operations, domestic and foreign, must be the same and must be the standard of measurement in the reports to outsiders of the company as a whole.

Thus, the proposed framework should enable headquarters management to better evaluate the relative performance of its subsidiaries since enterprise results would be comparable nationally as well as internationally. To the extent that the current cost reporting framework is universally adopted, local management decisions should be improved as intracountry comparisons of enterprise performance would also be facilitated. As managers were said to be concerned with the maintenance of physical capacity,[30] the proposal should also facilitate more equitable resource allocations within the corporate system — especially when general and specific price levels do not move in parallel fashion.

This proposal, while representing a rather marked departure from earlier formulations, finds support in the writings of Mueller,[31] Schoenfeld,[32] and, particularly, of Arthur Andersen and Co. in their *Accounting Standards for Business Enterprises Throughout the World*.[33] Those who are skeptical of the proposal's operationality should recognize the fact that the highly successful Netherlands-based multinational giant, the Philips Lamp Co., has utilized a variant of this consolidation and reporting framework for years. The company obviously feels that benefits of the approach far exceed the costs involved.[34]

LIMITATIONS OF THE MODEL

In view of the model's conceptual appeal, have we an approach, finally, that will quell the price-level adjustment–foreign currency translation controversy? Not by a long shot!

---

[29] Lorensen and Rosenfield, "Management Information," p. 102.

[30] Recall that this assumes that the margin between input and output prices remains constant.

[31] Gerhard G. Mueller, "Accounting for Multinational Companies," *Cost and Management* (July-August 1971): p. 5.

[32] H. M. Schoenfeld, "Comments on International Accounting in an Inflationary Economy," *Journal of International Accounting* (Fall 1968): 167.

[33] Arthur Andersen and Co., *Accounting Standards for Business Enterprises Throughout the World* (Chicago: Arthur Andersen and Co., 1974): 111-17.

[34] For a recent account of the Philips system see Geoffrey Holmes, "Replacement Value Accounting," *Accountancy* (March 1972): 4-8.

Notwithstanding implementation problems, the proposed approach is based on an assumption which many would question. In translating accounts of foreign subsidiaries at current rates of exchange, it was implicitly assumed that foreign currency translation was a neutral accounting process that merely converted foreign money to domestic currency equivalents. Some writers, however, question this neutrality suggesting that the current exchange rate to some extent mirrors price-level movements in both domestic and foreign countries.[35] To the extent that this is true, the currency translation process may produce results that are not entirely unambiguous.[36] It may even be argued that foreign exchange rates are a function of so many variables — political, economic, and random — that their use as a translation medium should be abandoned altogether!

It is apparent then that the proposed framework is far from a conceptual ideal. In fact, it is doubtful whether there ever will exist any "theoretically clean" solutions to the price-level adjustment–currency translation problem. However, limitations notwithstanding, the proposed framework provides information which is far more decision-relevant than existing constructs that focus on valuation norms not called for by investor decision models. In addition, it should be noted that the translation rate problem is not unique to the current proposal but is a common feature of all models utilizing exchange rates as translation factors.

CONCLUSIONS AND RECOMMENDATIONS: ARE THEY COMPATIBLE?

In view of its conceptual merit, will the proposed price-level adjustment–foreign currency translation combination become generally accepted in the United States? Probably not. The conventional accounting model in the United States and elsewhere appears wedded to the historical cost valuation framework, the logic of which has been well developed in the literature. And while the United States and other countries seriously are considering adjusting financial statements for inflation, they seem concerned primarily with general rather than

---

[35] Archie L. Monroe, "Experimenting with Price-Level Reporting," *Financial Executive* (December 1974): 48.

[36] Recognition of this problem has led some to suggest the use of "constructed" or "adjusted" foreign currency translation rates. For example, see Robert L. Gayton, "General Price Level Accounting and Foreign Operations," *Journal of Accountancy* (September 1971): 38-40; and Richard B. Klein, "Inter-Country Purchasing Power Index Numbers," *Management Accounting* (August 1972): 28-32.

specific price-level adjustments. Indeed, if there is one thing that is revealed by a study of accounting history, it is that the development of accounting principles is not so much a function of theoretical niceties as it is a function of political, institutional, and economic influences that make up the environment of the accounting process.[37] Thus, despite arguments to the contrary, it appears that recommendations advocated in APB statement 3 (and supported in literature by Lorensen and Rosenfield) will become the future norm in this area. That is, translating foreign accounts into U.S. dollars, and then restating for U.S. inflation, is headed for general acceptance in the United States regardless of whether they are really compatible!

Under the circumstances, it may very well be more realistic for us to recognize that, as long as policy prescriptions are valued for their pragmatic and practical appeal, there can be no way of arriving at theoretically sound solutions. In the absence of specific choice criteria derived from investor decision models, it is fruitless to argue the conceptual merits of competing constructs. It may be far more productive to admit that choices in the price-level adjustment–currency translation area are arbitrary at best and should be recognized as such. Readers of financial statements should be made aware that the reported price-level adjustment–foreign currency translation combination is one of several possible alternatives that exist and this information should be disclosed in the consolidated financial statements of multinational corporations. This approach would be more forthright and would minimize the possibility of misleading inferences being drawn by the investing public.

SELECTED BIBLIOGRAPHY

Robert L. Aliber and Clyde P. Stickney. "Accounting Measures of Foreign Exchange Exposure — The Long and Short of It." *Accounting Review,* January 1975, pp. 44-57.

American Institute of Certified Public Accountants. *Accounting Research Bulletin No. 43.* New York: AICPA, 1953, chap. 12, pars. 8 and 9.

———. "Status of Accounting Research Bulletins." *Accounting Principles Board Opinion No. 6.* New York: AICPA, 1965, par. 18.

———. "Financial Statements Restated for General Price Level Changes." *Statement of the Accounting Principles Board No. 3.* New York: AICPA, 1969.

[37] An excellent account in this regard is contained in Stephen A. Zeff's *Forging Accounting Principles in Five Countries: A History and an Analysis of Trends* (New York: Stipes Publishing Co., 1973).

240 ——. *Objectives of Financial Statements.* New York: American Institute of CPAs, October 1973.

Arthur Andersen and Co. *Accounting Standards for Business Enterprises Throughout the World.* Arthur Andersen and Co., 1974.

Edward C. Brusk, John Dearden, David F. Hawkins, and Victor M. Longstreet. *Financial Control of Multinational Operations.* New York: Financial Executives Research Foundation, 1971.

Frederick D. S. Choi. "Financial Disclosure in Relation to a Firm's Capital Costs." *Accounting and Business Research.* Autumn 1973, pp. 282-92.

Committee on International Accounting. *Report to the Financial Accounting Standards Board on Accounting for Foreign Currency Translation.* Florida: American Accounting Association, June 1974.

Thomas G. Evans, "Diversity in Foreign Currency Translation Methods: A Proposal for Uniformity." *CPA,* February 1974, pp. 41-45.

Robert L. Gayton. "General Price-Level Accounting and Foreign Operations." *Journal of Accountancy,* September 1971, pp. 38-40.

Samuel R. Hepworth. "Accounting Problems in Foreign Operations." *NAA Research Report No. 36.* New York: National Association of Accountants, 1960.

Geoffrey Holmes. "Replacement Value Accounting." *Accountancy,* March 1972, pp. 4-8.

Richard B. Klein. "Inter-Country Purchasing Power Index Numbers." *Management Accounting,* August 1972, pp. 28-32.

Leonard Lorensen and Paul Rosenfield. "Management Information and Foreign Inflation." *Journal of Accountancy,* December 1974, pp. 98-102.

Robert G. May, Gerhard G. Mueller, and Thomas H. Williams. *A New Introduction to Financial Accounting.* Englewood Cliffs, N.J.: Prentice-Hall, 1973.

Archie L. Monroe. "Experimenting with Price-Level Reporting." *Financial Executive,* December 1974, pp. 38-48.

Gerhard G. Mueller. *International Accounting.* New York: Macmillan Company, 1967.

——. "Accounting for Multinational Companies." *Cost and Management,* July-August 1971, pp. 28-34.

R. M. Parkinson. *Translation of Foreign Currencies.* Toronto: Canadian Institute of Chartered Accountants, 1972.

Lawrence Revsine. *Replacement Cost Accounting.* Englewood Cliffs, N.J.: Prentice-Hall, 1973.

Paul Rosenfield. "General Price-Level Accounting and Foreign Operations." *Journal of Accountancy,* February 1971, pp. 58-65.

R. W. Scapens. "The Treatment of Inflation Overseas." *Accountancy,* September 1973, pp. 10-16.

H. M. Schoenfeld. "Comments on International Accounting in an Inflationary Economy." *Journal of International Accounting,* Fall 1968, pp. 165-68.

Keith R. Schwayder. "Accounting for Exchange Rate Fluctuations." *Accounting Review,* October 1972, pp. 747-60.

Robert R. Sterling. "Decision-Oriented Financial Accounting." *Accounting and Business Research,* Summer 1972, pp. 198-208.

————. "Relevant Financial Reporting in an Age of Price Changes." *Journal of Accountancy,* February 1975, pp. 42-51.

David B. Zenoff and Jack Zwick. *International Financial Management.* Englewood Cliffs, N.J.: Prentice-Hall, 1969.

Stephen A. Zeff. *Forging Accounting Principles in Five Countries: A History and an Analysis of Trends.* New York: Stipes Publishing Co., 1972.

APPENDIX: PRICE-LEVEL ADJUSTMENTS AND FOREIGN CURRENCY TRANSLATION — A CASE STUDY*

The effects of accounting for inflation are shown by applying the restate-translate and translate-restate methods of accounting to the Esso Petroleum Company, Ltd., of England, a subsidiary of the American-based Exxon Corporation. The analysis is based on the following hypothesis: Use by a foreign subsidiary of a price-level adjusting index in conjunction with either the restate-translate or the translate-restate method of accounting affects the consolidated financial statements of the parent company. Our purpose is not (1) to propound the benefits of one translation method over another, (2) to suggest the best general price-level index, or (3) to establish the merits of the restate-translate over the translate-restate methodology or vice versa.

The general formula for the application of the restate-translate method was to use the U.K. consumer price index (CPI) for any restatements and combine it with the December 31, 1972, spot rate for translating all liabilities and assets in the British accounts into U.S. dollars. The general formula for the translate-restate method application was to use the monetary-nonmonetary method of translation according to the rules set forth in the 1973 Exxon annual report. This meant the application of historic exchange rates to nonmonetary items. The U.S. consumer price index (CPI) was then used for price-level-based restatements of the accounts. For consistency between the two methods (restate-translate and translate-restate), the consumer price index for both the United States and the United Kingdom was employed. The authors, however, recognize that there exists a general preference for the general index of retail prices (RPI) as an indicator of changes in the general purchasing power of the pound sterling. Yet since general purchasing power indexes of both the U.S. dollar and the British pound were needed, elimination of a source of possible bias

---

* Prepared by Rex Carlaw and Elizabeth Raleigh, both MBA students at the University of Washington.

through use of a comparable index was considered more important than preference for a particular index choice.

Several assumptions are made in this case either to facilitate analysis or to compensate for a lack of information. These assumptions are:

1. Esso Petroleum Company, Ltd., was purchased by Exxon Corporation in January 1969 (actual purchase year — 1951).
2. Fixed assets in 1969 are valued assuming acquisition that year. Incremental differences for years 1970-72 are interpreted as new fixed assets and valued accordingly.
3. Inventory listed on the balance sheet (12/31/72) is assumed to have been purchased within the fourth quarter of 1972.
4. Acceptances payable, overdrafts, and loans that are listed on the balance sheet (12/31/72) are assumed to have been acquired in 1972.
5. Loans from associated companies, share capital, and investments listed on the balance sheet (12/31/72) are assumed to have been acquired in 1969.
6. Deferred taxes and credits are assumed to be from the prior year 1971.
7. Reserves listed on the balance sheet is a "plug-in" figure.

Conclusion

In general, the results arrived at in exhibits 1 through 3 clearly show that use of either the restate-translate or translate-restate method has a rather significant differential effect on the parent company's consolidated financial statements.

Exhibit 1. Restate-Translate   243

Esso Petroleum Company, Ltd.*
Consolidated Income Statement 1972
(in thousands)

	1972	U.K. CPI	Restate	Rate	Translate
Turnover	723,953	A	735,613	I	1,727,293
Customs/excise	316,069	A	321,159	I	754,113
NET SALES	407,884		414,158		973,180
Trading profit (after depreciation)*	57,723	A	54,610	I	128,229
Interest and dividends receivable	4,989	A	5,069	I	11,903
Profit association company	48	A	49	I	115
TOTAL	62,760		59,728		140,247
Interest payable	15,707	No change	15,707	I	36,882
Taxation	19,116	A	19,116	I	44,886
Minority interest	12	A	12	I	28
Foreign exchange adjustment	d3,982	A	d4,046	I	d9,500
NET PROFIT	23,943		20,847		48,951
Depreciation expense*	20,210		24,578		57,712

Exhibit 1 (cont.)

Esso Petroleum Company, Ltd.*
Consolidated Balance Sheet, December 31, 1972
(in thousands)

ASSETS		1972	U.K. CPI	Restate	Rate	Translate
Cash and banks		5,823	No change	5,823	I	13,673
Receivables		73,758	No change	73,758	I	173,191
Inventory		65,924	B	66,115	I	155,245
TOTAL CURRENT		145,505		145,969		342,109
Accounts receivable		91,248	No change	91,248	I	214,259
Fixed assets	(1969)	238,076	C	276,065	I	648,228
(after deprecia-						
tion)*	(1970)	19,756	D	21,626	I	50,780
	(1971)	20,871	E	21,847	I	51,299
	(1972)	23,661	A	24,042	I	56,453
Investments		1,852	No change	1,852	I	4,349
TOTAL ASSETS		540,969		582,425		1,367,477
LIABILITIES						
Accounts payable and accrued		35,788	No change	35,788	I	84,403
Due subsidiaries		2,000	No change	2,000	I	4,696
Taxes		236	No change	236	I	554
Dividends (gross)		7,000	No change	7,000	I	16,437
Acceptances payable		18,950	No change	18,950	I	44,496
Overdrafts, loans		22,638	No change	22,638	I	53,156
TOTAL CURRENT		86,612		86,612		203,373
Share capital		100,000	C	115,957	I	272,279
Reserves		65,322	...	90,780	...	312,046
Loans from association		154,498	No change	154,498	I	362,777
Minority interest		256	C	297	I	697
Loans		83,734	No change	83,734	I	196,616
Deferred tax		37,410	No change	37,410	I	87,842
Deferred credits		9,434	No change	9,434	I	22,152
Employee benefit		3,703	No change	3,703	I	8,695
TOTAL LIABILITIES		540,969		582,425		1,367,477
Accumulated depreciation*		167,620		190,412		447,105

* Income and balance sheet figures were obtained from *Moody's Industrial Manual* 1972, p. 1,781.

Exhibit 2. Translate-Restate   245

Esso Petroleum Company, Ltd.
Consolidated Income Statement 1972
(in thousands)

	1972	Rate	Translate	U.S. CPI	Restate
Turnover	723,953	VI	1,699,480	a	1,760,558
Customs/excise	316,069	VI	741,972	a	768,638
NET SALES	407,884		957,508		991,920
Trading profit (after depreciation)*	57,723	I	132,254	a	125,849
Interest and dividends receivable	4,989	VI	11,712	a	12,133
Profit association company	48	VI	113	a	117
TOTAL	62,760		144,079		138,099
Interest payable	15,707	I	36,882	No change	36,882
Taxation	19,116	I	44,886	No change	44,886
Minority interest	12	I	28	a	29
Foreign exchange adjustment	d3,982	I	d9,350	a	d9,686
NET PROFIT	23,943		52,933		46,616
Depreciation expense*	20,210		50,740		63,722

Exhibit 2 (cont.)

Esso Petroleum Company, Ltd.
Consolidated Balance Sheet, December 31, 1972
(in thousands)

ASSETS	1972	Rate	Translate	U.S. CPI	Restate
Cash and banks	5,823	I	13,673	No change	13,673
Receivables	73,758	I	173,191	No change	173,191
Inventory	65,924	I	154,769	b	155,526
TOTAL CURRENT	145,505		341,633		342,390
Accounts receivable	91,248	I	214,259	No change	214,259
Fixed assets (1969)	238,076	III	571,525	c	738,220
(after (1970)	19,756	IV	47,292	d	57,428
depreciation)* (1971)	20,871	V	53,273	e	59,100
(1972)	23,661	VI	55,544	a	57,540
Investments	1,852	III	4,446	No change	4,446
TOTAL ASSETS	540,969		1,287,972		1,473,383

LIABILITIES

Accounts payable and accrued	35,788	VI	84,012	No change	84,012
Due subsidiaries	2,000	I	4,696	No change	4,696
Taxes	236	I	554	No change	554
Dividends (gross)	7,000	I	16,437	No change	16,437
Acceptances payable	18,950	VI	44,485	No change	44,485
Overdrafts, loans	22,638	VI	53,143	No change	53,143
TOTAL CURRENT	86,612		203,327		203,327
Share capital	100,000	III	240,060	c	310,077
Reserves	65,322	. . .	143,808	. . .	259,023
Loans from association	154,498	III	370,888	No change	370,888
Minority interest	256	III	615	c	794
Loans	83,734	III	201,012	No change	201,012
Deferred tax	37,410	V	95,489	No change	95,489
Deferred credits	9,434	V	24,080	No change	24,080
Employee benefit	3,703	VI	8,693	No change	8,693
TOTAL LIABILITIES	540,969		1,287,972		1,473,383
Accumulated depreciation*	167,620		403,384		505,511

* Income and balance sheet figures were obtained from *Moody's Industrial Manual* 1972, p. 1,781.

Exhibit 3. Comparative Results: Percentage Increases of both Restate-Translate and Translate-Restate Methods Over Exxon's Translation Method Alone

Income statement	Exxon's amount	R-T T-R	Change	Percent increase
Net profit	56,218	48,951 46,616	7,267 9,602	12.93 17.08
Net sales	957,508	973,180 991,920	15,672 34,412	1.64 3.60
Balance sheet				
Total assets	1,287,972	1,367,477 1,473,175	79,505 185,203	6.173 14.380
Current assets	341,633	342,109 342,390	476 757	0.139 0.220
Inventory	154,769	155,245 155,526	476 757	0.310 0.489
Fixed assets	727,634	806,760 912,288	79,126 184,654	10.870 25.377
Current liabilities	203,327	203,373 203,327	46 0	0.023 0.000

Exhibit 4. References and Notations

United Kingdom Consumer Price Indexes*		*Notation*
Dec. 31, 1972/1972 average = 138.8/136.6	= 1.016	A
Dec. 31, 1972/1972 fourth-quarter average = 138.8/138.4	= 1.00289	B
Dec. 31, 1972/1969 average = 138.8/119.7	= 1.1596	C
Dec. 31, 1972/1970 average = 138.8/126.8	= 1.0946	D
Dec. 31, 1972/1971 average = 138.8/132.6	= 1.0468	E

United States Consumer Price Indexes

Dec. 31, 1972/1972 average = 164.3/158.6	= 1.03594	a
Dec. 31, 1972/1972 fourth-quarter average = 164.3/163.5	= 1.004893	b
Dec. 31, 1972/1969 average = 164.3/127.2	= 1.292	c
Dec. 31, 1972/1970 average = 164.3/135.3	= 1.21434	d
Dec. 31, 1972/1971 average = 164.3/148.1	= 1.1094	e

Spot Rates

December 31, 1972	= 2.3481	I
1972 fourth-quarter average	= 2.3475	II
1969 average	= 2.4006	III
1970 average	= 2.3938	IV
1971 average	= 2.5525	V
1972 average	= 2.3475	VI

Exxon's Rules for Translation**

1. Translate at rate of acquisition: property, plant, equipment, investments, deferred charges, and credits; depreciation according to related asset.
2. Translate at year end rate: remaining assets and liabilities.
3. Translate at average rate during year: revenue and expenses.

---

* Indexes and spot rates were obtained from the International Monetary Fund's *International Financial Statistics*.
** 1973 Exxon Annual Report.

INFLATION ACCOUNTING

CHAPTER 17

A comparison of various international proposals on inflation accounting: a practitioner's view*
William P. Hauworth II

INTRODUCTION

Unfortunately, most countries now suffer from rampant inflation. This obviously has many adverse effects. It also has one effect that many consider beneficial. It has provided a stimulus for the accounting profession in many countries, and the governments in a few countries, to develop accounting systems that recognize effects of price changes. Some systems recognize effects of changes in the prices of specific items, some effects of changes in the general level of prices, and others effects of both types of changes.

This paper summarizes and compares the methods to give an accounting recognition to the effects of changing prices that are now required or have been proposed in a number of countries throughout the world.

PRICE-LEVEL ACCOUNTING

The methods now used in the primary or basic financial statements in three countries — Argentina, Brazil, and Chile — are based on price-level or general purchasing-power or constant-dollar accounting. These methods, with certain exceptions, retain the historical cost basis of accounting and reflect effects of changes in the general level of prices.

* William P. Hauworth II is a partner of Arthur Andersen & Co., Chicago. He has served as chairman of the International Practice Technical Standards Committee of the AICPA and is a member of that organization's Accountants International Study Group.

* This article is reprinted, with permission, from *The International Journal of Accounting: Education and Research* (Fall 1980) pp 63–82

Argentina

For a number of years, Argentina has had a high rate of inflation, frequently in three digits. As a result, the profession has actively promoted price-level accounting for some time. In 1971, a professional organization in Argentina published a recommendation advocating the presentation of price-level adjusted financial statements. A subsequent professional pronouncement required financial statements for periods ending on or after September 30, 1976, to include price-level adjusted financial statements as supplementary information in a second column next to the unadjusted balances or in a note.

In 1979, the Argentine accounting profession issued a further pronouncement that requires price-level adjusted financial statements to be presented as the primary financial statements for periods ending on or after September 30, 1979. To comply with legal requirements, unadjusted statements, which reflect price-level or appraisal adjustments of property and depreciation accounts but not of other accounts, must be presented as supplemental information. Argentine auditors now express opinions on the price-level adjusted statements in terms of fairness in accordance with generally accepted accounting principles and on the unadjusted statements in terms of compliance with legal requirements.

The price-level adjusted financial statements are required to reflect a comprehensive restatement that adjusts nonmonetary items for the change in the purchasing power of the peso from their date of origin to the balance-sheet date and presents the gain or loss in the purchasing power of net monetary items held during the period. Alternatively, a simplified approach can be used in restating certain nonmonetary items. Under this approach,

1. Marketable securities are stated at market value at the balance-sheet date.
2. Inventories are stated at current value.
3. Property, and plant and equipment accounts are stated at the restated amounts determined for book purposes in accordance with Argentine law or at appraised amounts.
4. Investments in business enterprises over which the investor exercises significant influence are stated at amounts determined by applying the equity method to the price-level adjusted financial statements of the investees.

Companies not listed on the stock exchange or not subject to special government regulation can follow a simplified approach in their adjusted income statements. Instead of restating individual items of income and expense and presenting the gain or loss from holding monetary items, they can present the effects of inflation in a single amount based on the change in restated net assets during the period. Any prior-period comparative financial statements presented are restated in terms of the purchasing power of the peso at the end of the current period.

Brazil

For some time, Brazilian legislation has required certain price-level adjustments to be reflected in financial statements. The method presently used in calculating the adjustments is specified in the 1976 Corporation Law, which requires three adjustments to be made.

The first restates permanent assets (which consist principally of property, plant and equipment, and long-term investments) and deferred charges based on the change during the year in a specified general price index. The second restates beginning net worth accounts based on the change in the same index. The third restates depreciation and amortization of permanent assets and deferred charges. The restatement of permanent assets is credited, and the restatements of the net worth accounts and depreciation and amortization are charged to current income.

These procedures are simple, and the results of applying them differ significantly from those obtained through comprehensive price-level adjustments only in that (1) inventory is treated as a monetary asset; and (2) no provision is made for updating prior-period financial statements.

Chile

For some years, Chilean law has required companies to restate their "invested capital" annually by applying the percentage increase in the consumer price index. The law also requires that property, and plant and equipment be restated in an amount equal to the lesser of (1) the amount by which invested capital is restated or (2) the amount determined by applying the percentage increase in the consumer price index to the property, and plant and equipment accounts. Depreciation is based on the restated amounts. If the restatement of invested capital exceeds the restatement of property, and plant and equipment, the excess or 20 percent of taxable income, whichever is less, must be charged to income.

In a number of countries, the accounting profession has issued standards, provisional standards, and exposure drafts dealing with the supplemental disclosure of current cost-accounting information. These countries include Australia, Canada, Germany, the Netherlands, New Zealand, South Africa, and the United Kingdom.

Australia

In Australia, the profession has issued a "provisional standard" that deals with "current-cost accounting" and "strongly recommends" that listed companies and public corporations include in their financial statements the following supplemental information on a current-cost basis: current cost of fixed assets and inventories, depreciation expense, and cost of goods sold.

The principal terms of the provisional standard are the following:

1. Nonmonetary assets are to be stated at the lower of current cost (less accumulated depreciation, where applicable) and recoverable amount as of the balance-sheet date. In this regard

a. Current cost is the lowest cost at which the asset's service potential, when the asset was first acquired by the entity, could currently be obtained by the entity in the normal course of business.

b. Recoverable amount is the amount expected to be recovered (i) from the total net cash revenues less all relevant cash expenses from the asset's continued use and/or (ii) through its sale.

2. A restatement of the current cost of an asset is to be credited or charged directly to a special surplus account, which is referred to as the "current-cost adjustment account."

3. Cost of goods sold is to be stated at the current cost of the goods at the time of sale or, if the goods had previously been written down to their recoverable amount, at that amount.

4. Depreciation is to be reported based on the average-for-the-period of the assets' current cost or, for assets carried at recoverable amounts, on the basis of that amount.

The Australian profession has issued two exposure drafts dealing with monetary items in the context of current-cost accounting. The latest provides for reporting "profit and gearing gains attributable to shareholders" and "entity net profits." The former reflects gains and losses in the purchasing power of all monetary items as well as adjustments to state depreciation and cost of sales at current cost. The latter reverses the gain or loss in the purchasing power of "loan capital."

The exposure draft provides for computing the purchasing-power gains and losses by:

1. Applying to trade receivables and trade payables the percentage change during the period in the current cost of the inputs of goods and services that are principally responsible for the balances of trade payables and the products whose sales generate the trade receivables.
2. Applying the percentage change during the year in the general price level to the monetary items of an enterprise whose business is the lending of money.
3. Applying to loan capital the percentage change in the general price level.
4. Applying to other monetary assets and liabilities the percentage change in a price-index representative of inputs of goods and services during the period or, if this is impracticable, in a general price index.

The gain or loss in the purchasing power of all monetary assets and liabilities is to be credited or charged to income with an offsetting entry to the current-cost adjustment account. Below the caption "profit and gearing gains attributable to shareholders," the gain or loss in the purchasing power of loan capital is to be reversed and taken to a "gearing gains reserve account" included in shareholders' equity. The final caption in the income statement, "entity net profits," excludes the gain or loss on loan capital.

In March 1980, the Australian profession issued a further exposure draft that deals with the extention of current-cost accounting to non-monetary items in addition to inventories and property. Its provisions are generally consistent with those of the provisional standard.

Canada

The Canadian Institute of Chartered Accountants issued a discussion paper on current-value accounting in 1976 and, after considering the responses to that paper, issued an exposure draft entitled "Current Cost Accounting" in December 1979. The draft proposes requiring certain enterprises to present supplementary current-cost information together with their annual historical cost financial statements. The enterprises affected are those whose securities are publicly traded and that have either (1) inventories and property, and plant and equipment (before deducting accumulated depreciation, depletion, and amortization) totalling at least $50 million or; (2) total assets of at least $350 million.

An enterprise presenting supplementary current-cost information is to present "current cost income of the enterprise" and "current cost income attributable to shareholders."

The "current cost income of the enterprise" is intended to present income after providing for the impact of specific price changes on the productive assets needed to maintain the enterprise's operating capability, whether they are financed by equity capital or debt. It is to be determined by making the following adjustments to historical cost income before deducting interest expense and income taxes.

1. A depreciation adjustment, representing the difference between depreciation for the period calculated on the current cost of property, plant and equipment, and the depreciation charged in the historical cost financial statements;

2. A cost of sales adjustment, representing the difference between the current cost, at the date of sale of goods sold during the period and the cost of goods sold charged in the historical cost financial statements;

3. A net-productive monetary-items adjustment to provide for the effect of specific price changes during the period on the net-productive monetary items required to support the operating capability of the enterprise; and

4. Any other material adjustments required to allow for the impact of specific price changes on the productive assets of the enterprise, for example, adjustments relating to disposals of items of property, and plant and equipment during the period.

The exposure draft defines current cost as the amount of cash or other consideration, measured in units of money, that would be needed to acquire an asset identical or equivalent to that owned. Acquisition might be either by purchase or production, as appropriate in the circumstances of the enterprise. The use of current cost as a measurement of an asset owned by an enterprise is subject to the restriction that:

1. In the case of assets held for sale, the measurement of the asset should not exceed net realizable value; and

2. In the case of assets held for use in the enterprise, the measurement of the asset should not exceed value in use, which is the net present value of future cash flows expected to result from the use of an asset in the enterprise and from its ultimate disposition.

The net productive monetary items with respect to which an adjustment is to be made are (1) short-term trade receivables, accruals, and prepaid expenses; (2) inventories not subject to a cost of sales adjustment; and (3) cash balances required for the conduct of day-to-day operating activities; net of (a) short-term trade payables and accruals; and (b) short-term loans required for the conduct of day-to-day operating activities.

The exposure draft states that calculation of the adjustment requires that relevant rates of price change be identified for each component of net productive monetary items. For example, the adjustment relating to receivables is to reflect changes in the current cost of goods or services sold that are attributable to changes in prices of the materials, labor, and other inputs, used to produce the goods. In many instances, changes in selling prices may provide an appropriate guide. Where payables are concerned, the adjustment is to reflect changes in the current cost of items that have been financed by those payables.

In addition to "current cost income of the enterprise," the supplementary information is to present "current cost income attributable to shareholders." This is intended to reflect the costs and benefits to the shareholders of financing a portion of the enterprise's productive assets with borrowed funds. It is determined by adjusting current-cost income of the enterprise to provide for income taxes and, when the productive assets of the enterprise are partly financed by net borrowings, to reflect the interest cost of debt, dividends on nonparticipating preferred shares, and a financing adjustment.

The financing adjustment is to reflect the realized cost or benefit to shareholders of financing productive assets with net borrowings. It is calculated by (1) determining the ratio of net borrowings to the sum of net borrowings and shareholders' equity, and (2) applying this ratio to the total of the current-cost adjustments reflected in the computation of current-cost income of the enterprise.

The exposure draft states that per share data should be presented for current-cost income attributable to the shareholders.

In addition to the income statement data, the supplementary information is to disclose the carrying value of inventory and property, and plant and equipment on a current-cost basis, compared with the corresponding net book amounts reported in the historical cost financial statements.

The exposure draft also provides for the presentation of a statement of changes in shareholders' equity giving effect to the restatement of inventory and property, and plant and equipment on a current-cost basis. The statement is to disclose separately the following items:

1. The change in the amount required to maintain the operating capability of the enterprise, distinguishing amounts attributable to:
   a. An increase/decrease in the current cost of property, and plant and equipment during the period;
   b. An increase/decrease in the current cost of inventory during the period; and
   c. An increase/decrease in net productive monetary items due to specific price changes during the period;
2. The amount of the financing adjustment; and
3. Current-cost income for the period attributable to shareholders.

Germany

In 1975, the German profession issued a pronouncement recommending that certain supplementary replacement-cost information be presented in a note to annual financial statements. The information relates to assets financed by equity, and the pronouncement is based on the assumption that equity is used first to finance property, and plant and equipment, then to finance inventories, and finally to finance other assets. The information to be disclosed is (1) the excess of replacement cost over historical cost depreciation, and (2) the amount required to maintain the operating capacity of inventory.

If the amount of equity is *less* than the amount of property, and plant and equipment, the excess of replacement cost over historical cost depreciation to be reported is the total excess multiplied by the ratio of equity to property, and plant and equipment. In that event, no amount is reported with respect to inventory.

If the amount of equity exceeds the amount of property, and plant and equipment, the amount required to maintain the operating capacity of inventory is determined by applying the percentage-price increase during the year relating to items included in ending inventory to the amount of the beginning inventory. If the ratio of (1) equity less property, and plant and equipment to (2) inventory is *less* than 1.0, this ratio is applied to the amount determined by applying the percentage price increase, and the result is the amount to be disclosed.

The German government is opposed to the presentation of accounting information that recognizes effects of price changes on the basis that presenting the information may increase inflation. Thus, the government has not supported the profession's recommendation, and relatively few companies have applied it.

The Netherlands

In the Netherlands, a commission composed of representatives from industry, the trade unions, and the accounting profession issues pronouncements on accounting matters. It has issued a recommendation that states that information that is more meaningful than historical cost is required with respect to property, and plant and equipment that has been held for a considerable length of time. The recommendation also states that more meaningful information can be provided either by revaluing the assets to current values or by disclosing current-value information in a note.

Leaders in the accounting profession generally recommend that assets, particularly depreciable fixed assets, be accounted for on the basis of replacement cost or appraised values, and a significant number of companies have adopted this basis of accounting for property, and plant and equipment.

A credit arising from a restatement of assets is generally reported in a separate reserve in the capital stock and surplus section of the balance sheet. Because the excess of depreciation based on replacement cost over depreciation based on original cost is not deductible for tax purposes, the reserve for revaluation is often recorded on a net-of-tax basis. A number of companies that state their property accounts at replacement cost also state their inventories on this basis.

New Zealand

In New Zealand, the accounting profession has issued a pronouncement that requires all listed companies to present a supplemental balance sheet and profit and loss account on a current-cost basis.

In the supplemental balance sheet, all nonmonetary assets are to be stated at their value to the business. The pronouncement states that the value to the business of an asset whose loss would materially impair the operating capability of the business is replacement cost less, where applicable, depreciation. The value to the business of an asset whose loss would not materially impair its operating capability is net realizable value.

The supplemental profit and loss account presents two measures of profitability: the "current cost operating profit of the enterprise" and the "profit attributable to the owners."

In arriving at the "current cost operating profit of the enterprise," the following principles are to be applied.

1. Depreciation is based on the current replacement cost of the related assets;

2. Cost of sales is based on the current cost of inventory at the time it is sold or consumed;

3. An adjustment is made to reflect the change in the purchasing power of "circulating monetary assets"; and

4. Interest on borrowed funds is *not* taken into consideration.

The circulating monetary assets of an enterprise are those monetary assets that must be maintained in order to service the production and selling activities in which the enterprise is engaged. These include cash (including deposits for a fixed term of up to twelve months), trade accounts receivable, installment receivables, notes receivable, refundable deposits paid, and contract work in process under fixed price contracts.

The adjustment to reflect the change in the purchasing power of circulating monetary assets is computed by multiplying the period's average investment in circulating monetary assets by the period's change in the general price index for the country.

The "profit attributable to the owners" is calculated by adjusting the "current cost operating profit of the enterprise" for the following items: (1) interest on borrowed funds; (2) the change in the value of those nonmonetary assets financed by borrowings; and (3) the change in the purchasing power of those circulating monetary assets financed by borrowing.

The change in the value of those nonmonetary assets financed by borrowings is calculated by multiplying the amount by which nonmonetary assets were revalued during the period by the ratio of average borrowings to average total assets during the period. Likewise, the change in the purchasing power of those circulating monetary assets that are financed by borrowings is calculated by multiplying the adjustment to reflect the change in the purchasing power of circulating monetary assets during the period by the ratio of average borrowings to average total assets during the period.

South Africa

In 1978, the profession in South Africa issued a guideline advocating the presentation of a supplemental current-cost income statement in which (1) depreciation is based on the current value to the business of its depreciable assets; (2) cost of sales is based on current value to the business of inventory on the date of sale; (3) a gain or loss on the disposition of a depreciable asset is based on its depreciated current cost; and (4) a gearing adjustment is reported.

The guideline states that the value to the business of a depreciable asset is the current cost that would have to be incurred to obtain and install an equivalent asset unless the asset will not be replaced upon the expiration of its useful life or it is no longer being used. If an asset will not be replaced, its value to the business is the higher of its recoverable amount and net realizable value; if an asset is no longer being used, its value to the business is net realizable value. The value to the business of inventory is the lower of current-cost and net realizable value.

If monetary assets exceed monetary liabilities, the gearing adjustment is computed by multiplying the average net monetary asset position by an index representative of the change in the price of the company's inputs.

If monetary liabilities exceed monetary assets, the gearing adjustment is computed by multiplying the sum of the difference between depreciation, cost of sales, and gains and losses on the disposition of depreciable assets on a current-cost basis and those amounts on the historical cost basis by the ratio of net monetary liabilities to the sum of net monetary liabilities, equity, deferred tax balances, and notes payable convertible into shares.

United Kingdom

More time has probably been spent on developing a system of inflation accounting in the United Kingdom than in any other country. In January 1973, the profession issued its first exposure draft on the subject, which proposed a system of general purchasing-power accounting. Following the publication of the Sandilands Report in 1975, the U.K. profession switched to current-cost accounting and issued a standard on the subject in March 1980, which is effective for years beginning after December 31, 1979.

The current-cost accounting standard applies to entities whose securities are listed on The Stock Exchange and to other entities that meet a size test. However, certain entities, including insurance companies and property investment companies, are exempted.

Affected enterprises are required to present a current-cost profit and loss account and balance sheet. This requirement can be complied with in any of three ways:

1. By presenting historical cost financial statements as the primary statements and supplementary current-cost statements;

2. By presenting current-cost financial statements as the primary statements and supplementary historical cost statements; or

3. By presenting current-cost financial statements as the only statements accompanied by adequate historical cost information.

The concept of value underlying the standard is value to the business which ordinarily is the net current cost of a replacement asset that has a similar useful output or service capacity as that of the existing asset when it was acquired. However, if a permanent diminution to a lower value has been recognized, the value to the business of an asset is the greater of its net realizable value and, if applicable, the amount recoverable from its further use.

The current-cost profit and loss account is to present two measures of profitability: the "current-cost operating profit" and the "current-cost profit attributable to the shareholders." The "current-cost operating profit" is stated before interest on net borrowings and income taxes and is to reflect three adjustments to the amounts reported on the historical cost basis.

1. The first adjusts depreciation to reflect the value to the business of depreciable assets consumed during the period.

2. The second adjusts cost of sales to the value to the business of inventory sold or consumed during the period.

3. The third is a monetary working capital adjustment.

Monetary working capital is defined as the aggregate of trade accounts and notes receivable, prepayments, and inventories not subject to the cost of sales adjustment less trade accounts and notes payable and accruals. That part of bank balances or overdrafts that fluctuates with the volume of these items as well as any cash floats required to support day-to-day operations of the business are to be included in monetary working capital if the effect of their inclusion on the "current-cost operating profit" is material.

The monetary working capital adjustment is to be computed by applying to each element of the monetary working capital the change in a relevant price index. The index for receivables should reflect the current cost of input costs applicable to the goods and services sold. The index for payables should reflect the cost of items financed by the payables.

"Current-cost profit attributable to shareholders" is determined after interest, income taxes, extraordinary items, and a gearing adjustment. The gearing adjustment is determined by multiplying the aggregate of the three adjustments reflected in "current-cost operating profit" by the ratio of net borrowings to net operating assets. Net borrowings are defined as the excess of:

the aggregate of all liabilities and provisions fixed in monetary terms (including convertible debentures and deferred tax but excluding proposed dividends) other than those included within monetary working capital and other than those that are, in substance, equity capital

over

the aggregate of all current assets other than those subject to a cost of sales adjustment and those included within monetary working capital.

Listed companies are required to disclose earnings per share based on the current-cost profit attributable to equity shareholders.

In the current-cost balance sheet, the following principles should be applied.

1. Property, and plant and equipment, and inventories are to be stated at their value to the business.

2. Investments to which the equity method applies are to be stated at equity in net assets stated on the current-cost basis or at the directors' best estimate thereof.

3. Other investments are to be stated at the directors' valuation.

4. Intangible assets other than goodwill are to be stated at the best estimate of their value to the business.

5. Goodwill is to be stated at the amount reported on the historical cost basis less any amount included therein that represents an excess of the value to the business over the historical cost of identifiable assets held by a subsidiary at the date of its acquisition.

6. Current assets not subject to the cost of sales adjustment and all liabilities are to be stated on the historical cost basis.

HYBRID METHODS

What might be referred to as hybrid methods of accounting for effects of price changes, because they combine features of both price-level and current-cost accounting, are now in effect in Mexico and the United States.

Mexico

The profession in Mexico issued an exposure draft on inflation accounting in November 1978 and a final statement in February 1980. This statement applies to all enterprises other than financial institutions, insurance companies, and not-for-profit entities. It is effective for years beginning after December 31, 1979.

The statement provides for the annual restatements of inventories; property, and plant and equipment; cost of sales; and depreciation expense. These restatements may be based on either current specific prices or the change in the consumer price index. If specific prices are used, they ordinarily are to be based on the replacement cost of inventory items and appraisals of property, and plant and equipment.

The statement permits the restatement of property, plant and equipment, and depreciation either to be recorded in the books and reflected in the basic financial statements or to be disclosed in a note or appendix to the statements. The restatement of inventories and cost of sales is to be disclosed in a note or appendix to the statements.

A statement of price-level adjusted shareholders' equity is to be included in the note or appendix. This is to report income for the period after the depreciation and cost of sales adjustments and the gain or loss during the period in the purchasing power of net monetary items.

Those companies using specific prices to restate nonmonetary assets are to compare the amount of the restatement with the amount computed by applying the change in the consumer price index to the nonmonetary assets. The difference is to be reported in the statement of price-level adjusted shareholders' equity as the gain or loss from holding nonmonetary assets.

United States

Inflation accounting has been discussed in the United States for at least thirty years. Finally, on December 25, 1979, the effective date of Statement of Financial Accounting Standards No. 33, inflation accounting became part of the reporting requirements applicable to certain large, publicly held companies.

These companies must disclose certain effects of changing prices as supplementary information to their basic financial statements. SFAS No. 33 requires each affected enterprise to report, for fiscal periods ending after December 25, 1979, income from continuing operations adjusted for changes in the general price level (that is, on the historical cost/constant dollar basis) and the purchasing-power gain (or loss) on net monetary items. The statement also requires disclosure of income from continuing operations measured using the current cost of inventories and property, plant and equipment, and the net increases (decreases) in the current costs of inventories and property, plant and equipment, and the amount of that increase (decrease) due to changes in the general price level. However, these current-cost amounts do not have to be reported until 1980 reports are issued.

Each affected company also must report a five-year summary of the following information stated in either the average of current-year constant dollars or dollars of the base year for the Consumer Price Index for All Urban Consumers.

1. Net sales and other operating revenues;
2. Income, including per share amounts, from continuing operations calculated on both historical cost/constant dollar and current-cost bases;
3. Purchasing-power gain or loss on net monetary items;
4. Net assets at fiscal year end at both current-cost and historical cost/constant dollar amounts;
5. Net increases (decreases) in the current-cost amounts of inventory and property, and plant and equipment, net of general price inflation;
6. Cash dividends per common share; and
7. Market price per common share at year end.

These disclosure requirements apply to public companies that have either (1) inventories and property, and plant and equipment before deducting accumulated depreciation, depletion, and amortization of more than $125 million, or (2) total assets net of accumulated depreciation, depletion, and amortization of more than $1 billion.

SFAS No. 33 imposes a limit on the amount at which assets are to be stated on both the historical cost/constant dollar and the current-cost bases. Amounts reported on these bases are not to exceed the assets' "recoverable amount," defined as the current worth of the net amount of cash expected to be recoverable from the use or sale of the assets. The statement provides that recoverable amounts may be taken to be net realizable value in the case of an asset that is about to be sold and value in use in the case of other assets. Value in use is the net present value of future cash flows (including the ultimate proceeds of disposal) expected to be derived from the use of an asset by the enterprise. "Recoverable amount" is calculated for asset groups (except in the case of an asset used independently of other assets) and need not be calculated unless it is judged to be materially and permanently below historical cost/constant dollars or current cost. If used, recoverable amount replaces historical cost/constant dollars and/or current cost in calculating the supplemental disclosures.

SFAS No. 33 does not require a comprehensive adjustment of all financial statement items to compute either historical cost/constant dollar or current-cost income from continuing operations although comprehensive restatement is permitted. SFAS No. 33 requires only cost of goods sold and depreciation, depletion, and amortization to be adjusted. Revenues, other operating expenses, and income taxes are assumed to be stated in amounts that are not materially different from current cost and constant dollars.

SFAS No. 33 differs significantly from the pronouncements issued in other countries in that it does not come to a bottom line. The purchasing-power gain or loss on net monetary items, the amount of the increase/decrease in the current costs of inventories and property, plant and equipment, and income from continuing operations are not required to be totalled.

INTERNATIONAL ACCOUNTING STANDARDS COMMITTEE

The International Accounting Standards Committee has taken an active interest in accounting for changing prices. In June 1977, it issued International Accounting Standard No. 6 which states:

> In complying with International Accounting Standard 1, Disclosure of Accounting Policies, enterprises should present in their financial statements information that describes the procedures adopted to reflect the impact on the financial statements of specific price changes, changes in the general level of prices, or of both. If no such procedures have been adopted that fact should be disclosed.

At its March 1980 meeting, the IASC approved the publication of an exposure draft of a possible replacement of International Accounting Standard No. 6. When published, this exposure draft will state that large enterprises whose securities are publicly traded should present supplementary information that adjusts cost of sales and depreciation for the effect of changing prices. It will leave the door open to the presentation of a financing or gearing adjustment.

COMPARISON OF METHODS

The methods of accounting for price changes that are presently in effect or being considered in twelve countries have now been reviewed. In what respects are these various methods similar? How do they differ? Focusing on a few key factors will facilitate a comparison of the various methods. These factors are listed below.

1. Is inflation accounting incorporated into the primary financial statements or presented as supplementary information?
2. What companies are to report inflation accounting information?
3. How are inventories, property, and plant and equipment stated?
4. What balance-sheet information is presented?
5. What concept of capital maintenance is implied?

Location of Information

It is interesting to note that in the three countries — Argentina, Brazil, and Chile — in which some variation of historical cost/constant dollar accounting is applied, inflation accounting is incorporated into the primary financial statements. On the other hand, in the countries using a current-cost or hybrid method, inflation accounting is presented as supplementary information, except in Mexico where it may be partially reported in the primary statements and in the Netherlands and the United Kingdom where it may be reported either in the primary statements or as supplementary information. Several years ago, the professions in Australia and the United Kingdom had contemplated a mandatory early incorporation of current-cost accounting into primary financial statements. This proved not to be feasible. It is also interesting that, of the countries reviewed, the three with the highest inflation rates are those using some variation of historical cost/constant dollar accounting.

One may conclude that with extreme inflation, historical cost/nominal dollar accounting becomes meaningless and price-level adjustments must be incorporated into the primary financial statements. However, because of resistance to change, a considerable period of time will be needed before current-cost accounting is likely to be required to be incorporated into primary financial statements.

Applicability of Requirements

In the countries in which some variation of historical cost/constant dollar accounting is used, all enterprises must follow the prescribed method. In the three current-cost countries in which compliance with the profession's suggestion regarding current-cost accounting is not mandatory — Germany, the Netherlands, and South Africa — those suggestions apply to all enterprises. In the other countries, the relevant pronouncements apply to only certain enterprises, such as large companies with publicly traded securities, or all listed companies, or all listed and certain other companies.

The limitations on the applicability of the relevant pronouncements presumably are based on cost/benefit considerations. The countries in which applicability is limited are countries in which the required information is or may be presented as supplementary information. It would not be logical to limit a requirement to incorporate current-cost accounting into primary financial statements to only some companies. Thus, cost/benefit considerations are likely to impede the incorporation of current-cost accounting into primary statements.

Valuation of Inventories and Property, and Plant and Equipment

Considerable variety exists with respect to the valuation of inventories, property, and plant and equipment in the three countries in which some variation of historical cost/constant dollar accounting is applied. In Argentina, both are stated at historical cost expressed in pesos of current purchasing power. In Brazil, property, and plant and equipment are stated on this basis while inventory is stated at historical cost in nominal cruzeiros. In Chile, property, and plant and equipment (to the extent they do not exceed equity) are stated at historical cost expressed in escudos of current purchasing power, while other property and inventories are stated at historical cost in nominal escudos.

There is more similarity with respect to the valuation of inventories and property, and plant and equipment among the various methods of current-cost accounting. The methods all focus on the current reproduction cost of existing assets. Most also provide for using some measure of recoverable amount when it is less than current cost. One difference in this regard is that when the recoverable amount is based on the future cash flows from the use and eventual disposition of an asset, the cash flows are to be discounted to their present value in Canada and the United States, but not in Australia, South Africa, or the United Kingdom. Particularly in view of today's interest rates, discounting appears to be required to produce meaningful amounts.

Balance-Sheet Information

In general, greater attention has been given to income-statement than to balance-sheet effects of price changes. Full balance sheets in which at least some assets are stated at amounts that reflect effects of price changes are provided for in the three countries using a system of historical cost/constant dollar accounting and in the Netherlands, New Zealand, and the United Kingdom. Disclosure of the current cost of property, plant and equipment, and inventories is provided for in Australia, Canada, Mexico, and the United States. The pronouncements in Germany and South Africa do not mention balance-sheet data.

Just as presentations of the results of operations that reflect effects of price changes often differ significantly from those that do not, presentations of financial position that reflect effects of price changes often differ significantly from those that do not. Restated balance sheets as well as restated income statements are needed to inform users of the statements of the impact of price changes on a business entity.

Capital Maintenance

The aspect of accounting for price changes that has been the most controversial has been which concept of capital maintenance to use and the related treatment of monetary items.

The concept underlying the systems of historical cost/constant dollar accounting being applied in Argentina, Brazil, and Chile is financial capital measured in units of constant purchasing power. That concept is consistent with the disclosures required in Mexico and by SFAS No. 33 in the United States. However, the FASB has avoided taking a position on the capital maintenance issue by not including a "bottom line" as part of its disclosures.

The concept of capital maintenance underlying the current-cost accounting systems in other countries is physical capital or operating capacity. However, considerable variations exist among countries on how this concept is applied:

1. In the Netherlands, the physical capital of an entity appears to be considered to be its property, and plant and equipment plus, perhaps, its inventory, regardless of how those assets are financed.
2. In Germany, the physical capital of an entity appears to be its property, plant and equipment, and inventory financed by equity; monetary items — including any financed by equity — are ignored.
3. In South Africa, the operating capacity of an entity appears to be its property, plant and equipment, and inventory financed by equity plus the purchasing power of any net monetary asset position financed by equity.
4. In Australia, Canada, New Zealand, and the United Kingdom, two measures of profitability are to be disclosed. The concept of capital to be maintained for the purpose of computing an entity's operating profit is the aggregate of the physical assets included in property, plant

and equipment, and inventories plus the purchasing power of circulating monetary assets or of net monetary working capital, regardless of how they are financed. Income attributable to the shareholders then reflects a gearing gain. In Australia, the gearing gain equals the decline in the purchasing power of loan capital. In New Zealand, it equals the increase in the value of nonmonetary assets financed by borrowings. In Canada and the United Kingdom, it equals the proportion of the current-cost adjustments for depreciation, cost of sales, and monetary working capital applicable to items financed by borrowings.

This author believes that the standard setters need to reconsider their conclusions regarding capital maintenance. Many of the existing pronouncements do not clearly articulate the concept to be applied but rather concentrate on explaining the mechanics of computing adjustments for gearing gains.

CONCLUSION

In most countries in which they exist, accounting systems that recognize effects of price changes have just recently been or are yet to be implemented. Thus, users of financial statements have yet to assess the utility of the information provided by these systems. A clear picture of the future of inflation accounting will become apparent only after users obtain experience with this information. Nevertheless, this author expects that the information will prove to be worthwhile and, unless inflation abates, will become a progressively more important part of financial reporting.

CHAPTER 18

Accounting for the effects of changing prices*
J. Timothy Sale and Robert W. Scapens

Accounting for the effects of changing prices

In the United Kingdom, the accounting profession has been grappling with accounting for the effects of changing prices since the late 1960s. Over a decade later, the Institute of Chartered Accountants in England and Wales published Statement of Standard Accounting Practice no. 16, *Current Cost Accounting*, seven months after the Financial Accounting Standards Board had issued its statement on inflation accounting (Statement no. 33, *Financial Reporting and Changing Prices*).

The May 1979 issue of the *Journal of Accountancy* contained a critique by Philip L. Defliese of the Financial Accounting Standards Board exposure draft on *Financial Reporting and Changing Prices*[1]. In his conclusions, Defliese suggested an approach to accounting for changing prices similar to the Hyde guidelines published by the Accounting Standards Committee (ASC) in the United Kingdom. On 31 March 1980, the ASC issued a standard, Statement of Standard Accounting Practice no. 16, *Current Cost Accounting*, which deals with accounting for price changes[2]. This standard not only builds on the foundations laid by the Hyde guidelines but it also includes some modifications. It is particularly significant to US accountants because there are important similarities and differences between FASB Statement no. 33, *Financial Reporting and Changing Prices*[3], issued last September, and SSAP 16.

To provide a better understanding of the provisions of Statement no. 33, this article discusses the following:

(1) The evolution of accounting for the effects of changing prices in the UK.
(2) The content of SSAP 16.
(3) The similarities and differences between SSAP 16 and SFAS no. 33
(4) Some implications for the US accounting profession based on the recent experience of the UK with inflation accounting.

The evolution of accounting for changing prices in the UK

To put the ASC's recent standard into perspective, it is appropriate to review some historical developments. In the late 1960s and early 1970s, the UK professional accounting bodies favoured a method of constant purchasing power accounting

* This article is reprinted, with permission, from *Journal of Accountancy* (July, 1980) pp 82–87

similar to the FASB's constant dollar accounting[4]. This culminated in the publication in 1974 of 'provisional' Statement of Standard Accounting Practice no. 7[5]. These proposals were suspended when a government-appointed committee, known as the Sandilands committee, recommended that the accounting profession move toward a system of current cost accounting that would ultimately replace historical cost accounting as the primary method of financial reporting[6].

The first attempt by the leadership of the Institute of Chartered Accountants in England and Wales to move toward current cost accounting, ED 18[7], turned out to be too radical a change for the accounting profession. In July 1977, the members of the institute voted to oppose any proposals that would replace historical cost financial statements. Even though the profession was still committed to implementing the Sandilands committee's recommendations, the experience of ED 18 suggested that progress could only be made slowly.

The next step came in November 1977, when the Hyde guidelines were published[8]. These guidelines encouraged large corporations to publish a supplementary income statement that included three adjustments restating historical cost income in terms of current costs; depreciation, cost of goods sold and financial leverage. The adjustment for financial leverage – the 'gearing' adjustment – created much controversy.

In an attempt to resolve this controversy, Exposure Draft 24, *Current Cost Accounting*, was issued in April 1979[9]. ED 24, the predecessor of SSAP 16, proposed a revision to the gearing adjustment in the Hyde guidelines and a further adjustment for monetary working capital. These adjustments will be discussed later.

In the latest step, SSAP 16 has implemented the proposals of ED 24, subject to minor modifications and clarifications. Historical cost will remain the normal basis for primary financial statements. For accounting periods beginning on or after January 1, 1980, however, most listed companies and those unlisted companies satisfying at least two of the following criteria will be required to publish supplementary current cost financial statements:

1 Annual sales in excess of £5 million.
2 Total assets on a historical basis in excess of £2.5 million.
3 Average number of UK employees in excess of 250 people[10].

Content of SSAP 16

Table 1, illustrates the current cost profit and loss account and the summarized current cost balance sheet proposed in SSAP 16. (A current cost balance sheet was not recommended by the Hyde guidelines.) Since there is no detailed list of valuation procedures in SSAP 16, each company is expected to compute the current cost of its assets in accordance with the principles used to compute the current cost adjustments included in the profit and loss account.

As can be seen from Table 1, the SSAP 16 profit and loss account is relatively simple. The historical cost profit is restated using the four adjustments mentioned earlier. An important distinction, however, is made between the "current cost operating profit" and the "current cost profit attributable to shareholders".

Table 1 Illustration of SSAP 16 current cost disclosures

Current cost profit and loss account – SSAP 16
(in thousands of pounds)

Sales		£20,000
Profit before interest and taxation on the historical cost basis		£ 2,900
Less: current cost adjustments		
Cost of goods sold	£ 460	
Monetary working capital	100	
Working capital	560	
Depreciation	950	1,510
Current cost operating profit		1,390
Gearing adjustment	(166)	
Interest payable less receivable	200	34
Current cost profit before taxation		1,356
Taxation		730
Current cost profit attributable to shareholders		626
Dividends		430
Retained current cost profit of the year		£ 196
Current cost earnings per share		20.9p
Operating profit return on the average of the net operating assets		6.0%

Summarized current cost balance sheet – SSAP 16
(in thousands of pounds)

Assets employed		
Fixed assets (net)		£19,530
Net current assets		
Inventory	£ 4,000	
Monetary working capital	800	
Total working capital	4,800	
Proposed dividends	(430)	
Other current liabilities	(570)	3,800
		£23,330
Financed by		
Capital and reserves		
Issued capital stock	3,000	
Current cost reserve	14,404	
Other reserves and retained profit	3,926	£21,330
Loan capital		2,000
		£23,330

Current cost operating profit is defined as the surplus arising from the ordinary activities of the business after allowing for the impact of price changes on the funds needed to continue the existing business and to maintain its operating capability, whether financed by capital stock or borrowings. It is calculated before interest and taxes[11].

The effects of financial leverage can be seen in the current cost profit attributable to shareholders. This is the surplus for the period after deducting the interest paid on borrowings and after making an adjustment for the effect of price changes on the portion of net operating assets that is financed by borrowings. It is calculated after taxes and extraordinary items[12].

In SSAP 16, three adjustments are applied to historical cost profit to obtain current cost operating profit. They are intended to maintain the operating capability of fixed assets, inventories and monetary working capital.

The first two adjustments, for the difference between the current and the historical costs of the depreciation expense and the cost of goods sold, were recommended in the Hyde guidelines and are also included in Statement no. 33[13].

The monetary working capital adjustment, which was first introduced in ED 24, recognizes that, in maintaining operating capability, it is just as important to maintain the monetary working capital as the fixed capital. The adjustment can be positive or negative, i.e., extending or reducing the cost of goods sold adjustment. SSAP 16 does not define the price changes to be used in the calculation of the adjustment. A consumer price index is unlikely to be appropriate in this case; the adjustment should reflect the price changes that affect payables and receivables[14].

The gearing adjustment

These three adjustments for depreciation, cost of goods sold and monetary working capital relate to the day-to-day operations of the business and are included in the calculation of current cost operating profit while the gearing adjustment is concerned with the effect of financing in a period of price changes. This adjustment adds back to current cost operating profit the portion of the three operating adjustments that relate to the loan-capital-financed assets. Its net effect is to maintain the stockholder-financed operating capability.

The gearing adjustment can be better explained by means of a simple illustration. Table 2 contains a comparative current cost balance sheet of a business that is neither growing nor declining and that always replaces assets as they are used up in generating sales. It makes an annual distribution of the current cost operating profit after paying interest on loan capital. The assets at the beginning and end of the year therefore represent identical operating capabilities; the difference of £100 is the increase in their current cost. It is assumed that this increase includes only the three operating adjustments shown in Table 1[15].

At the beginning of the year, the stockholders' equity represents 60% of the operating capability. To maintain this position at year-end, stockholders need 60% of £600, or £360. Their equity is £400 after they have received the distribution of current cost operating profit. The loan capital represents 40% at the beginning of the year – but this is fixed in money terms at £200. To maintain their proportion of the operating capability, they would need £240 at year-end. Because of the monetary nature of their claims, £40 of their operating capability has been

Table 2 Comparative current cost balance sheet

	Dec.31 1978	Dec. 31 1979
Net assets	£500	£600
Financed by		
Stockholders' equity	£300	£400
Loan capital	200	200
	£500	£600

transferred to stockholders' equity. This £40 is the amount which the gearing adjustment attempts to measure.

Formally, the gearing adjustment is calculated by multiplying the total of the current cost adjustments for depreciation, cost of goods sold and monetary working capital (£100) by the ratio of the net operating assets at current cost, financed by borrowings, to the total net operating assets at current cost (40%). Its purpose is to recognize the portion of the cost of increasing prices that must be borne by loan capital. For this purpose, the net operating assets should be measured in current costs. This approach, however, limits the gearing adjustment to a proportion of the realized increase in the current cost of the net operating assets (40% of £100, or £40).

The benefit to the stockholders represented by the gearing adjustment is obtained at the expense of lenders. It is not a benefit to the company as a whole and should not be seen as available for distribution – e.g., the £600 above represents the current cost of the assets required to maintain the operating capability of the entire business. Assets equal to the gearing adjustment of £40, therefore, cannot be distributed without reducing operating capability. Also, even if it was financially prudent, it may not be possible to raise loan capital in order to pay dividends.

The interest rate and the gearing adjustment can be considered together. In a period of increasing prices, interest rates may be high, but the interest payment will be offset (as far as the stockholders are concerned) by the gearing adjustment. As shown in Table 1, the interest expense can be associated with the gearing adjustment in computing the current cost profit for stockholders or the gearing adjustment can be shown separately as an adjustment to the current cost profit after interest and taxation.

Comparison of SSAP 16 with Statement no. 33

Before discussing the nature of the similarities and differences between SSAP 16 and Statement no. 33, two general observations need to be made. First, Statement no. 33 requires disclosure of information on income from continuing operations on both a constant dollar and a current cost basis[16], while SSAP 16 requires disclosure of this information on a current cost basis only.

Second, under Statement no. 33, information on income from continuing operations may be presented either in a statement format – disclosing revenues, expenses, gains and losses on a historical cost basis, a constant dollar basis and a current cost basis – or in a reconciliation format – disclosing adjustments to the income reported on a historical cost basis[17]. Although SSAP 16 is not explicit about format, its illustrative examples use the reconciliation format. Thus, this comparison between SSAP 16 and Statement no. 33 will be based on the reconciliation format.

The notion of current cost operating profit in SSAP 16 is comparable with income from continuing operations adjusted for changes in specific prices (current costs) required in Statement no. 33, with two exceptions. First, both have adjustments for depreciation and cost of goods sold, but SSAP 16 also has a monetary working capital adjustment. The FASB makes no distinction between short-term and long-term borrowings. The monetary working capital is included with other monetary items in a calculation of the "purchasing power gain or loss on net monetary items"[18]. SSAP 16, however, accounts for the effect of price changes on long-term monetary items through the gearing adjustment and on monetary working capital through the monetary working capital adjustment.

Second, Statement no. 33 separates adjustments for depreciation and cost of goods sold into two parts: (1) adjustments to historical cost to reflect the effects of general inflation (changes in general purchasing power) and (2) adjustments to reflect the difference between general inflation and changes in specific prices (current costs). The first set of adjustments is made to historical cost income from operations after interest and taxes to produce an intermediate figure representing income or loss from continuing operations adjusted for general inflation. The second set of adjustments is then made to this intermediate figure to produce income or loss from continuing operations adjusted for changes in specific prices, which, if interest and taxes are added back, is comparable to the current cost operating profit proposed in SSAP 16.

Both SSAP 16 and Statement no. 33 require the presentation of current cost balance sheet information, with SSAP 16 requiring a summarized current cost balance sheet and Statement no. 33 requiring disclosure of the current cost amounts of inventory and property, plant and equipment. The current cost income statement information is presented differently, however. SSAP 16 requires a complete statement (see Table 1) whereas Statement no. 33 requires a number of separate pieces of information (see Table 3,). Accordingly, the FASB income statement information has no "bottom line"; financial statement users are expected to combine the information in the way they consider most appropriate. The board wanted to allow enterprises to experiment with various methods before requiring any more comprehensive information.

The fundamental difference between SSAP 16 and Statement no. 33 arises from two different concepts of capital maintenance:

1 The financial concept of capital, which states that capital is maintained when the money value of net assets (measured either in nominal dollars or in units of purchasing power) remains constant.
2 The physical, productive (operating) capacity concept of capital, which states that capital is maintained when the net assets remain sufficient to produce a fixed quantity of goods and services[19].

Table 3 Statement of income from continuing operations adjusted for changing prices

For the year ended December 31, 1980*

(in thousands of average 1980 dollars)

Income from continuing operations, as reported in the income statement		$ 9,000
Adjustments to restate costs for the effect of general inflation		
Cost of goods sold	$(7,384)	
Depreciation and amortization expense	(4,130)	(11,514)
Loss from continuing operations adjusted for general inflation		(2,514)
Adjustments to reflect the difference between general inflation and changes in specific prices (current costs)		
Cost of goods sold	(1,024)	
Depreciation and amortization expense	(5,370)	(6,394)
Loss from continuing operations adjusted for changes in specific prices		$ (8,908)
Gain from decline in purchasing power of net amounts owed		$ 7,729
Increase in specific prices (current cost) of inventories and property, plant and equipment held during the year		$24,608
Effect of increase in general price level		18,959
Excess of increase in specific prices over increase in the general price level		$ 5,649

---

* At December 31, 1980, current cost of inventory was $65,700 and current cost of property, plant and equipment, net of accumulated depreciation, was $85,100.
Source: FASB Statement no. 33. Schedule A. p.32.

Statement no. 33 tries to embody both concepts while SSAP 16 has adopted the operating capacity concept.

The failure of Statement no. 33 to adjust current cost income from continuing operations for the effects of changing prices on monetary working capital (the monetary working capital adjustment in SSAP 16) is perhaps one indication that the FASB may, however, favour the financial concept. In fairness to the FASB, the board does state that, without this adjustment, current cost income from continuing operations does not measure the maintenance of operating capability exactly, indicating that to make the necessary adjustment would significantly increase the complexity of Statement no. 33[20].

This statement and the deduction of interest on long-term borrowings to compute historical cost income from continuing operations indicate a proprietary view of the business enterprise – a view which is consistent with the financial concept of capital maintenance. The operating capacity concept embodied in SSAP 16, however, reflects an entity view of the business.

Some implications of the UK experience

The obvious implication to be drawn from the recent UK experience is that it is difficult to bring about a rapid fundamental change in accounting methods. Current cost accounting is a new, untried system of accounting, and its benefits are not altogether clear. However, since SSAP 16 has developed through a process of evolution, it has generated more support than the first attempt to replace historical costs by current costs (ED 18).

This evolutionary process is illustrated by the amount of discussion and experiment which took place in the UK during the five years after the Sandilands report. During that time, there were many disagreements and various proposals and counterproposals, including the proposals of the Consultative Committee of Accountancy Bodies (CCAB;[21], ED 18, the Hyde guidelines and SSAP 16). This experience suggests that progress should be made slowly, through a process of building up experience and confidence in the new system, and the standard must be acceptable to both accountants and financial statement users.

Another, less obvious implication can be drawn from the change of preference in the UK from the financial concept of capital maintenance to the operating capacity concept. The financial concept favoured by the FASB was embodied in some of the earlier UK proposals, specifically provisional SSAP 7. This proposal came from the public accounting profession and, as such, probably reflected the views of the firms involved primarily in auditing. In light of the auditors' responsibilities for reporting to stockholders, this group should be expected to hold a proprietary view of the business, favouring the financial concept of capital maintenance[22].

The Sandilands committee, which included representatives of many sections of society, favoured the operating capacity concept. ED 18 was criticized by industrial accountants and controllers who prepared the current cost financial statements. They made it clear that the financial concept of capital maintenance was not generally acceptable. Such accountants, being involved with the business as a whole, were more likely to take an entity view rather than a proprietary view[23]. As more groups have become involved in the debate about current cost accounting, the balance of opinion has shifted in favour of the operating capacity concept.

The UK experience with current cost accounting tells us something about the standard-setting process. Standards cannot be imposed – they require compromise and consensus. For example, a body such as the ASC, with a substantial representation of auditors, will be permitted to produce and publish standards as long as they do not conflict with the interests of other members of the profession and of society in general. If they do conflict, influence may be exerted by other groups, such as financial statement preparers (changing the capital maintenance concept), members of small accounting practices (rejecting ED 18) and the government (constituting the Sandilands committee).

It cannot be concluded that an identical consensus will necessarily emerge in the US regarding accounting for the effects of changing prices. Different legal, social

nd cultural factors will affect the opinions and relative influence of the various
roups. Any imposition of a method of accounting for the effects of changing prices
nay create more problems than it solves – as with ED 18.

The FASB's preference for experimentation and flexibility should be supported
oy as many interest groups as possible. Furthermore, the discussion should not be
estricted to the methods described in Statement no. 33. All possible approaches
hould be evaluated. For instance, the various concepts of capital maintenance
hould be considered by both accountants and financial statement users. In this way
n acceptable method of accounting for the effects of changing prices should
merge.

References

1 Philip L. Defliese. Inflation Accounting: Pursuing the Elusive. *Journal of Accountancy*, May 1979, pp. 50–63.
2 Accounting Standards Committee, Statement of Standard Accounting Practice no. 16, *Current Cost Accounting* (London: ASC, March 1980)
3 Financial Accounting Standards Board Statement no. 33, *Financial Reporting and Changing Prices* (Stamford, Conn.: FASB, September 1979)
4 Ibid., paras. 39–50, 145–149 and 187–192
5 Accounting Standards Steering Committee, provisional Statement of Standard Accounting Practice no. 7, *Accounting for Changes in the Purchasing Power of Money* (London: ASSC, May 1974)
6 Inflation Accounting. *Report of the Inflation Accounting Committee*, Chairman. F. E. P. Sandilands, Cmnd 6225 (London: Her Majesty's Stationery Office, September 1975)
7 Accounting Standards Committee. Exposure Draft 18, *Current Cost Accounting* (London: ASC, 30 November 1976)
8 Inflation Accounting Steering Group of Accounting Standards Committee, *Interim Recommendation* (London: ASC, November 1977)
9 Accounting Standards Committee, ED 24, *Current Cost Accounting* (London: ASC, 30 April 1979)
10 It is estimated that these cut-off points will bring approximately 5,000 UK companies within the scope of the standard, as compared with an estimated 1,200 to 1,350 companies which will fall within the scope of FASB Statement no. 33
11 SSAP 16, par. 40
12 SSAP 16, par. 41
13 FASB Statement no. 33, par. 32
14 In practice there could be difficulties in identifying, on an objective basis, the items to be included in monetary working capital. SSAP 16 suggests that it would be reasonable to base the monetary working capital adjustment on the net of receivables, payables, cash change funds and any other bank balances or overdrafts which arise as a result of fluctuations in the values of inventories, receivables and payables.
15 Strictly, if fixed assets are included in the balance sheet, the increase in the undepreciated elements will not be charged in the income statement, but, for simplicity of the illustration, this effect is ignored
16 FASB Statement no. 33, pars. 29–30
17 Ibid. par. 32
18 FASB Statement no. 33, pars. 29b and 47–50
19 FASB Exposure Draft, *Financial Reporting and Changing Prices* (Stamford, Conn.: FASB, December 28, 1978), par. 59
20 FASB Statement no. 33, pars. 121 and 47–50
21 This proposal was similar to the FASB exposure draft on changing prices. See Consultative Committee of Accountancy Bodies, *Initial Reactions to the Report of the Inflation Accounting Committee* (London: CCAB, 30 October, 1975), reprinted in *Accountancy*, December 1975, pp. 92–96
22 Some indirect evidence for this expectation can be found in survey findings which indicated that UK auditors view financial reports primarily as a means of reporting to the stockholders about their investment. See Bryan Carsberg, Anthony Hope and R. W. Scapens, "The Objectives of Published Accounting Reports", *Accounting and Business Research*, Summer 1974, pp. 162–173
23 Ibid.

SOCIAL REPORTING

CHAPTER 19

Employees and the corporate social report: the Dutch case*
Hein Schreuder

ABSTRACT: Corporate social reporting is rapidly becoming normal business practice in the Netherlands. These reports are primarily addressed to the employee constituency and contain information on the personnel policy of the firm. This paper presents the results of a research project carried out to probe the reactions of employees toward the social reports actually published. The results are based on an analysis of 1,347 completed postal questionnaires and 240 additional interviews with employees of five corporations. The social report is perceived to be of medium importance as compared with other corporate means of communication. However, the respondents used the social reports more widely than was expected *a priori*. Their overall appreciation of the reports can be interpreted as "fairly adequate." The image of social reporting is not positive on all counts: the spirit in which it is provided is questioned by large groups of employees. An important outcome is that wide differences exist between the employees at various functional levels with respect to both their reading patterns and the importance attached to specific reporting items.

I N the last decade, corporate social reporting has become a widespread phenomenon in the Netherlands. Whereas before 1970 only a few companies published a social report, estimates of the number of such reports currently published run from 100 to well above 200. In the Dutch context "social reporting" refers to the provision of information on the relations between the organization and its employees. These reports are primarily addressed to the employee constituency.[1] The stated purpose of social reporting is "to provide information on" or (increasingly) "to account for" the social (personnel) policy. In addition, these reports are often distributed as well among other constituencies in order to provide a general insight into the social policy pursued by the organization. This paper reports on a research project which aimed at exploring the actual reactions of the main target group of social reporting: the employees.

The paper is organized as follows. First, some background information is presented regarding the state of the art of corporate social reporting in the Netherlands (Section 1). Then the methodology employed in this project will be

[1] In these respects, the Dutch social reports resemble those published, *e.g.*, in France [Rey, 1978] and West Germany [Schoenfeld, 1978; Schreuder, 1979]. In general, European social reports are more employee-oriented than their American counterparts, which contain more items of a general societal nature [Schreuder, 1978, pp. 40–41].

The author gratefully acknowledges the cooperation of Afke Schreuder-Sunderman and Frans Blommaert in the execution of this project and the helpful comments and suggestions from Professors Traas and Verburg as well as the anonymous reviewers and the Editor.

Hein Schreuder is Director of Business Research at the Economic and Social Institute of the Free University of Amsterdam.

Manuscript received December 1979.
Revision received April 1980.
Accepted June 1980.

* This article is reprinted, with permission, from *The Accounting Review* (April, 1981) pp 294–308

discussed (Section 2). The results obtained from an analysis of 1,347 questionnaires returned by the employees of five corporations as well as 240 additional interviews will be presented in Section 3. The paper concludes with a brief discussion of some implications and limitations of the author's research (Section 4).

SECTION 1

CORPORATE SOCIAL REPORTING IN THE NETHERLANDS

The pioneer in the field of corporate social reporting in the Netherlands seems to have been the chemical company Gist-Brocades. This company, which has a tradition of progressive social policies, published a social report as early as 1959. During the 1960s, this example was followed by only a few companies, but in the 1970s, corporate social reporting gained momentum. In 1977, the monthly magazine *PW* put up a prize for the "best social report" of the year. The number of participating companies rose from 75 in 1977 to 110 in 1979. Social reports are currently published by such diverse organizations as the state-owned post office, an accounting firm, a university, and corporate divisions.

A number of possible reasons for this trend can be mentioned. In the literature, the influence of the *Act on the Works Councils* has been stressed. The original version of this Act was passed in 1950. One of its articles stated that the entrepreneur was required to provide the Works Council with all information necessary to carry out the tasks within its competence and to inform the Works Council periodically on the economic course of affairs. The field of competence of the Works Council was, however, rather narrowly circumscribed. It was considerably enlarged in 1971 with the acceptance of a new version of the Act. In this version, it was explicitly stated

that the Works Council should be provided at least once a year with information pertaining to "the general policy with respect to recruitment, remuneration, training, promotion and dismissals." No provisions in this Act, however, specified the form in which this information should be presented, except that it should be in writing if requested by the Works Council.[2] Research carried out recently in 15 companies showed, however, that the Act on the Works Councils had not been the primary reason for the publication of the first social report in any company and had only been an additional reason in four companies [Dekker et al., 1980]. The 15 companies mentioned a variety of reasons, ranging from the social information needs of the employees and the desire to express the equivalence of the shareholders and the employees as corporate stakeholder groups (by providing both groups with their own report) to the wish not to be outdone in this development and even "following a fashion."

The fact to be stressed in the Dutch situation is that the overwhelming majority of the organizations publishing a social report do so voluntarily. Employers' federations have supported this trend. In 1974, the Federation of Employers in the Metallurgical Industry published a booklet in which an outspoken, favorable stand toward social reporting was taken:

Not only on formal grounds, but also from the viewpoint of a good general policy it should be considered just that in a community of people working together, each should have

[2] In the autumn of 1979, the Act on the Works Councils was revised again. If the distinction between a Works Council (emphasizing the corporate interest) and a Workers' Council (emphasizing the employees' interest) is accepted, it can be said that both the 1971 and the 1979 revisions represent a move from the former to the latter. In the 1979 version of the Act, social reporting is still not specifically mentioned.

an insight into the whole and should be involved in its functioning. Therefore, it is necessary that information is provided on a systematic and regular basis on all aspects of the conduct of business: the economic, the technical and the social aspects, both separately and integrated. An effective means for the provision of such information is the so-called personnel report, in which not only the social policies are discussed, but also the relations with the economic developments, the financial results and the prospects of the firm are brought out . . . [FME, 1974, unauthorized translation].

In 1975, the two general employers' federations, VNO and NCW, published a joint booklet expounding a similar, positive view [VNO/NCW, 1975]. The Dutch trade unions have not yet voiced their official view on corporate social reporting. They did, however, publish documents on the general information needs of employees [Overlegorgaan, 1974; FNV, 1976]. Content analysis of corporate social reports for the years 1975 and 1977 revealed that these information needs (taking the latter document as a standard of comparison) are not yet extensively met in the actual social reports, although some improvement is discernible [Van Hoorn and Dekker, 1979].

Several such content analyses have been performed, for instance by Van Ommeren [1974] and by Bouma and Feenstra [1975]. Van Hoorn and Dekker [1979] have conducted the most extensive content analyses of annual social reports to date. They examined the reports of 64 companies for the year 1975 and repeated this exercise on 57 of these reports for the year 1977. In Table 1, their research findings have been combined with those of Bouma and Feenstra [1975]. The list of items mentioned should give the reader some flavor of the informational content of Dutch social reports. With this background information in mind, attention can now be focused on the research reported in this article.

SECTION 2

THE RESEARCH PROJECT: STRUCTURE AND METHODOLOGY

The research carried out can be described as mainly exploratory in nature. The aim has been to probe the reactions of employees toward the corporate social reports actually being published and to solicit their opinions on some controversies in the literature. The basic approach taken in this project is a continuation of a line of research which is becoming rather common with respect to financial reporting. In several studies, individuals have been asked whether they have read corporate financial releases and whether they have found the information provided "useful" or "important" (see, e.g., Baker and Haslem [1973], Lee and Tweedie [1977] and Firth [1978]). It should be noted from the outset that the questions have not been framed in a specific decision-making context. This was not yet deemed possible, given the lack of prior research in this area. As a first step toward filling this gap, the present exploratory project was undertaken.

From a list of corporations which were known to have published a social report, five were selected.[3] Table 2 summarizes some features of the corporations in our sample. In each of these five corporations, the research project consisted of three parts: (a) introductory talks with company representatives involved in the process of social reporting, (b) a mailed questionnaire survey among employees, and (c) personal interviews with employees.

[3] Selection criteria were the nature of the corporations as well as their size, as measured by the number of employees. Only one corporation which was initially invited to participate in this project declined and had to be replaced.

TABLE 1

281

THE CONTENTS OF DUTCH SOCIAL REPORTS 1970–1977

	1970		1971		1972		1973		1975		1977	
Elements of Social Policy	nr	%	nr	%	nr	%	nr	%	nr	%	nr	%
I Composition of personnel												
1. Total number of employees	38	100	40	100	40	100	37	100	61	95	56	98
2. Classification factory workers—office workers	0	0	3	8	1	3	2	5	5	8	9	16
3. Classification foreigners—Dutchmen	4	11	8	20	7	18	7	19	19	33	15	26
4. Classification by educational level	1	3	1	3	1	3	1	3	5	8	5	9
5. Classification by length of tenure/contract	0	0	4	10	3	8	6	16	27	42	17	30
6. Age distribution	4	11	7	18	7	18	14	38	54	84	46	81
7. Sex distribution	3	8	6	15	6	15	12	32	40	63	38	67
8. List of executives	31	82	34	85	34	85	30	81	2	3	5	9
	81	(29.7)	103	(28.0)	99	(24.1)	109	(23.1)	213	(23.9)	191	(20.9)
II Other social aspects												
A. Financial												
9. Total wages paid	35	92	40	100	40	100	37	100	17	33	24	42
10. Collective Labor Agreement and reward systems	24	63	26	65	27	68	29	78	43	67	45	79
11. Costs of training and education	2	5	6	15	5	13	9	24	16	25	19	33
12. Types of internal training programs	16	42	21	53	20	50	22	59	45	70	46	81
13. Number of internal training programs	4	11	8	20	8	20	13	35	27	42	34	60
14. Types of external training programs	3	8	11	28	15	38	17	46	33	52	43	75
15. Number of external training programs	2	5	5	13	3	8	11	30	19	30	24	42
16. Housing	7	18	12	30	11	28	14	38	21	33	25	44
17. Costs of commuting facilities	0	0	0	0	2	5	5	14	8	13	18	32
18. Recreational facilities	7	18	9	23	10	25	13	35	33	52	25	44
19. Social funds (excl. pension funds)	7	18	11	28	13	33	18	49	32	50	37	65
	107	(39.2)	149	(40.5)	154	(37.5)	188	(39.8)	294	(33.1)	340	(37.2)
B. Communication												
20. Work consultation	11	29	11	28	20	50	16	43	38	59	37	65
21. Contacts with trade unions	15	39	17	43	20	50	23	62	41	64	47	82
22. Labor representation	26	68	35	88	36	90	35	95	48	75	46	81
23. Personnel magazine	8	21	12	30	20	50	19	51	22	34	23	40
24. Annual social or personnel report	7	18	12	30	17	43	20	54	64	100	57	100
	67	(24.5)	87	(23.6)	113	(27.5)	113	(23.9)	213	(24.0)	210	(23.0)
C. Miscellaneous												
25. Medical services	4	11	9	23	11	28	16	43	38	59	33	58
26. Safety	7	18	9	23	12	30	13	55	22	34	28	49
27. Number of accidents	2	5	4	10	7	18	9	24	21	33	28	49
28. Absenteeism due to sickness	4	11	6	15	13	33	19	51	46	72	34	60
29. Length of sickness leave	1	3	1	3	2	5	5	14	42	66	50	88
	18	(6.6)	29	(7.9)	45	(10.9)	62	(13.1)	169	(19.0)	173	(18.9)
Total number of companies studied (n)	38		40		40		37		64		57	
Total frequency of items	273	(100)	368	(100)	411	(100)	472	(100)	889	(100)	914	(100)
Maximum possible frequency (29 × n)	1102		1160		1160		1073		1836		1653	
Total frequency as % of maximum frequency		24.8		31.7		35.4		44.0		48.4		55.2

Notes: 1970–1973 calculated by Bouma and Feenstra [1975]; 1975 and 1977 by Van Hoorn and Dekker [1979].

Introductory Talks with Company Representatives

The purposes of these introductory talks were to get acquainted with the history of social reporting at the selected corporations, the actual procedures followed, and specifically, the *a priori* views of the company representatives involved in the process of social reporting. In sum, 38 individuals were interviewed, including 15 representatives of the Personnel

TABLE 2

SOME FEATURES OF THE CORPORATIONS SELECTED

Name	Industry	Number of Employees[a]	Circulation of Social Report	First Social Report on
AMRO-bank N.V.	banking	20,359	33,000	1962
Kluwer N.V.	publishing	3,648	5,500	1975
Koninklijke Wessanen N.V.	foods	3,167	8,600	1975
Naarden Int. Holland B.V.	chemical	999	1,250	1973
Stevin Groep N.V.	building	6,100	9,000	1975

[a] As of December 1977, excluding foreign subsidiaries. AMRO-bank N.V. exclusive of all subsidiaries.

TABLE 3

SAMPLE SIZE AND RESPONSE PER COMPANY (questionnaire survey)

Name	Number of Employees	Sample Size		Response	
		abs.	%	abs.	%
AMRO-bank N.V.	20,359	1,500	7.4	445	29.7
Kluwer N.V.	3,648	1,000	27.4	254	25.4
Koninklijke Wessanen N.V.	3,167	1,350	42.6	239	17.7
Naarden Int. Holland B.V.	999	950	95.1	218	22.9
Stevin Groep N.V.	6,100	1,049	17.2	191	18.2
Total	34,273	5,849	17.1	1,347	23.0

Department, 12 members of the Works Council, and four members of the Board of Directors. In all companies, the employees were considered to be the constituency toward which the social report was primarily addressed. The social report was mainly seen as an instrument to account for the social policies pursued by the company. However, no optimistic expectations existed as to the extent to which the social report performed this primary function. The general *a priori* view was that the social report was poorly read and not very much appreciated by the employees.

The Questionnaire Survey

At each company, a sample of employees was selected to receive a questionnaire. All samples were stratified by application of the following two charac-

teristics: (a) functional distribution and (b) departmental distribution.[4] Within these strata, random samples were obtained. The sample size was determined by the specific features of the company and by our research capacity. Table 3 shows the absolute and percentage sample sizes per company as well as the response obtained.

The questionnaires were mailed to the employees of four companies (and handed out at the fifth company) approximately ten days after publication of the social report. The questionnaires were accompanied by a letter of introduction by the Board of Directors or the Personnel Department as well as by a

[4] For two companies, an additional regional stratification was judged desirable and was technically feasible. For another company, the sample was also stratified by means of the distributions of age and the length of tenure.

postage-paid return envelope addressed to the Economic and Social Institute. In all letters, it was specifically stated that the Institute had taken the initiative to carry out this project at several companies in order to gain a broad view of the employees' reactions toward social reports. The employees were requested to return the questionnaire anonymously and complete confidentiality of the individual responses was guaranteed. The response obtained will be discussed below together with the interview response.

The Interviews with Employees

Finally, personal interviews were conducted with employees who had not received the questionnaire beforehand. The interview groups were selected according to the same criteria as discussed above. Each group consisted of about 50 employees. In sum, 240 employees were interviewed due to some absences and refusals.[5] The interviews were scheduled in the two-week period following the mailing or hand-out date of the questionnaire survey. The employees were not notified in advance in order to avoid "preparation" on their part. The interviews were semistructured. Each employee was first asked to complete the questionnaire. Then the interviewer encouraged the employee to air his or her views about the corporate social report. The interviewer did, however, possess a checklist to ensure that certain topics would be covered in each interview. The purpose of these interviews was threefold: (1) to test the employees' reactions to—and interpretation of—the questionnaire, (2) to delve more deeply into some issues and to gather additional information, and (3) to obtain a sample which could serve as control group. The interviews were considered to be indispensable as neither a pilot study nor a nonresponse survey was technically feasi-

ble.[6] As will become evident from an analysis of the results in Section 3, the control for nonresponse bias in the questionnaire survey by means of a separate interview sample has proven to be of great importance.

An Analysis of the Response

The questionnaires contained nine introductory questions regarding some background characteristics of the respondents. Table 4 lists these characteristics as well as the results of a chi-square test at the 0.05 significance level. In the first half of the table, all 1,587 postal and interview respondents are analyzed together, while in the second half the interview respondents are analyzed separately. The results are unequivocal: as far as can be tested, the total group of respondents is grossly nonrepresentative of the employee population of these five corporations. However, it is equally clear that the bias results from the postal respondents. The interview group is representative of the total population on seven of the eight characteristics which can be tested (albeit often incompletely). This result is far better than could be expected on the basis of our sample selection. A comparison of the results of the postal respondents with those of the interview group may, therefore, be regarded as a useful indication of the potential nonresponse

[5] These were distributed across the five companies as follows: AMRO-bank N.V. 49 (20.4 percent), Kluwer N.V. 48 (20.0 percent), Koninklijke Wessanen N.V. 49 (20.4 percent), Naarden Int. Holland B.V. 44 (18.3 percent) and Stevin Groep N.V. 50 (20.8 percent).

[6] A pilot study was technically infeasible, as the questionnaire was worded in accordance with the draft of the actual social report which was forthcoming, and many answers depended on the respondent's having read this social report. The interviews, however, provided evidence on the interpretation of the questions by the employees. Another benefit of the interview approach was that it allowed the interviewer to assess the answers given to the questionnaire in the course of the subsequent conversation. As a result, some mutually agreed changes were sometimes made.

TABLE 4

ANALYSIS OF THE CHARACTERISTICS OF THE RESPONDENTS (PER COMPANY)

Characteristics	All Respondents						Interview Group					
	1	2	3	4	5	1–5	1	2	3	4	5	1–5
Sex	NR	NR	R	R	R	NR(5)	R	R	R	R	R	R(5)
Age	NR	NR	R	R	NT	NR(4)	R	R	R	R	NT	R(4)
Educational Level	NT	NT	NT	NT	NT	NT	NT	NT	NT	NT	NT	NT
Length of Tenure	R	R	NT	R	NR	NR(4)	R	NR	NT	R	NR	NR(4)
Department	R	R	R	NA	R	R(4)	R	R	R	NA	R	R(4)
Region	NT	NR	R	NA	NT	NR(2)	NT	R	R	NA	NT	R(2)
Functional Level	NR	R	NR	NT	NR	NR(4)	R	R	R	NT	R	R(4)
Nature of Work	NT	NR	NT	NR	NT	NR(2)	NT	R	NT	R	NT	R(2)
Union Membership	NT	NT	NT	R	NT	R(1)	NT	NT	NT	R	NT	R(1)

Notes: The results of the chi-square test (at the 0.05 significance level) per characteristic are reported for each company and the five companies together by means of the following symbols:
R   = Representative.
NR = Non-Representative.
NT = Not Testable (population characteristics insufficiently specified for testing purposes).
NA = Not Asked.
This mode of reporting has been chosen because of the different degrees of freedom involved.
The 1–5 columns show the outcomes for the five companies together. The digit in parentheses indicates the number of firms for which the test was possible.

bias involved in applying postal questionnaires in this type of research.

In addition, cross-analyses have been conducted to examine the extent to which the responses to items covered in the questionnaire have been influenced by different background characteristics. These analyses revealed that, where different responses could be established, the functional distribution mostly served as the best explanation.[7] Especially in view of the exploratory nature of our research, these differences within the employee constituency were, of course, very interesting. Therefore, a reporting mode was chosen which would clearly bring out these differences. In the following section, all research results will, therefore, first be given for the postal and interview respondents separately, then for the total group of respondents, and finally for the three functional levels identified within this total group. The significance of the differences between the postal and interview response as well as the differences between the response at the three functional levels will be indicated by the significance levels (α) resulting from a chi-square test.

SECTION 3

AN ANALYSIS OF RESULTS

As a first step, the relative importance of the social report among other corporate means of communication was established. To this end, the employees were asked to indicate which medium contained the most important corporate information.[8] Table 5 shows that the corporate social report comes out in a middle position. Circulars and personnel magazines were perceived as more important sources of information. On the

[7] Which is to say that other explanations were mostly associated with the functional distribution, while the latter showed the greatest discriminating power.

[8] Again, it should be stressed that these questions were not framed in a decision context. Therefore, this exploratory study gives no indication in which respects or for what purpose the information was deemed important by the employees.

TABLE 5

THE IMPORTANCE OF CORPORATE MEANS OF COMMUNICATION

Means	Respondents			Functional Level		
	interview	postal	all	lower	middle	upper
Circulars	44.8	39.0	39.9	39.3	42.6	43.1
Personnel magazines	53.6	34.9	37.7	40.9	34.8	23.0
The social report	31.5	26.2	27.0	25.7	26.9	25.3
Reports of the Works Council	30.3	23.0	24.2	26.1	23.7	18.9
The annual financial report	19.4	16.3	16.8	9.8	21.4	44.9
Other	12.0	11.2	11.4	6.7	15.2	21.2
Significance level	$\alpha < 0.01$			$\alpha < 0.01$		

Note: All figures in this table and the following tables are expressed in percentages. As many respondents checked more than one possible answer to this question, the percentages here add up to over 100 percent.

other hand, the reports of the Works Council as well as the annual financial report were considered to be less informative. The differences between the answers obtained by means of the interviews and the postal questionnaires are highly significant. So are the answers given by employees at the various functional levels. Note especially the climb in perceived importance of the annual financial report and the other means of communication as the functional level rises.

Next, the question was posed: How important is information on the corporate social policies deemed to be? More than one third of all respondents considered such information to be "very important," and exactly one half answered "important." The percentage answering "not so important" or "unimportant" increased from 2.8 at the higher functional level to 14.1 at the lower level. Given this widespread interest in social information, the question of whether the corporate social report is the correct means to inform employees about the corporate social policy was addressed. More than 75 percent of all respondents answered affirmatively.

The actual use of the social report was then investigated. Here the importance of the interview control group is illustrated very clearly (see Table 6). While nearly half of all respondents reported to have read the social report rather thoroughly, the percentage is 52.8 for the postal respondents and 28.0 for the interviewees. Conversely, the percentages indicating no use of the report at all are 12.5 and 30.2, respectively. However, even taking the interview results as the better approximation of the real extent of usage, the outcome exceeded a priori expectations. On the basis of our introductory talks with company representatives, a lower extent of usage was anticipated. Even at the lower functional level, 64 percent of the interviewees reported they used the corporate report in some way, and 55.5 percent said they read more than one item.

Specific Reporting Items

An important part of our questionnaire consisted of a list of subjects covered in the social report.[9] Each list was specifically geared to the actual report. Thus, these lists varied somewhat in length (10–14 items) and in substance. We shall

[9] Those respondents who had not used the social report at all have been omitted from further analysis.

TABLE 6

RESPONDENTS' USE OF THE SOCIAL REPORT

	Respondents			Functional Level		
Extent	interview	postal	all	lower	middle	upper
Read rather thoroughly	28.0	52.8	48.9	23.6	32.6	41.7
Read some items	32.5	30.3	30.5	31.9	38.3	45.8
Read only one item	2.9	1.6	1.8	2.7	3.1	0.0
Leafed through	6.4	2.9	3.8	5.8	11.4	12.5
Not read at all	30.2	12.5	15.0	36.0	14.6	0.0
Significance level	$\alpha < 0.01$			$\alpha < 0.01$		

Note: The cross-tabulation with the functional level has been performed with the interview results.

TABLE 7

RANKING OF SUBJECTS OF SOCIAL REPORTS (ALL RESPONDENTS)

	Number of Reporting Companies	Rankings		
Subject		Reading	Importance	Treatment
Size and distribution of work force	5	1	10	1
Organization	4	2	4	4
Conditions of employment	5	3	2	2
Safety	3	4	1	8
Training and education	5	5	6	6
Financial information	4	6	5	3
Health and social services	3	7	7	5
Work consultation	3	8	8	9
Pensions	3	9	3	7
Labor representation	4	10	9	10

Note: "Work consultation" refers to on-the-job consultation about work programs etc. The rankings for all respondents are used, as the postal and interview results produced no significant differences in rankings. The Spearman and Kendall rank correlation coefficients (r_s and r_k) for the three sets of rankings are:

	r_s	r_k
Reading-Importance	0.19	0.20
Reading-Treatment	0.78	0.60
Importance-Treatment	0.05	0.06

report only on the items which appeared on at least three lists.

For each item, the following questions were asked:

(a) Have you *read* this subject?
(b) How *important* do you perceive it to be?
(c) How do you consider it to be *treated* in the report?

Table 7 summarizes the items, the number of reporting companies, and the rankings of items according to reading, importance, and treatment.

The rank correlation coefficients computed for the data in Table 7 show a very weak correspondence between the rankings for reading and importance. The degree of association between the rankings of reading and treatment is much higher. The employees' reading pattern thus seems more influenced by the treat

TABLE 8

RANKING OF SUBJECTS OF SOCIAL REPORTS PER FUNCTIONAL LEVEL

	Reading		Importance		Treatment	
Subject	lower	upper	lower	upper	lower	upper
Size and distribution of work force	2	8	10	10	1	2
Organization	5	1	3	1	2	4
Conditions of employment	3	4	2	4	3	1
Safety	1	5	1	6	8	9
Training and education	6	7	8	5	6	6
Financial information	9	6	7	3	4	3
Health and social services	4	9	6	7	5	5
Work consultation	7	3	4	8	10	10
Pensions	8	2	5	2	7	8
Labor representation	10	10	9	9	9	7
Rank correlation coefficients	$r_s = 0.05$ $r_k = 0.02$		$r_s = 0.49$ $r_k = 0.38$		$r_s = 0.90$ $r_k = 0.78$	

ment of subjects than by their importance. Table 7 also reveals some striking differences in the three rankings of individual items. For instance, the item perceived as most important (safety) is treated rather poorly, in the respondents' view. Conversely, the least important item (size and distribution of work force) is treated extremely well and is read most widely. Rather surprising is the low position of the items "work consultation" and "labor representation" on all three counts. These subjects have been considered as representing very significant social developments in recent years.

Whereas Table 7 presents the aggregate results for all employees, the question arises as to what degree certain groups of employees hold other views. Table 8 presents the results of a cross-analysis with the functional characteristic which was found to be most significant. It shows the three rankings for both the lower and the upper functional level. It is clearly brought out that the reading patterns of these two levels were not associated. The lower level read items such as "size and distribution of work force" and "health and social services" considerably more than the upper level, but, for example,

"pensions" was read considerably less. The lower level attached a much higher importance to "safety" and "work consultation" but much less to "financial information" than did the upper level. The appreciation of the subject treatment, on the other hand, is similar.[10]

General Appreciation of the Social Report

Several questions were designed to probe the employees' appreciation of the reporting mode. These questions were prompted by the widely held criticism that corporate social reports are incomprehensible to the large majority of employees. One aspect of this matter is the inclusion of tables and figures in the reports. More than 80 percent of all respondents (and 76.2 percent of those at lower functional levels) regarded these tables and figures as good amplifications of the text. Ninety percent of all respon-

[10] In their case study of a state-owned Swedish forestry enterprise, Anderson and Dahlberg [1977] found that the employee constituency valued the urgency of specific reporting items quite differently as compared with public authorities, citizens, and other forestry organizations. Therefore, social reporting possibly has to cope with both inter-group and intra-group differences in this respect.

TABLE 9

GENERAL APPRECIATION OF THE SOCIAL REPORTS

Point Value	Meaning	Respondents			Functional Level		
		interview	postal	all	lower	middle	upper
1	excellent	5.5	6.5	6.4	7.4	5.5	6.2
2	good	60.8	48.2	50.0	48.9	51.6	47.5
3	adequate	21.4	32.6	30.9	30.3	30.4	30.5
4	inadequate	3.6	6.7	6.3	5.3	6.9	10.3
5	poor	0.5	0.8	0.6	0.6	1.3	1.4
no information		8.3	5.2	5.7	7.5	4.4	4.1
Average score		2.27	2.44	2.41	2.38	2.45	2.51
Significance level		$\alpha < 0.01$			$0.05 < \alpha < 0.10$		

dents indicated that they understand these parts of the reports. The language used was described as "clear" by 83 percent of all respondents, with 13 percent preferring the description "not clear." The latter percentage increases to 18 for the employees at lower functional levels and to 22 for those with only elementary schooling. The main problem is indicated to be the difficult terminology used in corporate social reporting. An overall measure of the employees' appreciation of the social reports resulted from the question to judge the social report in its entirety. Here a five-point scale was used. Point values and choices available appear in Table 9. The individual reports each scored an average of between 2.2 and 2.6. The overall average was 2.4, which can be interpreted as "fairly adequate."[11] Interestingly, the overall average accorded to the social reports in their entirety shows a slight tendency to decrease as the functional level of the respondents increases; this average moves from 2.38 at the lower level to 2.45 and 2.51 at the middle and upper levels, respectively.

Some Opinions

The last sheet of the questionnaire contained opinion questions. Respondents were asked to indicate whether they agreed, disagreed, or, alternatively, had no opinion about a number of statements which were mainly derived from the literature. Table 10 summarizes some of the interesting results.[12] It shows, for instance, that a majority of employees wish to be informed about the corporate environmental effects in the social report. Only at the upper functional level do respondents rather reject than accept inclusion of such information. The response to this question differs widely per company. Of all bank employees, 38.0 percent agreed with the statement, while 34.1 percent disagreed. At the chemical company, these percentages are 74.5 and 15.4, respectively. These results are of considerable interest in the context of current European practices in which a separation of social information and

[11] All individual reports scored between "adequate" and "good" in the judgment of each functional level.
[12] Excluding the response to the first statement, the distribution over the choices available was remarkably stable per company. Note that the differences between the interview and postal results can be considered to be significant in five out of nine cases, while all differences between the answers of the three functional levels are highly significant.

TABLE 10

RESPONSE TO OPINION STATEMENTS

Opinion Statement	Choice	Respondents			Functional Level		
		interview	postal	all	lower	middle	upper
1. The social report should also contain information on corporate environmental effects.	agree	64.7	55.7	57.0	62.6	53.4	42.5
	disagree	23.7	23.5	23.3	15.1	27.4	45.2
	no opinion	10.3	16.7	16.0	18.3	14.8	9.4
		$0.01 < \alpha < 0.02$			$\alpha < 0.01$		
2. The social report is not critical enough, because conflicts and problems are insufficiently discussed	agree	34.6	44.1	42.8	44.0	42.4	41.4
	disagree	41.0	30.2	31.5	26.8	33.3	45.5
	no opinion	22.5	21.2	21.5	24.5	19.8	10.2
		$0.01 < \alpha < 0.02$			$\alpha < 0.01$		
3. The social report should ideally be written by the employees themselves	agree	16.4	18.8	18.3	18.6	19.2	11.5
	disagree	71.6	58.8	60.7	55.5	63.4	78.9
	no opinion	9.6	17.9	16.7	21.7	12.3	5.3
		$\alpha < 0.01$			$\alpha < 0.01$		
4. The social policy is discussed with great frankness in the social report	agree	35.7	33.9	34.1	33.7	31.7	45.2
	disagree	31.6	33.4	33.2	27.7	39.3	39.3
	no opinion	31.4	28.5	29.0	34.3	25.1	12.5
		$0.98 < \alpha < 0.99$			$\alpha < 0.01$		
5. The information contained in the social report is reliable	agree	69.9	59.9	61.7	58.2	60.0	78.0
	disagree	4.2	6.1	5.8	4.5	7.4	7.2
	no opinion	24.6	30.0	28.9	33.1	28.8	11.0
		$0.02 < \alpha < 0.05$			$\alpha < 0.01$		
6. The social report is used by the company to advertise its social policy	agree	23.2	27.8	27.1	24.2	28.5	35.5
	disagree	54.7	44.0	45.6	42.1	47.1	49.2
	no opinion	20.3	24.6	24.0	30.0	20.8	11.9
		$0.02 < \alpha < 0.05$			$\alpha < 0.01$		
7. The individual employee can recognize himself/herself in the social report	agree	28.6	24.0	24.5	25.7	21.8	24.6
	disagree	46.0	51.7	50.9	45.9	55.1	57.1
	no opinion	23.6	19.5	20.2	23.5	18.7	12.7
		$0.30 < \alpha < 0.50$			$\alpha < 0.01$		
8. The social report is not very interesting, as it is mainly retrospective	agree	12.0	14.8	14.4	12.7	16.0	14.8
	disagree	75.6	71.0	71.7	68.4	72.1	80.0
	no opinion	10.5	10.4	10.4	15.2	7.8	1.2
		$0.30 < \alpha < 0.50$			$\alpha < 0.01$		
9. The social report is an important addition to the information already provided by other means	agree	77.6	74.9	75.2	75.1	72.5	75.1
	disagree	10.9	13.6	13.5	10.0	17.0	17.9
	no opinion	10.3	8.0	8.1	11.3	7.0	2.5
		$0.50 < \alpha < 0.70$			$\alpha < 0.01$		

Note: The percentages do not add up to 100 percent; the difference indicates the number of respondents giving no information.

more general societal information often exists.

For the correct interpretation of Table 10, it should be pointed out that the respondents generally hold stronger views as their functional level increases. Thus, the percentage of respondents indicating "no opinion" decreases. For instance, while the percentage of employees which consider the social report not to be critical enough remains fairly stable at all functional levels, the percentage of those who disagreed with this statement rapidly increases as the functional level rises. The response to Statement 9 indicates again that the social report has been accepted by the employees as an additional corporate means of communication. At the same time, the image of corporate social reporting which appears from the opinions about Statements 2–8 provides some strong incentives to rethink current reporting policies. Although the information provided is mainly considered to be reliable,[13] in other respects it does not come out as well. Certainly, the spirit in which it is provided is questioned by the responding employees. Although about half of the respondents do not regard the social report as a public relations effort, a quarter do. In addition, its critical nature and frankness are perceived as questionable by large groups of respondents. Statement 7 conveys an often-suggested s andard of relevance for social reporting: Does the individual employee recognize his/her own working situation and problems in the social report? If this standard of relevance is accepted, the result is, of course, rather disappo nting. The answers to Statement 8 suggest that the problems do not stem mainly from the retrospective nature of the report, while the solution does not seem to lie in the employees writing the social report themselves, as indicated by the response to Statement 3.

SECTION 4

CONCLUDING OBSERVATIONS

The research results presented in this article should be regarded as not more than a first step toward the investigation of the effects of providing corporate social reports to employees. As far as the author knows, no prior research existed in this area (certainly not in the Dutch context). So, an exploratory approach was taken. This approach implied that the questions put to the employees were specific in the sense that they were geared to the actual reports published by the five corporations included in our study. On the other hand, the questions were general in the sense that they were not framed in a particular decision-making context. Further research is required to turn the balance toward the question of whether social report information, in general, affects specific decisions of employees.[14] For such further research, this exploratory investigation may suggest some hypotheses.

The main results of this research are twofold. First, the findings suggest that the social report has been accepted by employees as a corporate means of communication. Its importance *vis-à-vis* other means should not be overrated. However, nearly 70 percent of the employees inter-

---

[13] In the interviews, those responding with "no opinion" often correctly observed that they were not able to judge the veracity of this statement. (A similar remark pertains to statement 4.)

[14] The overall impression from the interviews was that the employees mainly did not use the social report for decision-making purposes. Rather, the report was used to gain a general overview of the corporate social field. In addition, the report may serve a "symbolic" function, which is appreciated by the employees. Of course, although a direct effect on decisions may be lacking, an indirect effect may still result from a changed corporate image.

2

291

viewed reported that they use the social report, and three-quarters of the respondents using the report indicated that it represents an important addition to the information provided by other means. Their general appreciation of the social report can be described as "fairly adequate." Second, it seems rather questionable whether the employees can be considered as a homogeneous target group for social reporting purposes. Differences exist both in reading patterns and in the importance attached to specific reporting items between the functional levels of employees. The opinions expressed with respect to certain statements about the social report vary significantly as well.

Another contribution of this paper may be in the methodological field. A control group of interviewees was used to obtain an indication of the potential nonresponse bias in the postal survey. A comparison of the postal and interview results reveals that the control group was essential for a correct interpretation of

many outcomes throughout the paper. The actual use of the social report would have been grossly overestimated on the basis of the postal survey only. Nonusers are apparently inadequately reached by a postal questionnaire. More surprising is the fact that the results relating only to the *users* of social reports (Tables 9 and 10) vary significantly in many cases as well. Thus, the use of a control group may be valuable not only for the interpretation of results sought for the entire population (users and nonusers), but also for only the actual user group.

Finally, it should be noted that our research was subject to methodological limitations as well. Apart from the absence of a decision-making context mentioned above, the main limitation is the reliance on self-reporting by the respondents. Although in the interviews some assessment of the response given was possible, future research should also apply other methodological approaches to ascertain the validity of these results.

REFERENCES

Anderson, B., and L. Dahlberg, *Towards a social report* (Swedish National Audit Bureau, 1977).

Baker, H. K., and J. A. Haslem, "Information Needs of Individual Investors," *Journal of Accountancy* (November 1973), pp. 64–69.

Bouma, J. L., and D. W. Feenstra, "Externe verslaggeving over personeel en personeelsbeheer in een aantal Nederlandse ondernemingen over de jaren 1970–1973," *Maandblad voor Bedrijfsadministratie en-Organisatie*, Vol. 74, No. 941 (1975), pp. 322–328.

Dekker, H. C. Th.P. van Hoorn and H. Schreuder, "Hoe komt sociale verslaggeving tot stand?", in H. Verhallen (editor), *Het Sociaal Verslag: Feiten en Meningen* (Samsom, 1980), pp. 109–162.

Firth, M., "A Study of the Consensus of the Perceived Importance of Disclosure of Individual Items in Corporate Annual Reports," *International Journal of Accounting* (Fall 1978), pp. 57–70.

FME, *Personeels—of sociaal jaarverslag*, (FME, 1974).

FNV, *Open Boek: Een nota over de behoefte van werknemers aan informatie over hun onderneming*, (FNV, 1976).

Lee, T. A., and D. P. Tweedie, *The Private Shareholder and the Corporate Report* (The Institute of Chartered Accountants in England and Wales, 1977).

Overlegorgaan NVV/NKV/CNV, *Informatie Behoefte Werknemers* (Overlegorgaan, 1974).

Rey, F., "Corporate Social Responsibility and Social Reporting in France," in H-M. Schoenfeld (compiler), *The Status of Social Reporting in Selected Countries*, Contemporary Issues in International Accounting, Occasional Paper No. 1 (University of Illinois, 1978), pp. 109–146.

292 Schoenfeld, H-M., "Social Reporting—Its Present Development in West Germany, Austria and Switzerland," in H-M. Schoenfeld (compiler), *The Status of Social Reporting in Selected Countries*, Contemporary Issues in International Accounting, Occasional Paper No. 1 (University of Illinois, 1978), pp. 1–71.

Schreuder, H., "Facts and Speculations on Corporate Social Reporting in France, Germany and Holland," Working-Paper 78-42 (European Institute for Advanced Studies in Management, 1978).

Schreuder, H., "Corporate Social Reporting in the Federal Republic of Germany: An Overview," *Accounting, Organizations and Society*, Vol. 4, No. 1/2 (1979), pp. 109–122.

Van Hoorn, Th.P., and H. C. Dekker, *Sociale verslaggeving op een tweesprong?* (Kluwer, 1979).

Van Ommeren, A. W., "Het sociaal jaarverslag: informatiebron of verantwoordingsstuk?", *Personeelbeleid*, Vol. 10, No. 9 (1974), pp. 432–437.

VNO/NCW, *Sociaal jaarverslag: informatie aan het personeel* (VNO/NCW, 1975).

CHAPTER 20

Management audit and social indicators: the MNC through the glasses of the LDC*
Hans B. Thorelli

The multinational corporation, (MNC) as we know it today, is essentially a product of the twentieth century. Young as MNCs are, many of them have had time to experience an entire life cycle from birth to death in one or several less developed countries (LDC), a drama proceeding from princely welcome to ignominious expulsion — with or without reasonable compensation (exhibit 1). It should be clear that nobody really "wins" from this outcome of the contest. The mutual interests of the participants call for not a drama but a partnership.

The very idea of partnership between government and business sounds unfamiliar or even vaguely suspect to many American ears. It tends to conjure up images of corruption and dictatorship in Nazi Germany or in Latin America. But, like marriage, partnership is an arrangement for good and evil. The potential for good is great where the arrangement is based on mutual respect and mutual responsibilities and is free from elements of conspiracy.

It has become customary to talk about the desirability of such a partnership in the last two decades. Yet it must be stated frankly that

*Hans B. Thorelli is E. J. Kelley Professor of Business Administration at Indiana University. Professor Thorelli headed the team which developed the International Operations Simulation (INTOP) at the University of Chicago fifteen years ago. His research and teaching in international business has taken him to western Europe, South Africa, Latin America and Thailand.

* This article is reprinted, with permission, from *The Multinational Corporation: Accounting and Social Implications* (Centre for International Education and Research in Accounting, University of Illinois, 1977) pp 1–19

Exhibit 1. Classical Drama of Multinational Business

Country Measures	Role of Country	Role of Company
Tax lures, concessions	Supplicant	Dictator
Import privileges on machinery, import restrictions on competitive goods	Junior partner	Master
"Strict" law enforcement	Arms-length	Arms-length
Discriminatory law enforcement, changes in concession contracts in favor of government	Master	Junior partner
Regulation, restrictions on remittance of profits or capital	Dictator	Supplicant

Note: The final state might be expulsion – with or without reasonable compensation

Source: Hans B. Thorelli, "The Multinational Corporation As A Change Agent," *Southern Journal of Business* (July 1966): 1-9.

during that same period the ante has been "upped" considerably on the MNC wishing to operate in the spirit of partnership. The prime factor has been the proliferation of nations (from about 100 in 1945 to about 150 today) and the concomitant intensification of nationalism, especially (and perhaps inevitably) in the new nations. Today more than ever before in modern times the world political scene reminds us of medieval Europe. A second factor has been the proliferation of MNCs themselves, a factor which has enhanced competition and further reduced the bargaining position of the individual MNC relative to any given host country. Naturally, the competition within its borders of scores of MNC subsidiaries is generally highly beneficial to an LDC, a fact completely forgotten in contemporary discussions in United Nation circles. We are just beginning to see the force of a third factor changing the climate of MNC operations perhaps even more drastically; namely, the emergence of the Third World as a bloc of nations ready to assert its will relative to both the industrially advanced countries and the MNCs, viewed as the offspring of the industrialized world.

Whatever the nature of the partnership or accommodation of the future, a periodic revaluation of the relationship is most likely to become a standard operating procedure. Interestingly, Cummins Engine Company, Inc., is one of the concerns which even now conducts an annual internal corporate responsibility audit for each overseas operation.

To get a background perspective different from our everyday environment in domestic operations this paper will deal with the evaluation of the MNC from the viewpoint of the LDC. It almost goes without saying that the MNC would be remiss if it did not also evaluate the LDC. Naturally, there are also many other stakeholders interested in evaluating the MNC, such as third-party LDC, the home country, stockholders, customers, employees, creditors in various countries, competitors, and so forth.

Performance audits involve measurement and recordkeeping. No more should have to be said to make clear that our topic concerns accounting and accountants. The discussion will be directed first to economic performance and practices, the area of almost exclusive interest in classic evaluation of managerial prowess. The "social indicators movement" suggests that the idea of a management audit must not be thus narrowly confined. This is certainly true in the LDCs. Thus, a second part of the paper is devoted to externalities and social indicators. We will conclude by suggesting some accounting challenges which seem to emerge from our inventory of factors to take into account.

ECONOMIC PERFORMANCE AND PRACTICES

Earnings and Remittances

Consolidated earnings per share or a statement of consolidated return on investment (ROI) as a measure of performance might satisfy a Milton Friedman but almost certainly not an LDC. Its authorities would naturally like to know about the profitability of operations of the local subsidiary stated in accordance with local accounting practice. But this is not nearly enough. First, it might look askance at very high rates of profit as presumed evidence of undue exploitation rather than of superior performance, especially so if most of the surplus has been remitted to the home country. Admittedly, nowadays this kind of a showing would be confined largely to companies using the strategy of FIFO — that is, "Fast In, Fast Out!" For better or worse, such firms literally may be able "to get away with it" before the ex-host country even becomes aware of what went on, much like some fly-by-night operators do inside our own country.

Second, the LDC is apt to be more impressed by a stable than by a great growth in earnings. In this respect they are more like Europeans than Americans.[1] Clearly, such an attribute may have implications as to inventory evaluation and the creation of hidden reserves of a distinctly un-American character. Third, the LDC will tend to evaluate earnings data relative to the extent of local participation in ownership of the MNC subsidiary. Too, remittances to the home county tend to be a good deal more palatable if local owners are also getting a share of profits.

Minimum Performance Specified by Host Country

In most industrialized nations there are few, if any, minimum requirements as to economic performance imposed by government on the great majority of companies operating in the "private" sector. Many LDCs, on the other hand, take the view that companies—or, at least, companies of foreign origin—should meet certain minimum performance requirements in areas of special interest to the host country in return for local operating privileges. As is typical of LDC approaches to regulation, such requirements usually are not applied in a uniform manner, the prescriptions varying not only on an industry-by-industry but also on a company-by-company basis.

Requirements of this kind involve such matters as minimum (occasionally maximum) level of physical output, minimum quotient of exports of processed goods, maximum quotient or quantity of exports of non-processed raw materials and minimum percentages of local materials and labor used in end products. Anyone the least familiar with the practical complexities of the "rules of origin" of the European Free Trade Association can easily see what a heyday the interpretation of such requirements can provide for those accountants, lawyers, and civil servants who derive pleasure (and personal gain) from maximizing bureaucracy. Yet it seems likely we shall see more of such requirements.

The host county is increasingly concerned also with some of the multinational business practices which in large measure influence the result of the local subsidiary. We are thinking primarily of a variety of corporate tax, currency translation, transfer, and pricing policies. Taken together, these are some of the principal everyday means by which the MNC tries to apply a global perspective of coordination in order to avoid country-by-country suboptimization in its far-flung

---

[1]The shift from growth to financial stability among prime objectives of the MNC is emphasized by the finance vice-president of Cummins Engine Company, Inc., John T. Hackett, in "New Financial Strategies for the MNC," *Business Horizons* (April 1975): 13-20.

operations. These are areas where the interests (at least, short-term) of the MNC and any single host country could be — and frequently are — at odds. The practices involved are sufficiently important to warrant separate comment.

Taxes

Barring undue political risks and constraints on remittances the natural preference of the MNC is to so regulate its internal relations and transactions that it shows high profits in countries with low tax rates and vice versa. This is a frequent empirical observation. Indeed in our own International Operations Simulation[2] — a sophisticated MNC strategy exercise in the management game form — the attention of participating student teams is generally quickly drawn to the possibilities inherent in the differences in local tax rates, loss carry-over provisions, and so forth, without any prodding from the administrator of the simulation. Occasionally, a veritable Ping-Pong game develops in discovering and eliminating loopholes and weaknesses in tax regulations between the teams and the administrator (representing the respective governments).

Be it in real life or in the context of a strategy exercise, what seems to the MNC like conservative management of resources in the "bonus pater familias" tradition to an LDC with a relatively high tax rate may appear as outrageous tax evasion. Clearly, there is room for legitimate differences of opinion as to what are reasonable tax behaviors and policies. The point is that the MNC is well advised not to take undue advantage of the skills of its own tax experts and the possible naiveté of the tax people in an LDC host country. Sooner or later the truth will come out, at which time it is only too easy — in the world in which we find ourselves — for the government to exercise its wrath.

Exchange Rates

European as well as American MNCs in recent years have had ample experience of the hazards of exchange rate fluctuations.[3]

---

[2] The simulation is documented in Hans B. Thorelli et al, *INTOP Player's Manual* (New York: Free Press-Macmillan, 1963) and Hans B. Thorelli and Robert L. Graves, *International Operations Simulation — with Comments on Design and Use of Management Games* (New York: Free Press-Macmillan, 1964).

[3] To take but one European example, the Ericsson Telephone Corporation of Sweden in 1974 reported $29 million and in 1975 some $18 million "exchange losses charged to operations," principally to the Brazilian subsidiary. These large figures should be seen in relation to consolidated earnings before taxes for this MNC, which in each of these years hovered around $100 million. (Figures from *Ericsson Annual Reports*).

The operations of a foreign subsidiary may be highly successful when measured in local currency but may actually involve losses to the multinational enterprise system because of devaluation. Action taken to reduce potential devaluation losses to the system may also reduce the income of the subsidiary in local currency.[4]

Clearly, the LDC will have an interest in how the MNC deals with currency fluctuations and in its way of reporting their impact.

Let us first recognize the distinction between translation and conversion. Translation refers to the process of restating financial accounts from one currency to another. Conversion is the actual sale of one currency for another. Being simulated rather than actual exchange of currency, translation is inherently a matter of judgment. Several conventions exist as to how translation may be executed, each with its set of advantages and disadvantages. Barring international agreement in the area, there is ample room for dialogue between the LDC and the MNC. Of special concern to the LDC should be the fact that unfavorable translation rates may impede the ability of the local subsidiary to obtain future allocations of MNC resources, at least in the short term.

Involving actual exchange, conversion may be less controversial. However, when conversion has taken place at black market rates—typically with the implicit acquiescence of the local government—the LDC may have an interest in the actual rate not being disclosed. This would be but another example of the fact that stakeholder pressures on accountants are not invariably in favor of greater publicity.

Intracompany Transfers

The conditions surrounding the transfer of materials, components, and finished products across national borders between various units of the MNC are in principle—though often not in practice—a matter of internal discretion, whether it be exercised centrally or locally. Too often we tend to think of absolute price as the only relevant variable here. But as in all other marketing activity—and this is what we are talking about in such transfers—there are other strategic considerations. Income, value-added and sales taxes, and tariff duties are examples.

The price of materials relative to components and final products, and of components relative to final products, is another important variable affecting local performance as well as the balance between

---

[4]Stefan H. Robock and Kenneth Simmonds, *International Business and Multinational Enterprises* (Homewood, Ill.: Richard D. Irwin, 1973), p. 484.

global optimization and local suboptimization. However irrational it may be from a global or even long-term local viewpoint, the pressure from LDCs is invariably in the direction of maximum local processing. MNCs in the future may expect increasingly to have to back up demonstrations of the reasonableness of relative prices with formal and sophisticated make-or-buy analyses in cases of imports of less than finally processed goods. Even so, we all know that strictly economic concerns will not always prevail.

Related to price is the use of accounts receivable (or, conversely, of prepayments) as means of extending intracompany credit, or to delay or advance international remittances and conversion of currencies. Here again, a strategy prompted by global considerations may not be viewed by an individual LDC as in its best interest.

Another aspect of intracompany marketing involves applications engineering, installation work, and the provision of patents and knowhow. Such transfer of technology may obviously be of great value to the LDC. Sometimes the services involved constitute part of the purchase of goods; sometimes they are paid for separately. This brings us to the general area of services payments.

Services Payments

Beyond the examples just mentioned payments are often made between units of an MNC (as indeed between units of many large domestic companies) for general management services, for marketing research, for executive development programs, for intracompany loans, and a plethora of other services. Many an LDC may wish to establish whether such payments really are for bona fide services, or merely represent means of withdrawing funds and/or avoiding local taxes.

At first glance this admittedly mushy area may seem in want of guidelines. When you contemplate the very legitimate need for intracorporate flexibility—a need which is certainly as great from the viewpoint of an LDC subsidiary as for the parent in the home country—you begin to think that maybe the area of services payments should be declared off limits to such organizations as International Coordination Committee for the Accounting Profession (ICCAP), International Accounting Standards (IASC), Financial Accounting Standards Board (FASB), and kindred alphabet bodies! [5]

---

[5] As yet no international body has made any pronouncement in this area, according to the United Nations Economic and Social Council, *Commission on Transnational Corporations Report* (E/C.10/AC.1/2), 28 July 1976.

Accounting and Financial Reporting Systems

The financial reporting systems of the MNC must respond to at least three related but distinct sets of needs. There are the needs of conforming to the accounting practices and the reporting expectations of host countries. There are the needs of the MNC headquarters for standardization in reporting systems in order to "really" know what is going on and to ensure comparability between subsidiaries. Finally, there are the needs of the MNC for its own sake and for that of tax authorities in the home country to issue consolidated reports.

There are different views of how reporting systems develop. We have argued in favor of an ecologic view of social institutions, implying that they develop in continuous interaction with the environment whose needs they are supposed to serve.[6] Given the fairly simple and highly secretive business environment, it is but natural that the development of accounting philosophy and systems has been a lag factor in most LDCs.[7] How different the complexity and sophistication of the reporting systems of the MNC—and how different the purposes which these systems serve!

Without for a moment questioning the need for the development of international accounting standards one may safely predict that for the foreseeable future the variegated needs and stages of economic development among nations will mitigate against any single-system approach to financial reporting in MNCs. Multiple systems are here to stay, although perhaps not for as long as death and taxes! Yet, in any given case, outside parties have a legitimate claim to know just *what* system has been used. For instance, if there be hidden reserves, we want to know the why and how.

The need for internal standardization of accounting systems is not confined to the reports themselves. A report is no better than the underlying data. In the absence of universal accounting standards there is a definite need for headquarters' monitoring of accounting methods and internal audits, no matter the sensitivities of local personnel.

Standardized internal reports constitute the backbone of consolidation. The need for consolidated reports is articulated by many home countries and by the financial community. There was a time

[6]Hans B. Thorelli, ed., *International Marketing Strategy* (Harmondsworth, England, and Baltimore: Penguin Books, 1973), reading 1, and Hans B. Thorelli, ed., *Strategy + Structure = Performance: The Strategic Planning Imperative* (Bloomington, Ind.: Indiana University Press, 1977), chap. 1.

[7]For an inventory of factors inhibiting a rapid emancipation of accounting in the LDCs see Alexander N. Keyserlingk, "International Public Accounting: An Underdeveloped Profession," *International Journal of Accounting* (Fall 1975): 15-22.

when this need was less pressingly felt by the MNCs themselves. Unscrupulous management could decide not only whether or not to consolidate but also what subsidiary accounts to consolidate. This left the avenue open to gross manipulation of short-term results. Éven many scrupulous managers until relatively recently rejected the idea of consolidation, on the grounds that it might give a misleadingly positive picture of results as long as there might be obstacles in the way of free remittances from one or several of the consolidated operations. It is true that there are as many obstacles to the free transfer of money as ever, and yet most MNC managements are now in favor of consolidation. There are two reasons for this. The investment community is now thoroughly aware of such obstructions. Equally important is the subtle shift in philosophy of the MNC from a multinational to global point of view. Given a global perspective, constraints on profit remittance are compatible with consolidation as long as investment of profits in the host country or in third countries is not precluded.

EXTERNALITIES AND SOCIAL INDICATORS

We now turn to social indicators and externalities, that is, areas of social costs and benefits occasioned by corporate action. The last ten years have witnessed a lively discussion of social indicators, externalities, the quality of life, and the associated "social responsiblities of business." The intensity of the debate has been directly correlated with the industrialization and per capita wealth of individual nations.

Beyond a few United Nations documents, surprisingly little of tangible import has been written about social indicators relevant to the LDCs in general and to locally harbored subsidiaries of MNCs in particular. For instance, there seems to be next to nothing on the subject in textbooks on international business, in the monographs of Business International and similar bodies and, I believe, in the literature of international accounting.

This lack of antecedents would be less disturbing if individual LDCs or the Third World as a group had clearly identified objectives and priorities in this area. As this is not the case, we shall have to impute them here. At least, this has the advantage that we can make our own selection!

And a selection there *has* to be. There is a virtually endless range of possible "social performances" of business from the macro to the micro level, from social aspects of the very core of business operations to the grant-in-aid of an art exhibit. Although some issues have been clarified by legislation, there are generally no hard and fast rules regarding accountability and responsibility here. Neither is there any consensus as to what *ought* to be. Short-term, at least, management is typically at liberty to lead or to lag relative to the actual or perceived needs of host countries in many of these areas.

We have chosen two such areas for discussion, both of which are relatively close to the "core" of business operations. One of them may be labeled loosely as "corporate citizenship" (or the MNC as resource transformer and employer) and the other "the MNC as a change agent." It almost goes without saying that there are no distinct borderlines between them.

CORPORATE CITIZENSHIP
Communications

The provision of information to local stakeholder groups is an important means for the MNC to build *trust* among these publics. In addition to annual reports, governments increasingly require confidential data from all areas of corporate activity. It is a miracle that Washington has not disappeared under the thousands of tons of forms it has commandeered from business. Even so, under the partnership concept it is often a good idea in the LDC voluntarily to furnish the government data that go beyond the requisite minimum. This is especially true in the area of future plans. Voluntary information programs should be directed also to stockholders, employees, the plant community, the press, and so on. Indeed, the more authoritarian and/or unstable the local government the greater the desirability of building rapport with other groups in society. The prudent MNC will increasingly undertake attitude surveys on a regular basis as a means of gauging how well it stays in tune with various publics.

Value Added

Conventionally, value added is reflected in the difference between the value of the company's sales and that of its purchased inputs on the income statement. This is definitely of interest to the LDC. However, the host country also might well take an interest in how much of all purchases were local in origin. (The need for standard rules for judging origin becomes apparent again.) A Nestlé Alimentana S. A. publication provides an example, as indicated in exhibit 2. This kind of tabulation could easily be broken down further by categories of expenses (and sales) and by individual countries.

Exhibit 2. Nestlé's Contribution to the Local Economy 1974
(in millions of Swiss francs)

	Latin America		Africa		Asia		Total	
Local expenses								
Purchases (goods and services)	1366.9		80.5		157.7		1605.1	
Salaries and labor (including social charges)	257.5		8.9		22.5		288.9	
Taxes	246.2		16.0		43.3		305.5	
TOTAL LOCAL EXPENSES	1870.6	81.2%	105.4	49.7%	223.5	43.9%	2199.5	72.7%
External expenses								
Imports	347.4		98.9		261.9		708.3	
Dividends, interests and royalties	85.8		7.8		23.5		117.1	
TOTAL EXTERNAL EXPENSES	433.2	18.8%	106.7	50.3%	285.4	56.1%	825.4	27.3%
GRAND TOTAL EXPENSES	2303.8	100.0%	212.1	100.0%	508.9	100.0%	3024.9	100.0%
EXPORTS	49.7		81.8		16.4		147.9	

Source: *Nestlé in the Developing Countries* (Vevey, Switzerland: Nestlé Alimentana S.A., 1975), p. 14.

Employer Practices

The creation of employment opportunities is vital in literally every LDC. Number, compensation, training, promotion, and stability of employment are matters of concern, as is the proportion of local relative to foreign management and professional personnel. Beyond working conditions and health and safety provisions many companies, notably in the extractive industries, face the challenge of providing schools, hospitals, stores, housing, and transportation facilities. In some of these areas the MNC must tread gently in order to avoid charges of paternalism.

Rensis Likert and Lee Brummet are names prominently associated with the effort to translate company practices in the employee relations area into benefits and costs to the company and to society. It is all to the good to assign a dollar tag to such practices when the magnitudes involved can be given reasonably precise monetary expression. But we should guard against the notion that all benefits are readily translated into hard currency. In 1974 more than 1,400 foreign nationals traveled to the Eastman Kodak Co. headquarters in the United States for advanced training.[8] Although reasonably precise estimates might be made of the costs involved here, it is clearly difficult to estimate the substantial total benefits, let alone their distribution between the company, the employees and the countries represented.

It is also important not to forget the employment multiplier effect of overseas operations. To quote Lee A. Iacocca on Ford Espana: "At last report, we had 244 Spanish suppliers, who had hired 11,000 new workers to handle our new business."[9]

Ownership

To some companies, such as Caterpillar Tractor Company and Ford Motor Company, control associated with full ownership of overseas subsidiaries appears as a practical necessity. It well may be. In such instances, local participation in ownership may be stimulated by offering for sale shares in the MNC itself, rather than in the subsidiary. Verily, this is in the spirit of a truly transnational enterprise. Realistically, however, most MNCs encounter strong pressure to

[8]International Management and Development Institute, *Top Management Report on Government — Business Cooperation in the Field of International Public Affairs,* (Washington, D.C.: IMDI, 1975), p.31.

[9]Lee A. Iacocca, address to the 63rd National Foreign Trade Convention, New York, 1976, p. 5.

provide local capital an opportunity to participate in ownership of local operations. This may take the form of shares in the local subsidiary but also in joint ventures of different types. It would take us too far to debate the relative merits of such arrangements. The prime short-term disadvantage is the loss of some measure of control; the prime long-term advantage may be the addition of a group of local stakeholders with a vested interest in the success of the MNC subsidiary. As is often the case, more is often to be gained by volunteer action than by postponing what is ultimately inevitable.

Pollution

At the United Nations Conference on the Environment in Stockholm in 1972 many spokesmen for the LDC — warmly applauded by Communist delegates — declared that environmental protection was for the rich and filthy (not necessarily the filthy rich), while development must have priority in the LDC. To the jester this would suggest that the MNC subsidiary generate as much smoke and effluent as convenient, as tangible indicators of industrial progress. Seriously, as the Union Carbide Corporation has noted,

Responsibility to the environment involves the selection of raw materials and manufacturing processes that have minimum polluting effects, the control of materials and processes to see that prescribed standards are met, and the installation of pollution abatement equipment.[10]

It must be clear, nevertheless, that the constellation of tradeoffs between economy and environmental protection may be different in an already highly industrialized country and in an LDC. Differences in climate, flora, and fauna may also well justify the use of more potent herbicides and pesticides in some LDCs than in the home countries of MNCs.[11] In situations like this the challenge to the MNC is to overcome by educational programs local suspicions that the pursuit of profits is more important to it than the welfare of host countries.

THE MNC AS A CHANGE AGENT
Value Structure

The cosmopolitan corporation should view itself as an agent of change, an agent of progress in LDC host countries. If it fails in this regard, it is likely to become the victim of nationalism. Yet to become

---

[10]*The International Responsibilities of a Multinational Corporation,* Union Carbide Corporation (New York: 1976), p. 4.

[11]"New Partners: Multinational Firms Help Poor Nations Grow More Food," *Wall Street Journal* (18 March 1975): 1-14.

an effective change agent the MNC must be a learner as well as a teacher, able to strike the delicate balance of constructive interaction.

By far the most important contribution the MNC can render to the host country is to contribute to a change in attitudes, a change in value structure among all the interest groups it encounters in the course of doing business. This is particularly true as regards consumers. Nothing could be more vital than introducing, and reenforcing, a customer oriented marketing concept. A basic prerequisite to economic development, at least in non-dictatorial nations, is a strengthened *individual need to achieve*. Modern marketing and merchandizing, by stimulating the individual to set *specific* goals in the area of property accumulation, and by dramatizing the relationship between effort, savings, and consumption, is a powerful vehicle in the creation of a climate of values conducive to growth.

Local stockholders frequently have to be educated to see the merit of long-term corporate perspectives and of some sacrifice in payout for corporate citizenship measures. Employees must be induced to learn new skills, respect the discipline of industry, be concerned with quality as well as quantity of output, respond to economic incentives, and so on. To object that this is the "imperialism of values" is utter nonsense: as all LDCs want economic development they had better adopt some of the values which have proven conducive to such growth.

Not all LDCs may show the proper concern for changes of this kind in the local value structure. Indeed, under the impact of the "heavy infrastructure" school of loose thinking which so tragically has dominated the world discussion of economic development for thirty years, the attitude of a majority of these countries may well be one of indifference or skepticism to such value changes. This must not discourage the MNC conscious of its role as change agent from attempting to set pioneering examples in this area. Sooner or later they will likely be recognized.

Corruption

A perennial issue in MNC-LDC relations is corruption. There is no way this huge topic can be given adequate treatment within the confines of this paper. We have, however, agreed to provide the panel on questionable international corporate payments with some appropriately controversial background remarks. They will take the form of a brief review of arguments pro and con and a tentative conclusion as regards subsidiaries of MNC operating in the LDC.

Arguments in favor of accepting the practice of corruption:

1. "When in Rome do as the Romans." This implies an abdication of the role of the MNC as a change agent insofar as ethics are concerned.
2. We should not practice "ethical imperialism," not "shove 'our' values down other people's throats." This argument is based on the questionable assumption that a majority of the population in the host country are in favor of corruption. Not only that: the argument also conveniently overlooks the fact that—for better or worse—the MNC brings pervasive changes in values in many other areas of life in the LDC.
3. We should simply be "neutral" relative to local values. Unfortunately, this argument is untenable. The average MNC subsidiary is a sufficiently major factor on the local scene that a neutral "going along" with the bribery system in effect means actively reenforcing it.
4. Corruption can play a positive role by building an invisible "web of trust" among participants. Maybe so. But the question is whether this is preferable to a visible web of trust based on functional merit.
5. Corruption can play a positive role as the "grease that lubricates" (German *Schmiergeld*) the local Establishment. Again we have the question whether a bureaucracy cannot be made to run along functional lines.
6. We can not afford to walk the straight and narrow as long as competitors bribe their way through the local bureaucracy. At the level of everyday realities this is probably the strongest reason in favor of accepting corruption as "a fact of life."[12] Of course, it does have a little of the flavor of the argumentation of several cadets in the recent West Point scandal: "You cannot get through here unless you cheat," or "Why should I be Simon pure when lots of my buddies are cheating?"

Arguments against corruption:

1. Corruption removes the causal relationship between honest effort and due reward. Thus the system is fundamentally counterproductive.
2. Corruption reenforces fatalism among the "little people" outside the bribery network.
3. Corruption reenforces existing inequalities and by definition involves discrimination. Thus, it tramples equal rights and is antidemocratic.
4. Corruption is a serious block against consumer emancipation in the LDC, as long as bribes can let you get away with selling imitation or

[12]A feature article in the *Wall Street Journal* (28 February 1977), "Crackdown on Bribery Hasn't Damaged Sales, Big Companies Report," does suggest, however, that at least in the short run American MNCs have not suffered by discontinuing corrupt practices.

fraudulent products, forget about quality control and the health and safety of your products, pollute the environment, use false weights and measures, and neglect warranties and consumer complaints.

Our own view is that while rich countries such as the United States can possibly absorb corruption as just another questionable business practice (and, indeed, we seem to have plenty of it), the LDC can ill afford the luxury. The dysfunctional effects of bribery are simply too great relative to the objectives of economic development. There is plenty of room for both individual and, not least, collective initiative among the MNCs active in a given host country to contribute to the gradual eradication of corruption. Let me suggest that in the long run this kind of initiative would help to restore the currently somewhat tarnished image of the MNC in both the LDCs and the industrialized world.

Technology Transfer

The emphasis on transfer of product and production technology (patents and technical knowhow) has been dangerously one-sided. From the viewpoint of balanced development, the transfer of marketing, accounting, and general management technology is at least as important. Prior conferences of this Center for International Education and Research in Accounting have emphasized that the transfer and indigenization of accounting techniques into the LDC is still a backward area. It is no great source of solace that things are equally antediluvian in marketing. High time it is that the MNC and the business professions make use of every opportunity offered by the LDC to get on with the enormous task of technical assistance in these fields.

Building Infrastructure

A great challenge of the local MNC is to foster the development of indigenous business infrastructure, such as local accounting firms, marketing research and advertising agencies, freight handlers, suppliers, and distributors. Clearly, this may also be viewed as an aspect of technology transfer. We have referred to Ford stimulating local sources of supply in Spain. Twenty years earlier Sears, Roebuck & Company did a truly pioneering job in Latin America by developing, training, and, frequently, financing hundreds of local suppliers and by introducing consumer credit on equitable terms. Nestlé's demonstration dairy farms in the state of Chiapas in Mexico furnish another fine example of activity which should be taken into account in any management audit of the performance of that company south of the border.

309

Reducing Dualism

Nowhere is the coexistence of a metropolitan growth sector and a rural stagnation sector as prevalent as in the LDCs. A striking and unfortunate fact of life is that typically both the government and the business community of the LDC pay little more than lip service to the crying need for integration of the rural population into the general thrust of development. Yet, sustained growth of the national economy usually calls for heroic effort to develop agriculture and associated processing activities as well as rural trading and small local manufacturing establishments. Unilever in Africa and, to some extent, Sears in Latin America are representative of MNCs which have accepted the need to bring the two halves of the dual economy together.[13] The LDCs would be well served by many more examples of this kind.

Consumer Protection, Education, and Information

Paradoxically, consumerism is strictly an affluent-country phenomenon. You will find nary a Ralph Nader in the Third World. Yet the average consumer is the true underdog of the LDC. Shoddy locally-made goods are the order of the day in every nation where sellers' markets, import substitution, and producer unconcern with quality prevail. Unconscionable interest rates and credit arrangements frequently create a buyer dependency that is more like serfdom than consumer sovereignty. Imitation, fraudulent and unsafe products galore permeate the marketplace. Their minds set on cement plants and heavy industry, LDC governments generally have no interest in consumers. The key to consumer emancipation is consumer protection, education, and information (in that order).[14]

As consumer emancipation is as much a cause as an effect of economic development, and as substandard competition is clearly not compatible with the modern MNC, it is difficult to imagine an area where the long-term interest of the MNC and that of the local population are more closely united. What we have here is the ideal

---

[13]That not every effort in this direction is an unqualified success is but natural. Thomas Rodolo's *A Business Guide for African Shopkeepers* (Durban: Unilever South Africa, Ltd., undated) is a guide written by a Black executive of Unilever for small Black retailers. However, the concepts used and problems discussed seem more appropriate to sizable metropolitan operations.

[14]Hans B. Thorelli and Sarah V. Thorelli, *Consumer Information Systems and Consumer Policy* (Cambridge, Mass.: Ballinger Publishing Co., 1977), pp. 279-81.

area for voluntary action by such corporations, proceeding singly or in unison.

THE CHALLENGE OF INTERNATIONAL ACCOUNTING

Our thesis is that the mutual interests of the LDC and the MNC call for a partnership or entente. The keystone of such an alliance is mutual trust and respect. One means of assuring that local operations are conducive to trust is a management audit ranging over the wide territory of managerial performance illustrated by our discussion. This audit may be an internal one, as is the case in Cummins Engine, or it may be carried out by consultants. The time may come also when host countries wish to undertake such audits under their own auspices, although this may be less likely where MNCs are already doing it on a voluntary basis.

In some instances it may be in the best interest of the parties to spell out the performance expected by the MNC in some detail in what might appropriately be called a social contract. This may, for example, be desirable when an MNC becomes engaged in a socialist country in a major way. It is true that the overall objectives of growth do not differ much between free enterprise and socialist countries. However, they frequently differ as to the *means* appropriate to reaching the ends. This implies that an MNC going into a socialist country had better bargain for maximum acceptable discretion and other rules of conduct at as early a stage as possible. Once the ground rules are spelled out it may be easier in some respects to operate in a socialist country, as the authoritarian power of the state will be behind you.

Whatever the performance aimed for, it has to be measured! This is precisely the key challenge of the accounting profession in a world where the number and complexity of relevant performance dimensions increase every day. As regards traditional economic performance and practices, the prime needs would seem to be standardization at the international level, while recognizing the need for both variations in local standards for domestic needs and homogeneity in standards when looking at the MNC from a global, headquarters point of view. Accountants working with and in the MNC must vastly increase the extension of technical assistance which the discipline is rendering to the LDCs. A special need is the perfectioning of project (and product) life cycle accounting, needed as a basis for strategic planning by both the MNC and the LDC.

Greater still, however, than the internationalization of classic accounting is the challenge confronting the profession in the evaluation

f corporate citizenship and social indicators. A whole host of
measures needs to be developed and implemented in this area. The
question is no longer whether this will be done, but whether accounting will be the discipline and profession accepting the challenge.
If you do, we may predict it will not be long before accounting is
deeply involved in qualitative as well as quantitative measurement.

A third major challenge is presented by the environmental scan-
ning information system MNC management will need for strategic
planning and performance control. Accounting may be called upon to
design a type of management information system (MIS) of which such
esoterics as futures research and periodic opinion surveys among all
relevant stakeholder interests may be important integral parts. That
kind of MIS will be needed to answer critical questions such as the following. Are we in tune with the demands of the operating environment
in our host countries? If not, what are the areas in which we need to
improve our performance?

But when all has been said and done at the local level, it is the
mission of accounting to retain and extend the global perspective of
the MNC. Never should we lose sight of the fact that it represents a
more successful instance of international cooperation and a closer approach to global thinking than we have thus far encountered among
governments. The MNC is the torchbearer of One World, and here in
the end lies its lasting service to humanity.

Undoubtedly it sounds incredible, but some nonaccountants have
been saying that accounting is dull. Whatever truth there may have
been to this saying in the past, one thing is clear. The future of accounting in international operations promises to be an exciting one.

PART V

Transnational financial decisions and control

CHAPTER 21

A synthesis of foreign direct investment theories and theories of the multinational firm*

A. Louis Calvet

Abstract. This paper first presents a taxonomy of the foreign direct investment theories following the market imperfections paradigm. It then focuses on recent developments pertaining to the theory of the multinational firm, specifically the appropriability, internalization, and diversification theories. Subsequently, the multinational phenomenon is seen as the result of an international differentiation of activities and an intrafirm integration across national borders — all this within a markets and hierarchies approach. Last, the paper points to areas for future research.

INTRODUCTION

■ It was twenty years ago that the late Stephen Hymer wrote his seminal thesis on foreign direct investment (FDI) and multinational enterprises (MNEs). Since then, the literature on these subjects has increased substantially and taken different directions, placing the multinational firm at the crossroads of many disciplines and of many debates as well.

Behind the proliferation of articles and books in this field, Hymer's theoretical contribution has remained unshaken and has led the way to further elaboration and refinement of the theory. One can hardly find a publication on FDI that does not make some reference to Hymer's work — which is highly indicative of its relevance. His early insights into the determinants of foreign direct investment have paved the way for further research, and major additions have taken place since, perhaps with increased frequency in the last five years. This renewed interest in the theory of the multinational firm (rather than foreign direct investment — a point to which this discussion shall return) results from various reasons, a major one being the parallel and growing interest in the economics of internal organization.

*A. L. Calvet is Assistant Professor at the Faculty of Administration at the University of Ottawa. This paper is based upon his doctoral dissertation completed at M.I.T. in 1980.

The author is much indebted to John H. Dunning of the University of Reading for many valuable suggestions. Two anonymous referees also provided valuable comments. All responsibility for errors remains with the author.

* This article is reprinted, with permission, from *The Journal of International Business Studies* (Spring/Summer 1981, Tenth Anniversary Special Issue) pp 43–59

The time seems ripe for reviewing the work done over the last few years in the direction pursued by Hymer and for identifying recent trends likely to guide the future research in the field. Such is the purpose of this paper. Section one presents a taxonomy of the determinants of foreign direct investment derived from the market imperfections paradigm. Section two singles out recent contributions to the theory of the MNE. In section three a new theoretical framework is proposed — the markets and hierarchies approach — in an attempt to encompass the various strands of current research on the MNE. Finally, section four discusses areas for further study.

FOREIGN DIRECT INVESTMENT IN THE CONTEXT OF THE THEORY OF THE MARKET: THE MARKET IMPERFECTIONS PARADIGM

Kindleberger provided the first comprehensive survey of the various theories of foreign direct investment along the lines expressed by Hymer.[1] He approached the question of direct investment from the standpoint of the perfectly competitive model of neoclassical economics by asserting that in a world of pure competition direct investment could not exist. [Kindleberger 1969, p. 13] Indeed, when all markets operate efficiently, when there are no external economies of production or marketing, when information is costless and there are no barriers to trade or competition, international trade is the only possible form of international involvement.[2] Logically, it follows that it is the departures from the model of perfect competition that must provide the rationale for foreign direct investment. The first deviation had been noted by Hymer [1960/1976], who postulated that local firms have better information about the economic environment in their country than do foreign companies. According to his argument, two conditions have to be fulfilled to explain the existence of direct investment: (1) foreign firms must possess a countervailing advantage over the local firms to make such investment viable, and (2) the market for the sale of this advantage must be imperfect. It was, thus, a natural step for Kindleberger later to suggest that market imperfections were the reason for the existence of foreign direct investment. Specifically, he came up with the following taxonomy: imperfections in goods markets, imperfections in factor markets, scale economies and government-imposed disruptions. [1969, p. 14] This classification may be called the 'market imperfections paradigm.' To encompass new developments in the field of determinants of foreign investment, a somewhat different taxonomy from that of Kindleberger may be proposed to distinguish among four classes: (1) market disequilibrium hypotheses, (2) government-imposed distortions, (3) market structure imperfections, and (4) market failure imperfections. Some brief comments are in order to elucidate the meaning of these four categories.

The common feature found in all the hypotheses in group (1) will be the transitory nature of foreign direct investment. FDI is an equilibrating force among segmented markets which eventually comes to an end when equilibrium is reestablished; that is, when rates of return are equalized among countries. The unifying characteristic in group (2) will be the role played by either host or home governments in providing the incentive to invest abroad. Group (3) will include theories in which the behavior of firms deviates from that assumed under conditions of perfect competition, through their ability to influence market prices. Finally, in group (4) will be classified theories which depart from the technical assumptions behind the model of perfect markets; that is, the assumptions about production techniques and commodity properties. This last category will deal basically with those phenomena which lead to market failure, or, cases where "the decentralizing efficiency of that regime of signals, rules and built-in sanctions which defines a price-market system" will fail. [Bator 1958, p. 352]

Several factors support this classification scheme. In the first place, the order in which the categories appear corresponds roughly to the chronological order in which new explanations of the FDI phenomenon have occurred. They range from the old view of an integrated approach to foreign direct investment and portfolio capital flows among countries, to the more recent versions of FDI as a spin-off of welfare economics. [Johnson 1970] Second, most, if not all of the early literature on FDI fits into this categorization. Third, the categories are roughly in the order of increasing need for control over foreign operations. The justification for controlling foreign firms becomes, as we will see, stronger as we go from (1) to (4). Finally, note that (1), (2), and (4) are compatible with profit-maximizing behavior while (3) requires a restricted version of the maximization argument, due to the typical interdependencies of oligopolistic industries. By being less restrictive, growth or sales maximization, profit satisficing, or any other mode of behavior can be accommodated in any of the four categories.

Market Disequilibrium Hypotheses

The notion of a perfect economy and perfect competition requires the assumption that prices everywhere are adjusted to bring supply and demand into equilibrium. It may well be that because of segmentation in world markets, rates of return are not equalized internationally. In a disequilibrium context flows of FDI would take place until markets returned to stability. Instances of disequilibrium conditions that provide incentives to invest abroad are numerous. They basically apply to factor markets and foreign exchange markets.

Currency overvaluation is perhaps the most salient example of these disequilibrium hypotheses. A currency may be defined as overvalued when at the prevailing rate of exchange production costs for tradable goods in the country are, on the average, higher than in other countries. [Ragazzi 1973, p. 491] Such an occurrence creates opportunities for profit-making by holding assets in undervalued currencies with the expectation that, once the equilibrium in the foreign exchange market is reestablished, capital gains will be realized. In the meantime, there is an incentive to locate production of internationally traded commodities in countries with undervalued currencies and to purchase income-producing assets with overvalued money. The important point is that, once exchange rates return to equilibrium, the flow of FDI should stop. Even more, foreign investors should sell their foreign assets, pocket the capital gains, and return to domestic operations.

Foreign direct investment may be attracted toward areas where the average rates of profit are higher. This is basically the capital markets disequilibrium hypothesis. It implies that, for a given level of risk, rates of return on assets are not equalized internationally by portfolio capital flows, due to inefficiencies in securities markets — such as, thinness or lack of disclosure. Therefore, the only way that rates of return on real assets can be brought to equilibrium is by flows of direct investment. The process is, however, self-destructive because firms from low yield countries will invest in countries with high yields until rates of return are brought to equilibrium. Then foreign direct investment will cease.[3]

The same approach has been used with respect to labor costs. Here foreign direct investment would flow from high-labor-cost countries to low-cost countries in the pursuit of cost minimization. This hypothesis is no exception to the transitory character of the FDI phenomenon, because the demand for labor in countries where wages are low will tend to hike up labor costs, while the lack of demand in source countries will drive wages down. The result: A finite life for direct investment.

Finally, disequilibrium situations may arise in technology markets. Rates of technical and technological innovation may vary among nations, thereby placing some countries in leadership positions with respect to new products and processes. The origins of superior knowledge can be traced back to superior R & D performance or merely chance factors — such as, a breakthrough in scientific knowledge. In any event, firms in countries where technology is relatively advanced would find profitable opportunities abroad and would, therefore, have an incentive to invest overseas.

The previous review covers basically all the situations where conventional economic disequilibrium conditions can give rise to FDI flows. The reader will have recognized in these hypotheses the old view of FDI as an equilibrating capital flow. It is not necessary to state at length the well-known shortcomings of this traditional view of FDI — shortcomings uncovered in Hymer's thesis, which showed that FDI can better be understood within the realm of industrial organization.[4] Prior to examining this latter approach, let us look at governmental policies and their relation to FDI.

Government-Imposed Distortions

At the outset, it should be mentioned that government policies could conceivably be responsible for some of the disequilibrium hypotheses previously considered. Fixed exchange rates, wage policies, and policies regulating the migration of labor create unstable conditions apt to foster foreign investing. The main difference, however, between the two categories is that there appear to be no equilibrating forces which would correct the distortions imposed by governments. That is to say, in order to nullify the incentive for direct investment, all governments would have to harmonize their policies or have no policies at all.

Tariffs, other trade barriers (for example, quotas), and, it might be added, nontariff barriers (for example, regulations for imported goods) are often regarded as a major cause of direct investment. Other things being equal, an increase in trade barriers (or the expectation of their rise) may be the necessary incentive for firms to establish a subsidiary inside the protected market, rather than export to it.

Another major government-induced distortion is the levy of taxes.[5] Not surprisingly, the incentive to invest abroad can originate in differences in the tax laws governing countries. After all, firms try to maximize rates of return after taxes. If, furthermore, the parent government tax laws encourage expatriation of capital (for example, via a deferral system), the incentive will be even stronger to set up foreign operations.

Government-related disruptions can take many other forms — from price and profit regulation to antitrust laws or any other change in the institutional setting in which business operates. All these actions can be used to rationalize the expatriation of domestic firms on the grounds that they restrict their autonomy.

Suffice it to say that when foreign direct investment is viewed as a package made up of capital, technology, and other forms of knowledge, the tariff argument indicates only that the movement of goods via exports is denied or restricted. In principle, tariffs do not prevent the licensing route nor does it necessarily follow that the foreign firm will be interested in setting up a subsidiary in the protected market. (Other conditions must be present; for example, the market must be large enough to allow the firm to recover the costs of its initial foreign investment.) As for the tax argument, it applies mainly to cases where a firm is able to generate profits abroad as a result of its foreign operations, given that local firms have an inherent advantage resulting from their institutional knowledge. This leads us directly into the oligopolistic approach to FDI.

Market Structure Imperfections

The previous cases of disequilibrium hypotheses and government-induced distortions are compatible with a "relatively" competitive market structure. Market structure imperfections, on the other hand, refer to deviations from purely market-determined prices brought about by the existence of monopolistic or oligopolistic market characteristics. In this perspective, foreign direct investment becomes the outgrowth of industrial organization.

The recognition that foreign direct investment belongs to the realm of industrial organization goes back to Hymer's writings. [1960/1976] Since then, it has received much attention and has become the most popular approach to date. [See for example: Bergsten, Horst, and Moran 1978.] There are two essential characteristics which set oligopolistic industries apart from competitive ones. First, the former are industries where maximizing decisions — whether of profit or growth — are interdependent; each firm must speculate on the reactions of the few other firms in the industry. Second, barriers to entry are essential, in order to prevent a surge of competition. As one would expect, both of these features have been used extensively to explain foreign direct investment.

Not all barriers to entry lend themselves to direct expansion abroad. Leaving aside vertical foreign investments which respond to barriers of a different kind, Caves considered product differentiation in the home market as being the critical element giving rise to foreign investment. [1971, p. 270] The successful firm, producing a differentiated product, controls knowledge about servicing the domestic market that can be used at little or no cost in other national markets. This provides the motivation for investing abroad, as long as the means to protect the product exist; such as, patents and copyrights.

Other contributions to the oligopolistic feature of direct investment include models which explicitly take into account the interdependence of firms in the industry. The most publicized is, perhaps, the product life cycle hypothesis [Vernon 1966] where firms react to the threat of losing markets — as the product matures — by expanding overseas and capturing the remaining rent from the product's development. Variations on this approach include the "follow the leader" case, where the investment moves of one firm trigger similar moves by other leading firms in the industry [Knickerbocker 1974], and the "exchange of threats" hypothesis, where oligopolists imitate each other by establishing subsidiaries in each other's markets. [Graham 1974]

Despite their success, the problems associated with the industrial organization hypotheses are many and serious. For one, there is too great an emphasis placed on sellers' concentration as being a main determinant of direct investment. Ragazzi reported that the degree of industrial concentration was, in general, much higher in Europe than in the U.S. in the 50s, although the bulk of FDI was from the U.S. to Europe. [1973, p. 489] Also, whereas FDI theories derived from industrial organization may explain the advantages of home country firms, they cannot predict the country or industry patterns of foreign investment. [Aliber 1970, p. 20] Nor can they adequately explain the apparent preference for takeovers of domestic firms over de novo investment. Furthermore, in many instances, neither are the causal factors in the investment decision isolated — for example, in Knickerbocker's thesis [1974] — nor is the decision integrated with the alternative methods — exports and licensing — of exploiting the foreign firms' advantages in the host country. Recent evidence based on Japan's direct investment abroad tends to confirm some of the shortcomings of the industrial organization approach, because the Japanese experience shows a compatibility of international investment with a relatively competitive market structure at home. [Kojima 1978; Ozawa 1979]

Finally, and particularly in Caves's argument, the static concept of product differentiation is related to the notion of intangible capital in the form of knowledge, yet the two do not imply the same form of international involvement. Indeed, "licensing of domestically controlled firms would be a feasible alternative in industries with an unchanging product mix since quality changes, brand changes, etc. pose no difficulties for agreements." [Baumann 1975, p. 683] However, as will be seen in the next section, the transfer of intangible capital in the form of knowledge does pose serious problems.

Market Failure Imperfections

As was pointed out earlier, market failure imperfections are characteristics in production techniques and commodity properties which prevent a market mechanism from allocating resources efficiently. There are basically three types of imperfections which lead to market failures: (1) external effects, (2) public goods, and (3) economies of scale (decreasing cost industries). Under any one of these conditions, the duality between social efficiency and market performance ceases to exist. [Bohm 1973, p. 19]

The significance of market failures as a potential explanation of FDI was not fully realized until 1970. At that time, Johnson related foreign direct investment to the welfare economics of technological and managerial knowledge as a factor of production — a typical case of market failure. [1970, p. 36] His ideas were based upon previous work done by Arrow on the accumulation of knowledge in society. [1962] Briefly, the peculiarities of knowledge which make its markets so imperfect are (1) the lumpiness of the inventive input necessary to produce it, and (2) the high degree of spillover or externality that accompanies the inventive process. [Nordhaus 1969, p. 36]

This in turn creates problems for both the production and international transfer of knowledge. First, reasons of social efficiency would dictate that existing knowledge be made available as a free good. Hence the dilemma: how is the production of new knowledge to be motivated, if no property rights are granted? Second, the natural characteristics of knowledge would favor its transfer within a single firm, hence 'justifying' foreign direct investment over other alternatives of exploiting foreign markets. Indeed, if markets for knowledge are difficult to organize, internalization within the firm achieves two objectives: (1) to provide channels for the transfer of this knowledge at lower costs than via external modes [Teece 1976]; and, (2) to avoid or slow down dissipation of this knowledge to competitors.

Before ending this section, it would be of interest to take a historical perspective in order to identify stages in the development of FDI theories. The author's view distinguishes among three phases in past and current thinking about foreign direct investment. The first one — perhaps the best known — began when Hymer linked FDI to industrial organization (the study of market imperfections) and thereby ended a period in which FDI had been associated with a capital flow.[6] The Hymer-Kindleberger school of thought found its roots in the traditional theory of the market; it dealt with market imperfections in a partial equilibrium setting and emphasized above all the monopolistic nature of FDI. A quotation from Kindleberger's writings [1969, pp. 13–14] adds additional support to the author's assertion: "the nature of the monopolistic advantages which produce direct investment can be indicated under a variety of headings:. . . departures from perfect competition in goods markets,. . . departures from perfect competition in factor markets,. . . internal and external economies of scale,. . . government limitations on output or entry." All these aspects belong to the theory of the market.

The second discontinuity — or change in direction — originated with Harry Johnson in 1970. In his well-known article he attempted to go beyond the Hymer-Kindleberger framework by investigating the welfare implications of the international transfer of knowledge — the central theme of FDI. He thereby placed the FDI debate at a different level of discourse, as he himself wrote: "This paper will be concerned with essentially the same possibilities as other authors have noted, but it seeks to place the issues in a broader and more fundamental perspective by relating them to the welfare economics of technological and managerial knowledge as a factor of production." [1970, p. 36] In so doing, he introduced FDI to a much richer area of economics where one studies not only the damaging effects of monopolies and oligopolies on market functioning, but also the failure of markets, including their non-existence — all within a global approach to the economic system and under the consideration of social efficiency. The direction taken by Johnson which attempts to place FDI in a global discussion of welfare economics has undoubtedly many advantages. Perhaps the most important one is showing how limited the monopolistic market imperfections perspective is. However, it also has a major disadvantage. Indeed, welfare economics has little to say in situations where prices are not taken as given, for then the resulting equilibrium need not be Pareto efficient. [Varian 1975, p. 234] In other words, whereas Johnson's ambitious perspective raises interesting questions (the production of knowledge, its appropriation, the effects on world's welfare, and so on), by the same token it raises more questions than economic theory can answer, at least at the present time. Hymer was already aware of this problem when he pointed out that to the extent that MNEs erode national power — that is, the effectiveness of governments' policies — they similarly prevent corrective governmental action in situations where it is necessary for achieving social efficiency. [Hymer 1970] The third and current stage in the thinking about FDI began with authors such as McManus [1972], Buckley and Casson [1976], and Magee [1976]. Their most salient feature: an emphasis on the theory of the MNE, rather than on the theory of FDI. This certainly reflects more than a choice of words; it is a purposive decision to go beyond the view that MNEs create market imperfections. It is also a "switch in attention from the act of foreign direct investment...to the institution making the investment." [Dunning 1979, p. 274]

MULTINATIONAL ENTERPRISES IN THE CONTEXT OF THE THEORY OF THE FIRM

Although market imperfections still underlie much of the thinking on MNEs, there has been a distinctive shift in the theoretical literature toward developing a global theory of the multinational firm.[7] It was not by chance that at approximately the same time the economic profession showed signs of a renewed interest in the economics of internal organization, a new terminology evolved for an old area of economics — the theory of the firm.[8]

This section will examine three major contributions in the field: the appropriability theory, the internalization theory, and the diversification theory. The three bring new insights to our understanding of the multinational phenomenon.

The Appropriability Theory

The appropriability theory of the multinational corporation, best represented in Magee's work [1976, 1977], is a consolidation of the views of two main streams of thought: on the one hand, the industrial organization approach to foreign direct investment; on the other hand, the neoclassical ideas on the private appropriability of the returns from investments in information. MNEs are at the crossroad of these two streams of thought for, as Magee states, the distinctive nature of these corporations resides in their being specialists in the production of 'information' [technology]. [1976, p. 317] Valuable information is generated by MNEs at five different stages: new product discovery, product development, creation of the production function, market creation, and appropriability.

The theory then postulates that, because sophisticated technologies are less prone to be imitated, MNEs are more successful in appropriating the returns from these technologies than from simple ones. Furthermore, sophisticated information is transferred more efficiently via internal channels than by market means. These two factors taken together enable Magee to assert that there is a built-in incentive in the economic system to generate sophisticated information — to the detriment, in some cases, of users' needs; for example, those of less developed countries. To complete the theory, Magee goes on to say that production is information-saving so that, ultimately, there is a decline in the production of new information. All these considerations generate a technology cycle at the industry level; that is, young industries are those where information is being created at a fast pace, which in turn implies that the size of the firm expands because of the internalization of the information produced. As the industry matures, the amount of information being created is minimal. Thus, optimum firm size diminishes accordingly. In terms of the international expansion of the firm, the assertion that optimum firm size declines after the innovation stage suggests that, after a certain point, licensing should increase relative to direct investment.

The propensity to engage in takeover activity is also an implication of the appropriability theory. On the subject of takeovers, Magee states that "takeovers of host country production facilities and mergers of multinationals with host country firms are normal consequences of the expansion in optimum size early in an industry's technology cycle." In addition, takeovers, according to Magee, "may be aimed at slowing the depreciation of the stock of information by absorbing the most likely interlopers." [1976, p. 333] Note that two arguments are being used: one is the higher efficiency of intrafirm transfers dictating an internal solution; the other one is the monopolistic argument of the industrial organization approach to FDI.

The Internalization Theory

Imperfect markets for knowledge is the basis of Buckley and Casson's theory of the multinational enterprise. [1976] It is perhaps in their work that the notion of the multinational firm as an entity is given the most attention. The starting point of their theory is the idea that the modern business sector carries out many activities apart from the routine production of goods and services. All these activities, including marketing, R & D, and training of labor, are interdependent and are related through flows of intermediate products — mostly in the form of knowledge and expertise. [Buckley and Casson 1976, p. 33] However, intermediate product markets are difficult to organize due to their imperfections — which provide an incentive to bypass them. This results in the creation of internal markets; that is, bringing the activities which are linked by the market under common ownership and control. [Buckley and Casson 1976, p. 33] Finally, it is the internalization of markets across national boundaries which gives rise to the multinational enterprise. A few years earlier, McManus [1972] had already shown that the essence of the phenomenon of international production is not the transfer of capital but rather the international extension of managerial control over foreign subsidiaries — control which is ownership-based and through which management replaces the market as the allocator of resources.

Dunning [1977], expanding on the internalization theory, stated that the incentives to internalize activities are to avoid the disadvantages, or capitalize on the advantages, of imperfections on external (markets and public) mechanisms of resource allocation [1977, p. 402]. Therefore, not only must firms possess superior resources — as in Hymer's argument — they must also have the desire and the ability to internalize the advantages which result from their possession.

The Diversification Theory

Up to now the imperfections with which this discussion has been concerned were imperfections in markets for products and for knowledge. Financial market imperfections have not been generally in the forefront of the literature, "presumably because financial markets are deemed to be more efficient than markets for real goods and services" [Lessard 1979]. However, the evidence that has accumulated recently tends to suggest that there are imperfections in financial markets, and hence advantages for the MNE in internalizing financial transactions. In his recent review of the internal financial transfers within MNEs, Lessard [1979] pointed to sources of gains stemming from exchange control arbitrage, credit market arbitrage and equity market arbitrage. Undoubtedly the most well-publicized advantage accruing to MNEs is that which derives from equity market arbitrage, i.e., risk reduction through diversification.

Although the mechanics of diversification are well known, the application of international diversification to the MNE has not always been properly substantiated.[9] Originally the argument had been put forward by international portfolio theorists that variations in security returns across countries show less correlation than within a single country. An immediate implication is that international diversification can be used as a means of reducing the average risk faced by investors. However, there is nothing in this argument which would justify corporate international diversification, for in an integrated and perfectly competitive world capital market, individual investors can diversify their holdings at no cost. The issue which was subsequently raised in the literature concerned the existence of barriers or costs to capital transfers and the potential benefits to be derived from the indirect diversification provided by MNEs. In one of the first attempts to deal with this issue, Agmon and Lessard [1977] argued that two conditions must be satisfied before attributing the diversification motive to the MNE: (1) there must exist greater barriers or costs to portfolio capital flows than to direct investment flows; and (2) investors must recognize that MNEs provide a diversification vehicle which would otherwise not be available. More recently, Errunza and Senbet [1980], taking a more general equilibrium perspective, have been able to show, however, that the existence of barriers *per se* does not yield price differentials among purely domestic and multinational stocks. Within a framework which allows for (1) supply adjustments by MNEs, and (2) interactions of barriers to international flows faced by both firms and investors, these authors have derived conditions under which the diversification services by MNEs get "priced out" in equilibrium. In other words, in a well-functioning domestic capital market, investors must accept a smaller equilibrium expected return on multinational stocks, and hence must pay a price premium to hold those stocks. Consequently, the pricing effects of international involvement by the MNE become hard to isolate empirically.

Tests on the diversification theory of the MNE had also, in the past, suffered from serious shortcomings. Agmon and Lessard [1977] provided limited evidence that investors "recognize" the international involvement of U.S. multinationals. Jacquillat and Solnik [1978] found, however, that portfolios made up of MNEs' shares are poor substitutes for international portfolio diversification, and that the extent of foreign influence on stock prices is very limited when compared to the extent of firms' foreign involvement. The difficulty with these and other tests on the behavior of MNEs' share prices is that (1) they rely on traditional risk-return generating processes and performance evaluation techniques which cannot assess whether FDI is beneficial to investors in terms of contributing to market value, and (2) more importantly, they are carried out without a fully developed theoretical model of the pricing of risky assets in an international context.[10] The recent work of Errunza and Senbet [1980] avoids some of the shortcomings of other studies by using a value-based — rather than a price-based — method to assess the effects of international operations. Briefly, they demonstrate that (1) there existed a positive and systematic relationship between the current degree of international involvement and the excess market value of U.S. multinationals over a ten-year time span, and (2) the monopoly rents derived by these firms were stronger during the sub-period in which barriers to capital flows were in effect. That is to say, the stronger relationship between international involvement and monopoly rents during the period characterized by barriers to capital flows (as compared to a later period with no restrictions) is indicative of the benefits to be derived from financial market imperfections, over and above those to be attributed to real market imperfections.

These three new approaches to the phenomenon of international production undoubtedly represent a step forward in explaining the propensity of firms to choose the foreign direct investment route over alternative ways, such as licensing, in order to exploit foreign markets. All three theories, however, offer a double-edged view of the MNE: on the one hand, multinationals appear to take advantage of imperfections to enhance their already impressive power[11]; on the other hand, they facilitate the transfer of factors, goods, and services, transfers which would otherwise be handled inefficiently, or not at all. Future empirical work comparable to Teece's [1976] may possibly shed further light on the question of whether MNEs create, extend, and/or perpetuate market imperfections, or whether they are a vehicle for overcoming natural imperfections to the benefit of all parties.

In spite of the progress that these approaches already represent, one can elucidate further the institutionalization of international production within the MNE by combining ideas drawn from these new explanations with earlier theoretical contributions to the FDI literature.

MARKETS AND HIERARCHIES: TOWARD A THEORY OF INTERNATIONAL BUSINESS

The early emphasis in FDI literature on departures from perfect markets was consistent with the historical development of economic theorizing. Economists approached the phenomenon of international production at first with a simple neoclassical view of the world. This led one of Kindleberger's students to state: "Paradoxically, the unifying concept for analysis of direct investment has been the static, profit maximizing, perfectly competitive market model of general equilibrium, with perfect information and no transactions costs." [McClain 1975, p. 181] Such an approach has, however, limited applicability for understanding the MNE because it is too general. In fact, justifying the role of MNEs solely on the basis of market imperfections is comparable to rationalizing the need for governmental allocation policies (such as, anti-trust laws and stabilization policies) because we live in an 'imperfect' economy. In other words, welfare economists as well as economists studying the MNE refer to the same imperfections (monopoly, oligopoly, natural imperfections) in their analysis, so that the rationalization of two phenomena so apparently distant — multinational firms and government intervention in the economy — rests upon the same theoretical basis. Upon reflection, this is no mere coincidence. What the market imperfections paradigm indicates is simply that firms and governments are substitutes for market allocations.

The efforts of Buckley and Casson [1976], Magee [1976], and Dunning [1977], discussed earlier, have gone in the direction of both negating some of the narrow assumptions of the early neoclassical approach and concentrating on the institution making the investment. Building upon these contributions, this section will elaborate further on a particular assumption of the neoclassical model which has come under renewed criticism[12] recently and the removal of which is crucial to understanding organizations: the assumption of zero transactions costs when operating a market. To see clearly the relevance of this assumption to international business a short digression is necessary.

Hardly anyone would deny that cooperative action is a necessity and that it involves interdependence between individuals. The necessary interdependence of individuals that underlies any productive activity calls for transactions or exchanges in which agents who supply capital, those who supply labor, and those who bring their expertise, and so on, receive something of value in return. Recognition of such basic facts makes the study of the various means by which these multiple transactions are organized an issue worth exploring. An investigation of the different modes of transacting becomes a central question for economics, to the extent that the interest resides in the efficiency with which transactions are carried out between individuals.

Economic theory showed long ago that competitive markets exhibit superior coordinating properties for the organization of economic exchanges. Specifically, provided that some important assumptions are met[13] (in particular, no transactional frictions), the allocation of resources which results under a system of competitive markets is Pareto optimal.

While providing a very powerful reason for justifying the organization of transactions through the mechanism of competitive markets, economic theory left itself exposed to a question first raised by Coase [1937] and since then taken up again by Malmgren [1961]: "why do multi-person, multi-process firms exist in a competitive economy?" and he went on to add: "to say that firms exist because co-ordination of production is required is to miss the point entirely. What has to be explained is why firms, in the form of willful entrepreneurs, organize production in areas where the market could do so also." [1961, pp. 400–401]

The answer to that question rests on the realization that the optimality of competitive markets in a Paretian sense does not necessarily hold true if there are non-negligible costs in using the markets. Transactions (enforcement) costs arise principally when (1) strategic or opportunistic behavior is present among agents to an exchange[14]; (2) the commodities or services traded are ambiguously defined; and (3) contractual obligations extend in time. In the typical cases where individuals are deprived of strategic behaviors (such as, shirking, gaming, cheating, or malingering) and exchange well-defined goods or services in discrete transactions, the superiority of the price mechanism may be irrefutable. However, insofar as transactions are allowed to be extended over time and refer to ambiguously defined commodities and services, and strategic behavior is allowed to be played out, enforcement and monitoring costs may become prohibitive. There is a broad consensus in the internal organization literature that, under these latter conditions, firms tend to substitute for markets, on the basis that the firms' internal control procedures are then better suited to organize transactions. [Williamson 1975]

These brief considerations, based mainly upon the work of Coase [1937] and Williamson [1975], lead to the main feature of their approach—that of treating markets on the one hand, and firms (hierarchies) on the other, as alternative modes of organizing production.[15] A much less emphasized outcome of this discussion, albeit by no means less important, is that the substitution of a hierarchy or bureaucracy for a market situation entails a profound change in the structure of interpersonal interactions and in the way in which economic exchange proceeds. In pure markets, transactions among individuals or groups are carried out at arm's length: participants share no relationships other than the ones required by the transactions themselves and can affect each other only via the market and the price system. In hierarchies, transactions take place among individuals or groups that are linked via an authority relation. (When companies are involved, the authority relation gets its legitimacy from ownership rights.) When seen in their purest forms, and from the standpoint of the degree of personal interaction required to accomplish the exchange, markets and firms can be considered as two extreme modes of organizing economic transactions. (Needless to say, many exchanges fall somewhere in between these two modes.[16] These purest cases are nevertheless interesting, because they constitute powerful categories for theorizing.)

Returning now to the subject of international production, the question of the particular form of involvement by firms outside their national boundaries can be put into a markets and hierarchies framework: why would a firm prefer to establish hierarchical links abroad rather than contract at arm's length? Stated differently, what advantages do firms find in hierarchical structures which make the latter preferable to the outright sale or license of proprietary assets to foreign-owned firms?

Phrasing the old licensing vs. direct investment question in this way is more than a semantical rearrangement of terms. First, it allows scholars who have worked on the MNE in a parallel fashion to economists, such as organizational theorists, to realize that organizations and markets are the two principal mechanisms for mediating transactions, and that organizations may be considered as examples of market failures. Therefore, our knowledge of organizations can be called upon to help us understand the reasons for their superiority in certain situations and thus complement our knowledge about markets. Second, by not assuming the primacy of one organizational mode over the other, the door is open to the investigation of the relative merits of each mode for a given environment and the kind of transaction involved. By merits are meant not only the efficiency of accomplishing the exchange but also the very fact that the transaction takes place and how it does so. This is a significant departure from economic theory which, in general, assigns an unjustified advantage to markets.

Firms do not expand abroad, though, simply because they can internalize transactions within their hierarchy. Their desire to operate internationally has to stem from other reasons too. Therefore, one must combine the hierarchies vs. markets paradigm with existing FDI hypotheses to arrive at a synthesis of the determinants of direct investment; thus, two facets of the foreign expansion of firms have to be explained. One is the foreign involvement — the multinational character; the other, the internalization within a single entity. In other words, certain factors must account for the differentiation of operations across national boundaries; other factors must explain the integration of operations within a hierarchical mode of economic organization.[17] The specification of these two sets of factors, as well as their interplay, is the subject of the remainder of this section.

Foreign involvement may occur for two basic reasons: (1) the firm possesses some valuable asset which it can use in other national jurisdictions; and (2) the host country owns resources attractive to the foreign firm. This can be restated by saying that there are firm- and country-specific factors to account for a firm's foreign involvement. A similar terminology was used by Dunning [1977; 1979] when he called the firm's internal factors 'ownership-specific endowments,' and its external factors 'location-specific endowments.' Location-specific factors refer not only to the endowments of countries, but also to gains arising from the geographical positioning of multiplant operations.[18]

Ownership-specific endowments have long been recognized as relevant to an understanding of foreign direct investment. The possession of proprietary intangible assets, such as technological expertise or entrepreneurial skills, confers to their owners the oft-cited advantage that foreign firms have over local enterprises. This is the crux of the industrial organization approach. The reason why certain firms should possess intangible assets not easily acquired by other firms, be they domestic or foreign, is not at all clear [Graham 1974, p. 85], although in a recent paper Dunning [1979] attributes them to country-specific factors. In any event, it gives rise to monopolistic power (as argued by Hymer [1960]) to be exploited abroad.

Akin to the 'superior' knowledge argument is the idea that monopolistic power arises in part from the property rights granted to firms to protect their assets and is translated into high rates of return on invested capital. To the extent that knowledge can be considered a public good, the property rights theory is undoubtedly relevant in explaining partially the monopolistic advantage that some firms have and indirectly the potential foreign involvement of a firm.

In short, the theories of industrial organization and of property rights must be considered when seeking explanations for the international involvement of firms. However, they both neglect the fact that production and distribution take place in geographical space where time, distance, and environmental differences are also of primary importance. The location-specific factors complement the firm-specific ones by adding the multinationality dimension — ignored by the latter. In this case, foreign involvement results from the advantages inherent in different geographical locations. In turn, the advantages to be gained are of two sorts: (1) those stemming from comparative cost as analyzed in international trade theory; and (2) those accruing to multiplant firms by means of multiplant economies. Hence, abundance of skilled labor, easy access to energy sources, cheap sources of capital, or protected markets — all these elements contribute to making a specific country attractive to foreign manufacturers. Also, multiplant economies give advantages to firms which locate in various countries, as shown recently by Scherer et al. [1975].

In summary, the author agrees with FDI literature that the theory of industrial organization, the theory of property rights, and the location theory are all related to the foreign involvement of firms. But nothing in these theories as yet shows that the involvement must be one of ownership control.

The choice of the mode of transacting (markets and hierarchies being the extreme forms) is a subsequent step in the international expansion of the firm. Hierarchical links must be weighed against other alternatives for servicing foreign markets, such as exporting, licensing, and joint-venturing. To illustrate the fact that the choice of a transacting mode obeys different rules from those which justify foreign involvement, consider the diversification theory as applied to FDI. This theory can be put to good use by showing the fallacy of many explanations of FDI. It has been argued that a firm diversifying its activities and assets internationally reduces the variance of its earnings, to the extent that cycles in various countries are not perfectly correlated. Assuming that firms are keen to diversify internationally, this strategy does not necessarily imply direct control.[19] One could imagine two or more firms from different countries doing so by means of a contract, which would stipulate a share of total earnings for each firm. In other words, suppose a firm from the U.S. locates a suitable partner in Britain, another one in Japan, and one more in West Germany willing to pool their earnings and divide the total according to a predetermined share. In so doing, fluctuations will be smoothed and the benefits of international diversification of the firm's operations reaped without the need to invest abroad. In pursuing this imaginary situation, one can easily see the kinds of problems which will be faced by the partners to such a deal: disagreements will arise as to the respective shares, the level of profits contributed by each partner, the enforcement of contract clauses, and other matters. The lack of control that each firm has over the activities of the others represents the sensitive issue in this imaginary situation. Moreover, one can identify more readily the role a hierarchy plays if one notices that the diversification that has been discussed is of a passive type: no attempts are made to alter the distribution of earnings (cash flows) in the example, only to reduce their average risk. The second facet of the diversification strategy is an active one, where a MNE tries to change the distribution of cash flows by modifying the real activities within the firm (that is, among subsidiaries and the parent firm).[20] The autonomy and flexibility with which a hierarchy can implement these changes cannot be attributed to a contractual, market-like agreement. No doubt, although hierarchical links may not be important for diversification, they are necessary for international risk alteration. To reiterate an argument stated earlier: the diversification motive is a reason for desiring foreign involvement, but it is not a sufficient reason for deciding on the mode of transacting. These are two separate issues.

In short, albeit firm– and location-specific factors determine the willingness of the firm to engage in foreign operations, the choice of the mode of transacting obeys institutional or organizational considerations. Here, internalization means the substitution of hierarchical relations for contractual modes.

An Eclectic Framework for the Multinational Phenomenon

The preceding discussion points to the rise of the multinational firm as the resultant of several forces that no single theory can encompass. Baumann [1975] clearly recognized the need for an eclectic approach, and Dunning unambiguously embraced the same position. In the latter's words: "In presenting the systemic theory [of ownership advantages], we accept we are in danger of being accused of eclectic taxonomy." [1977, p. 406] As shown earlier, an eclectic approach implies that location theory, industrial organization theory, and property rights theory all have something to contribute to an explanation of why firms decide to transact with foreign countries. To these must be added a hierarchies vs. markets theory, to account for the choice of mode of transacting. One could then argue that the international involvement of firms is best accounted for by: (1) location theory; (2) industrial organization theory; and, (3) property rights theory. For example, the higher the cost differentials between countries, the higher the advantages to be gained from multiple locations in different countries; the more R & D or advertising expenditures, the stronger the patent protection or the monopolistic returns of firms, the more important the degree of multinationalism would be.[21] In turn, the establishment of a multinational hierarchy is best accounted for by the markets and hierarchies theory, as was shown earlier.

Most common explanations for the existence of MNEs found in the FDI literature take for granted that markets are prevented from functioning efficiently — by monopolistic power, for instance. Hence, no institutional choice is necessary, for the domestic configuration of market power determines the international mode of transacting. In other words, industrial organization theory is a reason for both the international differentiation and the internal integration of the firm's activities.

The author's approach differs in that he is not satisfied with using the same arguments to explain multinationalism and the rise of multinational hierarchies. To arrive at a satisfactory answer, it has been assumed that transaction costs are ubiquitous and that their existence gives rise to a decision process regarding the appropriate institutional vehicle to transact internationally. It is therefore not obvious a priori which means of transacting will likely ensue, without specifying the nature of the transaction and the environment in which it will take place. Some transactions may best be handled by markets, others by hierarchies — in particular, when markets fail; that is, when they do not exist or are too costly to use. In so doing, the approach does not deny that certain firms may well 'create' market imperfections. But it is suggested that, by and large, it is the limitations of markets per se which enable us to understand the emergence of hierarchies in general and multinational hierarchies in particular. And these limitations have their roots in organizational factors. Briefly, the markets and hierarchies paradigm suggests that the technological determinism of FDI and MNE theories be replaced by one that is based upon transactional considerations where human and organizational behaviors play a central role.

FUTURE RESEARCH IN INTERNATIONAL BUSINESS

Putting into perspective the previous discussion, it is clear that the trend is toward investigating the nature of MNEs; that is, the reasons for their existence. It is also obvious that, although MNEs' operating modes are different, research on MNEs has to parallel research being made on the theory of the firm, at large.

Furthermore, the abandonment of the strict neoclassical framework, which assigns an undue advantage to the study of markets, enables one to investigate conditions—both at the environmental and organizational levels—which would favor either the establishment of markets or of hierarchies. Moreover, interfirm and intrafirm behaviors must be compared to ascertain some of their commonalities (for example, the use of shadow prices within firms) and their differences. More specifically, an interesting area of research is the investigation of the sharing of transactions between firms and markets, across industries, countries, and over time.

It should be noted that the markets and hierarchies framework, while being a powerful paradigm for discussing alternative modes of mediating transactions, is of a static nature.[22] More needs to be said about the forces which move economic transactions to be internalized or externalized. Only then would we be in a position to ascertain when MNEs create market imperfections and when they respond to them. Failure to develop the dynamic side of the paradigm would lead us to the dangerous road where all hierarchical or bureaucratical forms are de facto efficient responses to market failures. This need not be the case.

Behavioral issues within MNEs are also an area for further research. Managerial policies are indeed crucial for the successful operation of these large organizations, because they establish the control relationship on which the existence of a firm rests. And, the expansion of MNEs via acquisition activity deserves further study because it raises interesting questions concerning the valuation of assets in an international context.

The future of international business cannot be dissociated from an investigation of the possible arrangements of transacting internationally which fall between these two extreme forms—markets and hierarchies. Nor can it be cut off from much larger issues that have been carefully and purposely avoided, such as the political and social implications of the spread of hierarchical forms internationally. Finally, the future of international business cannot be understood without an awareness of changing trends in the sharing of decision making among the various groups in society and primarily within domestic hierarchies. For these changes cannot but affect the way international business will be conducted years hence.

FOOTNOTES

1. Several other surveys of the FDI literature appeared in the early and mid seventies discussing the respective merits of the various streams of economic theory (capital, trade, location, and investment theories) in explaining the phenomenon of international production. See for instance Ragazzi [1973], Dunning [1973], Stevens [1974], and Hufbauer [1975].

2. This assertion follows from the Heckscher-Ohlin theory of international trade. Trade of goods will equalize factor prices in a world of factor immobility. See Dunning [1977] for a discussion of this point.

3. Hufbauer [1975] provides a good criticism of this hypothesis, sometimes called 'the differential-return hypothesis.'

4. Most surveys have uncovered the many shortcomings of this approach to FDI and it is not necessary to repeat these well-known criticisms. The interested reader may refer to Dunning [1973; 1977; 1979].

5. See the work by Horst [1971; 1977; 1978].

6. The inappropriateness of international capital theory in explaining foreign direct investment comes from its ignorance of the composite nature of the international transfer of resources and the channels through which it takes place.

7. Recent attempts include those of Buckley and Casson [1976], Casson [1979], Hood and Young [1979], and Rugman [1979].

8. See for instance the Special Issues on the Economics of Internal Organization, *Bell Journal of Economics*, Spring and Autumn 1975.

9. Prachowny [1972] and Stevens [1972] concentrate on the risk-reducing benefits of diversification without explaining why these are uniquely realized through the MNE. See Lessard [1979] for a criticism of these approaches. Rugman [1975] emphasizes the higher stability of earnings achieved by MNEs, an argument which also conflicts with the 'homemade diversification theorem' which shows that firms need not diversify for individuals.

10. The interested reader may refer to Adler's comments [1980] and the reply by Agmon and Lessard [1980]. Also, a criticism of the two-factor world market model to assess the impact of foreign involvement is contained in Errunza and Yalovsky [1978].

11. Logically, a policy recommendation for MNEs is that they should scan the world environment in search of 'profitable' imperfections.

12. See McManus [1975] and Williamson [1975].

13. Economics does not have an immutable set of assumptions nor an indisputable definition for all concepts used when deriving the theorem about the optimality of a system of competitive markets in allocating scarce resources. Roughly, certain assumptions must be made about the technology, the availability of information, the characteristics of goods and services and the absence of monopoly power to prove that there exists a set of market prices such that profit-maximizing firms and utility-maximizing consumers who respond to these prices will automatically cause the economy to attain a Pareto optimal position. See Davis and Kamien [1969].

14. The concept of strategic behavior extends the considerations of self-seeking interest found in economics to encompass "false or empty, that is, self-disbelieved, threats and promises in the expectation that individual advantage will thereby be realized." [Goffman 1969, p. 105]

15. A good review of Williamson's approach within the context of other recent approaches to economic theorizing is Marris and Mueller [1980].

16. This point is developed in Calvet [1980].

17. This distinction is similar to that of Niehans [1977].

18. See on this subject Scherer et al. [1975].

19. The author also assumes that capital markets cannot be used by individual investors, so that the 'homemade diversification theorem' does not apply.

20. The author is indebted to Donald Lessard for this argument.

21. Multinationalism is here synonymous with international involvement.

22. The author owes this point to an anonymous referee.

REFERENCES

Adler, M. "Comment on: Agmon, T. and D. R. Lessard, Investor Recognition of Corporate International Diversification," 1980. (Forthcoming in *Journal of Finance*.)

Agmon, T. B., and Lessard, D. R. "Investor Recognition of Corporate International Diversification." *Journal of Finance*, September 1977, pp. 1049–1055.

Agmon, T. B., and Lessard, D. R. "Investor Recognition of Corporate International Diversification: Reply." 1980. (Forthcoming in *Journal of Finance*.)

Aho, C. M. "Foreign Direct Investment: Theories and Empirical Evidence." Manuscript of a paper written for the Council on International Economic Policy, 1974.

Aliber, R. Z. "A theory of Direct Foreign Investment." In *The International Corporation*, edited by C. P. Kindleberger. Cambridge, MA: MIT Press, 1970.

Arrow, K. J. "Economic Welfare and the Allocation of Resources for Invention." In *The Rate and Direction of Inventive Activity: Economic and Social Factors*, National Bureau of Economic Research. Princeton: Princeton University Press, 1962.

Bator, F. M. "The Anatomy of Market Failure." *Quarterly Journal of Economics*, August 1958, pp. 351-379.

Baumann, J. G. "Merger Theory, Property Rights and the Pattern of U. S. Direct Investment in Canada." *Weltwirtschaftliches Archiv* 7 (1975), pp. 676-698.

Bergsten, C. F.; Horst, T.; and Moran, T. H. *American Multinationals and American Interests*. Washington, DC: The Brookings Institution, 1978.

Bohm, P. *Social Efficiency: A Concise Introduction to Welfare Economics*. New York: John Wiley & Sons, 1973.

Buckley, P. J., and Casson, M. C. *The Future of the Multinational Enterprise*. London: The MacMillan Press, 1976.

Calvet, A. L. "Markets and Hierarchies: Towards a Theory of International Business." Doctoral dissertation, Sloan School of Management, M.I.T., 1980.

Casson, M. C. *Alternatives to the Multinational Enterprise*. London: MacMillan, 1979.

Caves, R. E. "International Corporations: The Industrial Economics of Foreign Investment." *Economica*, February 1971, pp. 1-27.

Coase, R. H. "The Nature of the Firm." *Economica*, November 1937, pp. 386-405.

Davis, O. A., and Kamien, M. I. "Externalities, Information and Alternative Collective Action." *The Analysis and Evaluation of Public Expenditure: The PPB System*. Joint Economic Committee, 91st Cong., 1st Session, 1969.

Dunning, J. H. "The Determinants of International Production." *Oxford Economic Papers*, November 1973, pp. 289-336.

_____. "Trade, Location of Economic Activity and the MNE: A Search for an Eclectic Approach." In *The International Allocation of Economic Activity*, edited by B. Ohlin, P. O. Hesselborn, and P. M. Wijkman. New York: Holmes and Meier Publishers Inc., 1977.

_____. "Explaining Changing Patterns of International Production: In Defence of the Eclectic Theory." *Oxford Bulletin of Economics and Statistics*, November 1979, pp. 269-295.

Errunza, V. R., and Yalovsky, M. "International Diversification and the Multinational Corporation." Working Paper, McGill University, Montreal, 1978.

Errunza, V. R., and Senbet, L. W. "The Effects of International Operations on the Market Value of the Firm: Theory and Evidence." Unpublished manuscript, September 1980. (Forthcoming in *Journal of Finance*.)

Goffman, I. *Strategic Interaction*. Philadelphia: University of Pennsylvania Press, 1969.

Graham, E. M. *Oligopolistic Imitation and European Direct Investment in the United States*. Doctoral dissertation, Harvard Business School, 1974.

Hood, N., and Young, S. *The Economics of Multinational Enterprise*. London: Longman, 1979.

Horst, T. O., "The Theory of the Multinational Firm: Optimal Behavior Under Different Tariff and Tax Rates." *Journal of Political Economy*, September/October 1971, pp. 1059-1072.

_____. "American Taxation of Multinational Corporations." *American Economic Review*, June 1977, pp. 376-389.

_____. "Tax Issues." In *American Multinationals and American Interests*, edited by C. F. Bergsten, T. O. Horst, and T. H. Moran. Washington, DC: The Brookings Institution, 1978, Chapter 6.

Hufbauer, G. C. "The Multinational Corporation and Direct Investment." In *International Trade and Finance*, edited by P. B. Kenen. Cambridge: Cambridge University Press, 1975.

Hymer, S. H. *The International Operations of National Firms: A Study of Direct Foreign Investment*. Cambridge, MA: MIT Press, 1976.

_____. "The Efficiency (Contradictions) of Multinational Corporations." *American Economic Review*, May 1970, pp. 441-448.

Jacquillat, B., and Solnik, B. "Multinationals are Poor Tools for Diversification." *The Journal of Portfolio Management*, Winter 1978, pp. 8-12.

Johnson, H. G. "The Efficiency and Welfare Implications of The International Corporation." In *The International Corporation*, edited by C. P. Kindleberger. Cambridge, MA: MIT Press, 1970

334 Kindleberger, C. P. *American Business Abroad: Six Lectures on Direct Investment.* New Haven: Yale University Press, 1969.

Knickerbocker, F. T. *Oligopolistic Reaction and Multinational Enterprise.* Cambridge, MA: Harvard Business School Division of Research, 1974.

Kojima, K. *Direct Foreign Investment: A Japanese Model of Multinational Business Operations.* London: Groom Helm, 1978.

Lessard, D. R. "Transfer Prices, Taxes and Financial Markets: Implications of Internal Financial Transfers within the Multinational Firm." In *Economic Issues of Multinational Firms,* edited by R. G. Hawkins. Greenwich, CT: JAI Press, 1979.

Magee, S. P. "Technology and the Appropriability Theory of the Multinational Corporation." In *The New International Economic Order,* edited by Jagdish Bhajwati. Cambridge MA: MIT Press, 1976.

_____. "Multinational Corporations, the Industry Technology Cycle and Development." *Journal of World Trade Law,* July/August 1977, pp. 297–321.

Malmgren, H. "Information, Expectations and the Theory of the Firm." *Quarterly Journal of Economics,* August 1961, pp. 399–421.

Marris, R., and Mueller, D. C. "The Corporation, Competition, and the Invisible Hand." *Journal of Economic Literature,* March 1980, pp. 32–63.

McClain, D. "The Determinants of Foreign Direct Investment in the U.S." Ph.D. Thesis, Department of Economics, M.I.T., 1975.

McManus, J. C. "The Theory of the International Firm." In *The Multinational Firm and the Nation State,* edited by C. Paquet. Toronto: Collier-Macmillan, 1972.

_____. "The Costs of Alternative Economic Organizations." *Canadian Journal of Economics,* August 1975, pp. 334–350.

Niehans, J. "Benefits of Multinational Firms for a Small Parent Economy: The Case of Switzerland." In *Multinationals from Small Countries,* edited by T. Agmon and C. P. Kindleberger. Cambridge, MA: MIT Press, 1977.

Nordhaus, W. D. *Invention, Growth, and Welfare.* Cambridge, MA: MIT Press, 1969.

Ozawa, T. "International Investment and Industrial Structure: New Theoretical Implications from the Japanese Experience." *Oxford Economic Papers,* March 1979, pp. 72–92.

Prachowny, M. F. J. "Direct Investment and the Balance of Payments of the United States: A Portfolio Approach." In *International Mobility and Movement of Capital,* edited by F. Machlup, et al. New York: Columbia University Press, 1972.

Ragazzi, G. "Theories of the Determinants of Direct Foreign Investment." *IMF Staff Papers,* July 1973, pp. 471–498.

Rugman, A. M. "Motives for Foreign Investment: The Market Imperfections and Risk Diversification Hypotheses." *Journal of World Trade Law,* September/October 1975, pp. 567–573.

_____. *International Diversification and the Multinational Enterprise.* Lexington, MA: Lexington Books, 1979.

Scherer, F. M.; Beckenstein, A. R.; Kaufer, E.; and Murphy, R. D. *The Economics of Multiplant Operation: An International Comparisons Study.* Cambridge, MA: Harvard University Press, 1975.

Stevens, G. V. "Capital Mobility and the International Firm." In *The International Mobility and Movement of Capital,* edited by F. Machlup, et al. New York, Columbia University Press, 1972.

_____. "Determinants of Investment." In *Economic Analysis and the Multinational Enterprise,* edited by J. H. Dunning. London; Allen & Unwin, 1974.

Teece, D. J. *The Multinational Corporation and the Resource Cost of International Technology Transfer.* Cambridge, MA: Ballinger, 1976.

Varian, H. R. "Distributive Justice, Welfare Economics, and the Theory of Fairness." *Philosophy & Public Affairs* 4 (1975), pp. 223–247.

Vernon, R. "International Investment and International Trade in the Product Cycle." *Quarterly Journal of Economics,* May 1966, pp. 190–207.

Williamson, O. E. *Markets and Hierarchies: Analysis and Antitrust Implications.* New York: Free Press, 1975.

CAPITAL BUDGETING AND LONG-TERM FINANCING

CHAPTER 22

Capital budgeting for the multinational corporation*
Alan C. Shapiro

Introduction

Multinational corporations (MNCs) evaluating foreign investments find their analyses complicated by a variety of problems rarely if ever encountered by domestic firms. This paper examines a number of such problems, including differences between project and parent company cash flows, foreign tax regulations, expropriation, blocked funds, exchange rate changes, inflation, and segmented capital markets. The major principle behind methods proposed to cope with these complications is to maximize the use of available information while reducing arbitrary cash flow and cost of capital adjustments. (A similar methodology, while not explicit, may lie behind some of the numerical examples in Rodriguez and Carter [13].) In practice, the methods usually involve adjusting a project's cash flows rather than its cost of capital. This is because there is normally more and better information on the specific impact of a given risk on a project's cash flows than on its cost of capital. Furthermore, adjusting a project's cost of capital to reflect incremental risk does not usually allow for adequate consideration of

the time pattern and magnitude of the risk being evaluated. As Robichek and Myers [12] point out, using a uniformly higher discount rate to reflect additional risk involves penalizing future cash flows relatively more heavily than present ones.

Parent vs. Project Cash Flows

Substantial differences can exist between project cash flows and cash flows back to the parent firm because of tax regulations and exchange controls, for example. Furthermore, many project expenses such as management fees and royalties are returns to the parent company. In addition, the *incremental* revenue contributed to the parent MNC by a project can differ from total project revenues if, for example, the project involves substituting local production for parent company exports. In general, incremental cash flows to the parent can be found by subtracting world-wide parent company cash flows (without the investment) from post-investment parent company cash flows. Given such differences, the question arises as to the relevant cash flows to use in project evaluation.

* This article is reprinted, with permission, from *Financial Management* (Spring 1978) pp 7–16

One suggested position is that "to the extent that the corporation views itself as a true multinational, the effect of restrictions on repatriation may not be severe" [13, p. 341]. According to economic theory, though, *the value of a project is determined by the net present value of future cash flows back to the investor.* Thus, the parent MNC should value only those cash flows *which are or can be repatriated,* since only accessible funds can be used to pay dividends and interest, amortize the firm's debt, and be reinvested. This principle also holds, of course, for a domestic firm. For example, dividends received by a parent firm from an unconsolidated domestic subsidiary (less than 80% ownership) are taxed at a 15% rate and hence should only be valued at .85 of the original dividend paid. While the principle itself is simple, it can be complicated to apply. The next several sections use this principle to analyze the impact of taxation, expropriation, and exchange controls on cash flows to the parent.

Tax Treatment of Foreign Source Income

Since only after-tax cash flows are relevant, it is necessary to determine when and what taxes must be paid on foreign-source profits. While the tax treatment of foreign-source earnings is quite complex, there are several stages in the taxation of all income from foreign investments. First, the local government involved taxes profits. If tax concessions are granted, however, the tax rate can be zero. Ordinarily, the company then pays a withholding tax to the local government on that portion of profits which is repatriated in the form of dividends, interest, and fees and royalties. These withholding taxes can sometimes be avoided, however, if the company remits profits in the form of loan repayments, for example, rather than as dividends. Furthermore, the dividend withholding rate can actually be negative (as in Germany, which taxes retained earnings at 51% while earnings paid out as dividends are taxed at only 15% [14]). In addition, many countries, including the United States, tax income remitted from overseas operations. The United States is the only country which will also tax certain unremitted profits known as subpart F income. To further complicate tax analysis, the U.S. taxes income arising from operations in developed countries differently from those in less-developed countries. (For a good description of U. S. taxation principles and practices, see Price-Waterhouse's "Information Guide for U.S. Corporations Doing Business Abroad" [11].)

To avoid double taxation, the U. S. government allows tax credits for foreign income and withholding taxes paid, but such credits can only be applied against U.S. taxes owed on other foreign-source income. The effective tax on foreign earnings thus depends on the local tax rate compared to the U.S. corporate income tax rate of 48%, the applicable withholding tax rate, and the availability of excess foreign tax credits. The actual withholding tax rate can still be substantially different from the nominal rate because of bilateral tax treaties.

To illustrate the complexities involved, assume an effective foreign income tax rate of t_f. Thus, each dollar of earnings abroad will provide $1 - t_f$ dollars of retained earnings. If these earnings are then repatriated in the form of dividends, with a dividend withholding tax rate of t_d, the amount of money that gets through, per dollar of original earnings, will equal:

\$.52, if either $T = t_f + t_d - t_f t_d < .48$ and no excess foreign tax credits are available, or if $T > .48$ and all foreign tax credits generated can be used elsewhere;

$1 - T$, if either $T < .48$ and excess foreign tax credits are available or if $T > .48$ and foreign tax credits are unusable. (These calculations only hold for developed countries. The applicable regulations for less developed countries can be found in the Price-Waterhouse guide [11].)

This computation becomes more complex if only some excess tax credits are available or if only a portion of the new tax credits generated can be used. The effective tax rate on repatriated dividends would then be a weighted average of .48 and T.

The actual tax on remitted funds would depend also on the transfer mechanism used, including adjustments in transfer prices, dividend flows, fee and royalty charges, and intracompany loan and credit arrangements. Ru ʳ˙erę [14] analyzes these various fund shifting methods and their associated costs.

Let M_t be the after-local tax dollar cash flow in year t. If τ is the marginal rate of additional taxation on remitted funds, then the present value of these cash flows to the parent if remitted immediately equals $M_t(1 - \tau)/(1 + k)^t$ where k is the project's cost of capital. If $T > .48$ and foreign tax credits are usable, then τ will be negative.

Reinvested profits are more difficult to value. Let r be the after-local tax rate of return on the reinvested funds. Suppose that cash generated in year t will be repatriated in year $t + s$ along with all incremental returns earned on these reinvested funds. Then the present value of cash generated in year t should equal

M_t $(1 + r)^a$ $(1 - \tau)/(1 + k)^{t + a}$ where the marginal tax rate τ on remitted funds can vary from year to year. If all cash flows are expected to be reinvested locally, then a terminal value for the project will have to be estimated based on the assumption that complete repatriation will occur at the end of the planning horizon.

The project cost of capital may also have to be adjusted to reflect these cross-border tax effects [10]. For example, retained earnings abroad need yield only $(1 - \tau)k_e$ where k_e is the parent company's required return on equity capital. This is because the parent company will receive $1 - \tau$ dollars for each dollar originally remitted. Thus each dollar of remitted funds must yield the parent company $(1 - \tau)k_e$ annually or, in equilibrium, the return on retained earnings. Parent company funds must yield the firm's marginal cost of capital (provided that the foreign investment doesn't change the MNC's overall riskiness), and hence their cost is unaffected by foreign tax factors. The after-tax cost of local debt is, of course, dependent on local taxes. Furthermore, the cost of debt raised abroad is affected not only by local tax rates but also by the tax treatment of exchange gains and losses arising from foreign currency-denominated debt (see [3] and [16] for elaboration of these effects).

Political and Economic Risk Analysis

There are several methods by which multinational corporations can account for the added political and economic risks of overseas operations. One is to use a higher discount rate for foreign operations, another to require a shorter payback period. Neither approach, however, lends itself to a careful evaluation of a particular risk's actual impact on investment returns. Thorough risk analysis requires assessment of the magnitude of the risk's effects on cash flows as well as an estimate of the time pattern of the risk. For example, an expropriation five years from now is likely to be much less threatening than one expected next year. Thus, using a uniformly higher discount rate just distorts the meaning of a project's present value without obviating the necessity for a careful risk evaluation. Furthermore, the choice of a risk premium (or risk premia if the discount rate is allowed to vary over time) is an arbitrary one, whether it is 2% or 10%. Instead, adjusting cash flows makes it possible to fully incorporate all available information about a specific risk's impact on an investment's future returns.

The cash flow adjustments presented in this paper employ only expected values; that is, the analysis reflects only the first moment of the probability distribution of a given risk's impact. While this procedure does not assume that shareholders are risk-neutral, it does assume either that risks such as expropriation, currency controls, inflation, and exchange rate changes are nonsystematic or that foreign investments tend to lower a firm's systematic risk. In the latter case, adjusting only the expected values of future cash flows will yield a lower bound on the investment's value to the firm.

According to modern capital asset pricing theory, the use of expected values to reflect incremental risks is justified as long as the systematic risk of a proposed investment remains unchanged [2]. To the extent that the risks dealt with in this paper are unsystematic, there is no theoretical reason to adjust a project's cost of capital to reflect them. In fact, though, foreign investments appear to reduce a firm's systematic risk by supplying international diversification [1]. If anything, therefore, this approach under- rather than overestimates a project's present value. (This would seem to be desirable both in its own right and also because the results presented by Agmon and Lessard [1] are just barely statistically significant.)

It is unlikely, however, that management will be concerned solely with the systematic component of total risk. Furthermore, the parent and subsidiary company are likely to have differing attitudes towards these risks. It is likely that ignorance of the former and bias of the latter may cause conflicts in recognition of these risks. An alternative approach is to use the Robichek and Myers [12] certainty-equivalent method where risk-adjusted cash flows are discounted at the risk-free rate. However, this method requires generating certainty-equivalent cash flows, for which no satisfactory procedure has yet been developed. Furthermore, it involves losing some information on the valuation of future cash flows that is provided by shareholders in the form of their required yield on a typical firm investment.

Expropriation

The extreme form of political risk is expropriation. This is of course an obvious case where project and parent company cash flows diverge. A sophisticated cash flow adjustment technique recommended by Stonehill and Nathanson [22] is to charge each year's flows a premium for political risk insurance whether or not such insurance is actually purchased. (The United States government sells political risk insurance through the Overseas Private Investment Corporation (OPIC). Other nations, as well as private insurance companies such as Lloyd's, will also insure overseas investments against certain types of political risk.) This solution, however, does not really measure the effect of a given political risk on a project's present value. In the case of expropriation, political risk insurance normally covers only the book value, not the economic value, of expropriated assets. The relationship between the book value of a project's assets and the project's economic value as measured by its future cash flows is tenuous at best. It is worthwhile, of course, to compare the cost of political risk insurance with its expected benefits. Insurance though is no substitute for a careful evaluation of the impact of political risk on a given project.

The approach suggested here directly examines the impact of expropriation on the project's present value to the parent. Let X_t be the parent's expected after-tax dollar cash flow from the project in year t. If I_o is the initial investment outlay, then the project's present value to the parent firm equals

$$-I_o + \sum_{t=1}^{n} \frac{X_t}{(1+k)^t},$$

where n is the life of the project and k the project cost of capital as before. Suppose now that an expropriation will take place with certainty during year h. Then, the new present value will equal

$$-I_o + \sum_{t=1}^{h-1} \frac{X_t}{(1+k)^t} + \frac{G_h}{(1+k)^h},$$

where G_h is the expected value of the net compensation provided. This compensation comes from several sources:

1. Direct compensation paid to the firm by the local government. (This compensation can be delayed, as in Chile, for example, where many MNCs were expropriated by the Allende government with little or no compensation. When Allende was overthrown, however, his successors began returning property and otherwise compensating these MNCs.).
2. Indirect compensation such as the management contracts received by oil companies whose properties were nationalized by the Venezuelan government. (Stephen Kobrin was gracious enough to point out to me the existence of these continuing arrangements.)
3. Payment received from political insurance. (Insurance payments may lag expropriation by several years as well.).
4. Tax deductions in the home country associated with such an extraordinary loss.
5. A reduction in the amount of capital that must be

repaid by the project equal to the unamortized portion of any local borrowing. It is inconceivable that a firm which has had a foreign operation expropriated would pay back any local borrowing except as part of a total compensation package worked out with the local government. Suppliers of capital from outside the host country would normally be repaid by the parent company (whether or not loans were guaranteed) in order to preserve the parent's credit reputation.

Since it is unlikely that compensation will be provided immediately or even simultaneously from the different sources, G_h must be adjusted to reflect the various delays possible. Uncertainty regarding the magnitude of G_h will require specification of the likely range and probability of this compensation. G_h is therefore an expected value rather than a number generated with certainty. For a given period h, a MNC can determine how large G_h must be to still undertake a project.

Similarly, for a given level of compensation, a firm can determine beyond what period h* expropriation will no longer affect the investment decision. For example, if $G = 0$, then h* is the minimum value of j for which

$$\sum_{t=1}^{h} \frac{X_t}{(1+k)^t} > I_o.$$

In this situation, h* can be considered the present value payback period.

If the probability of expropriation equals P_h in year h and 0 in all other years, then the project's expected net present value (NPV_p) would equal

$$-I_o + \sum_{t=1}^{h-1} \frac{X_t}{(1+k)^t} + (1-P_h) \sum_{t=h}^{n} \frac{X_t}{(1+k)^t}$$
$$+ P_h \frac{G_h}{(1+k)^h}.$$

The term $(1-P_h) \sum_{t=h}^{n} \frac{X_t}{(1+k)^t}$

reflects the fact that if there is no expropriation in period h, with probability $1 - P_h$, cash flows will continue to be generated as originally anticipated. If expropriation does occur, though, future cash flows will be zero, save for compensation.

Determining an exact value for P_h is likely to be difficult if not impossible. While a number of commercial and academic political risk forecasting models are available, there is little evidence they can sucessfully forecast these risks. These models normally apply country indices which attempt to quantify the level of political risk in each nation (see, for example, the Business International Risk Index [3] and the Political System Stability Index in Haendel and West [11]). Their common weakness is that they assume each firm in a country is facing the same degree of political risk. Empirical evidence on the post-World War II experiences of U.S. and British MNCs, however, clearly indicates that industries differ in their susceptibilities to political risk [8, 23]. For example, expropriation (or creeping expropriation) is more likely to occur in the extractive, utility, or financial service sectors of an economy than in the manufacturing sector. In general, it appears that the greater the perceived benefits to the local economy a given subsidiary provides, and the more expensive it would be to replace it with a purely local operation, the less risk it faces.

An alternative approach to use in incorporating information concerning the magnitude of P_h is break-even analysis. This involves determining the value of P* where P* is the solution to

$$NPV_p = 0 \text{ or } P^* = \frac{\displaystyle\sum_{t=1}^{n} \frac{X_t}{(1+k)^t} - I_o}{\displaystyle\sum_{t=h}^{n} \frac{X_t}{(1+k)^t} - \frac{G_h}{(1+k)^h}} .$$

If $P_h < P^*$, then the project will have a positive net present value, provided that the project would be acceptable in the absence of expropriation. This probability break-even analysis is useful, since it is normally easier and requires less information to ascertain whether $P_h < P^*$ or $P_h > P^*$ than to decide on the absolute level of P_h. For example, if $P^* = .30$, then it is unnecessary to argue whether $P_h = .50$ or .60, since the result will not affect the decision (provided the decision is based on the project's expected net present value). The same is true for an argument as to whether $P_h = .10$ or .20. This break-even analysis can also tell a company when it is worthwhile to invest in more precise data concerning P_h.

In addition, since the firm's own actions can affect the probability of expropriation, this analysis can help a firm to compare the value of trying to change P_h (by entering into a joint venture or switching to local suppliers) with the costs of such actions. The size of the ultimate compensation package is also likely to be affected by these policies and can be included in the analysis. Thus, management can use this procedure to value available alternative strategies both before and after undertaking the investment.

For the general case, let P_t be the probability of expropriation in period t, given no previous expropriation. Then the project's expected net present value equals

$$-I_o + \sum_{t=1}^{n} \prod_{i=1}^{t} (1-P_i)\frac{X_t}{(1+k)^t}$$

$$+ \sum_{t=1}^{n} \prod_{i=1}^{t-1} (1-P_i)\frac{P_t G_t}{(1+k)^t} .$$

If $P_t \equiv P$, this expression reduces to

$$-I + \sum_{t=1}^{n} (1-P)^t \frac{X_t}{(1+k)^t} + \sum_{t=1}^{n} (1-P)^{t-1} \frac{PG_t}{(1+k)^t} .$$

This model formulation lends itself naturally to simulation of various political risk alternatives.

Illustration. Suppose a firm wishes to analyze an investment with a five-year life. The initial investment required is $1,000,000, with five annual cash inflows of $500,000 expected. With a cost of capital equal to 20%, the present value of this investment is $495,500. However, an expropriation during year 3 is considered possible. If the expropriation does take place, it is believed that compensation equal to $200,000 will be paid. Then the break-even probability required for this investment to have a positive expected present value equals .80. If the probability of expropriation is less than .80, the investment should be undertaken (if the decision is based on expected values). The break-even probability drops to .68 if the net compensation is 0.

Suppose, instead, that the expropriation is expected during the second year. Then, even with compensation equal to $200,000, the investment should not be undertaken unless the probability of expropriation is less than .64. The break-even probability declines to .45, though, if $G_2 = 0$. Hence, the break-even probability P_2^* is much more sensitive to the degree of compensation than is P_3^*.

If an expropriation is not expected until year 4, the investment will automatically have a positive present value of $53,000 even if $P_4 = 1.0$ and $G_4 = 0$. (See Exhibit 1.)

Overall, the analysis reveals an investment that requires such a high probability of expropriation before it has a negative expected present value, particularly beyond the first year, that expropriation is probably not a relevant consideration. Any investment with a probability of expropriation of 45% in the second year,

Exhibit 1. Effects of Expropriation Timing and Compensation Package on Break-even Probabilities

Investment Cash Flows		Break-even Probability With Compensation of	
Initial Outlay —	$1,000,000	$200,000	0
Year 1	500,000	$P_1{}^* = .37$	$P_1{}^* = .33$
Year 2	500,000	$P_2{}^* = .64$	$P_2{}^* = .45$
Year 3	500,000	$P_3{}^* = .80$	$P_3{}^* = .68$
Year 4	500,000	$P_4{}^* = 1.0$	$P_4{}^* = 1.0$
Year 5	500,000	$P_5{}^* = 1.0$	$P_5{}^* = 1.0$
Present value discounted at 20%		$495,500	

for example, would very likely not be considered in the first place.

Blocked Funds

The same methodology developed above can be applied to analyze the effects of various exchange controls. In discussing blocked funds, it must be pointed out that if all funds are expected to be blocked in perpetuity, then the value of the project to the parent is zero.

Assume that in year j all funds become blocked. These exchange controls will be removed in year n, at which time all available funds can be remitted to the parent. As before, let the return on reinvested funds equal r. Then the net present value of the project will equal

$$-I_o + \sum_{t=1}^{j-1} \frac{X_t}{(1+k)^t} + \sum_{t=j}^{n} \frac{X_t(1+r)^{n-t}}{(1+k)^n} .$$

If the probability of exchange controls equals α_j in year j and 0 in all other years, then the project's new expected present value NPV_α equals

$$-I_o + \sum_{t=1}^{j-1} \frac{X_t}{(1+k)^t} + (1-\alpha_j) \sum_{t=j}^{n} \frac{X_t}{(1+k)^t}$$

$$+ \alpha_j \sum_{t=j}^{n} \frac{X_t(1+r)^{n-t}}{(1+k)^n} ,$$

assuming that all blocked funds can be repatriated in year n. The break-even value for α_j, α^*, can be found by setting $NPV_\alpha = 0$ and solving for α^*. Then,

$$\alpha^* = \frac{\sum\limits_{t=j}^{n} \dfrac{X_t}{(1+k)^t} - I_o}{\sum\limits_{t=j}^{n} \dfrac{X_t}{(1+k)^t} - \sum\limits_{t=j}^{n} \dfrac{X_t(1+r)^{n-t}}{(1+k)^n}} .$$

The same approach set forth in the expropriation example can be used to incorporate the likelihood of the imposition of exchange controls in any future period t with probability α_t, along with a probability distribution about lifting of these controls. If blocked funds cannot be repatriated, then a compensation value would have to be described and included in the analysis.

In actuality, firms have many ways to remove blocked funds. These methods include transfer price adjustments on intracorporate sales, loan repayments, and fee and royalty adjustments, so funds are likely to be only partially blocked.

If Y_t dollars can be repatriated even when exchange controls exist, then the previous formula presented would be modified as follows:

$$-I_o + \sum_{t=1}^{j-1} \frac{X_t}{(1+k)^t} + \sum_{t=j}^{n} \frac{Y_t}{(1+k)^t}$$

$$+ (1-\alpha_j) \sum_{t=j}^{n} \frac{X_t - Y_t}{(1+k)^t}$$

$$+ \alpha_j \sum_{t=j}^{n} \frac{(X_t - Y_t)(1+r)^{n-t}}{(1+k)^n} .$$

By using these formulas, a firm can see how sensitive its investment decision is to the probability and magnitude of blocked funds in any given year. If the present value turns out to be sensitive to the level of Y_t under exchange controls, the parent company can then structure its investment *in advance* so as to maximize the values of Y_t. This could include investing in the form of debt rather than equity, borrowing locally, and setting high transfer prices on goods sold to the subsidiary while buying goods produced by the subsidiary at lower prices where legally possible. Numerous other mechanisms available for using blocked funds are described in Shapiro [18]. The important thing to note is that many of these methods require planning *prior* to the initial commitment of funds.

Incidentally, the automatic inclusion of depreciation in computing cash flows from domestic operations is questionable when evaluating a foreign project. Dividend payments in excess of reported profits will decapitalize the enterprise, thereby inviting closer host government scrutiny. On the other hand, using depreciation cash flows to service parent company debt would be more acceptable. Thus, while parent company funds, whether called debt or equity, require the same return, the cash flow from foreign projects could very well be affected by the form of this investment. Ordinarily, the tax and repatriation flexibility advantages of debt will prove decisive.

Illustration. Consider, for example, an investment requiring an initial outlay of $1,000,000 with expected cash inflows of $350,000 annually for the next five years. The present value of this investment discounted at 20% is $46,850. If exchange controls are anticipated just before the second year remittance, then, with full repatriation at the end of year 5, $\alpha^* = .24$ if the blocked funds cannot be reinvested. In other words, the expected present value of the project is negative if the probability of exchange controls is greater than .24. If funds can be reinvested with an annual return of 5%, then α^* rises to .31 while $\alpha^* = .46$, if the reinvestment rate is 10%.

If exchange controls are not expected until year 3, then these probabilities rise to .52, .60, and 1.0, respectively. In the latter case, the possibility of currency controls will not affect the investment decision.

This break-even analysis can be extended still further. Suppose that the probability of exchange controls in year 2 is .5 and that reinvestment is impossible. Then at least 51% of the funds must be removable each year via fee remittances, loan repayments, and transfer price adjustments (for example) for the investment to have a positive expected present value. This remittance percentage declines to .37 with a reinvestment rate of 5% and to .08 if a 10% reinvestment rate is assumed.

Exchange Rate Change and Inflation

We now turn to the evaluation of two major economic risks facing multinationals — inflation and exchange rate changes. Inflation and exchange rate risk are opposite sides of the same coin. It is worthwhile, however, to analyze each effect separately since there is normally a lag between a given rate of inflation and the necessary exchange rate change [9]. This is particularly true when government intervention occurs, such as in a fixed rate system or a managed float. Furthermore, local price controls may not permit or may retard the effect of internal price adjustments.

Exchange Risk

As with political risk, many companies account for exchange risk by raising their discount rates. However, to the extent that exchange risk is unsystematic, the discount risk should not be adjusted. Rather, the expected value of cash flows should reflect the impact of exchange rate changes. The method advocated by Stonehill and Nathanson [22] is to adjust

each period's dollar cash flow, X_t, by the cost of an exchange risk management program. Thus, if d_t is the expected forward discount in period t, for example, then the present value of period t's cash flow will be set equal to $X_t (1 - d_t)/(1 + k)^t$. This technique is fine if local currency cash flows are fixed, as (for instance) in the case of interest on a foreign currency-dominated bond.

Where income is generated by an on-going business operation, however, local currency cash flows themselves will vary with the exchange rate. Thus, multiplying each period's projected local currency cash flow, L_t, by the forecasted exchange rate, e_t, will overlook the fact that L_t itself is a function, $L_t(e_t)$, of the expected exchange rate. In fact, several recent articles have set forth the systematic and predictable changes to local currency cost and revenue streams of an exchange rate change (see [5] and [15]). The major conclusions of this work are that the sector of an economy in which a firm is engaged (export, import-competing, purely domestic) and the sources of its inputs (imports, domestic traded, domestic non-traded) are the major determinants of its susceptibility to exchange risk.

The recommended approach here is to isolate the different sources of a project's cash flows and to analyze each stream separately. This would involve identifying the impact of an exchange rate change on the project's revenues (what percentage of its sales is local as opposed to exports), its costs (what percentage of its inputs is domestic) and on depreciation. It is also necessary to isolate those revenues and costs that are contractually fixed in either local or foreign currency from those inputs and sales whose prices can adjust to a changed exchange rate. For example, while local currency devaluation can increase dollar profits, dollar cash flows from depreciation will unambiguously decline by the devaluation percentage unless indexation of fixed assets is permitted. However, indexation, where it exists, is generally tied to an inflation index related to the exchange rate only to the extent that a devaluation will increase local currency prices [6]. Furthermore, working capital requirements will probably change because of the changed competitive situation the firm faces. These changes would have to be incorporated in the analysis. If R_t, C_t, and D_t are the local currency revenues, costs, and depreciation charges respectively of period t, then the project's expected after-local tax dollar cash flow in year t will equal $(1 - t_r) [R_t (e_t) - C_t (e_t)] e_t + D_t e_t + W_t (e_t) e_t$, where $W_t (e_t)$ is the net change in local currency working capital required with an exchange rate of e_t. In lieu of using expected exchange rates, it would be preferable to compute the above dollar cash flow for each possible exchange rate, assign a probability to each value, and then take the expected dollar cash flow over all possible exchange rates.

Illustration. Assume that a firm analyzing an overseas investment project anticipates a local currency (LC) devaluation of 10% at the end of the first year of plant operation. The relevant exchange risk factors are as follows: Output is sold in both domestic and export markets; imported and domestic raw materials are used; the unit cost of domestic raw materials will rise 8%; the unit cost of imported raw materials will increase 10%; the unit cost of labor will increase 4%; fixed costs will rise 5%; domestic and export prices will be raised 5% in local currency terms; both export and domestic sales will increase due to the lower price relative to foreign competitors' prices. (Since the initial dollar price is $10.00, a 5% price increase to LC105 will reduce the dollar price to $9.45.)

Taking all these factors into account, local currency cash flow will increase from LC 2,500,000 to LC 2,675,000. Dollar cash flow declines by $9,250 from $250,000 to $240,750. Much of this reduction is due to the $5,000 decrease in the dollar value of depreciation-generated cash flows $(.5 \times 1,000,000 \times .10 - .5 \times 1,000,000 \times .09)$. Exhibit 2 shows the calculation of these cash flows. The alternative method of reducing dollar cash flows by 10% would have led to a projected $25,000 reduction in cash flow.

In addition, working capital requirements are expected to increase by $50,000 to support the higher sales level. Therefore, the capital budget must be adjusted to reflect a yearly reduction in cash flow of $9,250 and a lump sum decrease of $50,000 at the end of the first year.

Inflation

Exchange rate changes are normally preceded by relatively higher or lower local rates of inflation than in the home country. As with exchange rate changes, a given inflation rate will not lead to a similar increase in profits or cash flows. Cash flows should be separated into their component parts to analyze each part on its own. The competitive as well as the cost effects of inflation can vary from firm to firm depending (as

Exhibit 2. Cash Flow Effect of a Currency Devaluation

	Exchange Rate	
	LC1 = $.10	LC1 = $.09
Revenues (Local Currency)		
Sales (Units)		
Domestic	100,000	105,000
Export	100,000	110,000
Price Per Unit	100	105
Gross Revenue	20,000,000	22,575,000
Costs (Local Currency)		
Raw materials (Cost per Unit)		
Domestic	25	27
Imported	20	22
Labor (Unit Cost)	25	26
Variable Cost Per Unit	70	75
Total Variable Costs	14,000,000	16,125,000
Fixed Costs	2,000,000	2,100,000
Depreciation	1,000,000	1,000,000
Total Costs	17,000,000	19,225,000
Profit Before Tax	3,000,000	3,350,000
Tax @ 50%	1,500,000	1,675,000
Net Profit after Tax	1,500,000	1,675,000
Depreciation	1,000,000	1,000,000
Total Local Currency Cash Flow	LC 2,500,000	LC 2,675,000
Dollar Cash Flow	$ 250,000	$ 240,750

with exchange rate changes) on the location of a firm's markets as well as on the sources of its inputs (see Shapiro [15] for elaboration of these effects). For example, a firm selling locally at inflated prices will find profits rapidly increasing if a large percentage of its costs is fixed in terms of either the local or a foreign currency. Items such as rent, power, labor, and imported inputs will exhibit either fixed prices or prices whose increases may lag increases in the firm's product prices.

One danger faced by firms in many countries is a price freeze imposed either during rapid inflation or following devaluation of the local currency. Generally these price freezes are more effective in controlling a firm's output prices than in controlling its input costs, thus leading to a profit squeeze. Furthermore, a foreign firm is less likely or able to flout local price control measures since it is under certain subtle pressures to be a "good corporate citizen." In such a situation, a firm could raise its prices in advance of an anticipated price freeze and take on the burden of competing with inflated prices. When the price freeze occurs, however, and costs inevitably rise afterwards, the firm would be in a better position to continue operating profitably. This is especially true if imported materials are being used and a devaluation has occurred. Local companies that are unable to raise their prices when production costs rise will probably start producing inferior merchandise and cut back on service, sustain considerable losses, and/or go out of business. All these factors would have to be reflected through an adjustment of future cash flows [19].

Inflation will normally influence a firm's cash flows by causing a rise in working capital requirements. This is due to higher costs, increases in its required cash balances, and an easing of credit terms leading to higher accounts receivable.

Where indexation is permitted, dollar cash flows from depreciation should increase in times of inflation. As noted above, however, this benefit will disappear or at least be reduced following a devaluation.

Capital Market Segmentation

Multinational firms often finance overseas investments with project-specific funds. There are two approaches to evaluating a project whose financing is partially arranged in a segmented capital market. One way is to adjust the project's weighted cost of capital to include the cost of this debt. If k is the firm's marginal cost of capital applicable to the project, then the project's total cost of capital is $I_o k$, where I_o is the total financing required. If F dollars of this total are

now raised in the form of debt at an interest rate of i_1 rather than at the firm's normal cost of debt, i_o, then the project's new total cost of capital equals $I_o k - F (i_o - i_1)$, which yields an adjusted marginal cost of

capital of $k - \dfrac{F}{I_o} (i_o - i_1) = k'$.

The assumption here is that the firm's cost of capital k is based on a target worldwide debt ratio and hence that each dollar of debt raised abroad replaces one dollar of domestic debt. The cost of capital adjustment required if a firm leverages itself more highly abroad than domestically is presented in [17]. Using this method, the present value of period t's cash flow would equal

$$\frac{X_t}{(1 + k')^t} .$$

The alternative method is to subtract the interest subsidy or penalty $F(i_o - i_1)$ from the project's cash flows in each period. These adjusted cash flows would then be discounted at the firm's marginal cost of capital k. Thus, the adjusted present value of period t's cash flow would equal

$$\frac{X_t - F (i_o - i_1)}{(1 + k)^t} .$$

Obviously, a firm would never borrow at $i_1 > i_o$ if it had the option of borrowing at i_o. Capital controls can lead to this result, however. For example, during the period 1968–1974, regulations established by the U.S. Office of Foreign Direct Investment (OFDI) and the Federal Reserve Board restricted access to the U.S. capital market if funds were intended for loans or investments in developed countries. This forced U.S. multinational firms to borrow in the Euro-dollar market at rates of interest higher than in the U.S. to finance their foreign operations.

In a recent paper [21], Stonehill and Shapiro show that the correct discount rate is the marginal cost of unrestricted funds, because this figure more accurately reflects the firm's opportunity cost of funds. To maximize the present value of shareholder wealth, project cash flows should be discounted at "the yield foregone on the most profitable investment opportunity rejected, or the required rate of return, whichever is the higher" [24, pp. 99]. This opportunity cost of funds will normally equal the firm's marginal cost of capital. Where capital market segmentation exists, however, the firm's opportunity cost of funds may well differ from the project's marginal cost of capital. Adjusting the cost of capital implicitly assumes that all cash

344 flows are reinvested at k', while the adjusted cash flow method correctly assumes that cash flows are being reinvested at k. Thus, in the case of an interest subsidy, *i.e.*, $i_1 < i_o$, the correct discount rate is k, and cash flows should be adjusted by $F(i_o - i_1)$.

This result appears to contradict previous sections of the paper involving the analysis of taxation and blocked funds, where the return on reinvested funds was assumed to equal r rather than k. It is necessary to differentiate here, however, between returns on retained earnings and parent company returns. *The capital budgeting model presented here only recognizes cash flows back to the parent, and it is the opportunity yield on these repatriated funds that is relevant.* This opportunity yield does equal K.

Summary and Conclusions

Capital budgeting for the multinational corporation presents many elements that rarely if ever exist in domestic capital budgeting. The primary thrust of this paper has been to adjust project cash flows instead of the discount rate to reflect the key political risks and economic risks that MNCs face abroad. Tax factors and segmented capital markets are also incorporated via cash flow instead of cost of capital adjustments. Cash flow adjustments are preferred on the pragmatic grounds that there is available more and better information on the effect of such risks on future cash flows than on the required discount rate.

References

1. Tamir Agmon and Donald Lessard, "International Diversification and the Multinational Corporation: An Investigation of the Price Behavior of the Shares of U.S. Based Multinational Corporations on the N.Y.S.E.," *Journal of Finance,* forthcoming
2. Harold Bierman, Jr., and Jerome E. Hass, "Capital Budgeting Under Uncertainty: A Reformulation," *Journal of Finance* (March 1973), p. 119.
3. Business International, *Business International Index of Environmental Risk,* Business International Corporation, New York, various dates.
4. Business International, *Business International Money Report,* Business International Corporation, New York, October 1, 1976.
5. Gunter Dufey, "Corporate Finance and Exchange Rate Variations," *Financial Management* (Summer 1972), p. 51.
6. David K. Eiteman and Arthur I. Stonehill, *Multinational Business Finance,* Reading, Massachusetts, Addison-Wesley Publishing Co., 1973.
7. Dan Haendel and Gerald West with Robert Meadow, *Overseas Investment and Political Risk,* Foreign Policy Research Institute Monograph Series, Philadelphia Pennsylvania, 1975.
8. Robert G. Hawkins, Norman Mintz, and Michael Provissiero, "Government Takeovers of U. S. Foreign Affiliates," *Journal of International Business Studies* (Spring 1976), p. 3.
9. John S. Hodgson and Patricia Phelps, "The Distributed Impact of Price-Level Variations on Floating Exchange Rates," unpublished working paper, Norman, Oklahoma, University of Oklahoma, 1973.
10. Walter N. Ness, Jr., "U. S. Corporate Income Taxation and the Dividend Remittance Policy of Multinational Corporations," *Journal of International Business Studies* (Spring 1975), p. 67.
11. Price-Waterhouse, "Information Guide for U. S. Corporations Doing Business Abroad," New York, March 1976.
12. Alexander A. Robichek and Stewart C. Myers, *Optimal Financing Decisions,* Englewood Cliffs, New Jersey, Prentice-Hall, Inc., 1965.
13. Rita M. Rodriquez and E. Eugene Carter, *International Financial Management,* Englewood Cliffs, New Jersey, Prentice-Hall, Inc., 1976.
14. David P. Rutenberg, "Maneuvering Liquid Assets in a Multinational Corporation," *Management Science* (June 1970), p. 671.
15. Alan C. Shapiro, "Exchange Rate Changes, Inflation and the Value of the Multinational Corporation," *Journal of Finance* (May 1975), p. 485.
16. Alan C. Shapiro, "Evaluating Financing Costs for Multinational Subsidiaries," *Journal of International Business Studies* (Fall 1975), p. 25.
17. Alan C. Shapiro, "Financial Structure and Cost of Capital in the Multinational Corporation," *Journal of Financial and Quantitative Analysis,* forthcoming.
18. Alan C. Shapiro, "Management of Blocked Funds," University of Pennsylvania working paper, 1976.
19. Alan C. Shapiro, "Protecting Against Anticipated Price Controls," University of Pennsylvania working paper, 1977.
20. Alan C. Shapiro and David P. Rutenberg, "Managing Exchange Risks in a Floating World," *Financial Management* (Summer 1976), p. 48.
21. Alan C. Shapiro and Arthur I. Stonehill, "Capital Budgeting With Segmented Capital Markets," University of Pennsylvania working paper, 1976.
22. Arthur I. Stonehill, and Leonard Nathanson, "Capital Budgeting and the Multinational Corporation," *California Management Review* (Summer 1968), p. 39.
23. J. Frederick Truitt, "Expropriation of Foreign Investment: Summary of the Post World War II Experience of American and British Investors in Less Developed Countries," *Journal of International Business Studies* (Fall 1970), p. 21.
24. James C. Van Horne, *Financial Management and Policy,* 4th ed., Englewood Cliffs, New Jersey, Prentice-Hall Inc., 1974.

CHAPTER 23

Financial structure and cost of capital in the multinational corporation*
Alan C. Shapiro

I. Introduction

As the multinational corporation (MNC) becomes the norm rather than the exception, the need to internationalize the tools of domestic financial analysis is apparent. A key question is: What cost-of-capital figure should be used in appraising the profitability of foreign investments? This paper seeks to provide a comprehensive approach to analyze the cost-of-capital question. It begins by extending the weighted cost-of-capital concept to the multinational firm. It then builds on previous research to address the following related topics: national or multinational financial structure norms; the role of parent company guarantees; the costing of various fund sources particularly when exchange risk is present; the impact of tax and regulatory factors; risk and diversification; and joint ventures.

II. The Weighted Cost of Capital--The Domestic Firm

The average incremental cost of funds which the domestic firm seeks to minimize by choosing an appropriate capital structure equals:

$$k_e(1-\lambda) + i_d\lambda$$

where k_e is the stockholders' risk-adjusted required return (the cost of new equity); i_d is the after-tax cost of new debt; and λ is the firm's target debt ratio (total debt/total assets). The target debt ratio, λ, is based on the financial structure which minimizes the average cost of new funds. If leverage is irrelevant in the absence of taxes, as Modigliani-Miller [13] argue, then λ would be based on institutional constraints. The general consensus today appaars to be that an optimal capital structure does exist, particularly when taxes are considered, but that the "average cost of capital curve is relatively

---

*
University of Pennsylvania.

* This article is reprinted, with permission, from the *Journal of Financial and Quantitative Analysis* (June 1978) pp 211–226

flat over a fairly wide range of leverage ratio" [28, p. 340]. Thus the cost of deviating from the optimum is likely to be minimal.

The cost-of-capital figure relevant for investment decisions is the marginal cost of capital. In this paper, the marginal cost of capital will be assumed constant and hence will equal the average cost of new funds $k_e(1-\lambda) + i_d\lambda$.

III. The Multinational Firm

The multinational corporation is assumed to finance its foreign subsidiaries in such a way as to minimize its incremental weighted cost of capital. As in the domestic firm, this figure will be assumed to equal the MNC's marginal cost of capital.

Following Adler [1, p. 120], suppliers of capital to the MNC will be assumed to associate the risk of default with the MNC's consolidated worldwide debt ratio λ.[1] This is primarily because bankruptcy or other forms of financial distress in an overseas subsidiary could seriously impair the parent company's ability to operate domestically. Any deviations from the MNC's target capital structure will cause adjustments in the mix of debt and equity used to finance future investments. The required adjustments and their cost implications are elaborated below.

IV. Costing Various Sources of Funds

Suppose a foreign subsidiary requires I dollars to finance a new investment, to be funded as follows:

P dollars by the parent; E_f dollars by the subsidiary's retained earnings, and D_f dollars by foreign debt with $P + E_f + D_f = I$.

In computing the subsidiary's weighted cost of capital, we will first examine the individual cost of each component as follows:

i) Parent Company Funds

The required rate of return on parent company funds (the rate used in capital budgeting) is the firm's marginal cost of capital. Hence, parent funds invested overseas should yield the parent's marginal cost of capital provided that the foreign investments undertaken do not change the overall riskiness of the MNC's operations. The effect of risk will be addressed in a later section.

---

[1]If the perceived risk of default is affected by the sources of funds in addition to the ratio of total debt to assets, then the multinational firm has a more complex optimization problem which may allow it to discriminate monopsonistically among lenders in different markets.

ii) Retained ,arnings

The cost of retained earnings overseas is an issue of current concern (see Ness [15], for example). The existence of dividend withholding taxes, tax deferral, and transfer costs could yield specific benefits to retaining earnings abroad. With an effective foreign tax rate of t_f, each dollar of earnings abroad will provide $1-t_f$ dollars of retained earnings. If these earnings are then remitted to parent headquarters in the form of dividends, though, only $\$.52 < 1-t_f$ will get through if $t_f < .48$ and no excess foreign tax credits are available.[2] Therefore, if the parent has a required rate of return on equity of k_e, retained earnings need yield only $\dfrac{.52k_e}{1-t_f} < k_e$ overseas to provide an equivalent return.[3] On the other hand, if the parent has an effective tax rate overseas in excess of 48 percent, then repatriated earnings will provide foreign tax credits. If these foreign tax credits can be used by the MNC, then the cost of retained earnings abroad, $\dfrac{.52k_e}{1-t_f}$ will be greater than k_e.[4]

The question arises as to whether a company should incorporate these adjustments in computing its cost of retained earnings. The major argument against such an approach is that since MNCs typically have other, lower cost, means of shifting funds from one country to another, the use of a uniform cost of equity would be more appropriate. These transfer mechanisms include adjustments in transfer prices, dividend flows, fee and royalty charges, and intracompany loan and credit arrangements. Rutenberg [19] analyzes these methods and the costs associated with each. A firm which operates through joint ventures or which has few intracorporate trade linkages will find that its ability to shift funds by means other than dividend payments is probably limited. Thus, the answer for a given firm to the question as to whether these tax adjustments should be incorporated depends upon how significant these tax and transfer cost effects are (i.e., if the cost of sending funds to headquarters is minimal, then the subsidiary's cost of equity should equal k_e; if not the cost of retained earnings

---

[2] These calculations only hold for subsidiaries in developed countries. The relevant tax rules for subsidiaries in less developed countries are reported in [16].

[3] For example, if k_e = 16 percent and t_f = .4, then the cost of retained earnings abroad would equal only 13.9 percent.

[4] These formulas also hold if there are dividend withholding taxes.

should be adjusted to reflect the minimum-cost means of transferring these funds).

iii) Depreciation

As in a purely domestic corporation, the cost of depreciation-generated funds equals the firm's incremental average cost of capital.

iv) Local Debt

Many firms borrow locally to provide offsetting liabilities for their exposed local currency assets. The after-tax dollar cost of borrowing locally equals the sum of the interest expense plus the exchange gain or loss. If e_o is the current dollar/local currency (LC) exchange rate, $(LC1 = \$e_o)$, e_1 is the expected exchange rate at the end of one year, and r_L is the local currency interest rate, then the effective dollar interest rate equals $r_L \dfrac{e_1}{e_o} (1-t_f) - \dfrac{e_o - e_1}{e_o}$ where, as before, t_f is the foreign tax rate. The first term is the after-tax dollar interest cost on $LC\dfrac{1}{e_o} = \$1$ (paid at year-end when the exchange rate is e_1) while the second term is the gain or loss involved in repaying a local currency loan of one dollar with local currency valued at year-end at $\dfrac{e_1}{e_o}$ dollars. The gain or loss has no tax implications since $LC\dfrac{1}{e_o}$ was borrowed and $LC\dfrac{1}{e_o}$ re-paid.[5] (See [21] and [24] for additional details on how to compute the cost of debt when exchange rate changes are likely.)

V. Computing with Weighted Cost of Capital

With no change in risk characteristics, the parent's cost of debt and equity remains at i_d and k_e respectively. Let the subsidiary's cost of retained earnings equal k_s and its after-tax dollar cost of foreign debt equal i_f.

Since the debt ratio for parent funds P already equals λ, an additional amount of equity, E, is required to bring the corporate debt ratio back to λ where E is the solution to:

---

[5] For example, if the annual cruzeiro cost of debt in Brazil is 35 percent, the Brazilian tax rate is 30 percent, and the cruzeiro is expected to depreciate 10 percent per annum, then the effective after-tax dollar cost of borrowing cruzeiros equals .7 (.90) 35 percent - 10 percent = 12.05 percent. This expression arises as follows: suppose $100 worth of cruzeiros are borrowed today. The cost of repaying the principal, at the end of one year, equals $90 since the exchange gain is not recognized by the Brazilian government (X cruzeiros were borrowed and X cruzeiros were repaid). In addition, the interest expense equals $35 (.90) (.07). The total cost then equals $12.05 for an effective dollar interest rate of 12.05 percent.

$$\frac{D_f}{D_f+E_f+E} = \lambda.$$

Then $E = \frac{D_f}{\lambda} - D_f - E_f$. The opportunity cost associated with this additional equity

is the difference between the cost of this equity $k_e E$ and the parent's weighted

cost of capital $[k_e(1-\lambda)+i_d\lambda]E$. By substituting and rearranging terms, this

cost is seen to equal

$$[D_f(1-\lambda)-E_f\lambda](k_e-i_d).$$

If $E = 0$ (i.e., $\frac{D_f}{D_f+E_f} = \lambda$), then this term also equals 0. The incremental weighted

cost of capital is then equal to

$$k_1 = \frac{P}{I}[k_e(1-\lambda)+i_d\lambda]+k_s\frac{E_f}{I} + \frac{i_fD_f}{I} +(k_e-i_d)[D_f(1-\lambda)-E_f\lambda].$$

The last term is the penalty (reward) for over-(under-) leveraging abroad.
If this investment changes the parent company risk characteristics, then the
parent's cost of equity capital must be adjusted.[6]

----

[6]A numerical example will illustrate some of the concepts presented here.
Assume that a new investment requires $100 million. Of this total, $20 million
will be provided by parent company funds, $25 million by retained earnings in
the subsidiary, and $55 million through the issue of new long-term debt by the
subsidiary. The parent's cost of equity equals 14 percent and its after-tax
cost of long-term debt equals 5 percent. However, this investment is expected
to increase the systematic risk of the firm, thereby requiring a rate of return
of 16 percent on new parent equity and 6 percent after-tax on new long-term debt.
With a foreign tax rate of 40 percent and no excess foreign tax credit available,
the cost of retained earnings will be set equal to 13.9 percent. Let the nominal
rate of interest on the subsidiary's debt be 16 percent with an anticipated average annual devaluation of 5 percent over the life of the loan. Then the effective after-tax dollar cost of this foreign debt equals 4 percent. Assume further
that the NMC's current debt/equity ratio, which is considered to be optimal,
equals 3/7 with present debt equal to $300 million and equity equal to $700 million. Then the new corporate D/E ratio equals 355/725. To return to a D/E
ratio of 3/7, additional equity in the amount of $103 million must be raised.
Ordinarily, $31 million of this $103 million would be in the form of debt. Thus,
an opportunity cost equal to $31,000,000 (.16 - .06) or $3,100,000 is paid for
the additional overseas leverage. The total annual risk-adjusted cost of the
parent company funds equals $20,000,000 (.16 x .7 + .06 x .3) = $2,600,000. The
annual cost of the retained earnings equals $25,000,000 (.139) = $3,500,000 and
the total annual expected cost of the foreign debt issued is $55,000,00 (.04) =
$2,200,000. Including the annual opportunity cost involved in over-leveraging
abroad, the average incremental cost of capital (and the marginal cost) equals
$\frac{2.6 + 3.5 + 2.2 + 3.1}{100}$ = 11.4 percent. This compares with the parent company's
cost of capital for this investment of 13 percent.

A simplified version of this formula is possible by redefining and reorganizing terms. If we set $k_o = k_e(1-\lambda) + i_d\lambda$, then k_1 reduces to:

$$k_o - \alpha(k_e - k_s) - \beta(i_d - i_f)$$

where $\alpha = \dfrac{E_f}{I}$ and $\beta = \dfrac{D_f}{I}$.

This formula ignores the possibility that the optimal D/E ratio may itself be dependent on the relative costs of debt and equity. It, therefore, provides an upper bound for estimating a subsidiary's cost of capital. Furthermore, this formula is appropriate whether or not an optimal capital structure exists. If it does exist, then λ should equal the optimal debt ratio. If not, then the cost of capital measured at λ remains constant over the entire range of leverage and the leverage penalty is exactly defined.

Using this formula, it is possible to settle one controversy in the literature. Zenoff and Zwick [29] argue for the use of the company-wide marginal cost-of-capital estimate as the discount factor to be used in evaluating foreign investments. On the other hand, Stonehill and Stitzel [26] claim that a firm should use the cost of capital appropriate to local firms operating in the same industry. Both these approaches are incorrect since they ignore the factor of multinationality. As the formula above indicates, in countries where the local cost of capital is high relative to an MNC's cost of funds, using the local cost of capital to evaluate investments will cause profitable ventures to be foregone. At the same time, it would be suboptimal for a multinational corporation to ignore the possibility that some of its subsidiaries may have access to lower cost funds than does the parent.

A related issue is the choice of subsidiary capital structure.

VI. Subsidiary Financial Structure

The question has been raised as to whether subsidiary financial structures should:

a) conform to parent company norms;

b) conform to the capitalization norms established in each country; or

c) vary, so as to take advantage of opportunities to minimize the cost of capital.

The third alternative appears to be the appropriate choice. As Adler [1, p. 122] points out, "Any accounting rendition of a separate capital structure for the subsidiary is therefore wholly illusory and should be ignored in planning foreign investments." Thus, within the constraints set by foreign statutory or minimum equity requirements and the need to maintain a worldwide financial structure, a multinational corporation should finance its requirements in such a manner as to minimize its incremental average cost of capital.

A subsidiary with a capital structure similar to its parent may miss out on profitable opportunities to lower its cost of funds. For example, rigid adherence to a fixed debt/equity ratio may not allow a subsidiary to take advantage of government-subsidized debt or low-cost loans from international agencies. On the other hand, forcing a subsidiary to borrow funds locally to meet parent norms may be quite expensive in a country with a high-cost capital market. The cost-minimizing approach would be to allow subsidiaries in low-cost countries to exceed the parent company capitalization norm while subsidiaries in high-cost nations would have lower target debt/equity ratios. This assumes that capital markets are at least partially segmented. While there are no definite conclusions on this issue at present, the variety and degree of governmental restrictions on capital market access lend credence to the segmentation hypothesis.[7] In addition, the behavior of MNCs in lobbying against regulations such as the OFDI restrictions indicates that they believe capital costs vary significantly among countries.

A counterargument by Stonehill and Stitzel [26] is that a subsidiary's financial structure should conform to local norms. Hence, subsidiaries based in Japan or West Germany should have much higher debt/equity ratios than the U.S. parent or a French subsidiary. As Naumann-Etienne [14, p. 8672] points out, the problem with this argument is that it ignores the strong linkage between U.S.-based multinationals and the U.S. capital market. Since most of its stock is owned and traded in the United States, it follows that the firm's target debt/equity ratio is dependent on U.S. shareholders' risk perceptions. Furthermore, the level of foreign debt/equity ratios is usually determined by institutional factors which have no bearing on U.S. multinationals. For example, Japanese and German banks own much of the equity as well as the debt issues of local corporations. Combining the functions of stockholder and lender may reduce the perceived risk of default on loans to captive corporations and increase the desirability of substantial leverage. This would not apply to a wholly-owned subsidiary. However, a joint venture with a corporation tied into the local banking system may enable an MNC to lower its local cost of capital by leveraging itself, without a proportional increase in risk, to a degree that would be impossible otherwise.

The basic hypothesis that underlies this paper thus far is that a

---

[7] A recent study by Dufey [5] for the U.S. Treasury classifies the rich variety of international constraints on international capital market efficiency.

subsidiary's capital structure is relevant only insofar as it affects the parent's consolidated worldwide debt ratio. The related issues of consolidation and parent company guarantees appear to indicate that at least some MNCs believe otherwise. The next section explores these issues at greater length.

VII. Parent Company Guarantees and Consolidation

Multinational firms are often thought to be reluctant to explicitly guarantee the debt of their subsidiaries even when a more advantageous interest rate can be negotiated. Their assumption appears to be that nonguaranteed debt would not be included in the parent company's worldwide debt ratio whereas guaranteed debt, as a contingent liability, would affect the parent's debt-raising capacity.

This assumption ignores certain realities. It is very unlikely that a parent company would allow a subsidiary to default on its debt, even if that debt were not guaranteed. In fact, a survey by Stobaugh [25] showed that not one of a sample of 20 medium and large multinationals (average foreign sales of $200 million and $1 billion annually, respectively) would allow their subsidiaries to default on debt which did not have a parent company guarantee. Of the small multinationals interviewed (average annual sales of $50 million), only one out of 17 indicated that it would allow a subsidiary to default on its obligations under some circumstances. It is reasonable, therefore, to assume that the multinationals feel a "moral" obligation, for very practical reasons, to implicitly, if not explicitly, guarantee their subsidiaries' debt. Since an explicit guarantee will generally lower subsidiary borrowing costs, it will usually be in the parent's best interest to issue such a guarantee provided that the parent is actually committed to making good on its subsidiaries' debt.[8]

Related to this issue of parent guaranteed debt is the belief, among some firms which do not consolidate their foreign affiliates, that unconsolidated (and nonguaranteed) overseas debt need not affect the MNC's debt ratio. Unless investors and analysts can be fooled permanently, though, unconsolidated overseas leveraging would not allow a firm to lower its cost of capital below the cost of capital for an identical firm which consolidated its foreign affiliates. Any overseas debt offering large enough to materially affect a firm's degree of

---

[8]It is likely that the market has already incorporated this practical commitment in its parent's worldwide debt capacity. An overseas creditor, on the other hand, may not be as certain regarding the firm's intentions. The fact that the parent doesn't guarantee its subsidiaries' debt may then convey some information, i.e., commitment to subsidiary debt is not that strong.

leverage would very quickly come to the attention of financial analysts.[9]

The effects of tax and regulatory factors on subsidiary capital structures will now be examined.

VIII. Tax and Regulatory Factors

Parent company funds, whether called equity or debt, require the same rate of return. However, the appropriate ratio of parent company loans to parent equity may be a crucial decision. Loans are generally preferred to equity by MNCs for a number of reasons. First of all, parent company loans to foreign subsidiaries are often regarded as equivalent to equity investments both by host countries and local creditors. A parent company loan is generally subordinated to all other kinds of debt and does not represent the same threat of insolvency as an external loan. Given this equivalence in the eyes of potential creditors and host governments, the tax and flexibility advantages of debt could become dominant considerations. A firm typically has wider latitude in repatriating funds in the form of interest and loan repayments than as dividends or reductions in equity, since the latter fund flows are usually more closely controlled by governments.

Another reason for the use of parent company loans as opposed to equity investments is the possibility of reducing taxes. If foreign tax rates are below U.S. rates, dividends will typically lead to increased taxes whereas loan repayments will not. If foreign tax rates are above 48 percent, and a withholding tax is assessed on dividends, paying out dividends will lead to higher taxes unless the excess foreign tax credits can be used elsewhere.

Firms do not have complete latitude in choosing their debt/equity ratios abroad. This is frequently a subject for negotiation with the host governments. In addition, dividends are often restricted to a fixed percentage of equity. A small equity base could also lead to a high return on equity, opening up a company to charges of exploitation.

It should be reiterated here that a firm's cost of capital is not affected by whether it calls its overseas investments debt or equity. However, the cash flow from foreign investments could very well be affected by the form of this

---

[9]Some evidence of market efficiency was provided through talks with bond raters at Moody's and Standard and Poor's. Individuals from both agencies stated that they would closely examine situations where nonguaranteed debt issued by unconsolidated foreign affiliates would noticeably affect a firm's worldwide debt equity ratio. In addition parent company guaranteed debt is included in bond rater analyses of a firm's contingent liabilities, whether this debt is consolidated or not. Thus, it appears that the growing financial sophistication of MNCs has been paralleled by increased sophistication among rating agencies and investors.

investment. According to Robbins and Stobaugh [17, p. 58], U.S. multinationals usually use more equity than is required to meet government regulations. As a result, total foreign plus U.S. taxes are greater than they need be.

Thus far, we have assumed that international investments will not affect a firm's risk characteristics. The next section examines this assumption both theoretically and empirically.

IX. Riskiness of Foreign Operations

The traditional approach to international investment considers foreign operations as adding to overall firm riskiness. Foreign exchange risk, the risks of expropriation and continued governmental intervention are pointed out as increasing the political and economic risks facing any firms operating abroad. However, this view is quite limited.

According to modern capital asset pricing theory, investors must be compensated only for their securities' systematic risk since nonsystematic risk can be diversified away by holding a market portfolio. Based on the pioneering work of Grubel [8] and Grubel and Fadnor [9] on international portfolios, this concept of systematic versus nonsystematic risk has been extended to the analysis of the riskiness of foreign operations. Although individual foreign investments may be riskier than comparable investments in the United States, the diversification effect due to operating in a number of countries whose economic cycles are not perfectly in phase could reduce the variation in a firm's earnings. We will now examine each of these sources of risk, concluding with evidence on the actual risk perceptions of investors.

X. Political Risk

Political risk is relevant to the MNC insofar as it results in a deprivation of wealth.[10] Empirical evidence by Truitt [27] on the expropriation experiences of U.S. and British MNCs since World War II indicates that industries can be ranked in terms of their susceptibilities to political risk. Expropriation or creeping expropriation is much more likely to happen in the extractive, utility, or financial service sectors of an economy than in the manufacturing sector although there is a trend toward increasing takeovers of manufacturing firms [11].

In general, the greater the benefits to the local economy provided by a given subsidiary, the lesser the degree of risk. Thus, political risk appears

------

[10] Any definition of political risk is arbitrary but in this paper it refers to expropriation, nationalization, and any other government interference with a subsidiary's operations which results in a loss of wealth to the MNC.

to be inversely related to a subsidiary's exports, the amount of local labor employed, the extent of capital and technology supplied by the firm, and the difficulty of replacement by local firms. In addition, joint ventures are less susceptible to political interference than are wholly-owned subsidiaries [6], perhaps because of the reduced perception of foreign control. Therefore, any arbitrary increase in a firm's cost of capital for political risk is likely to neglect the degree to which the firm can influence this risk. Furthermore, increasing a firm's discount rate to compensate for political risk will ignore the time pattern as well as the magnitude of this risk.

XI. Inflation and Exchange Risks

Foreign inflation will not affect the MNC's dollar cost of borrowing abroad [4]. However, exchange rate changes will affect these costs. To the extent that capital markets overseas are segmented, though, the cost of borrowing abroad may not fully reflect these exchange rate expectations.

Inflation and exchange rate changes will affect the future cash flows of a project. In fact, there are systematic and predictable changes to foreign currency cost and revenue streams, predictable both as to direction and magnitude. Recent studies have shown that the sector of the economy a firm operates in (export, import--competing, or purely domestic) and the sources of its inputs (imports, domestic traded, or nontraded goods) are the major determinants of a firm's exchange risk (for example, see [22]).

This means that the incremental effects of changes in currency values on the parent's risk characteristics and, hence, the parent's cost of capital, can only be determined by examining the impact of variations in foreign earnings on variations in the firm's worldwide consolidated earnings [23]. However, variations due to exchange rate changes will be difficult, if not empirically impossible, to separate out from variations due to other events such as changes in government policies, competitors' actions, etc. Nor need these exchange effects be isolated. The important factor to analyze is the simultaneous impact on firm earnings of the myriad of events to which a multinational firm is prone.

XII. Diversification

As we mentioned above, the greater riskiness of individual projects overseas could well be offset by beneficial portfolio effects. Supporting evidence is provided by Cohen [3] whose work indicates that there is little correlation between the earnings of the various national components of MNCs. To the extent that foreign cash flows are not perfectly correlated with those of domestic investments, the overall risk associated with variations in cash flows which confronts a stockholder might be reduced. Thus, the greater riskiness of individual projects overseas could well be offset by beneficial portfolio effects. However, international diversification by firms will benefit their stockholders only if there are barriers to direct international portfolio diversification by individual investors.[11] According to Agmon and Lessard [2] these barriers do exist. "Available evidence suggests that neither individual nor mutual funds are broadly diversified internationally, presumably at least in part due to institutional barriers to foreign investment" [2, p. 2]. Thus, the extent to which these portfolio effects are beneficial to an MNC is an empirical question.

Some tentative evidence is available. Severn [20] has found that the greater the foreign involvement of a firm, the lower the covariance of its earnings per share with the earnings per share of Standard and Poor's Composite Index. Gordon and Halpern [7] have demonstrated the close positive correlation between the systematic risk of a firm's earnings and its stock price β. Thus, Severn's conclusion that the higher the percentage of foreign to total earnings the lower the capitalization rate on its earnings appears reasonable. However, since multinationals are larger, on average, than are nonmultinationals, the reduction in earnings variability may be due to size, and a consequent increase in product diversification, rather than to the influence of foreign-source earnings. In fact, Haegele [10] has shown that while the stock price β's are slightly lower for MNC's, when corrected for size, there is no significant difference between the β's of MNCs and non-MNCs.

Rugman [18] does show that earning variability is a decreasing function of foreign-source earnings even when corrected for size. The relationship between this reduction in earnings variability and a reduction in the systematic risk of an MNC's earnings, however, is not demonstrated. This is an important distinction because there is no empirical evidence to suggest a correlation between a firm's stock price β and its degree of earnings variability. The only evidence available relates to a firm's systematic earnings risk. However, the risk of bankruptcy for a firm is dependent on total as opposed to only systematic earnings variability. Thus, a reduction in the total earnings variability could allow an MNC to leverage itself more highly leading to a reduction in its marginal cost of capital.

---

[11]Even if there are no barriers to individual diversification internationally, the reduced risk of bankruptcy associated with a more stable cash flow could lower an MNC's cost of capital.

Agmon and Lessard [2] have tested the proposition that investors recognize and reward the geographical diversification of U.S. multinationals by using a two-factor capital asset pricing model with the second factor being the percentage of foreign sales. According to the authors, "The results reported above support the hypothesis that the market (NYSE) behaves as if it recognizes the international composition of the activities of U.S. based corporations" [2, p. 12]. Taking a different approach, Kohers [12] has used the dividend valuation model (see [28] for an explanation of this model) to measure the cost of equity capital for MNCs. He found no statistically significant differences in the cost of equity capital for six of the seven industries studied including the oil and nonferrous metals industries.

Thus, while the evidence is scant, the available empirical research indicates that if multinationality alters a firm's perceived riskiness, the effect is slight for most firms and may well be beneficial.

XIV. Joint Ventures

Since many MNCs participate in joint ventures, either by choice or necessity, establishing the required rate of return for this form of investment is particularly important. Several problems arise. The most troublesome is the case where the MNC's required rate of return in a joint venture differs from its partner's cost of capital. Adler [1] suggests using a complex compensation principle whereby each partner is compensated on the basis of its opportunity cost of money. This will lead to a situation where each partner tries to declare as high a cost of capital as possible. Agreement on a joint venture cost of capital using this principle will then be even less likely. One solution is to set the required rate of return for the joint venture equal to the maximum cost of capital among the participants.

The firm can use the formula presented earlier to establish its marginal cost of capital in a joint venture. There is one caveat. A joint venture partner may have access to local sources of capital which enable the joint venture to be leveraged beyond what the subsidiary would be able to do on its own. The formula presented earlier penalized a subsidiary which leverages itself more than the parent itself is leveraged. This is due to the increased risk of financial distress associated with more highly leveraged firms. However, in countries such as Japan and Germany, increased leverage will not necessarily lead to increased financial risks due to the close relationship between the local banks and corporation. Thus, increased leverage in a joint venture in Japan, for example, may not req ire application of the leverage penalty. The assessment of the impact of leverage in a joint venture is a judgmental factor which requires an analysis of the partner's ties with the local financial community, particularly with the local banks.

XV. Summary and Conclusions

This paper has analyzed a number of factors related to an MNC's cost of capital. If capital markets are segmented or a subsidiary's risk characteristics are different from those of the parent, then the subsidiary's cost of capital must be adjusted to reflect these differences. It was decided that the issues of consolidation and parent-guaranteed debt are largely false ones--that the parent cannot significantly change its cost of capital by choosing whether to consolidate foreign earnings or guarantee local debt.

Analysis of the available evidence on the impact of foreign operations on firm riskiness suggests that, if there is an effect, it is generally to reduce both actual and perceived riskiness. However, some investments are more risk-prone than others and this must be accounted for. Much work remains to be done in empirically testing the proposition of international capital market segmentation. In addition, further empirical testing of invester perceptions of the riskiness of MNCs is required. These perceptions are likely to be affected by the location as well as the percentage of foreign-source earnings.

1]   Adler, M.   "The Cost of Capital and Valuation of a Two-Country Firm."
      Journal of Finance (March 1974), p. 119.

2]   Agmon, T., and D. Lessard.   "International Diversification and the Multi-
      national Corporation: An Investigation of Price Behavior of the Shares of
      U.S. Based Multinational Corporations on the N.Y.S.E."   Working Paper
      #804-75, Sloan School of Management, Massachusetts Institute of Technology
      (1975).

3]   Cohen, B. I.   *Multinational Firms and Asian Exports*.   New Haven, Conn.:
      Yale University Press (1975).

4]   de Faro, C., and J. V. Jucker.   "The Impact of Inflation and Devaluation
      on the Selection of an International Borrowing Source."   *Journal of Inter-
      national Business Studies* (Fall 1973), p. 97.

5]   Dufey, G.   "The Structure of Private Foreign Investment with Specific Ref-
      erence to Portfolio Investment."   Report prepared for U.S. Dept. of Treas-
      ury, OASIA/Research (January 31, 1976), cited with permission of author.

6]   Friedman; Dalmonoff; and Wolfgang.   *Joint International Business Ventures*.
      New York: Columbia University Press (1961).

7]   Gordon, M. J., and P. J. Halpern.   "Cost of Capital for the Division of a
      Firm."   *Journal of Finance* (September 1974), p. 1153.

8]   Grubel, H. G.   "internationally Diversified Portfolios: Welfare Gains
      and Capital Flows."   *American Economic Review* (December 1968), p. 1299.

9]   Grubel, H. G., and K. Fadner.   "The Interdependence of International
      Equity Markets."   *Journal of Finance* (March 1971), p. 89.

10]   Haegele, M. J.   "Exchange Rate Expectations and Security Returns."   Unpub-
      lished Ph.D. dissertation, The University of Pennsylvania (1974).

11]   Hawkins, R. G., and N. Mintz.   "Government Takeovers of U.S. Foreign
      Affiliates."   *Journal of International Business Studies* (Spring 1976),
      p. 3.

12]   Kohers, T.   "The Effect of Multinational Corporations on the Cost of
      Equity of U.S. Corporations: An Empirical Study."   *Management Internation-
      al Review* (2-3/1974), p. 121.

13]   Modigliani, F., and M. H. Miller.   "The Cost of Capital, Corporation
      Finance, and the Theory of Investment."   *American Economic Review* (June
      1958), p. 261.

14]   Naumann-Etienne, R.   "A Framework for Financial Decisions in Multinational
      Corporation-Summary of Recent Research."   *Journal of Financial and Quanti-
      tative Analysis* (November 1974), p. 859.

15]   Ness, W. L., Jr.   "U.S. Corporate Income Taxation and the Dividend Remit-
      tance Policy of Multinational Corporations."   *Journal of International
      Business Studies* (Spring 1975), p. 67.

16]   Price-Waterhouse.   "Information Guide on U.S. Corporations Doing Business
      Abroad."   (January 1972).

360   [17]   Robbins, S. M., and R. S. Stobaugh. "Financing Foreign Affiliates." *Financial Management* (Winter 1972), p. 56.

[18]   Rugman, A. M. "Risk Reduction by International Diversification." Paper presented at the Academy of International Business - INSEAD Conference, Fountainbleau, Paris (July 7, 1975).

[19]   Rutenberg, D. P. "Maneuvering Liquid Assets in a Multinational Corporation." *Management Science* (June 1970), p. 671.

[20]   Severn, A. K. "Investor Evaluation of Foreign and Domestic Risk." *Journal of Finance* (May 1974), p. 545.

[21]   Shapiro, A. C. "Evaluating Financing Costs for Multinational Subsidiaries." *Journal of International Business Studies* (Fall 1975), p. 25.

[22]   _____. "Exchange Rate Changes Inflation and the Value of the Multinational Corporation." *Journal of Finance* (May 1975), p. 485.

[23]   _____. "Defining Exchange Risk." *Journal of Business* (forthcoming).

[24]   Solnick, B. H., and J. Grall. "Eurobonds; Determinants of the Demand for Capital and the International Interest Rate Structure." *Journal of Bank Research* (Winter 1975), p. 218.

[25]   Stobaugh, R. S. "Financing Foreign Subsidiaries of U.S.-Controlled Multinational Enterprises." *Journal of International Business Studies* (Summer 1970), p. 43.

[26]   Stonehill, A., and T. Stitzel. "Financial Structure and Multinational Corporations." *California Management Review* (Fall 1969), p. 91.

[27]   Truitt, J. F. "Expropriation of Foreign Investment: Summary of the Post World War II Experience of American and British Investors in Less Developed Countries." *Journal of International Business Studies* (Fall 1970), p. 21.

[28]   Weston, J. F., and E. F. Brigham. *Managerial Finance*, 4th ed. New York: Holt, Rinehart and Winston (1972).

[29]   Zenoff, D. B., and J. Zwick. *International Financial Management*. Englewood Cliffs, N. J.: Prentice-Hall (1969).

FOREIGN EXCHANGE RISK MANAGEMENT

CHAPTER 24

Management of foreign exchange risk: a review article*
Laurent L. Jacque

Abstract. This paper reviews the literature on Foreign Exchange Risk Management (FERM) which has burgeoned during the last decade. Scholars' and practioners' emerging interest in Foreign Exchange Risk Management was spurred by the advent of fluctuating exchange rates in the early seventies as well as by the pronouncement of the infamous FASB Statement No. 8 in 1976 which laid down unambiguous guidelines for consolidating financial statements of multinational corporations. A normative (rather than a market) view of Foreign Exchange Risk Management is taken and accordingly the author reviews first the two key informational inputs necessary for any Foreign Exchange Risk Management program: forecasting exchange rates and measuring exposure to exchange risk. Available decision models for handling transaction and translation exposures are reviewed next. A concluding section identifies gaps in the existing literature and suggests directions for future research.

INTRODUCTION

> So much of barbarism, however, still remains in the transactions of most civilized nations, that almost all independent countries choose to assert their nationality by having, to their own inconvenience and that of their neighbors, a peculiar currency of their own.
>
> *John Stuart Mill, 1894*

■ Of all the winds of change that have buffeted multinational corporations (MNCs) in recent years, none has had a more pervasive impact upon their risk profile than the demise of the international monetary system of quasi-fixed exchange rates that had prevailed until March 1973 under the Bretton Woods agreement (1944–1971) and, later, under the short-lived Smithsonian accord (1971–1973). A somewhat chaotic system of floating exchange rates has emerged in its stead.

---

*Laurent L. Jacque is a Lecturer of International Business in the Management Department of the Wharton School, University of Pennsylvania. His research interests center on multinational financial management. He is the author of *Management of Foreign Exchange Risk: Theory and Praxis* (Lexington Books, 1978).

The author gratefully acknowledges the helpful comments from Gunter Dufey and Alan Shapiro.

* This article is reprinted, with permission, from the *Journal of International Business Studies* (Spring/Summer 1981, Tenth Anniversary Special Issue) pp 81–101

The resulting heightened volatility in currencies' prices has severely disrupted the steadiness of multinational corporations' foreign income streams. The recent implementation of the controversial and inflexible FASB Statement No. 8 has further exacerbated this seemingly erratic earnings pattern by doing away with the former widely used practice of *reserving* for foreign exchange gains and losses and forcing upon MNCs the periodic disclosure of such gains and losses even though no cash flows may be involved.

This unprecedented situation has stirred a considerable amount of interest among both academics and practitioners in Foreign Exchange Risk Management. This article reviews the literature on Foreign Exchange Risk Management published in the last decade to identify the conceptual weaknesses underlying the normative Foreign Exchange Risk Management decision models currently available and to suggest fruitful directions for future managerially oriented research.

MANAGEMENT OF FOREIGN EXCHANGE RISK: WHOSE VIEW?

Foreign Exchange Risk is commonly defined as the additional variability experienced by a multinational corporation in its worldwide consolidated earnings that results from unexpected currency fluctuations. It is generally understood that this considerable earnings variability can be eliminated — partially or fully — at a cost, the cost of Foreign Exchange Risk Management. Is such a cost warranted or, in other words, should corporate treasurers be concerned with the smooth period-to-period earnings pattern so cherished by security analysts, because a volatile earnings pattern is commonly believed to affect the firm's price-earnings ratio and, in turn, its ability to raise funds at a reasonable cost?

Modern capital market theory, which defines foreign exchange risk as "the systematic risk associated with a foreign currency denominated return (or cost) stream and measured by the covariance between the rate of change of the exchange rate and the domestic market return" [80, p. 25], answers in the negative. It argues that under certain assumptions of market efficiency (to be spelled out below) Foreign Exchange Risk Management is totally superfluous. This somewhat extreme point of view, detailed in Logue and Oldfield [48], holds that a firm's risky prospects are valued directly by the market on the basis of their expected profitability and their systematic risk (that is, the risk which cannot be "diversified away"); thus, it should make "no difference to the valuation of either the total market portfolio or the individual firm whether exchange risks . . . are passed through to the capital market as part of the risk of the firm's shares, or 'laid off,' or transferred directly to the market through forward exchange or foreign currency debt contracts."[1] In this somewhat hypothetical world, MNCs' treasurers abdicate the initiative of Foreign Exchange Risk Management whose responsibility is fully transferred to the firm's shareholders who, in turn, will manage the unsystematic portion of exchange risk through efficient portfolio diversification. The relevant question for scholarly investigation thus becomes that of exchange risk diversification from the viewpoint of the investor selecting claims on firms located in different countries or operating across national boundaries (MNCs), claims which are clearly denominated in different currencies. Normative research efforts in this direction are aimed at extending the Capital Asset Pricing

Model to a multicurrency world; however, existing International Capital Asset Pricing Models are based on extraordinarily restrictive assumptions. To wit, Fama and Farber [24] and Grauer, Litzenberger, and Stehle [33] assume away international capital market segmentation (that is, international capital markets are fully integrated). The former model presumes further that investors consume only one homogeneous good and that Purchasing Power Parity holds at all times. Solnik [72 a & b] similarly assumes full integration of international capital markets but allows for different consumption goods across countries; however, exchange rates are assumed to be uncorrelated with the corresponding local currency market returns, certainly a convenient simplifying premise. In sum, all three models acrobatically dispose of the exchange risk factor in their pricing of foreign currency denominated assets.

How to diversify exchange risk effectively at the investor level remains an unanswered question because existing International Asset Pricing Models require satisfaction of a strict set of conditions which are far removed from the current multicurrency institutional environment facing international investors. Therefore it should come as no surprise that most theoretical models of Foreign Exchange Risk Management and certainly all of current management practice have considered exchange risk from the viewpoint of a firm's treasurer aiming at minimizing the impact of exchange rate fluctuations upon earnings measured in some relevant numeraire, thus upholding the fundamental hypothesis behind Foreign Exchange Risk Management stated at the beginning of this section. Adoption of the firm total risk viewpoint is further warranted, as Makin [50b, p. 521] argues, when

> consideration is given to the time horizon of a typical manager which is likely to be considerably shorter than the time period required for the impact of exchange market disturbances on firm's profit to net to zero. Further, costs of capital can be influenced by the perceived riskiness of claims on multinationals and that perceived riskiness, relative to other multinationals, could be altered in the short run by heavy exposures in foreign currencies.

In a similar vein, Aliber [3, pp. 134–135] writes: "The question is whether the firm or individual investor can do a more effective job of diversifying against exchange risk . . . The firm may have superior knowledge, and may be able to protect itself against these risks at lower costs."

Indeed, to the extent that individual investors face exchange controls, high transaction costs, and taxation, MNCs, because they can lessen the burden of such market imperfections, are superiorly equipped to carry out currency diversification on behalf of their shareholders.

Having explained the logic behind the relevance of corporate Foreign Exchange Risk Management, this discussion next proceeds with a review of available methodologies for generating the two key informational inputs for effective Foreign Exchange Risk Management; namely, reliable probabilistic forecasts of future spot exchange rates as well as a projection of corporate exposures on a currency-by-currency basis.

FORECASTING EXCHANGE RATES

Although tremendous resources have been directed at forecasting exchange rate changes or establishing the irrelevance of such forecasting efforts (Market Efficiency hypothesis), little attention has been focused on the managerially more relevant issue of relating the forecastability of foreign exchange rates to Foreign Exchange Risk Management proper. Accordingly, this section will consider first, at some length, the general question of exchange rates forecasting independently from the praxis of Foreign Exchange Risk Management before attempting to reconcile the two.

The quantitative dimension of foreign exchange rates forecasting — that is, predicting expected future spot exchange rates — is traditionally emphasized by most forecasting models. However, the operational value of such predictions can be greatly enhanced if they can be supplemented by a qualitative forecast. Historically, parity changes have, in most cases, been tightly intermingled with a complex history of exchange restrictions running the gamut from selective controls on capital account transactions to indiscriminate controls on all exchange transactions.

The task of the currency forecaster is therefore twofold: (1) quantifying the magnitude of expected exchange rate changes (devaluations or revaluations in the context of pegged exchange rates; depreciation or appreciation in the context of floating exchange rates), and (2) anticipating the likelihood of imposition of exchange controls.

Forecasting Pegged Yet Adjustable Exchange Rates

The current international monetary system is best described as a system in which currencies within major trading blocs maintain their former pegged yet adjustable relationships with each other, but fluctuate continuously — or float in unison — against the currencies of the other major blocs. The European Monetary System, for example, is very much resurrecting, on a regional basis, the Bretton Woods system of quasi-fixed exchange rates through its tightly knit grid of par values.

Under such conditions, forecasting discrete change in parities is a relatively easy task, at least in direction if not in magnitude or timing. Jacque [39a, chapter 4] developed a four-step forecasting model.[2] First, through a review of selected economic indicators, the forecaster will identify which countries have balances of payments that are in fundamental disequilibrium. Second, for the currencies of such countries, the forecaster will measure the pressure that market forces are exercising on prevailing exchange rates. Third, the level of central banks' foreign exchange reserves gives an indication of the future point in time at which the central bank will no longer be in a position to defend the prevailing exchange rate. The fourth and crucial step is to predict the type of corrective policies that politically motivated decision-makers are likely to implement: will the country under pressure adjust through a manipulation of its exchange rate (devaluation or revaluation) or, instead, initiate, essentially for political reasons, deflationary or inflationary policies combined with exchange controls and extensive international borrowing?

An interesting attempt by Folks and Stansell [28] and Murenbeeld [53], based on the use of multivariate discriminant analysis, was made at identifying the likelihood and direction of potential changes in par values of countries maintaining pegged exchange rates (steps one and two of the above forecasting procedure); however, the forecasting outputs of such models is of limited value because they fail to provide any information as to the timing or magnitude of a potential exchange rate change.

For controlled exchange rates, black market rates will prove to be helpful leading gauges of subsequent devaluation of official (controlled) exchange rates. As a rule, the black market rate (generally available from *Pick's Currency Yearbook and Reports*) depends on the extent to which the official exchange rate overvalues the equilibrium exchange rate as well as on the extent to which illegal transactors (black marketeers) are apprehended and prosecuted. Indeed Culbertson [14] has shown that for an overvalued (controlled) exchange rate, the hypothetical equilibrium exchange rate will fall somewhere between the official and the black market rate.

Forecasting Floating Exchange Rates: Market-Based Forecasts

The return in early 1973 to floating exchange rates by a number of major currencies has generated considerable interest about the general question of whether foreign exchange markets do indeed constitute efficient markets. If clearly established, the Market Efficiency hypothesis would have far-ranging forecasting implications and could possibly establish the irrelevance of building elaborate forecasting models, but, before this critical last point is further elaborated, a careful statement of the efficient markets hypothesis is in order.

A foreign exchange market in which exchange rates always fully reflect all available information is said to be efficient.[3] Three degrees of Market Efficiency are customarily distinguished:[4] (1) the weakly[5] efficient market hypothesis says that series of historical exchange rates contain no information which can be used to forecast future spot exchange rates; (2) the semistrong version of market efficiency holds that a large and competitive group of market participants have access to all publicly available information relevant to the formation of expectations about future rates; finally, (3) if the set of available information also includes private or insiders' information, the market is said to be strongly efficient.

Let us now review the evidence for and against the efficiency of the foreign exchange market and explain the forecasting implications of the hypothesis. Tests of market efficiency have been characterized by the heterogeneity of the statistical tools used as well as of the sample periods and currencies selected. Furthermore, the testing methodologies used have generally been directly borrowed from analogous empirical studies of the stock markets and commodity futures markets, although it is not clear that they are appropriate for testing the efficiency of foreign exchange markets given the presence of major, nonprofit-maximizing participants, namely central banks. Finally, the lack of a comprehensive testing of an exhaustive and uniform data basis clearly precludes reaching clear cut conclusions for or against the efficiency hypothesis.[6]

Weak-form tests have received the most attention, probably because they are the easiest to carry out. These tests are concerned with two major issues: the extent of statistical dependence of successive changes in exchange rates and the profitability of trading rules. In essence, what is being investigated is whether past series of exchange rates contain useful information for the prediction of future spot prices, thus implying that general patterns would repeat themselves at regular intervals.

The assertion that current exchange rates reflect all publicly available information, as called for by the semistrong form of Market Efficiency, is so general that it has proven a difficult hypothesis to test empirically. Accordingly, empirical evidence for or against this form of market efficiency has been scant except for one recent study by Rogalski and Vinso [63] which provided conclusive evidence in its support.

Another forecasting model that has lately received increasing attention and that is intuitively consistent with the semistrong form of the Market Efficiency hypothesis concerns the predictive accuracy of forward exchange rates. Speculators who think that the forward rate is above their expectation of the future spot exchange rate will sell the foreign currency forward, thus bidding down the forward rate until it equals the expected future spot rate. Conversely, speculators who see the forward rate undervaluing the expected future spot rate will buy foreign currency forward, thus bidding the forward rate up until forward and expected future spot exchange rates become equal. If speculative demand for forward contracts were infinitely elastic and all speculators held homogeneous expectations with respect to the future spot exchange rate, the current forward exchange rate would be equal to the expected future spot exchange rate.

A number of theoretical arguments have been developed to establish that the forward exchange rate must necessarily be a biased predictor of the future spot exchange rate.[7,8] For instance, this simple forecasting model stands in apparent contradiction to the Modern Theory of forward exchange rates determination,[9] which generally suggests that the speculators' schedule is less than infinitely elastic and that, as a result, the equilibrium forward rate of exchange would be different from the future spot exchange rate. Only in the polar case (somewhat unrealistic) of risk-neutral speculators should the forward exchange rate be considered as an unbiased predictor of the future spot exchange rate.[10]

Extensive empirical testing of the Market Efficiency hypothesis, very ably surveyed by Kohlhagen [41a], has generally suffered from the joint hypothesis problem identified by Levich [45a]. Prominent studies include those of Poole [60], Dooley and Shafer [15], Giddy and Dufey [31], Logue and Sweeney [49], Cornell and Dietrich [13], Roll and Solnik [64] and Kohlhagen [41c], whose detailed critical evaluation is beyond the scope of this paper.

For fairly obvious reasons little attention has been devoted to the problem of long-term foreign exchange rate forecasts which are a much needed informational input into the selection of an optimal currency denomination for long-term debt financing or the even more puzzling question of debt refunding/debt refinancing in a multicurrency context.

The relationship between the term structure of interest rates and exchange rate expectations was explored by Porter [61]. The theoretical framework developed in this seminal study showed how the term structure of international interest rates can be used to make inferences as to the expected time path of the exchange rate adjustment between two currencies. This approach was subsequently operationalized very elegantly by Dufey and Giddy [17].

Econometric Modelling Approaches

Exchange rates econometric forecasting models are a systematic effort at uncovering a functional relationship between a set of explanatory (exogenous) variables — such as, price levels differential, interest rates differential, or differential in the rate of growth in money supplies — and a dependent (endogenous) variable — namely, the exchange rate. The functional relationship may involve only the current period values of the exogenous variables or may be of a lagged nature; that is, incorporate past periods values taken on by the exogenous variables. In this latter case econometric modelling is clearly inconsistent with the Market Efficiency hypothesis whereas in the former case it is not necessarily so. As a matter of fact, one may be tempted to argue that econometric forecasting disregarding lagged functional relationships is assisting the market in correctly interpreting all currently available information, thus making it more efficient.

The specification of the model itself — that is, the nature of the functional relationship (not necessarily linear) — as well as the choice of exogenous variables included generally blends economic theory (for example, a combination of the Purchasing Power Parity and Fisher theories) with the model builder's experience and intuition. In that sense, econometric building is as much an art as a science and accordingly the reader should expect the various forecasting services to be idiosyncratic.

Structural equations however (usually one for each currency forecasted) are extracted from time series of exogenous or endogenous variables — that is, from past observations. This means that if a drastic change in the structural relationship between independent and dependent variables were to occur and be disregarded in specifying functional relationships, the econometric model forecasting value would be adversely affected. Thus, if one accepts that the behavior of private and public market participants was markedly affected by the advent of floating exchanges rates, it is perhaps too early to forecast currency prices in the context of a floating exchange rates regime. The reason is that the observations available are still too few and far between (spanning only the 1973–1979 period) to derive meaningful functional relationships between exogenous and endogenous variables. Yet a number of econometricians have apparently felt otherwise because there are at least a dozen major econometric forecasting services that can be subscribed to for a fee.

One last additional feature of econometric forecasting models worth commenting upon is the random error term that is always incorporated in this type of model.[11] The inclusion of such a stochastic element allows probability statements to be made about the forecasted variable. This is indeed an attractive feature compared with a point estimate (as provided, for instance, by forward exchange rates) especially when it is recalled that the information is to be used in a risk management context. However, for econometric forecasting to be theoretically correct, several requirements must be met.[12] The major theoretical flaw of current forecasting efforts is probably the normality assumption (of exchange rates probability distribution) which is generally made. That exchange rates are not normally distributed has been established beyond doubt with Westerfield [77] and Vinso and Rogalski [76] providing empirical evidence to the effect that exchange rates are best described as non-normal members of the Pareto-Levy class of probability distribution.

As could be expected, there is some controversy as to the reliability of such econometric forecasts: in a recent examination of the track record of 6 major econometric forecasting services, Goodman [32] found that

The predictive accuracy of most — not all — of the economics-oriented foreign exchange rate forecasting services is so poor that they are likely to be of little use for corporations trying to manage their foreign exchange exposure.

The results are quite different for the technically-oriented services. Their consistently very strong predictive performance supports the view that speculative runs do occur in the exchange market and that the foreign market is not efficient.

However, Goodman's testing methodology is questionable given that his comparative criterion allows subscribers to economics-oriented forecasts to act only on the last day of the month; by contrast, subscribers to technically-oriented forecasting services are assumed to act on the day the forecast is received.

By contrast, a thorough and up-to-date appraisal of 9 forecasting advisory services by Levich [45c] indicates that some services have consistently beaten the forward rate and that the record of forecasting accuracy was too good to be explained by chance. These results are all the more interesting as they were established by a Chicago-trained economist whose doctoral effort was largely focused on establishing the efficiency of the foreign exchange market [45b].

Addressing himself to the more fundamental question of why a small but vigorously successful forecasting industry is competing with "free" market-based forecasts available daily from the financial press, Makin [50c] appropriately remarks that such ex post empirical evaluation of the accuracy of forecasting services is redundant. Indeed, the true market test is whether forecasters can coexist with the "free" market forecast and incur positive information gathering and processing costs while charging for their services a fee which allows them to earn a competitive rate of return. However, it would be surprising that the output of a permanently superior forecasting model be available commercially; in fact, a recent survey by Evans, Folks, and Jilling [21] indicated that 58.4 percent of the respondents felt that currency forecasting was the weakest link in their exchange risk management programs. One suspects that treasurers place only limited faith in commercially available forecasts but find them helpful for bureaucratic hedging purposes.

Forecasting and Foreign Exchange Risk Management

In sum, the lack of decisive answers to the general question of forecasting exchange rates remains probably the single most potent justification for undertaking costly, and at times highly constraining, protective policies against foreign exchange risk. More specifically, Dufey and Giddy [17] distinguish between two basically different forecasting situations:

(1) The foreign exchange market is efficient (floating exchange rates); the use of market-based forecasts is advocated. However, it should be recognized that the market's expected value will seldom be attained (that is, the actual exchange rate will generally differ from the one actually predicted by the forward exchange rate), hence the need to plan or attempt to forecast errors which are expected to occur. Further, it becomes imperative to assess what would be the impact of such unanticipated deviations from the expected rate on the net cash flows of the firm. (See the section on Managing Economic Exposure.)

(2) The foreign exchange market is inefficient because of stifling government controls on interest rates and exchange rates (pegged yet adjustable exchange

rates); multinational corporations should aim at capitalizing on the profit opportunities available because of market distortions in order to offset the cost of operating under government controls in real factor markets.

MEASURING EXPOSURE TO FOREIGN EXCHANGE RISK

An operationally viable — if conceptually weak — measure of exposure to foreign exchange risk is provided by accounting rules. A convenient dichotomy generally distinguishes between transaction and translation exposures.

Transaction Exposure

Wihlborg [79b] defines transaction exposure as an uncertain domestic currency value of an open position denominated in a foreign currency with respect to a known transaction; that is, a future foreign currency denominated flow. As expected, fluctuations in the exchange rate relationship over the life of the contract will result in windfall cash flow gains or losses with tax implications which are not necessarily symmetrical between gains and losses nor consistent across different types of underlying transactions. Jacque developed a simple exposure netting algorithm [39a, chapter 5] on an after-tax basis for subsidiaries of a multinational corporation which are not subjected to homogeneous tax laws with respect to exchange gains and losses.[13]

Translation Exposure

Foreign market entry through direct investment, by contrast, results in so-called translation exposure which Wihlborg [79b] defines as the uncertain domestic value of a net accounting position denominated in a foreign currency at a certain future date: that is, a future foreign currency denominated stock. The practice of periodically consolidating or aggregating parent's and affiliates' balance sheets will generally entail exchange gains or losses of a non-cash flow (paper) nature as exchange rates fluctuate over the accounting horizon. At the core of this consolidation process which allows multinational corporations to disclose earnings valued in a single numeraire (reference currency) lies the controversial question of how balance sheet accounts of foreign subsidiaries ought to be translated. Should the accounts of foreign subsidiaries be treated as exposed or non-exposed items — with exposed items translated at current exchange rates and non-exposed items translated at historical rates? Until 1976 (which marks the implementation of FASB Statement No. 8) multinational corporations were left free to use whatever methods they believed reflected most accurately their true economic performance. Most firms used either the current/non-current, monetary/non-monetary, or current method of translation, and there is an over abundance of accounting literature debating the merits and demerits of each method (cf. Hayes [36], Barrett and Spero [7], Olstein and O'Glove [57], and Pakkala [58], among the most prominent papers).

The mandatory translation guidelines put forward by Statement No. 8 (and subsequently No. 20) eliminated much of the flexibility that U.S.-based multinational corporations previously had in translating their foreign affiliates' financial statements into the reference currency. The most dramatic and perhaps most controversial ruling of Statement No. 8 is that exchange gains or losses resulting from both the conversion and translation processes are to be included in the net income for the accounting period in which the exchange rate change actually occurred. The distinction between realized and unrealized gains and losses was thus unequivocally discontinued as was the use of reserve accounts aimed at mitigating the erratic impact of exchange gains or losses on the earning profile. (For constructive suggestions on how such accounts could be reenacted see Ankrom [4a].) Also controversial are the provisions calling for the treatment of long-term debt as an exposed item (which led a number of U.S.-based MNCs' affiliates to shun local currency long-term funding in favor of dollar-denominated financing) whereas inventory would generally be considered as non-exposed. As a whole, Statement No. 8 has been severely criticized in a flurry of articles appearing in accounting magazines and journals. (See for instance Shank [67], Rodriguez [62a], and Aggarwal [1] for a limited but representative sample of the literature.) If Statement No. 8 has generally been received with skepticism by accountants, treasurers of U.S. multinational corporations have vehemently opposed it as surveys conducted by Choi, Lowe, and Worthley [11] and Stanley and Block [73] clearly establish. A major study commissioned by the FASB (Evans, Folks, and Jilling [21]) further reports that the implementation of Statement No. 8 resulted in increased Foreign Exchange Risk Management activities especially by firms which relied on translation methods most at variance with the guidelines laid down by the new ruling.

The logical consistency of segmenting foreign subsidiaries' financial statements between exposed and non-exposed categories has been questioned by Aliber and Stickney [2] who argue that if the Fisher effect holds, monetary items (generally treated as exposed items) are essentially non-exposed as cumulative interest revenue (exposure) over the maturity of the monetary asset (liability) and would offset the exchange loss (gain) from changes in the exchange rate. By contrast, treating non-monetary items as non-exposed items essentially assumes that Purchasing Power Parity will hold, which will generally not be true in the short term.

At the close of 1980, new controversy is about to be injected into this ongoing debate about what constitutes the optimal set of translation rules as the FASB is considering for adoption a new exposure draft which would supersede Statement no. 8. The new proposal would (1) impose the use of an all-current (or closing) rate method and (2) differentiate between transaction and translation gains or losses.

The first proposal would require all balance sheet accounts to be translated at the exchange rate prevailing at the time the consolidation is carried out; income statements would be translated at the average exchange rate for the reporting period.

Second, only transaction gains and losses (both realized and unrealized) would be charged to current income. By contrast, translation gains and losses would be accumulated in "a separate component of stockholders' equity." This is a major departure from FASB No. 8 rule and should reduce considerably the volatility in reported earnings. Although the new exposure draft should be welcome by U.S. multinationals, it is in clear contradiction with the concept of historical cost accounting. Finally, the use of an all-current rate method for translating the balance heets of overseas subsidiaries operating in hyperinflationary economies which do not use inflation accounting would clearly lead to exchange losses distorted beyond reason; overall, Giannotti and Walker [29] expect the new exposure draft to have a positive impact on the financial practices of multinational corporations as corporate attention is diverted from translation to transaction exposure management and foreign affiliates' financing is sourced from local currency denominated sources (rather than dollar denominated sources).

Economic Exposure

Although widely used, this accounting concept of exposure to foreign exchange risk is, by definition, misleading, because it fails to incorporate the longer-term impact of exchange rate changes on the economic valuation of the multinational corporation. Accordingly, Heckerman [37] outlines a net discounted cash-flow approach to the economic valuation of the foreign subsidiary of a multinational corporation but fails to recognize that future cash flows are themselves a function of exchange rates. A seminal paper by Dufey [16a] showed that exchange rate changes will predictably affect the nominal cash flows of the subsidiary of a multinational corporation; however, the net impact of such a devaluation or revaluation will not necessarily match in direction nor in magnitude the percentage change in the exchange rate. For example, a subsidiary operating in a devaluing country may find itself benefitting rather than suffering from such a devaluation if part of its revenues are derived from export sales.

A more systematic analysis of the impact of exchange rate changes on the foreign subsidiary's sourcing costs and sales revenue is found in Shapiro [68a]. On the revenue side, he distinguishes between domestic and foreign sales cashflows whereas on the cost side he identifies three partially substitutable inputs: namely, non-traded domestic goods and services, traded inputs, and imported goods.

Shapiro correctly concludes that economic exposure will be determined by the sector of the economy in which the subsidiary operates. As expected, the impact of changing exchange rates will markedly differ for export-oriented subsidiaries, strictly domestic-oriented subsidiaries facing no import competition, or subsidiaries meeting the challenge of stiff import-competition.[14]

Both Dufey's and Shapiro's papers fail to incorporate in their analyses the financial sector nor do they envision the potential use of currency denomination of debt for the purpose of neutralizing the economic exposure stemming from the real sector. Furthermore, the concept of economic exposure is strictly applied to the foreign subsidiary of a multinational corporation and generally assessed in nominal rather than real terms. The concept of economic exposure is obviously just as applicable to a strictly domestic firm (that is, selling to and procuring from domestic markets) which may find itself exposed, in spite of itself, to the vagaries of the international economy.

In a largely taxonomic paper, Wilhborg [79b] questions the relevance of an indiscriminate concept of economic exposure to foreign exchange risk by noting that there is no exposure when inflation is neutral and exchange rates are determined by the Purchasing Power Parity hypothesis. Indeed, real exposure will occur when inflation is not neutral (relative prices change with inflation and/or relative prices change with the exchange rate) and exchange rates deviate from their Purchasing Power Parity equilibria. The case of relative prices (including terms of trade) changing with the exchange rate is examined in depth by Shapiro [68a].

Cornell [12] concurs with this dichotomy between nominal and real cash flows by showing that, in a world in which exchange rates adjust instantaneously (Purchasing Power Parity holds at every point in time), there is, in real terms, no exchange risk as long as relative prices remain constant; thus, if contractual commitments in nominal terms are avoided (that is, contracts are written in terms of the price index), the firm will no longer be exposed to foreign exchange risk. By contrast, relative price risk remains the fundamental source of risk to which firms are exposed and it is equally faced by domestic and multinational corporations. Whether Purchasing Power Parity does hold is an empirical and controversial issue which has been extensively tested as illustrated in the comprehensive review article by Officer [56]. However, this theoretically attractive concept of economic exposure is difficult to turn into an operational index of exposure to exchange risk which could be readily used for Foreign Exchange Risk Management purposes.

THE MANAGEMENT OF FOREIGN EXCHANGE RISK

Normative models for Foreign Exchange Risk Management are few and far between and one cannot help but contrast the sparsely populated research space of international corporate finance (of which Foreign Exchange Risk Management is only one albeit major subset) with the overly prolific research effort in Market Efficiency testing (as applied to the foreign exchange market). The dichotomy between transaction exposure covering and translation exposure hedging will again provide a convenient framework for organizing our review.

Covering Transaction Exposure

Transaction exposure can be covered either through the use of forward contracts (available only for major trading currencies) or a combination of spot and money market transactions. If Interest Rate Parity fails to hold,[15] each option should be computed and the optimal covering route should be compared with the expected cost/revenue of retaining as uncovered the transaction exposure. This naive expected value criterion is discussed in Jacque [39a, chapter 7] and somewhat elaborated by Calderon-Rossel [10] who fails to recognize that both covering routes are fully consistent with the Interest Rate Parity theorem and certainly entail no residual randomness. If covering is to be undertaken on a recurring basis, Giddy [30b] questions the wisdom of such a practice as — over the longer run — the forward rate tends to be an unbiased predictor of the future spot exchange rate.

The case of contingent transaction exposures (resulting from competitive bidding) denominated in foreign currency is examined by Feiger and Jacquillat [26] who suggest covering such exposures through a combination of a forward sale contract and a foreign exchange call option; however, a market for call and put foreign exchange options has yet to materialize.

For the management of a vector of i transaction exposures, Kohlhagen [41b] develops a decision-theoretic payoff $(N)^{i-1} \times (N)^{i-1}$ matrix of profits over all sets of possible exchange rates (each currency can take N different values) and over all strategies (each of which is optimal for one set of future exchange rates). From such a payoff matrix, for a "conservative" firm aiming at protecting cash flows, a simple maximin strategy will be derived whereas a more aggressive firm will pursue a maximax strategy. Although theoretically inferior (no formal treatment of decision-makers' risk preference, no attempt at recognizing the statistical relationships among the exchange rates in which the transaction exposures are denominated), this model is appealing from a managerial point of view because it requires for informational inputs only estimates of reasonable ranges of future exchange rates rather than specific exchange rate projections with associated probability distributions.

In a seminal paper, Folks [27b] questions the validity of the cover/not cover paradigm and suggests that an optimal level of retained uncovered exposure can be found analytically by postulating a utility function as describing the risk preference of the decision-maker.[16] In a similar vein, Wheelwright [78] discusses the practical transaction exposure problem faced by a "big-ticket" item exporter. A preference curve is developed that explicitly shows the tradeoffs that the decision-maker is willing to make between the risk surrounding an uncertain situation and an amount to be received with certainty. The reader is left uncertain, however, as to how this preference curve should be derived; namely, what choice of a utility function is to be made for encoding the risk preference of the decision-maker? Preliminary empirical evidence on risk-preference of treasurers of MNCs is provided by Rodriguez [62b] who found asymmetrical attitudes toward foreign exchange risks.

Apportioning of exchange risk in bilateral transactions is generally thought to be achieved better by denominating the transaction in a third currency or mix of third currencies (artificial currency units) rather than by resorting to a combination of the domestic currencies of the two contracting parties. Using an expected utility framework of nominal return (cost), Schwab and Lusztig [65] show that the contracting parties will always achieve a superior sharing of exchange risk by limiting themselves to a combination of their own currencies. Thus, the use of a third currency or of artificial currency units such as SDRs, EURCOs, EUAs, or ARCRUs should be discouraged.[17] Only if the variability of real (rather than nominal) returns (costs) is to be minimized should bilateral transactions be denominated in third currencies or so-called "currency cocktails."

For a set of transaction exposures denominated in different currencies, Makin [50b] derives an efficient frontier of optimal portfolios of shares of exposures to be covered in a traditional mean-variance framework. Exchange rates are assumed to be normally distributed and the matrix of variance-covariance for future exchange rates available and stable. Although not stated, this model assumes the utility of the decision-maker to be quadratic. In a theoretical paper Levi [44a] shows that in a world where the matrix of cross-elasticities between exchange rate changes is fully known at the outset of the exposure horizon it is possible to fully cover the entire portfolio of transactions exposure through only one forward contract; this may perhaps explain why forward markets appear at times to be underutilized. Yet cross-elasticities between foreign currency movements are stochastic rather than deterministic thereby limiting the operational value of this approach.

The economic exposure problem of a trading firm which imports commodities for local sale is investigated by Hodder [38]. The mean-variance model developed by that author traces the optimal level of forward cover to be sought by the importer to the correlation between the local currency price of the imported commodities (in inventory) and the exchange rate (in which the accounts payable are denominated). This is the question of "currency pass-through" which economists are concerned with in attempting to explain balance of payments adjustment (or lack thereof) to changing exchange rates.

For affiliates of multinational corporations operating in hyperinflationary economies (underdeveloped countries), foreign short-term financing will generally result in major transaction exposure management challenges. Effective costs formulae reflecting anticipated exchange rate devaluations were developed by deFaro and Jucker [25] and Shapiro [68b] on an expected cost basis generally allowing for selection of the optimal source of financing on the basis of linear simulations of exchange rates devaluations. The technique of swap loans popular with a number of Latin American central banks allows the borrower to shelter loan principals from potentially large devaluation (see Eiteman and Stonehill [20]). None of these studies consider, on a risk adjusted basis, what would be the optimal portfolio of short-term financing sources as opposed to the cheapest borrowing source as determined on an expected cost basis.

Hedging Translation Exposure

The essence of hedging is to substitute, at the outset of the exposure horizon, a known cost of buying protection against foreign exchange risk for an unknown translation loss. In a sense, the hedger is trading the uncertainty of an accounting loss which may never materialize for the certainty of the cost of eliminating translation risks — a cost that bears some resemblance to an insurance premium. Thus, the rationale behind the concept of hedging is to substitute for exchange losses, footnoted in reported earnings statements, normal business costs (such hedging costs may include a substantial cash flow loss/gain component) that flow through the income statement.

The mechanics of hedging are set forth in Jacque [39a, chapter 9] who shows that, contrary to the widely held view, hedgers are not speculators but covered interest arbitragers in disguise. Liaeter [47a & b] develops a mean-variance framework which allows the hedger to find "a combination of financing and hedging operations that minimizes expected costs and strategy risk and does not violate a set of recognized operational constraints." Strategy risk is a combination of two types of risk — the business risk measures the risk generated from relying on future financing and hedging possibilities which are not known with certainty. The second strategy risk, the devaluation risk, is a combination of risks arising from "the possibility of wrong estimates in devaluation probabilities and devaluation amounts." This one-period (extended by Liaeter to a multiperiod model in [47b]), two-currency world model fails to recognize explicitly the possibly onerous cash flow cost component of pursuing an optimal hedging policy. Last but not least, Liaeter makes two assumptions in flagrant violation of accepted international financial economics: interest rates are independent of expected parity changes and exchange rates in various currencies are assumed to be uncorrelated. The former assumption ignores the Interest Rate Parity hypothesis whereas the latter assumption contradicts the underlying rationale of the portfolio approach to Foreign Exchange Risk Management.

Folks [27a] compares a mean-variance, minimax, expected monetary value and expected utility criteria as a basis for deriving an optimal hedging strategy when available Foreign Exchange Risk Management techniques are adjustment of fund flows, forward contracts, and exposure netting. None of these studies recognize that if the total cost of hedging is known with certainty at the outset of the exposure horizon, the mix of translation gains/losses plus cash flow losses/gains remains stochastic. An attempt at remedying this flaw is provided by Jacque [39b] who formulates an expected utility theoretic hedging model under an explicit chance constraint on the maximum cash-flow cost of hedging.

The only serious attempt at considering the set of translation exposures denominated in various currencies (held by a multinational corporation in the normal course of business) as a portfolio of statistically interdependent (correlated) elements is found in Gull [35] who formulated the optimization problem in a one-period mean-variance framework which fails to distinguish the (random) cash-flow component of hedging costs from unrealized (paper) translation losses. The major difficulty with such portfolio models is in generating the key informational input; namely, the variance-covariance matrix of exchange rate changes. Gull uses historical information to derive such a matrix in order to generate the optimal vector of pro forma residual exposures, thus implicitly assuming that the covariability structure of past exchange rate changes can be safely extrapolated into the next period. Finally, as with all normative hedging models no attempt is made at capturing the randomness of pro forma translation exposures which may be potentially as serious a source of risk as exchange risk itself.

The problem of selective hedging in a multi-period setting is solved by Shapiro and Rutenberg [69a]. The stochastic dynamic programming algorithm is formulated under somewhat restrictive assumptions. Given current hedging costs, expectations of future hedging costs (both of which are assumed to be linear) should a treasurer hedge a future period or should he wait? Hedging of a future period can be achieved by selling the suspect currency forward for τ periods and buying it forward for $(\tau-1)$ periods. One or several (discrete) devaluations are assumed throughout the exposure horizon. An expected value criterion, thus assuming risk neutrality on the part of the decision-maker, is used. No attention is paid to the cash-flow cost of deriving an optimal temporal hedging path.

Managing Economic Exposure

As a general rule, economic exposure management should aim at neutralizing the impact of unexpected exchange rate changes on net cash flows; this will generally be achieved by striving for a balanced currency mix of cash flows between the cost and revenue side.

An operational approach for implementing this concept of economic exposure management was developed by Nauman-Etienne [54]: (1) identify managerial policies, operational characteristics, and environmental parameters to which economic exposure is sensitive; (2) define protective steps to minimize adverse effects of unexpected exchange rate changes on future cash flows.

Optimally, the sales-inputs currency mix should be adjusted so that changes in future sales revenue will be neutralized by changes in the cost of inputs; however, such changes in the real sector of the firm will seldom bring about by themselves a neutral economic exposure. Generally, manipulation of the currency risk of short-term and long-term financing will be needed and this is generally the easier to implement of the two prescriptions because the currency composition of financing can be altered independently from the sources of inputs and destination of sales; as such, it plays a natural residual and offsetting role in equating sales revenue and input costs on a currency-by-currency basis. Carrying this argument to its logical conclusion Dufey [16b] summarized it as "finance in the currency where your profits are." The obvious flaw in this approach is that it fails to incorporate the dynamics of the currency composition of cash flow which generally respond to a variety of exogenous factors which are difficult to anticipate. Also disregarded in these studies is the simultaneous and offsetting change in price levels; that is, the analysis is strictly conducted in nominal terms rather than in real terms.

The Praxis of Foreign Exchange Risk Management

Last but not least, exposure measurement and exposure management have to be coordinated and integrated within an internally consistent set of guidelines acceptable to both subsidiaries' and headquarters' treasurers. Foremost is the question of apportioning equitably the responsibility of Foreign Exchange Risk Management without distorting the control/evaluation process of foreign operations [Korth 42b]. Lessard and Lorange [43] address the dilemma faced by MNCs attempting to reconcile the organizational decentralization necessary for an effective planning/control system in a large multinational/multidivisional corporation and the centralization imperative which is at the core of effective Foreign Exchange Risk Management. Specifically, the authors consider the possible combination of exchange rates — to be used in (1) setting the operating budget for a particular time period and (2) tracking realized performance relative to budgeted ones. The authors suggest that the dilemma can be resolved through the use of "internal forward rates"; that is, rates which are guaranteed by the corporate treasury irrespective of what actual exchange rates may turn out to be.

Organizational and control considerations will undoubtedly play a crucial role in setting up such a Foreign Exchange Risk Management program which will generally have to be centralized at the helm of the corporate treasurer if the synergistic benefits of multinationalism are to be taken advantage of [Ankrom 4b]. This is indeed one of the major findings of a survey of corporate Foreign Exchange Risk Management practices by Jilling [40].

One unresolved question remains: How to insure a consistent attitude toward risk (both over time and across currencies) which wouldn't reflect exclusively the treasurer's preferences but which would be firmly grounded in senior management's outlook toward risk.

Long-Term Debt Financing

This review would not be complete without mentioning promising yet embryonic research efforts aimed at the determination of the optimal currency (or artificial currency unit) of denomination in long-term debt financing. Jacque [39a, chapter

8] develops a break-even analysis methodological framework based upon expected net present value formulae (thus implicitly assuming risk neutrality on the part of the decision-maker). Using a similar framework Giddy [30d] derives a number of simplifying formulae expressing the effective cost of foreign currency denominated debt financing as a function of its nominal cost. Both approaches fail to recognize the dependency (in a probability sense) of the vector of exchange rates to prevail when interest and principal repayment will be made. Thus, future exchange rates ought to be modelled as belonging to a joint multivariate probability distribution and necessary parameters of such variates be computed accordingly.

FOREIGN EXCHANGE RISK MANAGEMENT AND THE MARKET EFFICIENCY HYPOTHESES

The emerging, yet embryonic, consensus among financial theoreticians is that exposure to foreign exchange risk may matter less than is commonly believed by multinational corporations' corporate treasurers, financial analysts, and investors. This jaundiced view of Foreign Exchange Risk Management is upheld by Logue and Oldfield [48] who argue that in efficient markets Foreign Exchange Risk Management is irrelevant and also relatively harmless. Theirs is loosely referred to as the Market Efficiency hypothesis and can be summarized in two propositions: in efficient capital markets, all available information is correctly impounded or reflected in stock prices. More specifically, investors are knowledgeable and sophisticated enough to be able to read beyond conventional accounting reports (balance sheets and income statements) to correctly assess the true economic value of the firm. This would mean, among other things, that hedging translation exposure to reduce or eliminate earnings variability is pure accounting gimmickry that shouldn't fool efficient investors.

Thus, in an efficient market, the multinational corporation's earning variability (resulting from translation gains or losses) would be placed in a proper economic perspective by investors and, therefore, should not affect its stock's price nor its cost of capital. However, such clearsightedness on the part of the market would require extensive and systematic disclosure by multinational corporations of their foreign subsidiaries' transaction, translation, and economic exposures.

This practice is clearly not yet accepted because multinational corporations generally disclose only consolidated financial statements.

This hypothesis seems to be contradicted in a recent empirical study by Makin [50a] which suggests (but doesn't necessarily prove) that, for instance, the first set of earnings reports prepared under FASB Statement No. 8 resulted for at least one group of firms (out of five) in the decline of their share prices that was not associated with overall market behavior. Thus the market would not be omniscient, and additional, albeit limited and imperfect, information (as that disclosed under FASB Statement No. 8) would lead investors to reevaluate their pricing of shares of corporations exposed to exchange risk. These preliminary results, however, failed to be upheld by the comprehensive study commissioned by the Financial Accounting Standards Board [Dukes, 18] which concluded that the issuance and implementation of FASB Statement No. 8 did not appear to have had significant detectable effects on the security returns of multinational firms.

Second, in efficient foreign exchange markets, currencies' prices adjust instantaneously to the inflation rates differential (Purchasing Power Parity hypothesis), thus leaving unchanged the true economic exposure to foreign exchange risk of a multinational corporation or of its foreign affiliates. The prescription in this case is simple: elaborate assessment of a firm's exposure to the inflation-cum-devaluation cycle is redundant and, a fortiori, managing economic exposure is about as irrelevant as managing accounting exposure. This point of view is elaborated upon by Aliber [3] and Giddy [30c].

Obviously, the operational value of such an extreme policy prescription will depend on the nature of the exchange rate system and the degree to which exchange rates reflect the relative internal purchasing power of any pair of currencies. Under a system of pegged yet adjustable exchange rates, par value adjustments may significantly lag price inflation differentials and the competitive position of the firm will be significantly and lastingly affected, thus calling for a strategic overhaul of the production and marketing policies. In the case of a domestic or an exporting company, an exchange rate adjustment that fails to reflect the true cost constraints of the sector in which the firm is operating will open new market horizons that would have been missed had the firm failed to recognize and/or anticipate correctly its true economic exposure.

Even in a world of floating exchange rates, which are being increasingly characterized as efficient, managing economic exposure may be a less dubious undertaking than implied by this second version of the Market Efficiency hypothesis. Instantaneous exchange rates adjustment to price levels differential will generally fail to capture the discrepancies among various sectorial price level movements that may indeed affect the true economic exposure of the firm. The sensitivity of the firm's cash flows to sectorial price movements should be carefully monitored and incorporated in marketing, production and financial plans. Even under strict conditions of foreign exchange market efficiency and positive bankruptcy costs, Dufey and Giddy [17] still prescribe that Management of Foreign Exchange Risk should aim at "structuring the firm's liabilities in such a way that any *unanticipated* change in the return on assets is offset, as far as possible, by a change in the effective cost of liabilities."

FOREIGN EXCHANGE RISK MANAGEMENT: DIRECTIONS FOR FURTHER RESEARCH

Nearly all normative research efforts in the area of foreign exchange risk management have focused exclusively on short-term decisions involving accounting exposure components of a firm's working capital and one may wonder why the case of stochastic transaction and translation exposures has altogether been ignored. Consider, for instance, the case of captive insurance companies which diversify their portfolio of underwriting activities by reinsuring a "layer" of foreign risk; clearly, the magnitude of the transaction exposure is unknown (stochastic). Bidding on foreign projects or acquisitions of foreign companies will similarly entail stochastic exposures whose magnitude can be characterized at best by a subjective probability distribution. Similarly, hedging translation exposure always assumes that the translation exposure is known with certainty whereas, in fact, it is extracted from pro forma statements and, thus, should be considered as a random variable for Foreign Exchange Risk Managment purposes.

Furthermore, the longer-term dimension of Foreign Exchange Risk Management — that is, long-term debt financing and debt refunding in a multicurrency world — has hardly been considered.

In addition, most research undertakings — with two exceptions [Gull 35 and Makin 50b] — were limited to a two-currency world (foreign currency in which the exposure is incurred and reference currency [$] in which the MNC's financial statements are disclosed) thereby ignoring the diversification effect of holding a portfolio of exposures denominated in currencies whose prices are correlated.

Moreover, transaction and translation exposures were handled separately with no attempt at reconciling the two constructs into an operationally meaningful single aggregate index of real exposure to foreign exchange risk.

Finally, all decision models — with one exception [Shapiro and Rutenberg 69a] — were one-period models, thereby disregarding the sequential nature of Foreign Exchange Risk Management problems. The creation of new financial instruments such as interest rate futures, however, is opening new opportunities for research in this area as it provides information on future forward exchange rates — indeed a critical informational input for such decision models.

FOOTNOTES

1. Donald R. Lessard, *International Financial Management* (Boston: Warren, Gorhan and Lamont, 1979), p. 353.

2. For an analogous, but strictly qualitative four-step sequence see Korth [42a].

3. This concept of market efficiency should be clearly distinguished from the concept of market perfection. Market perfection is certainly a sufficient condition of market efficiency but it is not a necessary one. As long as transactors take into account all available information, even large transaction costs that inhibit the flow of transactions do not in themselves imply that when transactions do take place, exchange rates will not "fully reflect" all available information.

4. This three-tier categorization of Market Efficiency was suggested by Eugene Fama [23] for empirical testing purposes in the context of stock prices.

5. Failure to establish the weak form of Market Efficiency would lend credence to the Price Dynamics view of exchange rates behavior. One version of the Price Dynamics hypothesis (the so-called "bandwagon" theory) asserts that a subset of market participants (market leaders) are known or simply perceived by the rest of market participants (market followers) to have earlier access to more timely and more accurate information concerning factors affecting future spot exchange rates and/or to have the use of more sophisticated forecasting models. Thus when the price of a currency begins to fall (to rise) market followers will "jump on the bandwagon"; that is, join in the selling (buying) pressure as they attribute the price change to a signal that market leaders (who know better) have themselves begun to sell (to buy). In so doing, market followers will be pushing the currency price down (up) further until it overshoots its equilibrium level and the trend eventually reverses itself. Clearly this view of exchange rates behavior supports the hypothesis that past exchange rates contain useful information in forecasting future exchange rates as information only disseminates itself slowly among market participants, thus disproving the Market Efficiency hypothesis.

6. For a critical evaluation of testing methodologies see Kohlhagen [41a, pp. 32-34].

7. A dissenting and somewhat unconventional opinion is offered by Papadia [59] who challenges the view that the forward exchange rate is equal to the future spot exchange rate and argues that:

> one of the two currencies which is exchanged in a forward transaction is riskier than the other. This implies that the party buying forward the riskier currency will require a premium to enter the contract. Such a premium will necessarily be expressed as a difference between the forward and the

expected spot rate. The two parties could agree on a future price and still enter the forward contract with a different one.

8. See for example Siegel's paradox [71] based on Jensen's inequality; McCulloch [52] suggests however that the bias introduced by looking at only one side of the market is negligible.

9. For an in depth discussion of the Modern Theory see Grubel [34] and Stoll [74].

10. Such an attitude toward risk by speculators would result into an infinitely elastic speculators' schedule.

11. An econometric model must contain a stochastic element to permit statistical inference from the data. The usual procedure is to hypothesize a model of varying degree of sophistication that should account for the phenomenon under review and then to add, almost as an after-thought, a disturbance or random error term to which convenient statistical properties are ascribed. This residual random error term represents in an undeterminate way all the factors that are ignored in the systematic part of the model.

12. Concerning the error term, e(t), the following six conditions for a correct use of multiregression analysis are all too often ignored: (1) $E[e(t)] = 0$, (2) $Var[e(t)]$ is constant and finite (homoscedasticity), (3) zero covariance between any two dependent variables (multicollinearity), (4) $Cov[e(t), e(t-k)] = 0$, (5) $Cov[e(t)$, dependent variable] $= 0$, and finally, (6) the error term is normally distributed $e(t) = N(0,s^2)$.

13. For a more limited attempt, see the model developed by Chemical Bank and discussed in Teck [75].

14. The concept of economic exposure is really the microeconomic analog of the well-known macroeconomic problem of balance of payments adjustment (or lack of) to changing exchange rates.

15. For reasons why the Interest Rate Parity theorem may fail to hold, see the comprehensive review monograph by Kohlhagen [41a], especially Section II. A primary explanation for observed deviations from Interest Rate Parity is transaction costs. For an attempt at measuring these costs, based on an ingenious device (trilateral arbitrage), see Levich [45b]. Levi [44a] shows that asymmetrical tax treatments of exchange capital gains/losses and interest income generally result in different after-tax Interest Rate Parity equilibria from the before-tax equilibria generally tested for in existing empirical work.

16. However no specific utility function model is used, which leaves the decision rules devoid of any operational content.

17. For a comprehensive discussion of artificial currency units, see Archeim and Park [5]. An empirical assessment of risk reduction provided by denominating contracts in artificial currency units is provided in Aubey and Cramer [6] as well as in Severn and Meinster [66] with the later study focusing exclusively on the use of SDRs.

REFERENCES

1. Aggarwal, Raj. "FASB No. 8 and Reported Results of Multinational Operations: Hazard for Managers and Investors." *Journal of Accounting, Auditing and Finance,* Spring 1978, pp. 197–217.

2. Aliber, Robert Z., and Stickney, Clyde P. "Accounting Measures of Foreign Exchange Exposure: The Long and Short of It." *The Accounting Review,* January 1975, pp. 44–57.

3. Aliber, Robert Z. *Exchange Risk and Corporate International Finance.* New York: John Wiley and Sons, 1979.

4a. Ankrom, Robert. "Why a Reserve is Cheaper than a Hedge." *Euromoney,* February 1979, pp. 56–61.

4b. _____. "Top-Level Approach to the Foreign Exchange Problem." *Harvard Business Review,* July–August 1974, pp. 70–90.

5. Archeim, J., and Park, Y. S. "Artificial Currency Units: The Functional Currency Areas." *Essays in International Finance* 114. Princeton, NJ: Princeton University, International Finance Section, April 1976.

6. Aubey, R. T., and Cramer, R. H. "The Use of International Currency Cocktails in the Reduction of the Exchange Rate Risk." *Journal of Economics and Business,* Winter 1977, pp. 128–134.

7. Barrett, Edgar M., and Spero, Leslie L. "Accounting Determinants of Foreign Exchange Gains and Losses. " *Financial Analysts Journal,* March–April 1975.

8. Biger, Nahum. "Exchange Risk Implications of International Portfolio Diversification." *Journal of International Business Studies,* Fall 1979, pp. 64–74.

9. Burns, Joseph M. *Accounting Standards and International Finance.* Washington, DC: American Enterprise Institute for Public Policy Research, 1976.

10. Calderon-Rossel, Jorge, R. "Covering Foreign Exchange Risk of Single Transactions: A Framework for Analysis. "*Financial Management,* Autumn 1979, pp. 78–85.

11. Choi, Frederick D. S.; Lowe, Howard D.; and Worthley, Reginald G. "Accountors, Accountants and Standard No. 8." *Journal of International Business Studies,* Fall 1978, pp. 81–87.

12. Cornell, Bradford. "Inflation, Relative Price Changes, and Exchange Risk." *Financial Management,* Autumn 1980, pp. 30–35.

13. _____., and Dietrich, J. Kimball. "The Efficiency of the Market for Foreign Exchange Under Floating Exchange Rates." *Review of Economics and Statistics,* February 1978, pp. 111–120.

14. Culbertson, William P. "Purchasing Power Parity and Black Market Exchange Rates." *Economic Inquiry,* June 1975, pp. 287–296.

15. Dooley, Michael P., and Shafer, Jeffrey R. "Analysis of Short-Run Exchange Rate Behavior: March 1973 to September 1975." *International Finance Discussion Papers.* New York: Federal Reserve System, 1976.

16a. Dufey, Gunter. "Corporate Finance and Exchange Rates Variations." *Financial Management,* Summer 1972, pp. 51–57.

16b. _____. "Corporate Financial Policies and Floating Exchange Rates." Address delivered to the Seventh Congress of the International Fiscal Association, 14 October 1974, Rome, Italy.

17. _____. and Giddy, Ian H. "International Financial Planning: The Use of Market Based Forecasts." *California Management Review,* Fall 1978, pp. 69–81.

18. Dukes, Ronald. *An Empirical Investigation of the Effects of Statement of Financial Accounting Standards No. 8 on Security Return Behavior.* Stamford, CT: Financial Standards Board 1978.

19. Eaker, Mark R. "Denomination Decision for Multinational Transactions." *Financial Management,* Autumn 1980, pp. 23–29.

20. Eiteman, David K., and Stonehill, Arthur I. *Multinational Business Finance.* 2d ed. Reading, MA: Addison-Wesley, 1978.

21. Evans, Thomas G.; Folks, William R., Jr.; and Jilling, Michael. *The Impact of Statement of Financial Accounting Standards No. 8 on the Foreign Exchange Risk Management Practices of American Multinationals: An Economic Impact Study.* Stamford, CT: Financial Accounting Standards Board, 1978.

22. Everett, Robert M.; Georges, Abraham M.; and Blumberg, Aryeh. "Appraising Currency Strengths and Weaknesses: An Operational Framework for Calculating Parity Exchange Rates." *Journal of International Business Studies,* Fall 1980, pp. 80–91.

23. Fama, Eugene. "Efficient Capital Markets: A Review of Theory and Empirical Work." *Journal of Finance,* December 1979, pp. 1129–1139.

24. _____., and Farber, Andre. "Money, Bonds and Foreign Exchange." *American Economic Review,* September 1979, pp. 639–649.

25. deFaro, Clovis, and Jucker, James V., "The Impact of Inflation and Devaluation on the Selection of an International Borrowing Source." *Journal of International Business Studies,* Fall 1973, pp. 97–104

26. Feiger, George, and Jacquillat, Bertrand. "Currency Option Bonds, Puts and Calls on Spot Exchange and the Hedging of Contingent Foreign Earnings." *The Journal of Finance,* December 1979, pp. 1129–1139.

27a. Folks, William R., Jr. "Decision Analysis for Exchange Risk Management." *Financial Management,* Winter 1972.

27b. _____. "The Optimal Level of Forward Exchange Transactions." *Journal of Financial and Quantitative Analysis*, January 1973.

28. _____., and Stansell, Stanley R. "The Use of Discriminant Analysis in Forecasting Exchange Rate Movements." *Journal of International Business Studies*, Spring 1975, pp. 33–50.

29. Gianotti, John B., and Walker, David P. "How the New FAS 8 Will Change Exposure Management." *Euromoney*, November 1980.

30a. Giddy, Ian H. "An Integrated Theory of Exchange Rate Equilibrium." *Journal of Financial and Quantitative Analysis*, December 1976, pp. 863–892.

30b. _____. "Why it Doesn't Pay to Make a Habit of Forward Hedging." *Euromoney*, December 1976.

30c. _____. "Exchange Risk: Whose View." *Financial Management*, Summer 1977, pp. 23–33.

30d. _____. "The Effective Cost of Foreign Currency Borrowing." *Journal of Financial and Quantitative Analysis*, forthcoming.

31. _____., and Dufey, Gunter. "The Random Behavior of Flexible Exchange Rates: Implications for Forecasting." *Journal of International Business Studies*, Spring 1975, pp. 1–32.

32. Goodman, Stephen H. "Foreign Exchange Rate Forecasting Techniques: Implications for Business and Policy." *The Journal of Finance*, May 1979, pp. 415–427.

33. Grauer, F. L. A.; Litzenberger, R. H.; and Stehle, R. H. "Sharing Rules and Equilibrium in an International Capital Market Under Uncertainty." *Journal of Financial Economics* 3 (1976), pp. 233–256.

34. Grubel, Herbert G. *Forward Exchange, Speculation, and the International Flow of Capital.* Palo Alto: Stanford University Press, 1966.

35. Gull, Don S. "Composite Foreign Exchange Risk," *Columbia Journal of World Business*, Fall 1975, pp. 51–69.

36. Hayes, Donald J. "Translating Foreign Currencies." *Harvard Business Review*, January–February 1972, pp. 6–18, 159–161.

37. Heckerman, Donald. "The Exchange Risks of Foreign Operations." *The Journal of Business*, January 1972, pp. 42–48.

38. Hodder, James. "Hedging of Exposure to Exchange-Rate Movements." Ph.D. dissertation, Stanford University, 1978.

39a. Jacque, Laurent L. *Management of Foreign Exchange Risk: Theory and Praxis.* Lexington, MA: D. C. Heath, 1978.

39b. _____. "Why Hedgers are not Speculators." *Columbia Journal of World Business*, Winter 1979.

40. Jilling, Michael. "Foreign Exchange Risk Management: Current Practices of U.S. Multinational Corporations." Ph.D. dissertation, University of South Carolina, 1976.

41a. Kohlhagen, Steven W. "The Behavior of Foreign Exchange Markets: A Critical Survey of the Empirical Literature." *Monograph 1978-3.* Salomon Brothers Center for the Study of Financial Institutions: New York University.

41b. _____. "A Model of Optimal Foreign Exchange Hedging Without Exchange Rate Projections." *Journal of International Business Studies*, Fall 1978, pp. 9–21.

41c. _____. "The Performance of the Foreign Exchange Markets: 1971–74. "*Journal of International Business Studies*, Fall 1975, pp. 33–39.

42a. Korth, Christopher M. "The Future of a Currency." *Business Horizons*, June 1972, pp. 67–76.

42b. _____. "Devaluation Dichotomy: Headquarters vs. Subsidiary." *MSU Business Topics*, Autumn 1972, pp. 52–58.

43. Lessard, Donald R., and Lorange, Peter. "Currency Changes and Management Control: Resolving the Centralization/Decentralization Dilemma." *Accounting Review*, July 1977, pp. 628–637.

44a. Levi, Maurice D. "Underutilization of Forward Markets or Rational Behavior." *Journal of Finance,* September 1979, pp. 1013–1017.

44b. _____. "Taxation and 'Abnormal' Capital Flows." *Journal of Political Economy,* June 1977, pp. 635–646.

45a. Levich, Richard M. "On the Efficiency of Markets for Foreign Exchange." In *International Economic Policy,* edited by Rudiger Dornbusch and Jacob A. Frankel. Baltimore: the Johns Hopkins University Press, 1978.

45b. _____. *The International Monetary Market: An Assessment of Forecasting Techniques and Market Efficiency.* Greenwich, CT: JAI Press, 1979.

45c. _____. "Analyzing the Accuracy of Foreign Exchange Forecasting Services: Theory and Evidence." Forthcoming in *Exchange Risk and Exposure: Current Development in International Financial Development,* co-edited with Clas Wilhborg. Lexington, MA: D. C. Heath, Lexington Books, 1980.

46. Levy, H., and Sarnat, M. "International Diversification of Investment Portfolios." *American Economic Review* (1970), pp. 668–675.

47a. Liaeter, Bernard A. "Managing Risks in Foreign Exchange." *Harvard Business Review,* March–April 1970, pp. 127–138.

47b. _____. *Financial Management of Foreign Exchange.* Cambridge, MA: The M.I.T. Press, 1971.

48. Logue, Dennis E., and Oldfield, George S. "Managing Foreign Assets When Foreign Exchange Markets are Efficient." *Financial Management,* Summer 1977, pp. 16–22.

49. _____. , and Sweeny, Richard J. "White Noise in Imperfect Markets: The Case of the Franc-Dollar Exchange Rate." *The Journal of Finance,* June 1977, pp. 761–768.

50a. Makin, John H. "Flexible Exchange Rates, Multinational Corporations and Accounting Standards." *Federal Reserve Bank of San Francisco Economic Review,* Fall 1977, pp. 44–45.

50b. _____. "Portfolio Theory and the Problem of Foreign Exchange Risk." *Journal of Finance,* May 1978, pp. 517–534.

50c. _____. "Techniques and Success in Forecasting Exchange Rates: Should it Be Done? Does it Matter? The Long and Short of It." Paper presented at the New York University Conference on Internationalization of Financial Market and National Economic Policy, 10–11 April 1980, New York, NY.

51. Malek, Talaat Abdel. "Managing Exchange Risks Under Floating Exchange Rates: The Canadian Experience." *Columbia Journal of World Business,* Fall 1976, pp. 41–52.

52. McCullock, J. Huston. "Operational Aspects of the Siegel Paradox." *Quarterly Journal of Economics,* February 1975, pp. 170–172.

53. Murenbeeld, Martin. "Economic Factors for Forecasting Foreign Exchange Rates." *Columbia Journal of World Business,* Summer 1975, pp. 81–95.

54. Nauman-Etienne, Ruediger. "Exchange Risk in Foreign Operations of Multinational Corporations." Ph.D. dissertation, University of Michigan, 1977.

55. Norr, David. "Currency Translation and the Analyst." *Financial Analysts Journal,* July–August 1976, pp. 46–54.

56. Officer, Lawrence H. "The Purchasing Power Parity of Exchange Rates: A Review Article." *I.M.F. Staff Paper 23,* no. 1, March 1976.

57. Olstein, Robert A., and O'Glove, Thorton L. "Devaluation and Multinational Reporting." *Financial Analysis Journal,* September–October 1973, pp. 65–84.

58. Pakkala, A. L. "Foreign Exchange Accounting of Multinational Corporations." *Financial Analysts Journal,* March–April 1975, pp. 32–41.

59. Papadia, Francesco. "It's Not an Error When the Forward Rate Differs From the Expected Spot." *Euromoney,* September 1979, pp. 94–96.

60. Poole, William. "Speculative Prices as Random Walk: An Analysis of Ten Time Series of Flexible Exchange Rates." *Southern Economic Journal,* April 1967, pp. 468–478.

61. Porter, Michael M. "A Theoretical and Empirical Framework for Analyzing the Term Structure of Exchange Rate Expectations." *International Monetary Fund Staff Papers,* November 1971, pp. 613–645.

384

62a. Rodriguez, Rita M. "FASB No. 8: What Has It Done For Us?" *Financial Analysts Journal*, March-April 1977, pp. 40-48.

62b. _____. *Foreign Exchange Management in U.S. Multinationals.* Lexington, MA: D. C. Heath, 1980.

63. Rogalski, Richard J., and Vinso, Joseph D. "Price Level Variations as Predictors of Flexible Exchange Rates." *Journal of International Business Studies*, Spring/Summer 1977, pp. 71-82.

64. Roll, Richard W., and Solnik, Bruno H. "A Pure Foreign Exchange Asset Pricing Model." *European Institute for Advanced Studies in Management*: Working Paper No. 75, August 1975.

65. Schwab, B., and Lusztig, P. "Apportioning Foreign Exchange Risk Through the Use of Third Currencies: Some Questions on Efficiency." *Financial Management*, Autumn 1978.

66. Severn, Alan K., and Meinster, D. R. "The Use of Multicurrency Financing by the Financial Manager." *Financial Management*, Winter 1978, pp. 45-53.

67. Shank, John K. "FASB Statement No. 8 Resolved Foreign Currency Accounting — or Did It?" *Financial Analysts Journal*, July-August 1976, pp. 55-61.

68a. Shapiro, Alan C. "Exchange Rate Changes, Inflation and the Value of the Multinational Corporation." *The Journal of Finance*, May 1975, pp. 485-502.

68b. _____. "Evaluating Financing Costs for Multinational Subsidiaries." *Journal of International Business Studies*, Fall 1975, pp. 25-32.

68c. _____. "Defining Exchange Risk," *Journal of Business,* January 1977, pp. 37-39.

69a. _____., and Rutenberg, David P. "When to Hedge." *Management Science,* August 1974, pp. 1514-1530.

69b. _____., and Rutenberg, David P. "Managing Exchange Risks in a Floating World." *Financial Management*, Summer 1976.

70. Shulman, Robert B. "Are Foreign Exchange Risks Measurable?" *Columbia Journal of World Business*, May-June 1970, pp. 55-60.

71. Siegel, Jeremy. "Risk, Interest, and Forward Exchange." *Quarterly Journal of Economics*, May 1972, pp. 303-309.

72a. Solnik, B. H. "International Pricing of Risk: An Empirical Investigation of World Capital Market Structure." *Journal of Finance*, December 1973, pp. 1151-1159.

72b. _____. "An Equilibrium Model of the International Capital Market." *Journal of Economic Theory*, August 1974, pp. 500-524.

73. Stanley, Marjorie T., and Block, Stanley B. "Response by United States Financial Managers to Financial Accounting Standard No. 8." *Journal of International Business Studies*, Fall 1978, pp. 89-99.

74. Stoll, Hans. "An Empirical Study of the Forward Exchange Market Under Fixed and Flexible Exchange Rate Systems." *Canadian Journal of Economics*, February 1968, pp. 55-78.

75. Teck, Alan. "Using Computers for Foreign Exchange Tax Planning." *The International Tax Journal*, Fall 1975, pp. 5-27.

76. Vinso, Joseph D., and Rogalski, Richard J. "Empirical Properties of Foreign Exchange Rates." *Journal of International Business Studies*, Fall 1978, pp. 69-80.

77. Westerfield, Janice M. "Empirical Properties of Foreign Exchange Rates Under Fixed and Floating Rate Regimes." *Journal of International Economics*, June 1977, pp. 181-200.

78. Wheelwright, Steven C. "Applying Decision Theory to Improve Corporate Management of Currency-Exchange Risks." *California Management Review*, Summer 1975, pp. 41-49.

79a. Wihlborg, Clas. *Currency Risks in International Financial Markets.* Princeton Study in International Finance, No. 44, December 1978.

79b. _____. "Currency Exposure: Taxonomy and Theory," forthcoming in *Exchange Risk and Exposure: Current Development in International Financial Development*, co-edited with Richard M. Levich. Lexington, MA: D. C. Heath, Lexington Books, 1980.

80. Wurster, Thomas S. "The Firm in the International Economy." Ph.D. dissertation, Yale University, 1978.

CHAPTER 25

American taxation of multinational firms*
Thomas Horst

Taxation of the multinational firm's foreign income has been debated continually over the last fifteen years. In the early 1950's the U.S. Treasury proposed to eliminate the deferral of *U.S.* taxes on foreign subsidiaries' retained earnings, in order to discourage the flow of direct investment capital abroad and to hasten the repatriation of direct investment income.[1] The Congress was unwilling to take so large a step, but in the Tax Reform Act of 1962 did require dividend income from developed countries to be "grossed up" and did limit the tax-haven abuse of deferral.[2] In the late 1960's the AFL-CIO grew increasingly concerned that *U.S.* multinationals were "exporting jobs" and called for the repeal of deferral and the foreign tax credit.[3] The New Economic Policy announced by President Nixon on August 15, 1971 sought to improve the balance of payments through a variety of measures including a tax preference for export income, the Domestic International Sales Corporation (*DISC*).[4] A primary argument in convincing Congress of the merits of *DISC* was that export income should enjoy a tax deferral comparable to foreign investment income. Although the union-backed Burke-Hartke Bill to repeal deferral and the foreign tax credit was voted down decisively in 1973, the Senate version of the Tax Reduction Act of 1975 would have eliminated deferral. Although this provision was dropped by the House-Senate conference committee, a special subcommittee chaired by Congressman Rostenkowski of the House Ways and Means Committee was established to study deferral and related issues more thoroughly. Finally, the Treasury implemented new guidelines for Sections 861–864 of the Internal Revenue Code which will create a strong tax incentive for *U.S.* investors to charge their foreign subsidiaries more for research and development undertaken by the parent. In opposing all these changes in *U.S.* policy, the multinationals have argued that higher taxes would undermine their competitiveness in world markets without helping *U.S.* exports, employment or the balance of payments.

This paper analyzes the profit-maximizing behavior of a multinational firm and explores the impact on that behavior of repealing deferral, compelling higher charges for *R & D* to foreign subsidiaries, and eliminating the foreign tax credit. My model is limited in obvious respects: the analysis is static, not dynamic; the "multinational" invests at home and in one foreign country; and exports between parent and subsidiary are ignored. Higher *U.S.* taxes on foreign investment income may encourage the firm to invest more at home and less abroad, but that substitution is not necessarily matched by an increase in the parent's ex-

*Fletcher School of Law and Diplomacy. Research was supported by a contract with the U.S. Treasury which endorses neither the methods nor the conclusions of this analysis. Thomas Pugel was instrumental in developing the mathematical analysis and the computer program used in empirical simulations. Gary Hufbauer, James Nunns, and George Kopits have devoted considerable time to earlier versions of the paper and made numerous constructive criticisms.

[1] "Deferral" means taxing the dividends, but not the retained earnings, of a subsidiary. The evolution of *U.S.* taxation of foreign-source income is more fully described in the forthcoming study by C. Fred Bergsten, Thomas Horst, and Theodore Moran, ch. 6. Gary Hufbauer and David Foster provide a thorough analysis of deferral and its relationship to other aspects of current *U.S.* tax policy.

[2] "Grossing up" means basing the tentative *U.S.* tax (i.e., before deducting the tax credit) on subsidiaries' dividends inclusive of the foreign income taxes allocable to those dividends.

[3] The foreign tax credit allows *U.S.* investors to reduce their *U.S.* income tax liability by the amount of foreign income and withholding taxes paid to foreign governments; see below.

[4] A *DISC* is essentially a dummy corporation established to receive tax-sheltered export income; half of

that income must be paid out as a dividend and thereby subject to *U.S.* taxation, but half may be reinvested in export-related assets, such as export accounts receivable.

* This article is reprinted, with permission, from the *American Economic Review* (June 1977) pp 376–389

ports or a decrease in its imports. The model's primary virtue is incorporating several complex features of *U.S.* tax policy into a coherent analysis of multinational investment behavior. I explore not only the location of real investment, but also the options for financing that investment. As I shall show, *U.S.* tax policy affects firms' financial behavior, and that behavior in turn mitigates the impact of tax policy on the location of new investment. Finally, I have kept the analysis simple enough to be able to construct rough estimates of its parameters and simulate the possible impact of various tax changes. In the following sections I set forth the basic model, describe the impact of various tax changes, and summarize the more important conclusions. To aid the reader, the mathematical notation is summarized in Appendix Table A1.

I. The Basic Model

It is assumed that a multinational firm starts with an existing stock of foreign and domestic investment and seeks the optimal change in its position over the next year. Because the earnings generated by existing investments are an important source of capital for new investment, we cannot ignore the role of the past in shaping the present. To be specific, assume that current revenues (net of labor and material costs, but gross of interest expenses and income taxes) R depend on the existing stock of investment I_0, plus new investment undertaken during the current period I.

(1) $$R = R(I_0 + I)$$
(2) $$R^* = R^*(I_0^* + I^*)$$

An asterisk differentiates the parent's domestic investment from its foreign subsidiary's. Presumably, the marginal and average return on investment at home or abroad declines as the level of investment expands.

The analysis focuses not only on the levels of foreign and domestic investment, but also on the financing of that investment. For simplicity's sake we ignore the market for new equity and concentrate on that for

debt. Rather than exploring directly the determinants of an optimal debt-equity ratio for the parent, subsidiary, and/or consolidated enterprise, it is merely assumed that new funds are available at home and overseas at increasing rates of interest. These increasing interest rates could reflect either the thinness of local capital markets or lenders' fears of the insolvency of the borrower. In either event, total borrowing costs B consist of those incurred by past borrowing L_0, plus those resulting from new borrowing, L:

(3) $$B = B(L_0 + L)$$
(4) $$B^* = B^*(L_0^* + L^*)$$

The levels of investment and borrowing are linked by balance sheet constraints. For the foreign subsidiary new investment I must equal new borrowing L, plus new funds obtained from the parent F, and the subsidiary's own retained earnings E_R:

(5) $$I = L + F + E_R$$

The parent's new investment I^* must equal its own new borrowing L^*, less new funds advanced to the subsidiary F, plus its own retained earnings:

(6) $$I^* = L^* - F + E_R^*$$

It is also assumed that the foreign subsidiary can deduct from its taxable income interest on *intra*firm debt as well as royalties, headoffice charges and other such payments for intrafirm services. Although I want to postpone for the moment the role of tax avoidance in determining such payments, let me note here that intrafirm interest expenses depend on the intrafirm interest rate i_p, and the ratio of debt to total intrafirm transfer of capital (debt plus equity) f. Total intrafirm interest payments equal those on past borrowing, $i_{p_0}f_0F_0$, plus those on new borrowing, i_pfF. Likewise, it will be assumed that royalties, headoffice, and other intrafirm charges vary at least in the short run in proportion h to the foreign subsidiary's total investment, $I_0 + I$. Thus, the foreign subsidiary's taxable income E_B equals the revenues from investment R, minus the interest paid to outside lenders B, the interest paid to the *U.S.* parent $i_{p_0} f_0 F_0 + i_p fF$, and payments for royalties, headoffice services, and the like, $h(I_0 + I)$:

(7) $E_B = R - B - (i_{p_0} f_0 F_0 + i_p fF)$
$- h(I_0 + I)$

Next it is assumed that the subsidiary pays income taxes at the rate t, and that the dividends paid to the parent D are some proportion p of income after taxes:

(8) $D = p(1 - t)E_B$

Thus, the retained earnings available for reinvestment by the foreign subsidiary E_R, as shown in equation (5) above, are

(9) $E_R = (1 - p)(1 - t)E_B$

Most foreign governments collect not just an income tax, but also withholding taxes (a typical rate would be 10 to 15 percent) on dividends, interest, royalties, and other payments to *U.S.* investors. Total withholding taxes paid W, equal:

(10) $W = w_D D + w_B (i_{p_0} f_0 F_0 + i_p fF)$
$+ w_H h(I_0 + I)$

where w_D, w_B, and w_H are the withholding tax rates for dividends, interest, and royalties, headoffice charges, etc., respectively.

We can now turn to *U.S.* tax policy. Rather than taxing foreign investment income net of foreign income and withholding taxes, the United States bases its tax on foreign-source income gross of foreign taxes and then grants a tax credit for foreign taxes paid. In my notation *U.S.* taxable income E_B^* equals domestic income net of interest costs $R^* - B^*$, plus interest, royalties, or other such receipts for intrafirm services and dividends:

(11) $E_B^* = R^* - B^* + (i_{p_0} f_0 F_0 + i_p fF)$
$+ h(I_0 + I) + D/(1 - t)$

Note that intrafirm income receipts are *not* reduced by the withholding tax and that dividends have been grossed up to include the foreign income taxes "deemed paid" on those dividends.[5] Foreign-source income for

[5]Legally speaking, the foreign subsidiary pays the income tax, and the *U.S.* parent is only deemed to have paid those taxes.

the purposes of determining *U.S.* taxes exceeds the cash actually received by the parent. Note further that *U.S.* taxable income includes the dividends, but not the retained earnings of the foreign subsidiary. That is the essence of deferral.

The taxes paid to the U.S. Treasury T^*, equal the *U.S.* tax rate t^* times taxable income E_B^*, less the foreign tax credit T_C^*:

(12) $T^* = t^* E_B^* - T_C^*$

The *U.S.* investor can claim a foreign tax credit equal to the *lesser* of two amounts: 1) the withholding taxes on dividends, interest, royalties, etc. plus the income taxes deemed paid on the dividends; and 2) the *U.S.* tax rate[6] times total foreign-source income:

(13) $T_C^* = min \left\{ W + \dfrac{tD}{1 - t}, t^* \cdot \right.$

$\left. [i_{p0} f_0 F_0 + i_p fF + h(I_0 + I) + D/(1 - t)] \right\}$

If foreign taxes paid or deemed paid are less than the maximum creditable—the *U.S.* taxes which would have been due on the foreign-source income—the investor is said to have a deficit of tax credits. Using the withholding tax formula (10), we can prove that the investor will have a deficit of foreign tax credits if and only if the share-weighted average of foreign tax rates is less than the *U.S.* income tax rate:

(14)

$s_B w_B + s_H w_H + s_D [w_D(1 - t) + t] < t^*$

where s_B, s_H, and s_D sum to unity and are the shares of interest, royalties, and other such fees, and dividends, respectively, in the *U.S.* investor's foreign-source income. Condition (14) indicates that even if the foreign tax burden on dividend income $w_D(1 - t) + t$ exceeds the *U.S.* tax rate t^*, the investor may yet avoid having surplus foreign tax credits by making sufficiently large interest and royalty payments. Let us rewrite the formula for the foreign tax credit as:

[6]Actually the foreign tax credit is limited not by the statutory tax rate but by the ratio of the firm's tentative *U.S.* taxes (i.e., before tax credits) to its total taxable income. If the firm has capital gains or certain other favorably taxed income, the statutory rate may exceed its average tax rate.

(15) $T_C^* = W + \dfrac{tD}{1-t} - x\{(w_B - t^*)$

$$(i_{p_0} f_0 F_0 + i_p fF)$$
$$+ (w_H - t^*)h(I_0 + I)$$
$$+ [w_D(1 - t) + t - t^*]$$
$$D/(1 - t)\}$$

where x is a binary variable equal to zero if and only if the investor has a deficit of foreign tax credits, i.e., condition (14) is satisfied. While equation (15) looks messier than (13), it is more tractable analytically.

The *U.S.* parent's after-tax income E_A^* equals its before-tax income E_B^*, less its *U.S.* taxes T^*, and the foreign taxes included in its taxable income:

(16) $E_A^* = E_B^* - T^* - [W + tD/(1 - t)]$

The consolidated, after-tax income of the multinational enterprise equals the parent's after-tax income (which includes dividend income from its foreign subsidiary) plus the subsidiary's retained earnings:

(17) $\qquad E_C^* = E_A^* + E_R$

To close out the model, we need to specify the parent's dividends and consequently its earnings available for reinvestment. It is assumed that the dividends paid to the ultimate shareholders D^* are some constant proportion p^* of *consolidated* after-tax earnings:

(18) $\qquad D^* = p^* E_C^*$

The parent's retained earnings are the difference between its after-tax income and its dividends:

(19) $E_R^* = E_A^* - D^* = (E_C^* - E_R)$
$\qquad\qquad - p^* E_C^* = (1 - p^*)E_C^* - E_R$

From (19) it is apparent that consolidated after-tax earnings E_C^* are proportionate to consolidated retained earnings available for investment:

(20) $\qquad E_C^* = \dfrac{1}{1 - p^*}(E_R^* + E_R)$

It is assumed that the multinational firm seeks to maximize either consolidated after-tax earnings or, equivalently, consolidated retained earnings available for investment.

I have little direct evidence on what, if anything, a multinational strives to maximize and have chosen consolidated after-tax earnings E_C^* because it seems to be as reasonable and as convenient an objective as any. I should note, however, that this objective function does *not* discount the value of earnings retained abroad despite the probable tax cost of repatriating those funds as dividends. Thus the behavioral assumption would most aptly characterize a management-controlled firm whose primary objective was the growth of the firm and for whom dividends to shareholders are comparable to a tax on consolidated earnings.

What should the firm do to maximize its consolidated earnings? To begin to answer this question, let us substitute several of the earlier formulas into equations (17) and (20) and rewrite consolidated after-tax earnings as:

(21) $E_C^* = \dfrac{E_R^* + E_R}{1 - p^*}$

$= (1 - t^*)(R^* - B^*) + (1 - t)(R - B)$
$\quad - [t^* - t + x(w_B - t^*)](i_{p_0} f_0 F_0 + i_p fF)$
$\quad - [t^* - t + x(w_H - t^*)]h(I_0 + I)$
$\quad - [t^* - t + x(w_D(1 - t) + t - t^*)]$
$\qquad\qquad\qquad pE_R/(1 - t)(1 - p)$

The multinational firm has *seven* degrees of freedom in maximizing consolidated income. It can set four intrafirm financial parameters—i_p, f, h, and p—plus the rates of new domestic and foreign investment I^* and I, and the rate of transferring new capital to its subsidiary F. All other variables in equation (21) are either predetermined or will be determined by these seven values.

We distinguish the four intrafirm financial parameters, i_p, f, h, and p, from the three remaining controls, I^*, I, and F, because the former should be minimized or maximized according to straightforward, tax-avoidance criteria, while the latter must satisfy standard first-order conditions. Let us look first at the intrafirm financial parameters for their optimal values can be determined by a close inspection of equation (21). We obviously need to differentiate between cases where an investor has a deficit, rather than a surplus, of foreign tax credits.

Deficit Case: A deficit of tax credits obtains when foreign tax rates are comparatively low, condition (14) can be satisfied, and thus $x = 0$. In this case the firm should *minimize* royalties, interest, dividends, and all other forms of repatriating income. Foreign investment should be financed insofar as possible out of retained earnings rather than new funds obtained from the parent. If funds must be repatriated in one form or another, the investor will, so far as taxes are concerned, be indifferent among interest, royalties, headoffice charges, or dividends. Each generates the same increase in total tax payments.

Surplus Case: A surplus of tax credits obtains when foreign tax rates are comparatively high, condition (14) is violated, and thus $x = 1$. In this case the firm should *maximize* royalties, headoffice charges, interest payments, and all other intrafirm charges deductible from the foreign subsidiary's income and *minimize* dividend payments. By substituting one form of income repatriation for another, the investor can reduce its foreign income taxes without a corresponding increase in its *U.S.* taxes. A multinational firm, in short, has a clear tax incentive to manipulate its intrafirm accounts to avoid generating excess tax credits.

Let me hasten to add that multinational firms have less than full flexibility in manipulating intrafirm accounts and that in actual practice tax avoidance is not the only criterion affecting the firm's behavior. National tax authorities strive to protect the local tax base: foreign governments may limit deductible payments to parent firms, and the United States applies its "arm's-length" standard to intrafirm interest rates, royalties, etc..[7] Likewise, foreign exchange authorities frequently limit intrafirm transactions to improve the balance of payments —witness the *U.S.* balance-of-payments

guidelines affecting dividend repatriation in the late 1960's. Furthermore, the multinational may be willing to pay higher taxes in order to withdraw its income from weak-currency countries or to minimize its exposure to expropriation. But taxes do matter. Sidney Robbins and Robert Stobaugh (pp. 28–29 and 77) found that intrafirm debt-equity ratios and the methods of income repatriation reflected tax considerations. George Kopits (1972, 1974) found that subsidiaries' dividend payout rates were higher the lower the tax cost of paying dividends and that royalty rates were manipulated to offset excess tax credits generated by dividends.

Consolidated income depends also on the rates of new domestic and foreign investment I^* and I, and new funds advanced to the foreign subsidiary F. The first-order condition obtained by taking the partial derivative of E_C^* with respect to domestic investment I^* is:[8]

$$(22) \qquad r^* = b^*$$

The marginal revenue from new domestic investment r^* should equal the marginal cost of newly borrowed funds in the United States, b^*. The analogous condition with respect to new foreign investment I is slightly more complicated:

$$(23) \qquad r = b + \frac{(t^* - t_f)h}{(1 - t_f)}$$

where t_f is defined to be the effective rate of global (foreign plus *U.S.*) taxation of the foreign subsidiary's income. Assuming the investor succeeds in avoiding a surplus of foreign tax credits, this effective rate of taxation is simply a weighted average of the foreign and *U.S.* income tax rates:

$$(24) \quad t_f = pt^* + (1 - p)t = t + p(t^* - t)$$

The portion of foreign subsidiary earnings paid out as dividends p, is taxed at the *U.S.*

389

---

[7]The arm's length standard obligates an American investor to use transfer prices equal to those which would have prevailed between an independent buyer and seller.

[8]The derivations of the first-order conditions and the equations of change are straightforward, but exceedingly cumbersome. Because they will be published in the Mathematical Appendix to Bergsten, Horst, and Moran, ch. 6, and are available from the author on request, they are not reproduced here.

rate t^*, while that portion retained by the subsidiary $1 - p$, is taxed at the foreign rate t. The second term on the right-hand side of condition (23) recognizes that increased foreign investment generates higher headoffice and other such charges and that such income will be taxed at the U.S., rather than the foreign, rate. Practically speaking, this second term on the right-hand side of condition (23) is small, and the foreign subsidiary equates the marginal revenue from new investment to the marginal cost of locally borrowed funds.

The third and most interesting first-order condition is obtained from the derivative of consolidated income with respect to new funds advanced to the subsidiary F:

$$(25) \qquad (1 - t^*)b^* = (1 - t_f)b - (t^* - t_f)i_p f$$

The significance of this condition is grasped more readily if we contrast two extreme cases, the equity-only and the debt-only investor. Suppose, first, that an American company invests overseas, borrows in local capital markets, but limits its own investment in its subsidiary to equity participation. That is to say, there is no intrafirm debt, only equity. This method of financing foreign investment is certainly encouraged by current U.S. tax policy, since debt gives rise to interest payments and thereby shifts income to the more highly taxed U.S. parent. In this equity-only case, $f = 0$, and condition (25) reduces to:

$$(26) \qquad (1 - t^*)b^* = (1 - t_f)b$$

The optimal transfer of new funds to the subsidiary equates the after-tax return on equity in the two countries. If the U.S. income tax rate t^* exceeds the foreign income tax rate t, it will also exceed t_f, and the foreign investor will have an implicit tax incentive to invest abroad rather than in the United States.

Suppose for the sake of contrast that the American investor disregards the tax advantages of equity and relies exclusively on debt to finance new foreign investment. Suppose further that it was willing and able to charge interest equal to the subsidiary's

marginal cost of newly borrowed funds b. In this case, $f = 1$, $i_p = b$, and condition (25) reduces to:

$$(27) \qquad b^* = b$$

The multinational has no tax incentive to favor foreign investment over domestic, for at the margin they both generate equal tax payments. While deferral may reduce U.S. taxes and thus leave the multinational with additional funds for global investment, it would not bias the location of that investment. Although condition (27) represents a hypothetical extreme, it points up an important conclusion: deferral encourages an American investor to favor foreign over domestic investment 1) the lower the foreign income tax rate, 2) the lower the rate of dividend repatriation, 3) the lower the ratio of debt to new capital (debt plus equity) transferred to the subsidiary, and 4) the lower the interest charged on intrafirm debt. Deferral thus encourages the American investor to use equity rather than debt in financing foreign investment, and the more equity used, the greater is the implicit bias towards foreign and against domestic investment.

II. The Impact of Changing U.S. Tax Policy

A. *Repealing Deferral*

In this section we will explore the impact of three proposed changes in current U.S. tax policy: repealing deferral; increasing $R\&D$ charges to foreign subsidiaries; and eliminating the foreign tax credit. If deferral were repealed, U.S. taxable income would include the grossed-up value of the foreign subsidiary's retained earnings $E_R/(1 - t)$ in addition to the income shown in equation (11) above. The U.S. taxable income and consolidated before-tax income now become one and the same:

$$(28) \qquad E_B^* = (R^* - B^*) + (R - B)$$

Assuming the foreign tax credit would be extended to include all foreign income taxes paid, not just those associated with dividends, consolidated after-tax income would equal:

$$(29) \quad E_C^* = (1 - t^*)(R^* - B^* + R - B)$$

$$- x \left\{ (w_B - t^*)(i_{p_0} f_0 F_0 + i_p fF) \right.$$

$$+ (w_H - t^*)h(I_0 + I)$$

$$\left. + [w_D p(1 - t) + t - t^*] \frac{E_R}{(1 - p)(1 - t)} \right\}$$

As long as foreign income and withholding tax rates are low enough, or royalties, interest, and other such charges can be kept high enough to avoid a surplus of tax credits, $x = 0$, and the multinational firm has no further tax incentives to minimize or maximize the use of debt, intrafirm interest rates, royalties, dividends, or the like. The only tax consideration affecting the intrafirm accounts would be the desire to avoid excess tax credits.

Turning from the intrafirm financial parameters to the rates of new domestic and foreign investment and new capital transferred to the subsidiary, the first-order conditions for maximizing consolidated income are:

$$(30) \qquad\qquad r^* = b^*$$
$$(31) \qquad\qquad r = b$$
$$(32) \qquad\qquad b^* = b$$

All the tax terms have cancelled each other out. Without deferral marginal revenue from new investment should equal the marginal cost of newly borrowed funds both within and between the two countries. Gone would be the implicit tax incentive to invest abroad rather than in the United States.[9]

To determine the amounts by which foreign and domestic investment might change, we must take the total derivatives of the original first-order conditions, (22), (23), and (25). Assuming for the moment that the intrafirm financial ratios i_p, f, h, and p remain fixed, we obtain three equations in three unknowns (dI^*, dI, and dF) and one

known $dt_f = (1 - p)(t^* - t)$. Rather than presenting the messy formulas,[10] let me describe the nature of the calculations and then proceed to some numerical examples. The impact of eliminating deferral can be decomposed into a *substitution* and *liquidity* effect. When U.S. taxes due on foreign investment income increase, the investor diverts fewer funds to foreign investment and more to domestic. This is the substitution effect. The liquidity effect derives from higher taxes: with fewer funds available for reinvestment and with outside funds becoming increasingly costly, the multinational cuts back on its global investment. The substitution and liquidity effects both reduce the rates of new foreign investment and new funds transferred to the foreign subsidiary. New domestic investment will increase if the positive substitution effect outweighs the negative liquidity effect.

My numerical examples are based upon the 1974 experience of American-owned manufacturing subsidiaries—see Appendix Table A2. Most of our model's parameters were roughly estimated from published statistical sources. For example, the average foreign income tax of 39 percent and average dividend payout rate of 42 percent implied an effective rate of global taxation of foreign subsidiary income of 42.8 percent. Thus, eliminating deferral would raise the effective rate of taxation from 42.8 percent to the U.S. rate of 48 percent, an increase of 5.2 percent. The parameters I could *not* estimate from any published sources were the elasticities of investment demand or borrowing costs implicit in equations (1) through (4) above. Accordingly, I arbitrarily assumed that the elasticities of the marginal revenue from new investment and marginal cost of new borrowing were equal to two and then compared those results with others based on higher or lower elasticities.

The numerical calculations of the impact of eliminating deferral are summarized in Table 1. Notice that I have scaled my example to make it appear that all new investment by foreign manufacturing affiliates of

---

[9] In actual practice, various nonneutralities would remain. For example, the U.S. investment tax credit does not apply to foreign investment, and state and local income taxes are only deductible from U.S. federal income taxes, while analogous foreign taxes would be creditable. These remaining nonneutralities are carefully evaluated by Hufbauer and Foster.

[10] See fn. 8 above.

TABLE 1—ESTIMATED IMPACT OF REPEALING DEFERRAL: ON NEW DOMESTIC
AND FOREIGN INVESTMENT, NEW FUNDS ADVANCED TO SUBSIDIARIES,
CONSOLIDATED AFTER-TAX INCOME, AND DOMESTIC AND FOREIGN TAXES
PAID BY U.S. MANUFACTURERS, 1974

	Initial Value	Case 1		Case 2 (More Elastic Investment)		Case 3 (Less Elastic Borrowing)	
		Absolute Change	Percentage Change	Absolute Change	Percentage Change	Absolute Change	Percentage Change
Domestic Investment	36,400	1,429	3.9	3,613	9.9	1,360	3.7
Foreign Investment	18,300	−1,549	−8.5	−3,789	20.7	−1,579	−8.6
New Funds for Subsidiary	2,710	−2,466	−91.0	−4,642	−171	−2,028	−75
Consolidated After-Tax Income	15,194	−532	−3.5	−477	−3.1	−534	−3.5
U.S. Taxes Paid	6,005	545	9.1	501	8.3	532	8.9
Foreign Taxes Paid	5,001	−80	−1.6	−148	−3.0	−65	−1.3

Note: Initial Values and Absolute Changes expressed in millions of dollars. Case 1 assumes the values for parameters shown in Appendix Table A2. Case 2 assumes the same values except the values of $r^{*\prime}$ and r' are two-fifths as large as those shown in Appendix Table A2. Case 3 assumes the same values as shown in Table A2 except the values of $b^{*\prime}$ and b' are twice as large as those shown.

U.S. corporations in 1974 was undertaken by the sole subsidiary of a large U.S. manufacturer. In Case 1 (where all investment and borrowing elasticities are assumed to equal two) eliminating deferral would increase the parent's investment by 3.9 percent and reduced the subsidiary's by 8.5 percent in 1974. Because of lost liquidity the rate of global investment would have been slightly lower than it actually was. The substantial reduction in intrafirm funds transferred reflects our implicit assumption that eliminating deferral would encourage multinational firms to borrow more abroad and less at home than they now do. That is to say, taxes affect the location of borrowing as well as the location of investment. Consolidated after-tax income would have been $532 million less than it was, which would represent a 3.5 percent decline for the large multinational manufacturer. These lowered earnings are the by-product, of course, of the higher taxes paid to the U.S. government. Foreign tax payments ease slightly because of the lower rate of new foreign investment and the higher rate of new borrowing by the foreign subsidiary.

In Case 2 all the parameters are identical to Case 1 except that we have assumed that new domestic and foreign *investment* are *more elastic* with respect to changes in the cost of capital than they were in Case 1 (the elasticities are equal to five rather than two). As can be seen, the more elastic domestic and foreign investment are, the greater is the substitution of domestic for foreign investment resulting from the loss of deferral. Case 3 differs from Case 1 only in assuming that new domestic and foreign *borrowing* are *less elastic* with respect to changes in the interest rate. As one can see, foreign investment falls by more and domestic rises by less than they did in Case 1. In short, the more elastic investment demand the greater the substitution effect is, and the more elastic the supply of external funds the smaller the liquidity effect is.

The estimates in Table 1 all assume that the intrafirm financial ratios i_p, f, h, and p remain fixed at their current values. As we noted above, however, eliminating deferral might also encourage investors to rely more on debt and less on equity in financing their foreign investment, to raise intrafirm interest and royalty rates, to expand charges for R&D and other headoffice expenses and to increase dividend payout rates. In the absence of deferral, all these changes except higher dividends would shift tax revenues from the foreign country to the United States. The statistics in Table 1 could thus understate the impact of eliminating de-

TABLE 2—ESTIMATED IMPACT OF DOUBLING HEADOFFICE, *R&D*, AND OTHER INTRAFIRM
SERVICE CHARGES: ON NEW DOMESTIC AND FOREIGN INVESTMENT, NEW FUNDS
ADVANCED TO SUBSIDIARIES, CONSOLIDATED AFTER-TAX INCOME, AND DOMESTIC AND
FOREIGN TAXES PAID BY *U.S.* MANUFACTURERS, 1974

	Initial Value	Case 1 (Deductions Allowed)		Case 2 (Deductions Disallowed)	
		Absolute Change	Percentage Change	Absolute Change	Percentage Change
Domestic Investment	36,400	149	0.4	1,393	3.8
Foreign Investment	18,300	−332	−1.8	−3,087	−16.9
New Funds for Subsidiary	2,710	444	16.4	−2,718	−100
Consolidated After-tax Income	15,194	−142	−0.9	−991	−6.5
U.S. Taxes Paid	6,005	688	11.5	981	16.3
Foreign Taxes Paid	5,001	−592	−11.8	−84	−1.7

Note: Initial Values and Absolute Changes expressed in millions of dollars. Both cases assume that headoffice and other such charges are raised from 1.1 to 2.2 percent of the foreign subsidiaries' total assets. In Case 1 the foreign government allows higher deductions from the subsidiaries' taxable income; in Case 2 they do not.

ferral on both domestic and foreign tax revenues.[11]

B. *Increasing R&D Charges to Foreign Subsidiaries*

As noted in the introduction, the Treasury has issued new guidelines for Sections 861–864 of the Internal Revenue Code. These new guidelines will require the multinationals to allocate a higher portion of their domestic *R&D* expenses to their foreign affiliates when determining their maximum allowable tax credit. Unless the investor has a deficit of tax credits, its *U.S.* tax payments will rise. The Treasury hopes that the multinationals would increase their *R&D* charges to avoid double taxation of this portion of their income. The multinationals claim that foreign tax authorities will not allow any additional deductions from the subsidiaries' income, so the disputed expenses would give rise to double taxation. We have used our microeconomic model to determine the impact of increasing *R&D* or other intrafirm charges assuming first that the foreign government would, and second that it would not, permit

[11]Of course, factors which we have ignored could reverse this conclusion. For example, foreign governments might retaliate by raising their taxes on *U.S.*-owned subsidiaries' income, which would increase their parents' *U.S.* tax credits and decrease their tax payments.

higher deductions from foreign subsidiary income.

Our findings are summarized in Table 2. Because there is no way of knowing how great the increase in intrafirm charges might be, we have arbitrarily assumed that all charges except for interest would be doubled. That is to say, headoffice, royalties, and all other intrafirm charges would increase from their current 1.1 percent to 2.2 percent of foreign subsidiaries' assets. Case 1 in Table 2 assumes that the foreign government would allow the multinational to deduct all such charges from the foreign subsidiaries' taxable income. As can be seen, the estimated impact on domestic and foreign investment would be minimal. The primary consequence would be a shift of taxable income from the foreign subsidiary to the *U.S.* parent. Foreign tax payments would fall by 12 percent while *U.S.* tax payments would increase by 11 percent. Because the *U.S.* income tax rate is higher than the foreign income tax rate, the global tax burden would rise and consolidated after-tax income would fall slightly.

This impact contrasts sharply with that in Case 2 where we have assumed that the foreign government would *not* allow increased deductions from the subsidiary's taxable income. The key to understanding this latter situation is recognizing that the new guidelines would subject foreign investment income to a disguised form of double taxation. Foreign investment would be cut by 17 percent, or twice the reduction from eliminating deferral. Likewise, U.S. taxes would increase by 16 percent, a gain based on the direct impact of the new guidelines and the induced cutback in funds advanced to the subsidiary (if more investable funds are retained by the parent, U.S. borrowing and interest expenses can be cut proportionately). But in this second case U.S. tax revenues gain at the expense of the American investor and not the foreign treasury. In short, by disallowing higher deductions for R&D expenses, the foreign government can protect its tax base. But in doing so, it permits the double taxation which inhibits new investment by American-owned subsidiaries.

C. Repealing the Foreign Tax Credit

Several critics of U.S. tax policy have proposed the repeal of the foreign tax credit as well as deferral. Taxable income in the United States would include all foreign investment income net of foreign income and withholding taxes:

(33)
$$E_B^* = (R^* - B^*) + (R - B - T - W)$$

U.S. taxes would equal the U.S. tax rate times the taxable income with no foreign tax credit:

(34) $$T^* = t^* E_B^*$$

Consolidated after-tax income would equal:

(35) $$E_C^* = (1 - t^*)(R^* - B^*)$$
$$+ (1 - t^*)(1 - w_D p)(1 - t)(R - B)$$
$$+ (1 - t^*)(t + w_D p(1 - t) - w_B) \cdot$$
$$(i_{p_0} f_0 F_0 + i_p f F)$$
$$+ (1 - t^*)(t + w_D p(1 - t) - w_H) h(I_0 + I)$$

Note the heavy taxation, $(1 - t^*)(1 - w_D p) \cdot (1 - t)$, of foreign investment income $R - B$. As is apparent from a close inspection of equation (35), the American investor can raise its consolidated after-tax earnings by increasing its use of intrafirm debt f, the rate of interest on that debt, i_p, or the rate of charging headoffice and other such expenses back to its subsidiary. Each of these measures shifts income from the subsidiary to the parent and relieves the double taxation of foreign investment income.

The new first-order conditions for maximizing after-tax income are:

(36) $$r^* = b^*$$

(37) $$r = b - \frac{t + w_D p(1 - t) - w_H}{(1 - t)(1 - w_D p)} h$$

(38) $$b^* = (1 - t)(1 - w_D p)b$$
$$+ (t + w_D p(1 - t) - w_B) i_p f$$

Once again, the most interesting of these first-order conditions is the third, and its significance becomes more apparent by contrasting an equity-only with a debt-only investor. If an American investor ignored the obvious tax incentives to finance foreign investment with debt and advanced only equity funds to its subsidiary, $f = 0$ and equation (38) becomes:

(39) $$b^* = (1 - t)(1 - w_D p) b$$

This is the mathematical formula for the AFL-CIO's dream and the multinationals' nightmare! Because of the double taxation of foreign equity income, the American manufacturer discriminates heavily against foreign investment and in favor of U.S. investment. By contrast, if an investor could rely wholly on debt in financing new investment and charge interest equal to its subsidiary's marginal cost of borrowing, $i_p f = b$ and equation (38) reduces to:

(40) $$b^* = (1 - w_B) b$$

Although the American investor would still discriminate against foreign investment, that discrimination would be much less than above. The firm's ability to substitute debt for equity in financing foreign investment will limit the substitution of domestic for foreign investment.

Our numerical examples bring out this point quite clearly. The estimates presented in Table 3 show the impact of repealing deferral and the foreign tax credit and allowing only a deduction for foreign taxes. In Case 1 the firm continues its traditional mix of debt and equity in financing foreign expansion; in Case 2 it uses only debt in fi-

TABLE 3—ESTIMATED IMPACT OF REPEALING DEFERRAL AND THE FOREIGN TAX CREDIT
AND ALLOWING ONLY A DEDUCTION FOR FOREIGN TAXES PAID: ON NEW DOMESTIC AND
FOREIGN INVESTMENT, NEW FUNDS ADVANCED TO SUBSIDIARIES, CONSOLIDATED
AFTER-TAX INCOME, AND DOMESTIC AND FOREIGN TAXES PAID BY *U.S.* MANUFACTURERS, 1974

	Initial Value	Case 1 (Initial Parameters)		Case 2 (Reliance on Debt)	
		Absolute Change	Percentage Change	Absolute Change	Percentage Change
Domestic Investment	36,400	9,291	25.5	3,970	10.9
Foreign Investment	18,300	−10,283	−56.2	−4,997	−27.3
New Funds for Subsidiary	2,710	−15,725	−580.3	−8,060	−297.4
Consolidated After-Tax Income	15,149	−2,974	−19.6	−3,107	−20.5
U.S. Taxes Paid	6,005	3,028	50.4	2,953	49.2
Foreign Taxes Paid	5,001	−504	−10.1	−144	−2.9

Note: Initial Values and Absolute Changes expressed in millions of dollars. Estimates include the repeal of deferral—see first three columns of Table 1. Both cases assume that the foreign tax credit is replaced by a deduction from taxable income. In Case 1 all parameters are as shown in Appendix Table A2; in Case 2 the investor raises the ratio of new debt to new funds f to unity, and the interest on that debt to equal the subsidiary's marginal cost of borrowing.

nancing new foreign investment and charges interest equal to the subsidiary's marginal cost of borrowing. The substitution of domestic for foreign investment is far greater in Case 1 (where the firm relies on its traditional debt-equity mix) than in Case 2 (where it shifts from equity to debt). Notice the substantial increase in *U.S.* taxes and the consequent decrease in consolidated corporate earnings and new investment. In fact, had the elasticities of investment demand and loanable funds been less than we supposed, the lost liquidity could more than offset the substitution effect, and domestic investment would *fall* with the repeal of the foreign tax credit. Finally, we note that the intrafirm flow of funds, already diminished by the repeal of deferral, would reverse its direction. The subsidiary either advances funds to the *U.S.* parent or repatriates previously received capital. In actual practice, this backflow of foreign direct investment might be blocked and the substitution of domestic for foreign investment diminished.[12]

[12]The foreign tax authorities, for example, might treat the repatriation of capital as dividends paid out of past earnings and thus subject to a withholding tax. Likewise, foreign subsidiaries' access to local capital markets might be curtailed if local borrowing exceeded local investment.

III. Conclusion

We have explored the effects of *U.S.* taxation of foreign investment income on foreign and domestic investment, the financing of that investment, the mix of debt and equity in advancing funds to a foreign subsidiary, and dividends, royalties, and other such intrafirm payments. Under existing *U.S.* policy, corporate income taxes on foreign income are deferred until the subsidiary formally pays a dividend to its *U.S.* parent, and the parent can claim a tax credit for income and withholding taxes paid to the foreign government. This policy encourages the use of equity rather than debt in financing foreign expansion and discourages the repatriation of foreign investment income; if income is repatriated, investors may want to make minimal interest, royalty, and other such payments to offset the excess tax credits generated by dividends. Current policy also offers an implicit tax incentive to investing overseas, and the size of the incentive increases the lower the foreign income tax, the lower the subsidiary's dividend payout rate, the less debt and the more equity used in financing foreign investment, and the lower the interest on intrafirm debt.

If deferral were repealed, so too would most of the tax incentives to invest abroad or to manipulate intrafirm accounts to avoid taxes. The impact of this and other tax changes can be disaggregated into a substitution and a liquidity effect. If the elasticities of investment opportunities at home and abroad are low, so too will be the induced substitution of domestic for foreign investment. Likewise, if the elasticities of the supply of outside funds are small, any tax increase will exercise a larger drag on the firm's rate of global investment.

We also explored the effects of compelling *U.S.* investors to charge their foreign subsidiaries with a higher proportion of current *R & D* expenses and of repealing the foreign tax credit. If foreign governments will allow higher deductions from the subsidiaries' taxable income, the United States would gain tax revenues at the expense of the foreign government. If higher deductions are disallowed, foreign investment income is subject to a disguised form of double taxation, *U.S.* tax payments rise, corporate after-tax income falls, and the rate of foreign investment contracts. Repealing the foreign tax credit would have a profound impact on a multinational's profitability and, if its ability to compensate for the lost liquidity with increased borrowing is small, on its rate of global investment. The substitution of domestic for foreign investment depends not only on the elasticities of investment opportunities, but also the firm's ability to substitute debt for equity in its internal financing of foreign investment.

This analysis can be extended in several directions. Additional foreign countries could be included; intrafirm exports might be taken into explicit account; other aspects of *U.S.* and foreign tax policy (for example, depreciation allowances, investment tax credits) could be explored; and better numerical estimates of the model's parameters could be developed. The analysis should incorporate the dynamics of investment planning even though the mathematics could become formidable. Finally, our characterization of a multinational's financial behavior was rudimentary. But the analysis showed that tax policy affects financial behavior, and financial behavior in turn mitigates the impact of tax policy on investment spending. This interaction between tax policy and multinational finance surely deserves further attention.

REFERENCES

C. **Fred Bergsten, Thomas Horst, and Theodore Moran,** *American Multinationals and American Interests,* Washington, forthcoming.

G. C. **Hufbauer and D. Foster,** "U.S. Taxation of the Undistributed Income of Controlled Foreign Corporations," Office of International Tax Affairs, Dept. of Treasury, Apr. 1976.

G. F. **Kopits,** "Dividend Remittance Behavior Within the International Firm: A Cross Country Analysis," *Rev. Econ. Statist.,* Aug. 1972, *54,* 339–42.

――――, "Intrafirm Royalties Crossing Frontiers and Transfer Pricing Behavior," unpub. manuscript, Nov. 1974.

M. E. **Kyrouz,** "Foreign Tax Rates and Tax Bases," *Nat. Tax. J.,* Mar. 1975, *28,* 61–80.

J. R. **Nunns and G. C. Hufbauer,** "The United States Balance of Tax Payments on Foreign Investment and Employment," *Colum. J. World Bus.,* Summer 1975, *10,* 12–20.

Sidney M. **Robbins and Robert V. Stobaugh,** *Money in the Multinational Enterprise,* New York 1973.

U.S. **Congress, Senate, Committee on Finance,** *Implications of Multinational Firms for World Trade and Investment and for United States Trade and Labor,* Washington 1973.

U.S. **Office of Business Economics,** "U.S. Direct Investment Abroad in 1974," *Surv. Curr. Bus.,* Oct. 1974, *55,* 43–63.

――――, "Capital Expenditures by Majority-Owned Foreign Affiliates of U.S. Companies: 1975 and 1976 and 1966–76 Trends," *Surv. Curr. Bus.,* Mar. 1976, *56,* 20–29.

U.S. **Office of Foreign Direct Investment,** *Foreign Affiliate Financial Survey,* Washington 1971.

TABLE A1—SUMMARY OF MATHEMATICAL NOTATION

Symbol	Meaning
R	Total return on investment net of labor and material costs, but gross of interest expense and income taxes
I	Investment
B	Total interest paid on external debt
L	Borrowing in external capital market
F	Transfer of investable funds (debt plus equity) from parent to subsidiary
E_R	Retained earnings available for new investment
i_p	Interest rate applied to intrafirm debt
f	Proportion of F which is debt rather than equity
h	Ratio of $R\&D$ and other headoffice charges to total foreign investment $I_0 + I$
E_B	Taxable income
T	Income taxes paid
t	Income tax rate
D	Dividends paid
p	Ratio of dividends paid to earnings after income taxes
E_A	Earnings after income taxes
W	Withholding taxes paid
w_D, w_B, w_H	Withholding tax rates applied to intrafirm dividends, interest, and headoffice charges, respectively
T_C	Foreign tax credit allowed
s_D, s_B, s_H	Relative shares of dividends, interest and headoffice charges in total foreign-source income
x	Binary variable equal to unity if and only if the investor has paid more foreign income and withholding taxes than are creditable
E^*_C	Consolidated (i.e., parent plus subsidiary) after-tax income
t_f	Effective global (i.e., foreign plus $U.S.$) rate of taxation of foreign-subsidiary income
r	Marginal revenue from additional investment, i.e., dR/dI
b	Marginal cost of additional outside borrowing, i.e., dB/dL

Notes: The * denotes the parent's $U.S.$ operations, the lack of one the subsidiary's foreign operations. The 0 subscript indicates a predetermined stock, the lack of one the current flow.

TABLE A2—VALUES AND SOURCES OF PARAMETER ESTIMATES USED IN SIMULATIONS

Parameter	Value	Definition and Source
b, b^*	.09	Assumed marginal cost of externally borrowed funds for parent or affiliate.
p	.42	Subsidiary's dividend payout ratio. According to the U.S. Office of Business Economics (1975), Table 4, p. 51, manufacturing affiliates had a gross dividends-earnings ratio of .40 in 1974. I have raised this estimate marginally to approximate a four- or five-year moving average.
p^*	.33	Parent's dividend payout ratio. This is the ratio of all $U.S.$ manufacturing firms' dividends to after-tax earnings. See U.S. Office of Business Economics (1975), p. S-20.
t	.391	Foreign income tax rate. This estimate is based on Kyrouz's realized tax rates; see Bergsten, Horst, and Moran, Table 6-2, col. 1.
t^*	.48	$U.S.$ statutory income tax rate.
E_B	10.67	Affiliate's before-tax earnings. According to the U.S. Office of Business Economics (1975), Table 11, p. 51, the after-tax earnings of manufacturing affiliates in 1974 was $6.498 billion. Since this is net of income taxes, I have grossed this figure up by dividing it by $1 - .391$.
h	.011	Ratio of fees and royalties to total affiliate investment. According to the U.S. Office of Business Economics (1975), Table 10, p. 49, manufacturing affiliates paid fees and royalties amounting to $1.855 billion in 1974. There is no reliable estimate of the total assets of $U.S.$ manufacturing affiliates to use in

TABLE A2—*continued*

Parameter	Value	Definition and Source
		deflating this figure. I consulted the U.S. Senate Committee on Finance, Table 12, p. 432 and obtained the estimate for $78 billion in total assets in 1970. I assumed that total assets grew at an annual growth rate of 16.7 percent per annum (the rate of growth of affiliate sales) between 1970 and 1974, which gives an estimated total assets for 1974 of $170 billion. Dividing the $1.85 billion in royalties and fees by the $170 billion total assets yields the value for h of .011.
w_D, w_H, w_B	.15	Withholding tax rates applied to dividends, fees, and interest payments, respectively. I have assumed that a 15 percent rate is applied to each type of payment.
F	2.71	Net capital outflow from parent to affiliate. See U.S. Office of Business Economics (1975), Table 3, p. 47.
$R^* - B^*$	12.73	Parent's domestic income before taxes. According to Bergsten, Horst, and Moran, Table 6-1, 24 multinational manufacturers reporting sufficient statistics earned 54.4 percent of their book income before taxes from domestic operations. The $12.73 billion equals 54.4 percent of $12.73 billion plus $10.67 billion (the latter being my estimate of the affiliate's pre-tax earnings above).
r'	−.0025	The slope of the marginal revenue from new investment by the foreign affiliate. This slope was chosen because it implied that an elasticity of 2 for the marginal-revenue-from-new-affiliate-investment schedule.
$r^{*'}$	−.0012	The slope of the marginal revenue from new investment by the U.S. parent. Lacking any more reliable estimate, I assumed that the elasticity of investment demand at home, 2, was the same as that abroad.
b'	.0049	The slope of the marginal cost of outside capital schedule for the foreign affiliate. Once again, lacking any better estimate I assumed a slope which would make the elasticity of the schedule equal to 2.
$b^{*'}$	.0024	Slope of the marginal cost of outside capital schedule for the U.S. parent. I chose a slope such that the elasticity would once again equal 2.
I_0	170.	Foreign affiliate's total assets. See note for h above.
F_0	34.	Total capital transferred from parent to affiliate. Robbins and Stobaugh, Table 4-1, Table 2, indicate that 20 percent of manufacturing affiliates' sources of funds between 1966 and 1969 came from their parents. My $34 billion estimate for F_0 is 20 percent of the $170 billion estimate for I_0.
f, f_0	.64	Ratio of intrafirm debt to total capital transfer for new and existing investment, respectively. Estimate obtained directly from U.S. Office of Business Economics (1975), Table 3, p. 47 for incorporated manufacturing affiliates.
i_p, i_{p_0}	.031	Intrafirm interest rate. James Nunns and Gary Hufbauer, Table 2, and U.S. Office of Foreign Direct Investment allows us to calculate the ratio of intrafirm interest payments to intrafirm debt. This low average interest rate reflects the use of interest-free trade credits.
I	18.3	Subsidiary's new investment in 1974. The U.S. Office of Business Economics (1976) Table 1, p. 21 indicates that manufacturing affiliates capital expenditures were $11.7 billion in 1974. This figure includes only property, plant, and equipment expenditures, so I have increased this figure by 56 percent to include short-term capital formation. This 56 percent increase is based on the ratio of the estimated increase in total assets between 1970 and 1974 (see note for h above) and the total value of property, plant, and equipment expenditures over that same interval.
I^*	36.4	According to the U.S. Senate Committee on Finance, Table 12, p. 432, the increase in the total assets of the U.S. parents between 1966 and 1970 was 1.99 times as large as that of their foreign affiliates. My value of I^* is 1.99 times 18.3, my estimate of the value of I.

CHAPTER 26

Imputation systems of corporation tax within the EEC*

C. W. Nobes

The design of the present UK system of corporation tax is sometimes misunderstood. It becomes clearer when it is compared to the systems operated in other countries. This article contrasts the workings of imputation in our own and other systems. Also, one of the Meade Committee's proposals for reform is examined. Then, the behaviour of our system during an inflationary period is briefly discussed. Finally, the purposes and current progress of the harmonisation of corporate taxation in the EEC are looked at.

Systems of corporation tax

Systems of corporation tax are often divided[1] into three types: imputation, classical and split-rate. The UK system in 1965–73 was a classical system. Under such systems, company profits are taxed without a deduction for dividends paid; then the dividends are fully taxed as investment income in the hands of the shareholders. The United States and the Netherlands are examples of countries which still have classical systems. These are described by other writers.[2]

The other two types of system (imputation and split-rate) are designed to mitigate the above 'economic double taxation' of dividends for the reasons mentioned below. Imputation systems approach this mitigation by imputing to the shareholders some or all of the tax paid by companies. For example, taxpayers in the UK are deemed to have paid tax at the basic rate on their dividends grossed up at the basic rate. Split-rate systems tax distributed profits at a lower rate

than retained profits. Such systems have a similar effect to imputation systems. Indeed, the present UK imputation system can be redesigned to look like a split-rate system with exactly the same corporation tax and income tax burdens (see the appendix).

There are other adjustments that can be made to mitigate double taxation. For example, in the USA the classical system is modified in that the first $100 of dividends received by an individual each year are exempted from personal income tax. Alternatively, the 'primary dividend' system allows companies to deduct some proportion of dividends in the calculation of their taxable incomes. Such a system has operated in Sweden and Iceland. We will return to different systems in the section on harmonisation. Meanwhile, attention will be directed to imputation systems.

The introduction of an imputation system in the UK in 1973 seems to have been the result of three main factors. First, there was the need to harmonise practice within the EEC. This will be discussed later. Second, there was an equity argument against the economic double taxation of dividends. This argument, also considered later, involves a comparison of incorporated and unincorporated businesses. The nature of the inequity depends on whether one is considering retained or distributed profit. This second argument was closely linked with a third: that an imputation system would encourage effective investment by reducing the classical system's bias against distribution of profits.

The purpose behind this third argument was a desire to improve the *quality* of investment. The theory is that there should be larger payments of dividends once economic double taxation is eased. This should lead to the movement of resources away from the many averagely profitable companies towards profit-maximising investors. These should direct the funds on to those companies which, because of their profit records, are most attractive and can use resources most effectively. Even if these larger dividend payments

---

[1] A. J. van den Tempel, *Corporation Tax and Individual Income Tax in the EEC*, Brussels, 1970; International Bureau of Fiscal Documentation, *European Taxation*, vol 12, nos 5 and 6, 1972; OECD, *Theoretical and Empirical Aspects of Corporate Taxation*, Paris, 1974.

[2] C. F. McCarthy, W. M. Mann and W. A. Gregory, *The Federal Income Tax*, Prentice-Hall, Englewood Cliffs, NJ, latest edition; J. F. Chown, *Taxation and Multinational Enterprise*, Longman, London, 1974, ch. 4; M. R. Saunders, *Tax Planning for Businesses in Europe*, Butterworth, London, 1977, ch. 8.

* This article is reprinted, with permission, from *Accounting and Business Research* (Spring 1980) pp 221–231

lead to smaller total investment, due to leakage into taxation and consumption, it can be argued that this should be more than compensated for by better quality investment.[3]

Unfortunately, it has not been possible to establish whether the imputation system in the UK would lead to greater dividends, because of such complicating factors since 1973 as high inflation and dividend restrictions. Also, it is not at all clear that it is possible for investors to tell which companies will make the best use of investment funds. A company's past record of profit does not reliably show that it will continue to be a more efficient user of investment resources.[4]

Having briefly introduced the imputation system, we should now look at how it works in the UK, France and West Germany.

The workings of the UK imputation system

One way of illustrating the workings of imputation is to make a comparison with the classical system. Suppose that a company earns net profits before tax of 10,000 every year. Suppose also that the rate of corporation tax under the UK classical system was 40% and under the imputation system is 52%. In each case, the basic rate of income tax is 33%. The tax credit *imputed* to unincorporated shareholders is linked to the basic rate of income tax for administrative simplicity. For this example, it is 33/67 of the cash dividend, as in 1978/79. Income tax is not deducted at source from dividends in the imputation system.

		Classical System		Imputation System	
Company:	Net profit before tax	10,000		10,000	
	less Corporation tax (40%)	4,000	(52%)	5,200	
	Profit available for distribution	6,000		4,800	
	Dividends (say)	2,000		1,340	
	Undistributed profit	4,000		3,460	

The 2,000 gross dividend under the classical system is equivalent to the 1,340 cash dividend under the imputation system:

Shareholder:	Dividend	2,000		1,340	
	less Basic rate income tax deducted at source (33%)		660		0
	Cash received		1,340		1,340
	Tax credit imputed (33/67 × 1340)		—		660
	Income to be taxed	2,000		2,000	
	Tax at basic rate (33%)	660		660	
	less Tax already paid	660		—	
	less Tax credit imputed	—		660	
	Tax due		0		0
	Net dividend after tax		1,340		1,340

This shows that, for the basic rate taxpayer, the payment of dividends causes no extra tax to be paid by either the company or the shareholder. (Advance Corporation Tax, ACT, is discussed below.) Consequently, when the tax on both company and shareholders is considered, companies

[3]OECD, *Theoretical and Empirical Aspects of Corporate Taxation*, Paris, 1974.
[4]G. Whittington, *The Prediction of Profitability*, Cambridge University Press, 1971, chs 4 and 5.

with large payout ratios suffer less tax than they would under a classical system. This is despite the higher rate of corporation tax under the imputation system. The precise proportion of dividend payout above which this is true depends on the levels of corporation tax and income tax.

So far, shareholders have been assumed to be unincorporated. For corporate shareholders, there is a *full* imputation of the corporation tax borne by the paying company on the profits out of which the dividends are paid. That is, the receiving company pays no tax on its dividend income.

Returning to unincorporated shareholders, those who pay no income tax because of low taxable incomes can claim 'repayment' of the tax credit. Those whose marginal rates are above the basic rate pay income tax on the 2,000 of the above example and can claim the tax credit. The effect on higher rate taxpayers is interesting. Let us use the above example but take 98% marginal income tax rate (i.e. 83% income tax and 15% investment income surcharge; the highest rates in 1978/79).

Shareholder:

Cash dividend		1,340
Imputed credit (33/67)	660	
	2,000	
Income tax (98%)	1,960	
Tax credit	660	
Tax to pay		1,300
Post-tax receipt		40

The tax rate here on the cash dividend is 97% (i.e. 1,300/1,340). This means that the so called 'tax credit' has merely reduced the individual's tax rate by 1%. Note that for basic rate taxpayers, the effective rate of income tax on *cash* dividends is 0%; but for 98% taxpayers it is 97% (rather than 98% less 33%, as might appear at first sight). For these latter taxpayers, there is little useful imputation of the 5,200 corporation tax borne by the paying company. There is full corporate taxation of the company's taxable profit, followed by 97% taxation on the cash dividend paid out of that taxed profit.

Under the 'classical' system of 1965–73, the 98% taxpayer would have been treated as follows,

using the same basic rate of income tax:

401

Gross dividend		2,000
Tax deducted at source (33%)		660
Net dividend received		1,340
Tax on 2,000 at 98%	1,960	
Tax already deducted	660	
Tax to pay		1,300
Post-tax receipt		40

This shows that, despite the remarks in the preceding paragraphs, the present partial imputation system is better for dividend recipients than the classical system, even for high rate taxpayers. To achieve a post-tax receipt of 40 under a classical system, the company has to pay out 2,000 rather than 1,340. Therefore, the bias against distribution has been lessened by the change to the imputation system. However, it has certainly not been removed, unless none of the shareholders pays tax at above the basic rate. As will be shown later, the bias *can* be removed by such an imputation system as that of West Germany.

If similar calculations to those above are performed for other rates of income tax, the table below can be constructed. It shows how the imputation system becomes steadily less useful as higher rates of personal taxation are reached. The general relationship is that the 'effective rate' is given by $(m - b)/(1 - b)$, where m is the marginal rate and b is the basic rate.[5]

Individual Marginal Tax Rate (m)%	Effective Rate on Cash Dividend %
33	0
50	25
70	55
98	97

This 'effective rate' is *negative* for those paying 0% or 25% marginal tax rates. This rate is relevant for dividend policy. Assuming that the company can reclaim ACT (see below), the 'effective rate' is the one that determines the extra tax which will be borne by the company-plus-shareholders as a result of the payment of dividend. In the case of non-taxpayers, the total tax borne by company-plus-shareholders will actually *fall* as a result of a payment of dividends.

It should be noted in summary that a partial imputation system *can* totally remove double taxation and the bias against distribution when the tax credit cancels the personal liability. Alterna-

---

[5] i.e. $\left(\dfrac{Dm}{1 - b} - \dfrac{Db}{1 - b} \right) \div D$, where D is the cash dividend.

tively, the double taxation can be removed by imputing all the corporation tax to shareholders; but even if there is no double taxation because there is no effective liability to corporation tax, there could still be some bias against distribution if personal income tax is larger than the underlying corporation tax and only operates when dividends are paid.

Advance corporation tax

A source of some confusion is the Advance Corporation Tax (ACT). This is an advance on the later payment of corporation tax (9–21 months after a company's year-end). It is not an essential part of an imputation system, as will be shown. It was designed mainly to improve the government's cash flow by speeding up tax payments. A second reason for it relates to those cases where there is no corporation tax liability (CTL) for there to be an advance of. This reason is discussed later.

ACT is related in size to the level of dividend payments: in 1978/79 it amounted to 33/67 of the dividend, when the basic rate of income tax was 33%. Any ACT paid[6] causes a set-off against the eventual CTL leaving only the difference (mainstream corporation tax) to be paid. ACT is *not*, therefore, an extra tax on dividends, assuming that there is an adequate CTL.

One supposes that, when the imputation system was planned, it was not clear that there would often be inadequate corporation tax liabilities to allow a full ACT set-off. This problem of 'unrelieved' ACT occurs because of low profits and high tax allowances. Particularly in inflationary periods, capital allowances and stock reliefs may greatly reduce taxable profits. In addition, despite low taxable profits, dividends have been rising in money terms. As far as has been possible within a period of dividend restraint, dividend policy seems to have been based on a desire to compensate shareholders for a fall in the real value of dividends rather than on estimates of changes in 'real' profit.[7] Therefore, there have been many examples of unrelieved ACT.[8]

This illustrates the second reason for ACT. That is, it ensures that imputation credits are not granted to recipients of dividends when there has been no underlying payment of corporation tax to impute. ACT is paid on dividends irrespective of a company's taxable profits and can normally only be relieved against CTL. Consequently, the shareholders' tax credits will always have been paid for.[9] In order to make this operate more exactly, the ACT set-off in any year is limited to the amount of ACT that would relate to a dividend that, when 'grossed up' for the ACT, would absorb all the taxable income. To reduce the harshness of this, unrelieved ACT can be carried back for 2 years or forward indefinitely against other years' CTL.

A prevalent misconception is that the reason that there are tax credits in the UK imputation system is because there is an ACT. We have seen that, for the above two good reasons, the tax credits amount to the same size as the ACT. However, in theory, the tax credits are not due to ACT but are a partial imputation of the CTL in order that double taxation of dividends is mitigated. This general point about imputation systems is made clear by two aspects of the French and German systems. These are that, in each case, the imputation tax credits are based on the rates of *corporation* tax and that there are no general equivalents of ACT. Perhaps even more revealing is the fact that the Irish imputation system, although it has a tax credit based on the basic rate of income tax and operates in other ways similarly to the UK system, also has no ACT.[10]

Having outlined the UK system, it is now time to draw contrasts with the French and German systems. In each case, the rules relating to the determination of taxable income, capital gains, tax collection, etc are interestingly different from UK practice.[11] However, our present purpose requires that attention be directed to the methods of imputation.

The French imputation system

Corporation tax in France is levied at a rate of 50% on taxable profit. Dividends are not deductible in the calculation of taxable profit; they are paid out of taxed profit. Also, these dividends are

---

[6]ACT is paid using a quarterly accounting system. The need to pay ACT is cancelled out to the extent that the company has received franked investment income which has caused ACT to be paid by the paying company.

[7]P. R. A. Kirkman and C. W. Nobes, 'Dividend policy and inflation', *Accountancy*, October 1976.

[8]e.g. 'Now institutional shareholders hit back', *Accountancy*, August 1975.

[9]Either by the paying company or another company; see note 6.

[10]*Corporation Tax Act 1976 (Ireland)*; SSAP, CCAB Accountancy Bodies, 1977, Appendix 3.

[11]J. F. Chown, *op. cit*, ch. 4; M. R. Saunders, *op. cit.*, chs 2 and 3.

subject to personal income tax in the hands of the recipients. However, there is a tax credit (*avoir fiscal*) which imputes to the shareholders some of the tax paid by the company. So far, the system is similar to the UK partial imputation system. An important difference is that the size of the tax credit is not linked to the basic rate of income tax, but is one half of the underlying corporation tax on the dividends. An example follows.

Company:	Taxable profits	10,000
	Corporation tax	5,000
	Distributable profit	5,000
	Dividend	4,000
	Undistributed profit	1,000
Shareholder:	Dividend	4,000
	Avoir fiscal	2,000
	Taxable income	6,000
	Tax credit available	2,000

This 50% imputation is of a similar size to the UK imputation (see section on harmonisation). However, because the top rates of French income tax are low compared to those in the UK, the imputation remains very useful for all unincorporated shareholders.

The French treatment of *corporate* shareholders is very different from UK practice. Instead of full imputation of corporation tax, the treatment depends on whether or not the recipient is a 'holding' company (one that owns at least 10% or FF 10m in the paying company). Holding companies pay tax on 5% of (grossed up) dividend income and take the tax credit appropriate to that proportion. Other companies pay corporation tax on all dividends. These dividends are grossed up by the tax credit which is then available to the company. In the above example, if the shareholder were a non-holding company, the corporation tax due on the 'net' dividend income of 4,000 would be 1,000 (i.e. 6,000 × 50%, less 2,000 tax credit).

As can be seen from the definition of a holding company, this disadvantageous tax treatment, under which dividends may partially bear corporation tax several times, only applies to small holdings not to subsidiaries or important trade investments. These latter holdings receive approximately full imputation, as mentioned above.

It should be noted that there is no general equivalent of ACT in the French imputation system. However, in cases where no French corporation tax has been borne on income out of which dividends are paid, a *précompte* of $33\frac{1}{3}$% is deducted at source from the dividend. This is charged in order to cover the net cost to the Revenue of the *avoir fiscal* available to the recipients. An example of this occurs where a French company receives dividend or branch income from abroad and has chosen to pay corporation tax on income from French sources only.[12] (An analogous option is not available to UK companies; and a *précompte* would not be necessary anyway because of ACT.)

The West German imputation system

By the corporation tax reform law of 1976, the split-rate system of corporation tax was replaced by an imputation system from 1st January 1977. However, the German imputation system continues to include different rates for distributed and undistributed profits: 36% for the former and 56% for the latter. Credit for the *full* amount of the underlying corporation tax is given to the recipients of dividends. There is also a withholding tax of 25% on dividends, which is a deduction of tax at source by the paying company on behalf of the Revenue authorities. It is designed to make evasion more difficult. Resident shareholders can claim credit for the withholding tax. These various points can be illustrated:

[12] M. R. Saunders, *op. cit.*, ch 2.

Company:			
	1.	Taxable income	10,000
	2.	Normal rate corporation tax (56%)	5,600
	3.	Balance before relief	4,400
	4.	Retained profit (e.g. $\frac{1}{4}$)	1,100
	5.	Distribution ($\frac{3}{4}$)	3,300
	6.	Reduction of corporation tax	1,500 i.e. (56% less 36%) of $\frac{3}{4}$ of 10,000
	7.	Total distribution	4,800
	8.	Withholding tax (25%)	1,200
	9.	Net distribution	3,600

Shareholder:

10.	Net distribution			3,600	
11.	Tax credits:	withholding	1,200		
12.		imputed	2,700		i.e. 36% of $\frac{1}{4}$ of
				3,900	10,000
13.	Taxable income			7,500	
14.	Income tax (e.g. 40%)			3,000	
15.	Tax credits			3,900	
16.	Refund			900	

Note that the reduction in corporation tax in line 6 means that distributed income bears only 36% tax. The shareholders receive the net distribution after a withholding tax (line 8), which can be treated as a tax credit (line 11). The imputed tax credit in line 12 is the full amount of corporation tax borne on the distributed income. The result of all this is that the company has paid 4,100 (i.e. 5,600 less 1,500) in corporation tax and has also deducted and paid 1,200 in withholding tax on the distribution. The shareholders pay no further tax and, moreover, they receive a refund of 900. The total received by the shareholders is, therefore, 4,500 (i.e. 3,600 + 900). This is 60% (because 40% has gone in income tax) of 7,500 (i.e. the distribution of $\frac{3}{4}$ of the income of 10,000).

This demonstrates that, as a result of full imputation, dividends bear no corporation tax but only income tax. The double taxation of dividend income has been completely removed for all unincorporated shareholders. This is very different in its effects from the UK system. Indeed, unlike a split-rate system, this German dual-rate imputation system cannot be re-expressed in order to behave identically to the British or French imputation systems. It is essentially a different kind of system. Ironically, although a move to an 'imputation' system appears to be a harmonising action, the previous German split-rate system was closer in effect to the British or French systems.

Turning to corporate shareholders, they also receive full imputation because dividend income is exempt from corporation tax when received by holding companies (those with at least a 25% holding). Alternatively, when the recipient is not a holding company, the treatment is similar to that for unincorporated shareholders. This includes the charging of a withholding tax and the process of imputation. The net result is that the dividend income only bears corporation tax once.

Again there is no ACT. However, there is a similar German provision to the French *précompte* in those cases where income paid out as

dividends has not borne German corporation ta due to double taxation treaties or other reasons.

The Meade Committee

The Meade Committee[13] devoted some attentio to the major problem in corporate taxation whic imputation is designed to solve, that is the diffe ent taxation of retained and distributed profit On the one hand, it might be argued that an double taxation of income (on the company an on the shareholder) is inequitable when compar sons are made with unincorporated businesse This argument is used to justify imputation c corporation tax to the shareholders. On the othe hand, it is argued that it is inequitable, agai compared to unincorporated businesses, to allo companies to accumulate retained profits whic have not borne tax at the shareholders' margin rates. This argument may justify a separate coporation tax at a higher rate than basic rat income tax, if shareholders are assumed to pa higher rates of tax.

One approach to solving these problems is tha of the split-rate systems, which have a lower rat of corporation tax for distributed income than fo retained income. Other approaches seen abov are to tax corporate profits at fairly high rate and then to impute all or part of this tax to share holders with their distributions.

The Meade Committee reasonably propose that the theoretically correct solution is fo retained profit to be apportioned to shareholder just as if they were partners ploughing profi back. This apportionment would be taxed wit the dividends at the shareholders' marginal ta rates. There would be a full imputation of corpor ation tax via a tax credit on both distributed an apportioned profit. In this way, the compan would effectively bear no tax, and corporation ta

[13]Meade Committee, *The Structure and Reform of Direc Taxation*, IFS/Allen and Unwin, London, 1978, chs 7 and 12.

Table A
The Value of Tax Allowances to UK Companies £m

	1974	1975	1976
Capital allowances	2,981	3,589	4,149
Stock relief	720	1,490	940
Taxes on company income	1,957	1,955	2,316

Notes: The 'value' of the capital allowances is taken to be 52% of their size. The figures for stock relief relate to fiscal years rather than calendar years. The table is drawn from several sources and, therefore, should be taken to give only a broad indication of magnitudes.

Sources: *National Income and Expenditure 1966–1976*, Central Statistical Office HMSO, 1978, pp 39 and 132; *Times Business News*, 30 March 1977, page 21; *Accountancy Age*, 3 March 1978, page 3.

would be a sort of withholding tax. This would solve the problems of double taxation and retained profits. Incidentally, it would be necessary to adjust capital gains tax in order to avoid a double taxation of the gains arising from retained profits.

Clearly, there would be some administrative problems with this system and some unfortunate implications for the cash flow of shareholders of companies which retain a high proportion of profits. However, the idea is very attractive theoretically. The present German system's treatment of *distributed* income is close to the Meade suggestions; and it taxes retained profits at a rate (56%) which is also the top marginal rate of income tax. The UK provisions that require close companies to apportion about half of their profits to shareholders so that they may bear income tax are also concerned with this problem.

Inflation

There are numerous detailed differences between the operations of the different corporation taxes discussed in this article. These are not so much differences of broad *system* but alternative ways of measuring taxable income, treating income from abroad, and so on. These matters are vital for many companies but must be left for tax books[14] and tax professionals. However, there are two particular differences between UK and Franco-German practice which might be said to amount to a difference of system with respect to inflation adjustments.

The first difference is that there has been a system of stock relief[15] in the UK since 1973, which approximately subjects taxable profit to a 'cost-of-sales adjustment'[16] by removing part of the holding gains on stocks. This is a very important adjustment (see Table A). In a similar way, US companies are allowed to use a last-in first-out (LIFO) system of inventory valuation as a partial correction. However, in France and Germany (and other continental European countries) there is no adjustment for stock holding gains.

The second difference is that in France and Germany (and indeed in most of the rest of the EEC and in the USA) depreciation is an allowable expense for tax purposes. Depreciation rates are generally prescribed and based on estimated useful lives of the appropriate assets. In contrast to this, the UK system of capital allowances means that the whole cost of plant and machinery and 54% of industrial buildings can be charged against profit in the year of purchase. In the year of purchase, the historic cost *is* the current cost. In this sense, there is also a 'depreciation adjustment'[16] to taxable profit (see Table A).

As a result of these two factors, the UK corporation tax system adjusts taxable income in a very approximate way towards a current cost operating profit figure. This reduces (or possibly even eliminates) the extent to which taxation is based on unrealistically high profit figures during inflationary periods. This is not the case with the French and German corporation taxes.

Harmonisation

The Treaty of Rome calls for the elimination of customs duties between member states, the introduction of common tariffs with third countries, and the removal of barriers to the free movement of persons, capital, goods and services. The interest in taxation shown by the EEC Commission, which is the guardian of the Treaty of Rome, stems from this desire to promote the free movement of persons, capital, goods and services. The free movement of goods and services implies par-

---

[14]J. F. Chown, *op. cit.*; M. R. Saunders, *op. cit.*

[15]S. R. James and C. W. Nobes, *The Economics of Taxation*, Philip Allan, Oxford, 1978, ch. 12.

[16]Accounting Standards Committee, *Current Cost Accounting*, ED18, London, 1976.

ticularly the harmonisation of indirect taxes. Similarly the free movement of people and capital implies the harmonisation of direct taxes. If there were no harmonisation of taxes and if barriers to movement were eliminated, there might then be encouragement or obstruction of flows of people, capital and so on to particular countries within the EEC for purely fiscal reasons.

It is the aim of harmonisation[17] that the conditions of competition and the returns to capital and effort should not be significantly affected by differences in effective tax burdens. Just by having looked at the corporate taxation systems in three EEC countries, it should be clear that the scope for harmonisation is considerable. However, there are much larger differences—for example, the Netherlands and Luxembourg have classical systems of corporation tax. The EEC Commission's activity in this area of tax harmonisation will now be charted.

In 1962, the Neumark Committee[18] recommended to the Commission that a split-rate system should be adopted. As has been said, this is similar to the pre-1977 German system and is designed to mitigate the effects of 'economic double taxation' of dividends by including a lower rate of corporation tax on distributed profits. In 1970, the van den Tempel Report[19] described the three types of corporation tax systems, and recommended the classical system.

However, the Commission's draft Directive[20] of 1975 on the harmonisation of corporate taxation proposes the imputation system. This must be partly due to the fact that a majority of EEC countries were already using such a system or had plans to introduce one. In 1975, Belgium, France and the UK were using an imputation system. Since then, Germany, Denmark, Ireland and Italy have introduced one. For rates of tax and tax credit see Table B.

Some of the reasons[21] for choosing an imputation system have been mentioned. They include the fact that the tax credit reduces the bias against

distribution and favours small investors (lower rate taxpayers). Also, the system should reduce the incentive for evasion by lowering the effective marginal rate of tax on dividends. In addition, since the corporation tax rate tends to be higher under an imputation system, there is a fairer comparison between the rates of tax borne on company retained profits and partnership profits.

The draft Directive proposes that there shall be imputation systems in operation with a single rate of tax between 45% and 55% (Article 3).[22] Also, Article 8 proposes that imputation credits shall be between 45% and 55% of the corporation tax that would have to be paid on a sum equal to the taxable income out of which the dividend could be paid (i.e. on the dividend increased by the corporation tax). For example, looking at the UK system in 1978/9:

Taxable income	1,000
Corporation tax	520
	480
Dividends	480
Undistributed profit	0
Recipients' income	480·00
Tax credit (33/67)	236·42
'Grossed up' dividend	716·42

$$\frac{\text{Tax credit}}{\text{Corporation tax}} = \frac{236·42}{520·00} = 45·47\%$$

Full distribution has been chosen so that it is easy to see that '520' is the corporation tax that would be paid on the dividends 'grossed up' at the corporation tax rate. The level of distribution will not affect this percentage.

It can be seen that, with the credit at 33/67, the UK system satisfies the above requirements. However, as was mentioned earlier, there are strong administrative reasons for linking the imputation credit directly with the basic rate of income tax. The lowering of the rate of 30% for 1979/80 reduces the credit percentage to 39·56%, which falls below the Directive's guidelines.

Another requirement of the draft Directive is that the corporation tax and imputation credits should not be discriminatory between companies or shareholders in different member states (Article 4). For example, the tax credit should be available to all. Further, the costs of the tax credit should be borne eventually by the state of the distributing corporation, even though another state may

---

[17]D. Dosser, *British Taxation and the Common Market*, Charles Knight, London, 1973, ch. 1, 4 and 6; and R. Burke, 'Harmonisation of Corporation Tax' *Intertax*, June–July, 1979.

[18]Neumark Committee, *EEC Reports on Tax Harmonisation*, International Bureau of Fiscal Documentation, Amsterdam, 1963.

[19]A. J. van den Tempel, *Corporation Tax and Individual Income Tax in the EEC*, Brussels, 1970.

[20]EEC Commission, *Proposal for a Directive concerning the Harmonization of Systems of Company Taxation and of Withholding Taxes on Dividends*, COM(75) 392 final, Brussels, 1975.

[21]International Bureau of Fiscal Documentation, *European Taxation*, Vol. 16, Nos. 2,3,4, 1976, pp. 41–51.

[22]C. W. Nobes, 'EEC imputation systems of corporation tax', *Journal of Business Law*, July 1979.

Table B

EEC imputation systems in 1979

Country	Imputation Introduced	National Corporation Tax rate %	Tax credit as proportion of dividend	Tax credit as % of underlying CT
Belgium	1963	48	57·5	62·29
France	1965	50	50	50
UK	1973	52	42.9 (i.e. 30/70)	39·56
Ireland	1976	45	42·9 (i.e. 30/70)	52·38
W. Germany	1977	56 & 36	56.25	100
Denmark	1977	37	15	25·54
Italy	1977	25²	33.33	100

Source for columns 3 and 4: Sections E of *The Taxation of Private Investment Income*, International Bureau of Fiscal Documentaion.

Notes: 1 Withholding taxes have been ignored throughout.
2 There is also a deductible local income tax of 15% making a total of 36.25%.

lose income tax revenue initially. There is to be a clearing house arrangement for settling such claims.

There was a discussion above on the usefulness of ACT as a means of ensuring that imputation credits cannot be granted without the payment of underlying corporation tax by the distributing company. The draft Directive is concerned with this area, and Article 9 proposes a *précompte* (or compensatory tax) for distributions where there is insufficient taxed profit in the present or preceding *five* years.

Also, Articles 14 to 17 propose a withholding tax of 25% on dividends. This is designed to discourage tax evasion by arranging for deduction of tax at source. The tax can be treated as a credit by EEC shareholders. This presents a significant disadvantage to investors in third countries. It is hoped that this problem will be alleviated before the Directive is passed.

The draft Directive has been criticised on many grounds. The omission of a proposed treatment for capital gains is important. Unless their taxation is also harmonised, there will be much wasteful manoeuvring in order to create capital gains in favourable member States rather than *income* in any State or capital gains in unfavourable States. Another criticism is that other corporate taxes, like net worth, turnover and local taxes, must be included in the harmonisation. More generally, the different rules relating to the calculation of taxable income need attention if total effective tax burdens are to be harmonised. A further criticism is that some countries in the EEC are intrinsically less attractive to companies for economic, geographical and political reasons; and that these countries need advantageous corporate tax regimes if they are to encourage investment and

employment. Therefore, to harmonise taxation without altering these other factors might give rise to unpleasant regional side-effects.

The 'opinion' of the European Parliament[23] on the draft Directive has stressed the need to include the problem of different tax bases as well as tax systems. Partly as a result of this and partly because member states are not enthusiastic about changing their tax systems or losing flexibility, the 1975 draft Directive (and that of 1978 concerning the taxation of financial institutions)[24] have been delayed and may need considerable amendment.

Meanwhile, little notice seems to have been taken of the draft Directive. For example, the new German system goes outside the proposals in a number of ways.[25] It has two rates rather than a single rate, both of which are outside the proposed range. Also, the tax credit is outside the range. Indeed, as far as rates are concerned, Table B shows that three out of the seven EEC countries with imputation systems had corporation tax rates outside the proposed range in 1979, and five out of the seven had tax credits outside the proposed range. These five include three of the systems introduced after the draft was issued.

So, harmonisation will probably be a slow process, and it needs to advance on a wider front than at present proposed. However, the proposals should give an indication of the direction of future changes in corporate taxation in the EEC.

[23] *Official Journal*, 1979, C 140.
[24] EEC Commission, *Proposal for a Directive on the Application to Collective Investment Institutions* [of the 1975 draft Directive], COM(78) 340 final, Brussels.
[25] R. T. Bartlett, 'The harmonization of company taxation within the EEC', *Journal of Business Law*, July 1977.

Summary

Corporation tax systems may be divided into three types with respect to their approaches to the taxation of distributed income. Imputation and split-rate systems are both designed to mitigate the economic double taxation of dividends which is inherent in classical systems. The former two systems can be viewed as different expressions of the same system. This article is mainly concerned with imputation systems, particularly those of the UK, France, West Germany and Ireland. Of these, only the German involves the full imputation to the shareholders of the corporation tax paid by the company. The others, therefore, still entail some double taxation of distributed income for higher rate taxpayers. In the UK for the highest rate taxpayers, there is almost complete double taxation.

The UK system is the only one in the EEC to include a general ACT. It is also unusual in that the tax credit attached to dividends is linked to the basic rate of income tax and has been contrived to be the same size as the ACT.

The French have one of the oldest imputation systems. It involves a tax credit of half the underlying rate of corporation tax. Unlike the UK system, the French system entails less than full imputation for incorporated shareholders. There is a *précompte* to pay for the tax credit where no French corporation tax has been paid.

The recent West German imputation system has two rates of tax, and full imputation to shareholders. This completely removes the economic double taxation of dividends. There is a similar provision to the *précompte*.

The Meade Committee recommended a system that would tax both distributed and retained profits at the shareholders' marginal rates of income tax. There would be full imputation of corporation tax. In this way, retained profits would not be allowed to accumulate without bearing income tax, but no profits would suffer economic double taxation.

An important difference between the UK and continental imputation systems is that the former is approximately adjusted for the effects of inflation.

Proposals for harmonisation of corporate taxation within the EEC date back almost as far as its foundation. The most recent proposals are contained in a draft Directive of 1975, which has yet to be approved by the Council of Ministers. It proposes an imputation system with rates and tax credits within certain bands. However, there seems little prospect of immediate progress in this area. The four EEC imputation systems introduced since the draft have all gone against it in some way. Also, the major differences in the determination of taxable income mean that the draft Directive would not harmonise tax burdens even if it harmonised some aspects of tax systems.

Appendix

The restating of the UK imputation system to resemble a split-rate system

Taking the same corporation tax rate as that used to illustrate the imputation system in the second section of the paper, let us redesign the system to make it look like a split-rate system without ACT.

	Imputation System
Net profit before tax	10,000
less Corporation tax (52%)	5,200 (ACT = 660, MCT = 4540)
Distributable profits	4,800
Dividends (say)	1,340
Undistributed profits	3,460
Cash dividends received by shareholder	1,340
Tax credit imputed (33/67)	660
Income to be taxed	2,000
Tax at basic rate (33%)	660
Tax credit	660
Tax due	0
or	
Tax at higher rate (e.g. 50%)	1,000
Tax credit	660
Tax due	340

Net profit before tax	10,000	
For distribution	2,000 ————————————→ 2,000	
	8,000 tax deducted at	
	source (33%)	660
Tax at 52% on 8,000 = 4,160		
	net cash dividend	1,340
Tax at 19% on 2,000 = 380		
	4,540	
Undistributed profit	3,460	
Gross taxable dividend	2,000	
Tax at basic rate (33%)	660	
Tax deducted at source	660	
Tax due	0	
Or Tax at higher rate	1,000	
(e.g. 50%)		
Tax deducted at source	660	
Tax due	340	

Let us now postulate a split-rate system with a corporation tax rate of 52% on undistributed profit, and 19% on distributed profit. Basic rate income tax is deducted at source under this system. Note that real split-rate systems usually work in the way illustrated, that is with the tax on the distributed income being paid out of the more highly taxed income (see above).

Notice that, in each case, the total tax paid by the company to the Revenue is 5,200. Also, the timing of the payments will be the same. The 660 paid in the split-rate system will be equivalent to ACT. The 4,540 will be equivalent to Mainstream Corporation Tax. Also, the net income tax due is the same for both 'systems'.

More generally, let

C_r = nominal rate applicable to retained profit
C_d = nominal rate applicable to distributed profit
t = rate of tax credit as proportion of dividend
m = marginal rate of income tax paid by shareholders
b = basic rate of income tax
Y = taxable income
D = cash dividend

Imputation System: $(C_r = C_d)$, Corporation tax liability $(CTL) = C_r.Y$

(i) $ACT = D.\dfrac{b}{1-b}$

Tax credit $= Dt$

(ii) Total income tax paid later
$= m.D.(1 + t) - Dt$

(iii) $MCT = CTL - ACT = C_r.Y - D.\dfrac{b}{1-b}$

Split-Rate System: Gross dividend $= D.\dfrac{1}{1-b}$

(iii) Total corporation tax

$= C_r.\left(Y - D.\dfrac{1}{1-b}\right) + C_d.D.\dfrac{1}{1-b}$

(i) Total income tax deducted at source

$= D.\left(\dfrac{1}{1-b}\right).b = D.\dfrac{b}{1-b}$

(ii) Total income tax paid later

$= mD.\dfrac{1}{1-b} - D.\dfrac{b}{1-b}$

Now, let particular rates be chosen so that $C_r = C_d + b$. Also, let us set $t = \dfrac{b}{1-b}$ as in the UK. A little algebraical manipulation will prove that the payments made at the same time are the same under both systems, that is (i) is the same under both systems, (ii) is the same, etc.

TRANSFER PRICING

CHAPTER 27

Transfer pricing by multinational manufacturing firms*

Sanjaya Lall

I. *Introduction*

This paper deals with the determinants and implications of the pricing of intra-firm trade by manufacturing firms operating in different countries. Intra-firm trade is defined here as transactions involving international shipments of commodities (including capital, intermediate and finished goods, but excluding technology or services) between branches or affiliates under the control of one firm. Only firms in the manufacturing sector (called multinational enterprises, MNEs, for short) are considered: while similar issues of transfer-pricing have arisen in primary sectors, they seem to have been understood more clearly and dealt with in an explicitly bargaining framework.

In the manufacturing sector the problem of transfer-pricing has remained a curious blind spot in the rapidly growing academic literature on the MNE and its effects on trade and development. The two major studies on the balance-of-payments effects of overseas investment on the capital-exporting countries (Hufbauer and Adler, 1968, on the US, and Reddaway, 1967, on the UK) have not even recognised the problem, while a great deal of the theoretical discussion of MNEs (for example, in Kindleberger, 1969 and 1970, or Johnson, 1969) has barely noted the existence of intra-firm trade[2]—the implication being either that such trade is very similar in its economic effects to inter-firm trade (between unrelated parties), or that it is quantitatively insignificant. Even some of economists who have recognised that intra-firm trade creates problems (Dunning, 1972; Vernon, 1971; Brooke and Remmers, 1970) seem to have underestimated its full extent.

[1] I am grateful for comments to Max Corden, Eprime Eshag, Ken Mayhew, George Richardson, Frances Stewart and Paul Streeten, and for discussions to Avigdor Meroz. I would also like to thank the New York office of UNCTAD for letting me use some data obtained in the course of research conducted for them, and Constantine Vaitsos for his help in getting access to these data and for stimulating an initial interest in this subject.

[2] A major exception is Vaitsos (1970 and 1972), whose work has not unfortunately been widely available till now.

* This article is reprinted, with permission, from the *Oxford Bulletin of Economics and Statistics* (August, 1973) pp 173–195

The argument of this paper is that the determination of prices in intra-firm trade takes place according to considerations rather different from those in inter-firm trade (Part II), that intra-firm trade is not an insignificant proportion of trade by MNEs or world manufactured trade (Part III), and that it raises serious issues about the effects of MNEs on trade, welfare and national control (Part IV). The discussion is conducted with special reference to the less-developed countries which play host to MNEs, and some data from Colombia is adduced to illustrate the potential impact of transfer-pricing.

II. *Determinants of Transfer-Pricing*

The fact that a transaction involving a transfer or sale of goods takes place *within* a firm, regardless of whether or not the firm spans different countries, and the firm is free within broad limits[1] to assign whatever price it likes to those goods, means that the traditional theory of pricing in competitive, oligopolistic or monopolistic markets ceases to apply to the process of transfer-pricing. The essential difference is simply that in transactions on the open market or between unrelated firms, the buyers and sellers are trying to maximise their profits at *each other's expense*, while in an intra-firm transaction the price is merely an accounting device and the two parties are trying to maximise *joint profits*. It is possible that the accounting price may approximate the arm's length price of the goods (the price which would obtain in an open market, or in a transaction between unrelated parties), but certainly there is no presumption that this should be so: any other price is equally plausible, and the conditions mentioned below will determine whether the actual transfer price will deviate from the arm's length price.

Any discussion of the transfer-pricing problem has to assume that there exists a yardstick by which the effect of the price can be measured; there must, in other words, be an arm's length price, and the goods may be 'overpriced' if transfer prices are higher, and 'underpriced' if they are lower, than this price.[2] It is not necessary for there to be an open market price; from the firm's point of view all that is required is that it should know at what price (or within what range) it would be prepared to sell to unrelated concerns. When a good is overpriced, therefore, the firm transfers funds *via* the pricing channel from the buying to the selling units; declared profits are thus understated and overstated respectively in comparison with the situation where no intra-firm transactions take place. The converse happens with underpricing.

Let us start with the case where a parent MNE in country A has a wholly owned subsidiary in country B, the goods transferred have an open market price, there is no official check on the transfer-prices set (though such prices may be assumed to be always positive), the same transfer price is declared in both A and B, and there is no internal constraint on declaring profits or losses in either place.

[1] The limits are discussed below in section II b.
[2] The terms 'over' and 'under-invoicing' may also be used, but these are sometimes used to denote the invoicing of trade between unrelated parties who act in collusion to transfer funds across national boundaries (Bhagwati, 1964 and 1967; Winston, 1970), and we shall keep this distinction.

Let us say that transfer-prices are being 'used' (to transmit profits) when they do not correspond to open market or arm's length prices, and consider in turn the inducements to and constraints on the 'use' of transfer-pricing in this way.[1] The simplifying assumptions are relaxed in the following sections.

A preliminary point to note is that the profits actually made in each country of the MNE's operation, given by the market conditions and costs of production (including the cost to the firm of intra-firm transfers), are not in any way directly affected by the level of transfer prices set.[2] We shall proceed on assumption that each unit maximises its real profits in its centre of operations, just as if it were an independent firm, and that the determination of transfer prices rests only on the question of where and how the profits are to be declared.

II.a.   *Inducements to the Use of Transfer Prices*

If the parent firm in A and the subsidiary in B both made profits, effective tax rates on remissible profits (taking into account withholding taxes) were equal, there were no restrictions on remissions and no price controls on the output in either country, import duties did not exceed the effective tax rates, the exchange rate of the two currencies was stable, and there were no political or other pressures on the level of declared, present or future, profits, then there would be no inducement to use transfer prices deliberately to move profits from one country to another. If transfer prices did diverge from their open market level, it would be the result of chance or lack of contact with the market rather than a conscious policy on the part of the MNE, since the conditions have been so defined that it makes no difference over the short or long term where profits are declared.[3]

Clearly these conditions are extremely restrictive, and many of them do not apply to less-developed host economies in particular, inducing MNEs to use intra-firm transactions to move profits to centres which are better for profit declaration. The inducements to such transfer-pricing may be grouped under two broad headings: those which maximise the present value of the MNE's overall profits, and those which minimise present and future risk or uncertainty about the value of profits.

Maximise Present Profits

Bearing in mind that the MNE is concerned to maximise the value of profits of *all its operations taken together*, and abstracting for the moment from the

---

[1] I have refrained from using the term 'misuse', because there is a very fine distinction to be drawn between tax 'avoidance', which is by convention legal and acceptable, and tax 'evasion', which is not. Transfer-pricing may be regarded as avoidance by the firms, and evasion by the host governments, concerned. On the firms' attitudes, see Green and Duerr, 1968.

[2] This is intuitively obvious, but is established at greater length by Copithorne, 1971.

[3] Copithorne (1971) has argued that a 'national corporation with foreign operations', as opposed to a truly multinational corporation, would have the objective of miximising profits in A subject to some (arbitrary) profit target in B, and thus would use transfer prices to ship the rest to A even in these conditions. It is not clear why this should happen, since the amount of profits sent back to A would be the same whether or not transfer prices were used; some threat to profit declaration in B has to be introduced if the preference for declaring them in A is not to be completely irrational.

problems of risk minimisation, we can postulate a number of conditions in which transfer-pricing will be used.

i. *Loss in one centre of operations.*—It may be argued that when the MNE makes losses in one of the countries it operates in, it would be induced to remit profits to that country so as to minimise its overall tax burden. Vaitsos (1972) has tried to construct a theory of transfer-pricing on the grounds that MNEs make losses in their home countries (in our example, country A) because of heavy overhead and research expenditures there. The firm in A will therefore overprice its exports to B or underprice imports from it. The argument is, however, of limited applicability. Besides the question of whether MNEs in fact make losses on their domestic operations, the inducement will operate only if A's government does not allow losses to be carried forward into the future for tax purposes or if the firm expects the losses to continue beyond the period of tax offsets.[1] Similarly, if the firm in B is making a loss, the MNE may move funds there if losses cannot be carried forward *and* if they cannot be offset against the tax burden in A. As most countries allow losses to be carried forward (but not indefinitely) and some capital exporting countries (notably the US) do allow tax offsets against losses made by subsidiaries, the incidence of this sort of inducement is probably rather small.

ii. *Taxes, tariffs and subsidies.*—The best known inducement to the use of transfer-pricing is international differences in tax and tariff rates (Horst, 1971; Copithorne, 1971; Tugendhat, 1971; Brooke and Remmers, 1970); export subsidies may also be introduced as a factor affecting the calculation. If tax rates are higher in B than in A, and the parent MNE supplies imports to the subsidiary, it would pay the firm to overprice these transactions and move profits to A as long as the difference in effective tax rates exceeds the tariff in B on those imports. If tariffs are higher, it would pay to underprice the imports.[2] Similarly, if the subsidiary is exporting to the parent it would pay to underprice the transactions as long as the tax rate differential plus the saving in import duty in A exceeded the export subsidy in B. If trade is taking place in both directions, the MNE may underprice imports into B to avoid duties and underprice its exports to A to take advantage of export subsidies in B and lower taxes in A.[3] The extent

[1] It may be argued that the cost of interest on losses in A would induce firms to minimise them, even if tax-offsets were available. Whether or not an MNE decides to use its profits in B to reduce interest payments in A depends, however, on the alternative returns available to the use of that money. It is only if the firm cannot invest it in more profitable ways in B or elsewhere that it would prefer to reduce its interest liabilities in A.

[2] The case of 'underinvoicing' imports to avoid duty has been noted by Bhagwati (1964, 1967), and that of overinvoicing by Winston (1970). Independent importers have to buy foreign exchange on the black market to make up the difference, and the profit calculation, like the one MNEs have to make for tax differentials and tariffs, is based on a comparison of black market premiums and tariffs. If the primary aim of the trader is to accumulate foreign exchange abroad, however, tariffs may not prove a substantial deterrent to overinvoicing. This is identical to the case where there are quantitative restrictions on remissions by MNEs, and transfer-pricing is used to ship funds abroad regardless of the tariff burden.

[3] The argument would apply even if the MNE wanted to re-invest profits in B. As long as tax rates on re-invested profits are the same as on remitted dividends it would pay the MNE to use transfer prices to minimise the tax burden, and re-invest in B by openly sending in addition to equity capital from A. If, as is often the case, the taxes on remissions were higher than on re-investments, the calculation would have to take into account the need for dividends versus re-investments and the appropriate tax differentials. The general effect would be to reduce the inducement to use the pricing channel.

to which profits can be moved around freely depends, of course, on the volume of intra-firm trade, the structure of the firm and the vigilance of the relevant authorities, discussed later.

iii. *Multiple exchange rates.*—In some countries which have multiple exchange rates (for instance, Colombia before 1966), the rate applicable to profit remittances tends to be unfavourable relative to the one applicable to capital or intermediate goods imports, effectively imposing an additional tax on declared profit remittances.

iv. *Quantitative restrictions.*—Limits imposed on the remittance of profits create a very strong inducement to use the transfer-pricing mechanism, especially when other channels, such as royalties and management and technical fees to the parent firm, are also controlled. If the subsidiary is exceptionally profitable, and the MNE does not wish to re-invest the profits in B, it may remit them by overpricing imports into B *regardless of the extra tariff cost*, since any gain in profits abroad would be a net benefit. Furthermore, if the amount of permissible dividends were calculated as a percentage of the MNE's net worth (equity plus re-investments),[1] the firm would be induced to overprice its initial equity contribution which took the form of capital equipment to inflate the capital base.

v. *Existence of local shareholders.*—The existence of local shareholders in the subsidiary in B may induce the MNE to overprice its imports into B for three reasons: first, to increase its own share of the total profits at the cost of the local shareholders; second, to inflate the initial value of capital equipment contributed by way of equity participation; and, third, to act in collusion with the local partners in order to provide funds for accumulation abroad or for resale in the black market.[2]

vi. *Exchange rate speculation.*—If the exchange rate of either A or B is expected to change and the MNE cannot or will not speculate openly, it may use transfer prices to reinforce the normal leads and lags which minimise its obligations in the devaluing currency. The profitability of such speculation would depend on the amount of devaluation expected and the cost of using transfer prices in terms of additional taxes and tariffs. There is a distinction to be drawn between active speculation for gain (as postulated here), which is basically short-term and liable to be reversed after the rates have been readjusted (or the crisis averted), and long-term hedging against a basically weak currency (mentioned below). The former is likely to be used by MNEs in developed countries (Brooke and Remmers, 1970 and 1972) in periods of exchange crises, while the latter is likely to occur in developing countries, particularly those with inflation.

[1] The limit in Colombia and other Andean Pact countries, for instance, is 14 per cent of net worth per annum, and includes re-invested profits which may be considered additions to foreign net worth. Excess profits may be held over for a less profitable future year, but not be remitted or added to net worth in that year.

[2] The temptation for such collusion would be particularly strong in countries where the government laid down strict requirements for local equity participation, which were fulfilled by the MNE selling shares to locals who were affluent nominees (traders, landowners, officials) rather than industrialists in their own right. While many leading MNEs may claim to be above this sort of behaviour, there is nothing unusual or surprising about it—the case of under or overinvoiced trade (*loc. cit.*) involves similar collusion between the local and foreign trading partners.

The long-term profitability of an MNE is subject to various pressures in the different areas it operates in, and the judicious use of transfer-pricing to show low levels of profits may well contribute to insuring its future earning, or even its existence, against all sorts of threats.

i. *Balance-of-payments and exchange rate pressures.*—Some countries may be deemed bad risks because of the threat of impending restrictions on remittances, periodic devaluations, and the like, and the MNE may adopt a long-term strategy of moving profits out *via* transfer-pricing.

ii. *Political and social pressures.*—These may range from trade union pressures for a larger share of declared profits to government threats to nationalisation because of 'exploitation'. In fact, any host country which tries to control or limit the activities of MNEs may be considered a more or less undesirable area to declare high profits in, and for long-term safety, regardless of tax-tariff or other short-term factors, the transfer-pricing mechanism may be used to send profits abroad. Expectation of individual firms are likely to differ considerably as far as this is concerned, however, and the built-in deterrent that the discovery of such a policy would itself exacerbate the situation may induce firms not to over-indulge. Nevertheless, the environment of a particular host country in the eyes of the MNE may well be one of the most important factors influencing the long-term use of the transfer-pricing channel; the inbuilt secrecy is ideal in situations where there are long-term threats to its operations arising from its profitability.

iii. *Direct threats to profits.*—The declaration of high profits may cause a number of reactions which directly reduce the MNE's profitability. First, the government may, where appropriate, lower the level of *protection* on the firm's final output. If the level of protection is determined by the government on the basis of the firm's cost of production plus some reasonable allowance for profit, the MNE can easily raise the protection, and its profits, by inflating its costs by overpricing intra-firm imports. The existence of such an instrument in the hands of the MNE gives it a strong weapon when bargaining for concessions with host governments, one which they may not even be aware of.

Second, a similar case arises when governments impose *price controls* on products manufactured by MNEs (pharmaceuticals is the most common example) the level at which prices are fixed being determined again by the costs of production. This happens most often when protection is granted by the banning of imports rather than by tariffs, and domestic prices are sought to be kept in check by direct means. There is evidence that overpricing of imports has been caused by this factor in India (Bhagwati, 1967) and Colombia (see below).

Third, the danger of increased *competition*, from other MNEs or local manufacturers, attracted by high declared profits, may also cause transfer-pricing to be used in exceptionally profitable countries (Vaitsos, 1970). A similar danger is that the host government may insist on profitable foreign enterprises *selling shares* to local investors, reducing both the rewards earned by the MNE as well as its control over the operation. If the process of gradual nationalisation has already started, high profits may speed it up. The government may also decide to take a larger share of the profits for itself by raising the level of *taxation* or imposing *special levies* on the firm.

These are the various inducements to the use of transfer-pricing by MNEs to transmit profits clandestinely from one country to another. Although there is no necessary presumption that the mechanism would be operated to the detriment of countries other than the home-country of the MNE, or of less-developed host countries generally—given exchange-rate instability, tax differentials, trade union pressures, and so on, it may well be worked against the home country[1]—the cards are in fact stacked heavily against the less-developed economies. Not only do their tax rates tend to be higher, their import duties on intermediate inputs relatively low, their balances-of-payments often in crisis, and quantitative restrictions often in force, but their political, social and economic environment also tends to be inimical to the free operation and expansion of MNEs. With a few exceptions, their governments try to limit and control MNE activities, to enlarge local shareholding in them, to lower their profits and ultimately even to get rid of them. It is difficult to imagine circumstances in which an MNE would want to ship profits *to* such countries (barring the few countries which are tax havens). In order to ensure that transfer-pricing was not used against it, a host economy would therefore have to conform politically and economically to many of the norms of the developed world—not an aim which most poor countries subscribe to, and certainly not one which should be demanded as a condition for increasing the activities of MNEs.

While many of the inducements to transfer-pricing have been noticed, most writers have assumed that the mechanism is not very much 'misused'. They have perhaps been impressed by limitations on its unrestricted use, mostly on the basis of evidence given by the firms themselves; some restrictions undoubtedly do exist, and we now examine what they are and how strictly they operate.

II.b.   *Limits to the Use of Transfer Prices*

There are in general two types of limits to the extent that transfer prices can be moved freely round to suit the overall objectives of the MNE, set, first, by the firms themselves (which we may term internal), and, second, by the authorities (external).

Internal Limits

The cohesion, adaptability and structure of the MNE may themselves impose certain constraints on the use of transfer prices. It may be noted that the 'motivation' of the firm, in the sense of whether it wants to maximise its dividends at the expense of growth or *vice versa*, or of whether it wants to maximise its

---

[1] It is important to note that the country which has taken most official action to control the use of transfer-pricing is the United States—the home of the largest MNEs—under section 482 of its Internal Revenue Code. The MNEs have reacted strongly against such interference, implying that the mechanism *is* valuable to them. See Keegan, 1969; Greene and Duerr, 1968; Duerr, 1972. Such action by capital exporting countries to raise their 'fair' share of taxes implies, of course, that less-developed host countries have even less chance of gaining fortuitously from transfer-pricing.

stock market valuation or some other objective of the management, is irrelevant to the question of transfer-pricing, which simply aims to *minimise taxes on and threats to profits which have already been earned, regardless of whether they are paid out in dividends or re-invested.*[1] A 'rational' use of transfer prices by an MNE is therefore compatible with different objectives concerning growth, dividends or even philanthropy.

While an MNE with local equity participation faces obvious internal checks to the use of transfer prices (subject to qualifications mentioned elsewhere) even an MNE with no local equity participation may face internal constraints at any of the following stages in the manipulation of transfer prices:

i the realisation at the level of the subsidiary's management that what is to be maximised is the profit of the MNE as a whole, perhaps at a cost to the subsidiary;

ii the communication of requisite knowledge (on taxes, tariffs, controls, policy) from subsidiary to parent;

iii the capacity in the parent firm to process the vast quantity of information on different subsidiaries and to arrive at a determinate set of transfer prices;

iv the capacity to implement the transfer prices, in terms of persuading the appropriate subsidiaries to put up with showing losses or low profits.

These constraints boil down to two: the degree of integration and central control in the MNE, and the psychological effects of requiring subsidiaries to conform to the profit declaration targets. As far as the first is concerned, it would appear that transfer-pricing can be used most effectively by very large corporations with tightly exercised central control, sophisticated computational facilities and a wide experience of world conditions and of dealing with governments, and not by investors with limited overseas operations and a great deal of autonomy between different units. The evolving structure of management in the largest firms has in fact tended to increasing rather than decreasing control from the centre (Williamson, 1971; Wells, 1971), with the crucial decisions regarding investment, pricing and research kept to the head office and minor production decisions delegated to individual units.[2] Moreover, as the great bulk of intra-firm trade is concentrated in the largest MNEs (see next section), the purely organisational constraint applicable to small firms cannot be very important from a quantitative point of view.

Firms make a great deal of the psychological constraint. One of their main arguments for retaining flexible transfer-pricing is to enable new subsidiaries to break into markets without showing large losses; some firms seem to operate on the concept of 'profit centres', with each centre required to show its true profit-

---

[1] This argument would have to be modified if the countries concerned did not have double-tax agreements. Thus, if the parent firm wanted to declare dividends in A, but taxes were lower in B, it would be useless to transfer profits to B via intra-firm trade, declare them there and bring them back to A, since A's government would levy additional tax to bring the overall tax up to its own level. To this extent, motivation would counteract the natural inducement to use transfer prices.

[2] The lack of freedom of subsidiaries in determining transfer prices is noted in a Ph.D. thesis by J. Shulman, quoted in Tugendhat (1971), chapter 10.

ability for the sake of morale as well as more effective control from the centre. It is difficult to take these arguments very seriously.[1] They revolve round the assumption that a local manager takes his performance as reported to the tax authorities or to local shareholders more seriously than his performance as judged by the parent firm. After all, his financial rewards come from the latter, and his loyalties may safely be presumed to lie more with his firm than with his tax authority. All that is required is that the MNE keep two sets of accounts, one showing 'real' profits and the other taxable profits; keeping two account books is one of the oldest business practices in the world and certainly not beyond the capacity of MNEs.

We have assumed till now that the firm knows the 'right' prices for all commodities involved in intra-firm trade, and is able to work the pricing mechanism with precision to achieve its objectives. In fact a large number of such commodities do not have a free-market reference price at all, because they are not traded on open markets or because they are the monopoly of the firm concerned and subject to discriminatory pricing in different markets. It is, moreover, very difficult in many such cases to assign a correct arm's length price due to the existence of joint overhead (especially R and D) costs, and any particular price used by the firms, or assigned by a host government, may be criticised for being arbitrary. This does not reduce the usefulness of the transfer-pricing mechanism: on the contrary, it makes it easier for the MNE to maximise its overall profit without having to keep double sets of accounts, while rendering it more difficult for host governments to calculate costs and profits for individual subsidiaries.[2] Let us now consider the problems faced by the authorities in checking the use of transfer prices.

External Limits

There are two sets of authorities in the countries of MNE operations which are immediately concerned with transfer prices: the customs and the tax authorities. The former are chiefly concerned to see that shipments are not obviously underpriced, so that they receive a fair amount of tariff revenue. They are not particularly well-equipped to check in a routine manner whether the prices charged are correct or not; the task of checking transfer prices is a complex and difficult one, and requires specialised technical knowledge over a broad range of commodities. Customs officials may get suspicious if prices are changed very often and in large amount, but the Colombian experience shows that individual items may be marked at 3,000 per cent above prices charged in world markets or by other firms and escape routine notice (Vaitsos, 1970), while the Roche Products case in the UK shows that a highly developed country is equally

[1] The recent investigation of Hoffman-La Roche, the Swiss pharmaceutical firm, by the British Monopolies Commission (1973) reveals an absolutely unconstrained use of transfer prices. In the company's own words, transfer prices are determined by 'what is reasonable for tax purposes' (para. 138).
[2] On the problems faced by the US tax authorities in assigning correct transfer prices, and the various rules-of-thumb used, see Keegan (1969) and Duerr (1972). See also the Monopolies Commission (1973) reports on similar problems for Roche Products in the UK.

vulnerable. Though many countries do question customs valuations of firms, the procedure is unsystematic, arbitrary and inadequate.[1]

Tax authorities face similar difficulties. They do not, with the exception of the US, normally enquire into transfer prices directly, and, like customs officials, are not equipped to do so. They may question a firm which is declaring 'too little' profits, and even assign an arbitrarily higher figure, but this is hardly an effective check to a clever manipulation of prices and profits. Such procedures may also be unfair to firms which are making genuine losses, and while permitting firms which show reasonable profits to remit large sums undetected.

While it is very likely that the day-to-day workings of the tax-customs administration will not show up any but the most blatant or careless use of transfer prices, even closer direct checks such as those exercised by the US tax authorities, and the relatively isolated ones by other governments, are fraught with difficulties. We have mentioned above that it is inherently problematical to assign arm's length prices to goods with joint costs which are not traded openly: there are no easy reference prices and marginal cost pricing will not be accepted as 'fair' where heavy R and D expenditures are involved. Many commodities in intrafirm trade do not fall into this category, but for those which do the host governments must negotiate a fair rate of profit with the MNEs concerned after taking into account all the direct and indirect costs of production. As long as some such task is not undertaken, however, and transfer prices are left to the discretion of the MNEs, it is clear that the latter will have the upper hand and deliberately use the mechanism to their own advantage.

III. *Evidence on Intra-Firm Trade and Transfer-Pricing*

As most countries do not collect data on intra-firm trade as distinct from inter-firm trade, and transfer prices are rarely checked, we have to rely for evidence on some surveys carried out in the USA and the UK for the former and on an investigation by the Colombian government for the latter.

III.a. *US and UK Intra-Firm Trade*

The US Government's Department of Commerce has conducted surveys and published figures on intra-firm trade by a sample of US-owned MNEs. The figures cover the period 1962 to 1970,[2] though the years 1967–69 are missing; details are given in the Appendix, which cites the sources and defines the samples and terms used. The Department of Commerce also carried out a comprehensive survey of *all* US firms with foreign investments for the year 1966, the so-called 'benchmark' survey, which enables us to judge the size of the sample coverage in that year; the benchmark-survey figures are also shown in the Appendix. Unfortunately, I was unable to get a copy of the original benchmark survey and had to rely on secondary sources (Foster, 1972).

---

[1] It is possible that intra-firm trade in finished goods is easier to check, and thus less subjected to misuse, than trade in intermediate and capital goods. However, we have no evidence on this.

[2] There are no data on infra-firm trade before 1962.

The following points must be noted about the US data:

i. There is no evidence on the amount of US trade accounted for by non-US MNEs; private direct manufacturing investment in the US by foreigners is quite substantial, and came to $3.0 billion in 1963, rising to over $5.3 billion in 1969 (over 18 per cent of US manufacturing investment abroad).

ii. The definition of 'affiliated firms' was changed for the 1966–70 sample, with the requirement raised from 25 per cent US shareholding to 51 per cent US shareholding.

iii. The 1962–64 figures were for a sample (256 MNEs and 25,000 affiliates) extrapolated to represent total MNE trade; later years were not adjusted in this way.

iv. The 1965 sample included 271 manufacturing firms of which 257 reported exports (1,869 affiliates); the 1966–70 sample covered 223 firms and 3,752 majority-owned affiliates.

v. Earnings (dividends, interest, royalties and fees) figures for sample firms were not given, so that the tables show earnings of all US foreign manufacturing investment.

The data are thus neither complete nor fully comparable between different years. Despite this, the facts that emerge about the magnitude of intra-firm trade are extremely interesting, and we may make some very rough adjustments to see the overall impact of such trade. Table I shows various relationships derived from the Appendix table.

Intra-firm exports of sample firms rose from 18 per cent of US manufactured exports in 1962 to 24 per cent in 1970; if we inflate the 1970 figure by the same extent that the 1966 benchmark figure exceeds the 1966 survey figure, we get a ratio of 35 per cent. If we add another 6 per cent non-US MNE's (18 per cent on the basis of book-value of investments) we get a figure of over 40 per cent. Similarly, for intra-firm imports we arrive at a final figure of over 25 per cent, and for total affiliate trade as a percentage of total US manufactured trade we get approximately 34 per cent. In other words, about *one-third of total US trade*

TABLE I

United States: Intra-Firm Manufacturing Trade by US MNEs 1962–70
(percentages)

	Sample Data						1966 Benchmark Survey	1970 Blown-up (1966 basis)
	1962	1963	1964	1965	1966	1970		
	(1)	(2)	(3)	(4)	(5)	(6)	(7)	(8)
Exports to Affiliates/Total US manufactured Exports	17.9	19.7	20.3	22.5	21.1	23.5	31.6	35.1
Imports from Aff./Total US manufactured Imports	14.4	15.5	18.5	15.9	14.5	15.6	20.1*	21.6*
Total Aff. Trade/Total US manufactured Trade	16.6	18.2	19.7	19.9	18.3	19.8	26.7*	28.8*
Dividends and Interest/ Total Aff. Trade	20.0	15.5	17.4	18.5	17.5	16.6	12.0*	11.4*
Dividends and Interest + Royalties and Fees/Total Aff. Trade	28.2	24.3	26.7	27.9	27.1	25.5	18.5*	17.5*

* Based on approximate figure for affiliated imports for 1966 benchmark survey.

in manufactured trade was intra-firm in 1970, and the general trend seemed to rise over time.

The value of declared earnings on foreign manufacturing investment was far exceeded by the value of intra-firm trade, and a mere 12 per cent change in transfer prices in 1970 would have equalled the entire dividends and interest earned abroad. If we included royalties and management fees, an 18 per cent change in prices would (ignoring tax-tariff problems) suffice to exceed the total sum of earnings abroad.

Intra-firm exports in the samples grew by 178 per cent (total US manufactured exports by 112 per cent), imports by 261 per cent (234 per cent), and total trade by 204 per cent (155 per cent) during 1962–70. At the same time, the book value of US manufacturing investments grew by 144 per cent, and dividends and interest by 151 per cent. In absolute sums, the value of total affiliate trade for the 1970 sample came to $11 billion, and to approximately $16 billion on a blown-up basis.

The 1965 sample survey reveals a *very high degree of concentration* between the 251 manufacturing firms in terms of their intra-firm exports: 18 parent firms (7 per cent) accounted for 65 per cent of the exports,while at the other end 150 firms (60 per cent) accounted for only 6 per cent.[1] It is very likely, though evidence is not at hand to prove it, that the degree of concentration has increased over time with the increasing importance of large MNEs (Wells, 1971). In any case, if about 50 US MNEs and a similar number of non-US MNEs controlled between them all but a minor proportion of world intra-firm trade, these 100 or so firms would be the ones controlling not only an immense quantity of resources but also the means to move its rewards around practically at will.

Let us consider the UK data, which cover only 1966 but include both British and foreign MNEs.[2] A survey of 1,466 manufacturing firms showed that of their total exports of £3,360 million, exports to 'related' firms accounted for £1,030 million, or 30 per cent. Total British manufactured exports for 1966 came to £4,272 million; thus intra-firm exports came to 24 per cent of the total.[3]

The intra-firm exports of US owned firms in the sample accounted for a much higher proportion of their total exports (56 per cent) than of non-US foreign firms (37 per cent) or British firms (27 per cent). The point frequently made that US affiliates in the UK export a larger proportion of their output than British firms should be accompanied by the point that a far higher proportion of such exports are within those firms themselves.

There are no figures available for the amount of intra-firm imports into the UK, but the picture shown by exports seems rather similar to that of the US.

---

[1] Bradshaw, 1969. The industrial composition of US intra-firm trade also reflects the pattern of MNE investment, with the sectors having over 50 per cent of their exports going to affiliates being the ones with most rapid expansion of MNEs, e.g. pharmaceuticals, rubber, transport equipment, non-electrical machinery, office equipment. Traditional industries (like food, paper, metal products) have a relatively small incidence of intra-firm exports from the US.

[2] *Board of Trade Journal*, 1968.

[3] Unfortunately, there are no figures available for the earnings of the sample firms, or even of UK manufacturing investments abroad as distinct from total overseas investments.

The degree of concentration in the UK is even higher than that of the US: 32 (less than 2 per cent) of the firms account for 52 per cent of intra-firm exports, while the last 1,499 (76 per cent) account only for 6 per cent.

It may plausibly be argued that the pattern of intra-firm trade as shown in these two countries is roughly representative of the pattern among the developed countries as a whole. Thus, a quarter to a third of their trade in manufactured products takes place within MNEs: the exact figure does not matter for present purposes, but it is clear that the magnitudes involved are vast, and cannot continue to be disregarded as they have been in the literature.

As far as less developed countries are concerned, there are no figures on the extent of intra-firm trade. It is probably much more important for their imports than for their exports; the bulk of manufacturing investment in these areas, especially by MNEs, is heavily dependent on imported components, and to a large extent these imports are from related firms. Given that many developing countries control the foreign sector, however, it is likely that the incidence of MNE trade is smaller as a percentage of their total imports of manufactures than in developed countries. Similarly, MNE exports are a relatively new phenomenon, and, though expanding rapidly (Helleiner, 1973), still account for a small portion of total manufactured exports.

This is not, however, to argue that such trade is insignificant and its implications inconsequential for less-developed countries. The absolute magnitude of intra-firm trade may still be very large, and the implications of transfer-pricing far more serious, than for the developed world, first because there are many more reasons why this mechanism should be operated against the interests of less-developed countries, and, second, because they can afford far less to lose resources (in foreign exchange) in this way. We shall return to the implications of transfer-pricing in section IV; let us first look at the evidence from Colombia.

III.b. *Transfer-Pricing in Colombia*

The evidence on the use of transfer-pricing in Colomba is especially valuable because of the extreme scarcity of information on this practice in almost all the countries in which MNEs operate. Without such evidence arguments about the dangers of transfer-pricing could simply be dismissed as unfounded or propogandist;[1] even the selective and limited investigations as conducted by the Colombian government provide some proof of its potentialities.

After the Colombian government passed Decree 444 in 1967, imposing various exchange controls and restrictions on the flows of exchange by foreign investors, an examination of the transfer-pricing mechanism was undertaken in the belief that it was pointless to control dividends and royalties when such a wide channel as intra-firm trade was left open. The main sector studied was *pharmaceuticals*, the industry with the largest number of foreign firms in the country: the rubber, chemical and electrical industries were also investigated,

---

[1] Perhaps some indirect support for our case could be adduced from the evidence on tied aid, which is believed to raise the cost of imports by 20 per cent to the aid recipients (Pearson Commission, 1969). Since intra-firm trade is simply an extreme form of tying of purchases, it is easy to imagine how much more prices can be pushed up.

but much less intensively. The research, carried out for 1968 by the Planning Office (Planeación) and for 1967–70 by the Import Control Board (INCOMEX), employed qualified chemists and technicians, and compared the prices actually charged on imports with prices paid for comparable commodities by locally owned firms, by other Latin American countries, and in world markets generally. The objective was to discover the extent of overpricing,[1] and to reduce its incidence by legal action, including the imposition of heavy fines.

In arriving at the world market price, the investigators took the average of available quotations rather than the lowest one, and allowed for transportation costs and a 20 per cent margin for error. Thus, the calculations were, if anything, unduly generous to the foreign firms. Planeación discovered a weighted average of over-pricing for a wide range of pharmaceutical imports of 155 per cent (for 1968)[2] and INCOMEX of 87 per cent (for 1967–70), the difference in findings being accounted for by differences in coverage over time and products, with the latter being more comprehensive. The savings achieved by the government's action came to US $3.3 million annually in the pharmaceutical sector, out of a total import bill of $15 million.

It was also found that some rubber imports had been overpriced by 44 per cent, some chemical imports by 25 per cent and electrical components by 54 per cent. Moreover, studies on transfer-pricing undertaken in other neighbouring countries, especially Chile, showed that the pattern was similar (UNCTAD, 1971). The scope of the investigations was more limited, but the tenor of the results was unmistakable. It is clear that unless the mechanism were attacked directly, there are few inbuilt constraints, of the nature discussed previously, to its use.

It may be of interest to consider the evidence for 14 foreign firms in Colombia in rather more detail; these firms are part of a sample studied by the present author in the course of research conducted for UNCTAD. Using the evidence uncovered by Planeación and INCOMEX, and combining it with balance-sheet figures for these firms (which must, of course, remain anonymous), we can see the effect that overpricing has had on their profitability (Table 2). The figures pertain to the period before the government's legal action against overpricing took effect. There are 11 pharmaceutical, 1 rubber and 2 electrical firms, and the period covered is 1966–70, and the figures express averages for these years. There are 12 wholly foreign-owned firms (marked A) and 2 foreign majority-owned firms (marked B).

Column 2 shows that the weighted average of overpricing ranged from 33 per cent to over 300 per cent for the imports investigated in the pharmaceutical sector, and from 24 per cent to 81 per cent in the other sectors. The difference made to profitability from proved overpricing (column 4) ranges from 2 per cent to 112 per cent of net worth in the former, and from 0.3 per cent to 6 per cent in

---

[1] Overpricing is defined as $(P_c - P_w)/P_w \times 100$, where P_c stands for the price actually paid in Colombia and P_w the comparable world market price. For details of the findings see Vaitsos (1970) and DANE (1971).

[2] Overpricing on individual products was sometimes as high as 3000 per cent (Vaitsos, 1970). When brought to court, the firms were unable to justify the prices charged (*El Tiempo*, 1971).

TABLE 2

Overpricing by and Profitability of 14 Foreign Firms in Colombia (1966–70)

Industries and Firms	(1) % Imports Investigated	(2) % Proved Overpricing	(3) Declared Profits as % net Worth	(4) Profits on Proved Over-pricing as % Net Worth	(5) Profits on Overpricing % N.W. (Imputed)	(6) (3) + (5)
Pharmaceutical						
1 (A)	52.1	158.3	7.6	41.5	79.6	87.2
2 (B)	20.1	39.5	11.2	2.0	10.0	21.2
3 (A)	100.0	56.6	16.5	19.6	19.6	36.1
4 (A)	28.1	81.0	6.3	5.6	19.9	26.2
5 (A)	32.4	288.9	6.3	19.2	59.3	65.6
6 (A)	39.1	33.5	0.1	2.5	63.9	64.0
7 (A)	35.2	33.7	12.4	3.1	8.8	21.2
8 (A)	54.1	95.4	−7.4	17.9	33.1	26.1
9 (A)	48.6	83.7	42.8	111.7	229.8	272.6
10 (A)	44.2	313.8	27.5	39.6	89.6	117.1
11 (A)	30.9	138.9	5.9	9.9	32.0	37.9
Rubber						
12 (B)	60.0	40.0	8.3	6.1	10.2	**18.5**
Electrical						
13 (A)	22.3	24.1	8.1	0.3	1.3	9.4
14 (A)	30.4	81.1	0.7	1.8	5.9	6.6

Notes: 1. (A) indicates that the firm is wholly foreign owned, and (B) that foreign investors hold 51–99 per cent of the equity.

2. Per cent of overpricing is defined as in footnote above, and is for the weighted average of all imports investigated (shown in column 1).

3. Declared profits comprises after-tax profits net of depreciation and interest. Minus shows loss.

4. Net worth calculated in terms of constant US dollars.

5. Column (4) shows profits from proved, and column (5) from imputed, overpricing.

the latter, industries; such profits exceed the value of declared profits for 9 of the 14 firms. If we impute the proved level of overpricing to total imports of the firms, including the imports not investigated, we find that profits on overpricing rise substantially in pharmaceuticals, but not so dramatically in the other industries. Imputed overpricing profits exceed declared profits for 11 of the 14 firms.[1]

It is impossible to generalise from a sample of such a small size and with such variability. Clearly, different foreign firms have different attitudes to transfer-pricing as opposed to declaring profits openly. The inducements to use transfer-pricing in Colombia are obvious enough: there are quantitative limits on profit remittances abroad as well as price controls on pharmaceutical and rubber products; duties on imports of intermediate products are quite low, especially in pharmaceuticals (a nominal 1–2 per cent); there is considerable suspicion of foreign enterprise and restriction on their activities; and some of the foreign firms are exceptionally profitable. Colombia seems to have been almost a laboratory case for the exercise of transfer-pricing. Many other less-developed

[1] In this context, it is interesting to note the Monopolies Commission (1973) findings on Roche Products that profits from transfer-pricing accounted for 76 per cent of total profits in 1966–72, and came to over six times the amount of declared profits (Para. 164). The calculation of arm's length prices of the two relevant products made ample allowance for overhead and R and D costs; the extent of overpricing came to 123 per cent for Librium and 161 per cent for Valium in 1970.

host countries are in a similar situation, but have not started to react to it effectively.

To reiterate the main points of this section: first, intra-firm trade in manufactures today accounts for a substantial part of world trade, and will account for a larger proportion in the future if MNEs continue to grow; second, such trade is highly concentrated within a relatively few MNEs which also control an immense quantity of world resources and production; third, the declared earnings of MNEs are very much smaller than the value of intra-firm trade, so that a relatively minor change in transfer prices can cause a very large change in MNE's profitability; and, fourth, the available evidence indicates that transfer-pricing *is* deliberately used to transfer profits from less desirable to more desirable areas, and the existing inbuilt constraints to its use are ineffective. Let us now consider some of the implications of this situation.

IV   *Implications of Transfer-Pricing*

This section is divided into three parts, dealing with the implications of transfer-pricing for trade theory, for the welfare of host economies and for government policy.

IV.a.   *Transfer-Pricing and Trade Theory*

The size and growth of international investment in the modern world has important effects on the determination of trade patterns, both in the traditional Hecksher-Ohlin framework (by altering relative factor endowments) as well as in the more recent technological/oligopolistic theories of comparative advantage (by transmitting technology, changing skills and tastes, extending product differentiation, using various market imperfections and economies of scale).[1] In fact, many of these new theories, of which the product cycle model is a good example, use the MNE as a central agent of dynamic comparative advantage (Johnson, 1969). Moreover, the proponents of the free flow of capital see the MNE ushering in a new era of world-wide efficiency in the allocation of resources and even an international equalisation of factor prices (Kindleberger, 1969).

The assumption implicit in all such reasoning, and its accompanying recommendations for policy, is that trade controlled by MNEs is governed by the same principles of valuation as other forms of trade. Thus, the value of intra-firm trade is taken to be determined by the same factors as inter-firm trade, and the gains arising from the former are assumed to accrue to the various trading countries in the same way as from the latter. If our argument about intra-firm trade and transfer-pricing has any validity, however, it is clear that this sort of assumption is not tenable. In fact, a strong attack may be mounted on both the positive and normative aspects of trade theory for that part of trade which is intra-firm.

As far as its *positive aspects* are concerned, the existence of transfer-pricing introduces a divergence between the explanation of the *quantities* of goods involved in intrafirm trade as distinct from their stated *values*, and thus renders

[1] For a summary and preliminary empirical testing of various theories, see Hufbauer, 1970.

the existing comparative cost doctrines, of both the traditional Hecksher-Ohlin and the modern technological/oligopolistic types, all of which are couched in terms of market values of trade, inapplicable to such trade. The quantities of goods in intra-firm trade may well be determined on considerations of comparative cost, at least from the MNE's point of view, but the values stated may be quite different from those in open-market conditions. Since positive trade theory seeks to explain stated values, however, and assumes some sort of competitive market framework to establish a determinate relationship between market prices and quantities, it cannot hope to explain trade which takes place essentially outside any market.

It is true that in quantitative terms the validity of the comparative cost doctrine remains unimpaired. Its empirical testing, however, becomes practically impossible for intra-firm trade, and undoubtedly the theory loses a great deal of its interest and significance by being unable to deal with its valuation. What is needed now is for economists to construct an adjunct to traditional theories of trade to encompass intra-firm trade. This would attempt to assess the 'trade creating' and 'trade diverting' effects of transfer-pricing, to stipulate when and how a country becomes a favourable place for profit declaration and thus enjoys a relatively stronger current visible trade account, and to investigate whether commodities specialised in by MNEs (say, those which are technologically advanced or heavily differentiated) are more prone to intra-firm rather than inter-firm trade over time. It may also be worth discovering whether MNEs try to protect or expand intra-firm trade more between countries which differ considerably, as opposed to those which are similar, in their relative attractiveness as centres for profit declaration; and, more basically, to know how MNEs judge such attractiveness, and how individual assessments differ. Certainly, existing trade theory needs new direction if it is to be fully relevant.

The implications for the *normative aspects* of trade theory may be considered more serious. Most economists recommend more and freer trade in the implicit belief that all the trading partners receive due benefits from such trade when their goods are sold in world markets. Clearly, the potential benefits of trade are considerably diminished if the traded products are not priced in competitive markets, but valued in such a way that one factor of production, foreign capital, is able to deprive a country of part of its due share and remit it abroad. Intra-firm trade makes it quite likely that *the benefits of trading are distributed haphazardly between trading partners*, with some countries (the home bases of MNEs in particular) gaining at the expense of others (especially the developing host countries) in such trade.

Furthermore, it may be argued that when the use of transfer-pricing enables the MNE to extract more protection from the government, the host economy is not only deprived of its share in 'fair' profits (including allowances for risk and oligopoly), but the profits made are themselves too high. If the MNE is a dynamic agent of comparative advantage, therefore, it also has the power to extract a high price for its services, to conceal this price and to send its rewards to places of its own choosing.

If a host country cannot be sure of capturing a fair share of the benefits from the resources used by foreign investors, and from the induced changes in patterns of trade and production, the conventional arguments about welfare gains from foreign investment need considerable modification. Regardless of whether the MNE has been induced to invest for defensive purposes in protected and in-efficient facilities or has come in for reasons of efficient resource allocation, *the use of transfer-pricing means that the net gains from foreign investment are less, or losses more, than they otherwise would have been.*

The loss caused by transfer-pricing may be borne by various groups in the host economy: the government (loss of taxes), local shareholders (loss of legiti-mate share of profits), trade unions (if it deprives them of higher wages), con-sumers (from higher prices, if it enables firms to get more protection), and even other producers (if by worsening the foreign exchange situation it causes a shortage of maintenance imports).[1] This is only the immediate impact. Over the long run, it deprives the economy of the benefits of investment foregone, and may distort the pattern of investment (or worsen the existing distortions) by raising levels of real effective protection. At the same time, if the low level of declared profits deters prospective local competitors, it perpetuates the economy's dependence on foreigners.

It is clear that the welfare implications are more serious for less-developed than for developed host countries. Insofar as the terms on which MNEs enter less-developed countries, and their effect on welfare, is the result of a bargaining process, the existence of intra-firm trade acts as a *powerful bargaining counter in the MNE's favour*, enabling it to conceal from the government a crucial item of information. And the advantage is a permanent one, at least as long as intra-firm trade exists.

IV.c. IMPLICATIONS FOR HOST GOVERNMENT POLICY

The preceding argument has assumed that host governments do nothing special to check the transfer-pricing mechanism. This is indeed the case with most host countries, which act in the belief that world prices in the manufacturing sector are somehow determined by objective market forces, or which have trust in the intentions of MNEs. Neither may be justified. Certainly the concern shown in recent literature with the control of MNEs shows that even some proponents of MNEs are worried about the amount of power wielded by them (e.g. Vernon, 1971). The existence and growth of intra-firm trade increases this power and correspondingly diminishes the ability of governments to regulate and control them. The exercise of effective government regulation must include methods of monitoring intra-firm trade and enforcing reasonable transfer prices.

We shall not enter into a detailed discussion here of the methods available of countering transfer-pricing, but it may be useful to mention the main altern-

---

[1] The gains from transfer-pricing would accrue similarly to the other country's govern-ment, shareholders in the firm, and possibly trade unions. There would also be numerous favourable dynamic effects, on investment, innovation, and growth.

atives. The presumption is that governments are not willing to adapt their policies in such a way as to make them attractive to MNEs for declaring profits.

First, the government may set tariffs and tax rates at the same levels, so that it realises the same amount of revenue whichever way funds are remitted. This has the drawbacks that it would not stop transfer-pricing in cases where its main inducement is not tax differentials but other factors, and that it would limit tariffs to use as tax instruments rather than for a flexible protectionist policy.

Second, it may try to break the link between imports and parent companies by channeling all imports through an independent (possibly state) agency or forcing firms to buy elsewhere. This would involve a large administrative commitment and the risk of red-tapism and inefficiency.

Third, the tax authority may try to judge the profits of MNEs on evidence other than declared accounts, say, by their profitability abroad, or their sales, or some such measure. This may become extremely arbitrary, contentious and liable to corruption.

Fourth, the government may decide to check transfer prices directly and compare them with world prices. This would be a difficult task, and, as the US experience shows, subject to some dispute and arbitrariness when items not openly traded on world markets are being assessed. The use of consultants or international agencies may be of great help here.

Fifth, all the governments playing host to MNEs may get together and tax them jointly, rendering the whole process of profit transfer irrelevant. This may be the ideal solution—meeting international threats with international action— but it seems highly impracticable.

Sixth, the government may encourage internal checks to the use of transfer-pricing by enlarging the share of local equity in MNEs. This would be effective only if local shareholders had the technical and business capacity to check transfer prices, and if they did not themselves collude with their foreign partners. If requirements were too stringent, some MNEs would be deterred from investing at all.

Thus, all such policies face difficulties. The most practicable one at present seems to be direct official checks of the sort started in Colombia; its effectiveness can be increased by inter-government co-operation and exchange of information (as in the Andean Pact). If the transfer-pricing mechanism is really important to MNEs, it may be expected that they would resist any encroachment upon it, especially from less-developed countries where it is most useful. *Some* control seems to be essential, however, if MNEs are to be allowed to expand and benefit the host countries; unfortunately, the existing body of trade and investment theory is at best inadequate, and, at worst, completely misleading, as a guide to forming policies in this field.

Institute of Economics and Statistics,
Oxford

1. Barker, B. L., 1972, 'US Foreign Trade Associated with US Multinational Companies', *Survey of Current Business*, December.

2. Bhagwati, J., 1964, 'On the Underinvoicing of Imports', *BOUIES*.

3. Bhagwati, J., 1967, 'Fiscal Policies, the Faking of Foreign Exchange Declarations and the Balance of Payments', *BOUIES*.

4. *Board of Trade Journal*, 1968, 'Overseas Transactions in 1966–Trade Credits and Exports', London.

5. Bradshaw, M. T., 1969, 'US Exports to Foreign Affiliates of US Firms', *Survey of Current Business*, May.

6. Brooke, M. Z., and Remmers, H. L., 1970, *The Strategy of Multinational Enterprise*, Longman, London.

7. Brooke, M. Z. and Remmers, H. L., 1972, *The Multinational Company in Europe*, Longman, London.

8. Copithorne, L. W., 1971, 'International Corporate Transfer Prices and Government Policy', *Canadian Journal of Economics*, Vol. IV.

9. DANE (Departamento Administrativo Nacional de Estadística), 1971, 'Survey of Foreign Investment in Colombia', (in Spanish), *Boletín Mensual de Estadística*, No. 239, June, Bogota.

10. Duerr, M. G., 1972, *Tax Allocations and International Business*, The Conference Board, New York.

11. Dunning, J. F., 1972, Introduction to *International Investment*, Penguin.

12. *El Tiempo*, 1971, 'Incomex Rebajá Precios', Bogota newspaper, 15 September.

13. Foster, S. B., 1972, 'Impact of Direct Investment Abroad by US Multinational Companies on the Balance of Payments', *Federal Reserve Bank of New York Monthly Review*, July.

14. Greene, J. and Duerr, M. G., 1968, *Intercompany Transfers in Multinational Firms*, The Conference Board, New York.

15. Helleiner, G. K., 1973, 'Manufactured Exports from Less Developed Countries and Multinational Firms', *Economic Journal*, March.

16. Horst, T., 1971, 'The Theory of the Multinational Firm: Optimal Behaviour under Different Tariff and Tax Rates', *Journal of Political Economy*, Vol. 79.

17. Hufbauer, G. C. and Adler, F. M., 1968, *Overseas Manufacturing Investment and the Balance of Payments*, US Treasury Department, Washington, D.C.

18. Hufbauer, G. C., 1970, 'The Impact of National Characteristics and Technology on the Commodity Composition of Trade in Manufactured Goods', in R. Vernon (ed.), *The Technology Factor in International Trade*, National Bureau of Economic Research, New York.

19. Johnson, H. G., 1969, 'The Theory of International Trade', in P. A. Samuelson (ed.), *International Economic Relations*, Macmillan, New York.

430

20. Keegan, W. J., 1969, 'Multinational Pricing: How Far is Arm's Length?', *Columbia Journal of World Business*, Vol. IV, No. 3.

21. Kindleberger, C. P., 1969, *American Business Abroad*, Yale University Press, New Haven.

22. Kindleberger, C. P., 1970, (ed.), *The International Corporation*, MIT Press, Cambridge, Mass.

23. Monopolies Commission, 1973, *Chlordiazepoxide and Diazepam*, HMSO, London.

24. Pearson Commission, 1969, *Partners in Development*, Praeger, New York.

25. Reddaway, W. B., *et al*, 1967, *Effects of UK Direct Investment Overseas, An Interim Report*, Cambridge University Press.

26. Tugendhat, C., 1971, *The Multinationals*, Eyre and Spottiswoode, London.

27. UNCTAD, 1971, *Policies Relating to Technology in the Countries of the Andean Pact: Their Foundations*, Santiago, TD/107.

28. US Department of Commerce, 1972, *Special Survey of US Multinational Companies* 1970, Bureau of Economic Analysis, Washington, D.C.

29. Vaitsos, C. V., 1970, *Transfer of Resources and Preservation of Monopoly Rents*, (Mimeo.), Harvard Development Advisory Service.

30. Vaitsos, C. V., 1972, *Inter-Country Income Distribution and Trans-national Corporations*, (Mimeo.), Lima.

31. Vernon, R., 1971, *Sovereignty at Bay*, Longman, London.

32. Wells, L. T., 1971, 'The Multinational Business Enterprise: What Kind of International Organization?', *International Organization*, Summer.

33. Williamson, O. E., 1971, 'Managerial Discretion, Organization Form and the Multi-Division Hypothesis', in R. Marris and A. Wood (ed.), *The Corporate Economy*, Macmillan, London.

34. Winston, G. C., 1970, 'Overinvoicing, Underutilization and Distorted Industrial Growth', *Pakistan Development Review*.

Appendix: *US Intra-Firm Manufacturing Trade and Total Trade in Manufactures: 1962–70 (In US $ millions)*
MNE Data Based on Samples[1]

	1962	1963	1964	1965		1966		1970		1966[2] Benchmark Survey	
				Total by MNEs	With Affiliates	Total	With Aff.	Total	With Aff.	Total	With Aff.
A. Data on US Mfg. MNEs											
1. Exports	2,549	2,945	3,490	7,866	4,057	9,975	4,208	16,139	7,079	12,600	6,300
2. Industry:											
a. Food	—	—	—	381	79	307	124	363	144	—	—
b. Chemicals and Allied	—	—	—	1,468	756	1,560	679	2,075	981	—	—
c. Metals	—	—	—	873	285	768	180	1,471	204	—	—
d. Machinery	—	—	—	1,956	1,121	2,965	1,153	4,762	2,270	—	—
e. Transport Equipment	—	—	—	2,214	3,093	3,093	1,508	5,376	2,588	—	—
f. Other	—	—	—	974	435	1,290	565	2,092	892	—	—
3. Imports	1,150	1,301	1,636	—	1,856	5,707	2,161	9,393	4,153	—	3,000
4. Total Trade	3,699	4,246	5,126	—	5,913	15,682	6,369	25,532	11,232	—	9,300
B. Data on Total US Mfg. Trade and Remittances											
5. Total US Exports[3]	14,265	14,928	17,188	18,043		19,940		30,177			
6. " " Imports	7,970	8,415	8,851	11,671		14,943		26,627			
7. Dividends and Interest Earned[4]	741	660	893	1,094		1,116		1,859			
8. Royalties and Fees Earned	303	371	479	568		609		1,002			
9. Total Earnings (8+9)	1,044	1,031	1,372	1,652		1,725		2,861			

432

Sources: 1 Foster, 1972; Hufbauer and Adler, 1968.

2 *Statistical Abstracts* (various years), US Department of Commerce.

3 *Survey of Current Business*, December 1965; May 1969; November 1972; and December 1972.

4 US Department of Commerce, *Special Survey of US Multinational Companies* 1970, Washington, D.C., 1972.

Notes: 1. Sample coverages, which vary from time to time, are as follows: a. 1962–64: sample of 256 parent MNEs and about 2,500 affiliates, with 'affiliates' defined to cover firms with 25 per cent or more US equity. The sample figures were 'blown up' to represent all foreign investors. b. 1965: sample of 271 manufacturing firms, of which 257 reported exports to 1,869 affiliates (defined as before). There was *no* blowing up of sample figures. c. 1966–70: sample of 223 manufacturing firms with 3,752 affiliates, which were redefined to cover only 'majority owned' foreign affiliates. There was no blowing up of sample figures.

2. Based on Foster, 1972, because original survey, *US Direct Investments Abroad* 1966, Part II, was not available here. The figures are rounded, and import figures are approximations, probably too low. This survey covered *all* foreign investors—3,300 parent companies and about 23,000 affiliates, which were defined as 1962–65 above.

3. Total US exports and imports include: tobacco manufactures and cigarettes, alcohol, chemicals, machinery, transport equipment and other manufactured goods. Military shipments are excluded. Figures are from various *Statistical Abstracts*.

4. Earnings are on *all* manufacturing investments abroad, since data on sample MNEs are not available separately. They include branch earnings but exclude reinvested profits.

CHAPTER 28

Transfer pricing decisions in US multinational corporations*

Jane O. Burns

Abstract. This paper provides information about the effect 14 variables have on transfer pricing decisions in 62 MNCs. Questionnaire data is factor analyzed and evaluated to determine whether significant differences exist when respondents are grouped alternately into five dichotomous categories: (1) those assessed compared with those not assessed additional U.S. federal income taxes because of transfer pricing methods, (2) those among the first 150 compared with those among the remaining 500 largest U.S. industrial firms, (3) those whose export sales exceed $25 million compared with those whose export sales do not, (4) those whose export sales to subsidiaries exceed 50 percent of total exports compared with those whose export sales to subsidiaries do not, and (5) those unable to use a market-based transfer price compared with those who are able to do so. By means of Student's t-test and .10 level of significance, it is determined that some variables and factors do have greater influence on transfer pricing decisions for some types of companies.

INTRODUCTION

■ Although most foreign subsidiaries are separate legal entities, many U.S.-based multinational corporations (MNCs) consider them to be integral parts of one economic organization. Consequently, the success of the total organization may be stressed even to the extent that some decisions are not in the best interest of an individual unit. Becuse intracompany transfers are often numerous and involve substantial values, prices assigned to goods and services are exceedingly important to the buying and selling units and, because of external pressures, to the total organization.

Few business decisions have greater impact on the operations of MNCs than those involving pricing between related units located in different countries. Numerous articles and books discuss pricing strategies of intracompany exports for

*Jane O. Burns, CPA, is Associate Professor of Accounting at Indiana University. She received a Ph.D. degree in Business Administration from the Pennsylvania State University. Dr. Burns' research and publications concentrate on international taxation.

The author gratefully acknowledges the valuable assistance provided by Franklin Acito, Assistant Professor of Marketing, Indiana University.

* This article is reprinted, with permission, from the *Journal of International Business Studies* (Fall 1980) pp 23–39

MNCs.[1] These strategies are generally influenced by various business objectives such as maximizing organizational profits, optimizing cash flows, penetrating new markets, and avoiding conflicts with foreign host governments. The literature commonly assumes that MNCs incorporate many of these interrelated variables into transfer pricing decisions.[2] Much of this assumption is speculation however, because information on intracompany policies generally is not publicly available. This study was undertaken in order to help alleviate this deficiency in data and to explore possible interrelationships. Financial executives from a sample of U.S.-based MNCs were asked to provide information about the extent that their firms' transfer pricing decisions are influenced by certain external factors. The results of the survey are summarized and analyzed in this article.

RESEARCH PARTICIPANTS

The sample population for this study was chosen from the largest U.S.-based industrial corporations. A total of 210 companies was selected from the *Fortune* 500 largest industrial corporations in the United States[3] that met at least one of the following criteria: (1) participants in a study on Domestic International Sales Corporations,[4] (2) participants in a study on investments abroad,[5] or (3) supporting companies of the Special Committee for U.S. Exports. Whereas the selection process was designed to identify companies that were likely to have exports to foreign subsidiaries, its lack of randomness prevents any generalization being made about all such intracompany sales.

TABLE 1

Responses to the Questionnaire

	Number of Companies	Percent[a]	
Companies completing questionnaire	62	54	30
Reasons given by companies responding but not participating:			
No exports to subsidiaries	21	18	
Do not complete questionnaires	14	12	
Subject is too sensitive	9	8	
Exports to subsidiaries are insignificant	5	4	
Tax audit is in progress	3	3	
Total companies responding but not participating	52	46	25
Total companies responding	114	100	55
Companies not responding	96		46
Total companies contacted	210		100

[a]Percentages may not total one hundred because of rounding.

A questionnaire was mailed to the senior financial officer of each of the 210 companies selected; 55 percent replied, and 62 (54 percent of those responding) usable questionnaires were received. Of the remaining 46 percent responding, 18 percent stated their organizations did not export goods to foreign subsidiaries, and, therefore, had no information to provide. In addition, 28 percent declined to participate because: (1) they do not complete questionnaires as a matter of policy (12 percent), (2) the subject matter and data requested is too sensitive (8 percent), (3) exports to foreign subsidiaries are insignificant (4 percent), or (4) a tax audit of their firm's transfer prices is in progress (3 percent) (Table 1).

Based on the usable questionnaires received, average export sales represent 11 percent of the firms' gross sales and about 42 percent of their exports are to subsidiaries. Consequently, these 62 U.S.-based MNCs are transferring in excess of $7 billion annually through intracompany sales to foreign subsidiaries. Because it is estimated that 40 percent of all international trade occurs between related parties,[6] participants in this study account for approximately 16 percent of all U.S. company exports to foreign related parties. In 97 percent of these companies, most pricing decisions for intracompany export transactions are made by U.S. personnel.

Participating MNCs funnel 70 percent of their export dollar sales through one of two export incentive tax corporations—63 percent through a Domestic International Sales Corporation (DISC) and 7 percent through a Western Hemisphere Trade Corporation (WHTC).[7] Seventeen companies utilize the DISC for all exports. Surprisingly, 9 companies do not export through either of the special corporations. Also, only 4 of the participating companies have exports with a subsidiary organized as a U.S. Possession Corporation.

INFLUENCES ON INTRACOMPANY PRICES

Participants were asked to evaluate the importance that each of 14 variables has on export pricing decisions for their firms. One question required that respondents consider each variable and either (1) strongly agree, (2) agree, (3) be undecided, (4) disagree, or (5) strongly disagree that it had a substantial influence on their firms' transfer pricing decisions. A second question requested respondents to refer to the list of 14 variables and select the 5 they believed most important to their organization. Although the second question requested that 5 variables be chosen, several participants recorded fewer. A mean of the responses was calculated for each variable in each question. Based on the mean, the 14 variables were ranked in the order of importance for each question (Table 2). Spearman's rank correlation coefficient reveals that rankings for the two questions are highly correlated.[8]

Responses to the first question indicate that most participants believe that, in their organization, intracompany prices for exports are influenced substantially by 10 of the 14 variables. Based on the mean, the 10, in order of importance, are: (1) market conditions in the foreign country, (2) competition in the foreign country, (3) reasonable profit for foreign affiliate, (4) U.S. federal income taxes, (5) economic conditions in the foreign country, (6) import restrictions, (7) customs duties, (8) price controls, (9) taxation in the foreign country, and (10) exchange controls. A majority of the participants believe 4 of the listed variables are not im portant to their firms when establishing intracompany export prices. Continuin in order of importance determined by the mean, the four are: (11) U.S. export i centives, (12) floating exchange rates, (13) management of cash flows, an (14) other U.S. federal taxes.

TABLE 2

Influences on Transfer Pricing Decisions

Intracompany transfer prices for exports are influenced substantially by:	Question 1			Question 2	
	Rank	Mean[a]	Standard Deviation	Rank	Percent Selecting[b]
U.S. federal income taxes	4	2.57	1.190	4	49.2
Other U.S. federal taxes	14	3.64	.876	14	4.9
Taxation in the foreign country	9	2.84	1.143	5	39.3
U.S. export incentives	11	3.10	1.121	10/11	18.0
Competition in the foreign country	2	2.26	.964	1	65.6
Market conditions in the foreign country	1	2.15	.872	2/3	63.9
Customs duties	7	2.70	.937	10/11	18.0
Exchange controls	10	2.92	.954	9	19.7
Price controls	8	2.80	.997	8	21.3
Import restrictions	6	2.62	.986	7	24.6
Economic conditions in the foreign country	5	2.61	1.037	6	36.1
Floating exchange rates	12	3.16	.916	13	8.2
Management of cash flows	13	3.20	.928	12	13.1
Reasonable profit for foreign affiliate	3	2.31	.975	2/3	63.9

[a]The mean for each variable is based on a scale of 1—strongly agree—through 5—strongl' disagree.

[b]The percent selecting is calculated by dividing the number of respondents selecting the variable by the total number of respondents.

When responses to the second question are tabulated, only 3 variables are se lected as being among the most important by more than half the participants. O these 3, competition in the foreign country is selected by 66 percent, and bot market conditions in the foreign country and reasonable profit for foreign affiliate are selected by 64 percent. A comparison of responses for the two questions reveals that most variables are ranked similarly in both questions; however, there are two exceptions. One, whereas taxation in the foreign country is ranked ninth in the first question, it is ranked fifth in the second question. Conversely, cus toms duties ranks higher in importance in the first question (seventh) than in the second question (tenth/eleventh).

Responses to the two questions support the literature; transfer pricing decisions for most of the participating companies are influenced substantially by several external factors. Table 2 does not reveal, however, which variables are considered to be closely related nor what types of companies are influenced more by which variables. Statistical analysis of the data provides insight to these questions.

DATA ANALYSIS

In the initial stage of data analysis, the 14 variables were factor analyzed. The purpose of this investigation was to identify the existence of underlying dimensions that account for the commonality of preferences for different variables. A varimax rotated factor analysis after rotation with Kaiser normalization yielded five factors. Standard criteria were followed in extracting the factors: all five had an eigenvalue greater than 1, each explained more than 5 percent of the variance, and collectively they explained a substantial portion (80 percent) of the total variance of the variables. The variable listed last, reasonable profit for foreign affiliate, was eliminated from the analysis. It was spread across the five factors with all loadings below .4, indicating a lack of relationship for this variable with the underlying factors (Table 3).

Factor one, internal foreign environment, indicates that 2 variables are very closely related. Those respondents who are inclined to consider market conditions in the foreign country important (or unimportant) also tend to consider competition in the foreign country important (or unimportant). This relationship was expected. Not expected, however, is the fact that the loading on this factor for a third variable, economic conditions in the foreign country, is low.

The second factor, influences on cash flows, accounts for 4 variables: management of cash flows, exchange controls, floating exchange rates, and U.S. export incentives. Although intuitively it might be suggested that variable loadings on this factor should be closely associated with loadings on factor three, artificial barriers, the analysis indicates such a relationship does not exist for respondents in this study. Only one of the variables—exchange controls—receives a high loading for both factors. In addition to exchange controls, other variables closely related as artificial barriers are price controls, customs duties, and import restrictions.

Three variables dealing with taxation are accounted for by the fourth factor, taxes: U.S. federal income taxes, taxation in the foreign country, and other U.S. federal taxes. The loading for customs duties, a variable also dealing with taxation, is quite low for this factor; instead, it is more highly identified with artificial barriers, as was expected.

Even though the analysis indicates the presence of five underlying dimensions, the final factor, economic structure, is less clearly defined than the four preceding factors. It accounts for two variables: economic conditions in the foreign country and U.S. export incentives. Neither of these variables has a very high loading. It is possibly the underlying dimension most difficult to understand. When individual responses to the two variables are considered together, however, the relationship is evident. One possible interpretation of this factor from the tabulation is that when economic conditions in the foreign country are strong, they are not influential in pricing decisions and U.S. export incentives are not par-

TABLE 3

Factor Loadings[a]

Intracompany transfer prices for exports are influenced substantially by:	Factor 1 Internal Foreign Environment	Factor 2 Influences on Cash Flows	Factor 3 Artificial Barriers	Factor 4 Taxes	Factor 5 Economic Structure
U.S. federal income taxes				.761	
Other U.S. federal taxes				.469	
Taxation in the foreign country				.724	.452
U.S. export incentives		.426			
Competition in the foreign country	.891				
Market conditions in the foreign country	.898				
Customs duties			.519		
Exchange controls		.637	.427		
Price controls			.654		
Import restrictions			.459		
Economic conditions in the foreign country					.510
Floating exchange rates		.503			
Management of cash flows		.696			
Reasonable profit for foreign affiliate					

[a]Only factor loadings exceeding .4 are shown for clarity.

ticularly relevant to exporting; however, when economic conditions in the foreign country are unstable or weak, this fact becomes more influential in pricing as does the availability of U.S. export incentives to help offset negative economic aspects. Unfortunately, it is not possible to evaluate this interpretation with the present data.

In order to analyze the data further, respondents are arranged into five dichotomous categories. It is hypothesized that variables influencing export prices charged subsidiaries are more important for: (1) those assessed compared with those not assessed additional U.S. federal income taxes because of transfer pricing methods, (2) those among the first 150 compared with those among the remaining 500 largest U.S. industrial firms, (3) those whose export sales exceed $25 million compared with those whose export sales do not exceed $25 million, (4) those whose export sales to subsidiaries exceed 50 percent of total exports compared with those whose export sales to subsidiaries do not exceed 50 percent of total exports, and (5) those unable to use a market-based transfer price compared with those able to use a market-based transfer price. In each of the five categories, companies are separated into two groups. The mean for each of the 14 variables and five factors is calculated for each group. Using Student's t-test for the separate variance estimate, the means are analyzed to determine whether significant levels of differences exist for any of the variables or factors.

Analysis of Responses Based on Tax Reallocations Under Internal Revenue Code Section 482

Although composed of numerous legally separate entities, MNCs often operate as one economic unit. In contrast, Section 482 of the Internal Revenue Code requires that each entity operate as an economically separate unit. Conflict arises when entities are taxed differently. As a result, transfer prices between U.S.-based MNCs and their foreign subsidiaries are often adjusted by the Internal Revenue Service (IRS) during a tax audit.

All corporations with assets of $50 million or more and most corporations with international transactions are audited by the IRS annually.[9] Consequently, tax returns of all participating firms were audited for the twelve years—1966 through 1977—included in this study. During these audits, 53 percent of the firms had transfer prices for exports adjusted by the IRS for at least two of the twelve years. The number of years with adjustments averaged between four and five. Transfer prices used by the remaining 47 percent were not adjusted.

There are a number of possible explanations of why prices were adjusted for the first group of companies but not for the second group. One of these relevant to this study is that firms in the first group may have allowed transfer prices to be influenced more by external pressures. Decisions substantially affected by such pressures could produce artificial prices that would not withstand an IRS audit. To test this possibility, responses for those companies that were assessed additional U.S. federal income taxes because of transfer pricing methods (Group 1) were separated from those not assessed such additional taxes (Group 2). Prior to analyzing the data, it was hypothesized that transfer pricing decisions are influenced more by the 14 variables for Group 1 firms than for Group 2 firms. Table 4

TABLE 4

Analysis of Responses Based on Tax Reallocations Under Internal Revenue Code Section 482

Intracompany transfer prices for exports are influenced substantially by:	Group 1 Reallocations Made			Group 2 Reallocations Not Made			Level of Significance[b]
	Rank	Mean[a]	Standard Deviation	Rank	Mean[a]	Standard Deviation	
Variables:							
U.S. Federal income taxes	7	2.81	1.256	2	2.31	1.072	.048
Other U.S. Federal taxes	14	3.84	.884	14	3.41	.825	.027
Taxation in the foreign country	10	3.06	1.134	6/7	2.59	1.119	.052
U.S. export incentives	13	3.38	1.129	10	2.79	1.048	.020
Competition in the foreign country	2	2.12	.907	4	2.41	1.018	—
Market conditions in the foreign country	1	2.06	.914	1	2.24	.830	—
Customs duties	6	2.78	1.039	9	2.62	.820	—
Exchange controls	8	2.94	.982	11	2.90	.939	.085
Price controls	9	2.97	1.092	8	2.62	.862	—
Import restrictions	4	2.66	.937	6/7	2.59	1.053	—
Economic conditions in the foreign country	5	2.69	1.120	5	2.52	.949	—
Floating exchange rates	12	3.28	.991	12	3.03	.823	—
Management of cash flows	11	3.19	.965	13	3.21	.902	—
Reasonable profit for foreign affiliate	3	2.28	.958	3	2.34	1.010	—
Factors:							
Internal foreign environment		−.146	.902		.161	.948	—
Influences on cash flows		.022	.849		−.025	.671	—
Artificial barriers		.089	.745		−.098	.674	—
Taxes		.177	.839		−.195	.765	.038
Economic structure		.120	.555		−.132	.671	.058

[a] The mean for each variable is based on a scale of 1—strongly agree—through 5—strongly disagree. The mean for each factor is based on standardized scores used in factor analysis. Therefore, the lower the mean the more influence it has on the intracompany pricing decision. Because the means for the factors ignore both level and dispersion differences, they are not appropriate for ranking.

reveals this hypothesis is not supported by the data. Thus, the hypothesis must be rejected for all 14 variables and five factors.

Table 4 indicates this exploratory study provides an interesting alternate hypothesis for future research. Mean values actually indicate the reverse of the hypothesis tested in this study may be true—that is, transfer pricing decisions may be influenced more by some of the variables for Group 2 firms than for Group 1 firms. Significant levels of differences are reported in the Table for 5 variables and 2 factors. The 5 variables are U.S. federal income taxes, other U.S. federal taxes, taxation in the foreign country, U.S. export incentives, and price controls. The two factors are taxes and economic structure.

With regard to the data reported in Table 4, several points should be noted. Only one of the five variables—U.S. federal income taxes—has a very high rank. Group 2 rankings for the remaining four variables range from six to fourteen. Thus, while some differences may exist, they generally are for variables believed to have little or no influence on the pricing decision.

This qualification should not overshadow the fact that differences are indicated by the responses. Because the 5 variables were assigned to three separate factors, it may be assumed that most respondents believed their effect on pricing was dissimilar. What is the relationship between these respondent differences and the fact that Group 2 firms had no Section 482 reallocations for the twelve-year period? Some possible answers to this question are:

1. There is no relationship. Instead, differences may be due to one or more of the limitations applicable to this type of research.

2. The influence exerted by U.S. federal income taxes may have caused Group 2 firms to adhere more closely to the requirements of Section 482.

3. Group 2 firms may have understated transfer prices and overstated U.S. income to avoid possible Section 482 reallocations and because use of U.S. export incentives allowed sufficient profit on exports.

4. These two groups may differ on some other, more important point. For example, other elements examined in this study to provide insight to this interpretation were dollar sales, dollar export sales, and percentage of total exports that were to subsidiaries. None of these three, however, revealed significant differences.

Whether greater emphasis on some of the listed variables actually benefited Group 2 firms during tax audits cannot be determined with certainty in the present tax environment. In fact, because of the ambiguity that surrounds transfer pricing, it is probably not possible to determine whether the adjusted price for those firms assessed additional taxes is more or less "reasonable" or "fair" than those not assessed additional taxes.

Analysis of Responses Based on MNC size

Frequently, it is assumed that the larger the MNCs, the more power they have and the more likely it is that their decisions, including transfer pricing, are substantially influenced by external pressures. The belief that larger MNCs have more power is based partially on the fact that their gross sales often exceed the gross national products of countries in which many of their subsidiaries are located.[10]

TABLE 5

Analysis of Responses Based on Fortune 500 Ranking

Intracompany transfer prices for exports are influenced substantially by:	Group 1 Ranked From 1–150			Group 2 Ranked From 151–500			
	Rank	Mean[a]	Standard Deviation	Rank	Mean[a]	Standard Deviation	Level of Significance[b]
Variables:							
U.S. Federal income taxes	6	2.60	1.070	4	2.55	1.312	—
Other U.S. Federal taxes	14	3.63	.765	14	3.65	.985	—
Taxation in the foreign country	11	2.90	1.155	8	2.77	1.146	—
U.S. export incentives	10	2.87	1.074	13	3.32	1.137	.056
Competition in the foreign country	2	2.03	.718	3	2.48	1.122	.034
Market conditions in the foreign country	1	1.93	.740	2	2.35	.950	.029
Customs duties	8/9	2.77	.971	5	2.65	.915	—
Exchange controls	8/9	2.77	.858	10	3.06	1.031	—
Price controls	7	2.67	.844	9	2.94	1.124	—
Import restrictions	5	2.57	.774	6	2.68	1.166	—
Economic conditions in the foreign country	4	2.47	.973	7	2.74	1.094	—
Floating exchange rates	12	3.07	.868	11/12	3.26	.965	—
Management of cash flows	13	3.13	.937	11/12	3.26	.930	—
Reasonable profit for foreign affiliate	3	2.30	.877	1	2.32	1.077	—
Factors:							
Internal foreign environment		−.208	.752		.201	1.046	.042
Influences on cash flows		−.096	.752		.092	.775	—
Artificial barriers		−.025	.731		.024	.705	—
Taxes		.031	.756		−.030	.889	—
Economic structure		−.091	.608		.088	.630	—

[a] The mean for each variable is based on a scale of 1—strongly agree—through 5—strongly disagree. The lower the mean the more influence it has on the intracompany pricing decision. The mean for each factor is based on standardized scores used in factor analysis. Therefore, the mean for the factors ignore both level and dispersion differences, they are not appropriate for ranking. Because the means for the factors ignore both level and dispersion differences, they are not appropriate for ranking.

Whereas MNC size is equated traditionally with gross sales, this study employs three separate measures of size: gross sales, gross exports to subsidiaries, and percentage of gross exports to subsidiaries. The hypothesis for each of these three dimensions is that transfer pricing decisions are influenced more by the 14 variables for larger firms than for the remaining firms.

Because approximately half the participants are listed among the 150 industrial companies with the largest gross sales in the United States, their responses are separated from those of the other companies. Prior to analyzing the data, it was hypothesized that transfer pricing decisions are influenced more by the 14 variables for these 150 firms (Group 1) than for the remaining firms (Group 2). Based on a .10 level of significance, this hypothesis is supported for 3 variables and one factor (Table 5). The 3 variables considered more important by Group 1 are U.S. export incentives, competition in the foreign country, and market conditions in the foreign country. Because the latter 2 variables have high loadings on the internal foreign environment factor, it is not surprising that the data indicate further that Group 1 is influenced more by this factor than is Group 2.

A second approach to analyzing the data by MNC size classifies responses based on gross exports to subsidiaries. Because approximately half the firms have gross exports of $25 million or more, responses for these companies are separated from those participants with exports less than $25 million. Prior to analyzing the data, it was hypothesized that transfer pricing decisions are influenced more by the 14 variables for those firms with larger dollar volume of exports to subsidiaries (Group 1) than for the other firms (Group 2). At a .10 level of significance, this hypothesis is supported for 6 of the variables and two of the factors (Table 6). Those companies with a larger dollar volume of exports to subsidiaries consider U.S. federal income taxes, taxation in the foreign country, customs duties, exchange controls, floating exchange rates, and management of cash flows to be of greater importance than do those companies with a smaller dollar volume of exports. The data further indicate that Group 1 is influenced more by factors relating to influences on cash flows and taxes than is Group 2.

The third measure used for MNC size is based on the percentage of gross exports that are made to subsidiaries. Participant companies with at least half their gross exports to subsidiaries are separated from those with a lower percentage. Prior to analysis, it was hypothesized that transfer pricing decisions are influenced more by the 14 variables for those firms with a greater percentage of gross exports to subsidiaries (Group 1) than for those with a lower percentage of gross exports to subsidiaries (Group 2). At a .10 level of significance, this hypothesis is supported for 4 of the variables and two of the factors (Table 7). Respondents in Group 1 consider U.S. federal income taxes, other U.S. federal taxes, taxation in the foreign country, and customs duties to be more important. Responses indicate further that Group 1 is influenced more by artificial barriers and taxes than is Group 2. It also should be noted that whereas U.S. federal income taxes is ranked as the most important variable by Group 1, it is ranked in a tie for sixth place by Group 2. Similarly, although taxation in the foreign country is ranked in a tie for third by Group 1, it is ranked tenth by Group 2. These are two of the most significant differences in rankings found in the study; however, Spearman's rank correlation coefficient reveals that rankings of all variables for these two groups are highly correlated.

TABLE 6

Analysis of Responses Based on Total Export Sales to Subsidiaries

Intracompany transfer prices for exports are influenced substantially by:	Group 1 Exports to Subsidiaries of $25 Million or More			Group 2 Exports to Subsidiaries Under $25 Million			
	Rank	Mean[a]	Standard Deviation	Rank	Mean[a]	Standard Deviation	Level of Significance[b]
Variables:							
U.S. Federal income taxes	4	2.35	.950	6	2.80	1.375	.074
Other U.S. Federal taxes	14	3.58	.807	14	3.70	.952	—
Taxation in the foreign country	8	2.61	.955	9	3.07	1.285	.062
U.S. export incentives	11	2.97	1.110	10	3.23	1.135	—
Competition in the foreign country	2	2.13	.718	3	2.40	1.163	—
Market conditions in the foreign country	1	2.06	.772	1	2.23	.971	.095
Customs duties	5	2.55	.768	7	2.87	1.074	.002
Exchange controls	6/7	2.58	.672	11	3.27	1.081	—
Price controls	9	2.68	.832	8	2.93	1.143	—
Import restrictions	6/7	2.58	.807	5	2.67	1.155	—
Economic conditions in the foreign country	10	2.71	1.006	4	2.50	1.075	.078
Floating exchange rates	12	3.00	.894	12	3.33	.922	.081
Management of cash flows	13	3.03	.875	13	3.37	.964	—
Reasonable profit for foreign affiliate	3	2.29	.824	2	2.33	1.124	—
Factors:							
Internal foreign environment		−.081	.842		.083	1.019	—
Influences on cash flows		−.194	.734		.201	.752	.021
Artificial barriers		−.102	.647		.105	.770	—
Taxes		−.168	.614		.173	.969	.054
Economic structure		.099	.609		−.102	.627	—

[a]The mean for each variable is based on a scale of 1—strongly agree—through 5—strongly disagree. Therefore, the lower the mean the more influence it has on the intracompany pricing decision. The mean for each factor is based on standardized scores used in factor analysis. Because the means for the factors ignore both level and dispersion differences, they are not appropriate for ranking.

Intracompany transfer prices for exports are influenced substantially by:	Group 1—50% or More of Exports are to Subsidiaries			Group 2—Under 50% of Exports are to Subsidiaries			Level of Significance[b]
	Rank	Mean[a]	Standard Deviation	Rank	Mean[a]	Standard Deviation	
Variables:							
U.S. Federal income taxes	1	2.00	.866	6/7	2.80	1.231	.004
Other U.S. Federal taxes	13/14	3.35	.862	14	3.75	.866	.059
Taxation in the foreign country	3/4	2.35	.931	10	3.02	1.171	.012
U.S. export incentives	11/12	3.24	.970	11	3.04	1.180	—
Competition in the foreign country	3/4	2.35	.862	2	2.23	1.008	—
Market conditions in the foreign country	2	2.29	.849	1	2.09	.884	—
Customs duties	6/7	2.47	.514	6/7	2.80	1.047	.056
Exchange controls	10	2.94	.659	9	2.91	1.053	—
Price controls	9	2.71	.588	8	2.84	1.119	—
Import restrictions	5	2.41	.795	5	2.70	1.047	—
Economic conditions in the foreign country	8	2.65	.786	4	2.59	1.127	—
Floating exchange rates	11/12	3.24	.664	12/13	3.14	1.002	—
Management of cash flows	13/14	3.35	.862	12/13	3.14	.955	—
Reasonable profit for foreign affiliate	6/7	2.47	.943	3	2.25	.991	—
Factors:							
Internal foreign environment		-.081	.842		-.050	.920	—
Influences on cash flows		-.194	.734		-.053	.801	—
Artificial barriers		-.102	.647		.062	.804	.070
Taxes		-.168	.614		.157	.862	.002
Economic structure		.099	.609		.000	.670	—

[a]The mean for each variable is based on a scale of 1—strongly agree—through 5—strongly disagree. The mean for each factor is based on standardized scores used in factor analysis. Therefore, the lower the mean the more influence it has on the intracompany pricing decision. Because the means for the factors ignore both level and dispersion differences, they are not appropriate for ranking.

[b]Level of significance is based on a one-tailed Student's t-test. Only levels below .10 are shown for clarity.

TABLE 8

Summary of Level of Significance for Responses Based on Size[a]

| | Levels of Significance[b] | | |
Intracompany transfer prices for exports are influenced substantially by:	Gross Sales	Gross Exports to Subsidiaries	Percentage of Gross Exports to Subsidiaries
Variables:			
U.S. Federal income taxes		.074	.004
Other U.S. Federal taxes			.059
Taxation in the foreign country		.062	.012
U.S. export incentives	.056		
Competition in the foreign country	.034		
Market conditions in the foreign country	.029		
Customs duties		.095	.056
Exchange controls		.002	
Price controls			
Import restrictions			
Economic conditions in the foreign country			
Floating exchange rates		.078	
Management of cash flows		.081	
Reasonable profit for foreign affiliate			
Factors:			
Internal foreign environment	.042		
Influences on cash flows		.021	
Artificial barriers			.070
Taxes		.054	.002
Economic structure			

[a]Data are taken from Tables 5, 6, and 7.

[b]All levels of significance are based on a one-tailed Student's t-test and indicate the larger firms are influenced more by the variables and factors.

Table 8, a summary of the levels of significance reported in Tables 5–7, reveals several interesting points:

1. Transfer pricing decisions of larger participant firms apparently are influenced more by some of the variables than are transfer pricing decisions of the other participants.

2. Which variables have more influence on the larger firms' transfer pricing decisions depends on the definition of large; in fact, there is considerable inconsistency across definitions. Only 3 of the variables have significant differences for more than one of the size groupings.

3. Significant differences do not exist for 4 of the variables regardless of which of the three definitions of large is used. These 4 are price controls, import restrictions, economic conditions in the foreign country, and reasonable profit for foreign affiliate.

4. According to levels of significance for the factors, some consistency among responses for different definitions of size does exist; however, there is inconsistency across factors. For example, companies with larger gross sales are influenced substantially by the internal foreign environment but this difference is not revealed for the other two size groupings.

5. Taxes is the only factor with significant differences for more than one of the size groupings.

6. Significant differences do not exist for the last factor, economic structure, regardless of which of the three definitions of large is used.

Analysis of Responses Based on Ability to Use Market-Based Prices

In the United States, authority to reallocate income and deductions for tax purposes between related parties is granted to the Treasury by Section 482 of the Internal Revenue Code. According to the Treasury, intracompany transfer prices must be determined at arm's length. The Regulations establish three methods for determining arm's length prices applicable to intracompany transactions—comparable uncontrolled prices, resale price, and cost plus.[11]

According to the Regulations, the comparable uncontrolled price method provides the most accurate representation of an arm's length price. Uncontrolled prices exist when: (1) sales are made by members of the MNC to unrelated parties, (2) purchases are made by members of the MNC from unrelated parties, and (3) sales are made between two unrelated parties, neither of which are members of the MNC.[12]

The resale price method must be evaluated after the comparable uncontrolled price method is rejected as inapplicable to the situation.[13] Generally, the resale method is most appropriate for transfers to sales subsidiaries for ultimate distribution to unrelated parties. The equivalent to an arm's length price is obtained by subtracting the subsidiary's profit from the uncontrolled selling price.

The cost-plus method must be evaluated after the comparable uncontrolled and resale price methods are rejected as inapplicable to the situation.[14] The cost-plus method is most appropriate for transfers of components or unfinished goods to foreign subsidiaries. In determining an arm's length price under the cost-plus method, an appropriate markup for profit is added to the seller's total cost of the product. Cost is to be "computed in a consistent manner in accordance with sound accounting practices for allocating or apportioning costs, which neither favors nor burdens controlled sales in comparison with uncontrolled sales."[15] Requirements for uncontrolled sales for the cost-plus method are similar to those of the resale method except when viewed from the seller's perspective rather than from that of the buyer.

If requirements for any one of the three pricing methods are met, that method must be used unless the taxpayer presents an alternate method that "is clearly more appropriate."[16] In situations where none of the three methods are available,

TABLE 9

Analysis of Responses Based on Ability to Use Market-Based Prices

Intracompany transfer prices for exports are influenced substantially by:	Group 1 Market-Based Prices Unreasonable			Group 2 Market-Based Prices Reasonable			Level of Significance[b]
	Rank	Mean[a]	Standard Deviation	Rank	Mean[a]	Standard Deviation	
Variables:							
U.S. Federal income taxes	2	2.32	1.056	9	2.79	1.269	.061
Other U.S. Federal taxes	14	3.39	.916	14	3.85	.795	.022
Taxation in the foreign country	5	2.50	1.072	10/11	3.12	1.139	.016
U.S. export incentives	10	3.00	1.122	13	3.18	1.131	—
Competition in the foreign country	4	2.46	1.036	2	2.09	.879	.070
Market conditions in the foreign country	1	2.25	.887	1	2.06	.864	—
Customs duties	6	2.75	.887	6	2.67	.990	—
Exchange controls	11	3.14	.891	7/8	2.73	.977	.044
Price controls	9	2.89	.832	7/8	2.73	1.126	—
Import restrictions	8	2.82	.983	4/5	2.45	.971	.075
Economic conditions in the foreign country	7	2.79	.995	4/5	2.45	1.063	—
Floating exchange rates	12	3.21	.876	10/11	3.12	.960	—
Management of cash flows	13	3.32	.983	12	3.09	.879	—
Reasonable profit for foreign affiliate	3	2.39	1.100	3	2.24	.867	—
Factors:							
Internal foreign environment		.145	.987		-.123	.873	—
Influences on cash flows		.136	.765		-.116	.754	—
Artificial barriers		.087	.541		-.074	.832	—
Taxes		-.253	.736		.215	.836	.012
Economic structure		-.002	.718		.002	.536	—

[a]The mean for each variable is based on a scale of 1—strongly agree—through 5—strongly disagree. The mean for each factor is based on standardized scores used in factor analysis. Therefore, the lower the mean the more influence it has on the intracompany pricing decisions. Because the means for the factors ignore both level and dispersion differences, they are not appropriate for ranking.

variations of one of these methods or some other appropriate method may be adopted. Regulations offer no other guidelines for approximating arm's length prices. Presumably, the Treasury anticipated that the three methods would cover all but a few intracompany transfers. In fact, from August 1966 until 1968, IRS agents were instructed to use one of the three methods with no fourth option.[17]

Only 43 percent of the respondents believe the comparable uncontrolled price is reasonable for their firms' intracompany exports; 30 percent believe the resale price is reasonable; and 64 percent believe the cost-plus price is reasonable. Only 5 percent indicate none of the three prices are reasonable for most of their intracompany export sales.

The Regulations state the three methods of determining a transfer price must be considered in the order in which they are listed. When the survey responses are analyzed in terms of the Regulations, 43 percent should use the comparable uncontrolled price, 15 percent the resale price, 37 percent the cost-plus price, and 5 percent may use some other appropriate method.

The comparable uncontrolled price and resale price are market-based methods; the transfer price is determined by referring to transactions between unrelated parties. In comparison, the cost-plus price is not based on market-determined prices and therefore potentially more susceptible to external pressures. Based on the Regulations, responses of firms that qualify for the cost-plus method or for some other appropriate method form Group 1. Responses of the remaining firms that qualify for one of the two market-based prices form Group 2. It was hypothesized that transfer pricing decisions are influenced more by the 14 variables for Group 1 firms than for Group 2 firms. At a .10 level of significance, this hypothesis is supported for the factor taxes and for all 3 variables with high loadings on this factor: U.S. federal income taxes, other U.S. federal taxes, and taxation in the foreign country (Table 9).

Table 9 indicates also that the reverse of the hypothesis tested in this study may be true for some variables; that is, transfer pricing decisions may be influenced more by some of the variables for Group 2 firms than for Group 1 firms. Significant levels of differences are reported in the table for three variables: competition in the foreign country, exchange controls, and import restrictions. Some possible reasons for the apparent conflict are: 1) Differences may be due, as noted earlier, to one or more of the limitations applicable to this type of research; 2) Group 2 companies may not be using market-based prices even though the Regulations seem to require them to do so; and 3) Group 2 companies may be in a position that enables them to establish market prices that are influenced by some of the variables.

CONCLUSIONS

This exploratory study provides information about influences external pressures have on intracompany export pricing decisions for 62 U.S.-based MNCs. Although survey research is subject to a number of limitations, several interesting conclusions with further research potential can be drawn from the findings for these companies:

1. Participants support an assumption frequently appearing in the literature that intracompany export pricing decisions are substantially influenced by several external pressures.

2. The use of factor analysis indicates the existence of underlying dimensions that account for the commonality of preferences for different variables.

3. The fact that transfer pricing decisions for exports are substantially influenced by external pressures may not increase the likelihood that an adjustment will be made in these prices during an IRS audit.

4. Several external pressures apparently have more influence on intracompany export pricing decisions for larger participant firms than for the remaining firms; however, which external pressures are more influential depends on whether large is defined in terms of gross sales, gross exports to subsidiaries, or percentage of gross exports to subsidiaries.

5. U.S. and foreign income taxes apparently have more influence on intracompany export pricing decisions for participants not qualifying under Section 482 Regulations for market-based prices than for those qualifying for market-based prices.

FOOTNOTES

1. For example see: Jeffrey S. Arpan, "International Intra-Corporate Pricing: Non-American Systems and Views" (DBA Diss., Indiana University, 1971), pp. 130–131; Frederick D. S. Choi and Gerhard G. Mueller, *An Introduction to Multinational Accounting* (Englewood Cliffs, NJ: Prentice-Hall, Inc., 1978), pp. 302–314; John D. Daniels, Ernest W. Ogram, Jr., and Lee H. Radebaugh, *International Business: Environments and Operation* (Reading, MA: Addison-Wesley Publishing Company, 1976), pp. 43–44, 173, 435–436; Endel J. Kolde, *International Business Enterprise* (Englewood Cliffs, NJ: Prentice-Hall, Inc., 1973), pp. 234–236; Russell M. Moore and George M. Scott, eds., *An Introduction to Financial Control and Reporting in Multinational Enterprises,* Studies in International Business No. 1 (Austin, TX: University of Texas at Austin, 1973), pp. 62–65; Sidney M. Robbins and Robert B. Stobaugh, *Money in the Multinational Enterprise* (NY: Basic Books, Inc., 1973), pp. 91–92, 162–164, 184–186; Franklin R. Root, *International Trade and Investment* (Cincinnati, OH: South-Western Publishing Co., 1978), pp. 551–553; James S. Shulman, "Transfer Pricing in Multinational Business" (DBA Diss., Harvard University, 1966), pp. 36–55; Constantine V. Vaitsos, *Intercompany Distribution and Transnational Enterprises* (Oxford: Clarendon Press, 1974), pp. 50, 88–118; and Raymond Vernon, *Sovereignty at Bay* (NY: Basic Books, Inc., 1971), pp. 137–139.

2. For example see: Business International, *Setting Intercorporate Pricing Policies* (NY: Business International Corporation, 1973), pp. 37–51; James Greene, "Intercorporate Pricing Across National Frontiers," *The Conference Board Record,* October 1969, pp. 44–45; "Multinational Corporations and Income Allocation Under Section 482 of the Internal Revenue Code," *Harvard Law Review,* April 1976, pp. 1217–1219; Arpan, pp. 130–131; and Shulman, p. 1.

3. "The Fortune Directory of the 500 Largest Industrial Corporations," *Fortune,* May 1978, pp. 264–265.

4. Jane O. Burns, "Domestic International Sales Corporation: An Empirical Investigation" (Ph.D. Diss., The Pennsylvania State University, 1976) and Burns, "Accounting for the DISC: An Empirical Investigation," *The International Tax Journal,* April 1978, pp. 882–891.

5. Business International, *The Effects of US Corporate Foreign Investment, 1974–75* (NY: Business International Corporation, 1977).

6. Moore and Scott, p. 62.

7. The Tax Reform Act of 1976 provided for the elimination of all advantages of the Western Hemisphere Trade Corporation by 1 January 1980.

8. The formula for Spearman's rank correlation coefficient is:

$$r' = 1 - \frac{6(\Sigma d_i^2)}{n(n^2 - 1)}$$

Where d_i = difference between the rankings of each variable for the two questions; n = size of sample.

9. *IRS Can Improve Its Process for Deciding Which Corporate Returns to Audit,* Report to the Congress of the United States (Washington, DC: United States General Accounting Office, 1979), pp. 10, 32.

10. *Multinational Corporations: Hearings Before the Subcommittee on International Trade of the Committee on Finance, United States Senate,* 93d Congress, 1st Session (Washington, DC: U.S. Government Printing Office, 1973), pp. 404, 448, 452, 465, 475–476.

11. Tres. Regs., §1.482-2.

12. Ibid., §1.482-2(e)(2).

13. Ibid., §1.482-2(e)(3).

14. Ibid., §1.482-2(e)(4).

15. Ibid., §1.482-2(e)(4)(ii).

16. Ibid., §1.482-2(e)(1)(iii).

17. Michael G. Duerr, *Tax Allocations and International Business* (NY: The Conference Board, Inc., 1972), p. 24.

PERFORMANCE EVALUATION AND CONTROL SYSTEMS

CHAPTER 29

Evaluation and control of foreign operations*
Alan C. Shapiro

INTRODUCTION

A major responsibility faced by the financial executives of multinational corporations (MNCs) is to design and implement an evaluation and control system for overseas operations. This system must incorporate the influence of numerous factors which are rarely, if ever, encountered by purely domestic corporations. These factors include exchange-rate changes, differing rates of inflation, currency controls, foreign tax regulations, cross-border transfer pricing, and the differences between subsidiary and parent-company cash flows.

Unfortunately, developing an evaluation and control system is still an art, relying on judgment more than theory. No universal principles have yet appeared to use in designing such a system for domestic operations, much less for foreign operations. Therefore, this article has the modest goal of suggesting a set of reasonable guidelines, based on a mixture of economic theory, behavioral science and empirical evidence, to use in accounting for a variety of international elements while measuring, evaluating, and controlling the performance of foreign operations and their managers.

* Alan C. Shapiro is associate professor at the University of Southern California Graduate School of Business Administration and is head of the international financial management component of the new International Business Education and Research Program.

The author wishes to acknowledge the financial support of the Institute of International Business of the Stockholm School of Economics and the encouragement and assistance of its director, Dr. Lars Otterbeck.

* This article is reprinted, with permission, from *The International Journal of Accounting: Education and Research* (Fall 1978) pp 83–104

Designing an evaluation system involves four stages. The critical first stage must be to specify its purpose(s). While trivial perhaps, many companies have gotten into trouble by failing to distinguish, for example, between the evaluation of subsidiary performance and managerial performance. As we will see, it is possible for a manager to do an excellent job while his subsidiary is doing very poorly and vice versa.

The next stage involves determining what decisions will be made on the basis of these evaluations and the information necessary to support such decisions. For example, when evaluating managerial performance, it is necessary to separate the effects of uncontrollable variables, such as inflation, from those which are controllable, such as credit extension. Furthermore, capital allocation decisions require very different measures of subsidiary performance than does ensuring the smooth functioning of current operations.

The third stage is the design of a reporting or information system to provide the necessary information or at least a reasonable approximation. Many companies will probably find that their reporting system is inadequate for the purposes specified.

The final stage involves conducting a cost/benefit analysis of the evaluation system. *This analysis does not have to be quantitative but it should be comprehensive.* Some benefits might be (1) greater control over current operations, (2) more rigorous capital budgeting decisions, and (3) greater awareness of managerial effectiveness. Against these benefits must be weighed the costs which might arise including (1) time and money involved in redesigning the information system, and (2) behavioral problems which might be associated with the new evaluation system. The latter cost might include reduced initiative on the part of local managers who feel they are being overly controlled. This need not occur since one of the goals of an evaluation system should be to provide the information necessary to reward managers for their performance. An evaluation system which does not motivate a manager to work in the company's best interest will not be an effective one, regardless of its other attributes.

Exhibit 1 shows the design of an evaluation system diagrammatically. It is all too evident, however, that many multinational, as well as domestic, corporations have not fully considered this design process. Complaints by subsidiary managers that too much information is being demanded while management at headquarters complains that too much data, but too little good information, are being supplied by the subsidiaries is evidence enough of dissonance between system design and goals.

The main purposes of the evaluation system discussed in this paper include

1. To provide a rational basis for global resource allocation;
2. To have an early warning system if something is wrong with current operations;
3. To evaluate the performance of individual managers; and
4. To provide a set of standards that will motivate managers.

We will now explore each of these purposes in turn and comment on some of the methods currently used by MNCs in achieving these goals.

Resource Allocation

A key decision problem continually faced by multinationals is allocation of capital among their various subsidiaries on a worldwide basis. To aid in this process, companies often use the return on existing investments as a guide. This approach is fine if returns on past investments are *indicative* of *future returns*. There may be problems, though, if proposed investments are not comparable to existing ones or if the relevant returns on past investments are incorrectly measured. Obviously, to the extent that new investments are unrelated to previous ones, using historical subsidiary returns to allocate capital globally will be successful only by chance.

The more interesting, and probably more likely, occurrence in multinational capital budgeting is where potential investments are comparable to past ones, for example, replacement of depreciated assets, but it is difficult to decide on the *relevant selection criteria*. For example, a number of nonfinancial criteria such as market share, sales growth, and stability of production, are often used in comparing investments. Ultimately, though, most firms are interested in the return on their capital employed. A 1970 Conference Board study indicated that some version of *return on investment* (ROI) is the most typical means of measuring the long-run profit performance of foreign subsidiaries.[1] However, there are a number of pitfalls involved in allowing return on past investments to guide this process. These problems fall into two areas: first, problems associated with measuring the correct investment base, and second, difficulties in determining the relevant returns.

The investment base can include:

1. Parent's equity
2. Fixed assets
   a. Gross
   b. Net of depreciation
3. Working capital
   a. Total
   b. Net of supplier credits
   c. Net of intracompany accounts

In addition, these assets can be valued on an historical or current cost basis.

Fortunately, financial theory pinpoints the *relevant investment* base. It equals the incremental value of all capital required. Thus, the investment must be measured on a *current or replacement cost*, rather than historical cost, basis and should include gross fixed assets as well as total working capital requirements net of external supplier credits. Using historical rather than replacement costs in a period of inflation will understate true capital requirements leading to an unrealized increase in the projected return on investment. The working capital figure should include inventory valued on a current cost basis. Intracompany receivables should be excluded since these accounts cancel on a corporate-wide basis; for instance, increasing one subsidiary's intracompany receivables by a dollar will lead to a dollar reduction in another unit's working capital requirements. Furthermore, these accounts are arbitrary and subject to corporate manipulation.

Measuring the *relevant returns* on foreign operations is a more

---

[1] Irene W. Meister, *Managing the International Financial Function* (New York: The Conference Board, 1970).

difficult task. Substantial differences can arise between subsidiary cash flows and cash flows back to the parent firm due to tax regulations and exchange controls, for example. Further, adjustments in transfer prices and intersubsidiary credit arrangements can distort the true profitability of a given investment or subsidiary by shifting profits and liquidity from one unit to another. In addition, fees and royalties are costs to a subsidiary but benefits to the parent company.

Studies by The Conference Board and Business International revealed considerable variation among firms in measuring returns.[2] Measured returns included different combinations of foreign earnings, royalties, fees, dividends, rentals, interest, commissions, and export profits. Some firms included only repatriated profits while others included most or all of these return elements. Some measured only before-tax returns, others only returns after foreign taxes, and still others took into account both U.S. and foreign taxes paid.

The correct approach again relies on economic theory. According to this theory, *the value of an investment is determined by the net present value of incremental cash flows back to the investor.* The key concept here is incremental cash flow. Determining incremental cash flows for a MNC involves taking the difference between worldwide cash flows with the investment and worldwide cash flows in the investment's absence. Thus, all royalties, fees, and overhead allocations paid by a subsidiary should be included in its profit calculation as would be all profits earned by other units due to the subsidiary's existence. This would include profits arising from the adjustment of transfer prices on goods bought from or sold to the subsidiary, as well as all profits on exports to the subsidiary which would not have occurred in the subsidiary's absence. However, any profits on sales or any licensing fees and royalties which would have been earned by another unit of the MNC are not economically attributable to the subsidiary. Further, *the parent MNC should value only those cash flows which are or can be repatriated* since only funds accessible to the parent can be used to pay dividends and interest, amortize the firm's debt, and be reinvested. In addition, since only after-tax cash flows are relevant, it is necessary to determine the taxes that must be paid on foreign-source income and when such payment will occur.

The actual tax on remitted funds will depend on the transfer mechanism used, as well as on the tax regulations involved. These transfer

---

[2] Ibid., and Business International Corporation, "Evaluating Foreign Operations: The Appropriate Rates for Comparing Results with Budgets," *Business International Money Report* (20 May 1977), p. 154.

mechanisms include adjustments in transfer prices, dividend flows, fee and royalty charges, overhead allocation, and intracompany loan and credit arrangements.[3] For example, repaying a parent company loan would normally entail no additional withholding taxes.

The cost of carrying intracompany receivables should be excluded from the subsidiary's profit and loss calculation since this cost is offset elsewhere in the corporation by a corresponding reduction in working capital requirements. By the same logic, the subsidiary should be charged for the cost of any intracorporate payables on its balance sheet.

Return on Investment Criteria

A variety of comparisons are possible with a subsidiary's return on investment (ROI) figure. These include comparisons with local competitors, with the firm's subsidiaries and/or competitors on a regional or global basis, and with parent-company operations. In addition, comparisons can be made with the firm's original investment plans. We will now examine the information content of these comparisons to see what decisions are likely to be affected, and how, by the data generated.

Even if caution is exercised, comparisons with local or regional competitors can be meaningless. Different accounting and disclosure requirements leading to different depreciation and earnings reports under similar operating circumstances may not permit comparisons to be made with any degree of certainty. Some foreign firms, for example, do not separate nonrecurring income arising out of the sale of assets from operating income. Even if comparisons were limited to home-country competitors, it is usually impossible to determine the actual profitability of local operations because of the high degree of integration and the less-than-arms-length dealings between units of a multinational corporation.

Cross-country comparisons with other affiliates of the multinational corporation are possible, but to what purpose? Ex post, some investments will always be more profitable than others. Thus, in evaluating new investments, *a comparison of historical returns is useful only if these returns are indicative of the relative returns to be expected on future investments in these countries.* Even if expected ROIs differ across countries, it is necessary to consider the element of risk as well. Certain low risk-low return investments may well be preferable to some high risk-high return investments.

[3] David P. Rutenberg, "Maneuvering Liquid Assets in a Multinational Corporation," *Management Science* (June 1970): 671.

Furthermore, as Robbins and Stobaugh point out, multinationals have many *strategic motivations* for going abroad which are not necessarily expressed in ROI calculations.[4] For example, a firm may willingly forego economies of scale in production to achieve greater security of supply by having multiple and redundant production facilities.[5] In addition, operating in several nations may give a firm greater bargaining leverage in dealing with local governments or labor unions. Being multinational may also lower the *firm's risk profile* by reducing its dependence on the state of just one nation's economy. In fact, both Cohen and Rugman have found that earnings variability decreases as foreign activities increase[6] while research by Agmon and Lessard indicates that investors value the international diversification supplied by the multinational firm.[7]

It is true that ROI comparisons across subsidiaries might identify potential problems with current operations. However, as we will see in the next section, more direct methods of receiving early warnings of trouble are possible.

Perhaps the most important comparison that can be made is between *actual results and ex ante budgeted figures*. A postinvestment audit can help a firm learn from its mistakes as well as its successes. In the multinational corporation, where so many additional complexities enter into the capital budgeting decision, it is easier to make errors due to a lack of experience. Reviewing the record of past investments can enable a firm to determine whether there is any consistency in its estimation errors such as generally under- or overestimating the impact of inflation on costs or of devaluations on dollar revenues from foreign sales. Correction factors can then be included in future investment analyses. Even if estimation errors are random, a firm may be able to place limits on the relative magnitudes of these errors and thereby supply useful inputs to an investment simulation model.

In analyzing actual results, it is necessary to recall the previously mentioned nonfinancial strategic rationale that may have prompted the

[4] Sidney M. Robbins and Robert B. Stobaugh, *Money in the Multinational Enterprise* (New York: Basic Books, Inc., 1973).

[5] David P. Rutenberg and Ram Rao, "Robust Plant Location for the Stochastic World of a Multi-National Manufacturer" (GSIA Working Paper, Carnegie-Mellon University, 1973).

[6] Benjamin I. Cohen, *Multinational Firms and Asian Exports* (New Haven: Yale University Press, 1975); and Alan M. Rugman, "Risk Reduction by International Diversification," *Journal of International Business Studies* (Fall-Winter 1976): 75.

[7] Tamir Agmon and Donald R. Lessard, "Invester Recognition of Corporate International Diversification," *Journal of Finance* (September 1977).

original investment. Otherwise, an investment undertaken for one reason may be judged on the basis of different criteria resulting in a misleading comparison.

Evaluation of Current Subsidiary Performance

Frequent monitoring of operations in an uncertain environment is useful to determine whether any tactical or strategic changes are warranted. The appropriate measure(s) to use in controlling foreign operations, though, will vary by company and subsidiary. For marketing-oriented companies, market share, sales growth, or cost/sales dollar may be the most relevant measures. A manufacturing subsidiary may be most concerned about unit production costs, quality control, or the labor turnover rate. Others may find return on assets or a working capital to sales ratio most helpful. The important thing is to use those measures which experience has determined are the key leading indicators as to when an operation is out of control. In evaluating foreign operations, though, it may be necessary to employ different standards than those used in controlling the domestic business.

Inventory turnover may be lower overseas due to the larger inventory stocks required to cope with longer lead times to delivery and more frequent delays in intracompany shipments of goods. Where foreign production occurs, it may be necessary to stockpile additional supplies of imported raw material and components given the possibility of a dock strike, import controls, or some other supply disruption.[8]

Receivables may also be greater abroad, particularly in countries experiencing rapid rates of inflation. During times of inflation, consumers normally prefer to purchase on longer credit terms, expecting to repay their debt with less valuable future money. Furthermore, local credit standards are often more relaxed than in the home market, especially in countries lacking in alternative credit arrangements. To remain competitive, MNCs may feel compelled to loosen their own credit standards. This is not always the best policy, however. The multinational corporation should weigh the profit on incremental credit sales against the additional carrying costs, including devaluation losses and bad debts, associated with an easier credit policy.[9]

[8] Alan C. Shapiro, Howard C. Kunreuther, and Pascal E. Lang, "Planning Horizons for Inventory Stockpiling" (University of Pennsylvania Working Paper, 1977).
[9] Alan C. Shapiro, "Optimal Inventory and Credit-Granting Strategies under Inflation and Devaluation," *Journal of Financial and Quantitative Analysis* (January 1973): 37.

Different cost standards are usually necessary for foreign operations due to local value-added requirements (which mandate the use of more expensive local goods and services), import tariffs, government limitations on the choice of production processes, and a frequent inability to lay off or fire workers. In the latter case, labor becomes a fixed rather than a variable cost.

Most firms find it helpful to design budgets based on explicit assumptions on the internal and external environment. In a foreign environment, with greater uncertainty, *flexible budgeting* will probably be even more useful than it is domestically. Flexible budgeting involves computing alternative budgets based on different projections of the future rate of inflation, exchange rate changes, wage settlements, and so forth.

It is obviously impossible to develop a different budget for each potential future scenario. Instead, a limited number of the most likely scenarios should be selected for further study. If the firm selects these scenarios carefully, it should have an advantage in coping with foreseeable changes in its operating environment. Furthermore, these alternative budgets will provide a firm with a more reasonable and reliable basis for evaluating the performance of its overseas managers. This is the subject of the next section.

Evaluating Managerial Performance

The standards used to evaluate managers will also serve to motivate them. A key goal, therefore, in designing a management evaluation system is to ensure that the resulting managerial motivation will be congruent with overall corporate objectives. A good strategy which managers are not motivated to follow will be of little value. Thus, it is necessary to anticipate the likely response of a rational manager to a particular set of evaluation criteria.

For example, managers evaluated on the basis of current earnings will likely emphasize short-run profits to the detriment of longer-term profitability. This is particularly true if executives are frequently transferred, enabling them to escape the long-run consequences of their actions. These actions might include reducing advertising and maintenance, cutting back on research and development (R&D) expenditures, and investing less money on employee training. Managers judged according to return on investment will also concentrate on short-run profits. Furthermore, they will likely be slower to replace used equipment, particularly during a period of rapid inflation, even when economically justifiable. This is both because new investments will increase the investment base and also because ROI measured on an historical cost basis will be greater than ROI on a replacement cost basis. If return on equity is used as the measure of performance, managers will have an incentive to substitute local debt for retained earnings and parent-company equity. The effect of this will be to increase the MNC's worldwide debt ratio causing a deterioration in the parent company's credit rating and an increase in its cost of capital.

Consistent with the goal of properly motivating employees is the principle that *a manager's performance should be judged on the basis of results in those areas over which he has control.* Assigning responsibility without authority will lead to frustrated and disgruntled employees. Furthermore, it is unreasonable, as well as dysfunctional, to reward or penalize a manager for the impact of economic events beyond his control. Thus, headquarters must carefully distinguish between managerial performance and subsidiary performance.

As noted earlier, *a subsidiary can be doing quite well despite the poor performance of its management* and vice versa. For example, during a time of rapid inflation, a subsidiary selling to local customers will show a proportional increase in its dollar profitability. Poor management will just hold down the increase in profits. After the inevitable devaluation, though, dollar profitability will invariably decline even with good management in control. Furthermore, a consistently poor profit performance by a manager may simply be evidence of a past mistake in approving the original investment.

Rather than evaluate managerial performance on the basis of a subsidiary's profitability or ROI which are subject to uncontrollable events, it would be more useful to compare *actual results* with the *budgeted figures.* Revenue and cost variances can then be examined to determine whether these were likely to have been caused by external economic factors (such as inflation or devaluation), by corporate policy shifts (such as transfer price adjustments), or by managerial decisions (a new product strategy).

The keys to this analysis are the explicit assumptions which are incorporated in the budget and the knowledge of how changes in these assumptions are likely to affect the budgeted numbers. Exhibit 2 illustrates the likely impact of exchange rate changes. As the exhibit points out, the main factors which determine this impact are the sector of the economy in which a firm is operating (export, domestic import-competing, domestic nonimport-competing) and the source of its inputs (imports, domestic traded goods and services, domestic nontraded goods and services).

Exhibit 2. Characteristic Economic Effects of Exchange Rate Changes on MNCs

Cash-flow categories	Relevant economic factors	Devaluation impact	Revaluation impact
Revenue		*Parent-currency revenue impact*	*Parent-currency revenue impact*
Export sales	Price sensitive demand	Increase (+ +)	Decrease (− −)
	Price insensitive demand	Slight increase (+)	Slight decrease (−)
Local sales	Weak prior import competition	Sharp decline (− −)	Increase (+)
	Strong prior import competition	Decrease (−) (less than de-valuation %)	Slight increase
Costs		*Parent-currency cost impact*	*Parent-currency cost impact*
Domestic inputs	Low import content	Decrease (− −)	Increase (+ +)
	High import content/ inputs used in ex-port or import competing sectors	Slight decrease (−)	Slight increase (+)
Imported inputs	Small local market	Remain the same (0)	Remain the same (0)
	Large local market	Slight decrease (−)	Slight increase (+)
Depreciation		*Cash-flow impact*	*Cash-flow impact*
Fixed assets	No asset valuation adjustment	Decrease by de-valuation % (− −)	Increase by re-valuation % (+ +)
	Asset valuation adjustment	Decrease (−)	Increase (+)

Note: To interpret the above chart, and taking the impact of a devaluation on local demand as an example, it is assumped that if import competition is weak, local prices will climb slightly, if at all; in such a case there would be a sharp contraction in parent-company revenue. If imports generate strong competition, local-currency prices are expected to increase, although not to the full extent of the devaluation; in this instance only a moderate decline in parent-company revenue would be registered.

By including allowances for training programs, research and development, and other vital functions in the budget, the natural tendency to neglect these areas can be reduced. However, it is necessary to consider other, less tangible, factors as well when evaluating performance.

A profit-oriented manager may allow relations with the host country to deteriorate. A study by Negandhi and Baliga indicates that, in contrast to the typical American MNC's concentration on profits, European and Japanese multinationals emphasize cultivating and maintaining harmonious relations with host government officials and others in the local environment.[10] Given the difficulties facing multinationals abroad, qualitative determinants of long-run profitability and viability are likely to be more important in the future and should be included in any performance evaluation. The inability to objectively measure the state of host country relations is not a reason to ignore it. Ultimately, any performance measure is subjective, even if it is quantitative, since the choice of which measure(s) to stress is a matter of judgment.

The next section deals with three areas of current concern in performance evaluation: transfer pricing, adjusting intracorporate fund flows, and the choice of appropriate exchange rates for internal use.

Transfer pricing. In a decentralized profit center, transfer prices on goods and services (fees and royalties) can be a significant determinant of a manager's performance. Therefore, unless the manager is not held accountable for the influence of transfer prices on his reported profits, he is likely to react in ways which are counterproductive to the organization as a whole. Cases have arisen, for example, where managers selling to subsidiaries which are forced to buy from them behaved as monopolists and attempted to gouge their captive customers. On the other hand, purchasers of goods and services from other units of the MNC may try to act as monopsonists and underpay their suppliers.

Even if a manager wanted to act in the best interests of the corporation, his perspective would be too limited. Thus, individual managers are likely to ignore or be ignorant of the broader legal, tax, and liquidity calculations involved in setting a corporate-wide transfer pricing policy.[11] For these reasons, transfer pricing is too important to be left to subsidiaries. However, budgeted profit requirements for individual subsidiaries should recognize and adjust for the distorting influence of less-than-arm's-length transfer prices. In other words, managerial evaluations should be decoupled from the particular transfer prices being used. This can be done by charging managers who are buying goods

[10] Anant R. Negandhi and B. R. Baliga, "Quest for Survival and Growth: A Study of American, European, and Japanese Multinational Corporations" (International Institute of Management Working Paper, 1976).
[11] Edgar M. Barrett, "Case of the Tangled Transfer Price," *Harvard Business Review* (May-June 1977): 20; and Rutenberg, "Liquid Assets," p. 671.

the marginal cost of production and shipping while managers who are selling goods would be credited with a reasonable profit on their sales. Managers of subsidiaries only producing for sale to other units of the corporation should be evaluated on the basis of their costs of production rather than profits since they have no control over their revenues.

One manufacturing firm which set transfer prices on the basis of cost plus an allocation for overhead and then used these prices for evaluation purposes found that its sales managers were pushing low, rather than high, margin products. Due to their high overhead costs, the high margin products were less profitable to the sales managers than to the company. Further investigation showed that demand for these high margin products was quite elastic and that significant potential profits were being lost due to the transfer pricing strategy in effect.

Decoupling may present problems at times, however. For example, the transfer prices of multinational drug companies are closely monitored worldwide, and this information is shared by a number of governments. Thus, it may be necessary to keep transfer prices at the same level worldwide. Given the low elasticity of demand for many branded pharmaceuticals, these prices are normally set quite high. However, due to competitive circumstances, some individual subsidiaries may be penalized by the necessity to market these drugs at high prices. To sell to these subsidiaries at lower prices, though, would jeopardize the firm's worldwide pricing strategy since other countries would wonder why they had to pay higher prices. These effects would have to be considered to evaluate management performance fairly, particularly when making comparisons across subsidiaries.

Exchange rates for evaluation purposes. Firms must choose the exchange rate(s) to use when setting budgets and evaluating performance.[12] When setting the operating budget, for example, two exchange rates are possible — the actual spot rate at the time or the forecast rate. In addition, if the budget is revised when exchange rate changes occur, the updated rate can be used. In evaluating performance relative to the budget, there are three alternative rates that can be used: the actual rate at the time the budget is set, the projected end-of-period rate, or the actual end-of-period rate. There are, thus, six exchange rate combinations possible.

A study of 200 MNCs, however, revealed that only three budget

[12] Donald R. Lessard and Peter Lorange, "Currency Changes and Management Control: Resolving the Centralization/Decentralization Dilemma," *Accounting Review* (July 1977): 628.

valuation combinations were actually used.[13] Half of the firms surveyed used a projected rate for budgeting but measured performance with the end of period rate, 30 percent used a projected rate both for budgeting and performance evaluation, while the remaining 20 percent used the spot rate for budgeting and the end-of-period rate for tracking performance.

In choosing the appropriate combination of budgeting and evaluation rates to use, it is necessary to consider the behavioral consequences involved. If at the one extreme, the budget and evaluation rates assume no exchange rate change (by using the actual beginning-of-period rate for both purposes), then managers will have no incentive to incorporate anticipated exchange rate changes in their decisions. For example, a marketing manager rewarded on the basis of the spot rate prevailing at the date of sale rather than the anticipated rate upon collection of the receivables generated will likely engage in an uneconomical expansion of credit sales. At the other extreme, if exchange rate changes are ignored in the budget, but the end-of-period rate is used for evaluation, the manager will probably behave in an overly risk averse manner since he or she will bear the full consequences of any exchange rate fluctuations. The harmful effects of such a system will likely include "padding" of the budgets as well as decentralized hedging by managers to reduce their perceived risks.

The use of forecast rates at both the budgeting and evaluation stages appear to be the most desirable combination since it excludes unplanned currency fluctuations but recognizes expected fluctuations at the budgeting stage. Clearly this combination will dominate all other combinations which hold managers responsible for unforeseen exchange fluctuations but do not force them to consider likely currency changes at the budgeting stage. This standard seems most fair since the local decision maker receives no blame or credit for anticipated currency fluctuations. It is also most realistic since it serves to make decentralized decision making congruent with corporate-wide goals and information. Lessard and Lorange call these projected rates internal forward rates.[14] One means of constructing these internal forward rates, which may differ considerably from the actual forward rate, is presented by Shapiro and Rutenberg.[15]

---

[13] Business International Corporation, "Evaluating Foreign Operations," p. 154.
[14] Lessard and Lorange, "Currency Changes," p. 628.
[15] Alan C. Shapiro and David P. Rutenberg, "When to Hedge against Devaluation," *Management Science* (August 1974): 1514.

If the exchange rate changes dramatically, it may be necessary to adjust the projected rate during the operating cycle. The need for adjustment will depend on the magnitude of these changes as well as the degree of exposed assets and local currency earnings. Most importantly, it will depend on the extent to which operating decisions can be changed in response to a new exchange rate. Lessard and Lorange point out that if decisions are irreversible, then the evaluation rate should not be adjusted.[16] Such a change would violate the principle of insulating operating managers from random currency changes. If decisions are reversible, albeit at a cost, new plans should be drawn with updated rates. However, any change in budget and evaluation rates should apply only for the remainder of the period — the time during which new operating decisions can be made. In all cases, it would appear that updating the projected rates when appropriate is preferable to holding operating managers responsible for actual exchange rate changes whether anticipated or not. Furthermore, adjusting these rates would permit sharing the results of unforeseen developments rather than imposing them on operating units.

Adjusting intracorporate fund flows. The ability to adjust intracorporate fund flows by speeding or slowing payments on intracorporate accounts is a valuable and widely used technique in liquidity and exchange risk management. However, use of this tool, known as leading and lagging, is likely to distort the various working capital ratios of subsidiaries. For example, a subsidiary ordered to extend longer credit terms to another unit will show an increase in its receivables to sales ratio. Furthermore, its interest expenses will increase while its customer's working capital costs will decline. Since leading and lagging is a corporate policy, its effects should not be included in any evaluation of subsidiary management. It would be advisable, of course, to consider these effects when evaluating the financial staff at headquarters.

Motivating managers. Implicit in the comments in this section is *the idea that these evaluations will serve as inputs for promotion and salary decisions. The connection should be made obvious to managers.* Otherwise, these evaluations become irrelevant data, useful neither for motivational purposes nor for selecting and promoting a highly qualified cadre of international executives.

Managers who feel they are not rewarded (or penalized) for their

---

[16] Lessard and Lorange, "Currency Changes," p. 628.

job performances may put less effort into the work. However, the real damage is the loss of the entreprenurial spirit that appears to be necessary to cope with a rapidly changing environment. The incentive to take risks is encouraged by the existence of significant rewards for success. Without these rewards, a manager's initiative may be severely diminished, perhaps resulting in work as hard as before but only in more traditional areas rather than embarking on new ventures which offer great potential but are risky.

To implement these evaluations, an effective reporting and control system is necessary. This is the subject of the next section.

REPORTING AND CONTROL SYSTEMS

Many multinationals have found it useful and sometimes necessary to require more frequent reporting by their affiliates due to the increased likelihood of problems arising overseas. Different methods of reporting and communications may also be useful, such as a worldwide telex system and more personal visits with headquarters staff both in the field and at the home office.

Choosing an Appropriate Exchange Rate

Almost by definition, multinational firms have transactions in more than one currency. Thus, MNCs face the problem of which exchange rate(s) to use when reporting the results of foreign operations. A number of alternative exchange rates possibilities exist but interviews with a number of MNCs disclose certain distinct preferences.

Multinational corporations appear to use either the end-of-period rate to book all transactions during the period or else a predetermined rate. This predetermined rate is revised only when the actual exchange rate differs from it by more than a given percentage, usually between 2½ and 5 percent. Another possibility, the average rate during the period, is rarely used because of the additional complexity involved. It should be noted, however, that each of these methods could present measurement problems if care is not taken in the application.

The end-of-period rate, for example, could seriously distort actual profitability if a major exchange rate change occurs during the period unless most sales take place at the new exchange rate. Otherwise, if sales are uniformly distributed throughout the period, an average rate could most accurately represent the period's income. On the other hand, use of an average rate is inappropriate if sales are bunched and a major currency change occurs.

When using a predetermined rate, the limits within which fluctuations are permitted must be set so that changes within these margins will not seriously distort the period's income. Clearly, a firm with a 5 percent profit margin on its sales should not use a predetermined rate with 5 percent fluctuation limits.

Capital goods manufacturers or other firms which usually have only a few large sales during a period should probably use the actual exchange rates at which each transaction took place. The basic criterion then in deciding on which reporting rate to use should be that the approach chosen will not seriously distort the period's actual income.

Centralization versus Decentralization

A key concept in the design of a reporting system is responsibility reporting. This involves flowing information from each decision area to the manager accountable for the results of these decisions. A general rule of thumb in organizational design appears to be to decentralize responsibility as much as possible. The fewer the linkages between activity areas, the better decentralization will function. However, in the multinational corporation, the interactions among various units is often so great because of tax factors or economies of scale in risk management (to be discussed later), for example, that complete decentralization will be suboptimal.

Some firms have partially decentralized operations by establishing regional headquarters for the different geographical areas of the world. This shortens the lines of communication and enhances the dispersal of geographically-centered information. The more similar business conditions are within, as compared with between, geographical regions, the more valuable regional headquarters are likely to be.

In companies with a dearth of experienced international financial managers, there is an added incentive to centralize decisions. It is often felt that the talents of this limited number of experienced managers can best be utilized at headquarters where fullest advantage can be taken of their knowledge. Working against centralization is the complexity and size of the multinational corporation which makes it difficult, if not impossible, for any headquarters group to completely coordinate financial activities worldwide.

A Conference Board study on the level of corporate involvement in certain key multinational financial decision areas indicated that the wider the perspective required, the more likely it was that a particular decision would be controlled by headquarters.[17] The following are some of the results of the Conference Board study.

---
[17] Meister, *Financial Function.*

Repatriation of funds. Of the companies surveyed, 85 percent indicated that decisions involving repatriation of funds were made at the corporate level. However, respondents appeared to have little control of the repatriation decision in joint ventures where they were minority partners.

Intersubsidiary financing. In most companies, either the chief financial executive of the parent company or the treasurer, with the advice of tax counsel, decided on which intracorporate fund flows should take place.

Acquisition of funds. Of the firms studied, 85 percent indicated that all medium and long-term financing was approved at corporate headquarters. Many firms, though, allowed their subsidiaries much more leeway with regard to short-term financing.

Protection of assets. Many of the firms questioned did not have any formal plans for asset protection although a number indicated that they were beginning to change toward greater centralization. The advent of FASB 8 has accelerated the centralization of exposure management.[18]

Planning and control. The responses here were quite varied. The more financially oriented (as opposed to marketing oriented, for example) that firms were, the more likely they were to have a centralized planning and control function.

A more recent study by Stobaugh indicated significant differences in attitudes towards centralization among small (average annual foreign sales of $50 million), medium (average foreign sales of $200 million annually), and large (average of $1 billion in annual foreign sales) multinationals.[19] Small MNCs generally allowed subsidiaries considerable leeway in financial management, perhaps because of the lack of sophistication in international financial management at headquarters. The tendency among medium-sized firms was to try to optimize worldwide results, treating each subsidiary as just one unit in a global system. These firms required very sophisticated control and reporting systems. Large MNCs appeared to reverse the centralization trend somewhat, providing subsidiaries with formal guidelines but allowing them con-

[18] Financial Accounting Standards Board, "Accounting for the Translation of Foreign Currency Transactions and Foreign Currency Financial Statements," Statement of Financial Accounting Standards No. 8 (Stamford, Conn.: FASB, 1975).

[19] Robert B. Stobaugh, "Financing Foreign Subsidiaries of U.S.-Controlled Multinational Enterprises," *Journal of International Business Studies* (Summer 1970): 43.

siderable initiative within those guidelines. This was apparently due to a recognized inability to optimize in such a complex system. The author will now examine two particular areas — currency and cash management — where controversy has developed over the optimal degree of headquarters control.

International Cash and Foreign Exchange Risk Management

In the areas of cash and foreign exchange risk management, there are good arguments for both centralization and decentralization. Arguing for centralization is the reasonable assumption that local treasurers want to optimize their own financial and exposure positions, regardless of the overall corporate situation. To a local treasurer, a subsidiary's cash reserves may appear too low while to the corporate treasurer, the subsidiary is holding excess liquidity relative to the corporation's ability to supply liquidity from its worldwide reserves. Similarly, a study by Rodriguez has concluded that *foreign exchange risk aversion increased with decentralization of the financial function.*[20] Local treasurers ignored the possibilities available to the corporation to *trade off positive and negative currency exposure* positions by consolidating exposure worldwide. A further benefit of centralized exposure management is the ability to take advantage of the economies of scale in risk management effect,[21] that is, the fact that the *total variability or risk of a currency exposure portfolio is less than the sum of the individual variabilities of each currency exposure considered in isolation.* This is due to the less-than-perfect positive correlation that exists between the various currencies. Thus, centralization of exchange risk management should reduce the amount of hedging required to achieve a given level of safety. This can be valuable given the high costs of hedging. The company can then select the cheapest option(s) worldwide to hedge its remaining exposure. Tax effects can be crucial at this stage,[22] but only headquarters will have the required global perspective.

These are all powerful arguments for centralization of cash and currency risk management. Against these benefits, though, must be weighed the loss of local knowledge and the lack of incentive for local managers to take advantage of particular situations with which only

[20] Rita M. Rodriguez, "Management of Foreign Exchange Risk in the U.S. Multinationals," *Journal of Financial and Quantitative Analysis* (November 1974): 849.
[21] Harry Markowitz, "Portfolio Selection," *Journal of Finance* (March 1952): 89.
[22] Alan C. Shapiro and David P. Rutenberg, "Managing Exchange Risks in a Floating World," *Financial Management* (Summer 1976): 48.

they may be familiar. However, this conflict between centralization and decentralization is more apparent than real.

As the section on evaluation noted, the use of internal forward rates can enhance the advantages and suppress the disadvantages of both centralization and decentralization. Similar advantages can be achieved by using internal interest rates. This can be done by providing local managers with interest rates and forward rates which reflect the opportunity costs of money and exposure to the parent corporation. Thus, headquarters can make full use of local knowledge while ensuring that local managers act in the company's best interests. With regard to exchange risk, headquarters, in effect, is offering to *sell insurance* to local managers to cover their exposure. If a manager decides it is cheaper to hedge locally, fine. At least he has taken into consideration the cost of hedging to the corporation.

In setting internal interest rates, the corporate treasurer, in effect, is *acting as a bank,* offering to borrow or lend currencies at given rates. By examining these internal rates, local treasurers will have a greater awareness of the opportunity cost of their idle cash balances as well as an added incentive to act on this information. In many instances, they will prefer to transfer at least part of their cash balances (where permitted) to a central pool in order to earn a greater return. To make pooling of funds work, though, it is essential that managers have access to the central pool whenever they require funds.

Mechanisms of Control

When designing a control system for use overseas, there may be a tendency to use the most sophisticated system available due to the complexity of the problems encountered abroad. Furthermore, since headquarters is not bearing the most of furnishing subsidiary reports, it is likely to demand a good deal of information which is rarely, if ever, used merely on the off chance that it might be needed. However, *a sophisticated and complex system may yield worse results than a simpler, less ambitious system* if local managers are not top caliber or local operations are of small size. A system which is more sophisticated than the managers it is supposed to control can lead to suspicions, frustration, and, ultimately, to sabotage attempts. Where operations are small, a complex reporting system can become burdensome and take managers away from their primary function which is to manage.

According to Zenoff and Zwick, a new and relatively sophisticated management group took control of Singer Corp. in the early 1960s. Despite their desire to bring more sophistication to Singer's international business, though, the new management felt that the quality of many of their field managers precluded the adoption of a complex system of performance standards and evaluation criteria. Instead, they opted for a system of simple standards and reports that were comprehensible and provided some degree of control.[23] Over time, a simple system can evolve into a successful sophisticated system. However, local managers must understand the system. Otherwise, they will defeat it, either deliberately or inadvertently.

Even with sophisticated managers, however, a relatively small operation may not warrant the reporting requirements and elaborate control mechanism of a larger affiliate. *The value of gathering additional information must be balanced against its cost in terms of taking up scarce management time.* A small company may not have the resources to hire additional personnel to fill out reports, and thus the job is left to the existing managers, adding to their workload.

A possible solution is to require fewer reports from smaller subsidiaries while at the same time monitoring several key performance indicators. As long as these indicators remain within bounds, a subsidiary is allowed considerable freedom. If problems appear, then additional controls can be imposed. In effect, this is reporting and control by exception. The danger here is that these additional controls may be perceived as punishment and reacted to accordingly. Tact and a truly helpful attitude will be necessary to convince a manager that these new reports and controls are designed to help him do a better job.

A zero-base information system would aid in this process of reducing information requirements. This would involve an audit of all the information which is currently being provided and the uses of that information. Unless information is being used in decision making, it should be discarded.

Traveling teams of auditors are another device used to facilitate communications and control with the multinational corporation. Quite often, though, it is difficult to find qualified people willing to be constantly on the go, living out of suitcases. Furthermore, these teams may be perceived as spies and met with hostility, unless they demonstrate their helpfulness to the local managers. The attitudes of the team members will be dependent on whether headquarters actually is using them as spies or instead intends for them the more constructive role of assistants and consultants to managers in the field.

Feedback is an important element in any evaluation and control

---

[23] David B. Zenoff and Jack Zwick, *International Financial Management* (Englewood Cliffs, N.J.: Prentice Hall, 1969), p. 457.

system. Local managers, sophisticated or not, from large or small operations, are likely to complain about overreporting and overcontrol if they feel that headquarters demands information without providing a commensurate amount of feedback. Since the reporting system is normally tailored to the needs of headquarters alone, preparing reports is seen as a waste of time for subsidiary management. Redesigning the reporting system so that it provides more useful information to subsidiary management along with more feedback from headquarters will increase the incentive of local management to cooperate with headquarters.

Sometimes only negative feedback is received. According to some managers, "I only hear from headquarters when I am doing poorly, never when I am doing well." This lack of symmetry is difficult to understand since praise can be an equally effective motivating force. After all, almost everyone likes to feel that his or her work is recognized and appreciated.

Many of the problems referred to in this paper are caused by a lack of communications between headquarters and its subsidiaries. One suggested approach to facilitate headquarters-subsidiary communications is to require all top headquarters staff personnel to spend at least two years in the field becoming acquainted with the problems faced by subsidiaries. At the same time, subsidiary managers would be required to spend time at headquarters to gain a broader perspective of the corporation's activities.

CONCLUSIONS

As stated at the beginning of this paper, there is no set of scientific principles that can guarantee the development of a successful evaluation and control system. However, a truly geocentric system, to use Perlmutter's terminology,[24] should encourage a free flow of ideas and information worldwide. Headquarters must avoid the temptation of trying to overcontrol field operations or else run the risk of stifling local initiative. In addition, local managers should have the opportunity to explain their operating results and seek help for their problems. The lack of such a safety mechanism will cause the kinds of problems associated with a too rigid adherence to strictly numerical criteria. In the final analysis, it appears that in the multinational corporation, as in any social institution, a system characterized by mutual understanding works best.

[24] Howard V. Perlmutter, "The Tortuous Evolution of the Multinational Corporation," *Columbia Journal of World Business* (January-February 1969).

CHAPTER 30

Currency changes and management control: resolving the centralization/decentralization dilemma*

Donald R. Lessard and Peter Lorange

ABSTRACT: Multinational corporations with decentralized responsibility for operations face a serious dilemma. If financial policies, including the treatment of foreign exchange risks, are set centrally, the performances of operating groups will be influenced by exchange risk policies over whose effect they have little control. If financial decisions are left to the operating units, on the other hand, they are likely to overreact to exchange risks and thus suboptimize from a corporate perspective. This article suggests that this dilemma can be resolved through the use of "internal forward rates"—rates at which the corporate treasury agrees to translate future foreign currency revenue and expense items. It illustrates the impact of differing treatments of exchange rate changes in budgeting and tracking the performance of decentralized operating units. The article concludes with a discussion of how internal forward rates should be set and updated.

E FFECTIVE control systems for decentralized operations require that operating management has a significant degree of control over the variables affecting the performance on which they are evaluated. Changes in exchange rates are one set of variables which affect the performance of foreign divisions. Many multinationals' policies to cope with changes in exchange rates are set at the corporate level and, thus, are not under control of the foreign divisional manager.

This situation reflects a complex organizational dilemma. On the one hand, pressures of time, distance, market and product differentials, as well as complex business-government relations, point toward the advantages of a decentralized organizational structure.[1] On the other hand, many normative models suggest that an appropriate response to fluctuating exchange rates, taxation differentials, controls on currency flows and variations in financial markets require highly centralized financial decision making[2] (for example, Horst [1971]; Lietaer [1970]; Robbins and Stobaugh, [1973]; Rutenberg [1970]; and Shapiro

[1] A marked evolution of corporate structure towards decentralized operations has taken place over the last four decades. For the classical discussion of this development, see Chandler [1962]; for the case of multinational corporations, see Stopford and Wells [1972] and Channon [1973]; for a summary of planning and control tools in decentralized corporations, see Lorange and Vancil [1977].

[2] Although Robbins and Stobaugh [1973] provide extensive examples and analyses supporting the benefits of centralized financial decision making, they find that the largest corporations have backed off from complete centralization of this function. This may be due to the difficulties of coordinating it with the management control process.

We are grateful to Frederick Kelly, Steven Kohlhagen, Morris McInnes, Stuart Traver and two reviewers for this journal for a number of helpful comments.

Donald R. Lessard and Peter Lorange are Associate Professors of Management at Massachusetts Institute of Technology.

* This article is reprinted, with permission, from *The Accounting Review* (July, 1977) pp 628–637.

[1973]). If centralized financial decisions are imposed on operating managers and if the effects of such decisions are not somehow eliminated from the reported operating results, accounting profits will not provide accurate guides for control, and the motivational consequences may be undesirable. On the other hand, if operating managers are given the responsibility for financial decisions, it is unlikely that they will follow policies which are optimal from a corporate viewpoint,[3] even though the policies may decrease their own profits. In addition, they may overreact to risks of potential exchange rate fluctuations which appear large from their limited perspective.

In this article, first we introduce the question of an appropriate exchange rate for use in the budgeting process and through a simple example illustrate the effects of alternative approaches on management decisions. Then we discuss the benefits of using the same set of exchange rates in both setting the budget and tracking performance relative to the budget. We conclude with a discussion of how such rates should be set and whether and how often they should be updated to reflect new information. Throughout the discussion we focus on the control process over the operating cycle, with a time horizon of one year or less.

EXCHANGE RATES AND THE CONTROL PROCESS

Implicit in the control process of firms with foreign operations are assumptions about the future course of exchange rates and their impact on the firm. Operating decisions in any particular time period reflect a manager's anticipations regarding future exchange rates and their impact on performance. Exchange rates are incorporated in the control process at two points: (1) in setting the operating budget for a particular time period and

(2) in tracking realized performance relative to the budget. When setting the operating budget, two sets of exchange rates can be used: the actual (spot) rates at that time or rates projected at that time for the end of the period. Further, if the budget is updated when exchange rates change, the actual rate at the end of the period can be used for the budget. In tracking performance relative to the budget, three sets of rates can be used: the actual rate when the budget was set, the rate projected at that time for the end of the period and the actual rate at the end of the period. The range of logical combinations of these rates is outlined in Table 1. Four cells are shaded out since they appear to be undesirable combinations.

In combination A-1, the exchange rate existing at the time the budget is developed is used in the budget as well as in tracking results relative to the budget. The implicit assumption is that the exchange rate will not change, but if it does, it will have no effect on the evaluation of the manager's performance. Combination A-3, where the exchange rate used to develop the budget is the actual rate at that time, while the actual rate at the end of the period is used to track results, excludes exchange rate forecasts from budgeting but places the full effect of any changes that take place on the operating manager. Combination P-2 involves a projected exchange rate both for budget preparation and for

[3] The idea of holding operating managers responsible only for anticipated exchange rate fluctuations and assigning responsibility for unanticipated fluctuation to the financial function is valid whether operating decisions are centralized or decentralized. However, centralized operations will not encounter the same difficulties as decentralized operations where the operating divisions are evaluated on a performance measure that may be influenced not only by currency changes but also by corporate financial decisions which are outside the control of these operating managers.

TABLE 1

POSSIBLE COMBINATIONS OF EXCHANGE RATES IN THE CONTROL PROCESS

Rate Used for Determining Budget \ Rate Used to Track Performance Relative to Budget	Actual at Time of Budget	Projected at Time of Budget	Actual at End of Period
Actual at time of budget	A-1	A-2	A-3
Projected at time of budget	P-1	P-2	P-3
Actual at end of period (through updating)	E-1	E-2	E-3

subsequent tracking of performance. Thus, P-2 introduces exchange rate forecasts into budgeting and holds the manager responsible for performance defined at that rate regardless of the actual outcome. We refer to the projected rates used in this fashion as internal forward rates (IFRs) since their use is analogous to the treasurer acting as a banker and "buying forward" receipts in foreign currencies at guaranteed rate.

Combination P-3 makes use of projected exchange rate when determining the budget and the actual rate at the end of the period rate for tracking performance. This again incorporates a projection but holds the manager responsible for the impact on performance of deviations from the projected rate. Thus, in this case the treasurer does not "guarantee" the forward rate. Combination E-3 employs the actual exchange rate at the end of the period, both for determining the budget as well as for tracking actual performance relative to the budget. Consequently, E-3 does not incorporate a projection of exchange rate in the budget, but neither does it hold the manager responsible for any exchange rate fluctuation since the budget is always updated as the exchange rate changes.

The three shaded cells in the lower left of Table 1 (P-1—projected rate for setting the budget, actual rate at the time of the budget for tracking subsequent performance; E-1—actual end-of-period rate for setting the budget and actual rate at the time of budget preparation for tracking performance; E-2—actual rate at the end of the period for budget determination and projected rate at budget determination time for performance tracking) require exchange rate forecasts or updates for determining the budget but ignore these when tracking performance relative to the budget. The other shaded cell, A-2, requires the use of a projected rate (set at the time of the budget preparation) in measuring actual performance but does not use this rate for the preparation of the budget. Instead, the actual rate at that time is used. Hence, these four combinations are ruled out as inefficient.

A recent study of ten multinational corporations [Traver, 1975] showed that five used variants of P-3 (budgeting with a projected rate but tracking performance with the actual rate at end of period), three used variants of P-2 (projected rate at time of budget preparation both for preparing the budget and for performance tracking), and two had systems

TABLE 2

BUDGETED PERFORMANCE AT DIFFERENT
EXCHANGE RATES

	Option A	Option B	Option C
Local Currency Budget (stated in LC terms)			
Sales	80,000	100,000	150,000
Cost of goods sold	60,000	80,000	125,000
Operating expenses	4,000	5,000	7,500
Profit	16,000	15,000	17,500
[Exposed assets]	[75,000]	[100,000]	[200,000]
Dollar Budget I (LC 1 = $0.10)			
Sales	8,000	10,000	15,000
Cost of goods sold	6,000	8,000	12,500
Operating expenses	400	500	750
Profit	1,600	1,500	1,750
Dollar Budget II (LC 1 = $0.0833)			
Sales	6,664	8,333	12,495
Cost of goods sold	4,998	6,664	10,413
Operating expenses	333	417	625
Loss on exposed assets*	1,252	1,670	3,340
Profit	81	−418	−1,883
Dollar Budget III (LC 1 = $0.09165)			
Sales	7,332	9,165	13,748
Cost of goods sold	5,499	7,332	11,456
Operating expenses	367	458	687
Loss on exposed assets**	625	835	1,670
Profit	841	540	−65

* Loss on exposed assets for budget II are calculated as follows:

Option A: $(75,000 \times 0.10) - (75,000 \times 0.0833)$
$$= 7,500 - 6,248 = \underline{1,252}$$

Option B: $(100,000 \times 0.10) - (100,000 \times 0.0833)$
$$= 10,000 - 8,330 = \underline{1,670}$$

Option C: $(200,000 \times 0.10) - (200,000 \times 0.0833)$
$$= 20,000 - 16,660 = \underline{3,340}$$

** Losses on exposed assets for budget III are calculated as follows:

Option A: $(75,000 \times 0.10) - (75,000 \times 0.09165)$
$$= 7,500 - 6,874 = \underline{625}$$

Option B: $(100,000 \times 0.10) - (100,000 \times 0.09165)$
$$= 10,000 - 9,165 = \underline{835}$$

Option C: $(200,000 \times 0.10) - (200,000 \times 0.09165)$
$$= 20,000 - 18,330 = \underline{1,670}$$

resembling A-3 (actual rate at beginning of period for budgeting and actual rate at end of period for tracking).

An Illustration

The likely effect of each of these different approaches on the decisions of managers of foreign responsibility centers can be illustrated with a simple example. Assume that the current dollar price of the foreign local currency (LC) is $0.10 and that there are two equally likely possibilities for the dollar value of the local currency in the next period—a 50 percent chance that it will move to $0.0833 and a 50 percent chance that it will remain the same, $0.10. Thus the expected dollar value of the local currency is $0.09165.[4] Assuming for the moment that the firm requires no risk-premium for bearing the risk of foreign exchange fluctuations, we can use the expected rate of $0.09165 as an appropriate IFR. Further assume that the manager is faced with an operating decision regarding three options which are not mutually exclusive. As is typically the case, the computations of adjustments to dollar profit due to currency fluctuations will involve adjustments of the foreign asset values as well as adjustment of foreign operating profits. Finally, we assume that the accounting results of the foreign responsibility center are translated from local currency into the parent company's currency according to the monetary/nonmonetary method.[5]

In Table 2, option "A" involves sales

[4] Throughout the paper we use the dollar as the parent company's home currency. All other currencies are lumped under the heading local currency (LC).

[5] In this paper we are not concerned with the definition of exposure, although the adjustments in our example are consistent with the latest FASB statement [1975]. Our proposal can be used in conjunction with a wide variety of exposure definitions, many of which would reflect economic reality more closely than current accounting conventions. See, for example, Dufey [1972] and First National City Bank [1975].

of LC 80,000 and requires LC 75,000 of "exposed" assets.[6] Option "B" gives sales of LC 100,000 and requires LC 100,000 of exposed assets. Option "C" gives sales of LC 150,000 but requires LC 200,000 of exposed assets. The remaining details of each option as well as the budgeted performance at each of the possible exchange rates are shown in Table 2. For simplicity, we assume that changes in the exchange rate will have no impact on LC operating results. Therefore, the actual performance at each rate will equal the budgeted performance for that rate. Also for simplicity we ignore the effect of taxes. It is easy to see how the treatment of foreign exchange fluctuations will affect a manager's budgeted and reported profits and, therefore, his or her incentives. If, at the one extreme, the budget implicitly assumes that there will be no exchange rate change, and if foreign exchange fluctuations are considered to be outside of the realm of the operating manager (as is the case with combination A-1 in Table 1), the results will be recorded as if the beginning and ending exchange rate is LCI = $0.10 (Budget 1 of Table 2), regardless of the actual outcome. All three options will appear profitable, including C which involves an expected loss. At the other extreme, if possible exchange rates are ignored in the budget but actual exchange fluctuations are imposed on the manager (case A-3 in Table 1), he or she probably will avoid option B as well as option C because of the high probability of a very poor performance relative to the budget (Budget II, Table 2). However, B has an expected profit and therefore is a sound option for all but the most risk-averse firms.

If the budget and reported profit are based on the internal forward exchange rate, LCI = $0.09165 (Case P-2, Table 1), the division manager clearly will accept

Plans A and B and avoid Plan C (Budget III, Table 2). If the budget is based on the internal forward exchange rate but if performance is measured at the actual rate at the end of the period, the manager will clearly accept Plan A and reject Plan C, but the decision regarding Plan B will depend upon the extent to which the manager is averse to taking risks. The differences between actual and budgeted profits for the various budget-rate/tracking-rate combinations are illustrated in Table 3. Note that in all combinations along the diagonal, that is, those in which the same type of rates are used in both budget preparation and performance tracking, there will be no deviations due to exchange rate variations. However, the various combinations along the diagonal do have quite different implications for operating decisions. The combinations involving actual rates at the time of the budget or the actual rates at the end of the period for both budgeting and tracking (A-1 and E-3) allow the manager to ignore the effect of both anticipated and unanticipated fluctuations in exchange rates.

The combination of actual beginning of period rates for budgeting and actual end of period rates for tracking, A-3, although used in practice, appears to represent the worst of all possible worlds [Traver, 1975]. In the budgeting stage, no account will be taken of possible exchange fluctuations, yet their full impact will be attributed to the manager at the tracking stage. The harmful effects of such a system can be expected to include "padding" of budgets or decentralized hedging actions by managers to reduce exchange risks which are likely to loom

---

[6] "Exposed assets" under the monetary/nonmonetary translation method are defined as the *excess* of cash plus LC receivables plus other LC financial assets over all forms of LC obligations.

TABLE 3

EFFECTS ON PERFORMANCE IN OUR EXAMPLE FROM POSSIBLE COMBINATIONS
OF EXCHANGE RATES IN BUDGETING PROCESS

Rate Used for Determining Budget / Rate Used to Track Performance Relative to Budget	Actual at Time of Budget		Projected at Time of Budget		Actual at End of Period	
	Actual Outcome LC1 = $.10	Actual Outcome LC1 = $.0833	Actual Outcome LC1 = $.10	Actual Outcome LC1 = $.0833	Actual Outcome LC1 = $.10	Actual Outcome LC1 = $.0833
Actual at time of Budget (LC1: $.10)	*A-1*				*A-3*	
Option A Profit	1600	1600			1600	81
Budget	1600	1600			1600	1600
Deviation	0	0			0	−1519
Option B Profit	1500	1500			1500	−418
Budget	1500	1500			1500	1500
Deviation	0	0			0	−1918
Option C Profit	1750	1750			1750	−1883
Budget	1750	1750			1750	1750
Deviation	0	0			0	−3633
Projected at time of Budget (LC1: $.09165)			*P-2*		*P-3*	
Option A Profit			841	841	1600	81
Budget			841	841	841	841
Deviation			0	0	+759	−760
Option B Profit			540	540	1500	−418
Budget			540	540	540	540
Deviation			0	0	+960	−958
Option C Profit			−65	−65	1750	−1883
Budget			−65	−65	−65	−65
Deviation			0	0	+1815	−1818
Actual rate at end of Period (LC1: $.10 or LC1: $.0833)					*E-3*	
Option A Profit					1600	81
Budget					1600	81
Deviation					0	0
Option B Profit					1500	418
Budget					1500	418
Deviation					0	0
Option C Profit					1750	−1883
Budget					1750	−1883
Deviation					0	0

very large from their narrower local perspective.

Combination P-2, involving IFRs at the budgeting and tracking stages, excludes unplanned exchange fluctuations but acknowledges expected fluctuations at the budgeting stage. Thus, it will dominate the other alternatives which expose managers to unforeseen exchange fluctuations but fail to force managers to consider them at the budgeting stage. These dominated combinations are A-1 and E-3. Based on these observations, we believe that combination P-2 generally will be superior to all others. Combination P-3 may appear equally attractive in situations where operating plans should and can be changed in response to exchange rate shifts. However, in a later section we argue that even under these circumstances P-2 is superior.

The suggested procedure of using internal forward exchange rates as the basis for decision making and performance evaluation goes a long way towards satisfying two major criteria for good management control systems, goal-congruence and fairness. Goal-congruence is restored because a corporate-wide point of view has been brought to bear on the currency exchange rate, eliminating decisions taken on the basis of the expectations and risk-preferences of local managers who necessarily will have a narrower horizon on the currency risk problem than the corporate headquarters. Fairness is restored, at least in regard to the exchange rate fluctuations, by the establishment of a standard under which the local decision maker gets no blame or credit for currency fluctuations outside of the division manager's control.

An examination of the foreign operations of the ten corporations referred to above confirms our approach. For those firms where both operating and financial decisions were decentralized, imposing exchange risk fluctuations on operating managers by tracking performance at actual end of period rates seemed to cause little concern since local management had authority to control the risk. However, of those firms with decentralized operations which attempted to centralize financial management, the ones which were most successful in eliciting local management behavior consistent with corporate goals combined consistent budgeting and tracking rates in their control systems.

SETTING INTERNAL FORWARD EXCHANGE RATES

. One possible objection to the use of IFRs is the need for exchange rate forecasts. This requirement may appear to be particularly onerous in view of evidence that current exchange rate fluctuations are large relative to fundamental factors such as inflation differentials and interest rate differentials. Also, exchange markets appear to be efficient; therefore, the fluctuations can be characterized as a random process [Giddy and Dufey, 1975; Kohlhagen, 1976]. However, forecasts of some type, whether implicit or explicit, are required for proper planning regardless of the particular control system. Further, in precisely this type of environment, in which there are large random exchange rate fluctuations, it is important to shield operating managers from these unforeseeable exchange rate variations.

Even in this environment some forecasting of exchange rates, at least in terms of long-term trends, is possible, and forecasts are available from major banks and econometric firms. Rather than dwell on the issue of forecasting exchange rates, we focus here on how IFRs should relate to the firms' forecasts. The value to a firm of flows in a particular currency in the future will not necessarily be equal to the expected value of the currency. Many firms seek to limit exchange rate risk by hedging their exposure through actions such as restructuring their financial assets and liabilities, changing the timing of international cash flows or entering into forward exchange contracts. Further, the value of currency flows to or from particular units of the firm depends upon their tax treatment. This will be a function of the firm's overall tax position as well as the range of mechanisms it has at its disposal for shifting profits and/or funds among subsidiary firms.[7]

A further question regarding IFRs is to what extent operating managers should have a role in setting them.

The most important reason for involving operating managers in setting IFRs is that these rates not only will reflect the corporation's best estimates of future exchange rate movements, but also they will reflect the extent to which the corporation can alter its business or financial decisions in anticipation of or in response to exchange rate changes. Decisions open to the firm might include changing prices or currencies in which sales are invoiced, sources of inputs, production schedules, markets for outputs and borrowing sources, in addition to hedging as a means of shifting some funds from one currency to another or leading and lagging certain receipts and/or disbursements. That is, IFRs cannot be determined properly without a schedule of receipts and disbursements because of the simultaneous nature of the problem. This problem can be modelled formally as a decomposed mathematical programming problem which allows a centralized finance function and decentralized control over operations. However, we consider the most realistic method to be the use of one or more iterations between the two related problems. Beginning with a set of

provisional IFRs, operating managers could prepare rough, highly aggregated sets of operating plans for their divisions. In turn, these would serve as input for a first solution of the centralized funds management problem. Then the resulting IFRs could be used to produce a final set of operating plans and budgeting rates to guide subsequent decisions. This iterative process points out the need for close coordination between the two activities.

Of course, another important consideration is to incorporate all relevant information available on a timely basis. To the extent that operating managers in particular countries have access to information not available to central financial personnel, they must be drawn into the process. This is unlikely for most major currencies, but it may be significant for smaller or less-developed countries about which information is not readily available. A final consideration is that managers should be incorporated in the process to assure understanding and acceptance of the IFRs, which are important inputs into business plans as well as reported performance. An honored convention for minimizing dysfunctionali-

---

[7] It might be useful to think of the IFRs as shadow prices from a model for centralized international funds management. Scott [1973] provides a concise description of the key elements in this type of model. Robbins and Stobaugh [1973] formulate it as a linear programming problem, Lietaer [1970] describes it as a quadratic programming problem, and Rutenberg [1970] depicts it as a network problem. The inputs into such a model include the schedules of current and anticipated exposure as well as cash budgets which reflect variables such as planned activity, tax rates, interest rates, current and forecasted exchange rates and internal and external constraints on financial alternatives. Such a model should reflect the firm's willingness to bear exchange rate risks either through constraints limiting total risk exposure or through more explicit risk-reward tradeoffs. Since the objective of the model is to maximize the value of future flows or minimize the cost of funding future requirements, taking risk preferences into account, the shadow prices associated with future flows in various currencies may be interpreted as IFRs, representing the best estimate of their value to the firm.

ties in control systems is that managers should have a role in the negotiation of any performance budget relevant to their own units. Confidence in the system undoubtedly would be strengthened if there were a procedure for appealing unacceptable IFRs to a higher level of management and a procedure for revising the IFRs when unforeseen events dramatically change the exchange rate.

ADJUSTING TO EXCHANGE RATE CHANGES WITHIN THE OPERATING CYCLE

To this point we have avoided the question of whether IFRs should be adjusted within the operating cycle if exchange rates change dramatically. The need for adjustment will depend on several factors, including the volatility of exchange rates and the relative sizes of exposed assets and LC earnings streams within the corporate total. Most critically, it will depend on the extent to which operating decisions can be changed in response to the new exchange rates. Clearly, if the operating cycle corresponds to a period over which decisions are not reversible, IFRs should not be changed under even the most extreme circumstances. Such a change would violate the basic concept of insulating operating managers from random exchange rate shifts. In other cases, decisions may be reversible at some cost. These cases call for new operating plans with some adjustment in the manager's reported profits to offset the costs involved. If the operating cycle is sufficiently long relative to the duration of particular operating decisions, IFRs can and should be updated. However, even here the change should apply only to the remainder of the period—the period for which new operating decisions can be made. In all cases, it would appear that updating the IFRs when appropriate would be preferable to making the operating subsidiaries

responsible for actual exchange rate outcomes, whether reflected in the IFRs or not. Further, the coordination required for adjusting IFRs would create an environment of "sharing" the results of unforeseen developments instead of capriciously imposing them on operating units.

SUMMARY

We have outlined an approach for handling the treatment of currency changes within the multinational corporation's planning and control systems. This approach incorporates decentralized operating control of individual foreign subsidiaries and centralized control of the firm's finances. A set of currency rates which reflect the best judgment of not only currency developments but also the corporation's position vis-a-vis these changes, called IFRs, were suggested to be an appropriate basis for the development of budgets, as well as for tracking the operating performance of the foreign subsidiaries relative to the budget. Local management will be expected to take actions congruent with corporate objectives on the basis of these rates and will be held responsible for their performances relative to these rates. At the same time, financial decisions can be handled centrally, allowing a more effective and coordinated set of policies without impinging on the decentralized operating decisions.

The logic of using IFRs to deal with foreign exchange risks can be extended readily to other risks including price and interest rate fluctuations. As some form of inflation accounting is adopted, for example, a similar treatment of domestic price level risks will be called for. We have singled out exchange risks because we believe that their current treatment is a major source of conflict and distortion in decentralized multinational organizations.

Chandler, A. D., *Strategy and Structure* (M.I.T. Press, 1972).

Channon, D. F., *The Strategy and Structure of British Enterprise* (Division of Research, Harvard Business School, 1973).

Dufey, G., "Corporate Finance and Exchange Variations," *Financial Management* (Summer 1972), pp. 51–57.

Financial Accounting Standards Board, Statement No. 8: *Accounting for the Translation of Foreign Currency Transactions and Foreign Currency Financial Statements* (1975).

First National City Bank, *Corporate Foreign Exposure Management* (1975).

Giddy, I. and G. Dufey, "The Random Behavior of Flexible Exchange Rates: Implications for Forecasting," *Journal of International Business Studies* (Spring 1975), pp. 1–32.

Horst, T., "The Theory of Multinational Firm: Optimal Behavior Under Different Tariffs and Tax Rates," *Journal of Political Economy* (September-October 1971), pp. 1059–1072.

Kohlhagen, S. W., "The Foreign Exchange Markets—Models, Tests, and Empirical Evidence" working paper (U.C. Berkeley, 1976).

Lietaer, B. A., *Financial Management of Foreign Exchange: An Operational Technique to Reduce Risk* (M.I.T. Press, 1970).

Lorange, P. and R. F. Vancil, *Strategic Planning Systems* (Prentice-Hall, 1977).

Robbins, S. M. and R. B. Stobaugh, *Money in the Multinational Enterprise* (Basic Books, 1973).

Rutenberg, D. P., "Maneuvering Liquid Assets in a Multinational Company: Formulation and Deterministic Solution Procedures," *Management Science* (June 1970), pp. 671–684.

Scott, G. M., *An Introduction to Financial Control and Reporting in Multinational Enterprises* (University of Texas at Austin, 1973).

Shapiro, A. C., "Exchange Risk Management for the Multinational Corporation," paper presented at Financial Management Association (1973).

Stopford, J. and L. T. Wells, *Managing the Multinational Enterprise: Organization of the Firm and Ownership of the Subsidiaries* (Basic Books, 1972).

Traver, S., "Setting 'Smart' Budgeting Rates in the Control Process" (Masters' Thesis, M.I.T., Sloan School of Management, 1975).

Index